SOFTWARE TESTING AND QUALITY ASSURANCE

SOFTWARE TESTING AND QUALITY ASSURANCE
Theory and Practice

KSHIRASAGAR NAIK

Department of Electrical and Computer Engineering
University of Waterloo, Waterloo

PRIYADARSHI TRIPATHY

NEC Laboratories America, Inc.

A JOHN WILEY & SONS, INC., PUBLICATION

Published by John Wiley & Sons, Inc., Hoboken, New Jersey
Published simultaneously in Canada

For general information on our other products and services or for technical support, please contact our
Customer Care Department within the United States at (800) 762-2974, outside the United States at
(317) 572-3993 or fax (317) 572-4002.

Wiley also publishes its books in a variety of electronic formats. Some content that appears in print
may not be available in electronic formats. For more information about Wiley products, visit our web
site at www.wiley.com.

Library of Congress Cataloging-in-Publication Data:

Naik, Kshirasagar, 1959–
  Software testing and quality assurance / Kshirasagar Naik and Priyadarshi Tripathy.
      p. cm.
  Includes bibliographical references and index.
  ISBN 978-0-471-78911-6 (cloth)
1. Computer software—Testing. 2. Computer software—Quality control. I. Tripathy,
  Piyu, 1958–II. Title.
    QA76.76.T48N35 2008
    005.14—dc22

                                                          2008008331

10 9

To our parents
Sukru and Teva Naik
Kunjabihari and Surekha Tripathy

CONTENTS

CHAPTER 9 *FUNCTIONAL TESTING*   **222**

CHAPTER 10   *TEST GENERATION FROM FSM MODELS*   265

CHAPTER 11   *SYSTEM TEST DESIGN*   321

PREFACE

karmany eva dhikaras te; ma phalesu kadachana; ma karmaphalahetur bhur; ma
te sango stv akarmani.
Your right is to work only; but never to the fruits thereof; may you not be
motivated by the fruits of actions; nor let your attachment to be towards inaction.
— *Bhagavad Gita*

We have been witnessing tremendous growth in the software industry over the past
25 years. Software applications have proliferated from the original data processing
and scientific computing domains into our daily lives in such a way that we do not
realize that some kind of software executes when we do even something ordinary,
such as making a phone call, starting a car, turning on a microwave oven, and
making a debit card payment. The processes for producing software must meet two
broad challenges. First, the processes must produce low-cost software in a short
time so that corporations can stay competitive. Second, the processes must produce
usable, dependable, and safe software; these attributes are commonly known as
quality attributes. Software quality impacts a number of important factors in our
daily lives, such as economy, personal and national security, health, and safety.

Twenty-five years ago, testing accounted for about 50% of the total time
and more than 50% of the total money expended in a software development
project—and, the same is still true today. Those days the software industry was a
much smaller one, and academia offered a single, comprehensive course entitled
Software Engineering to educate undergraduate students in the nuts and bolts of
software development. Although software testing has been a part of the classical
software engineering literature for decades, the subject is seldom incorporated into
the mainstream undergraduate curriculum. A few universities have started offering
an *option* in software engineering comprising three specialized courses, namely,
Requirements Specification, *Software Design*, and *Testing and Quality Assurance*.
In addition, some universities have introduced full undergraduate and graduate
degree programs in software engineering.

Considering the impact of software quality, or the lack thereof, we observe
that software testing education has not received its due place. Ideally, research
should lead to the development of tools and methodologies to produce low-cost,
high-quality software, and students should be educated in the testing fundamentals.
In other words, software testing research should not be solely academic in nature
but must strive to be practical for industry consumers. However, in practice, there

is a large gap between the testing skills needed in the industry and what are taught and researched in the universities.

Our goal is to provide the students and the teachers with a set of well-rounded educational materials covering the fundamental developments in testing theory and common testing practices in the industry. We intend to provide the students with the "big picture" of testing and quality assurance, because software quality concepts are quite broad. There are different kinds of software systems with their own intricate characteristics. We have not tried to specifically address their testing challenges. Instead, we have presented testing theory and practice as broad stepping stones which will enable the students to understand and develop testing practices for more complex systems.

We decided to write this book based on our teaching and industrial experiences in software testing and quality assurance. For the past 15 years, Sagar has been teaching software engineering and software testing on a regular basis, whereas Piyu has been performing hands-on testing and managing test groups for testing routers, switches, wireless data networks, storage networks, and intrusion prevention appliances. Our experiences have helped us in selecting and structuring the contents of this book to make it suitable as a textbook.

Who Should Read This Book?

We have written this book to introduce students and software professionals to the fundamental ideas in testing theory, testing techniques, testing practices, and quality assurance. Undergraduate students in software engineering, computer science, and computer engineering with no prior experience in the software industry will be introduced to the subject matter in a step-by-step manner. Practitioners too will benefit from the structured presentation and comprehensive nature of the materials. Graduate students can use the book as a reference resource. After reading the whole book, the reader will have a thorough understanding of the following topics:

- Fundamentals of testing theory and concepts
- Practices that support the production of quality software
- Software testing techniques
- Life-cycle models of requirements, defects, test cases, and test results
- Process models for unit, integration, system, and acceptance testing
- Building test teams, including recruiting and retaining test engineers
- Quality models, capability maturity model, testing maturity model, and test process improvement model'

How Should This Book be Read?

The purpose of this book is to teach how to *do* software testing. We present some essential background material in Chapter 1 and save the enunciation of software quality questions to a later part of the book. It is difficult to intelligently discuss for beginners what software quality *means* until one has a firm sense of what software testing *does*. However, practitioners with much testing experience can jump to Chapter 17, entitled "Software Quality," immediately after Chapter 1.

There are three different ways to read this book depending upon someone's interest. First, those who are exclusively interested in software testing concepts and want to apply the ideas should read Chapter 1 ("Basic Concepts and Preliminaries"), Chapter 3 ("Unit Testing"), Chapter 7 ("System Integration Testing"), and Chapters 8–14, related to system-level testing. Second, test managers interested in improving the test effectiveness of their teams can read Chapters 1, 3, 7, 8–14, 16 ("Test Team Organization"), 17 ("Software Quality"), and 18 ("Maturity Models"). Third, beginners should read the book from cover to cover.

Notes for Instructors

The book can be used as a text in an introductory course in software testing and quality assurance. One of the authors used the contents of this book in an undergraduate course entitled Software Testing and Quality Assurance for several years at the University of Waterloo. An introductory course in software testing can cover selected sections from most of the chapters except Chapter 16. For a course with more emphasis on testing techniques than on processes, we recommend to choose Chapters 1 ("Basic Concepts and Preliminaries") to 15 ("Software Reliability"). When used as a supplementary text in a software engineering course, selected portions from the following chapters can help students imbibe the essential concepts in software testing:

- Chapter 1: Basic Concepts and Preliminaries
- Chapter 3: Unit Testing
- Chapter 7: System Integration Testing
- Chapter 8: System Test Category
- Chapter 14: Acceptance Testing

Supplementary materials for instructors are available at the following Wiley website: http:/www.wiley.com/sagar.

Acknowledgments

In preparing this book, we received much support from many people, including the publisher, our family members, and our friends and colleagues. The support has been in many different forms. First, we would like to thank our editors, namely, Anastasia Wasko, Val Moliere, Whitney A. Lesch, Paul Petralia, and Danielle Lacourciere who gave us much professional guidance and patiently answered our various queries. Our friend Dr. Alok Patnaik read the whole draft and made numerous suggestions to improve the presentation quality of the book; we thank him for all his effort and encouragement. The second author, Piyu Tripathy, would like to thank his former colleagues at Nortel Networks, Cisco Systems, and Airvana Inc., and present colleagues at NEC Laboratories America.

Finally, the support of our parents, parents-in-law, and partners deserve a special mention. I, Piyu Tripathy, would like to thank my dear wife Leena, who has taken many household and family duties off my hands to give me time that I needed to write this book. And I, Sagar Naik, would like to thank my loving wife Alaka for her invaluable support and for always being there for me. I would also like to thank my charming daughters, Monisha and Sameeksha, and exciting son, Siddharth, for their understanding while I am writing this book. I am grateful to my elder brother, Gajapati Naik, for all his support. We are very pleased that now we have more time for our families and friends.

Kshirasagar Naik
University of Waterloo
Waterloo

Priyadarshi Tripathy
NEC Laboratories America, Inc.
Princeton

LIST OF FIGURES

LIST OF TABLES

CHAPTER 1

Basic Concepts and Preliminaries

Software is like entropy. It is difficult to grasp, weighs nothing, and obeys the second law of thermodynamics, i.e., it always increases.

— *Norman Ralph Augustine*

1.1 QUALITY REVOLUTION

People seek quality in every man-made artifact. Certainly, the concept of quality did not originate with software systems. Rather, the quality concept is likely to be as old as human endeavor to mass produce artifacts and objects of large size. In the past couple of decades a quality revolution, has been spreading fast throughout the world with the explosion of the Internet. Global competition, outsourcing, off-shoring, and increasing customer expectations have brought the concept of quality to the forefront. Developing quality products on tighter schedules is critical for a company to be successful in the new global economy. Traditionally, efforts to improve quality have centered around the end of the product development cycle by emphasizing the detection and correction of defects. On the contrary, the new approach to enhancing quality encompasses all phases of a product development process—from a requirements analysis to the final delivery of the product to the customer. Every step in the development process must be performed to the highest possible standard. An effective quality process must focus on [1]:

- Paying much attention to customer's requirements
- Making efforts to continuously improve quality
- Integrating measurement processes with product design and development
- Pushing the quality concept down to the lowest level of the organization
- Developing a system-level perspective with an emphasis on methodology and process
- Eliminating waste through continuous improvement

Software Testing and Quality Assurance: Theory and Practice, Edited by Kshirasagar Naik and Priyadarshi Tripathy
Copyright © 2008 John Wiley & Sons, Inc.

A quality movement started in Japan during the 1940s and the 1950s by William Edwards Deming, Joseph M. Juran, and Kaoru Ishikawa. In circa 1947, W. Edwards Deming "visited India as well, then continued on to Japan, where he had been asked to join a statistical mission responsible for planning the 1951 Japanese census" [2], p. 8. During his said visit to Japan, Deming invited statisticians for a dinner meeting and told them how important they were and what they could do for Japan [3]. In March 1950, he returned to Japan at the invitation of Managing Director Kenichi Koyanagi of the Union of Japanese Scientists and Engineers (JUSE) to teach a course to Japanese researchers, workers, executives, and engineers on statistical quality control (SQC) methods. Statistical quality control is a discipline based on measurements and statistics. Decisions are made and plans are developed based on the collection and evaluation of actual data in the form of metrics, rather than intuition and experience. The SQC methods use seven basic quality management tools: Pareto analysis, cause-and-effect diagram, flow chart, trend chart, histogram, scatter diagram, and control chart [2].

In July 1950, Deming gave an eight-day seminar based on the Shewhart methods of statistical quality control [4, 5] for Japanese engineers and executives. He introduced the *plan–do–check–act* (PDCA) cycle in the seminar, which he called the Shewhart cycle (Figure 1.1). The Shewhart cycle illustrates the following activity sequence: setting goals, assigning them to measurable milestones, and assessing the progress against those milestones. Deming's 1950 lecture notes formed the basis for a series of seminars on SQC methods sponsored by the JUSE and provided the criteria for Japan's famed Deming Prize. Deming's work has stimulated several different kinds of industries, such as those for radios, transistors, cameras, binoculars, sewing machines, and automobiles.

Between circa 1950 and circa 1970, automobile industries in Japan, in particular Toyota Motor Corporation, came up with an innovative principle to compress the time period from customer order to banking payment, known as the "lean principle." The objective was to minimize the consumption of resources that added no value to a product. The lean principle has been defined by the National Institute of Standards and Technology (NIST) Manufacturing Extension Partnership program [61] as "a systematic approach to identifying and eliminating waste through continuous improvement, flowing the product at the pull of the customer in pursuit of perfection," p.1. It is commonly believed that lean principles were started in Japan by Taiichi Ohno of Toyota [7], but Henry Ford

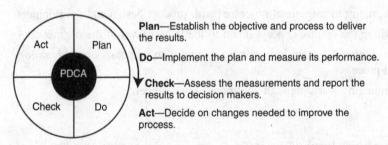

Plan—Establish the objective and process to deliver the results.

Do—Implement the plan and measure its performance.

Check—Assess the measurements and report the results to decision makers.

Act—Decide on changes needed to improve the process.

Figure 1.1   Shewhart cycle.

had been using parts of lean as early as circa 1920, as evidenced by the following quote (Henry Ford, 1926) [61], p.1:

One of the noteworthy accomplishments in keeping the price of Ford products low is the gradual shortening of the production cycle. The longer an article is in the process of manufacture and the more it is moved about, the greater is its ultimate cost.

This concept was popularized in the United States by a Massachusetts Institute of Technology (MIT) study of the movement from mass production toward production, as described in *The Machine That Changed the World*, by James P. Womack, Daniel T. Jones, and Daniel Roos, New York: Rawson and Associates, 1990. Lean thinking continues to spread to every country in the world, and leaders are adapting the principles beyond automobile manufacturing, to logistics and distribution, services, retail, health care, construction, maintenance, and software development [8].

Remark: Walter Andrew Shewhart was an American physicist, engineer, and statistician and is known as the father of statistical quality control. Shewhart worked at Bell Telephone Laboratories from its foundation in 1925 until his retirement in 1956 [9]. His work was summarized in his book *Economic Control of Quality of Manufactured Product*, published by McGraw-Hill in 1931. In 1938, his work came to the attention of physicist W. Edwards Deming, who developed some of Shewhart's methodological proposals in Japan from 1950 onward and named his synthesis the Shewhart cycle.

In 1954, Joseph M. Juran of the United States proposed raising the level of quality management from the manufacturing units to the entire organization. He stressed the importance of systems thinking that begins with product requirement, design, prototype testing, proper equipment operations, and accurate process feedback. Juran's seminar also became a part of the JUSE's educational programs [10]. Juran spurred the move from SQC to TQC (total quality control) in Japan. This included companywide activities and education in quality control (QC), audits, quality circle, and promotion of quality management principles. The term TQC was coined by an American, Armand V. Feigenbaum, in his 1951 book *Quality Control Principles, Practice and Administration*. It was republished in 2004 [11]. By 1968, Kaoru Ishikawa, one of the fathers of TQC in Japan, had outlined, as shown in the following, the key elements of TQC management [12]:

- Quality comes first, not short-term profits.
- The customer comes first, not the producer.
- Decisions are based on facts and data.
- Management is participatory and respectful of all employees.
- Management is driven by cross-functional committees covering product planning, product design, purchasing, manufacturing, sales, marketing, and distribution.

Remark: A quality circle is a volunteer group of workers, usually members of the same department, who meet regularly to discuss the problems and make presentations to management with their ideas to overcome them. Quality circles were started in Japan in 1962 by Kaoru Ishikawa as another method of improving quality. The movement in Japan was coordinated by the JUSE.

One of the innovative TQC methodologies developed in Japan is referred to as the *Ishikawa* or *cause-and-effect* diagram. Kaoru Ishikawa found from statistical data that dispersion in product quality came from four common causes, namely *materials*, *machines*, *methods*, and *measurements*, known as the 4 Ms (Figure 1.2). The bold horizontal arrow points to quality, whereas the diagonal arrows in Figure 1.2 are probable causes having an effect on the quality. Materials often differ when sources of supply or size requirements vary. Machines, or equipment, also function differently depending on variations in their parts, and they operate optimally for only part of the time. Methods, or processes, cause even greater variations due to lack of training and poor handwritten instructions. Finally, measurements also vary due to outdated equipment and improper calibration. Variations in the 4 Ms parameters have an effect on the quality of a product. The Ishikawa diagram has influenced Japanese firms to focus their quality control attention on the improvement of materials, machines, methods, and measurements.

The total-quality movement in Japan has led to pervasive top-management involvement. Many companies in Japan have extensive documentation of their quality activities. Senior executives in the United States either did not believe quality mattered or did not know where to begin until the National Broadcasting Corporation (NBC), an America television network, broadcast the documentary "If Japan Can ... Why Can't We?" at 9:30 P.M. on June 24, 1980 [2]. The documentary was produced by Clare Crawford-Mason and was narrated by Lloyd Dobyns. Fifteen minutes of the broadcast was devoted to Dr. Deming and his work. After the

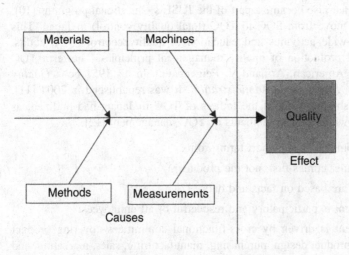

Figure 1.2 Ishikawa diagram.

broadcast, many executives and government leaders realized that a renewed emphasis on quality was no longer an option for American companies but a necessity for doing business in an ever-expanding and more demanding competitive world market. Ford Motor Company and General Motors immediately adopted Deming's SQC methodology into their manufacturing process. Other companies such as Dow Chemical and the Hughes Aircraft followed suit. Ishikawa's TQC management philosophy gained popularity in the United States. Further, the spurred emphasis on quality in American manufacturing companies led the U.S. Congress to establish the Malcolm Baldrige National Quality Award—similar to the Deming Prize in Japan—in 1987 to recognize organizations for their achievements in quality and to raise awareness about the importance of quality excellence as a competitive edge [6]. In the Baldrige National Award, quality is viewed as something defined by the customer and thus the focus is on *customer-driven quality*. On the other hand, in the Deming Prize, quality is viewed as something defined by the producers by conforming to specifications and thus the focus is on *conformance to specifications*.

Remark: Malcolm Baldrige was U.S. Secretary of Commerce from 1981 until his death in a rodeo accident in July 1987. Baldrige was a proponent of quality management as a key to his country's prosperity and long-term strength. He took a personal interest in the quality improvement act, which was eventually named after him, and helped draft one of its early versions. In recognition of his contributions, Congress named the award in his honor.

Traditionally, the TQC and lean concepts are applied in the manufacturing process. The software development process uses these concepts as another tool to guide the production of quality software [13]. These concepts provides a framework to discuss software production issues. The software capability maturity model (CMM) [14] architecture developed at the Software Engineering Institute is based on the principles of product quality that have been developed by W. Edwards Deming [15], Joseph M. Juran [16], Kaoru Ishikawa [12], and Philip Crosby [17].

1.2 SOFTWARE QUALITY

The question "What is software quality?" evokes many different answers. Quality is a complex concept—it means different things to different people, and it is highly context dependent. Garvin [18] has analyzed how software quality is perceived in different ways in different domains, such as philosophy, economics, marketing, and management. Kitchenham and Pfleeger's article [60] on software quality gives a succinct exposition of software quality. They discuss five views of quality in a comprehensive manner as follows:

1. *Transcendental View:* It envisages quality as something that can be recognized but is difficult to define. The transcendental view is not specific to software quality alone but has been applied in other complex areas

of everyday life. For example, In 1964, Justice Potter Stewart of the U.S. Supreme Court, while ruling on the case *Jacobellis v. Ohio*, 378 U.S. 184 (1964), which involved the state of Ohio banning the French film *Les Amants* ("The Lovers") on the ground of pornography, wrote "I shall not today attempt further to define the kinds of material I understand to be embraced within that shorthand description; and perhaps I could never succeed in intelligibly doing so. But *I know it when I see it*, and the motion picture involved in this case is not that" (emphasis added).

2. *User View*: It perceives quality as fitness for purpose. According to this view, while evaluating the quality of a product, one must ask the key question: "Does the product satisfy user needs and expectations?"

3. *Manufacturing View*: Here quality is understood as conformance to the specification. The quality level of a product is determined by the extent to which the product meets its specifications.

4. *Product View*: In this case, quality is viewed as tied to the inherent characteristics of the product. A product's inherent characteristics, that is, internal qualities, determine its external qualities.

5. *Value-Based View*: Quality, in this perspective, depends on the amount a customer is willing to pay for it.

The concept of software quality and the efforts to understand it in terms of measurable quantities date back to the mid-1970s. McCall, Richards, and Walters [19] were the first to study the concept of software quality in terms of *quality factors* and *quality criteria*. A quality factor represents a behavioral characteristic of a system. Some examples of high-level quality factors are *correctness*, *reliability*, *efficiency*, *testability*, *maintainability*, and *reusability*. A quality criterion is an attribute of a quality factor that is related to software development. For example, modularity is an attribute of the architecture of a software system. A highly modular software allows designers to put cohesive components in one module, thereby improving the maintainability of the system.

Various software quality models have been proposed to define quality and its related attributes. The most influential ones are the ISO 9126 [20–22] and the CMM [14]. The ISO 9126 quality model was developed by an expert group under the aegis of the International Organization for Standardization (ISO). The document ISO 9126 defines six broad, independent categories of quality characteristics: *functionality, reliability, usability, efficiency, maintainability*, and *portability*. The CMM was developed by the Software Engineering Institute (SEI) at Carnegie Mellon University. In the CMM framework, a development process is evaluated on a scale of 1–5, commonly known as level 1 through level 5. For example, level 1 is called the initial level, whereas level 5—optimized—is the highest level of process maturity.

In the field of software testing, there are two well-known process models, namely, the test process improvement (TPI) model [23] and the test maturity Model (TMM) [24]. These two models allow an organization to assess the current state of their software testing processes, identify the next logical area for improvement, and recommend an action plan for test process improvement.

1.3 ROLE OF TESTING

Testing plays an important role in achieving and assessing the quality of a software product [25]. On the one hand, we improve the quality of the products as we repeat a *test–find defects–fix* cycle during development. On the other hand, we assess how good our system is when we perform system-level tests before releasing a product. Thus, as Friedman and Voas [26] have succinctly described, software testing is a verification process for software quality assessment and improvement. Generally speaking, the activities for software quality assessment can be divided into two broad categories, namely, *static analysis* and *dynamic analysis*.

- **Static Analysis:** As the term "static" suggests, it is based on the examination of a number of documents, namely requirements documents, software models, design documents, and source code. Traditional static analysis includes code review, inspection, walk-through, algorithm analysis, and proof of correctness. It does not involve actual execution of the code under development. Instead, it examines code and reasons over all possible behaviors that might arise during run time. Compiler optimizations are standard static analysis.
- **Dynamic Analysis:** Dynamic analysis of a software system involves actual program execution in order to expose possible program failures. The behavioral and performance properties of the program are also observed. Programs are executed with both typical and carefully chosen input values. Often, the input set of a program can be impractically large. However, for practical considerations, a finite subset of the input set can be selected. Therefore, in testing, we observe some representative program behaviors and reach a conclusion about the quality of the system. Careful selection of a finite test set is crucial to reaching a reliable conclusion.

By performing static and dynamic analyses, practitioners want to identify as many faults as possible so that those faults are fixed at an early stage of the software development. Static analysis and dynamic analysis are complementary in nature, and for better effectiveness, both must be performed repeatedly and alternated. Practitioners and researchers need to remove the boundaries between static and dynamic analysis and create a hybrid analysis that combines the strengths of both approaches [27].

1.4 VERIFICATION AND VALIDATION

Two similar concepts related to software testing frequently used by practitioners are *verification* and *validation*. Both concepts are abstract in nature, and each can be realized by a set of concrete, executable activities. The two concepts are explained as follows:

- **Verification:** This kind of activity helps us in evaluating a software system by determining whether the product of a given development phase satisfies the requirements established before the start of that phase. One may note that a product can be an intermediate product, such as requirement specification, design specification, code, user manual, or even the final product. Activities that check the correctness of a development phase are called *verification activities*.

- **Validation:** Activities of this kind help us in confirming that a product meets its intended *use*. Validation activities aim at confirming that a product meets its customer's expectations. In other words, validation activities focus on the final product, which is extensively tested from the customer point of view. Validation establishes whether the product meets overall expectations of the users.

    Late execution of validation activities is often risky by leading to higher development cost. Validation activities may be executed at early stages of the software development cycle [28]. An example of early execution of validation activities can be found in the eXtreme Programming (XP) software development methodology. In the XP methodology, the customer closely interacts with the software development group and conducts acceptance tests during each development iteration [29].

The verification process establishes the correspondence of an implementation phase of the software development process with its specification, whereas validation establishes the correspondence between a system and users' expectations. One can compare verification and validation as follows:

- Verification activities aim at confirming that one is *building the product correctly*, whereas validation activities aim at confirming that one is *building the correct product* [30].

- Verification activities review interim work products, such as requirements specification, design, code, and user manual, during a project life cycle to ensure their quality. The quality attributes sought by verification activities are consistency, completeness, and correctness at each major stage of system development. On the other hand, validation is performed toward the end of system development to determine if the entire system meets the customer's needs and expectations.

- Verification activities are performed on interim products by applying mostly static analysis techniques, such as inspection, walkthrough, and reviews, and using standards and checklists. Verification can also include dynamic analysis, such as actual program execution. On the other hand, validation is performed on the entire system by actually running the system in its real environment and using a variety of tests.

1.5 FAILURE, ERROR, FAULT, AND DEFECT

In the literature on software testing, one can find references to the terms *failure*, *error*, *fault*, and *defect*. Although their meanings are related, there are important distinctions between these four concepts. In the following, we present first three terms as they are understood in the fault-tolerant computing community:

- **Failure:** A failure is said to occur whenever the external behavior of a system does not conform to that prescribed in the system specification.

- **Error:** An error is a *state* of the system. In the absence of any corrective action by the system, an error state could lead to a failure which would not be attributed to any event subsequent to the error.

- **Fault:** A fault is the adjudged cause of an error.

A fault may remain undetected for a long time, until some event activates it. When an event activates a fault, it first brings the program into an intermediate error state. If computation is allowed to proceed from an error state without any corrective action, the program eventually causes a failure. As an aside, in fault-tolerant computing, corrective actions can be taken to take a program out of an error state into a desirable state such that subsequent computation does not eventually lead to a failure. The process of failure manifestation can therefore be succinctly represented as a behavior chain [31] as follows: fault → error → failure. The behavior chain can iterate for a while, that is, failure of one component can lead to a failure of another interacting component.

The above definition of failure assumes that the given specification is acceptable to the customer. However, if the specification does not meet the expectations of the customer, then, of course, even a fault-free implementation fails to satisfy the customer. It is a difficult task to give a precise definition of fault, error, or failure of software, because of the "human factor" involved in the overall acceptance of a system. In an article titled "What Is Software Failure" [32], Ram Chillarege commented that in modern software business software failure means "the customer's expectation has not been met and/or the customer is unable to do useful work with product," p. 354.

Roderick Rees [33] extended Chillarege's comments of software failure by pointing out that "failure is a matter of function only [and is thus] related to purpose, not to whether an item is physically intact or not" (p. 163). To substantiate this, Behrooz Parhami [34] provided three interesting examples to show the relevance of such a view point in wider context. One of the examples is quoted here (p. 451):

> Consider a small organization. *Defects* in the organization's staff promotion policies can cause improper promotions, viewed as *faults*. The resulting ineptitudes & dissatisfactions are *errors* in the organization's state. The organization's personnel or departments probably begin to *malfunction* as result of the errors, in turn causing an overall *degradation* of performance. The end result can be the organization's *failure* to achieve its goal.

There is a fine difference between defects and faults in the above example, that is, execution of a defective policy may lead to a faulty promotion. In a software context, a software system may be defective due to design issues; certain system states will expose a defect, resulting in the development of faults defined as incorrect signal values or decisions within the system. In industry, the term defect is widely used, whereas among researchers the term fault is more prevalent. For all practical purpose, the two terms are synonymous. In this book, we use the two terms interchangeably as required.

1.6 NOTION OF SOFTWARE RELIABILITY

No matter how many times we run the test–find faults–fix cycle during software development, some faults are likely to escape our attention, and these will eventually surface at the customer site. Therefore, a quantitative measure that is useful in assessing the quality of a software is its *reliability* [35]. *Software reliability* is defined as the probability of failure-free operation of a software system for a specified time in a specified environment. The level of reliability of a system depends on those inputs that cause failures to be observed by the end users. Software reliability can be estimated via *random testing*, as suggested by Hamlet [36]. Since the notion of reliability is specific to a "specified environment," test data must be drawn from the input distribution to closely resemble the future usage of the system. Capturing the future usage pattern of a system in a general sense is described in a form called the *operational profile*. The concept of operational profile of a system was pioneered by John D. Musa at AT&T Bell Laboratories between the 1970s and the 1990s [37, 38].

1.7 OBJECTIVES OF TESTING

The stakeholders in a test process are the programmers, the test engineers, the project managers, and the customers. A stakeholder is a person or an organization who influences a system's behaviors or who is impacted by that system [39]. Different stakeholders view a test process from different perspectives as explained below:

- **It does work:** While implementing a program unit, the programmer may want to test whether or not the unit works in normal circumstances. The programmer gets much confidence if the unit works to his or her satisfaction. The same idea applies to an entire system as well—once a system has been integrated, the developers may want to test whether or not the system performs the basic functions. Here, for the psychological reason, the objective of testing is to show that the system works, rather than it does not work.

- **It does not work:** Once the programmer (or the development team) is satisfied that a unit (or the system) works to a certain degree, more tests are conducted with the objective of finding faults in the unit (or the system). Here, the idea is to try to make the unit (or the system) fail.

- **Reduce the risk of failure:** Most of the complex software systems contain faults, which cause the system to fail from time to time. This concept of "failing from time to time" gives rise to the notion of *failure rate*. As faults are discovered and fixed while performing more and more tests, the failure rate of a system generally decreases. Thus, a higher level objective of performing tests is to bring down the risk of failing to an acceptable level.

- **Reduce the cost of testing:** The different kinds of costs associated with a test process include

    the cost of designing, maintaining, and executing test cases,

    the cost of analyzing the result of executing each test case,

    the cost of documenting the test cases, and

    the cost of actually executing the system and documenting it.

Therefore, the less the number of test cases designed, the less will be the associated cost of testing. However, producing a small number of arbitrary test cases is not a good way of saving cost. The highest level of objective of performing tests is to produce low-risk software with fewer number of test cases. This idea leads us to the concept of *effectiveness of test cases*. Test engineers must therefore judiciously select fewer, effective test cases.

1.8 WHAT IS A TEST CASE?

In its most basic form, a *test case* is a simple pair of < input, expected outcome >. If a program under test is expected to compute the square root of nonnegative numbers, then four examples of test cases are as shown in Figure 1.3.

In stateless systems, where the outcome depends solely on the current input, test cases are very simple in structure, as shown in Figure 1.3. A program to compute the square root of nonnegative numbers is an example of a stateless system. A compiler for the C programming language is another example of a stateless system. A compiler is a stateless system because to compile a program it does not need to know about the programs it compiled previously.

In state-oriented systems, where the program outcome depends both on the current state of the system and the current input, a test case may consist of a

TB_1:	< 0, 0 >,
TB_2:	< 25, 5 >,
TB_3:	< 40, 6.3245553 >,
TB_4:	< 100.5, 10.024968 >.

Figure 1.3 Examples of basic test cases.

TS$_1$: < check balance, $500.00 >, < withdraw, "amount?" >,
      < $200.00, "$200.00" >, < check balance, $300.00 > .

Figure 1.4 Example of a test case with a sequence of < input, expected outcome >.

sequence of < input, expected outcome > pairs. A telephone switching system and an automated teller machine (ATM) are examples of state-oriented systems. For an ATM machine, a test case for testing the *withdraw* function is shown in Figure 1.4. Here, we assume that the user has already entered validated inputs, such as the cash card and the personal identification number (PIN).

In the test case TS$_1$, "check balance" and "withdraw" in the first, second, and fourth tuples represent the pressing of the appropriate keys on the ATM keypad. It is assumed that the user account has $500.00 on it, and the user wants to withdraw an amount of $200.00. The expected outcome "$200.00" in the third tuple represents the cash dispensed by the ATM. After the withdrawal operation, the user makes sure that the remaining balance is $300.00.

For state-oriented systems, most of the test cases include some form of decision and timing in providing input to the system. A test case may include loops and timers, which we do not show at this moment.

1.9 EXPECTED OUTCOME

An *outcome* of program execution is a complex entity that may include the following:

- Values produced by the program:

    Outputs for local observation (integer, text, audio, image)

    Outputs (messages) for remote storage, manipulation, or observation

- State change:

    State change of the program

    State change of the database (due to add, delete, and update operations)

- A sequence or set of values which must be interpreted together for the outcome to be valid

An important concept in test design is the concept of an *oracle*. An oracle is any entity—program, process, human expert, or body of data—that tells us the expected outcome of a particular test or set of tests [40]. A test case is meaningful only if it is possible to decide on the acceptability of the result produced by the program under test.

Ideally, the expected outcome of a test should be computed while designing the test case. In other words, the test outcome is computed before the program is executed with the selected test input. The idea here is that one should be able to compute the expected outcome from an *understanding* of the program's requirements. Precomputation of the expected outcome will eliminate any implementation bias in case the test case is designed by the developer.

In exceptional cases, where it is extremely difficult, impossible, or even undesirable to compute a single expected outcome, one should identify expected outcomes by examining the actual test outcomes, as explained in the following:

1. Execute the program with the selected input.
2. Observe the actual outcome of program execution.
3. Verify that the actual outcome is the expected outcome.
4. Use the verified actual outcome as the expected outcome in subsequent runs of the test case.

1.10 CONCEPT OF *COMPLETE* TESTING

It is not unusual to find people making claims such as "I have exhaustively tested the program." Complete, or exhaustive, testing means *there are no undiscovered faults at the end of the test phase*. All problems must be known at the end of complete testing. For most of the systems, complete testing is near impossible because of the following reasons:

- The domain of possible inputs of a program is too large to be completely used in testing a system. There are both valid inputs and invalid inputs. The program may have a large number of states. There may be timing constraints on the inputs, that is, an input may be valid at a certain time and invalid at other times. An input value which is valid but is not properly timed is called an *inopportune* input. The input domain of a system can be very large to be completely used in testing a program.

- The design issues may be too complex to completely test. The design may have included implicit design decisions and assumptions. For example, a programmer may use a global variable or a *static* variable to control program execution.

- It may not be possible to create all possible execution environments of the system. This becomes more significant when the behavior of the software system depends on the real, outside world, such as weather, temperature, altitude, pressure, and so on.

1.11 CENTRAL ISSUE IN TESTING

We must realize that though the outcome of complete testing, that is, discovering all faults, is highly desirable, it is a near-impossible task, and it may not be attempted. The next best thing is to select a subset of the input domain to test a program.

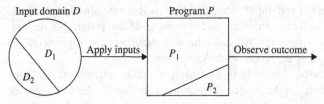

Figure 1.5 Subset of the input domain exercising a subset of the program behavior.

Referring to Figure 1.5, let D be the input domain of a program P. Suppose that we select a subset D_1 of D, that is, $D_1 \subset D$, to test program P. It is possible that D_1 exercises only a part P_1, that is, $P_1 \subset P$, of the *execution behavior* of P, in which case faults with the other part, P_2, will go undetected.

By selecting a subset of the input domain D_1, the test engineer attempts to deduce properties of an entire program P by observing the behavior of a part P_1 of the entire behavior of P on selected inputs D_1. Therefore, *selection* of the subset of the input domain must be done in a systematic and careful manner so that the deduction is as accurate and complete as possible. For example, the idea of *coverage* is considered while selecting test cases.

1.12   TESTING ACTIVITIES

In order to test a program, a test engineer must perform a sequence of testing activities. Most of these activities have been shown in Figure 1.6 and are explained in the following. These explanations focus on a single test case.

- **Identify an objective to be tested:** The first activity is to identify an *objective* to be tested. The objective defines the intention, or *purpose*, of designing one or more test cases to ensure that the program supports the objective. A clear purpose must be associated with every test case.

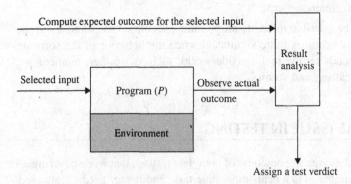

Figure 1.6 Different activities in program testing.

- **Select inputs:** The second activity is to select test inputs. Selection of test inputs can be based on the requirements specification, the source code, or our expectations. Test inputs are selected by keeping the test objective in mind.

- **Compute the expected outcome:** The third activity is to compute the expected outcome of the program with the selected inputs. In most cases, this can be done from an overall, high-level understanding of the test objective and the specification of the program under test.

- **Set up the execution environment of the program:** The fourth step is to prepare the right execution environment of the program. In this step all the assumptions external to the program must be satisfied. A few examples of assumptions external to a program are as follows:

  Initialize the local system, external to the program. This may include making a network connection available, making the right database system available, and so on.

  Initialize any remote, external system (e.g., remote partner process in a distributed application.) For example, to test the client code, we may need to start the server at a remote site.

- **Execute the program:** In the fifth step, the test engineer executes the program with the selected inputs and observes the actual outcome of the program. To execute a test case, inputs may be provided to the program at different physical locations at different times. The concept of *test coordination* is used in synchronizing different components of a test case.

- **Analyze the test result:** The final test activity is to analyze the result of test execution. Here, the main task is to compare the actual outcome of program execution with the expected outcome. The complexity of comparison depends on the complexity of the data to be observed. The observed data type can be as simple as an integer or a string of characters or as complex as an image, a video, or an audio clip. At the end of the analysis step, a test verdict is assigned to the program. There are three major kinds of test verdicts, namely, *pass*, *fail*, and *inconclusive*, as explained below.

  If the program produces the expected outcome and the purpose of the test case is satisfied, then a pass verdict is assigned.

  If the program does not produce the expected outcome, then a fail verdict is assigned.

  However, in some cases it may not be possible to assign a clear pass or fail verdict. For example, if a timeout occurs while executing a test case on a distributed application, we may not be in a position to assign a clear pass or fail verdict. In those cases, an inconclusive test verdict is assigned. An inconclusive test verdict means that further tests are needed to be done to refine the inconclusive verdict into a clear pass or fail verdict.

A *test report* must be written after analyzing the test result. The motivation for writing a test report is to get the fault fixed if the test revealed a fault. A test report contains the following items to be informative:

Explain how to reproduce the failure.

Analyze the failure to be able to describe it.

A pointer to the actual outcome and the test case, complete with the input, the expected outcome, and the execution environment.

1.13   TEST LEVELS

Testing is performed at different levels involving the complete system or parts of it throughout the life cycle of a software product. A software system goes through four stages of testing before it is actually deployed. These four stages are known as *unit*, *integration*, *system*, and *acceptance* level testing. The first three levels of testing are performed by a number of different stakeholders in the development organization, where as acceptance testing is performed by the customers. The four stages of testing have been illustrated in the form of what is called the classical V model in Figure 1.7.

In unit testing, programmers test individual program units, such as a procedures, functions, methods, or classes, in isolation. After ensuring that individual units work to a satisfactory extent, modules are assembled to construct larger subsystems by following integration testing techniques. Integration testing is jointly performed by software developers and integration test engineers. The objective of

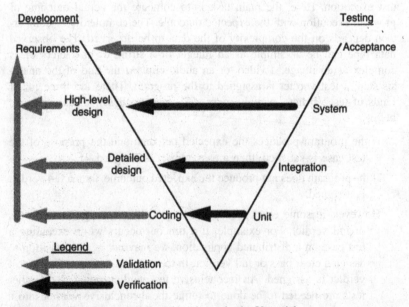

Figure 1.7   Development and testing phases in the V model.

integration testing is to construct a reasonably stable system that can withstand the rigor of system-level testing. System-level testing includes a wide spectrum of testing, such as functionality testing, security testing, robustness testing, load testing, stability testing, stress testing, performance testing, and reliability testing. System testing is a critical phase in a software development process because of the need to meet a tight schedule close to delivery date, to discover most of the faults, and to verify that fixes are working and have not resulted in new faults. System testing comprises a number of distinct activities: creating a test plan, designing a test suite, preparing test environments, executing the tests by following a clear strategy, and monitoring the process of test execution.

Regression testing is another level of testing that is performed throughout the life cycle of a system. Regression testing is performed whenever a component of the system is modified. The key idea in regression testing is to ascertain that the modification has not introduced any new faults in the portion that was not subject to modification. To be precise, regression testing is not a distinct level of testing. Rather, it is considered as a subphase of unit, integration, and system-level testing, as illustrated in Figure 1.8 [41].

In regression testing, new tests are not designed. Instead, tests are selected, prioritized, and executed from the existing pool of test cases to ensure that nothing is broken in the new version of the software. Regression testing is an expensive process and accounts for a predominant portion of testing effort in the industry. It is desirable to select a subset of the test cases from the existing pool to reduce the cost. A key question is how many and which test cases should be selected so that the selected test cases are more likely to uncover new faults [42–44].

After the completion of system-level testing, the product is delivered to the customer. The customer performs their own series of tests, commonly known as *acceptance testing*. The objective of acceptance testing is to measure the quality of the product, rather than searching for the defects, which is objective of system testing. A key notion in acceptance testing is the customer's *expectations* from the system. By the time of acceptance testing, the customer should have developed their acceptance criteria based on their own expectations from the system. There are two kinds of acceptance testing as explained in the following:

- User acceptance testing (UAT)
- Business acceptance testing (BAT)

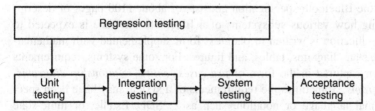

Figure 1.8 Regression testing at different software testing levels. (From ref. 41. © 2005 John Wiley & Sons.)

User acceptance testing is conducted by the customer to ensure that the system satisfies the contractual acceptance criteria before being signed off as meeting user needs. On the other hand, BAT is undertaken within the supplier's development organization. The idea in having a BAT is to ensure that the system will eventually pass the user acceptance test. It is a rehearsal of UAT at the supplier's premises.

1.14   SOURCES OF INFORMATION FOR TEST CASE SELECTION

Designing test cases has continued to stay in the foci of the research community and the practitioners. A software development process generates a large body of information, such as requirements specification, design document, and source code. In order to generate effective tests at a lower cost, test designers analyze the following sources of information:

- Requirements and functional specifications
- Source code
- Input and output domains
- Operational profile
- Fault model

Requirements and Functional Specifications   The process of software development begins by capturing user needs. The nature and amount of user needs identified at the beginning of system development will vary depending on the specific life-cycle model to be followed. Let us consider a few examples. In the Waterfall model [45] of software development, a requirements engineer tries to capture most of the requirements. On the other hand, in an agile software development model, such as XP [29] or the Scrum [46–48], only a few requirements are identified in the beginning. A test engineer considers all the requirements the program is expected to meet whichever life-cycle model is chosen to test a program.

The requirements might have been specified in an informal manner, such as a combination of plaintext, equations, figures, and flowcharts. Though this form of requirements specification may be ambiguous, it is easily understood by customers. For example, the Bluetooth specification consists of about 1100 pages of descriptions explaining how various subsystems of a Bluetooth interface is expected to work. The specification is written in plaintext form supplemented with mathematical equations, state diagrams, tables, and figures. For some systems, requirements may have been captured in the form of *use cases*, *entity–relationship diagrams*, and *class diagrams*. Sometimes the requirements of a system may have been specified in a formal language or notation, such as Z, SDL, Estelle, or finite-state machine. Both the informal and formal specifications are prime sources of test cases [49].

Source Code Whereas a requirements specification describes the *intended behavior* of a system, the source code describes the *actual behavior* of the system. High-level assumptions and constraints take concrete form in an implementation. Though a software designer may produce a detailed design, programmers may introduce additional details into the system. For example, a step in the detailed design can be "sort array A." To sort an array, there are many sorting algorithms with different characteristics, such as iteration, recursion, and temporarily using another array. Therefore, test cases must be designed based on the program [50].

Input and Output Domains Some values in the input domain of a program have special meanings, and hence must be treated separately [5]. To illustrate this point, let us consider the *factorial* function. The factorial of a nonnegative integer n is computed as follows:

```
factorial(0) = 1;
factorial(1) = 1;
factorial(n) = n * factorial(n-1);
```

A programmer may wrongly implement the factorial function as

```
factorial(n) = 1 * 2 * ... * n;
```

without considering the special case of $n = 0$. The above wrong implementation will produce the correct result for all positive values of n, but will fail for $n = 0$.

Sometimes even some output values have special meanings, and a program must be tested to ensure that it produces the special values for all possible causes. In the above example, the output value 1 has special significance: (i) it is the minimum value computed by the factorial function and (ii) it is the only value produced for two different inputs.

In the integer domain, the values 0 and 1 exhibit special characteristics if arithmetic operations are performed. These characteristics are $0 \times x = 0$ and $1 \times x = x$ for all values of x. Therefore, all the special values in the input and output domains of a program must be considered while testing the program.

Operational Profile As the term suggests, an *operational profile* is a quantitative characterization of how a system will be used. It was created to guide test engineers in selecting test cases (inputs) using samples of system usage. The notion of operational profiles, or *usage profiles*, was developed by Mills et al. [52] at IBM in the context of Cleanroom Software Engineering and by Musa [37] at AT&T Bell Laboratories to help develop software systems with better reliability. The idea is to infer, from the observed test results, the future reliability of the software when it is in actual use. To do this, test inputs are assigned a probability distribution, or profile, according to their occurrences in actual operation. The ways test engineers assign probability and select test cases to operate a system may significantly differ from the ways actual users operate a system. However, for accurate estimation of the reliability of a system it is important to test a system by considering the ways it will actually be used in the field. This concept is being used to test web applications, where the user session data are collected from the web servers to select test cases [53, 54].

Fault Model Previously encountered faults are an excellent source of information in designing new test cases. The known faults are classified into different classes, such as initialization faults, logic faults, and interface faults, and stored in a repository [55, 56]. Test engineers can use these data in designing tests to ensure that a particular class of faults is not resident in the program.

There are three types of fault-based testing: error guessing, fault seeding, and mutation analysis. In error guessing, a test engineer applies his experience to (i) assess the situation and guess where and what kinds of faults might exist, and (ii) design tests to specifically expose those kinds of faults. In fault seeding, known faults are injected into a program, and the test suite is executed to assess the effectiveness of the test suite. Fault seeding makes an assumption that a test suite that finds seeded faults is also likely to find other faults. Mutation analysis is similar to fault seeding, except that mutations to program statements are made in order to determine the fault detection capability of the test suite. If the test cases are not capable of revealing such faults, the test engineer may specify additional test cases to reveal the faults. Mutation testing is based on the idea of fault simulation, whereas fault seeding is based on the idea of fault injection. In the fault injection approach, a fault is inserted into a program, and an oracle is available to assert that the inserted fault indeed made the program incorrect. On the other hand, in fault simulation, a program modification is not guaranteed to lead to a faulty program. In fault simulation, one may modify an incorrect program and turn it into a correct program.

1.15 WHITE-BOX AND BLACK-BOX TESTING

A key idea in Section 1.14 was that test cases need to be designed by considering information from several sources, such as the specification, source code, and special properties of the program's input and output domains. This is because all those sources provide complementary information to test designers. Two broad concepts in testing, based on the sources of information for test design, are *white-box* and *black-box* testing. White-box testing techniques are also called *structural testing* techniques, whereas black-box testing techniques are called *functional testing* techniques.

In structural testing, one primarily examines *source code* with a focus on control flow and data flow. Control flow refers to flow of control from one instruction to another. Control passes from one instruction to another instruction in a number of ways, such as one instruction appearing after another, function call, message passing, and interrupts. Conditional statements alter the normal, sequential flow of control in a program. Data flow refers to the propagation of values from one variable or constant to another variable. Definitions and uses of variables determine the data flow aspect in a program.

In functional testing, one does not have access to the internal details of a program and the program is treated as a black box. A test engineer is concerned only with the part that is accessible outside the program, that is, just the input and the externally visible outcome. A test engineer applies input to a program, observes the externally visible outcome of the program, and determines whether or not the program outcome is the expected outcome. Inputs are selected from the program's requirements specification and properties of the program's input and output domains. A test engineer is concerned only with the functionality and the features found in the program's specification.

At this point it is useful to identify a distinction between the scopes of structural testing and functional testing. One applies structural testing techniques to individual units of a program, whereas functional testing techniques can be applied to both an entire system and the individual program units. Since individual programmers know the details of the source code they write, they themselves perform structural testing on the individual program units they write. On the other hand, functional testing is performed at the external interface level of a system, and it is conducted by a separate software quality assurance group.

Let us consider a program unit U which is a part of a larger program P. A program unit is just a piece of source code with a well-defined objective and well-defined input and output domains. Now, if a programmer derives test cases for testing U from a knowledge of the internal details of U, then the programmer is said to be performing structural testing. On the other hand, if the programmer designs test cases from the stated objective of the unit U and from his or her knowledge of the special properties of the input and output domains of U, then he or she is said to be performing functional testing on the same unit U.

The ideas of structural testing and functional testing do not give programmers and test engineers a choice of whether to design test cases from the source code or from the requirements specification of a program. However, these strategies are used by different groups of people at different times during a software's life cycle. For example, individual programmers use both the structural and functional testing techniques to test their own code, whereas quality assurance engineers apply the idea of functional testing.

Neither structural testing nor functional testing is by itself good enough to detect most of the faults. Even if one selects all possible inputs, a structural testing technique cannot detect all faults if there are *missing paths* in a program. Intuitively, a path is said to be missing if there is no code to handle a possible condition. Similarly, without knowledge of the structural details of a program, many faults will go undetected. Therefore, a combination of both structural and functional testing techniques must be used in program testing.

1.16   TEST PLANNING AND DESIGN

The purpose of system test planning, or simply test planning, is to get ready and organized for test execution. A test plan provides a framework, scope, details of resource needed, effort required, schedule of activities, and a budget. A framework is a set of ideas, facts, or circumstances within which the tests will be conducted. The stated scope outlines the domain, or extent, of the test activities. The scope covers the managerial aspects of testing, rather than the detailed techniques and specific test cases.

Test design is a critical phase of software testing. During the test design phase, the system requirements are critically studied, system features to be tested are thoroughly identified, and the objectives of test cases and the detailed behavior of test cases are defined. Test objectives are identified from different sources, namely, the requirement specification and the functional specification, and one or more test cases are designed for each test objective. Each test case is designed as a combination of modular test components called *test steps*. These test steps can be combined together to create more complex, multistep tests. A test case is clearly specified so that others can easily borrow, understand, and reuse it.

It is interesting to note that a new test-centric approach to system development is gradually emerging. This approach is called test-driven development (TDD) [57]. In test-driven development, programmers design and implement test cases before the production code is written. This approach is a key practice in modern agile software development processes such as XP. The main characteristics of agile software development processes are (i) incremental development, (ii) coding of unit and acceptance tests conducted by the programmers along with customers, (iii) frequent regression testing, and (iv) writing test code, one test case at a time, before the production code.

1.17 MONITORING AND MEASURING TEST EXECUTION

Monitoring and measurement are two key principles followed in every scientific and engineering endeavor. The same principles are also applicable to the testing phases of software development. It is important to monitor certain metrics which truly represent the progress of testing and reveal the quality level of the system. Based on those metrics, the management can trigger corrective and preventive actions. By putting a small but critical set of metrics in place the executive management will be able to know whether they are on the right track [58]. Test execution metrics can be broadly categorized into two classes as follows:

- Metrics for monitoring test execution
- Metrics for monitoring defects

The first class of metrics concerns the process of executing test cases, whereas the second class concerns the defects found as a result of test execution. These metrics need to be tracked and analyzed on a periodic basis, say, daily or weekly. In order to effectively control a test project, it is important to gather valid and accurate information about the project. One such example is to precisely know when to trigger revert criteria for a test cycle and initiate root cause analysis of the problems before more tests can be performed. By triggering such a revert criteria, a test manager can effectively utilize the time of test engineers, and possibly money, by suspending a test cycle on a product with too many defects to carry out a meaningful system test. A management team must identify and monitor metrics while testing is in progress so that important decisions can be made [59]. It is important to analyze and understand the test metrics, rather than just collect data and make decisions based on those raw data. Metrics are meaningful only if they enable the management to make decisions which result in lower cost of production, reduced delay in delivery, and improved quality of software systems.

Quantitative evaluation is important in every scientific and engineering field. Quantitative evaluation is carried out through measurement. Measurement lets one evaluate parameters of interest in a quantitative manner as follows:

- Evaluate the effectiveness of a technique used in performing a task. One can evaluate the effectiveness of a test generation technique by counting the number of defects detected by test cases generated by following the technique and those detected by test cases generated by other means.

- Evaluate the productivity of the development activities. One can keep track of productivity by counting the number of test cases designed per day, the number of test cases executed per day, and so on.

- Evaluate the quality of the product. By monitoring the number of defects detected per week of testing, one can observe the quality level of the system.

- Evaluate the product testing. For evaluating a product testing process, the following two measurements are critical:

    Test case effectiveness metric: The objective of this metric is twofold as explained in what follows: (1) measure the "defect revealing ability" of the test suite and (2) use the metric to improve the test design process. During the unit, integration, and system testing phases, faults are revealed by executing the planned test cases. In addition to these faults, new faults are also found during a testing phase for which no test cases had been designed. For these new faults, new test cases are added to the test suite. Those new test cases are called test case escaped (TCE). Test escapes occur because of deficiencies in test design. The need for more testing occurs as test engineers get new ideas while executing the planned test cases.

    Test effort effectiveness metric: It is important to evaluate the effectiveness of the testing effort in the development of a product. After a product is deployed at the customer's site, one is interested to know the effectiveness of testing that was performed. A common measure of test effectiveness is the number of defects found by the customers that were not found by the test engineers prior to the release of the product. These defects had escaped our test effort.

1.18   TEST TOOLS AND AUTOMATION

In general, software testing is a highly labor intensive task. This is because test cases are to a great extent manually generated and often manually executed. Moreover, the results of test executions are manually analyzed. The durations of those tasks can be shortened by using appropriate tools. A test engineer can use a variety of tools, such as a *static code analyzer*, a *test data generator*, and a *network analyzer*, if a network-based application or protocol is under test. Those tools are useful in increasing the efficiency and effectiveness of testing.

Test automation is essential for any testing and quality assurance division of an organization to move forward to become more efficient. The benefits of test automation are as follows:

- Increased productivity of the testers
- Better coverage of regression testing
- Reduced durations of the testing phases
- Reduced cost of software maintenance
- Increased effectiveness of test cases

Test automation provides an opportunity to improve the skills of the test engineers by writing programs, and hence their morale. They will be more focused on developing automated test cases to avoid being a bottleneck in product delivery to the market. Consequently, software testing becomes less of a tedious job.

Test automation improves the coverage of regression testing because of accumulation of automated test cases over time. Automation allows an organization to create a rich library of reusable test cases and facilitates the execution of a consistent set of test cases. Here consistency means our ability to produce repeated results for the same set of tests. It may be very difficult to reproduce test results in manual testing, because exact conditions at the time and point of failure may not be precisely known. In automated testing it is easier to set up the initial conditions of a system, thereby making it easier to reproduce test results. Test automation simplifies the debugging work by providing a detailed, unambiguous log of activities and intermediate test steps. This leads to a more organized, structured, and reproducible testing approach.

Automated execution of test cases reduces the elapsed time for testing, and, thus, it leads to a shorter time to market. The same automated test cases can be executed in an unsupervised manner at night, thereby efficiently utilizing the different platforms, such as hardware and configuration. In short, automation increases test execution efficiency. However, at the end of test execution, it is important to analyze the test results to determine the number of test cases that passed or failed. And, if a test case failed, one analyzes the reasons for its failure.

In the long run, test automation is cost-effective. It drastically reduces the software maintenance cost. In the sustaining phase of a software system, the regression tests required after each change to the system are too many. As a result, regression testing becomes too time and labor intensive without automation.

A repetitive type of testing is very cumbersome and expensive to perform manually, but it can be automated easily using software tools. A simple repetitive type of application can reveal memory leaks in a software. However, the application has to be run for a significantly long duration, say, for weeks, to reveal memory leaks. Therefore, manual testing may not be justified, whereas with automation it is easy to reveal memory leaks. For example, stress testing is a prime candidate for automation. Stress testing requires a worst-case load for an extended period of time, which is very difficult to realize by manual means. Scalability testing is another area that can be automated. Instead of creating a large test bed with hundreds of equipment, one can develop a simulator to verify the scalability of the system.

Test automation is very attractive, but it comes with a price tag. Sufficient time and resources need to be allocated for the development of an automated test suite. Development of automated test cases need to be managed like a programming project. That is, it should be done in an organized manner; otherwise it is highly likely to fail. An automated test suite may take longer to develop because the test suite needs to be debugged before it can be used for testing. Sufficient time and resources need to be allocated for maintaining an automated test suite and setting up a test environment. Moreover, every time the system is modified, the modification must be reflected in the automated test suite. Therefore, an automated test suite should be designed as a modular system, coordinated into reusable libraries, and cross-referenced and traceable back to the feature being tested.

It is important to remember that test automation cannot replace manual testing. Human creativity, variability, and observability cannot be mimicked through automation. Automation cannot detect some problems that can be easily observed by a human being. Automated testing does not introduce minor variations the way a human can. Certain categories of tests, such as usability, interoperability, robustness, and compatibility, are often not suited for automation. It is too difficult to automate all the test cases; usually 50% of all the system-level test cases can be automated. There will always be a need for some manual testing, even if all the system-level test cases are automated.

The objective of test automation is not to reduce the head counts in the testing department of an organization, but to improve the productivity, quality, and efficiency of test execution. In fact, test automation requires a larger head count in the testing department in the first year, because the department needs to automate the test cases and simultaneously continue the execution of manual tests. Even after the completion of the development of a test automation framework and test case libraries, the head count in the testing department does not drop below its original level. The test organization needs to retain the original team members in order to improve the quality by adding more test cases to the automated test case repository.

Before a test automation project can proceed, the organization must assess and address a number of considerations. The following list of prerequisites must be considered for an assessment of whether the organization is ready for test automation:

- The test cases to be automated are well defined.
- Test tools and an infrastructure are in place.

- The test automation professionals have prior successful experience in automation.

- Adequate budget should have been allocated for the procurement of software tools.

1.19   TEST TEAM ORGANIZATION AND MANAGEMENT

Testing is a distributed activity conducted at different levels throughout the life cycle of a software. These different levels are unit testing, integration testing, system testing, and acceptance testing. It is logical to have different testing groups in an organization for each level of testing. However, it is more logical—and is the case in reality—that unit-level tests be developed and executed by the programmers themselves rather than an independent group of unit test engineers. The programmer who develops a software unit should take the ownership and responsibility of producing good-quality software to his or her satisfaction. System integration testing is performed by the system integration test engineers. The integration test engineers involved need to know the software modules very well. This means that all development engineers who collectively built all the units being integrated need to be involved in integration testing. Also, the integration test engineers should thoroughly know the build mechanism, which is key to integrating large systems.

A team for performing system-level testing is truly separated from the development team, and it usually has a separate head count and a separate budget. The mandate of this group is to ensure that the system requirements have been met and the system is acceptable. Members of the system test group conduct different categories of tests, such as functionality, robustness, stress, load, scalability, reliability, and performance. They also execute business acceptance tests identified in the user acceptance test plan to ensure that the system will eventually pass user acceptance testing at the customer site. However, the real user acceptance testing is executed by the client's special user group. The user group consists of people from different backgrounds, such as software quality assurance engineers, business associates, and customer support engineers. It is a common practice to create a temporary user acceptance test group consisting of people with different backgrounds, such as integration test engineers, system test engineers, customer support engineers, and marketing engineers. Once the user acceptance is completed, the group is dismantled. It is recommended to have at least two test groups in an organization: integration test group and system test group.

Hiring and retaining test engineers are challenging tasks. Interview is the primary mechanism for evaluating applicants. Interviewing is a skill that improves with practice. It is necessary to have a recruiting process in place in order to be effective in hiring excellent test engineers. In order to retain test engineers, the management must recognize the importance of testing efforts at par with development efforts. The management should treat the test engineers as professionals and as a part of the overall team that delivers quality products.

1.20   OUTLINE OF BOOK

With the above high-level introduction to quality and software testing, we are now in a position to outline the remaining chapters. Each chapter in the book covers technical, process, and/or managerial topics related to software testing. The topics have been designed and organized to facilitate the reader to become a software test specialist. In Chapter 2 we provide a self-contained introduction to the theory and limitations of software testing.

Chapters 3–6 treat unit testing techniques one by one, as quantitatively as possible. These chapters describe both static and dynamic unit testing. Static unit testing has been presented within a general framework called *code review*, rather than individual techniques called *inspection* and *walkthrough*. Dynamic unit testing, or execution-based unit testing, focuses on control flow, data flow, and domain testing. The JUnit framework, which is used to create and execute dynamic unit tests, is introduced. We discuss some tools for effectively performing unit testing.

Chapter 7 discusses the concept of integration testing. Specifically, five kinds of integration techniques, namely, top down, bottom up, sandwich, big bang, and incremental, are explained. Next, we discuss the integration of hardware and software components to form a complete system. We introduce a framework to develop a plan for system integration testing. The chapter is completed with a brief discussion of integration testing of off-the-shelf components.

Chapters 8–13 discuss various aspects of system-level testing. These six chapters introduce the reader to the technical details of system testing that is the practice in industry. These chapters promote both qualitative and quantitative evaluation of a system testing process. The chapters emphasize the need for having an independent system testing group. A process for monitoring and controlling system testing is clearly explained. Chapter 14 is devoted to acceptance testing, which includes acceptance testing criteria, planning for acceptance testing, and acceptance test execution.

Chapter 15 contains the fundamental concepts of software reliability and their application to software testing. We discuss the notion of *operation profile* and its application in system testing. We conclude the chapter with the description of an example and the time of releasing a system by determining the additional length of system testing. The additional testing time is calculated by using the idea of software reliability.

In Chapter 16, we present the structure of test groups and how these groups can be organized in a software company. Next, we discuss how to hire and retain test engineers by providing training, instituting a reward system, and establishing an attractive career path for them within the testing organization. We conclude this chapter with the description of how to build and manage a test team with a focus on teamwork rather than individual gain.

Chapters 17 and 18 explain the concepts of software quality and different maturity models. Chapter 17 focuses on quality factors and criteria and describes the ISO 9126 and ISO 9000:2000 standards. Chapter 18 covers the CMM, which was developed by the SEI at Carnegie Mellon University. Two test-related models, namely the TPI model and the TMM, are explained at the end of Chapter 18.

We define the key words used in the book in a glossary at the end of the book. The reader will find about 10 practice exercises at the end of each chapter. A list of references is included at the end of each chapter for a reader who would like to find more detailed discussions of some of the topics. Finally, each chapter, except this one, contains a literature review section that, essentially, provides pointers to more advanced material related to the topics. The more advanced materials are based on current research and alternate viewpoints.

REFERENCES

1. B. Davis, C. Skube, L. Hellervik, S. Gebelein, and J. Sheard. *Successful Manager's Handbook*. Personnel Decisions International, Minneapolis, 1996.
2. M. Walton. *The Deming Management Method*. The Berkley Publishing Group, New York, 1986.
3. W. E. Deming. Transcript of Speech to GAO Roundtable on Product Quality—Japan vs. the United States. *Quality Progress*, March 1994, pp. 39–44.
4. W. A. Shewhart. *Economic Control of Quality of Manufactured Product*. Van Nostrand, New York, 1931.
5. W. A. Shewhart. The Application of Statistics as an Aid in Maintaining Quality of a Manufactured Product. *Journal of American Statistical Association*, December 1925, pp. 546–548.
6. National Institute of Standards and Technology, *Baldridge National Quality Program*, 2008. Available: http://www.quality.nist.gov/.
7. J. Liker and D. Meier. *The Toyota Way Fieldbook*. McGraw-Hill, New York, 2005.
8. M. Poppendieck and T. Poppendieck. *Implementing Lean Software Development: From Concept to Cash*. Addison-Wesley, Reading, MA, 2006.
9. A. B. Godfrey and A. I. C. Endres. The Evolution of Quality Management Within Telecommunications. *IEEE Communications Magazine*, October 1994, pp. 26–34.
10. M. Pecht and W. R. Boulton. *Quality Assurance and Reliability in the Japanese Electronics Industry*. Japanses Technology Evaluation Center (JTEC), Report on Electronic Manufacturing and Packaging in Japan, W. R. Boulton, Ed. International Technology Research Institute at Loyola College, February 1995, pp. 115–126.
11. A. V. Feigenbaum. *Total Quality Control*, 4th ed. McGraw-Hill, New York, 2004.
12. K. Ishikawa. *What Is Total Quality Control*. Prentice-Hall, Englewood Cliffs, NJ, 1985.
13. A. Cockburn. What Engineering Has in Common With Manufacturing and Why It Matters. *Crosstalk, the Journal of Defense Software Engineering*, April 2007, pp. 4–7.
14. S. Land. *Jumpstart CMM/CMMI Software Process Improvement*. Wiley, Hoboken, NJ, 2005.
15. W. E. Deming. *Out of the Crisis*. MIT, Cambridge, MA, 1986.
16. J. M. Juran and A. B. Godfrey. *Juran's Quality Handbook*, 5th ed. McGraw-Hill, New York, 1998.
17. P. Crosby. *Quality Is Free*. New American Library, New York, 1979.
18. D. A. Garvin. What Does "Product Quality" Really Mean? *Sloan Management Review*, Fall 1984, pp. 25–43.
19. J. A. McCall, P. K. Richards, and G. F. Walters. Factors in Software Quality, Technical Report RADC-TR-77-369. U.S. Department of Commerce, Washington, DC, 1977.
20. International Organization for Standardization (ISO). Quality Management Systems—Fundamentals and Vocabulary, ISO 9000:2000. ISO, Geneva, December 2000.
21. International Organization for Standardization (ISO). Quality Management Systems—Guidelines for Performance Improvements, ISO 9004:2000. ISO, Geneva, December 2000.
22. International Organization for Standardization (ISO). Quality Management Systems—Requirements, ISO 9001:2000. ISO, Geneva, December 2000.
23. T. Koomen and M. Pol. *Test Process Improvement*. Addison-Wesley, Reading, MA, 1999.

24. I. Burnstein. *Practical Software Testing*. Springer, New York, 2003.

25. L. Osterweil et al. Strategic Directions in Software Quality. *ACM Computing Surveys*, December 1996, pp. 738–750.

26. M. A. Friedman and J. M. Voas. *Software Assessment: Reliability, Safety, Testability*. Wiley, New York, 1995.

27. Michael D. Ernst. Static and Dynamic Analysis: Synergy and Duality. Paper presented at ICSE Workshop on Dynamic Analysis, Portland, OR, May 2003, pp. 24–27.

28. L. Baresi and M. Pezzè. *An Introduction to Software Testing*, Electronic Notes in Theoretical Computer Science. Elsevier, Vol. 148, Feb. 2006, pp. 89–111.

29. K. Beck and C. Andres. *Extreme Programming Explained: Embrace Change*, 2nd ed. Addison-Wesley, Reading, MA, 2004.

30. B. W. Boehm. *Software Engineering Economics*. Prentice-Hall, Englewood Cliffs, NJ, 1981.

31. J. C. Laprie. Dependability—Its Attributes, Impairments and Means. In *Predictably Dependable Computing Systems*, B. Randall, J. C. Laprie, H. Kopetz, and B. Littlewood, Eds. Springer-Verlag, New York, 1995.

32. R. Chillarege. What Is Software Failure. *IEEE Transactions on Reliability*, September 1996, pp. 354–355.

33. R. Rees. What Is a Failure. *IEEE Transactions on Reliability*, June 1997, p. 163.

34. B. Parhami. Defect, Fault, Error, . . . , or Failure. *IEEE Transactions on Reliability*, December 1997, pp. 450–451.

35. M. R. Lyu. *Handbook of Software Reliability Engineering*. McGraw-Hill, New York, 1995.

36. R. Hamlet. Random Testing. In *Encyclopedia of Software Engineering*, J. Marciniak, Ed. Wiley, New York, 1994, pp. 970–978.

37. J. D. Musa. Software Reliability Engineering. *IEEE Software*, March 1993, pp. 14–32.

38. J. D. Musa. A Theory of Software Reliability and Its Application. *IEEE Transactions on Software Engineering*, September 1975, pp. 312–327.

39. M. Glinz and R. J. Wieringa. Stakeholders in Requirements Engineering. *IEEE Software*, March–April 2007, pp. 18–20.

40. A. Bertolino and L. Strigini. On the Use of Testability Measures for Dependability Assessment. *IEEE Transactions on Software Engineering*, February 1996, pp. 97–108.

41. A. Bertolino and E Marchelli. *A Brief Essay on Software Testing*. In *Software Engineering, Vol. 1, The Development Process*, 3rd ed., R. H. Thayer and M. J. Christensen, Eds. Wiley–IEEE Computer Society Press, Hoboken, NJ, 2005.

42. D. Jeffrey and N. Gupta. Improving Fault Detection Capability by Selectively Retaining Test Cases during Test Suite Reduction. *IEEE Transactions on Software Engineering*, February 2007, pp. 108–123.

43. Z. Li, M. Harman, and R. M. Hierons. Search Algorithms for Regression Test Case Prioritization. *IEEE Transactions on Software Engineering*, April 2007, pp. 225–237.

44. W. Masri, A. Podgurski, and D. Leon. An Empirical Study of Test Case Filtering Techniques Based on Exercising Information Flows. *IEEE Transactions on Software Engineering*, July 2007, pp. 454–477.

45. W. W. Royce. Managing the Development of Large Software Systems: Concepts and Techniques. In *Proceedings of IEEE WESCON*, August 1970, pp. 1–9. Republished in ICSE, Monterey, 1987, pp. 328–338.

46. L. Rising and N. S. Janoff. The Scrum Software Development Process for Small Teams. *IEEE Software*, July/August 2000, pp. 2–8.

47. K. Schwaber. *Agile Project Management with Scrum*. Microsoft Press, Redmond, WA, 2004.

48. H. Takeuchi and I. Nonaka. The New Product Development Game. *Harvard Business Review*, Boston, January-February 1986, pp. 1–11.

49. A. P. Mathur. *Foundation of Software Testing*. Pearson Education, New Delhi, 2007.

50. P. Ammann and J. Offutt. *Introduction to Software Testing*. Cambridge University Press, 2008.

51. M. Pezzè and M. Young. *Software Testing and Analysis: Process, Principles, and Techniques*. Wiley, Hoboken, NJ, 2007.

52. H. D. Mills, M. Dyer, and R. C. Linger. Cleanroom Software Engineering. *IEEE Software*, September 1987, pp. 19–24.

53. S. Elbaum, G. Rothermel, S. Karre, and M. Fisher II. Leveraging User Session Data to Support Web Application Testing. *IEEE Transactions on Software Engineering*, March 2005, pp. 187–202.

54. S. Sampath, S. Sprenkle, E. Gibson, L. Pollock, and A. S. Greenwald. Applying Concept Analysis to User-Session-Based Testing of Web Applications. *IEEE Transactions on Software Engineering*, October 2007, pp. 643–657.

55. A. Endress. An Analysis of Errors and Their Causes in System Programs. *IEEE Transactions on Software Engineering*, June 1975, pp. 140–149.

56. T. J. Ostrand and E. J. Weyuker. Collecting and Categorizing Software Error Data in an Industrial Environment. *Journal of Systems and Software*, November 1984, pp. 289–300.

57. K. Beck. *Test-Driven Development*. Addison-Wesley, Reading, MA, 2003.

58. D. Lemont. *CEO Discussion—From Start-up to Market Leader—Breakthrough Milestones*. Ernst and Young Milestones, Boston, May 2004, pp. 9–11.

59. G. Stark, R. C. Durst, and C. W. Vowell. Using Metrics in Management Decision Making. *IEEE Computer*, September 1994, pp. 42–48.

60. B. Kitchenham and S. L. Pfleeger. Software Quality: The Elusive Target. *IEEE Software*, January 1996, pp. 12–21.

61. J. Kilpatrick. Lean Principles. http://www.mep.org/textfiles/LeanPrinciples.pdf, 2003, pp. 1–5.

Exercises

1. Explain the principles of statistical quality control. What are the tools used for this purpose? Explain the principle of a control chart.

2. Explain the concept of lean principles.

3. What is an "Ishikawa" diagram? When should the Ishikawa diagram be used? Provide a procedure to construct an Ishikawa diagram.

4. What is total quality management (TQM)? What is the difference between TQM and TQC?

5. Explain the differences between *validation* and *verification*.

6. Explain the differences between *failure, error*, and *fault*.

7. What is a test case? What are the objectives of testing?

8. Explain the concepts of *unit, integration, system, acceptance*, and *regression* testing.

9. What are the different sources from which test cases can be selected?

10. What is the difference between *fault injection* and *fault simulation*?

11. Explain the differences between *structural* and *functional* testing.

12. What are the strengths and weaknesses of automated testing and manual testing?

CHAPTER 2

Theory of Program Testing

He who loves practice without theory is like the sailor who boards [a] ship without a rudder and compass and never knows where he may cast.
— *Leonardo da Vinci*

2.1 BASIC CONCEPTS IN TESTING THEORY

The idea of program testing is as old as computer programming. As computer programs got larger and larger since their early days in the 1960s, the need for eliminating defects from them in a systematic manner received more attention. Both the research community and the practitioners became more deeply involved in software testing. Thus, in the 1970s, a new field of research called *testing theory* emerged. Testing theory puts emphasis on the following:

- Detecting defects through execution-based testing
- Designing test cases from different sources, namely, requirement specification, source code, and the input and output domains of programs
- Selecting a subset of test cases from the set of all possible test cases [1, 2]
- Effectiveness of the test case selection strategy [3–5]
- Test oracles used during testing [6, 7]
- Prioritizing the execution of the selected test cases [8]
- Adequacy analysis of test cases [9–15]

A theoretical foundation of testing gives testers and developers valuable insight into software systems and the development processes. As a consequence, testers design more effective test cases at a lower cost. While considering testing theory, there may be a heightened expectation that it lets us detect all the defects in a computer program. Any testing theory must inherit the fundamental limitation of testing. The limitation of testing has been best articulated by Dijkstra: *Testing can only reveal the presence of errors, never their absence* [16]. In spite of the

---

said limitation, testing remains as the most practical and reliable method for defect detection and quality improvement.

In this chapter, three well-known testing theories are discussed. These are Goodenough and Gerhart's theory [17], Weyuker and Ostrand's theory [18], and Gourlay's theory [19]. Goodenough and Gerhart introduced some key concepts such as *an ideal test*, *reliability* and *validity* of a test, *test selection criteria*, *thorough test*, and five categories of program errors. Weyuker and Ostrand refined some of the above ideas in the form of *uniformly reliable criterion*, *uniformly valid criterion*, and *uniformly ideal test*. Gourlay introduced the concept of a *test system* and a general method for comparing different test methods.

2.2 THEORY OF GOODENOUGH AND GERHART

Goodenough and Gerhart published a seminal paper [17] in 1975 on test data selection. This paper gave a fundamental testing concept, identified a few types of program errors, and gave a theory for selecting test data from the input domain of a program. Though this theory is not without critiques, it is widely quoted and appreciated in the research community of software testing.

2.2.1 Fundamental Concepts

Let D be the input domain of a program P. Let $T \subseteq D$. The result of executing P with input $d \in D$ is denoted by $P(d)$ (Figure 2.1):

OK(d): Define a predicate OK(d) which expresses the acceptability of result $P(d)$. Thus, OK(d) = *true* if and only if $P(d)$ is an acceptable outcome.

SUCCESSFUL(T): For a given $T \subseteq D$, T is a *successful* test, denoted by SUCCESSFUL(T), if and only if, $\forall t \in T$, OK(t). Thus, SUCCESSFUL(T) = true if and only if, $\forall t \in T$, OK(t).

Ideal Test: T constitutes an *ideal test* if

$$OK(t) \ \forall t \in T \Rightarrow OK(d) \ \forall d \in D$$

An ideal test is interpreted as follows. If from the successful execution of a sample of the input domain we can conclude that the program contains no errors, then the sample constitutes an ideal test. Practitioners may

Input domain D

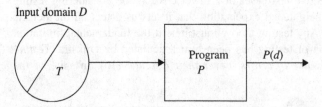

Figure 2.1   Executing a program with a subset of the input domain.

loosely interpret "no error" as "not many errors of severe consequences." The validity of the above definition of an ideal test depends on how "thoroughly" T exercises P. Some people equate *thorough test* with exhaustive or complete test, in which case $T = D$.

COMPLETE(T, C): A *thorough test* T is defined to be one satisfying COMPLETE(T,C), where COMPLETE is a predicate that defines how some test *selection criteria* C is used in selecting a particular set of test data T from D. COMPLETE(T, C) will be defined in a later part of this section. Essentially, C defines the properties of a program that must be exercised to constitute a thorough test.

Reliable Criterion: A selection criterion C is *reliable* if and only if either every test selected by C is successful or no test selected is successful. Thus, reliability refers to consistency.

Valid Criterion: A selection criterion C is *valid* if and only if whenever P is incorrect C selects at least one test set T which is not successful for P. Thus, validity refers to the ability to produce meaningful results.

Fundamental   Theorem. $(\exists T \subseteq D)(\text{COMPLETE}(T, C) \wedge \text{RELIABLE}(C) \wedge \text{VALID}(C) \wedge \text{SUCCESSFUL}(T)) \Rightarrow (\forall d \in D)\text{OK}(d)$

Proof. Let P be a program and D be the set of inputs for P. Let d be a member of D. We assume that P fails on input d. In other words, the actual outcome of executing P with input d is not the same as the expected outcome. In the form of our notation, $\neg\text{OK}(d)$ is true. VALID(C) implies that there exists a complete set of test data T such that $\neg\text{SUCCESSFUL}(T)$. RELIABLE(C) implies that if one complete test fails, all tests fail. However, this leads to a contradiction that there exists a complete test that is successfully executed.

One may be tempted to find a reliable and valid criterion, if it exists, so that all faults can be detected with a small set of test cases. However, there are several difficulties in applying the above theory, as explained in the following:

- Since faults in a program are unknown, it is impossible to prove the reliability and validity of a criterion. A criterion is guaranteed to be both reliable and valid if it selects the entire input domain D. However, this is undesirable and impractical.
- Neither reliability nor validity is preserved during the debugging process, where faults keep disappearing.
- If the program P is correct, then any test will be successful and every selection criterion is reliable and valid.
- If P is not correct, there is in general no way of knowing whether a criterion is ideal without knowing the errors in P.

2.2.2 Theory of Testing

Let D be the input domain of a program P. Let C denote a set of test predicates. If $d \in D$ satisfies test predicate $c \in C$, then $c(d)$ is said to be true. Selecting data to satisfy a test predicate means selecting data to exercise the condition combination in the course of executing P.

With the above idea in mind, COMPLETE(T, C), where $T \subseteq D$, is defined as follows:

$$\text{COMPLETE}(T, C) \equiv (\forall c \in C)(\exists t \in T)c(t) \wedge (\forall t \in T)(\exists c \in C)c(t)$$

The above theory means that, for every test predicate, we select a test such that the test predicate is satisfied. Also, for every test selected, there exists a test predicate which is satisfied by the selected test. The definitions of an ideal test and thoroughness of a test do not reveal any relationship between them. However, we can establish a relationship between the two in the following way.

Let B be the set of faults (or bugs) in a program P revealed by an ideal test T_I. Let a test engineer identify a set of test predicates C_1 and design a set of test cases T_1, such that COMPLETE(T_1, C_1) is satisfied. Let B_1 represent the set of faults revealed by T_1. There is no guarantee that T_1 reveals all the faults. Later, the test engineer identifies a larger set of test predicates C_2 such that $C_2 \supset C_1$ and designs a new set of test cases T_2 such that $T_2 \supset T_1$ and COMPLETE(T_2, C_2) is satisfied. Let B_2 be the set of faults revealed by T_2. Assuming that the additional test cases selected reveal more faults, we have $B_2 \supset B_1$. If the test engineer repeats this process, he may ultimately identify a set of test predicates C_I and design a set of test cases T_I such that COMPLETE(T_I, C_I) is satisfied and T_I reveals the entire set of faults B. In this case, T_I is a thorough test satisfying COMPLETE(T_I, C_I) and represents an ideal test set.

2.2.3 Program Errors

Any approach to testing is based on assumptions about the way program faults occur. Faults are due to two main reasons:

- Faults occur due to our inadequate understanding of all conditions with which a program must deal.
- Faults occur due to our failure to realize that certain combinations of conditions require special treatments.

Goodenough and Gerhart classify program faults as follows:

- **Logic Fault:** This class of faults means a program produces incorrect results independent of resources required. That is, the program fails because of the faults present in the program and not because of a lack of resources. Logic faults can be further split into three categories:

    Requirements fault: This means our failure to capture the real requirements of the customer.

Design fault: This represents our failure to satisfy an understood requirement.

Construction fault: This represents our failure to satisfy a design. Suppose that a design step says "Sort array A." To sort the array with N elements, one may choose one of several sorting algorithms. Let

```
for (i = 0; i < N; i++) {
    :
}
```

be the desired for loop construct to sort the array. If a programmer writes the for loop in the form

```
for (i = 0; i <= N; i++){
    :
}
```

then there is a construction error in the implementation.

- **Performance Fault:** This class of faults leads to a failure of the program to produce expected results within specified or desired resource limitations.

A thorough test must be able to detect faults arising from any of the above reasons. Test data selection criteria must reflect information derived from each stage of software development. Since each type of fault is manifested as an improper effect produced by an implementation, it is useful to categorize the sources of faults in implementation terms as follows:

Missing Control Flow Paths: Intuitively, a control flow path, or simply a path, is a feasible sequence of instructions in a program. A path may be missing from a program if we fail to identify a condition and specify a path to handle that condition. An example of a missing path is our failure to test for a zero divisor before executing a division. If we fail to recognize that a divisor can take a zero value, then we will not include a piece of code to handle the special case. Thus, a certain desirable computation will be missing from the program.

Inappropriate Path Selection: A program executes an inappropriate path if a condition is expressed incorrectly. In Figure 2.2, we show a desired behavior and an implemented behavior. Both the behaviors are identical except in the condition part of the if statement. The if part of the implemented behavior contains an additional condition B. It is easy to see that

Desired behavior	Implemented behavior
if (A) proc1();	if (A && B) proc1();
else proc2();	else proc2();

Figure 2.2 Example of inappropriate path selection.

both the desired part and the implemented part behave in the same way for all combinations of values of A and B except when $A = 1$ and $B = 0$.

Inappropriate or Missing Action: There are three instances of this class of fault:

- One may calculate a value using a method that does not necessarily give the correct result. For example, a desired expression is $x = x \times w$, whereas it is wrongly written as $x = x + w$. These two expressions produce identical results for several combinations of x and w, such as $x = 1.5$ and $w = 3$, for example.
- Failing to assign a value to a variable is an example of a missing action.
- Calling a function with the wrong argument list is a kind of inappropriate action.

The main danger due to an inappropriate or missing action is that the action is incorrect only under certain combinations of conditions. Therefore, one must do the following to find test data that reliably reveal errors:

- Identify all the conditions relevant to the correct operation of a program.
- Select test data to exercise all possible combinations of these conditions.

The above idea of selecting test data leads us to define the following terms:

Test Data: Test data are actual values from the input domain of a program that collectively satisfy some test selection criteria.

Test Predicate: A test predicate is a description of conditions and combinations of conditions relevant to correct operation of the program:

- Test predicates describe the *aspects* of a program that are to be tested. Test data cause these aspects to be tested.
- Test predicates are the motivating force for test data selection.
- Components of test predicates arise first and primarily from the specifications for a program.
- Further conditions and predicates may be added as implementations are considered.

2.2.4   Conditions for Reliability

A set of test predicates must at least satisfy the following conditions to have any chance of being reliable. These conditions are key to meaningful testing:

- Every individual branching condition in a program must be represented by an equivalent condition in C.
- Every potential termination condition in the program, for example, an overflow, must be represented by a condition in C.
- Every condition relevant to the correct operation of the program that is implied by the specification and knowledge of the data structure of the program must be represented as a condition in C.

2.2.5   Drawbacks of Theory

Several difficulties prevent us from applying Goodenough and Gerhart's theory of an *ideal test* as follows [18]:

- The concepts of reliability and validity have been defined with respect to the entire input domain of a program. A criterion is guaranteed to be both reliable and valid if and only if it selects the entire domain as a single test. Since such exhaustive testing is impractical, one will have much difficulty in assessing the reliability and validity of a criterion.

- The concepts of reliability and validity have been defined with respect to a program. A test selection criterion that is reliable and valid for one program may not be so for another program. The goodness of a test set should be independent of individual programs and the faults therein.

- Neither validity nor reliability is preserved throughout the debugging process. In practice, as program failures are observed, the program is debugged to locate the faults, and the faults are generally fixed as soon as they are found. During this debugging phase, as the program changes, so does the idealness of a test set. This is because a fault that was revealed before debugging is no more revealed after debugging and fault fixing. Thus, properties of test selection criteria are not even "monotonic" in the sense of being either always gained or preserved or always lost or preserved.

2.3   THEORY OF WEYUKER AND OSTRAND

A key problem in the theory of Goodenough and Gerhart is that the reliability and validity of a criterion depend upon the presence of faults in a program and their types. Weyuker and Ostrand [18] provide a modified theory in which the validity and reliability of test selection criteria are dependent only on the program *specification*, rather than a program. They propose the concept of a *uniformly ideal* test selection criterion for a given output specification. In the theory of Goodenough and Gerhart, implicit in the definitions of the predicates OK(d) and SUCCESS-FUL(T) is a program P. By abbreviating SUCCESSFUL() as SUCC(), the two predicates are rewritten as follows:

OK(P, d): Define a predicate OK(P, d) which expresses the acceptability of result $P(d)$. Thus, OK(P, d) = true if and only if $P(d)$ is an acceptable outcome of program P.

SUCC(P, T): For a given $T \subseteq D$, T is a *successful* test for a program P, denoted by SUCC(P, T), if and only if, $\forall t \in T$, OK(P, t). Thus, SUCC(T) = true if and only if, $\forall t \in T$, OK(P, t).

With the above definitions of OK(P, d) and SUCC(P, T), the concepts of *uniformly valid* criterion, *uniformly reliable* criterion, and *uniformly ideal* test selection are defined as follows.

Uniformly Valid Criterion C: Criterion C is uniformly valid iff

$$(\forall P)[(\exists d \in D)(\neg OK(P, d)) \Rightarrow (\exists T \subseteq D)(C(T) \& \neg SUCC(P, T))]$$

Uniformly Reliable Criterion C: Criterion C is uniformly reliable iff

$$(\forall P)(\forall T_1, \forall T_2 \subseteq D)[(C(T_1) \& C(T_2)) \Rightarrow (SUCC(P, T_1)$$
$$\Leftrightarrow SUCC(P, T_2))]$$

Uniformly Ideal Test Selection: A uniformly ideal test selection criterion for a given specification is both uniformly valid and uniformly reliable.

The external quantifier $(\forall P)$ binding the free variable P in the definition of uniformly valid criterion C essentially means that the rest of the predicate holds for all programs P for a given output specification. Similarly, the external quantifier $(\forall P)$ binding the free variable P in the definition of uniformly reliable criterion C means that the rest of the predicate holds for all programs P for a given output specification.

Since a uniformly ideal test selection criterion is defined over *all* programs for a given specification, it was intended to solve all the program-dependent difficulties in the definitions given by Goodenough and Gerhart. However, the concept of uniformly ideal test selection also has several flaws. For example, for any significant program there can be no uniformly ideal criterion that is not trivial in the sense of selecting the entire input domain D. A criterion C is said to be *trivially valid* if the union of all tests selected by C is D. Hence, the following theorems.

Theorem. A criterion C is uniformly valid if and only if C is trivially valid.

Proof. Obviously a trivially valid criterion is valid. Now we need to show that a criterion C which is not trivially valid cannot be uniformly valid for a given output specification. For any element d not included in any test of C, one can write a program which is incorrect for d and correct for $D - \{d\}$.

Theorem. A criterion C is uniformly reliable if and only if C selects a single test set.

Proof. If C selects only one test, it is obviously reliable for any program. Now, assume that C selects different tests T_1 and T_2 and that $t \in T_1$ but $t \notin T_2$. A program P exists which is correct with respect to test inputs in T_2 but incorrect on t. Thus, the two tests yield different results for P, and C is not reliable.

Now, we can combine the above two theorems to have the following corollary.

Corollary. A criterion C is uniformly valid and uniformly reliable if and only if C selects only the single test set $T = D$.

An important implication of the above corollary is that uniform validity and uniform reliability lead to *exhaustive testing* —and exhaustive testing is considered to be impractical. Next, the above corollary is reformulated to state that irrespective of test selection criterion used and irrespective of tests selected, except the entire D, one can always write a program which can defeat the tests. A program P is said to defeat a test T if P passes T but fails on some other valid input. This is paraphrasing the well-known statement of Dijkstra that *testing can only reveal the presence of errors, never their absence* [16].

Reliability and validity of test selection criterion are ideal goals, and ideal goals are rarely achieved. It is useful to seek less ideal but usable goals. By settling for less ideal goals, we essentially accept the reality that correctness of large programs is not something that we strive to achieve.

Weyuker and Ostrand [18] have introduced the concept of a *revealing criterion* with respect to a subdomain, where a *subdomain* S is a subset of the input domain D. A test selection criterion C is *revealing* for a subdomain S if whenever S contains an input which is processed incorrectly then every test set which satisfies C is unsuccessful. In other words, if any test selected by C is successfully executed, then every test in S produces correct output. A predicate called REVEALING(C, S) captures the above idea in the following definition:

$$\text{REVEALING}(C, S) \text{ iff } (\exists d \in S)(\neg\text{OK}(d)) \Rightarrow (\forall T \subseteq S)(C(T) \Rightarrow \neg\text{SUCC}(T))$$

The key advantage in a revealing criterion is that it concerns only a subset of the input domain, rather than the entire input domain. By considering a subset of the input domain, programmers can concentrate on local errors. An important task in applying the idea of a revealing criterion is to partition the input domain into smaller subdomains, which is akin to partitioning a problem into a set of subproblems. However, partitioning a problem into subproblems has been recognized to be a difficult task.

2.4   THEORY OF GOURLAY

An ideal goal in software development is to find out whether or not a program is correct, where a correct program is void of faults. Much research results have been reported in the field of program correctness. However, due to the highly constrained nature of program verification techniques, no developer makes any effort to prove the correctness of even small programs of, say, a few thousand lines, let alone large programs with millions of lines of code. Instead, testing is accepted in the industry as a practical way of finding faults in programs. The flip side of testing is that it cannot be used to settle the question of program correctness, which is the ideal goal. Even though testing cannot settle the program correctness issue, there is a need for a testing theory to enable us to compare the power of different test methods.

To motivate a theoretical discussion of testing, we begin with an ideal process for software development, which consists of the following steps:

- A customer and a development team specify the needs.
- The development team takes the specification and attempts to write a program to meet the specification.
- A test engineer takes both the specification and the program and selects a set of test cases. The test cases are based on the specification and the program.
- The program is executed with the selected test data, and the test outcome is compared with the expected outcome.
- The program is said to have faults if some tests fail.
- One can say the program to be ready for use if it passes all the test cases.

We focus on the selection of test cases and the interpretation of their results. We assume that the specification is correct, and the specification is the sole arbiter of the correctness of the program. The program is said to be correct if and only if it satisfies the specification. Gourlay's testing theory [19] establishes a relationship between three sets of entities, namely, *specifications*, *programs*, and *tests*, and provides a basis for comparing different methods for selecting tests.

2.4.1   Few Definitions

The set of all programs are denoted by $\mathcal{P}$, the set of all specifications by $\mathcal{S}$, and the set of all tests by $\mathcal{T}$. Members of $\mathcal{P}$ will be denoted by p and q, members of $\mathcal{S}$ will be denoted by r and s, and members of $\mathcal{T}$ will be denoted by t and u.

Uppercase letters will denote subsets of $\mathcal{P}$, $\mathcal{S}$, and $\mathcal{T}$. For examples, $p \in P \subseteq \mathcal{P}$ and $t \in T \subseteq \mathcal{T}$, where t denotes a single test case. The correctness of a program p with respect to a specification s will be denoted by p corr s. Given s, p, and t, the predicate p ok(t) s means that the result of testing p under t is judged successful by specification s. The reader may recall that T denotes a set of test cases, and p ok(T) s is true if and only if p ok(t) s $\forall t \in T$.

We must realize that if a program is correct, then it will never produce any unexpected outcome with respect to the specification. Thus, p corr $s \Rightarrow p$ ok(t) s $\forall t$.

Definition.   A *testing system* is a collection $< \mathcal{P}, \mathcal{S}, \mathcal{T}, \text{corr}, \text{ok} >$, where $\mathcal{P}$, $\mathcal{S}$, and $\mathcal{T}$ are arbitrary sets, corr $\subseteq \mathcal{P} \times \mathcal{S}$, sets, ok $\subseteq \mathcal{T} \times \mathcal{P} \times \mathcal{S}$, and $\forall p \forall s \forall t (p$ corr $s \Rightarrow p$ ok$(t)s)$.

Definition.   Given a testing system $< \mathcal{P}, \mathcal{S}, \mathcal{T}, \text{corr}, \text{ok} >$ a new system $< \mathcal{P}, \mathcal{S}, \mathcal{T}', \text{corr}, \text{ok}' >$ is called a *set construction*, where $\mathcal{T}'$ is the set of all subsets of $\mathcal{T}$, and where p ok$'(T)s \Leftrightarrow \forall t (t \in T \Rightarrow p$ ok$(t)s)$. (The reader may recall that T is a member of $\mathcal{T}'$ because $T \subseteq \mathcal{T}$.)

Theorem. $< \mathcal{P}, \mathcal{S}, \mathcal{T}', \text{corr}, \text{ok}' >$, a set construction on a testing system $< \mathcal{P}, \mathcal{S}, \mathcal{T}, \text{corr}, \text{ok} >$, is itself a testing system.

Proof.   We need to show that p corr $s \Rightarrow p$ ok$'(T)$ s. Assume that p corr s holds. By assumption, the original system is a testing system. Thus, $\forall t$, p ok(t) s. If we choose a test set T, we know that, $\forall t \in T$, p ok(t) s. Therefore, p ok$'(T)$ s holds.

The set construction is interpreted as follows. A test consists of a number of trials of some sort, and success of the test as a whole depends on success of all the trials. In fact, this is the rule in testing practice, where a test engineer must run a program again and again on a variety of test data. Failure of any one run is enough to invalidate the program.

Definition.   Given a testing system $< \mathcal{P}, \mathcal{S}, \mathcal{T}, \text{corr}, \text{ok} >$ a new system $< \mathcal{P}, \mathcal{S}, \mathcal{T}', \text{corr}, \text{ok}' >$ is called a *choice construction*, where $\mathcal{T}'$ is the set of subsets of $\mathcal{T}$, and where p ok$'(T)$ $s \Leftrightarrow \exists t(t \in T \wedge p$ ok(t) $s)$. (The reader may recall that T is a member of $\mathcal{T}'$ because $T \subseteq \mathcal{T}$.)

Theorem. $< \mathcal{P}, \mathcal{S}, \mathcal{T}', \text{corr}, \text{ok}' >$, a choice construction on a testing system $< \mathcal{P}, \mathcal{S}, \mathcal{T}, \text{corr}, \text{ok} >$, is itself a testing system.

Proof.   Similar to the previous theorem, we need to show that p corr $s \Rightarrow p$ ok$'(T)$ s. Assume that p corr s. Thus, $\forall t$, p ok(t) s. If we pick a nonempty test set T, we know that $\exists t \in T$ such that p ok(t) s. Thus, we can write $\forall T(T \neq \phi \Rightarrow \exists t(t \in T \wedge p$ ok(t) $s))$, and $\forall T(T \neq \phi \Rightarrow p$ ok$'(T)$ $s)$. The empty test set ϕ must be excluded from $(\mathcal{T}')$ because a testing system must include at least one test.

The choice construction models the situation in which a test engineer is given a number of alternative ways of testing the program, all of which are assumed to be equivalent.

Definition.   A test method is a function $M : \mathcal{P} \times \mathcal{S} \rightarrow \mathcal{T}$.

That is, in the general case, a test method takes the specification S and an implementation program P and produces test cases. In practice, test methods are predominantly program dependent, specification dependent, or totally dependent on the expectations of customers, as explained below:

- **Program Dependent:** In this case, $T = M(P)$, that is, test cases are derived solely based on the source code of a system. This is called *white-box* testing. Here, a test method has complete knowledge of the internal details of a program. However, from the viewpoint of practical testing, a white-box method is not generally applied to an entire program. One applies such a method to small *units* of a given large system. A unit refers to a function, procedure, method, and so on. A white-box method allows a test engineer to use the details of a program unit. Effective use of a program unit requires a thorough understanding of the unit. Therefore, white-box test methods are used by programmers to test their own code.

- **Specification Dependent:** In this case, $T = M(S)$, that is, test cases are derived solely based on the specification of a system. This is called *black-box* testing. Here, a test method does not have access to the internal details of a program. Such a method uses information provided in the specification of a system. It is not unusual to use an entire specification in the generation of test cases because specifications are much smaller in size than their corresponding implementations. Black-box methods are generally used by the development team and an independent system test group.

- **Expectation Dependent:** In practice, customers may generate test cases based on their *expectations* from the product at the time of taking delivery of the system. These test cases may include *continuous-operation* tests, *usability* tests, and so on.

2.4.2   Power of Test Methods

A tester is concerned with the methods to produce test cases and to compare test methods so that they can identify an appropriate test method. Let M and N be two test methods. For M to be *at least as good as* N, we must have the situation that whenever N finds an error, so does M. In other words, whenever a program fails under a test case produced by method N, it will also fail under a test case produced by method M, with respect to the same specification. Therefore, $F_N \subseteq F_M$, where F_N and F_M are the sets of faults discovered by test sets produced by methods N and M, respectively.

Let T_M and T_N be the set of test cases produced by methods M and N, respectively. Then, we need to follow two ways to compare their fault detection power.

Case 1: $T_M \supseteq T_N$. In this case, it is clear that method M is at least as good as method N. This is because method M produces test cases which reveal all the faults revealed by test cases produced by method N. This case is depicted in Figure 2.3a.

Case 2: T_M and T_N overlap, but $T_M \not\supseteq T_N$. This case suggests that T_M does not totally contain T_N. To be able to compare their fault detection ability, we execute the program P under both sets of test cases, namely T_M and T_N. Let F_M and F_N be the sets of faults detected by test sets T_M and T_N, respectively. If $F_M \supseteq F_N$, then we say that method M is at least as good as method N. This situation is explained in Figure 2.3b.

2.5   ADEQUACY OF TESTING

Testing gives designers and programmers much confidence in a software component or a complete product if it passes their test cases. Assume that a set of test cases

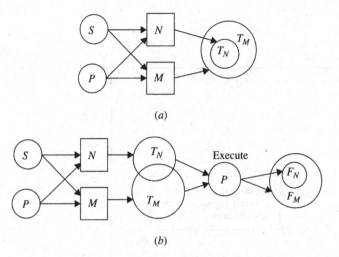

Figure 2.3   Different ways of comparing power of test methods: (*a*) produces all test cases produced by another method; (*b*) test sets have common elements.

T has been designed to test a program P. We execute P with the test set T. If T reveals faults in P, then we modify the program in an attempt to fix those faults. At this stage, there may be a need to design some new test cases, because, for example, we may include a new procedure in the code. After modifying the code, we execute the program with the new test set. Thus, we execute the test-and-fix loop until no more faults are revealed by the updated test set. Now we face a dilemma as follows: Is P really fault free, or is T not good enough to reveal the remaining faults in P? From testing we cannot conclude that P is fault free, since, as Dijkstra observed, testing can reveal the presence of faults, but not their absence. Therefore, if P passes T, we need to know that T is "good enough" or, in other words, that T is an adequate set of tests. It is important to evaluate the adequacy of T because if T is found to be not adequate, then more test cases need to be designed, as illustrated in Figure 2.4. Adequacy of T means whether or not T thoroughly tests P.

Ideally, testing should be performed with an *adequate* test set T. Intuitively, the idea behind specifying a criterion for evaluating test adequacy is to know whether or not sufficient testing has been done. We will soon return to the idea of test adequacy. In the absence of test adequacy, developers will be forced to use ad hoc measures to decide when to stop testing. Some examples of ad hoc measures for stopping testing are as follows [13]:

- Stop when the allocated time for testing expires.
- Stop when it is time to release the product.
- Stop when all the test cases execute without revealing faults.

Figure 2.4 depicts two important notions concerning test design and evaluating test adequacy as follows:

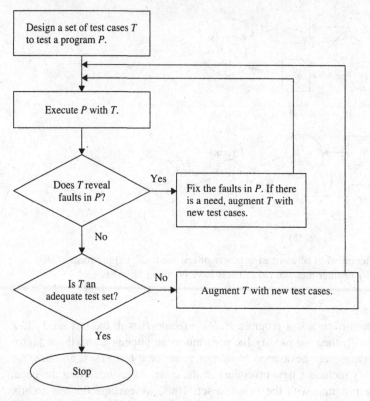

Figure 2.4   Context of applying test adequacy.

- Adequacy of a test set T is evaluated *after* it is found that T reveals no more faults. One may argue: Why not design test cases to meet an adequacy criterion? However, it is important to design test cases independent of an adequacy criterion because the primary goal of testing is to locate errors, and, thus, test design should not be constrained by an adequacy criterion. An example of a test design criteria is as follows: Select test cases to execute all statements in a program at least once. However, the difficulty with such a test design criterion is that we may not be able to know whether every program statement can be executed. Thus, it is difficult to judge the adequacy of the test set selected thereby. Finally, since the goal of testing is to reveal faults, there is no point in evaluating the adequacy of the test set as long as faults are being revealed.

- An adequate test set T does not say anything about the correctness of a program. A common understanding of correctness is that we have found and fixed all faults in a program to make it "correct." However, in practice, it is not realistic—though very much desirable—to find and fix all faults in a program. Thus, on the one hand, an adequacy criterion may not try to aim for program correctness. On the other hand, a fault-free program should not turn any arbitrary test set T into an adequate test.

The above two points tell us an important notion: that the adequacy of a test set be evaluated independent of test design processes for the programs under test. Intuitively, a test set T is said to be adequate if it covers all aspects of the actual computation performed by a program and all computations intended by its specification. Two practical methods for evaluating test adequacy are as follows:

- **Fault Seeding:** This method refers to implanting a certain number of faults in a program P and executing P with test set T. If T reveals k percent of the implanted faults, we assume that T has revealed only k percent of the original faults. If 100% of the implanted faults have been revealed by T, we feel more confident about the adequacy of T. A thorough discussion of fault seeding can be found in Chapter 13.

- **Program Mutation:** Given a program P, a *mutation* is a program obtained by making a small change to P. In the program mutation method, a series of mutations are obtained from P. Some of the mutations may contain faults and the rest are equivalent to P. A test set T is said to be adequate if it causes every faulty mutation to produce an unexpected outcome. A more thorough discussion of program mutation can be found in Chapter 3.

2.6   LIMITATIONS OF TESTING

Ideally, all programs should be correct, that is, there is no fault in a program. Due to the impractical nature of proving even small programs to be correct, customers and software developers rely on the efficacy of testing. In this section, we introduce two main limitations of testing:

- Testing means executing a program with a generally small, proper subset of the input domain of the program. A small, proper subset of the input domain is chosen because cost may not allow a much larger subset to be chosen, let alone the full input set. Testing with the full input set is known as exhaustive testing. Thus, the inherent need to test a program with a small subset of the input domain poses a fundamental limit on the efficacy of testing. The limit is in the form of our inability to extrapolate the correctness of results for a proper subset of the input domain to program correctness. In other words, even if a program passes a test set T, we cannot conclude that the program is correct.

- Once we have selected a subset of the input domain, we are faced with the problem of verifying the correctness of the program outputs for individual test input. That is, a program output is examined to determine if the program performed correctly on the test input. The mechanism which verifies the correctness of a program output is known as an *oracle*. The concept of an oracle is discussed in detail in Chapter 9. Determining the correctness of a program output is not a trivial task. If either of the following two conditions hold, a program is considered *nontestable* [20]:

There does not exist an oracle.

It is too difficult to determine the correct output.

If there is no mechanism to verify the correctness of a program output or it takes an extraordinary amount of time to verify an output, there is not much to be gained by running the test.

2.7 SUMMARY

The ideal, abstract goal of testing is to reveal all faults in a software system without exhaustively testing the software. This idea is the basis of the concept of an ideal test developed by Goodenough and Gerhart [17]. An ideal test is supposed to be a small, proper subset of the entire input domain, and we should be able to extrapolate the results of an ideal test to program correctness. In other words, in an abstract sense, if a program passes all the tests in a carefully chosen test set, called an ideal test, we are in a position to claim that the program is correct.

Coupled with the concept of an ideal test is a test selection criterion which allows us to pick members of an ideal test. A test selection criterion is characterized in terms of reliability and validity. A reliable criterion is one which selects test cases such that a program either passes all tests or fails all tests. On the other hand, a valid criterion is one which selects at least one test set which fails in case the program contains a fault. If a criterion is both valid and reliable, then any test selected by the criterion is an ideal test. The theory has a few drawback. First, the concepts of reliability and validity have been defined with respect to one program and its entire input domain. Second, neither reliability nor validity is preserved throughout the debugging phase of software development.

Faults occur due to our inadequate understanding of all conditions that a program must deal with and our failure to realize that certain combinations of conditions require special treatments. Goodenough and Gerhart categorize faults into five categories: logic faults, requirement faults, design faults, construction faults, and performance faults.

Weyuker and Ostrand [18] tried to eliminate the drawbacks of the theory of Goodenough and Gerhart by proposing the concept of a uniformly ideal test. The concept is defined with respect to *all* programs designed to satisfy a specification, rather than just one program—hence the concept of "uniformity" over all program instances for a given specification. Further, the idea of uniformity was extended to test selection criteria in the form of a uniformly reliable and uniformly valid criterion. However, their theory too is impractical because a uniformly valid and uniformly reliable criterion selects the entire input domain of a program, thereby causing exhaustive testing. Next, the idea of an ideal test was extended to a proper subset of the input domain called a subdomain, and the concept of a revealing criterion was defined.

Though testing cannot settle the question of program correctness, different testing methods continue to be developed. For example, there are specification-based testing methods and code-based testing methods. It is important to develop a theory to compare the power of different testing methods. Gourlay [19] put forward a theory to compare the power of testing methods based on their fault detection abilities.

A software system undergoes multiple test–fix–retest cycles until, ideally, no more faults are revealed. Faults are fixed by modifying the code or adding new code to the system. At this stage there may be a need to design new test cases. When no more faults are revealed, we can conclude this way: either there is no fault in the program or the tests could not reveal the faults. Since we have no way to know the exact situation, it is useful to evaluate the adequacy of the test set. There is no need to evaluate the adequacy of tests so long as they reveal faults. Two practical ways of evaluating test adequacy are fault seeding and program mutation.

Finally, we discussed two limitations of testing. The first limitation of testing is that it cannot settle the question of program correctness. In other words, by testing a program with a proper subset of the input domain and observing no fault, we cannot conclude that there are no remaining faults in the program. The second limitation of testing is that in several instances we do not know the expected output of a program. If for some inputs the expected output of a program is not known or it cannot be determined within a reasonable amount of time, then the program is called nontestable [20].

LITERATURE REVIEW

Weyuker and Ostrand [18] have shown by examples how to construct revealing subdomains from source code. Their main example is the well-known triangle classification problem. The triangle classification problem is as follows. Let us consider three positive integers A, B, and C. The problem is to find whether the given integers represent the sides of an equilateral triangle, the sides of a scalene right triangle, and so on.

Weyuker [13] has introduced the notion of *program inference* to capture the notion of test data adequacy. Essentially, program inference refers to deriving a program from its specification and a sample of its input–output behavior. On the other hand, the testing process begins with a specification S and a program P and selects input–output pairs that characterize every aspect of the actual computations performed by the program and the intended computations performed by the specification. Thus, program testing and program inference are thought of as inverse processes. A test set T is said to be adequate if T contains sufficient data to infer the computations defined by both S and P. However, Weyuker [13] explains that such an adequacy criterion is not pragmatically usable. Rather, the criterion can at best be used as a guide. By considering the difficulty in using the criterion, Weyuker defines two weaker adequacy criterion, namely *program adequate* and *specification adequate*. A test set T is said to be program adequate if it contains sufficient data to infer the computations defined by P. Similarly, the test set T is said to be specification adequate if it contains sufficient data to infer the computations defined by S. It is suggested that depending upon how test data are selected, one of the two criteria can be eased out. For example, if T is derived from S, then it is useful to evaluate if T is program adequate. Since T is selected from S, T is expected to contain sufficient data to infer the computations defined by S, and there is no need to evaluate T's specification adequacy. Similarly, if T is derived from P, it is useful to evaluate if T is specification adequate.

The students are encouraged to read the article by Stuart H. Zweben and John S. Gourlay entitled "On the Adequacy of Weyuker's Test Data Adequacy Axioms" [15] The authors raise the issue of what makes an axiomatic system as well as what constitutes a proper axiom. Weyuker responds to the criticism at the end of the article. Those students have never seen such a professional interchange; this is worth reading for this aspect alone. This article must be read along with the article by Elaine Weyuker entitled "Axiomatizing Software Test Data Adequacy" [12].

Martin David and Elaine Weyuker [9] present an interesting notion of *distance between programs* to study the concept of test data adequacy. Specifically, they equate adequacy with the capability of a test set to be able to successfully distinguish a program being tested from all programs that are sufficiently close to it and differ in input–output behavior from the given program.

Weyuker [12, 21] proposed a set of properties to evaluate test data adequacy criteria. Some examples of adequacy criteria are to (i) ensure coverage of all branches in the program being tested and (ii) ensure that boundary values of all input data have been selected for the program under test. Parrish and Zweben [11] formalized those properties and identified dependencies within the set. They formalized the adequacy properties with respect to criteria that do not make use of the specification of the program under test.

Frankl and Weyuker [10] compared the relative fault-detecting ability of a number of structural testing techniques, namely, data flow testing, mutation testing, and a condition coverage technique, to branch testing. They showed that the former three techniques are better than branch testing according to two probabilistic measures.

A good survey on test adequacy is presented in an article by Hong Zhu, Patrick A. V. Hall, and John H. R. May entitled "Software Unit Test Coverage and Adequacy" [14]. In this article, various types of software test adequacy criteria proposed in the literature are surveyed followed by a summary of methods for comparison and assessment of adequacy criteria.

REFERENCES

1. R. Gupta, M. J. Harrold, and M. L. Soffa. *An Approach to Regression Testing Using Slicing*. Paper presented at the IEEE-CS International Conference on Software Maintenance, Orlando, FL, November 1992, pp. 299–308.
2. G. Rothermel and M. Harrold. Analyzing Regression Test Selection Techniques. *IEEE Transactions on Software Engineering*, August 1996, pp. 529–551.

3. V. R. Basili and R. W. Selby. Comparing the Effectiveness of Software Testing. *IEEE Transactions on Software Engineering*, December 1987, pp. 1278–1296.

4. W. E. Howden. Weak Mutation Testing and Completeness of Test Sets. *IEEE Transactions on Software Engineering*, July 1982, pp. 371–379.

5. D. S. Rosenblum and E. J. Weyuker. Using Coverage Information to Predict the Cost-effectiveness of Regression Testing Strategies. *IEEE Transactions on Software Engineering*, March 1997, pp. 146–156.

6. L. Baresi and M. Young. Test Oracles, Technical Report CIS-TR-01–02. University of Oregon, Department of Computer and Information Science, Eugene, OR, August 2002, pp. 1–55.

7. Q. Xie and A. M. Memon. Designing and Comparing Automated Test Oracles for Gui Based Software Applications. *ACM Transactions on Software Engineering amd Methodology*, February 2007, pp. 1–36.

8. G. Rothermel, R. Untch, C. Chu, and M. Harrold. Prioritizing Test Cases for Regression Testing. *IEEE Transactions on Software Engineering*, October 2001, pp. 929–948.

9. M. Davis and E. J. Weyuker. Metric Space-Based Test-Data Adequacy Criteria. *Computer Journal*, January 1988, pp. 17–24.

10. P. G. Frankl and E. J. Weyuker. Provable Improvements on Branch Testing. *IEEE Transactions on Software Engineering*, October 1993, pp. 962–975.

11. A. Parrish and S. H. Zweben. Analysis and Refinement of Software Test Data Adequacy Properties. *IEEE Transactions on Software Engineering*, June 1991, pp. 565–581.

12. E. J. Weyuker. Axiomatizing Software Test Data Adequacy. *IEEE Transactions on Software Engineering*, December 1986, pp. 1128–1138.

13. E. J. Weyuker. Assessing Test Data Adequacy through Program Inference. *ACM Transactions on Programming Languages and Systems*, October 1983, pp. 641–655.

14. H. Zhu, P. A. V. Hall, and J. H. R. May. Software Unit Test Coverage and Adequacy. *ACM Computing Surveys*, December 1997, pp. 366–427.

15. S. H. Zweben and J. S. Gourlay. On the Adequacy of Weyuker's Test Data Adequacy Axioms. *IEEE Transactions on Software Engineering*, April 1989, pp. 496–500.

16. E. W. Dijkstra. Notes on Structured Programming. In *Structured Programming*, O.-J. Dahl, E. W. Dijkstra, and C. A. R. Hoare, Eds. Academic, New York, 1972, pp. 1–81.

17. J. B. Goodenough and S. L. Gerhart. Toward a Theory of Test Data Selection. *IEEE Transactions on Software Engineering*, June 1975, pp. 26–37.

18. E. J. Weyuker and T. J. Ostrand. Theories of Program Testing and the Application of Revealing Subdomains. *IEEE Transactions on Software Engineering*, May 1980, pp. 236–246.

19. J. S. Gourlay. A Mathematical Framework for the Investigation of Testing. *IEEE Transactions on Software Engineering*, November 1983, pp. 686–709.

20. E. J. Weyuker. On Testing Non-Testable Programs. *Computer Journal*, Vol. 25, No. 4, 1982, pp. 465–470.

21. E. J. Weyuker. The Evaluation of Program-Based Software Test Data Adequacy Criteria. *Communications of the ACM*, June 1988, pp. 668–675.

Exercises

1. Explain the concept of an ideal test.

2. Explain the concept of a selection criterion in test design.

3. Explain the concepts of a valid and reliable criterion.

4. Explain five kinds of program faults.

5. What are the drawbacks of Goodenough and Gerhart's theory of program testing?

6. Explain the concepts of a uniformly ideal test as well as the concepts of uniformly valid and uniformly reliable criteria.

7. Explain how two test methods can be compared.

8. Explain the need for evaluating test adequacy.

9. Explain two practical methods for assessing test data adequacy.

10. Explain the concept of a nontestable program.

CHAPTER 3

Unit Testing

Knowledge is of no value unless you put it into practice.
— *Anton Chekhov*

3.1 CONCEPT OF UNIT TESTING

In this chapter we consider the first level of testing, that is, unit testing. Unit testing refers to testing program units in isolation. However, there is no consensus on the definition of a unit. Some examples of commonly understood units are functions, procedures, or methods. Even a class in an object-oriented programming language can be considered as a program unit. Syntactically, a program unit is a piece of code, such as a function or method of class, that is invoked from outside the unit and that can invoke other program units. Moreover, a program unit is assumed to implement a well-defined function providing a certain level of abstraction to the implementation of higher level functions. The function performed by a program unit may not have a direct association with a system-level function. Thus, a program unit may be viewed as a piece of code implementing a "low"-level function. In this chapter, we use the terms unit and module interchangeably.

Now, given that a program unit implements a function, it is only natural to test the unit before it is integrated with other units. Thus, a program unit is tested in isolation, that is, in a stand-alone manner. There are two reasons for testing a unit in a stand-alone manner. First, errors found during testing can be attributed to a specific unit so that it can be easily fixed. Moreover, unit testing removes dependencies on other program units. Second, during unit testing it is desirable to verify that each distinct execution of a program unit produces the expected result. In terms of code details, a distinct execution refers to a distinct path in the unit. Ideally, all possible—or as much as possible—distinct executions are to be considered during unit testing. This requires careful selection of input data for each distinct execution. A programmer has direct access to the input vector of the unit by executing a program unit in isolation. This direct access makes it easier to execute as many distinct paths as desirable or possible. If multiple units are put together for testing, then a programmer needs to generate test input with indirect relationship with the input vectors of several units under test. The said indirect relationship makes it difficult to control the execution of distinct paths in a chosen unit.

Unit testing has a limited scope. A programmer will need to verify whether or not a code works correctly by performing unit-level testing. Intuitively, a programmer needs to test a unit as follows:

- Execute every line of code. This is desirable because the programmer needs to know what happens when a line of code is executed. In the absence of such basic observations, surprises at a later stage can be expensive.
- Execute every predicate in the unit to evaluate them to true and false separately.
- Observe that the unit performs its intended function and ensure that it contains no known errors.

In spite of the above tests, there is no guarantee that a satisfactorily tested unit is functionally correct from a systemwide perspective. Not everything pertinent to a unit can be tested in isolation because of the limitations of testing in isolation. This means that some errors in a program unit can only be found later, when the unit is integrated with other units in the integration testing and system testing phases. Even though it is not possible to find all errors in a program unit in isolation, it is still necessary to ensure that a unit performs satisfactorily before it is used by other program units. It serves no purpose to integrate an erroneous unit with other units for the following reasons: (i) many of the subsequent tests will be a waste of resources and (ii) finding the root causes of failures in an integrated system is more resource consuming.

Unit testing is performed by the programmer who writes the program unit because the programmer is intimately familiar with the internal details of the unit. The objective for the programmer is to be satisfied that the unit works as expected. Since a programmer is supposed to construct a unit with no errors in it, a unit test is performed by him or her to their satisfaction in the beginning and to the satisfaction of other programmers when the unit is integrated with other units. This means that all programmers are accountable for the quality of their own work, which may include both new code and modifications to the existing code. The idea here is to push the quality concept down to the lowest level of the organization and empower each programmer to be responsible for his or her own quality. Therefore, it is in the best interest of the programmer to take preventive actions to minimize the number of defects in the code. The defects found during unit testing are internal to the software development group and are not reported up the personnel hierarchy to be counted in quality measurement metrics. The source code of a unit is not used for interfacing by other group members until the programmer completes unit testing and checks in the unit to the version control system.

Unit testing is conducted in two complementary phases:

- Static unit testing
- Dynamic unit testing

In static unit testing, a programmer does not execute the unit; instead, the code is examined over all possible behaviors that might arise during run time. Static unit testing is also known as non-execution-based unit testing, whereas dynamic unit testing is execution based. In static unit testing, the code of each unit is validated against requirements of the unit by reviewing the code. During the review process, potential issues are identified and resolved. For example, in the C programming language the two program-halting instructions are abort() and exit(). While the two are closely related, they have different effects as explained below:

- **Abort():** This means abnormal program termination. By default, a call to abort() results in a run time diagnostic and program self-destruction. The program destruction may or may not flush and close opened files or remove temporary files, depending on the implementation.
- **Exit():** This means graceful program termination. That is, the exit() call closes the opened files and returns a status code to the execution environment.

Whether to use abort() or exit() depends on the context that can be easily detected and resolved during static unit testing. More issues caught earlier lead to fewer errors being identified in the dynamic test phase and result in fewer defects in shipped products. Moreover, performing static tests is less expensive than performing dynamic tests. Code review is one component of the defect minimization process and can help detect problems that are common to software development. After a round of code review, dynamic unit testing is conducted. In dynamic unit testing, a program unit is actually executed and its outcomes are observed. Dynamic unit testing means testing the code by actually running it. It may be noted that static unit testing is not an alternative to dynamic unit testing. A programmer performs both kinds of tests. In practice, partial dynamic unit testing is performed concurrently with static unit testing. If the entire dynamic unit testing has been performed and a static unit testing identifies significant problems, the dynamic unit testing must be repeated. As a result of this repetition, the development schedule may be affected. To minimize the probability of such an event, it is required that static unit testing be performed prior to the final dynamic unit testing.

3.2   STATIC UNIT TESTING

Static unit testing is conducted as a part of a larger philosophical belief that a software product should undergo a phase of inspection and correction at each milestone in its life cycle. At a certain milestone, the product need not be in its final form. For example, completion of coding is a milestone, even though coding of all the units may not make the desired product. After coding, the next milestone is testing all or a substantial number of units forming the major components of the product. Thus, before units are individually tested by actually executing them, those are subject to usual review and correction as it is commonly understood. The idea behind review is to find the defects as close to their points of origin as possible so that those defects are eliminated with less effort, and the interim product contains fewer defects before the next task is undertaken.

In static unit testing, code is reviewed by applying techniques commonly known as *inspection* and *walkthrough*. The original definition of inspection was coined by Michael Fagan [1] and that of walkthrough by Edward Yourdon [2]:

- **Inspection:** It is a step-by-step peer group review of a work product, with each step checked against predetermined criteria.
- **Walkthrough:** It is a review where the author leads the team through a manual or simulated execution of the product using predefined scenarios.

Regardless of whether a review is called an inspection or a walkthrough, it is a systematic approach to examining source code in detail. The goal of such an exercise is to assess the quality of the software in question, *not* the quality of the process used to develop the product [3]. Reviews of this type are characterized by significant preparation by groups of designers and programmers with varying degree of interest in the software development project. Code examination can be time consuming. Moreover, no examination process is perfect. Examiners may take shortcuts, may not have adequate understanding of the product, and may accept a product which should not be accepted. Nonetheless, a well-designed code review process can find faults that may be missed by execution-based testing. The key to the success of code review is to divide and conquer, that is, having an examiner inspect small parts of the unit in isolation, while making sure of the following: (i) nothing is overlooked and (ii) the correctness of all examined parts of the module implies the correctness of the whole module. The decomposition of the review into discrete steps must assure that each step is simple enough that it can be carried out without detailed knowledge of the others.

The objective of code review is to review the code, not to evaluate the author of the code. A clash may occur between the author of the code and the reviewers, and this may make the meetings unproductive. Therefore, code review must be planned and managed in a professional manner. There is a need for mutual respect, openness, trust, and sharing of expertise in the group. The general guidelines for performing code review consists of six steps as outlined in Figure 3.1: readiness, preparation, examination, rework, validation, and exit. The input to the readiness step is the criteria that must be satisfied before the start of the code review process, and the process produces two types of documents, a change request (CR) and a report. These steps and documents are explained in the following.

Step 1: Readiness The author of the unit ensures that the unit under test is ready for review. A unit is said to be ready if it satisfies the following criteria:

- **Completeness:** All the code relating to the unit to be reviewed must be available. This is because the reviewers are going to read the code and try to understand it. It is unproductive to review partially written code or code that is going to be significantly modified by the programmer.

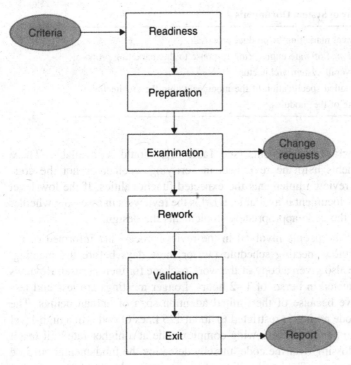

Figure 3.1   Steps in the code review process.

- **Minimal Functionality:** The code must compile and link. Moreover, the code must have been tested to some extent to make sure that it performs its basic functionalities.

- **Readability:** Since code review involves actual reading of code by other programmers, it is essential that the code is highly readable. Some code characteristics that enhance readability are proper formatting, using meaningful identifier names, straightforward use of programming language constructs, and an appropriate level of abstraction using function calls. In the absence of readability, the reviewers are likely to be discouraged from performing the task effectively.

- **Complexity:** There is no need to schedule a group meeting to review straightforward code which can be easily reviewed by the programmer. The code to be reviewed must be of sufficient complexity to warrant group review. Here, complexity is a composite term referring to the number of conditional statements in the code, the number of input data elements of the unit, the number of output data elements produced by the unit, real-time processing of the code, and the number of other units with which the code communicates.

- **Requirements and Design Documents:** The latest approved version of the low-level design specification or other appropriate descriptions

TABLE 3.1 Hierarchy of System Documents

Requirement: High-level marketing or product proposal.
Functional specification: Software engineering response to the marketing proposal.
High-level design: Overall system architecture.
Low-level design: Detailed specification of the modules within the architecture.
Programming: Coding of the modules.

of program requirements (see Table 3.1) should be available. These documents help the reviewers in verifying whether or not the code under review implements the expected functionalities. If the low-level design document is available, it helps the reviewers in assessing whether or not the code appropriately implements the design.

All the people involved in the review process are informed of the group review meeting schedule two or three days before the meeting. They are also given a copy of the work package for their perusal. Reviews are conducted in bursts of 1–2 hours. Longer meetings are less and less productive because of the limited attention span of human beings. The rate of code review is restricted to about 125 lines of code (in a high-level language) per hour. Reviewing complex code at a higher rate will result in just glossing over the code, thereby defeating the fundamental purpose of code review. The composition of the review group involves a number of people with different roles. These roles are explained as follows:

- **Moderator:** A review meeting is chaired by the moderator. The moderator is a trained individual who guides the pace of the review process. The moderator selects the reviewers and schedules the review meetings. Myers suggests that the moderator be a member of a group from an unrelated project to preserve objectivity [4].

- **Author:** This is the person who has written the code to be reviewed.

- **Presenter:** A presenter is someone other than the author of the code. The presenter reads the code beforehand to understand it. It is the presenter who presents the author's code in the review meeting for the following reasons: (i) an additional software developer will understand the work within the software organization; (ii) if the original programmer leaves the company with a short notice, at least one other programmer in the company knows what is being done; and (iii) the original programmer will have a good feeling about his or her work, if someone else appreciates their work. Usually, the presenter appreciates the author's work.

- **Recordkeeper:** The recordkeeper documents the problems found during the review process and the follow-up actions suggested. The person should be different than the author and the moderator.

- **Reviewers:** These are experts in the subject area of the code under review. The group size depends on the content of the material under review. As a rule of thumb, the group size is between 3 and 7. Usually this group does not have manager to whom the author reports. This is because it is the author's ongoing work that is under review, and neither a completed work nor the author himself is being reviewed.

- **Observers:** These are people who want to learn about the code under review. These people do not participate in the review process but are simply passive observers.

Step 2: **Preparation** Before the meeting, each reviewer carefully reviews the work package. It is expected that the reviewers read the code and understand its organization and operation before the review meeting. Each reviewer develops the following:

- **List of Questions:** A reviewer prepares a list of questions to be asked, if needed, of the author to clarify issues arising from his or her reading. A general guideline of what to examine while reading the code is outlined in Table 3.2.

- **Potential CR:** A reviewer may make a formal request to make a change. These are called change requests rather than defect reports. At this stage, since the programmer has not yet made the code public, it is more appropriate to make suggestions to the author to make changes, rather than report a defect. Though CRs focus on defects in the code, these reports are not included in defect statistics related to the product.

- **Suggested Improvement Opportunities:** The reviewers may suggest how to fix the problems, if there are any, in the code under review. Since reviewers are experts in the subject area of the code, it is not unusual for them to make suggestions for improvements.

Step 3: **Examination** The examination process consists of the following activities:

- The author makes a presentation of the procedural logic used in the code, the paths denoting major computations, and the dependency of the unit under review on other units.

- The presenter reads the code line by line. The reviewers may raise questions if the code is seen to have defects. However, problems are not resolved in the meeting. The reviewers may make general suggestions on how to fix the defects, but it is up to the author of the code to take corrective measures after the meeting ends.

- The recordkeeper documents the change requests and the suggestions for fixing the problems, if there are any. A CR includes the following details:

  1. Give a brief description of the issue or action item.
  2. Assign a priority level (major or minor) to a CR.
  3. Assign a person to follow up the issue. Since a CR documents a potential problem, there is a need for interaction between the author

TABLE 3.2 Code Review Checklist

1. Does the code do what has been specified in the design specification?
2. Does the procedure used in the module solve the problem correctly?
3. Does a software module duplicate another existing module which could be reused?
4. If library modules are being used, are the right libraries and the right versions of the libraries being used?
5. Does each module have a single entry point and a single exit point? Multiple exit and entry point programs are harder to test.
6. Is the cyclomatic complexity of the module more than 10? If yes, then it is extremely difficult to adequately test the module.
7. Can each atomic function be reviewed and understood in 10–15 minutes? If not, it is considered to be too complex.
8. Have naming conventions been followed for all identifiers, such as pointers, indices, variables, arrays, and constants? It is important to adhere to coding standards to ease the introduction of a new contributor (programmer) to the development of a system.
9. Has the code been adequately commented upon?
10. Have all the variables and constants been correctly initialized? Have correct types and scopes been checked?
11. Are the global or shared variables, if there are any, carefully controlled?
12. Are there data values hard coded in the program? Rather, these should be declared as variables.
13. Are the pointers being used correctly?
14. Are the dynamically acquired memory blocks deallocated after use?
15. Does the module terminate abnormally? Will the module eventually terminate?
16. Is there a possibility of an infinite loop, a loop that never executes, or a loop with a premature exit?
17. Have all the files been opened for use and closed at termination?
18. Are there computations using variables with inconsistent data types? Is overflow or underflow a possibility?
19. Are error codes and condition messages produced by accessing a common table of messages? Each error code should have a meaning, and all of the meanings should be available at one place in a table rather than scattered all over the program code.
20. Is the code portable? The source code is likely to execute on multiple processor architectures and on different operating systems over its lifetime. It must be implemented in a manner that does not preclude this kind of a variety of execution environments.
21. Is the code efficient? In general, clarity, readability, or correctness should not be sacrificed for efficiency. Code review is intended to detect implementation choices that have adverse effects on system performance.

of the code and one of the reviewers, possibly the reviewer who made the CR.

4. Set a deadline for addressing a CR.

- The moderator ensures that the meeting remains focused on the review process. The moderator makes sure that the meeting makes progress at a certain rate so that the objective of the meeting is achieved.

- At the end of the meeting, a decision is taken regarding whether or not to call another meeting to further review the code. If the review process leads to extensive rework of the code or critical issues are identified in the process, then another meeting is generally convened. Otherwise, a second meeting is not scheduled, and the author is given the responsibility of fixing the CRs.

Step 4: **Rework**   At the end of the meeting, the recordkeeper produces a summary of the meeting that includes the following information:

- A list of all the CRs, the dates by which those will be fixed, and the names of the persons responsible for validating the CRs

- A list of improvement opportunities

- The minutes of the meeting (optional)

A copy of the report is distributed to all the members of the review group. After the meeting, the author works on the CRs to fix the problems. The author documents the improvements made to the code in the CRs. The author makes an attempt to address the issues within the agreed-upon time frame using the prevailing coding conventions [5].

Step 5: **Validation**   The CRs are independently validated by the moderator or another person designated for this purpose. The validation process involves checking the modified code as documented in the CRs and ensuring that the suggested improvements have been implemented correctly. The revised and final version of the outcome of the review meeting is distributed to all the group members.

Step 6: **Exit**   Summarizing the review process, it is said to be complete if all of the following actions have been taken:

- Every line of code in the unit has been inspected.

- If too many defects are found in a module, the module is once again reviewed after corrections are applied by the author. As a rule of thumb, if more than 5% of the total lines of code are thought to be contentious, then a second review is scheduled.

- The author and the reviewers reach a consensus that when corrections have been applied the code will be potentially free of defects.

- All the CRs are documented and validated by the moderator or someone else. The author's follow-up actions are documented.

- A summary report of the meeting including the CRs is distributed to all the members of the review group.

The effectiveness of static testing is limited by the ability of a reviewer to find defects in code by visual means. However, if occurrences of defects depend on some actual values of variables, then it is a difficult task to identify those defects by visual means. Therefore, a unit must be executed to observe its behaviors in response to a variety of inputs. Finally, whatever may be the effectiveness of static tests, one cannot feel confident without actually running the code.

Code Review Metrics   It is important to collect measurement data pertinent to a review process, so that the review process can be evaluated, made visible to the upper management as a testing strategy, and improved to be more effective. Moreover, collecting metrics during code review facilitates estimation of review time and resources for future projects. Thus, code review is a viable testing strategy that can be effectively used to improve the quality of products at an early stage. The following metrics can be collected from a code review:

- Number of lines of code (LOC) reviewed per hour
- Number of CRs generated per thousand lines of code (KLOC)
- Number of CRs generated per hour
- Total number of CRs generated per project
- Total number of hours spent on code review per project

3.3   DEFECT PREVENTION

It is in the best interest of the programmers in particular and the company in general to reduce the number of CRs generated during code review. This is because CRs are indications of potential problems in the code, and those problems must be resolved before different program units are integrated. Addressing CRs means spending more resources and potentially delaying the project. Therefore, it is essential to adopt the concept of defect prevention during code development. In practice, defects are inadvertently introduced by programmers. Those accidents can be reduced by taking preventive measures. It is useful to develop a set of guidelines to construct code for defect minimization as explained in the following. These guidelines focus on incorporating suitable mechanisms into the code:

- Build internal diagnostic tools, also known as *instrumentation code*, into the units. Instrumentation codes are useful in providing information about the internal states of the units. These codes allow programmers to realize built-in tracking and tracing mechanisms. Instrumentation plays a passive role in dynamic unit testing. The role is passive in the sense of observing and recording the internal behavior without actively testing a unit.
- Use standard controls to detect possible occurrences of error conditions. Some examples of error detection in the code are divides by zero and array index out of bounds.
- Ensure that code exists for all return values, some of which may be invalid. Appropriate follow-up actions need to be taken to handle invalid return values.
- Ensure that counter data fields and buffer overflow and underflow are appropriately handled.
- Provide error messages and help texts from a common source so that changes in the text do not cause inconsistency. Good error messages

identify the root causes of the problems and help users in resolving the problems [7].

- Validate input data, such as the arguments, passed to a function.
- Use assertions to detect impossible conditions, undefined uses of data, and undesirable program behavior. An assertion is a Boolean statement which should never be false or can be false only if an error has occurred. In other words, an assertion is a check on a condition which is assumed to be true, but it can cause a problem if it not true. Assertion should be routinely used to perform the following kinds of checks:

  1. Ensure that preconditions are satisfied before beginning to execute a unit. A precondition is a Boolean function on the states of a unit specifying our expectation of the state prior to initiating an activity in the code.

  2. Ensure that the expected postconditions are true while exiting from the unit. A postcondition is a Boolean function on the state of a unit specifying our expectation of the state after an activity has been completed. The postconditions may include an invariance.

  3. Ensure that the invariants hold. That is, check invariant states— conditions which are expected not to change during the execution of a piece of code.

- Leave assertions in the code. You may deactivate them in the released version of code in order to improve the operational performance of the system.
- Fully document the assertions that appear to be unclear.
- After every major computation, reverse-compute the input(s) from the results in the code itself. Then compare the outcome with the actual inputs for correctness. For example, suppose that a piece of code computes the square root of a positive number. Then square the output value and compare the result with the input. It may be needed to tolerate a margin of error in the comparison process.
- In systems involving message passing, buffer management is an important internal activity. Incoming messages are stored in an already allocated buffer. It is useful to generate an event indicating low buffer availability before the system runs out of buffer. Develop a routine to continually monitor the availability of buffer after every use, calculate the remaining space available in the buffer, and call an error handling routine if the amount of available buffer space is too low.
- Develop a timer routine which counts down from a preset time until it either hits zero or is reset. If the software is caught in an infinite loop, the timer will expire and an exception handler routine can be invoked.
- Include a loop counter within each loop. If the loop is ever executed less than the minimum possible number of times or more than the maximum possible number of times, then invoke an exception handler routine.

- Define a variable to indicate the branch of decision logic that will be taken. Check this value after the decision has been made and the right branch has supposedly been taken. If the value of the variable has not been preset, there is probably a fall-through condition in the logic.

3.4   DYNAMIC UNIT TESTING

Execution-based unit testing is referred to as dynamic unit testing. In this testing, a program unit is actually executed in isolation, as we commonly understand it. However, this execution differs from ordinary execution in the following way:

1. A unit under test is taken out of its actual execution environment.

2. The actual execution environment is emulated by writing more code (explained later in this section) so that the unit and the emulated environment can be compiled together.

3. The above compiled aggregate is executed with selected inputs. The outcome of such an execution is collected in a variety of ways, such as straightforward observation on a screen, logging on files, and software instrumentation of the code to reveal run time behavior. The result is compared with the expected outcome. Any difference between the actual and expected outcome implies a failure and the fault is in the code.

An environment for dynamic unit testing is created by emulating the context of the unit under test, as shown in Figure 3.2. The context of a unit test consists of two parts: (i) a caller of the unit and (ii) all the units called by the unit. The environment of a unit is emulated because the unit is to be tested in isolation and the emulating environment must be a simple one so that any fault found as a result of running the unit can be solely attributed to the unit under test. The caller unit is known as a *test driver*, and all the emulations of the units called by the unit under test are called *stubs*. The test driver and the stubs are together called *scaffolding*. The functions of a test driver and a stub are explained as follows:

- **Test Driver:** A test driver is a program that invokes the unit under test. The unit under test executes with input values received from the driver and, upon termination, returns a value to the driver. The driver compares the actual outcome, that is, the actual value returned by the unit under test, with the expected outcome from the unit and reports the ensuing test result. The test driver functions as the *main* unit in the execution process. The driver not only facilitates compilation, but also provides input data to the unit under test in the expected format.

- **Stubs:** A stub is a "dummy subprogram" that replaces a unit that is called by the unit under test. Stubs replace the units called by the unit under test. A stub performs two tasks. First, it shows an evidence that the stub was,

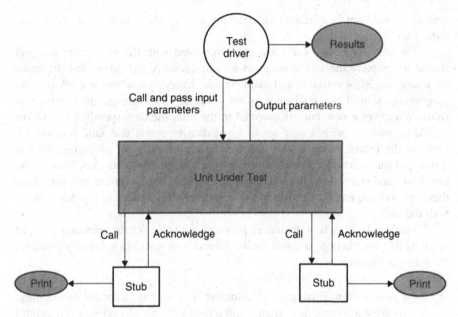

Figure 3.2   Dynamic unit test environment.

in fact, called. Such evidence can be shown by merely printing a message. Second, the stub returns a precomputed value to the caller so that the unit under test can continue its execution.

The driver and the stubs are never discarded after the unit test is completed. Instead, those are reused in the future in regression testing of the unit if there is such a need. For each unit, there should be one dedicated test driver and several stubs as required. If just one test driver is developed to test multiple units, the driver will be a complicated one. Any modification to the driver to accommodate changes in one of the units under test may have side effects in testing the other units. Similarly, the test driver should not depend on the external input data files but, instead, should have its own segregated set of input data. The separate input data file approach becomes a very compelling choice for large amounts of test input data. For example, if hundreds of input test data elements are required to test more than one unit, then it is better to create a separate input test data file rather than to include the same set of input test data in each test driver designed to test the unit.

The test driver should have the capability to automatically determine the success or failure of the unit under test for each input test data. If appropriate, the driver should also check for memory leaks and problems in allocation and deallocation of memory. If the module opens and closes files, the test driver should check that these files are left in the expected open or closed state after each test. The test driver can be designed to check the data values of the internal variable that normally would not be available for checking at integration, system, or acceptance testing levels.

The test driver and stubs are tightly coupled with the unit under test and should accompany the unit throughout its life cycle. A test driver and the stubs for a unit should be reusable and maintainable. Every time a unit is modified, the programmer should check whether or not to modify the corresponding driver and stubs. Whenever a new fault is detected in the unit, the corresponding test driver should be updated with a new set of input data to detect that fault and similar faults in the future. If the unit is expected to run on different platforms, the test driver and stubs should also be built to test the unit on new platforms. Finally, the test driver and stubs should be reviewed, cross-referenced with the unit for which these are written, and checked in to the version control system as a product along with the unit.

The low-level design document provides guidance for the selection of input test data that are likely to uncover faults. Selection of test data is broadly based on the following techniques:

- **Control Flow Testing:** The following is an outline of control flow testing: (i) draw a control flow graph from a program unit; (ii) select a few control flow testing criteria; (iii) identify paths in the control flow graph to satisfy the selection criteria; (iv) derive path predicate expressions from the selected paths; and (v) by solving the path predicate expression for a path, generate values of the inputs to the program unit that are considered as a test case to exercise the corresponding path. A thorough discussion of control flow testing is given in Chapter 4.

- **Data Flow Testing:** The following is an outline of data flow testing: (i) draw a data flow graph from a program unit; (ii) select a few data flow testing criteria; (iii) identify paths in the data flow graph to satisfy the selection criteria; (iv) derive path predicate expressions from the selected paths; and (v) by solving the path predicate expression, generate values of the inputs to the program unit that are considered as a test case to exercise the corresponding path. Chapter 5 discusses data flow testing in greater detail.

- **Domain Testing:** In control flow and data flow testing, no specific types of faults are explicitly considered for detection. However, domain testing takes a new approach to fault detection. In this approach, a category of faults called *domain errors* are defined and then test data are selected to catch those faults. It is discussed in detail in Chapter 6.

- **Functional Program Testing:** In functional program testing one performs the following steps: (i) identify the input and output domains of a program; (ii) for a given input domain, select some *special* values and compute the expected outcome; (iii) for a given output domain, select some *special* values and compute the input values that will cause the unit to produce those output values; and (iv) consider various combinations of the input values chosen above. Chapter 9 discusses functional testing.

3.5 MUTATION TESTING

Mutation testing has a rich and long history. It can be traced back to the late 1970s [8–10]. Mutation testing was originally proposed by Dick Lipton, and the article by DeMillo, Lipton, and Sayward [9] is generally cited as the seminal reference. Mutation testing is a technique that focuses on measuring the adequacy of test data (or test cases). The original intention behind mutation testing was to expose and locate weaknesses in test cases. Thus, mutation testing is a way to measure the quality of test cases, and the actual testing of program units is an added benefit. Mutation testing is not a testing strategy like control flow or data flow testing. It should be used to supplement traditional unit testing techniques.

A mutation of a program is a modification of the program created by introducing a single, small, legal syntactic change in the code. A modified program so obtained is called a *mutant*. The term mutant has been borrowed from biology. Some of these mutants are equivalent to the original program, whereas others are faulty. A mutant is said to be *killed* when the execution of a test case causes it to fail and the mutant is considered to be *dead*.

Some mutants are *equivalent* to the given program, that is, such mutants always produce the same output as the original program. In the real world, large programs are generally faulty, and test cases too contain faults. The result of executing a mutant may be different from the expected result, but a test suite does not detect the failure because it does not have the right test case. In this scenario the mutant is called *killable* or *stubborn*, that is, the existing set of test cases is insufficient to kill it. A *mutation score* for a set of test cases is the percentage of nonequivalent mutants killed by the test suite. The test suite is said to be *mutation adequate* if its mutation score is 100%. Mutation analysis is a two-step process:

1. The adequacy of an existing test suite is determined to distinguish the given program from its mutants. A given test suite may not be adequate to distinguish all the nonequivalent mutants. As explained above, those nonequivalent mutants that could not be identified by the given test suite are called stubborn mutants.

2. New test cases are added to the existing test suite to kill the stubborn mutants. The test suite enhancement process iterates until the test suite has reached a desired level of mutation score.

Let us consider the following program *P* that finds rank corresponding to the first time the maximum value appears in the array. For simplicity, we assume that the program *P* reads three input arguments and prints the message accordingly:

```
1. main(argc,argv)
2. int argc, r, i;
3. char *argv[];
4. { r = 1;
5.    for i = 2 to 3 do
6.       if (atoi(argv[i]) > atoi(argv[r])) r = i;
```

```
7. printf("Value of the rank is %d \n", r);
8. exit(0); }
```

Now let us assume that we have the following test suite that tests the program P:

> Test case 1:
>
> > Input: 1 2 3
> >
> > Output: Value of the rank is 3
>
> Test case 2:
>
> > Input: 1 2 1
> >
> > Output: Values of the rank is 2
>
> Test case 3:
>
> > Input: 3 1 2
> >
> > Output: Value of the rank is 1

Now, let us mutate the program P. We can start with the following changes:

> Mutant 1: Change line 5 to

```
for i = 1 to 3 do
```

> Mutant 2: Change line 6 to

```
if (i > atoi(argv[r])) r = i;
```

> Mutant 3: Change line 6 to

```
if (atoi(argv[i]) >= atoi(argv[r])) r = i;
```

> Mutant 4: Change line 6 to

```
if (atoi(argv[r]) > atoi(argv[r])) r = i;
```

If we run the modified programs against the test suite, we will get the following results:

> Mutants 1 and 3: The programs will completely pass the test suite. In other words, mutants 1 and 3 are not killed.
>
> Mutant 2: The program will fail test case 2.
>
> Mutant 4: The program will fail test case 1 and test case 2.

If we calculate the mutation score, we see that we created four mutants, and two of them were killed. This tells us that the mutation score is 50%, assuming that mutants 1 and 3 are nonequivalent.

The score is found to be low. It is low because we assumed that mutants 1 and 3 are nonequivalent to the original program. We have to show that either mutants

1 and 3 are equivalent mutants or those are killable. If those are killable, we need to add new test cases to kill these two mutants. First, let us analyze mutant 1 in order to derive a "killer" test. The difference between P and mutant 1 is the starting point. Mutant 1 starts with $i = 1$, whereas P starts with $i = 2$. There is no impact on the result r. Therefore, we conclude that mutant 1 is an equivalent mutant. Second, we add a fourth test case as follows:

Test case 4:

Input: 2 2 1

Then program P will produce the output "Value of the rank is 1" and mutant 3 will produce the output "Value of the rank is 2." Thus, this test data kills mutant 3, which give us a mutation score of 100%.

In order to use the mutation testing technique to build a robust test suite, the test engineer needs to follow the steps that are outlined below:

Step 1: Begin with a program P and a set of test cases T known to be correct.

Step 2: Run each test case in T against the program P. If a test case fails, that is, the output is incorrect, program P must be modified and retested. If there are no failures, then continue with step 3.

Step 3: Create a set of mutants $\{P_i\}$, each differing from P by a simple, syntactically correct modification of P.

Step 4: Execute each test case in T against each mutant P_i. If the output of the mutant P_i differs from the output of the original program P, the mutant P_i is considered incorrect and is said to be killed by the test case. If P_i produces exactly the same results as the original program P for the tests in T, then one of the following is true:

- P and P_i are *equivalent*. That is, their behaviors cannot be distinguished by any set of test cases. Note that the general problem of deciding whether or not a mutant is equivalent to the original program is undecidable.

- P_i is *killable*. That is, the test cases are insufficient to kill the mutant P_i. In this case, new test cases must be created.

Step 5: Calculate the mutation score for the set of test cases T. The mutation score is the percentage of nonequivalent mutants killed by the test data, that is, Mutation score $= 100 \times D/(N - E)$, where D is the dead mutants, N the total number of mutants, and E the number of equivalent mutants.

Step 6: If the estimated mutation adequacy of T in step 5 is not sufficiently high, then design a new test case that distinguishes P_i from P, add the new test case to T, and go to step 2. If the computed adequacy of T is more than an appropriate threshold, then accept T as a good measure of the correctness of P with respect to the set of mutant programs P_i, and stop designing new test cases.

Mutation testing makes two major assumptions:

1. *Competent Programmer Hypothesis*: This assumption states that programmers are generally competent, and they do not create "random" programs. Therefore, we can assume that for a given problem a programmer will create a correct program except for simple errors. In other words, the mutants to be considered are the ones falling within a small deviation from the original program. In practice, such mutants are obtained by systematically and mechanically applying a set of transformations, called *mutation operators*, to the program under test. These mutation operators are expected to model programming errors made by programmers. In practice, this may be only partly true.

2. *Coupling Effect*: This assumption was first hypothesized in 1978 by DeMillo et al. [9]. The assumption can be restated as complex faults are coupled to simple faults in such a way that a test suite detecting all simple faults in a program will detect most of the complex faults. This assumption has been empirically supported by Offutt [11] and theoretically demonstrated by Wah [12]. The fundamental premise of mutation testing as coined by Geist et al. [13] is: *If the software contains a fault, there will usually be a set of mutants that can only be killed by a test case that also detect that fault*.

Mutation testing helps the tester to inject, by hypothesis, different types of faults in the code and develop test cases to reveal them. In addition, comprehensive testing can be performed by proper choice of mutant operations. However, a relatively large number of mutant programs need to be tested against many of the test cases before these mutants can be distinguished from the original program. Running the test cases, analyzing the results, identifying equivalent mutants [14], and developing additional test cases to kill the stubborn mutants are all time consuming. Robust automated testing tools such as Mothra [15] can be used to expedite the mutation testing process. Recently, with the availability of massive computing power, there has been a resurgence of mutation testing processes within the industrial community to use as a white-box methodology for unit testing [16, 17]. Researchers have shown that with an appropriate choice of mutant programs mutation testing is as powerful as path testing, domain testing [18], and data flow testing [19].

3.6 DEBUGGING

The programmer, after a program failure, identifies the corresponding fault and fixes it. The process of determining the cause of a failure is known as *debugging*. Debugging occurs as a consequence of a test revealing a failure. Myers proposed three approaches to debugging in his book *The Art of Software Testing* [20]:

- **Brute Force:** The brute-force approach to debugging is preferred by many programmers. Here, "let the computer find the error" philosophy is used.

Print statements are scattered throughout the source code. These print statements provide a crude trace of the way the source code has executed. The availability of a good debugging tool makes these print statements redundant. A dynamic debugger allows the software engineer to navigate by stepping through the code, observe which paths have executed, and observe how values of variables change during the controlled execution. A good tool allows the programmer to assign values to several variables and navigate step by step through the code. Instrumentation code can be built into the source code to detect problems and to log intermediate values of variables for problem diagnosis. One may use a memory dump after a failure has occurred to understand the final state of the code being debugged. The log and memory dump are reviewed to understand what happened and how the failure occurred.

- **Cause Elimination:** The cause elimination approach can be best described as a process involving *induction* and *deduction* [21]. In the induction part, first, all pertinent data related to the failure are collected , such as what happened and what the symptoms are. Next, the collected data are organized in terms of behavior and symptoms, and their relationship is studied to find a pattern to isolate the causes. A cause hypothesis is devised, and the above data are used to prove or disprove the hypothesis. In the deduction part, a list of all possible causes is developed in order of their likelihoods, and tests are conducted to eliminate or substantiate each cause in decreasing order of their likelihoods. If the initial tests indicate that a particular hypothesis shows promise, test data are refined in an attempt to isolate the problem as needed.

- **Backtracking:** In this approach, the programmer starts at a point in the code where a failure was observed and traces back the execution to the point where it occurred. This technique is frequently used by programmers, and this is useful in small programs. However, the probability of tracing back to the fault decreases as the program size increases, because the number of potential backward paths may become too large.

Often, software engineers notice other previously undetected problems while debugging and applying a fix. These newly discovered faults should not be fixed along with the fix in focus. This is because the software engineer may not have a full understanding of the part of the code responsible for the new fault. The best way to deal with such a situation is to file a CR. A new CR gives the programmer an opportunity to discuss the matter with other team members and software architects and to get their approval on a suggestion made by the programmer. Once the CR is approved, the software engineer must file a defect in the defect tracking database and may proceed with the fix. This process is cumbersome, and it interrupts the debugging process, but it is useful for very critical projects. However, programmers often do not follow this because of a lack of a procedure to enforce it.

A Debugging Heuristic   The objective of debugging is to precisely identify the cause of a failure. Once the cause is identified, corrective measures are taken to fix the fault. Debugging is conducted by programmers, preferably by those who wrote the code, because the programmer is the best person to know the source code well enough to analyze the code efficiently and effectively. Debugging is usually a time consuming and error-prone process, which is generally performed under stress. Debugging involves a combination of systematic evaluation, intuition, and, sometimes, a little bit of luck. Given a symptom of a problem, the purpose is to isolate and determine its specific cause. The following heuristic may be followed to isolate and correct it:

Step 1: Reproduce the symptom(s).

- Read the troubleshooting guide of the product. This guide may include conditions and logs, produced by normal code, or diagnostics code specifically written for troubleshooting purpose that can be turned on.

- Try to reproduce the symptoms with diagnostics code turned on.

- Gather all the information and conduct *causal analysis* The goal of causal analysis is to identify the root cause of the problem and initiate actions so that the source of defects is eliminated.

Step 2: Formulate some likely hypotheses for the cause of the problem based on the causal analysis.

Step 3: Develop a test scenario for each hypothesis to be proved or disproved. This is done by designing test cases to provide unambiguous results related to a hypothesis. The test cases may be static (reviewing code and documentation) and/or dynamic in nature. Preferably, the test cases are nondestructive, have low cost, and need minimum additional hardware needs. A test case is said to be destructive if it destroys the hardware setup. For example, cutting a cable during testing is called destructive testing.

Step 4: Prioritize the execution of test cases. Test cases corresponding to the highly probable hypotheses are executed first. Also, the cost factor cannot be overlooked. Therefore, it is desirable to execute the low-cost test cases first followed by the more expensive ones. The programmer needs to consider both factors.

Step 5: Execute the test cases in order to find the cause of a symptom. After executing a test case, examine the result for new evidence. If the test result shows that a particular hypothesis is promising, test data are refined in an attempt to isolate the defect. If necessary, go back to earlier steps or eliminate a particular hypothesis.

Step 6: Fix the problem.

- Fixing the problem may be a simple task, such as adding a line of code or changing a variable in a line of code, or a more complex task such as modifying several lines of code or designing a new unit. In the complex case, defect fixing is a rigorous activity.

- If code review has already been completed for the module which received a fix, then code review must be done once again to avoid any side effects (collateral damage) due to the changes effected in the module.

- After a possible code review, apply the fix.

- Retest the unit to confirm that the actual cause of failure had been found. The unit is properly debugged and fixed if tests show that the observed failure does not occur any more.

- If there are no dynamic unit test cases that reveal the problem, then add a new test case to the dynamic unit testing to detect possible reoccurrences or other similar problems.

- For the unit under consideration, identify all the test cases that have passed. Now, perform a regression test on the unit with those test cases to ensure that new errors have not been introduced. That is why it is so important to have archived all the test cases that have been designed for a unit. Thus, even unit-level test cases must be managed in a systematic manner to reduce the cost of software development.

Step 7: Document the changes which have been made. Once a defect is fixed, the following changes are required to be applied:

- Document the changes in the source code itself to reflect the change.

- Update the overall system documentation.

- Changes to the dynamic unit test cases.

- File a defect in the defect tracking database if the problem was found after the code was checked in to the version control system.

3.7 UNIT TESTING IN EXTREME PROGRAMMING

A TDD approach to code development is used in the XP methodology [22, 23]. The key aspect of the TDD approach is that a programmer writes low-level tests before writing production code. This is referred to as *test first* [24] in software development. Writing test-driven units is an important concept in the XP methodology. In XP, a few unit tests are coded first, then a simple, partial system is implemented to pass the tests. Then, one more new unit test is created, and additional code is written to pass the new test, but not more, until a new unit test is created. The process is continued until nothing is left to test. The process is illustrated in Figure 3.3 and outlined below:

Step 1: Pick a requirement, that is, a story.

Step 2: Write a test case that will verify a small part of the story and assign a fail verdict to it.

Step 3: Write the code that implements a particular part of the story to pass the test.

Step 4: Execute all tests.

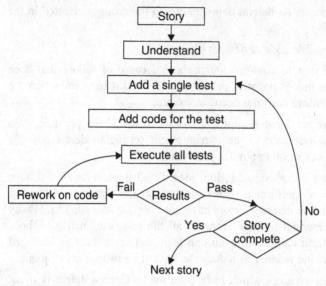

Figure 3.3   Test-first process in XP. (From ref. 24. © 2005 IEEE.)

Step 5: Rework the code, and test the code until all tests pass.

Step 6: Repeat **steps 2–5** until the story is fully implemented.

The simple cycle in Figure 3.3 shows that, at the beginning of each cycle, the intention is for all tests to pass except the newly added test case. The new test case is introduced to *drive* the new code development. At the end of the cycle, the programmer executes all the unit tests, ensuring that each one passes and, hence, the planned task of the code still works. A TDD developer must follow the three laws proposed by Robert C. Martin [25]:

- One may not write production code unless the first failing unit test is written.
- One may not write more of a unit test than is sufficient to fail.
- One may not write more production code than is sufficient to make the failing unit test pass.

These three laws ensure that one must write a portion of a unit test that fails and then write just enough production code to make that unit test pass. The goal of these three laws is not to follow them strictly—it is to decrease the interval between writing unit tests and production code.

Creating unit tests helps a developer focus on what needs to be done. Requirements, that is, user stories, are nailed down firmly by unit tests. Unit tests are released into the code repository along with the code they test. Code without unit tests may not be released. If a unit test is discovered to be missing, it must be created immediately. Creating unit tests independently before coding sets up checks and balances and improves the chances of getting the system right the first time.

Unit tests provide a safety net of regression tests and validation tests so that XP programmers can refactor and integrate effectively.

In XP, the code is being developed by two programmers working together side by side. The concept is called pair programming. The two programmers sit side by side in front of the monitor. One person develops the code tactically and the other one inspects it methodically by keeping in mind the story they are implementing. It is similar to the two-person inspection strategy proposed by Bisant and Lyle [26]. Code inspection is carried out by an author–examiner pair in discrete steps, examining a small part of the implementation of the story in isolation, which is key to the success of the code review process.

3.8 JUNIT: FRAMEWORK FOR UNIT TESTING

The JUnit is a unit testing framework for the Java programming language designed by Kent Beck and Erich Gamma. Experience gained with JUnit has motivated the development of the TDD [22] methodology. The idea in the JUnit framework has been ported to other languages, including C# (NUnit), Python (PyUnit), Fortran (fUnit) and C++ (CPPUnit). This family of unit testing frameworks is collectively referred to as xUnit. This section will introduce the fundamental concepts of JUnit to the reader.

Suppose that we want to test the individual methods of a class called Planet-Class. Let Move() be a method in PlanetClass such that Move() accepts only one input parameter of type *integer* and returns a value of type integer. One can follow the following steps, illustrated using pseudocode in Figure 3.4, to test Move():

- Create an object instance of PlanetClass. Let us call the instance Mars. Now we are interested in testing the method Move() by invoking it on object Mars.
- Select a value for all the input parameters of Move()—this function has just one input parameter. Let us represent the input value to Move() by x.
- Know the expected value to be returned by Move(). Let the expected returned value be y.

```
:
Planet Mars = new Planet(); // Instantiate class Planet to create
                            // an object Mars.
x = ... ; // Select a value for x.
y = ... ; // The expected value to be returned by the call Move(x).
z = Mars.Move(x); // Invoke method Mars() on object Mars.
if (z == y) print("Test passed");
else print("Test failed.");
:
```

Figure 3.4 Sample pseudocode for performing unit testing.

- Invoke method Move() on object Mars with input value x. Let z denote the value returned by Move().
- Now compare y with z. If the two values are identical, then the method Move() in object Mars passes the test. Otherwise, the test is said to have failed.

In a nutshell, the five steps of unit testing are as follows:

- Create an object and select a method to execute.
- Select values for the input parameters of the method.
- Compute the expected values to be returned by the method.
- Execute the selected method on the created object using the selected input values.
- Verify the result of executing the method.

Performing unit testing leads to a programmer consuming some resources, especially time. Therefore, it is useful to employ a general programming framework to code individual test cases, organize a set of test cases as a *test suite*, initialize a test environment, execute the test suite, clean up the test environment, and record the result of execution of individual test cases. In the example shown in Figure 3.4, creating the object Mars is a part of the initialization process. The two print() statements are examples of recording the result of test execution. Alternatively, one can write the result of test execution to a file.

The JUnit framework has been developed to make test writing simple. The framework provides a basic class, called TestCase, to write test cases. Programmers need to *extend* the TestCase class to write a set of individual test cases. It may be noted that to write, for example, 10 test cases, one need not write 10 subclasses of the class TestCase. Rather, one subclass, say MyTestCase, of TestCase, can contain 10 methods—one for each test case.

Programmers need to make assertions about the state of objects while extending the TestCase class to write test cases. For example, in each test case it is required to compare the actual outcome of a computation with the expected outcome. Though an if() statement can be used to compare the equality of two values or two objects, it is seen to be more elegant to write an assert statement to achieve the same. The class TestCase extends a utility class called Assert in the JUnit framework. Essentially, the Assert class provides methods, as explained in the following, to make assertions about the state of objects created and manipulated while testing.

assertTrue(Boolean condition): This assertion passes if the condition is *true*; otherwise, it fails.

assertEquals(Object expected, Object actual): This assertion passes if the expected and the actual objects are equal according to the equals() method; otherwise, the assertion fails.

assertEquals(int expected, int actual): This assertion passes if expected and actual are equal according to the $==$ operator; otherwise, the assertion fails. For each primitive type int, float, double, char, byte, long, short, and boolean, the assertion has an overloaded version.

assertEquals(double expected, double actual, double tolerance): This assertion passes if the absolute value of the difference between expected and actual is less than or equal to the tolerance value; otherwise, the assertion fails. The assertion has an overloaded version for float inputs.

assertSame(Object expected, Object actual): This assertion passes if the expected and actual values refer to the same object in memory; otherwise, the assertion fails.

assertNull(Object testobject): This assertion passes if testobject is null; otherwise the assertion fails.

assertFalse(Boolean condition): This is the logical opposite of assertTrue().

The reader may note that the above list of assertions is not exhaustive. In fact, one can build other assertions while extending the TestCase class. When an assertion fails, a programmer may want to know immediately the nature of the failure. This can be done by displaying a message when the assertion fails. Each assertion method listed above accepts an optional *first* parameter of type String—if the assertion fails, then the String value is displayed. This facilitates the programmer to display a desired message when the assertion fails. As an aside, upon failure, the assertEquals() method displays a customized message showing the expected value and the actual value. For example, an assertEquals() method can display the following:

```
junit.framework.AssertionFailedError: expected: <2006> but
    was:<2060>.
```

At this point it is interesting to note that only failed tests are reported. Failed tests can be reported by various means, such as displaying a message, displaying an identifier for the test case, and counting the total number of failed test cases. Essentially, an assertion method throws an exception, called AssertionFailedError, when the assertion fails, and JUnit catches the exception. The code shown in Figure 3.5 illustrates how the assertTrue() assertion works: When the JUnit framework catches an exception, it records the fact that the assertion failed and proceeds to the next test case. Having executed all the test cases, JUnit produces a list of all those tests that have failed.

In Figure 3.6, we show an example of a test suite containing two test cases. In order to execute the two test cases, one needs to create an object instance of

```
static public void assertTrue(Boolean condition) {
        if (!condition)
                throw new AssertionFailedError();
}
```

Figure 3.5   The assertTrue() assertion throws an exception.

```
import TestMe; // TestMe is the class whose methods are going
             //to be tested.
import junit.framework.*; // This contains the TestCase class.

public class MyTestSuite  extends  TestCase { // Create a subclass
                                              //of TestCase

    public void MyTest1() { // This method is the first test case
         TestMe object1 = new TestMe( ... ); // Create an
                                      //instance of TestMe with
                                      //desired parameters
         int x = object1.Method1(...); //  invoke Method1
                                   //on object1
         assertEquals(365, x); // 365 and x are expected and
                             //actual values, respectively
    }

    public void MyTest2() { // This method is the second test case
         TestMe object2 = new TestMe( ... ); // Create another
                                      //instance of TestMe
                                      //with desired parameters
         double y = object2.Method2(...); //  invoke Method2
                                     //on object2
         assertEquals(2.99, y, 0.0001d); // 2.99 is the expected
                               // value; y is the actual
                               // value; 0.0001 is tolerance
                               // level
    }
}
```

Figure 3.6   Example test suite.

MyTestSuite and invoke the two methods MyTest1() and MyTest2(). Whether or not the two methods, namely Method1() and Method()2, are to be invoked on two different instances of the class TestMe depends on the individual objectives of those two test cases. In other words, it is the programmer who decides whether or not two instances of the class TestMe are to be created.

This section is by no means a thorough exposition of the capabilities of the JUnit framework. Readers are referred to other sources, such as *JUnit Recipes* by Rainsberger [27] and *Pragmatic Unit Testing* by Hunt and Thomas [28]. In addition, tools such as Korat [29], Symstra [30], and Eclat [31] for Java unit testing are being developed and used by researchers.

3.9   TOOLS FOR UNIT TESTING

Programmers can benefit from using tools in unit testing by reducing testing time without sacrificing thoroughness. The well-known tools in everyday life are an editor, a compiler, an operating system, and a debugger. However, in some cases, the real execution environment of a unit may not be available to a programmer while the code is being developed. In such cases, an emulator of the environment is useful in testing and debugging the code. Other kinds of tools that facilitate effective unit testing are as follows:

1. *Code Auditor:* This tool is used to check the quality of software to ensure that it meets some minimum coding standards. It detects violations of programming, naming, and style guidelines. It can identify portions of code that cannot be ported between different operating systems and processors. Moreover, it can suggest improvements to the structure and style of the source code. In addition, it counts the number of LOC which can be used to measure productivity, that is, LOC produced per unit time, and calculate defect density, that is, number of defects per KLOC.

2. *Bound Checker:* This tool can check for accidental writes into the instruction areas of memory or to any other memory location outside the data storage area of the application. This fills unused memory space with a signature pattern (distinct binary pattern) as a way of determining at a later time whether any of this memory space has been overwritten. The tool can issue diagnostic messages when boundary violations on data items occur. It can detect violation of the boundaries of array, for example, when the array index or pointer is outside its allowed range. For example, if an array z is declared to have a range from $z[0]$ to $z[99]$, it can detect reads and writes outside this range of storage, for example, $z[-3]$ or $z[10]$.

3. *Documenters:* These tools read source code and automatically generate descriptions and caller/callee tree diagram or data model from the source code.

4. *Interactive Debuggers:* These tools assist software developers in implementing different debugging approaches discussed in this chapter. These tools should have the trace-back and breakpoint capabilities to enable the programmers to understand the dynamics of program execution and to identify problem areas in the code. Breakpoint debuggers are based on deductive logic. Breakpoints are placed according to a heuristic analysis of code [32]. Another popular kind of debugger is known as omniscient debugger (ODB), in which there is no deduction. It simply follows the trail of "bad" values back to their source—no "guessing" where to put the breakpoints. An ODB is like "the snake in the grass," that is, if you see a snake in the grass and you pull its tail, sooner or later you get to its head. In contrast, breakpoint debuggers suffer from the "lizard in the grass" problem, that is, when you see the lizard and grab its tail, the lizard breaks off its tail and gets away [33].

5. *In-Circuit Emulators:* An in-circuit emulator, commonly known as ICE, is an invaluable software development tool in embedded system design. It provides a high-speed Ethernet connection between a host debugger and a target microprocessor, enabling developers to perform common source-level debugging activities, such as watching memory and controlling large numbers of registers, in a matter of seconds. It is vital for board bring-up, solving complex problems, and manufacturing or testing of products. Many emulators have advanced features, such as

performance analysis, coverage analysis, buffering of traces, and advance trigger and breakpoint possibilities.

6. *Memory Leak Detectors:* These tools test the allocation of memory to an application which requests for memory, but fails to deallocate. These detect the following overflow problems in application programs:

- Illegal read, that is, accesses to memory which is not allocated to the application or which the application is not authorized to access.

- Reads memory which has not been initialized.

- Dynamic memory overwrites to a memory location that has not been allocated to the application.

- Reading from a memory location not allocated, or not initialized, prior to the read operation.

The tools watch the heap, keep track of heap allocations to applications, and detect memory leaks. The tools also build profiles of memory use, for example, which line-of-code source instruction accesses a particular memory address.

7. *Static Code (Path) Analyzer:* These tools identify paths to test, based on the structure of the code such as McCabe's cyclomatic complexity measure (Table 3.3). Such tools are dependent on source language and require the source code to be recompiled with the tool. These tools can be used to improve productivity, resource management, quality, and predictability by providing complexity measurement metrics.

8. *Software Inspection Support:* Tools can help schedule group inspections. These can also provide status of items reviewed and follow-up actions and distribute the reports of problem resolution. They can be integrated with other tools, such as static code analyzers.

9. *Test Coverage Analyzer:* These tools measure internal test coverage, often expressed in terms of the control structure of the test object, and report the coverage metric. Coverage analyzers track and report what paths were exercised during dynamic unit testing. Test coverage analyzers are powerful tools that increase confidence in product quality by assuring that tests cover all of the structural parts of a unit or a program. An important aspect in test coverage analysis is to identify parts of source code that were never touched by any dynamic unit test. Feedback from the coverage reports to the source code makes it easier to design new unit test cases to cover the specific untested paths.

10. *Test Data Generator:* These tools assist programmers in selecting test data that cause a program to behave in a desired manner. Test data generators can offer several capabilities beyond the basics of data generation:

- They have generate a large number of variations of a desired data set based on a description of the characteristics which has been fed into the tool.

- They can generate test input data from source code.

- They can generate equivalence classes and values close to the boundaries.

- They can calculate the desired extent of boundary value testing.

TABLE 3.3   McCabe Complexity Measure

McCabe's complexity measure is based on the cyclomatic complexity of a programe graph for a module. The metric can be computed using the formula $v = e - n + 2$,
where
v = cyclomatic complexity of graph,
e = number of edges (program flow between nodes)
n = number of nodes (sequential group of program statements)
If a strongly connected graph is constructed (one in which there is an edge between the exit node and the entry node), the calculation is $v = e - n + 1$.
Example: A program graph, illustrated below, is used to depict control flow. Each circled node represents a sequence of program statements, and the flow of control is represented by directed edges. For this graph the cyclomatic complexity is $v = 9 - 8 + 2 = 3$

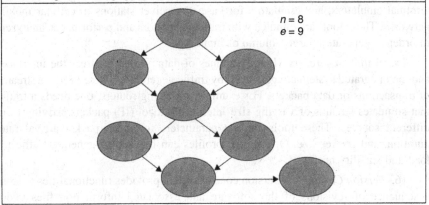

$n = 8$
$e = 9$

Source: From ref. 6.

- They can estimate the likelihood of the test data being able to reveal faults.

- They can generate data to assist in mutation analysis.

Automatic generation of test inputs is an active area of research. Several tools, such as CUTE [34], DART [35], and EGT system [36], have been developed by researchers to improve test coverage.

11. *Test Harness:* This class of tools supports the execution of dynamic unit tests by making it almost painless to (i) install the unit under test in a test environment, (ii) drive the unit under test with input data in the expected input format, (iii) generate stubs to emulate the behavior of subordinate modules, and (iv) capture the actual outcome as generated by the unit under test and log or display it in a usable form. Advanced tools may compare the expected outcome with the actual outcome and log a test verdict for each input test data.

12. *Performance Monitors:* The timing characteristics of software components can be monitored and evaluated by these tools. These tools are essential for any real-time system in order to evaluate the performance characteristics of the system, such as delay and throughput. For example, in telecommunication systems, these tools can be used to calculate the end-to-end delay of a telephone call.

13. *Network Analyzers:* Network operating systems such as software that run on routers, switches, and client/server systems are tested by network analyzers. These tools have the ability to analyze the traffic and identify problem areas. Many of these networking tools allow test engineers to monitor performance metrics and diagnose performance problems across the networks. These tools are enhanced to improve the network security monitoring (NSM) capabilities to detect intrusion [37].

14. *Simulators and Emulators:* These tools are used to replace the real software and hardware that are currently not available. Both kinds of tools are used for training, safety, and economy reasons. Some examples are flight simulators, terminal emulators, and emulators for base transceiver stations in cellular mobile networks. These tools are bundled with traffic generators and performance analyzers in order to generate a large volume of input data.

15. *Traffic Generators:* Large volumes of data needed to stress the interfaces and the integrated system are generated by traffic generators. These produce streams of transactions or data packets. For example, in testing routers, one needs a traffic that simulates streams of varying size Internet Protocol (IP) packets arriving from different sources. These tools can set parameters for mean packet arrival rate, duration, and packet size. Operational profiles can be used to generate traffic for load and stability testing.

16. *Version Control:* A version control system provides functionalities to store a sequence of revisions of the software and associated information files under development. A system release is a collection of the associated files from a version control tool perspective. These files may contain source code, compiled code, documentation, and environment information, such as version of the tool used to write the software. The objective of version control is to ensure a systematic and traceable software development process in which all changes are precisely managed, so that a software system is always in a well-defined state. With most of the version control tools, the repository is a central place that holds the master copy of all the files.

The configuration management system (CMS) extends the version control from software and documentation to control the changes made to hardware, firmware, software, documentation, test, test fixtures, test documentation, and execution environments throughout the development and operational life of a system. Therefore, configuration management tools are larger, better variations of version control tools. The characteristics of the version control and configuration management tools are as follows:

- **Access Control:** The tools monitor and control access to components. One can specify which users can access a component or group of components. One can also restrict access to components currently undergoing modification or testing.

- **Cross Referencing:** The tools can maintain linkages among related components, such as problem reports, components, fixes, and documentations.

One can merge files and coordinate multiple updates from different versions to produce one consolidated file.

- **Tracking of Modifications:** The tools maintain records of all modifications to components. These also allow merging of files and coordinate multiple updates from different versions to produce one consolidated file. These can track similarities and differences among versions of code, documentation, and test libraries. They also provide an audit trail or history of the changes from version to version.

- **Release Generation:** The tools can automatically build new system releases and insulate the development, test, and shipped versions of the product.

- **System Version Management:** The tools allow sharing of common components across system versions and controlled use of system versions. They support coordination of parallel development, maintenance, and integration of multiple components among several programmers or project teams. They also coordinate geographically dispersed development and test teams.

- **Archiving:** The tools support automatic archiving of retired components and system versions.

3.10 SUMMARY

This chapter began with a description of unit-level testing, which means identifying faults in a program unit analyzed and executed in isolation. Two complementary types of unit testing were introduced: static unit testing and dynamic unit testing. Static unit testing involves visual inspection and analysis of code, whereas a program unit is executed in a controlled manner in dynamic unit testing.

Next, we described a code review process, which comprises six steps: readiness, preparation, examination, rework, validation, and exit. The goal of code review is to assess the quality of the software in question, not the quality of the process used to develop the product. We discussed a few basic metrics that can be collected from the code review process. Those metrics facilitate estimation of review time and resources required for similar projects. Also, the metrics make code review visible to the upper management and allow upper management to be satisfied with the viability of code review as a testing tool.

We explained several preventive measures that can be taken during code development to reduce the number of faults in a program. The preventive measures were presented in the form of a set of guidelines that programmers can follow to construct code. Essentially, the guidelines focus on incorporating suitable mechanisms into the code.

Next, we studied dynamic unit testing in detail. In dynamic unit testing, a program unit is actually executed, and the outcomes of program execution are observed. The concepts of test driver and stubs were explained in the context of a unit under test. A test driver is a caller of the unit under test and all the "dummy modules" called by the unit are known as stubs. We described how mutation analysis can be used to locate weaknesses in test data used for unit testing. Mutation analysis should be used in conjunction with traditional unit testing techniques such as domain analysis or data flow analysis. That is, mutation testing is not an alternative to domain testing or data flow analysis.

With the unit test model in place to reveal defects, we examined how programmers can locate faults by debugging a unit. Debugging occurs as a consequence of a test revealing a defect. We discussed three approaches to debugging: brute force, cause elimination, and backtracking. The objective of debugging is to precisely identify the cause of a failure. Given the symptom of a problem, the purpose is to isolate and determine its specific cause. We explained a heuristic to perform program debugging.

Next, we explained dynamic unit testing is an integral part of the XP software development process. In the XP process, unit tests are created prior to coding—this is known as test first. The test-first approach sets up checks and balances to improve the chances of getting things right the first time. We then introduced the JUnit framework, which is used to create and execute dynamic unit tests.

We concluded the chapter with a description of several tools that can be useful in improving the effectiveness of unit testing. These tools are of the following types: code auditor, bound checker, documenters, interactive debuggers, in-circuit emulators, memory leak detectors, static code analyzers, tools for software inspection support, test coverage analyzers, test data generators, tools for creating test harness, performance monitors, network analyzers, simulators and emulators, traffic generators, and tools for version control.

LITERATURE REVIEW

The Institute of Electrical and Electronics Engineers (IEEE) standard 1028-1988 (*IEEE Standard for Software Reviews and Audits: IEEE/ANSI Standard*) describes the detailed examination process for a technical review, an inspection, a software walkthrough, and an audit. For each of the examination processes, it includes an objective, an abstract, special responsibilities, program input, entry criteria, procedures, exit criteria, output, and auditability.

Several improvements on Fagan's inspection techniques have been proposed by researchers during the past three decades. Those proposals suggest ways to enhance the effectiveness of the review process or to fit specific application domains. A number of excellent articles address various issues related to software inspection as follows:

S. Biffl, and M. Halling, "Investigating the Defect Effectiveness and Cost Benefit of Nominal Inspection Teams," *IEEE Transactions on Software Engineering*, Vol. 29, No. 5, May 2003, pp. 385–397.

A. A. Porter and P. M. Johnson, "Assessing Software Review Meeting: Results of a Comparative Analysis of Two Experimental Studies," *IEEE*

Transactions on Software Engineering, Vol. 23, No. 3, March 1997, pp. 129–145.

A. A. Porter, H. P. Siy, C. A. Toman, and L. G. Votta, "An Experiment to Assess the Cost-Benefits of Code Inspection in Large Scale Software Development," *IEEE Transactions on Software Engineering*, Vol. 23, No. 6, June 1997, pp. 329–346.

A. A. Porter and L. G. Votta, "What Makes Inspection Work," *IEEE Software*, Vol. 14, No. 5, May 1997, pp. 99–102.

C. Sauer, D. Jeffery, L. Land, and P. Yetton, "The Effectiveness of Software Development Technical Reviews: A Behaviorally Motivated Program of Search," *IEEE Transactions on Software Engineering*, Vol. 26, No. 1, January 2000, pp. 1–14.

An alternative non-execution-based technique is formal verification of code. Formal verification consists of mathematical proofs to show that a program is correct. The two most prominent methods for proving program properties are those of Dijkstra and Hoare:

E. W. Dijkstra, *A Discipline of Programming*, Prentice-Hall, Englewood Cliffs, NJ, 1976.

C. A. R. Hoare, "An Axiomatic Basis of Computer Programming," *Communications of the ACM*, Vol. 12, No. 10, October 1969, pp. 576–580.

Hoare presented an axiomatic approach in which properties of program fragments are described using preconditions and postconditions. An example statement with a precondition and a postcondition is {PRE} P {POST}, where PRE is the precondition, POST is the postcondition, and P is the program fragment. Both PRE and POST are expressed in first-order predicate calculus, which means that they can include the universal quantifier $\forall$ ("for all") and existential quantifier $\exists$ ("there exists"). The interpretation of the above statement is that if the program fragment P starts executing in a state satisfying PRE, then if P terminates, P will do so in a state satisfying POST.

Hoare's logic led to Dijkstra's closely related "calculus of programs," which is based on the idea of weakest preconditions. The weakest preconditions R with respect to a program fragment P and a postcondition POST is the set of all states that, when subject to P, will terminate and leave the state of computation in POST. The weakest precondition is written as WP(P, POST).

While mutation testing systematically implants faults in programs by applying syntactic transformations, *perturbation testing* is performed to test a program's robustness by changing the values of program data during run time, so that the subsequent execution will either fail or succeed. Program perturbation is based on three parts of software hypothesis as explained in the following:

- **Execution:** A fault must be executed.
- **Infection:** The fault must change the data state of the computation directly after the fault location.

- **Propagation:** The erroneous data state must propagate to an output variable.

In the perturbation technique, the programmer injects faults in the data state of an executing program and traces the injected faults on the program's output. A fault injection is performed by applying a perturbation function that changes the program's data state. A perturbation function is a mathematical function that takes a data state as its input, changes the data state according to some specified criteria, and produces a modified data state as output. For the interested readers, two excellent references on perturbation testing are as follows:

M. A. Friedman and J. M. Voas, *Software Assessment—Reliability, Safety, Testability*, Wiley, New York, 1995.

J. M. Voas and G. McGraw, *Software Fault Injection—Inoculating Programs Against Errors*, Wiley, New York, 1998.

The paper by Steven J. Zeil ("Testing for Perturbation of Program Statement," *IEEE Transactions on Software Engineering*, Vol. 9, No. 3, May 1983, pp. 335–346) describes a method for deducing sufficient path coverage to ensure the absence of prescribed errors in a program. It models the program computation and potential errors as a vector space. This enables the conditions for nondetection of an error to be calculated. The above article is an advanced reading for students who are interested in perturbation analysis.

Those readers actively involved in software configuration management (SCM) systems or interested in a more sophisticated treatment of the topic must read the article by Jacky Estublier, David Leblang, André V. Hoek, Reidar Conradi, Geoffrey Clemm, Walter Tichy, and Darcy Wiborg-Weber ("Impact of Software Engineering Research on the Practice of Software Configuration Management," *ACM Transactions on Software Engineering and Methodology*, Vol. 14, No. 4, October 2005, pp. 383–430). The authors discussed the evolution of software configuration management technology, with a particular emphasis on the impact that university and industrial research has had along the way. This article creates a detailed record of the critical value of software configuration management research and illustrates the research results that have shaped the functionality of SCM systems.

REFERENCES

1. M. E. Fagan. Design and Code Inspections to Reduce Errors in Program Development. *IBM Systems Journal*, July 1976, pp. 182–211; reprinted 1999, pp. 258–287.
2. E. Yourdon. *Structured Walkthroughs*. Prentice-Hall, Englewood Cliffs, NJ, 1979.
3. D. Parnas and M. Lawford. The Role of Inspection in Software Quality Assurance. *IEEE Transactions on Software Engineering*, August 2003, pp. 674–676.
4. G. Myers. A Controlled Experimentat in Program Testing and Code Walk-throughs/Inspections. *Communications of the ACM*, September 1978, pp. 760–768.
5. H. Sutter and A. Alexandrescu. *C++ Coding Standards: 101 Rules, Guidelines, and Best Practices*. Addison-Wesley, Reading, MA, 2004.

6. T. J. McCabe. A Complexity Measure. *IEEE Transactions on Software Engineering*, December 1976, pp. 308–320.

7. A. Davis. *Disecting Error Messages*. Dr. Dobb's Journal, June 2005, pp. 34–41.

8. T. Budd and F. Sayward. Users Guide to the Pilot Mutation System, Technical Report 114. Department of Computer Science, Yale University, 1977.

9. R. A. DeMillo, R. J. Lipton, and F. Sayward. Hints on Test Data Selection: Help for the Practicing Programmer. *IEEE Computer*, April 1978, pp. 34–41.

10. R. G. Hamlet. Testing Programs with the Aid of Compiler. *IEEE Transactions on Software Engineering*, July 1977, pp. 279–290.

11. A. J. Offutt. Investigations of the Software Testing Coupling Effect. *ACM Transactions on Software Engineering Methodology*, January 1992, pp. 3–18.

12. K. S. H. T. Wah. A Theoretical Study of Fault Coupling. *Journal of Software Testing, Verification, and Reliability*, March 2000, pp. 3–46.

13. R. Geist, A. J. Offutt, and F. Harris. Estimation and Enhancement of Real-Time Software Reliability through Mutation Analysis. *IEEE Transactions on Computers*, May 1992, pp. 550–558.

14. A. J. Offutt and J. Pan. Automatically Detecting Equivalent Mutants and Infeasible Paths. *Journal of Software Testing, Verification, and Reliability*, September 1997, pp. 165–192.

15. R. A. DeMillo, D. S. Guindi, K. N. King, W. M. McCracken, and A. J. Offutt. An Extended Overview of the Mothra Software Testing Environment. In *Proceedings of the Second Workshop on Software Testing, Verification, and Analysis*, Banff, Alberta. IEEE Computer Society Press, New York, July 1988, pp. 142–151.

16. P. Chevalley and P. Thevenod-Fosse. A Mutation Analysis Tool for Java Programs. *International Journal on Software Tools for Technology Transfer (STTT)*, Springer Berlin /Heidelberg, November 2003, pp. 90–103.

17. A. Kolawa. Mutation Testing: A New Approach to Automatic Error-Detection. *STAR-EAST*, www.StickyMinds.com, 1999.

18. P. G. Frankl and E. J. Weyuker. An Applicable Family of Data Flow Testing Criteria. *IEEE Transactions on Software Engineering*, March 1993, pp. 202–213.

19. A. P. Mathur and W. E. Wong. An Empirical Comparison of Data Flow and Mutation-Based Test Adequacy Criteria. *Journal of Software Testing, Analysis, and Verification*, March 1994, pp. 9–31.

20. G. Myers. *The Art of Software Testing*, 2nd ed. Wiley, New York, 2004.

21. R. S. Pressman. *Software Engineering: A Practitioner's Approach*. McGraw-Hill, New York, 2005.

22. K. Beck. *Test-Driven Development*. Addison-Wesley, Reading, MA, 2003.

23. R. Jeffries and G. Melnik. TDD: The Art of Fearless Programming. *IEEE Software*, May/June 2007, pp. 24–30.

24. H. Erdogmus, M. Morisio, and M. Torchiano. On the Effectiveness of the Test-First Approach to Programming. *IEEE Transactions on Software Engineering*, March 2005, pp. 226–237.

25. R. C. Martin. *Professionalism and Test-Driven Development. IEEE Software*, May/June 2007, pp. 32–36.

26. D. B. Bisant and J. R. Lyle. Two Person Inspection Method to Improve Programming Productivity. *IEEE Transactions on Software Engineering*, October 1989, pp. 1294–1304.

27. J. B. Rainsberger. *JUnit Recipes*. Manning Publications, Greenwich, Connecticut 2005.

28. A. Hunt and D. Thomas. *Pragmatic Unit Testing in Java with JUnit*. The Pragmatic Bookshelf, Lewisville, Texas, 2004.

29. C. Boyapati, S. Khurshid, and D. Marinov. Korat: Automated Testing Based on Java Predicates. Paper presented at the ACM International Symposium on Software Testing and Analysis (ISSTA), Rome, Italy, 2002, pp. 123–133.

30. T. Xie, D. Marinov, W. Schulte, and D. Notkin. Symstra: A Framework for Generating Object-Oriented Unit Tests using Symbolic Execution. In *Proceedings of the 11th International Conference on Tools and Algorithms for the Construction and Analysis of Systems*, Edinburgh, U.K., Springer Berlin/Hiedelberg, 2005, pp. 365–381.

31. C. Pacheco and M. D. Ernst. Eclat: Automatic Generation and Classification of Test Inputs. Paper presented at ECOOP 2005 Object-Oriented Programming, 19th European Conference, Glasgow, Scotland, July 2005, pp. 504–527.

32. D. Spinellis. Debuggers and Logging Frameworks. *IEEE Software*, September 2006, pp. 98–99.

33. B. Lewis. Omniscient Debugging. *Dr. Dobb's Journal*, June 2005, pp. 16–24.
34. K. Sen, D. Marinov, and Gul Agha. CUTE: A Concolic Unit Testing Engine for C. In *Proceedings of the 10th European Software Engineering Conference*, held jointly with 13th ACM SIGSOFT International Symposium on Foundations of Software Engineering, Lisbon, Portugal, September 2005, pp. 263–272.
35. P. Godefroid, N. Klarlund, and K. Sen. DART: Directed Automated Random Testing. In *Proceedings of the 2005 ACM SIGPLAN Conference on Programming Language Design and Implementation*, Chicago IL, ACM Press, New York, 2005, pp. 213–223.
36. C. Cadar and D. Engler. Execution Generated Test Cases: How to Make Systems Code Crash Itself. *Lecture Notes in Computer Science (LNCS)*, Vol. 3639, 2005, pp. 2–23.
37. R. Bejtlich. *The Tao of Network Security Monitoring: Beyond Intrusion Detection*. Addison-Wesley, Boston, MA, 2005.

Exercises

1. Study the Yourdon [2] concept of a design walkthrough and the IBM concept [1] of a design inspection. Discuss the similarities and the differences between them.

2. A software engineering group is developing a mission-critical software system that will launch laser-guided missiles to its destinations. This is a new kind of product that was never built by the company. As a quality assurance manager, which code review methodology—walkthrough or inspection—would you recommend? Justify your answer.

3. What size of a review team would you recommend for the project in exercise 2, and why? What are the different roles of each member of the review team? What groups should send representatives to participate in code review?

4. Suppose that the C programming language is chosen in the project in exercise 2. Recommend a detailed code review checklist to the review team.

5. In addition to code review, what other static unit testing techniques would you recommend for the project in exercise 3? Justify your answer.

6. Describe the special role of a recordkeeper.

7. Discuss the importance of code review rework and validation.

8. Draw a control flow graph for the following sample code. Determine the cyclomatic complexity of the graph.

```
(a) sum_of_all_positive_numbers(a, num_of_entries, sum)
(b) sum = 0
(c) init = 1
(d)    while(init <= num_of_entries)
(e)        if a[init] > 0
(f)            sum = sum + a[init]
           endif
(g)        init = init + 1
       endwhile
(h) end sum_of_all_positive_numbers
```

9. A test engineer generates 70 mutants of a program P and 150 test cases to test the program P. After the first iteration of mutation testing, the tester finds 58 dead mutants and 4 equivalent mutants. Calculate the mutation score for this test suite. Is the test suite adequate for program P? Should the test engineer develop additional test cases? Justify your answer.

10. There is some debate as to whether code should be compiled before it is reviewed and vice versa. Based on your experience, give an opinion on this matter.

11. Attempt to draw a control flow graph for a module that you have recently developed. Determine the cyclomatic complexity for the module. Is the module too complex?

12. For your current software project, conduct a formal code review as described in Section 3.2.

13. For your current software project, develop dynamic unit test cases for each of the units in the JUnit framework if the code is in Java or in an appropriate xUnit framework.

CHAPTER 4

Control Flow Testing

He who controls the present, controls the past. He who controls the past, controls the future.
— *George Orwell*

4.1 BASIC IDEA

Two kinds of basic statements in a program unit are *assignment* statements and *conditional* statements. An assignment statement is explicitly represented by using an assignment symbol, " = ", such as x = 2*y;, where *x* and *y* are variables. Program *conditions* are at the core of conditional statements, such as if(), for() loop, while() loop, and goto. As an example, in if(x! = y), we are testing for the inequality of *x* and *y*. In the absence of conditional statements, program instructions are executed in the sequence they appear. The idea of successive execution of instructions gives rise to the concept of *control flow* in a program unit. Conditional statements alter the default, sequential control flow in a program unit. In fact, even a small number of conditional statements can lead to a complex control flow structure in a program.

Function calls are a mechanism to provide *abstraction* in program design. A call to a program function leads to control entering the called function. Similarly, when the called function executes its *return* statement, we say that control exits from the function. Though a function can have many return statements, for simplicity, one can restructure the function to have exactly one return. A program unit can be viewed as having a well-defined entry point and a well-defined exit point. The execution of a sequence of instructions from the entry point to the exit point of a program unit is called a program *path*. There can be a large, even infinite, number of paths in a program unit. Each program path can be characterized by an input and an expected output. A specific input value causes a specific program path to be executed; it is expected that the program path performs the desired computation, thereby producing the expected output value. Therefore, it may seem natural to execute as many program paths as possible. Mere execution of a large number of

Software Testing and Quality Assurance: Theory and Practice, Edited by Kshirasagar Naik and Priyadarshi Tripathy
Copyright © 2008 John Wiley & Sons, Inc.

paths, at a higher cost, may not be effective in revealing defects. Ideally, one must strive to execute fewer paths for better effectiveness.

The concepts of *control flow* in computer programs [1], program paths [2], and control flow testing [2–8] have been studied for many decades. Tools are being developed to support control flow testing [9]. Such tools identify paths from a program unit based on a user-defined criterion, generate the corresponding input to execute a selected path, and generate program stubs and drivers to execute the test. Control flow testing is a kind of structural testing, which is performed by programmers to test code written by them. The concept is applied to small *units* of code, such as a function. Test cases for control flow testing are derived from the source code, such as a program unit (e.g., a function or method), rather than from the entire program.

Structurally, a path is a sequence of statements in a program unit, whereas, semantically, it is an execution instance of the unit. For a given set of input data, the program unit executes a certain path. For another set of input data, the unit may execute a different path. The main idea in control flow testing is to appropriately select a few paths in a program unit and observe whether or not the selected paths produce the expected outcome. By executing a few paths in a program unit, the programmer tries to assess the behavior of the entire program unit.

4.2 OUTLINE OF CONTROL FLOW TESTING

The overall idea of generating test input data for performing control flow testing has been depicted in Figure 4.1. The activities performed, the intermediate results produced by those activities, and programmer preferences in the test generation process are explained below.

> *Inputs*: The *source code* of a program unit and a set of *path selection criteria* are the inputs to a process for generating test data. In the following, two examples of path selection criteria are given.

> **Example.** Select paths such that every statement is executed at least once.

> **Example.** Select paths such that every conditional statement, for example, an if() statement, evaluates to *true* and *false* at least once on different occasions. A conditional statement may evaluate to true in one path and false in a second path.

> *Generation of a Control Flow Graph*: A control flow graph (CFG) is a detailed graphical representation of a program unit. The idea behind drawing a CFG is to be able to visualize all the paths in a program unit. The process of drawing a CFG from a program unit will be explained in the following section. If the process of test generation is automated, a compiler can be modified to produce a CFG.

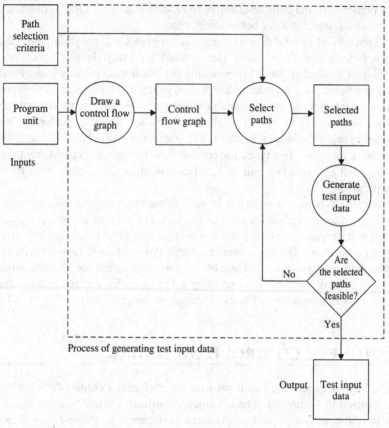

Figure 4.1 Process of generating test input data for control flow testing.

Selection of Paths: Paths are selected from the CFG to satisfy the path selection criteria, and it is done by considering the structure of the CFG.

Generation of Test Input Data: A path can be executed if and only if a certain instance of the inputs to the program unit causes all the conditional statements along the path to evaluate to true or false as dictated by the control flow. Such a path is called a *feasible* path. Otherwise, the path is said to be *infeasible*. It is essential to identify certain values of the inputs from a given path for the path to execute.

Feasibility Test of a Path: The idea behind checking the feasibility of a selected path is to meet the path selection criteria. If some chosen paths are found to be infeasible, then new paths are selected to meet the criteria.

4.3 CONTROL FLOW GRAPH

A CFG is a graphical representation of a program unit. Three symbols are used to construct a CFG, as shown in Figure 4.2. A rectangle represents a sequential

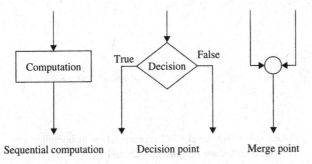

Figure 4.2   Symbols in a CFG.

computation. A maximal sequential computation can be represented either by a single rectangle or by many rectangles, each corresponding to one statement in the source code.

We label each computation and decision box with a unique integer. The two branches of a decision box are labeled with **T** and **F** to represent the true and false evaluations, respectively, of the condition within the box. We will not label a merge node, because one can easily identify the paths in a CFG even without explicitly considering the merge nodes. Moreover, not mentioning the merge nodes in a path will make a path description shorter.

We consider the openfiles() function shown in Figure 4.3 to illustrate the process of drawing a CFG. The function has three statements: an assignment statement int i = 0;, a conditional statement if(), and a return(i) statement. The reader may note that irrespective of the evaluation of the if(), the function performs the same action, namely, null. In Figure 4.4, we show a high-level representation of

```
FILE *fptr1, *fptr2, *fptr3; /* These are global variables. */

int openfiles(){
    /*
        This function tries to open files "file1", "file2", and
        "file3" for read access, and returns the number of files
        successfully opened. The file pointers of the opened files
        are put in the global variables.
    */
    int i = 0;
    if(
        ((( fptr1 = fopen("file1", "r")) != NULL) && (i++)
                                            && (0)) ||
        ((( fptr2 = fopen("file2", "r")) != NULL) && (i++)
                                            && (0)) ||
        ((( fptr3 = fopen("file3", "r")) != NULL) && (i++))
    );
    return(i);
}
```

Figure 4.3   Function to open three files.

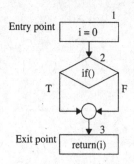

Figure 4.4   High-level CFG representation of openfiles().
The three nodes are numbered 1, 2, and 3.

the control flow in openfiles() with three nodes numbered 1, 2, and 3. The flow graph shows just two paths in openfiles().

A closer examination of the condition part of the if() statement reveals that there are not only Boolean and relational operators in the condition part, but also assignment statements. Some of their examples are given below:

Assignment statements: fptr1 = fopen("file1", "r") and i++

Relational operator: fptr1! = NULL

Boolean operators: && and ||

Execution of the assignment statements in the condition part of the if statement depends upon the component conditions. For example, consider the following component condition in the if part:

```
((( fptr1 = fopen("file1", "r")) != NULL) && (i++) && (0))
```

The above condition is executed as follows:

- Execute the assignment statement fptr1 = fopen("file1", "r").
- Execute the relational operation fptr1! = NULL.
- If the above relational operator evaluates to false, skip the evaluation of the subsequent condition components (i++) && (0).
- If the relational operator evaluates to true, then first (i) is evaluated to true or false. Irrespective of the outcome of this evaluation, the next statement executed is (i++).
- If (i) has evaluated to true, then the condition (0) is evaluated. Otherwise, evaluation of (0) is skipped.

In Figure 4.5, we show a detailed CFG for the openfiles() function. The figure illustrates a fact that a CFG can take up a complex structure even for a small program unit.

We give a Java method, called ReturnAverage(), in Figure 4.6. The method accepts four parameters, namely value, AS, MIN, and MAX, where value is an integer array and AS is the maximum size of the array. The array can hold fewer number of elements than AS; such a scenario is semantically represented by having the value -999 denoting the end of the array. For example, AS = 15,

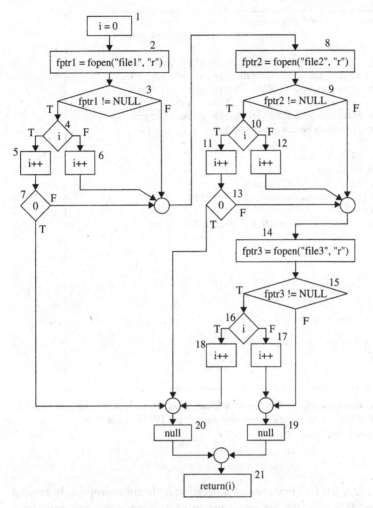

Figure 4.5   Detailed CFG representation of openfiles(). The numbers 1–21 are the nodes.

whereas the 10th element of the array is −999, which means that there are 10 elements—0–9–in the array. MIN and MAX are two integer values that are used to perform certain computations within the method. The method sums up the values of all those elements of the array which fall within the closed range [MIN, MAX], counts their number, and returns their average value. The CFG of the method is shown in Figure 4.7.

4.4   PATHS IN A CONTROL FLOW GRAPH

We assume that a control flow graph has exactly one *entry* node and exactly one *exit* node for the convenience of discussion. Each node is labeled with a unique

```
public static double ReturnAverage(int value[],
                           int AS, int MIN, int MAX){
  /*
  Function: ReturnAverage Computes the  average
  of all  those  numbers in the  input array  in
  the  positive  range  [MIN, MAX]. The  maximum
  size  of the array is AS. But, the  array size
  could be smaller than AS in which case the end
  of input is represented by -999.
  */
      int i, ti, tv, sum;
      double av;
      i = 0; ti = 0; tv = 0; sum = 0;
      while (ti < AS && value[i] != -999) {
          ti++;
          if (value[i] >= MIN && value[i] <= MAX) {
              tv++;
              sum = sum + value[i];
          }
          i++;
      }
      if (tv > 0)
          av = (double)sum/tv;
      else
          av = (double) -999;
      return (av);
}
```

Figure 4.6   Function to compute average of selected integers in an array. This program is an adaptation of "Figure 2. A sample program" in ref. 10. (With permission from the Australian Computer Society.)

integer value. Also, the two branches of a decision node are appropriately labeled with true (T) or false (F). We are interested in identifying entry–exit paths in a CFG. A path is represented as a sequence of computation and decision nodes from the entry node to the exit node. We also specify whether control exits a decision node via its true or false branch while including it in a path.

In Table 4.1, we show a few paths from the control flow graph of Figure 4.7. The reader may note that we have arbitrarily chosen these paths without applying any path selection criterion. We have unfolded the loop just once in **path 3**, whereas **path 4** unfolds the same loop twice, and these are two distinct paths.

4.5   PATH SELECTION CRITERIA

A CFG, such as the one shown in Figure 4.7, can have a large number of different paths. One may be tempted to test the execution of each and every path in a program unit. For a program unit with a small number of paths, executing all the paths may

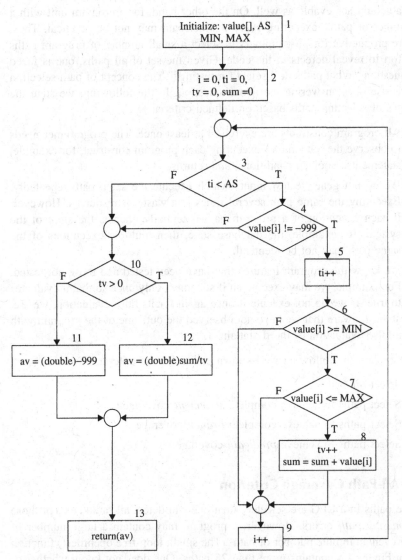

Figure 4.7   A CFG representation of ReturnAverage(). Numbers 1–13 are the nodes.

TABLE 4.1   Examples of Path in CFG of Figure 4.7

Path 1	1-2-3(F)-10(T)-12-13
Path 2	1-2-3(F)-10(F)-11-13
Path 3	1-2-3(T)-4(T)-5-6(T)-7(T)-8-9-3(F)-10(T)-12-13
Path 4	1-2-3(T)-4(T)-5-6(T)-7(T)-8-9-3(T)-4(T)-5-6(T)-7(T)-8-9-3(F)-10(T)-12-13

be desirable and achievable as well. On the other hand, for a program unit with a large number of paths, executing every distinct path may not be practical. Thus, it is more productive for programmers to select a small number of program paths in an effort to reveal defects in the code. Given the set of all paths, one is faced with a question "What paths do I select for testing?" The concept of path selection criteria is useful is answering the above question. In the following, we state the advantages of selecting paths based on defined criteria:

- All program constructs are exercised at least once. The programmer needs to observe the outcome of executing each program construct, for example, statements, Boolean conditions, and returns.

- We do not generate test inputs which execute the same path repeatedly. Executing the same path several times is a waste of resources. However, if each execution of a program path potentially updates the *state* of the system, for example, the database state, then multiple executions of the same path may not be identical.

- We know the program features that have been tested and those not tested. For example, we may execute an if statement only once so that it evaluates to true. If we do not execute it once again for its false evaluation, we are, at least, aware that we have not observed the outcome of the program with a false evaluation of the if statement.

Now we explain the following well-known path selection criteria:

- Select *all* paths.
- Select paths to achieve complete *statement* coverage.
- Select paths to achieve complete *branch* coverage.
- Select paths to achieve *predicate* coverage.

4.5.1 All-Path Coverage Criterion

If *all* the paths in a CFG are selected, then one can detect all faults, except those due to *missing path* errors. However, a program may contain a large number of paths, or even an infinite number of paths. The small, loop-free openfiles() function shown in Figure 4.3 contains more than 25 paths. One does not know whether or not a path is feasible at the time of selecting paths, though only eight of all those paths are feasible. If one selects all possible paths in a program, then we say that the *all-path* selection criterion has been satisfied.

Let us consider the example of the openfiles() function. This function tries to open the three files file1, file2, and file3. The function returns an integer representing the number of files it has successfully opened. A file is said to be successfully opened with "read" access if the file exists. The existence of a file is either "yes" or "no." Thus, the input domain of the function consists of eight combinations of the existence of the three files, as shown in Table 4.2.

We can trace a path in the CFG of Figure 4.5 for each input, that is, each row of Table 4.2. Ideally, we identify test inputs to execute a certain path in a

TABLE 4.2   Input Domain of openfiles()

Existence of file1	Existence of file2	Existence of file3
No	No	No
No	No	Yes
No	Yes	No
No	Yes	Yes
Yes	No	No
Yes	No	Yes
Yes	Yes	No
Yes	Yes	Yes

TABLE 4.3   Inputs and Paths in openfiles()

Input	Path
< No, No, No >	**1-2-3(F)-8-9(F)-14-15(F)-19-21**
< Yes, No, No >	**1-2-3(T)-4(F)-6-8-9(F)-14-15(F)-19-21**
< Yes, Yes, Yes >	**1-2-3(T)-4(F)-6-8-9(T)-10(T)-11-13(F)-14-15(T)-16(T)-18-20-21**

program; this will be explained later in this chapter. We give three examples of the paths executed by the test inputs (Table 4.3). In this manner, we can identify eight possible paths in Figure 4.5. The all-paths selection criterion is desirable since it can detect faults; however, it is difficult to achieve in practice.

4.5.2   Statement Coverage Criterion

Statement coverage refers to executing individual program statements and observing the outcome. We say that 100% statement coverage has been achieved if *all* the statements have been executed at least once. Complete statement coverage is the *weakest* coverage criterion in program testing. Any test suite that achieves less than statement coverage for new software is considered to be unacceptable.

All program statements are represented in some form in a CFG. Referring to the ReturnAverage() method in Figure 4.6 and its CFG in Figure 4.7, the four assignment statements

```
i   = 0;
ti  = 0;
tv  = 0;
sum = 0;
```

have been represented by node **2**. The while statement has been represented as a loop, where the loop control condition

```
(ti < AS && value[i] != -999)
```

has been represented by nodes **3** and **4**. Thus, covering a statement in a program means visiting one or more nodes representing the statement, more precisely, selecting a **feasible** entry–exit path that includes the corresponding nodes. Since a single entry–exit path includes many nodes, we need to select just a few paths to cover all the nodes of a CFG. Therefore, the basic problem is to select a few feasible paths to cover all the nodes of a CFG in order to achieve the complete statement coverage criterion. We follow these rules while selecting paths:

- Select short paths.
- Select paths of increasingly longer length. Unfold a loop several times if there is a need.
- Select arbitrarily long, "complex" paths.

One can select the two paths shown in Figure 4.4 to achieve complete statement coverage.

4.5.3 Branch Coverage Criterion

Syntactically, a branch is an outgoing edge from a node. All the rectangle nodes have at most one outgoing branch (edge). The exit node of a CFG does not have an outgoing branch. All the diamond nodes have two outgoing branches. Covering a branch means selecting a path that includes the branch. Complete branch coverage means selecting a number of paths such that every branch is included in at least one path.

In a preceding discussion, we showed that one can select two paths, **SCPath 1** and **SCPath 2** in Table 4.4, to achieve complete statement coverage. These two paths cover *all* the nodes (statements) and most of the branches of the CFG shown in Figure 4.7. The branches which are not covered by these two paths have been highlighted by bold dashed lines in Figure 4.8. These uncovered branches correspond to the three independent conditions

```
value[i] != -999
value[i] >= MIN
value[i] <= MAX
```

evaluating to false. This means that as a programmer we have not observed the outcome of the program execution as a result of the conditions evaluating to false. Thus, complete branch coverage means selecting enough number of paths such that every condition evaluates to true at least once and to false at least once.

We need to select more paths to cover the branches highlighted by the bold dashed lines in Figure 4.8. A set of paths for complete branch coverage is given in Table 4.5.

TABLE 4.4 Paths for Statement Coverage of CFG of Figure 4.7

SCPath 1	1-2-3(F)-10(F)-11-13
SCPath 2	1-2-3(T)-4(T)-5-6(T)-7(T)-8-9-3(F)-10(T)-12-13

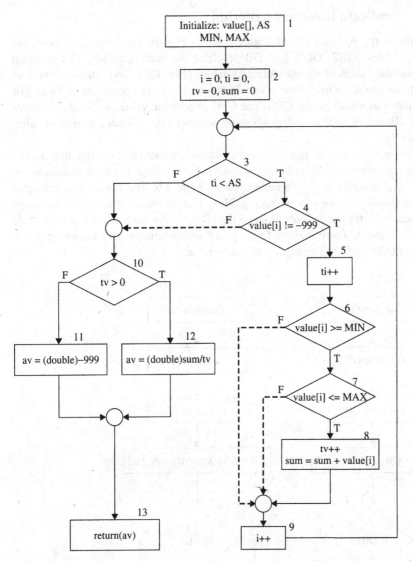

Figure 4.8   Dashed arrows represent the branches not covered by statement covering in Table 4.4.

TABLE 4.5   Paths for Branch Coverage of CFG of Figure 4.7

BCPath 1	1-2-3(F)-10(F)-11-13
BCPath 2	1-2-3(T)-4(T)-5-6(T)-7(T)-8-9-3(F)-10(T)-12-13
BCPath 3	1-2-3(T)-4(F)-10(F)-11-13
BCPath 4	1-2-3(T)-4(T)-5-6(F)-9-3(F)-10(F)-11-13
BCPath 5	1-2-3(T)-4(T)-5-6(T)-7(F)-9-3(F)-10(F)-11-13

4.5.4 Predicate Coverage Criterion

We refer to the partial CFG of Figure 4.9*a* to explain the concept of predicate coverage. OB1, OB2, OB3, and OB are four Boolean variables. The program computes the values of the individual variables OB1, OB2, and OB3— details of their computation are irrelevant to our discussion and have been omitted. Next, OB is computed as shown in the CFG. The CFG checks the value of OB and executes either OBlock1 or OBlock2 depending on whether OB evaluates to true or false, respectively.

We need to design just two test cases to achieve both statement coverage and branch coverage. We select inputs such that the four Boolean conditions in Figure 4.9*a* evaluate to the values shown in Table 4.6. The reader may note that we have shown just one way of forcing OB to true. If we select inputs so that these two cases hold, then we do not observe the effect of the computations taking place in nodes **2** and **3**. There may be faults in the computation parts of nodes **2** and **3** such that OB2 and OB3 always evaluate to false.

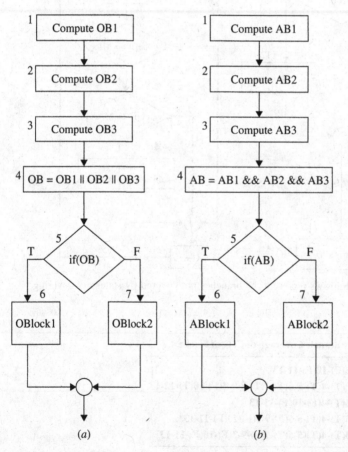

Figure 4.9 Partial CFG with (*a*) OR operation and (*b*) AND operation.

TABLE 4.6 Two Cases for Complete Statement and Branch Coverage of CFG of Figure 4.9a

Cases	OB1	OB2	OB3	OB
1	T	F	F	T
2	F	F	F	F

Therefore, there is a need to design test cases such that a path is executed under all possible conditions. The False branch of node 5 (Figure 4.9a) is executed under exactly one condition, namely, when OB1 = False, OB2 = False, and OB3 = False, whereas the true branch executes under *seven* conditions. If all possible combinations of truth values of the conditions affecting a selected path have been explored under some tests, then we say that *predicate coverage* has been achieved. Therefore, the path taking the true branch of node 5 in Figure 4.9a must be executed for all seven possible combinations of truth values of OB1, OB2, and OB3 which result in OB = True.

A similar situation holds for the partial CFG shown in Figure 4.9b, where AB1, AB2, AB3, and AB are Boolean variables.

4.6 GENERATING TEST INPUT

In Section 4.5 we explained the concept of path selection criteria to cover certain aspects of a program with a set of paths. The program aspects we considered were all statements, true and false evaluations of each condition, and combinations of conditions affecting execution of a path. Now, having identified a path, the question is how to select input values such that when the program is executed with the selected inputs, the chosen paths get executed. In other words, we need to identify inputs to force the executions of the paths. In the following, we define a few terms and give an example of generating test inputs for a selected path.

1. *Input Vector:* An input vector is a collection of all data entities read by the routine whose values must be fixed prior to entering the routine. Members of an input vector of a routine can take different forms as listed below:

- Input arguments to a routine
- Global variables and constants
- Files
- Contents of registers in assembly language programming
- Network connections
- Timers

A file is a complex input element. In one case, mere existence of a file can be considered as an input, whereas in another case, contents of the file are considered to be inputs. Thus, the idea of an input vector is more general than the concept of input arguments of a function.

Example. An input vector for openfiles() (Figure 4.3) consists of individual presence or absence of the files file1, file2, and file3.

Example. The input vector of the ReturnAverage() method shown in Figure 4.6 is < value [], AS, MIN, MAX > .

2. *Predicate:* A predicate is a logical function evaluated at a decision point.

Example. The construct ti < AS is the predicate in decision node **3** of Figure 4.7.

Example. The construct OB is the predicate in decision node **5** of Figure 4.9.

3. *Path Predicate:* A path predicate is the set of predicates associated with a path.

The path in Figure 4.10 indicates that nodes **3, 4, 6, 7,** and **10** are decision nodes. The predicate associated with node **3** appears twice in the path; in the first instance it evaluates to true and in the second instance it evaluates to false. The path predicate associated with the path under consideration is shown in Figure 4.11.

We also specify the intended evaluation of the component predicates as found in the path specification. For instance, we specify that value[i] ! = −999 must evaluate to true in the path predicate shown in Figure 4.11. We keep this additional information for the following two reasons:

- In the absence of this additional information denoting the intended evaluation of a predicate, we will have no way to distinguish between the two instances of the predicate ti < AS, namely **3(T)** and **3(F)**, associated with node **3**.

1-2-3(T)-4(T)-5-6(T)-7(T)-8-9-3(F)-10(T)-12-13

Figure 4.10   Example of a path from Figure 4.7.

```
        ti < AS  ≡ True
value[i] != -999  ≡ True
 value[i] >= MIN  ≡ True
 value[i] <= MAX  ≡ True
        ti < AS  ≡ False
        tv > 0   ≡ True
```

Figure 4.11   Path predicate for path in Figure 4.10.

- We must know whether the individual component predicates of a path predicate evaluate to true or false in order to generate path forcing inputs.

4. *Predicate Interpretation:* The path predicate shown in Figure 4.11 is composed of elements of the input vector $< \text{value}[], \text{AS}, \text{MIN}, \text{MAX} >$, a vector of local variables $< i, ti, tv >$, and the constant -999. The local variables are not visible outside a function but are used to

- hold intermediate results,
- point to array elements, and
- control loop iterations.

In other words, they play no roles in selecting inputs that force the paths to execute. Therefore, we can easily substitute all the local variables in a predicate with the elements of the input vector by using the idea of symbolic substitution. Let us consider the method shown in Figure 4.12. The input vector for the method in Figure 4.12 is given by $< x1, x2 >$. The method defines a local variable y and also uses the constants 7 and 0.

The predicate

```
x1 + y >= 0
```

can be rewritten as

```
x1 + x2 + 7 >= 0
```

by symbolically substituting y with $x_2 + 7$. The rewritten predicate

```
x1 + x2 + 7 >= 0
```

has been expressed solely in terms of the input vector $< x1, x2 >$ and the constant vector $< 0,7 >$. Thus, *predicate interpretation* is defined as the process of symbolically substituting operations along a path in order to express the predicates solely in terms of the input vector and a constant vector.

In a CFG, there may be several different paths leading up to a decision point from the initial node, with each path doing different computations. Therefore, a predicate may have different interpretations depending on how control reaches the predicate under consideration.

```
public static int SymSub(int x1, int x2){
int y;
y = x2 + 7;
if (x1 + y >= 0)
      return (x2 + y);
else return (x2 - y);
}
```

Figure 4.12 Method in Java to explain symbolic substitution [11].

5. *Path Predicate Expression:* An interpreted path predicate is called a path predicate expression. A path predicate expression has the following properties:

- It is void of local variables and is solely composed of elements of the input vector and possibly a vector of constants.

- It is a set of constraints constructed from the elements of the input vector and possibly a vector of constants.

- Path forcing input values can be generated by solving the set of constraints in a path predicate expression.

- If the set of constraints cannot be solved, there exist no input which can cause the selected path to execute. In other words, the selected path is said to be *infeasible*.

- An infeasible path does not imply that one or more components of a path predicate expression are unsatisfiable. It simply means that the total combination of all the components in a path predicate expression is unsatisfiable.

- Infeasibility of a path predicate expression suggests that one considers other paths in an effort to meet a chosen path selection criterion.

Example.   Consider the path shown in Figure 4.10 from the CFG of Figure 4.7. Table 4.7 shows the nodes of the path in column 1, the corresponding description of each node in column 2, and the interpretation of each node in column 3. The

TABLE 4.7   Interpretation of Path Predicate of Path in Figure 4.10.

Node	Node Description	Interpreted Description
1	Input vector: < value[], AS, MIN, MAX >	
2	i = 0, ti = 0, tv = 0, sum = 0	
3(T)	ti < AS	0 < AS
4(T)	value[i]! = − 999	value[0]! = − 999
5	ti++	ti = 0 + 1 = 1
6(T)	value[i] > = MIN	value[0] > = MIN
7(T)	value[i] < = MAX	value[0] < = MAX
8	tv++ sum = sum + value[i]	tv = 0 + 1 = 1 sum = 0 + value[0] = value[0]
9	i++	i = 0 + 1 = 1
3(F)	ti < AS	1 < AS
10(T)	tv > 0	1 > 0
12	av = (double) sum/tv	av = (double) value[0]/1
13	return(av)	return(value[0])

Note: The bold entries in column 1 denote interpreted predicates.

intended evaluation of each interpreted predicate can be found in column 1 of the same row.

We show the path predicate expression of the path under consideration in Figure 4.13 for the sake of clarity. The rows of Figure 4.13 have been obtained from Table 4.11 by combining each interpreted predicate in column 3 with its intended evaluation in column 1. Now the reader may compare Figures 4.11 and 4.13 to note that the predicates in Figure 4.13 are interpretations of the corresponding predicates in Figure 4.11.

Example. We show in Figure 4.14 an infeasible path appearing in the CFG of Figure 4.7. The path predicate and its interpretation are shown in Table 4.8, and the path predicate expression is shown in Figure 4.15. The path predicate expression is unsolvable because the constraint $0 > 0 \equiv$ True is unsatisfiable. Therefore, the path shown in Figure 4.14 is an infeasible path.

```
         0 < AS   ≡ True    ........ (1)
value[0] != -999  ≡ True    ........ (2)
  value[0] >= MIN ≡ True    ........ (3)
  value[0] <= MAX ≡ True    ........ (4)
         1 < AS   ≡ False   ........ (5)
         1 > 0    ≡ True    ........ (6)
```

Figure 4.13   Path predicate expression for path in Figure 4.10.

```
1-2-3(T)-4(F)-10(T)-12-13.
```

Figure 4.14   Another example path from Figure 4.7.

TABLE 4.8   Interpretation of Path Predicate of Path in Figure 4.14.

Node	Node Description	Interpreted Description
1	Input vector: $< value[], AS, MIN, MAX >$	
2	i = 0, ti = 0, tv = 0, sum = 0	
3(T)	ti < AS	0 < AS
4(F)	value[i]! = − 999	value[0]! = − 999
10(T)	tv > 0	0 > 0
12	av = (double)sum/tv	av = (double)value[0]/0
13	return(av)	return((double) value[0]/0)

Note: The bold entries in column 1 denote interpreted predicates.

```
        0 < AS    ≡ True  ........ (1)
value[0] != -999   ≡ True  ........ (2)
        0 > 0     ≡ True  ........ (3)
```

Figure 4.15   Path predicate expression for path in Figure 4.14.

```
     AS    = 1
     MIN   = 25
     MAX   = 35
value[0]   = 30
```

Figure 4.16   Input data satisfying constraints of Figure 4.13.

6. *Generating Input Data from Path Predicate Expression:* We must solve the corresponding path predicate expression in order to generate input data which can force a program to execute a selected path. Let us consider the path predicate expression shown in Figure 4.13. We observe that constraint 1 is always satisfied. Constraints 1 and 5 must be solved together to obtain AS = 1. Similarly, constraints 2, 3, and 4 must be solved together. We note that MIN $<$ = value[0] $<$ = MAX and value[0]! = −999. Therefore, we have many choices to select values of MIN, MAX, and value[0]. An instance of the solutions of the constraints of Figure 4.13 is shown in Figure 4.16.

4.7   EXAMPLES OF TEST DATA SELECTION

We give examples of selected test data to achieve complete statement and branch coverage. We show four sets of test data in Table 4.9. The first two data sets cover all statements of the CFG in Figure 4.7. However, we need all four sets of test data for complete branch coverage.

If we execute the method ReturnAverage shown in Figure 4.6 with the four sets of test input data shown in Figure 4.9, then each statement of the method is executed at least once, and every Boolean condition evaluates once to true and

TABLE 4.9   Test Data for Statement and Branch Coverage

Test Data Set	Input Vector			
	AS	MIN	MAX	value[]
1	1	5	20	[10]
2	1	5	20	[−999]
3	1	5	20	[4]
4	1	5	20	[25]

once to false. We have thoroughly tested the method in the sense of complete branch coverage. However, it is possible to introduce simple faults in the method which can go undetected when the method with the above four sets of test data is executed. Two examples of fault insertion are given below.

Example. We replace the correct statement

```
av = (double) sum/tv;
```

with a faulty statement

```
av = (double) sum/ti;
```

in the method. Here the fault is that the method computes the average of the total number of inputs, denoted by ti, rather than the total number of valid inputs, denoted by tv.

Example. We replace the correct statement

```
sum = sum + value[i];
```

with a faulty statement

```
sum = value[i];
```

in the method. Here the fault is that the method no more computes the sum of all the valid inputs in the array. In spite of the fault, the first set of test data produce the correct result due to *coincidental correctness*.

The above two examples of faults lead us to the following conclusions:

- One must generate test data to satisfy certain selection criteria, because those selection criteria identify the aspects of a program that we want to cover.
- Additional tests, which are much longer than the simple tests generated to meet coverage criteria, must be generated after the coverage criteria have been met.
- Given a set of test data for a program, we can inject faults into the program which go undetected by those test cases.

4.8 CONTAINING INFEASIBLE PATHS

Woodward, Hedley, and Hennell [12] have identified some practical problems in applying the idea of path testing. First, a CFG may contain a very large number of paths; therefore, the immediate challenge is to decide which paths to select to derive test cases. Second, it may not be feasible to execute many of the selected paths. Thus, it is useful to apply a path selection strategy: First, select as many short paths as feasible; next choose longer paths to achieve better coverage of statements, branches, and predicates. A large number of infeasible paths in a CFG complicate the process of test selection. To simplify path-based unit testing, it is useful to reduce the number of infeasible paths in a program unit through language design, program design, and program transformation. Brown and Nelson [13] have demonstrated the possibility of writing code with no infeasible paths.

Bertolino and Marre [14] have given an algorithm to generate a set of paths, to cover all the branchs of a CFG, to reduce the number of infeasible paths in the chosen set. Their algorithm is based on the idea of a *reduced* flow graph, called a *ddgraph*. The algorithm uses the concepts of *dominance* and *implications* among the arcs of a ddgraph.

Yates and Malevris [15] have suggested a strategy to reduce the number of infeasible paths in a set of paths to achieve branch coverage. They suggest selecting a path cover, that is, a set of paths, whose constituent paths each involve a *minimum number of predicates*. On the contrary, if a path involves a large number of predicates, it is less likely that all the predicates simultaneously hold, thereby making the path infeasible. They have statistically demonstrated the efficacy of the strategy.

McCabe's [16] *cyclomatic complexity* measure (Table 3.3) gives an interesting graph-theoretic interpretation of a program flow graph. If we consider cyclomatic complexity measures as paths in a flow graph, it is likely that a few infeasible paths will be constructed. The above discussion leads us to conclude that though the idea of statement coverage and branch coverage appear simple and straightforward, it is not easy to fully achieve those coverage criteria even for small programs.

4.9 SUMMARY

The notion of a path in a program unit is a fundamental concept. Assuming that a program unit is a function, a path is an executable sequence of instructions from the start of execution of the function to a return statement in the function. If there is no branching condition in a program unit, then there is just one path in the function. Generally, there are many branching conditions in a program unit, and thus there are numerous paths. One path differs from another path by at least one instruction. A path may contain one or more loops, but, ultimately, a path is expected to terminate its execution. Therefore, a path is of finite length in terms of number of instructions it executes. One can have a graphical representation of a program unit, called a control flow graph, to capture the concept of control flow in the program unit.

Each path corresponds to a distinct behavior of the program unit, and therefore we need to test each path with at least one test case. If there are a large number of paths in a program, a programmer may not have enough time to test all the paths. Therefore, there is a need to select a few paths by using some path selection criteria. A path selection criterion allows us to select a few paths to achieve a certain kind of coverage of program units. Some well-known coverage metrics are statement coverage, branch coverage, and predicate coverage. A certain number of paths are chosen from the CFG to achieve a desired degree of coverage of a program unit. At an abstract level, each path is composed of a sequence of predicates and assignment (computation) statements. The predicates can be functions of local variables, global variables, and constants, and those are called path predicates. All the predicates along the path must evaluate to true when control reaches the predicates for a path to be executable. One must select inputs, called path forcing inputs, such that the path predicates evaluate to true in order to be able to execute the path. The process of selecting path forcing inputs involves transforming the path predicates into a form that is void of local variables. Such a form of path predicates is called a path predicate expression. A path predicate expression is solely composed of the input vector and possibly a vector of constants. One can generate values of the input vector, which is considered as a test case, to exercise a path by solving the corresponding path predicate expression. Tools are being designed for generating test inputs from program units.

If a program unit makes function calls, it is possible that the path predicates are functions of the values returned by those functions. In such a case, it may be difficult to solve a path predicate expression to generate test cases. Path testing is more applicable to lower level program units than to upper level program units containing many function calls.

LITERATURE REVIEW

Clarke [3] describes an automated system to generate test data from FORTRAN programs. The system is based on the idea of selecting program paths, identifying path conditions, and solving those conditions to generate inputs. When the program is executed with the selected inputs, the corresponding paths are executed. Automatically generating test inputs is a difficult task. The general problem of test generation from source code is an unsolvable problem. To mitigate the problem, there have been suggestions to select paths in certain ways. For example, select paths that execute loops for a restricted number of times. Similarly, select paths that are restricted to a maximum statement count. This is because longer paths are likely to have more predicates and are likely to be more complex. The system generates test inputs for paths that can be described by a set of linear path constraints.

The students are encouraged to read the tutorial by J. C. Huang entitled "An Approach to Program Testing," *ACM Computing Surveys*, Vol. 8, No. 3, September 1975, pp. 113–128. This article discusses a method for determining path conditions to enable achievement of branch coverage. It introduces the reader to the predicate calculus notation for expressing path conditions.

Ramamoorthy, Ho, and Chen [7] discuss the usefulness of symbolic substitution in generating path predicates for testing a path. Array referencing is a major problem in symbolic substitution because index values may not be known during symbolic execution. References to arrays are recorded in a table while performing symbolic execution, and ambiguities are resolved when test input are generated to evaluate the subscript expressions. Another major problem is determination of the number of times to execute a loop.

Considering that symbolic execution requires complex algebraic manipulations, Korel [17] suggested an alternative idea based on actual execution of the program under test, function minimization methods, and data flow analysis. Test data are gathered for the program using concrete values of the input variables. A program's control flow is monitored while executing the program. If an execution, that is, a program path, is an undesirable one, then function minimization algorithms are used to locate the values of input variables which caused the undesirable path to be executed. In this approach, values of array indexes and pointers are known at each step of program execution. Thus, this approach helps us in overcoming the difficulties in handling arrays and pointers.

An excellent book on path-based program testing is *Software Testing Techniques* by Beizer [5]. The reader can find a more through treatment of the subject in the said book.

The test tool from *ParaSoft* [9] allows programmers to perform flow-based testing of program units written in C, C++, and Java. If a program unit under test calls another program unit, the tool generates a stub replacing the called unit. If a programmer wants to control what return values are used, he or she can create a stub table specifying the input–outcome mapping.

REFERENCES

1. F. E. Allen and J. Cocke. Graph Theoretic Constructs for Program Control Flow Analysis, Technical Report RC3923. IBM T. J. Watson Research Center, New York, 1972.
2. J. B. Goodenough and S. L. Gerhart. Toward a Theory of Test data Selection. *IEEE Transactions on Software Engineering*, June 1975, pp. 26–37.
3. L. A. Clarke. A System to Generate Test Data and Symbolically Execute Programs. *IEEE Transactions on Software Engineering*, September 1976, pp. 215–222.
4. W. E. Howden. Reliability of the Path Analysis Testing Strategy. *IEEE Transactions on Software Engineering*, September 1976, pp. 38–45.
5. B. Beizer. *Software Testing Techniques*, 2nd ed. Van Nostrand Reinhold, New York, 1990.
6. G. J. Myers. *The Art of Software Testing*. Wiley, New York, 1979.
7. C. V. Ramamoorthy, S. F. Ho, and W. T. Chen. On the Automated Generation of Program Test Data. *IEEE Transactions on Software Engineering*, December 1976, pp. 293–300.
8. H. Zhu, P. A. V. Hall, and J. H. R. May. Software Unit Test Coverage and Adequacy. *ACM Computing Surveys*, December 1997, pp. 366–427.
9. Parasoft Corporation, available: http://www.parasoft.com/. Parasoft Application Development Quality Solution, 1996-2008.
10. P. M. Herman. A Data Flow Analysis Approach to Program Testing. *Australian Computer Journal*, November 1976, pp. 92–96.
11. J. C. King. Symbolic Execution and Program Testing. *Communications of the ACM*, July 1976, pp. 385–394.
12. M. R. Woodward, D. Hedley, and M. A. Hennell. Experience with Path Analysis and Testing of Programs. *IEEE Transactions on Software Engineering*, May 1980, pp. 278–286.
13. J. R. Brown and E. C. Nelson. Functional programming, TRW Defence and Space Systems Group for Rome Air Development Center, Technical Report on Contract F30602-76-C-0315, July 1977.
14. A. Bertolino and M. Marre. Automatic Generation of Path Covers Based on the Control Flow Analysis of Computer Programs. *IEEE Transactions on Software Engineering*, December 1994, pp. 885–899.
15. D. F. Yates and N. Malevris. Reducing the Effects of Infeasible Paths in Branch Testing. *ACM SIGSOFT Software Engineering Notes*, December 1989, pp. 48–54.
16. T. J. McCabe. A complexity Measure. *IEEE Transactions on Software Engineering*, December 1976, pp. 308–320.
17. B. Korel. Automated Software Test Data Generation. *IEEE Transactions on Software Engineering*, August 1990, pp. 870–879.

```
int binsearch(int X, int V[], int n){
   int low, high, mid;
   low = 0;
   high = n - 1;
   while (low <= high) {
      mid = (low + high)/2;
      if (X < V[mid])
           high = mid - 1;
      else if (X > V[mid])
           low = mid + 1;
      else
           return mid;
   }
   return -1;
}
```

Figure 4.17   Binary search routine.

Exercises

You are given the binary search routine in C shown in Figure 4.17. The input array V is assumed to be sorted in ascending order, n is the array size, and you want to find the index of an element X in the array. If X is not found in the array, the routine is supposed to return -1.

The first eight questions refer to the binary search() function.

1. Draw a CFG for binsearch().

2. From the CFG, identify a set of entry–exit paths to satisfy the complete statement coverage criterion.

3. Identify additional paths, if necessary, to satisfy the complete branch coverage criterion.

4. For each path identified above, derive their path predicate expressions.

5. Solve the path predicate expressions to generate test input and compute the corresponding expected outcomes.

6. Are all the selected paths feasible? If not, select and show that a path is infeasible, if it exists.

7. Can you introduce two faults in the routine so that these go undetected by your test cases designed for complete branch coverage?

8. Suggest a general way to detect the kinds of faults introduced in the previous step.

9. What are the limitations of control flow–based testing?

10. Show that branch coverage includes statement coverage.

CHAPTER 5

Data Flow Testing

An error does not become truth by reason of multiplied propagation, nor does truth become error because nobody sees it.
— *Mohandas Karamchand Gandhi*

5.1 GENERAL IDEA

A program unit, such as a function, accepts input values, performs computations while assigning new values to local and global variables, and, finally, produces output values. Therefore, one can imagine a kind of "flow" of data values between variables along a path of program execution. A data value computed in a certain step of program execution is expected to be used in a later step. For example, a program may open a file, thereby obtaining a value for a file pointer; in a later step, the file pointer is expected to be used. Intuitively, if the later use of the file pointer is never verified, then we do not know whether or not the earlier assignment of value to the file pointer variable is all right. Sometimes, a variable may be defined twice without a use of the variable in between. One may wonder why the first definition of the variable is never used. There are two motivations for data flow testing as follows. First, a memory location corresponding to a program variable is accessed in a desirable way. For example, a memory location may not be read before writing into the location. Second, it is desirable to verify the correctness of a data value generated for a variable—this is performed by observing that all the uses of the value produce the desired results.

The above basic idea about data flow testing tells us that a programmer can perform a number of tests on data values, which are collectively known as data flow testing. Data flow testing can be performed at two conceptual levels: *static data flow testing* and *dynamic data flow testing*. As the name suggests, static data flow testing is performed by analyzing the source code, and it does not involve actual execution of source code. Static data flow testing is performed to reveal potential defects in programs. The potential program defects are commonly known as *data flow anomaly*. On the other hand, dynamic data flow testing involves identifying program paths from source code based on a class of *data flow testing criteria*.

The reader may note that there is much similarity between control flow testing and data flow testing. Moreover, there is a key difference between the two approaches. The similarities stem from the fact that both approaches identify program paths and emphasize on generating test cases from those program paths. The difference between the two lies in the fact that control flow test selection criteria are used in the former, whereas data flow test selection criteria are used in the latter approach.

In this chapter, first we study the concept of data flow anomaly as identified by Fosdick and Osterweil [1]. Next, we discuss dynamic data flow testing in detail.

5.2 DATA FLOW ANOMALY

An anomaly is a deviant or abnormal way of doing something. For example, it is an abnormal situation to successively assign two values to a variable without using the first value. Similarly, it is abnormal to use a value of a variable before assigning a value to the variable. Another abnormal situation is to generate a data value and never use it. In the following, we explain three types of abnormal situations concerning the generation and use of data values. The three abnormal situations are called **type 1**, **type 2**, and **type 3** anomalies [1]. These anomalies could be manifestations of potential programming errors. We will explain why program anomalies need not lead to program failures.

> *Defined and Then Defined Again (Type 1)*: Consider the partial sequence of computations shown in Figure 5.1, where f1(y) and f2(z) denote functions with the inputs y and z, respectively. We can interpret the two statements in Figure 5.1 in several ways as follows:
>
> - The computation performed by the first statement is redundant if the second statement performs the intended computation.
>
> - The first statement has a fault. For example, the intended first computation might be w = f1(y).
>
> - The second statement has a fault. For example, the intended second computation might be v = f2(z).
>
> - A fourth kind of fault can be present in the given sequence in the form of a missing statement between the two. For example, v = f3(x) may be the desired statement that should go in between the two given statements.

```
    :
  x = f1(y)
  x = f2(z)
    :
```

Figure 5.1 Sequence of computations showing data flow anomaly.

It is for the programmer to make the desired interpretation, though one can interpret the given two statements in several ways, However, it can be said that there is a data flow anomaly in those two statements, indicating that those need to be examined to eliminate any confusion in the mind of a code reader.

Undefined but Referenced (Type 2): A second form of data flow anomaly is to use an undefined variable in a computation, such as $x = x - y - w$, where the variable w has not been *initialized* by the programmer. Here, too, one may argue that though w has not been initialized, the programmer intended to use another initialized variable, say y, in place of w. Whatever may be the real intention of the programmer, there exists an anomaly in the use of the variable w, and one must eliminate the anomaly either by initializing w or replacing w with the intended variable.

Defined but Not Referenced (Type 3): A third kind of data flow anomaly is to define a variable and then to undefine it without using it in any subsequent computation. For example, consider the statement $x = f(x, y)$ in which a new value is assigned to the variable x. If the value of x is not used in any subsequent computation, then we should be suspicious of the computation represented by $x = f(x, y)$. Hence, this form of anomaly is called "defined but not referenced."

Huang [2] introduced the idea of "states" of program variables to identify data flow anomaly. For example, initially, a variable can remain in an "undefined" (U) state, meaning that just a memory location has been allocated to the variable but no value has yet been assigned. At a later time, the programmer can perform a computation to define (d) the variable in the form of assigning a value to the variable—this is when the variable moves to a "defined but not referenced" (D) state. At a later time, the programmer can reference (r), that is, read, the value of the variable, thereby moving the variable to a "defined and referenced" state (R). The variable remains in the R state as long as the programmer keeps referencing the value of the variable. If the programmer assigns a new value to the variable, the variable moves back to the D state. On the other hand, the programmer can take an action to undefine (u) the variable. For example, if an opened file is closed, the value of the file pointer is no more recognized by the underlying operating system, and therefore the file pointer becomes undefined. The above scenarios describe the normal actions on variables and are illustrated in Figure 5.2.

However, programmers can make mistakes by taking the wrong actions while a variable is in a certain state. For example, if a variable is in the state U—that is, the variable is still undefined—and a programmer reads (r) the variable, then the variable moves to an abnormal (A) state. The abnormal state of a variable means that a programming anomaly has occurred. Similarly, while a variable is in the state D and the programmer undefines (u) the variable or redefines (d) the variable, then the variable moves to the abnormal (A) state. Once a variable enters the abnormal state, it remains in that state irrespective of what action—d, u, or r—is taken. The actions that take a variable from a desired state, such as U or D, to an abnormal state are illustrated in Figure 5.2.

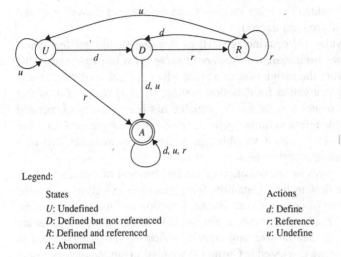

Legend:

States

U: Undefined
D: Defined but not referenced
R: Defined and referenced
A: Abnormal

Actions

d: Define
r: Reference
u: Undefine

Figure 5.2   State transition diagram of a program variable. (From ref. 2. © 1979 IEEE.)

Now it is useful to make an association between the **type 1**, **type 2**, and **type 3** anomalies and the state transition diagram shown in Figure 5.2. The **type 1**, **type 2**, and **type 3** anomalies are denoted by the action sequences *dd*, *ur*, and *du*, respectively, in Figure 5.2.

Data flow anomaly can be detected by using the idea of *program instrumentation*. Intuitively, program instrumentation means incorporating additional code in a program to monitor its execution status. For example, we can write additional code in a program to monitor the sequence of *states*, namely the *U*, *D*, *R*, and *A*, traversed by a variable. If the state sequence contains the *dd*, *ur*, and *du* subsequence, then a data flow anomaly is said to have occurred.

The presence of a data flow anomaly in a program does not necessarily mean that execution of the program will result in a failure. A data flow anomaly simply means that the program *may* fail, and therefore the programmer must investigate the cause of the anomaly. Let us consider the *dd* anomaly shown in Figure 5.1. If the real intention of the programmer was to perform the second computation and the first computation produces no side effect, then the first computation merely represents a waste of processing power. Thus, the said *dd* anomaly will not lead to program failure. On the other hand, if a statement is missing in between the two statements, then the program can possibly lead to a failure. The programmers must analyze the causes of data flow anomalies and eliminate them.

5.3   OVERVIEW OF DYNAMIC DATA FLOW TESTING

In the process of writing code, a programmer manipulates variables in order to achieve the desired computational effect. Variable manipulation occurs in several ways, such as initialization of the variable, assignment of a new value to the variable, computing a value of another variable using the value of the variable, and controlling the flow of program execution.

Rapps and Weyuker [3] convincingly tell us that one should not feel confident that a variable has been *assigned the correct value* if no test case causes the execution of a path from the assignment to a point where the value of the variable is *used*. In the above motivation for data flow testing, (i) assignment of a correct value means whether or not a value for the variable has been correctly generated and (ii) use of a variable refers to further generation of values for the same or other variables and/or control of flow. A variable can be used in a predicate, that is, a condition, to choose an appropriate flow of control.

The above idea gives us an indication of the involvement of certain kinds of program paths in data flow testing. Data flow testing involves selecting entry–exit paths with the objective of covering certain data definition and use patterns, commonly known as data flow testing criteria. Specifically, certain program paths are selected on the basis of data flow testing criteria. Following the general ideas in control flow testing that we discussed in Chapter 4, we give an outline of performing data flow testing in the following:

- Draw a data flow graph from a program.
- Select one or more data flow testing criteria.
- Identify paths in the data flow graph satisfying the selection criteria.
- Derive path predicate expressions from the selected paths and solve those expressions to derive test input.

The reader may recall that the process of deriving a path predicate expression from a path has been explained in Chapter 4. The same idea applies to deriving a path predicate expression from a path obtained from a data flow graph. Therefore, in the rest of this chapter we will explain a procedure for drawing a data flow graph from a program unit, and discuss data flow testing criteria.

5.4 DATA FLOW GRAPH

In this section, we explain the main ideas in a data flow graph and a method to draw it. In practice, programmers may not draw data flow graphs by hand. Instead, language translators are modified to produce data flow graphs from program units. A data flow graph is drawn with the objective of identifying data definitions and their uses as motivated in the preceding section. Each occurrence of a data variable is classified as follows:

Definition: This occurs when a value is moved into the memory location of the variable. Referring to the C function VarTypes() in Figure 5.3, the assignment statement i = x; is an example of definition of the variable *i*.

Undefinition or Kill: This occurs when the value and the location become unbound. Referring to the C function VarTypes(), the first

```
(iptr = malloc(sizeof(int)));
```

```
int VarTypes(int x, int y){
    int i;
    int *iptr;
    i = x;
    iptr = malloc(sizeof(int));
    *iptr = i + x;
    if (*iptr > y)
        return (x);
    else {
        iptr = malloc(sizeof(int));
        *iptr = x + y;
        return(*iptr);
    }
}
```

Figure 5.3   Definition and uses of variables.

statement initializes the integer pointer variable iptr and

```
iptr = i + x;
```

initializes the value of the location pointed to by iptr. The second

```
iptr = malloc(sizeof(int));
```

statement redefines variable iptr, thereby undefining the location previously pointed to by iptr.

Use: This occurs when the value is fetched from the memory location of the variable. There are two forms of *uses* of a variable as explained below.

- **Computation use (c-use):** This directly affects the computation being performed. In a c-use, a potentially new value of another variable or of the same variable is produced. Referring to the C function VarTypes(), the statement

```
*iptr = i + x;
```

gives examples of c-use of variables i and x.

- **Predicate use (p-use):** This refers to the use of a variable in a predicate controlling the flow of execution. Referring to the C function VarTypes(), the statement

```
if (*iptr > y) ...
```

gives examples of p-use of variables y and iptr.

A data flow graph is a directed graph constructed as follows:

- A sequence of *definitions* and c-uses is associated with each node of the graph.
- A set of p-uses is associated with each edge of the graph.

- The entry node has a definition of each parameter and each nonlocal variable which occurs in the subprogram.
- The exit node has an *undefinition* of each local variable.

Example: We show the data flow graph in Figure 5.4 for the ReturnAverage() example discussed in Chapter 4, The initial node, node **1**, represents initialization of the input vector < value, AS, MIN, MAX > . Node **2** represents the initialization of the four local variables *i*, ti, tv, and sum in the routine. Next we introduce a NULL node, node **3**, keeping in mind that control will come back to the beginning of the while loop. Node **3** also denotes the fact that program control exits from the while loop at the NULL node. The statement ti++ is represented by node **4**. The predicate associated with edge **(3, 4)** is the condition part of the while loop, namely,

```
((ti < AS) && (value[i] != -999))
```

Statements tv++ and sum = sum + value[i] are represented by node **5**. Therefore, the condition part of the first if statement forms the predicate associated with edge **(4, 5)**, namely,

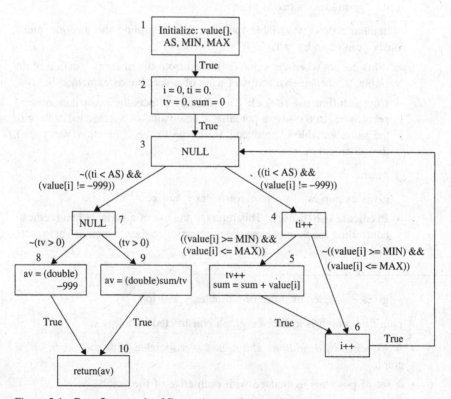

Figure 5.4   Data flow graph of ReturnAverage() example.

```
((value[i] >= MIN) && (value[i] <= MAX))
```

The statement i++ is represented by node **6**. The predicate associated with edge **(4, 6)** is the negation of the condition part of the if statement, namely,

```
((value[i] >= MIN) && (value[i] <= MAX)).
```

The predicate associated with edge **(5, 6)** is true because there is an unconditional flow of control from node **5** to node **6**. Execution of the while loop terminates when its condition evaluates to false. Therefore, the predicate associated with edge **(3, 7)** is the negation of the predicate associated with edge **(3, 4)**, namely,

```
~((ti < AS) && (value[i] != -999))
```

It may be noted that there is no computation performed in a NULL node. Referring to the second if statement, av = (double) − 999 is represented by node **8**, and av = (double) sum/tv is represented by node **9**. Therefore, the predicate associated with edge **(7, 9)** is

```
(tv > 0),
```

and the predicate associated with edge **(7, 8)** is

```
~(tv > 0).
```

Finally, the return(av) statement is represented by node **10**, and the predicate True is associated with both the edges **(7, 8)** and **(7, 9)**.

5.5 DATA FLOW TERMS

A variable *defined* in a statement is *used* in another statement which may occur immediately or several statements after the definition. We are interested in finding *paths* that include pairs of definition and use of variables. In this section, we explain a family of path selection criteria that allow us to select paths with varying strength. The reader may note that for every feasible path we can generate a test case. In the following, first we explain a few terms, and then we explain a few selection criteria using those terms.

> *Global c-use*: A c-use of a variable x in node i is said to be a *global c-use* if x has been defined before in a node other than node i.

> **Example:** The c-use of variable tv in node **9** is a global c-use since tv has been defined in nodes **2** and **5** (Figure 5.4).

> *Definition Clear Path*: A path $(i - n_1 - \cdots - n_m - j)$, $m \geq 0$, is called a definition clear path (def-clear path) with respect to variable x
> - from node i to node j and
> - from node i to edge (n_m, j)

if x has been neither *defined* nor *undefined* in nodes $n_1, \ldots, n_m$. The reader may note that the definition of a def-clear path is unconcerned about the status of x in nodes i and j. Also, a def-clear path does not preclude loops. Therefore, the path **2-3-4-6-3-4-6-3-4-5**, which includes a loop, is a def-clear path.

Example: The paths **2-3-4-5** and **2-3-4-6** are def-clear paths with respect to variable tv from node **2** to **5** and from node **2** to **6**, respectively (Figure 5.4).

Global Definition: A node i has a global definition of a variable x if node i has a definition of x and there is a def-clear path with respect to x from node i to some

- node containing a global c-use or
- edge containing a p-use of

variable x. The reader may note that we do not define *global* p-use of a variable similar to global c-use. This is because every p-use is associated with an edge—and not a node.

In Table 5.1, we show all the global definitions and global c-uses appearing in the data flow graph of Figure 5.4; def(i) denotes the set of variables which have global definitions in node i. Similarly, c-use(i) denotes the set of variables which have global c-uses in node i. We show all the predicates and p-uses appearing in the data flow graph of Figure 5.4 in Table 5.2; predicate(i,j) denotes the predicate associated with edge (i, j) of the data flow graph in Figure 5.4; p-use(i, j) denotes the set of variables which have p-uses on edge (i, j).

Simple Path: A simple path is a path in which all nodes, except possibly the first and the last, are distinct.

TABLE 5.1 Def() and c-use() Sets of Nodes in Figure 5.4

Nodes i	def(i)	c-use(i)
1	{value, AS, MIN, MAX}	{}
2	{i, ti, tv, sum}	{}
3	{}	{}
4	{ti}	{ti}
5	{tv, sum}	{tv, i, sum, value}
6	{i}	{i}
7	{}	{}
8	{av}	{}
9	{av}	{sum, tv}
10	{}	{av}

TABLE 5.2   Predicates and p-use() Set of Edges in Figure 5.4

Edges (i, j)	predicate(i, j)	p-use(i, j)
(1, 2)	True	{}
(2, 3)	True	{}
(3, 4)	(ti < AS) && (value[i] ! = −999)	{i, ti, AS, value}
(4, 5)	(value[i] < = MIN) && (value[i] > = MAX)	{i, MIN, MAX, value}
(4, 6)	~((value[i] < = MIN) && (value[i] > = MAX))	{i, MIN, MAX, value}
(5, 6)	True	{}
(6, 3)	True	{}
(3, 7)	~((ti < AS) && (value[i] ! = −999))	{i, ti, AS, value}
(7, 8)	~(tv > 0)	{tv}
(7, 9)	(tv > 0)	{tv}
(8, 10)	True	{}
(9, 10)	True	{}

Example: Paths **2-3-4-5** and **3-4-6-3** are simple paths (Figure 5.4).

Loop-Free Path: A loop-free path is a path in which *all* nodes are distinct.

Complete Path: A complete path is a path from the entry node to the exit node.

Du-path: A path $(n_1 - n_2 - \cdots - n_j - n_k)$ is a definition-use path (du-path) with respect to (w.r.t) variable x if node n_1 has a global definition of x and *either*

- node n_k has a global c-use of x and $(n_1 - n_2 - \cdots - n_j - n_k)$ is a def-clear simple path w.r.t. x *or*
- edge (n_j, n_k) has a p-use of x and $(n_1 - n_2 - \cdots - n_j)$ is a def-clear, loop-free path w.r.t. x.

Example: Considering the global definition and global c-use of variable tv in nodes **2** and **5**, respectively, **2-3-4-5** is a du-path.

Example: Considering the global definition and p-use of variable tv in nodes **2** and on edge **(7, 9)**, respectively, **2-3-7-9** is a du-path.

5.6   DATA FLOW TESTING CRITERIA

In this section, we explain seven types of data flow testing criteria. These criteria are based on two fundamental concepts, namely, definitions and uses—both c-uses and p-uses—of variables.

All-defs: For each variable x and for each node i such that x has a global definition in node i, select a complete path which includes a def-clear path from node i to

- node j having a global c-use of x or
- edge (j,k) having a p-use of x.

Example: Consider the variable tv, which has global definitions in nodes **2** and **5** (Figure 5.4 and Tables 5.1 and 5.2). First, we consider its global definition in node **2**. We find a global c-use of tv in node **5**, and there exists a def-clear path **2-3-4-5** from node **2** to node **5**. We choose a complete path **1-2-3-4-5-6-3-7-9-10** that includes the def-clear path **2-3-4-5** to satisfy the all-defs criterion. We also find p-uses of variable tv on edge **(7, 8)**, and there exists a def-clear path **2-3-7-8** from node **2** to edge **(7, 8)**. We choose a complete path **1-2-3-7-8-10** that includes the def-clear path **2-3-7-8** to satisfy the all-defs criterion. Now we consider the definition of tv in node **5**. In node **9** there is a global c-use of tv, and in edges **(7, 8)** and **(7, 9)** there are p-uses of tv. There is a def-clear path **5-6-3-7-9** from node **5** to node **9**. Thus, we choose a complete path **1-2-3-4-5-6-3-7-9-10** that includes the def-clear path **5-6-3-7-9** to satisfy the all-defs criterion. The reader may note that the complete path **1-2-3-4-5-6-3-7-9-10** covers the all-defs criterion for variable tv defined in nodes **2** and **5**. To satisfy the all-defs criterion, similar paths must be obtained for variables i, ti, and sum.

> *All-c-uses*: For each variable x and for each node i, such that x has a global definition in node i, select complete paths which include def-clear paths from node i to *all* nodes j such that there is a global c-use of x in j.

Example: Let us obtain paths to satisfy the all-c-uses criterion with respect to variable ti. We find two global definitions of ti in nodes **2** and **4**. Corresponding to the global definition in node **2**, there is a global c-use of ti in node **4**. However, corresponding to the global definition in node **4**, there is no global c-use of ti. From the global definition in node **2**, there is a def-clear path to the global c-use in node **4** in the form of **2-3-4**. The reader may note that there are *four* complete paths that include the def-clear path **2-3-4** as follows:

1-2-3-4-5-6-3-7-8-10,

1-2-3-4-5-6-3-7-9-10,

1-2-3-4-6-3-7-8-10, and

1-2-3-4-6-3-7-9-10.

One may choose one or more paths from among the four paths above to satisfy the all-c-uses criterion with respect to variable ti.

> *All-p-uses*: For each variable x and for each node i such that x has a global definition in node i, select complete paths which include def-clear paths from node i to *all* edges (j,k) such that there is a p-use of x on edge (j,k).

Example: Let us obtain paths to satisfy the all-p-uses criterion with respect to variable tv. We find two global definitions of tv in nodes **2** and **5**. Corresponding to the global definition in node **2**, there is a p-use of tv on edges **(7, 8)** and **(7, 9)**. There are def-clear paths from node **2** to edges **(7, 8)** and **(7, 9)**, namely **2-3-7-8** and **2-3-7-9**, respectively. Also, there are def-clear paths from node **5** to edges

(7, 8) and **(7, 9)**, namely, **5-6-3-7-8** and **5-6-3-7-9**, respectively. In the following, we identify *four* complete paths that include the above four def-clear paths:

1-2-3-7-8-10,

1-2-3-7-9-10,

1-2-3-4-5-6-3-7-8-10, and

1-2-3-4-5-6-3-7-9-10.

All-p-uses/Some-c-uses: This criterion is identical to the all-p-uses criterion except when a variable x has no p-use. If x has no p-use, then this criterion reduces to the some-c-uses criterion explained below.

Some-c-uses: For each variable x and for each node i such that x has a global definition in node i, select complete paths which include def-clear paths from node i to *some* nodes j such that there is a global c-use of x in node j.

Example: Let us obtain paths to satisfy the all-p-uses/some-c-uses criterion with respect to variable i. We find two global definitions of i in nodes **2** and **6**. There is no p-use of i in Figure 5.4. Thus, we consider some c-uses of variable i. Corresponding to the global definition of variable i in node **2**, there is a global c-use of i in node **6**, and there is a def-clear path from node **2** to node **6** in the form of **2-3-4-5-6**. Therefore, to satisfy the all-p-uses/some-c-uses criterion with respect to variable i, we select the complete path **1-2-3-4-5-6-3-7-9-10** that includes the def-clear path **2-3-4-5-6**.

All-c-uses/Some-p-uses: This criterion is identical to the all-c-uses criterion except when a variable x has no global c-use. If x has no global c-use, then this criterion reduces to the some-p-uses criterion explained below.

Some-p-uses: For each variable x and for each node i such that x has a global definition in node i, select complete paths which include def-clear paths from node i to *some* edges (j,k) such that there is a p-use of x on edge (j,k).

Example: Let us obtain paths to satisfy the all-c-uses/some-p-uses criterion with respect to variable AS. We find just one global definition of AS in node **1**. There is no global c-use of AS in Figure 5.4. Thus, we consider some p-uses of AS. Corresponding to the global definition of AS in node **1**, there are p-uses of AS on edges **(3, 7)** and **(3, 4)**, and there are def-clear paths from node **1** to those two edges, namely, **1-2-3-7** and **1-2-3-4**, respectively. There are many complete paths that include those two def-clear paths. One such example path is given as **1-2-3-4-5-6-3-7-9-10**.

All-uses: This criterion is the conjunction of the all-p-uses criterion and the all-c-uses criterion discussed above.

All-du-paths: For each variable x and for each node i such that x has a global definition in node i, select complete paths which include *all* du-paths from node i

- to *all* nodes j such that there is a global c-use of x in j and
- to *all* edges (j,k) such that there is a p-use of x on (j,k).

In Chapter 4, we explained a procedure to generate a test input from an entry–exit program path. There is much similarity between the control flow–based testing and the data flow–based testing. Their difference lies in the ways the two techniques select program paths.

5.7 COMPARISON OF DATA FLOW TEST SELECTION CRITERIA

Having seen a relatively large number of test selection criteria based on the concepts of data flow and control flow, it is useful to find relationships among them. Given a pair of test selection criteria, we should be able to compare the two. If we cannot compare them, we realize that they are incomparable. Rapps and Weyuker [3] defined the concept of an *includes* relationship to find out if, for a given pair of selection criteria, one includes the other. In the following, by a *complete* path we mean a path from the entry node of a flow graph to one of its exit nodes.

Definition: Given two test selection criteria c_1 and c_2, c_1 *includes* c_2 if for every def/use graph any set of complete paths of the graph that satisfies c_1 also satisfies c_2.

Definition: Given two test selection criteria c_1 and c_2, c_1 *strictly includes* c_2, denoted by $c_1 \rightarrow c_2$, provided c_1 includes c_2 and for some def/use graph there is a set of complete paths of the graph that satisfies c_2 but not c_1.

It is easy to note that the "$\rightarrow$" relationship is a transitive relation. Moreover, given two criteria c_1 and c_2, it is possible that neither $c_1 \rightarrow c_2$ nor $c_2 \rightarrow c_1$ holds, in which case we call the two criteria *incomparable*. Proving the strictly includes relationship or the incomparable relationship between two selection criteria in a programming language with arbitrary semantics may not be possible. Thus, to show the strictly includes relationship between a pair of selection criteria, Rapps and Weyuker [3] have considered a restricted programming language with the following syntax:

Start statement:	**start**
Input statement:	**read** $x_1, \ldots, x_n$, where $x_i, \ldots, n$ are variables.
Assignment statement:	$y \leftarrow f(x_1, \ldots, x_n)$, where $y, x_i, \ldots, n$ are variables, and f is a function.
Output statement:	**print** $e_1, \ldots, e_n$, where $e_1, \ldots, e_n$ are output values.
Unconditional transfer statement:	**goto** m, where m is a label.
Conditional transfer statement:	**if** $p(x_1, \ldots, x_n)$, **then goto** m, where p is a predicate.
Halt statement:	**stop**

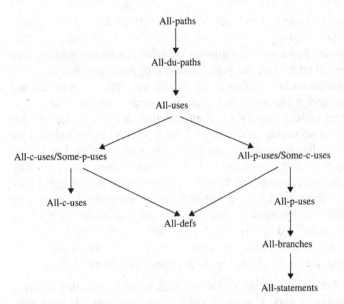

Figure 5.5   Relationship among DF (data flow) testing criteria. (From ref. 4. © 1988 IEEE.)

Frankl and Weyuker [4] have further extended the relationship; what they have proved has been summarized in Figure 5.5. For example, the all-paths selection criterion strictly includes the all-du-paths criterion. Similarly, the all-c-uses/some-p-uses criterion strictly includes the all-defs criterion.

However, we cannot find a strictly includes relationship between the pair all-c-uses and all-p-uses. Let P_x^c be a set of paths selected by the all-c-uses criterion with respect to a variable x. Now we cannot say with certainty whether or not the path set P_x^c satisfies the all-p-uses criterion with respect to the same variable x. Similarly, let P_x^p be a set of paths selected by the all-p-uses criterion with respect to the variable x. Now we cannot say with certainty whether or not the path set P_x^p satisfies the all-c-uses criterion with respect to the same variable x. Thus, the two criteria all-c-uses and all-p-uses are incomparable.

Note the relationship between data flow–based test selection criteria and control flow–based test selection criteria, as shown in Figure 5.5. The two control flow–based test selection criteria in Figure 5.5 are all-branches and all-statements. The all-p-uses criterion strictly includes the all-branches criterion, which implies that one can select more paths from a data flow graph of a program unit than from its control flow graph.

5.8 FEASIBLE PATHS AND TEST SELECTION CRITERIA

Given a data flow graph, a path is a sequence of nodes and edges. A complete path is a sequence of nodes and edges starting from the initial node of the graph to one of its exit nodes. A complete path is executable if there exists an assignment of values to input variables and global variables such that all the path predicates evaluate to true, thereby making the path executable. *Executable* paths are also known as *feasible* paths. If no such assignment of values to input variables and global variables exists, then we call the path *infeasible* or *inexecutable*.

Since we are interested in selecting inputs to execute paths, we must ensure that a test selection criterion picks executable paths. Assume that we want to test a program by selecting paths to satisfy a certain selection criterion C. Let P_C be the set of paths selected according to criterion C for a given program unit. As an extreme example, if all the paths in P_C are infeasible, then the criterion C has not helped us in any way. For a criterion C to be useful, it must select a set of executable, or feasible, paths. Frankl and Weyuker [4] have modified the definitions of the test selection criteria so that each criterion selects only feasible paths. In other words, we modify the definition of criterion C to obtain a criterion $C*$ which selects only feasible paths, and $C*$ is called a feasible data flow (FDF) testing criterion. As an example, the criterion (All-c-uses)* is an adaptation of All-c-uses such that only feasible paths are selected by (All-c-uses)*, as defined below.

> *(All-c-uses)**: For each variable x and for each node i, such that x has a global definition in node i, select feasible complete paths which include def-clear paths from node i to *all* nodes j such that there is a global c-use of x in j.

Thus, test selection criteria (All-paths)*, (All-du-paths)*, (All-uses)*, (All-c-uses/Some-p-uses)*, (All-p-uses/Some-c-uses)*, (All-c-uses)*, (All-p-uses)*, (All-defs)*, (All-branches)*, and (All-statements)* choose only feasible paths, and, therefore, these are called feasible data flow (FDF) testing criteria. Frankl and Weyuker [4] have shown that the strictly includes relationships among test selection criteria, as shown in Figure 5.5, do not hold if the selection criteria choose only feasible paths. The new relationship among FDF test selection criteria is summarized in Figure 5.6. Though it is seemingly useful to select only feasible paths, and therefore consider only the FDF test selection criteria, we are faced with the decidability problem. More specifically, it is undecidable to know if a given set of paths is executable. We cannot automate the application of an FDF test selection criterion, if we do not know the executability of the path. On the other hand, a data flow testing criterion may turn out to be inadequate if all its selected paths are infeasible, in which case the criterion is considered to be inadequate. Consequently, a test engineer must make a choice between using an inadequate selection criterion and one that cannot be completely automated.

5.9 COMPARISON OF TESTING TECHNIQUES

So far we have discussed two major techniques for generating test data from source code, namely control flow–based path selection and data flow–based path selection. We also explained a few criteria to select paths from a control flow graph and data flow graph of a program. Programmers often randomly select test data based on their own understanding of the code they have written. Therefore, it is natural to

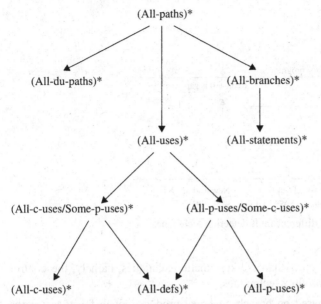

Figure 5.6   Relationship among FDF (feasible data flow) testing criteria. (From ref. 4. ©
1988 IEEE.)

compare the effectiveness of the three test generation techniques, namely random
test selection, test selection based on control flow, and test selection based on data
flow. Comparing those techniques does not seem to be an easy task. An acceptable,
straightforward way of comparing them is to apply those techniques to the same
set of programs with known faults and express their effectiveness in terms of the
following two metrics:

- Number of test cases produced
- percentage of known faults detected

Ntafos [5] has reported on the results of an experiment comparing the effectiveness of three test selection techniques. The experiment involved seven mathematical programs with known faults. For the control flow–based technique, the
branch coverage criterion was selected, whereas the *all-uses* criterion was chosen for data flow testing. Random testing was also applied to the programs. The
data flow testing, branch testing, and random testing detected 90%, 85.5%, and
79.5%, respectively, of the known defects. A total of 84 test cases were designed
to achieve all-uses coverage, 34 test cases were designed to achieve branch coverage, and 100 test cases were designed in the random testing approach. We interpret
the experimental results as follows:

- A programmer can randomly generate a large number of test cases to find
  most of the faults. However, one will run out of test cases to find some of
  the remaining faults. Random testing does not look to be ineffective, but

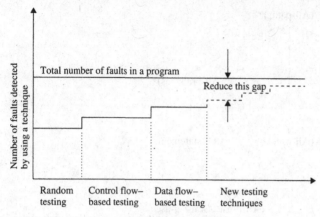

Figure 5.7   Limitation of different fault detection techniques.

it incurs higher costs than the systematic techniques, namely, the control flow and the data flow techniques.

- Test selection based on branch coverage produces much fewer test cases than the random technique, but achieves nearly the same level of fault detection as the random technique. Thus, there is significant saving in the cost of program testing.

- The all-uses testing criterion gives a programmer a new way to design more test cases and reveal more faults than the branch coverage criterion.

- All these techniques have inherent limitations which prevent them from revealing all faults. Therefore, there is a need to use many different testing techniques and develop new techniques. This idea is depicted in Figure 5.7. Our goal is to reduce the gap between the total number of faults present in a program and the faults detected by various test generation techniques.

5.10   SUMMARY

Flow of data in a program can be visualized by considering the fact that a program unit accepts input data, transforms the input data through a sequence of computations, and, finally, produces the output data. Therefore, one can imagine data values to be flowing from one assignment statement defining a variable to another assignment statement or a predicate where the value is used.

Three fundamental actions associated with a variable are *undefine* (u), *define* (d), and *reference* (r). A variable is implicitly undefined when it is created without being assigned a value. On the other hand, a variable can be explicitly undefined. For example, when an opened file is closed, the variable holding the file pointer becomes undefined. We have explained the idea of "states" of a variable, namely, *undefined* (U), *defined* (D), *referenced* (R), and *abnormal* (A), by considering the three fundamental actions on a variable. The A state represents the fact that the variable has been accessed in an *abnormal* manner causing data flow anomaly.

Individual actions on a variable do not cause data flow anomaly. Instead, certain sequences of actions lead to data flow anomaly, and those three sequences of actions are *dd*, *ur*, and *du*. A variable continues to remain in the abnormal state irrespective of subsequent actions once it enters that state. The mere presence of data flow anomaly in a program may not lead to program failure. The programmer must investigate the cause of an anomaly and modify the code to eliminate it. For example, a missing statement in the code might have caused a *dd* anomaly, in which case the programmer needs to write new code.

The program path is a fundamental concept in testing. One test case can be generated from one executable path. The number of different paths selected for execution is a measure of the extent of testing performed. Path selection based on statement coverage and branch coverage lead to a small number of paths being chosen for execution. Therefore, there exists a large gap between control flow testing and exhaustive testing. The concept of data flow testing gives us a way to bridge the gap between control flow testing and exhaustive testing.

The concept of data flow testing gives us new selection criteria for choosing more program paths to test than what we can choose by using the idea of control flow testing. Specifically, the data flow test selection criteria are all-du-paths, all-defs, all-c-uses, all-p-uses, all-uses, all-c-uses/some-p-uses, and all-p-uses/some-c-uses. To compare two selection criteria, the concept of a strictly includes relationship is found to be useful.

LITERATURE REVIEW

Osterweil and Fosdick [6] have implemented a system, called DAVE, to analyze FORTRAN programs and detect *ur*, *dd*, and *du* types of data flow anomalies. DAVE detects those anomalies by performing a flow graph search for each variable in a given program unit. For programs with subprogram invocations, the system works in a bottom-up manner, that is, the called subprograms are analyzed before analyzing the caller.

Programmers need to be aware that it is difficult to apply the idea of data flow analysis to all kinds of data structures and program constructs. The analysis of arrays is one such difficulty. Fosdick and Osterweil [1] have noted that problems arise when different elements of the same array are acted upon in different ways, thereby giving rise to different patterns of definition, reference, and undefinition. Static data flow analysis systems, such as DAVE, do not evaluate index expressions and therefore cannot tell us what array element is being referenced in a given expression. Such systems try to get around this problem by treating an entire array as one single variable, rather than a set of different variables of the same type. Fosdick and Osterweil have shown that recursive programs pose difficulty in data flow analysis. A programming style that can pose a difficulty in data flow analysis is to pass a single variable as an argument more than once. This is because DAVE assumes that all subprogram parameters are distinct variables.

Laski and Korel [7] argue that data flow testing bridges the gap between branch testing and all-paths testing. On the one hand, in branch testing, one selects a set of paths to cover all branches of the control flow graph of a program unit; one needs to select a small number of paths to satisfy the criterion. On the other hand, all-paths testing is the same as exhaustive testing. Data flow testing allows programmers to select many more paths than chosen by branch testing. Essentially, in data flow testing, loops are unfolded to exercise the definition–use pairs.

Herman [8] had a programmer apply data flow testing to a number of medium-sized program units of about 800 statements. It is interesting to note that faults detected during testing were usually found while attempting to devise test data to satisfy the chosen paths, rather than while examining the test run output. The fact that program faults were found during the process of test design is significant in the sense that system development and selection of tests can simultaneously be done in producing a better quality system.

The article by Ural [9] presents a method for generating test cases from the specifications of communications protocols given in the Estelle language. The method involves static data flow analysis of specifications. The method is summarized as follows: (i) transform a specification into a graph containing both the control flow and the data flow aspects; (ii) detect data flow anomalies in the specification; and (iii) generate test cases to cover all definition–use pairs.

The article by Ntafos [10] explains an extended overview of data flow testing strategies in terms of their relative coverage of a program's structure and the number of test cases needed to satisfy each strategy. In addition, the article extends the subsumption hierarchy introduced by Rapps and Weyuker [3] by including $TER_n = 1$. For details about testing hierarchy levels, denoted by n above and test effectiveness ratio (TER), the reader is referred to the article by Woodward, Hedley, and Hennell [11].

The concept of selecting program paths based on data flow has been studied in different ways by different researchers, namely, Laski and Korel [7], Ntafos [5], and Rapps and Weyuker [3]. To facilitate the comparison and simplify the discussion, Clarke, Podgurski, Richardson, and Zeil [12] define all the data flow criteria using a single set of terms. They give a new subsumption hierarchy of the data flow test selection criteria by modifying the subsumption hierarchy of Rapps and Weyuker [7] shown in Figure 5.5.

Koh and Liu [3] have presented a two-step approach for generating paths that test both the control flow and the data flow in implementations of communication protocols based on the idea of extended finite-state machines. First, select a set of paths to cover a data flow selection criterion. Second, selectively augment the state transitions in the chosen set of paths with state check sequences so that control flow can be ensured and data flow coverage can be preserved. The test design methodology of Sarikaya, Bochmann, and Cerny [14] also generates paths to achieve joint coverage of control flow and data flow in the Estelle specifications of communication protocols.

Researchers have extended the classical data flow testing approach to the testing of object-oriented programs [15–18]. Harrold and Rothermel [16] have applied the concept of data flow testing to the testing of classes in object-oriented programs. The three levels of testing that they have proposed are *intramethod* testing, *intermethod* testing, and *intraclass* testing. Intermethod testing is the same as data flow testing performed on a unit in a procedural programming language, such as C. Intermethod testing is similar to integrating program units in a procedural programming language. Finally, intraclass testing refers to calling the public methods of a class in a random, acceptable sequence.

The concept of classical data flow testing that is applied to one program unit at a time has been extended to *interprocedural* data flow testing. The idea of interprocedural data flow has been extensively studied in the literature (see ref. 19 and the bibliography of the article by Harrold and Soffa [20]).

Often programmers utilize the capability of pointers in the C and C++ languages. Data flow analysis becomes difficult when pointers are passed between procedures. Pande, Landi, and Ryder [21] have defined a term called *reaching definitions*, which is the set of all points where a value of a variable was last written. For one level of pointer indirection, they give a polynomial time algorithm for the problem. To develop the algorithm, the authors have introduced the concept of an *interprocedural control flow graph*, which is a hybrid of the control flow graph and call graph. They prove that the general problem of identifying interprocedural reaching definitions is *NP*-hard.

Lemos, Vincenzi, Maldonado, and Masiero [22] have applied the idea of data flow testing to aspect-oriented programs [23]. The concept of aspect-oriented programming was developed to address the difficulty in clearly capturing certain high-level design decisions at the code level. The properties of those design decisions are called *aspects*, and hence the name *aspect-oriented programming*. The reason some design decisions are difficult to represent at the code level is that they cross-cut the system's basic functionality [23]. Naturally, an aspect that is difficult to code is likely to be more difficult to test and verify. To this end, the work of Lemos et al. [22] gains significance. They have proposed the concept of an *aspect-oriented def-use* (AODU) graph, based on the idea of a data flow instruction graph [24], and identified new coverage criteria, such as *all-exception-independent-uses*, *all-exception-dependent-uses*, and *all-crosscutting-uses*. Zhao [25] has applied the idea of data flow testing at a coarse-grain level in aspect-oriented programs. The author extended the concept of class testing studied by Harrold and Rothermel [16].

The 1990 book *Software Testing Techniques* by Beizer [26] gives an excellent exposition of the concept of data flow testing.

REFERENCES

1. L. D. Fosdick and L. J. Osterweil. Data Flow Analysis in Software Reliability. *Computing Surveys*, September 1976, pp. 305–330.
2. J. C. Huang. Detection of Data Flow Anomaly through Program Instrumentation. *IEEE Transactions on Software Engineering*, May 1979, pp. 226–236.
3. S. Rapps and E. J. Weyuker. Selecting Software Test Data Using Data Flow Information. *IEEE Transactions on Software Engineering*, April 1985, pp. 367–375.
4. P. G. Frankl and E. J. Weyuker. An Applicable Family of Data Flow Testing Criteria. *IEEE Transactions on Software Engineering*, October 1988, pp. 1483–1498.
5. S. C. Ntafos. On Required Element Testing. *IEEE Transactions on Software Engineering*, November 1984, pp. 795–803.

6. L. J. Osterweil and L. D. Fosdick. Dave—A Validation, Error Detection, and Documentation System for Fortran Programs. *Software—Practice and Experience*, October/December 1976, pp. 473–486.

7. J. W. Laski and B. Korel. A Data Flow Oriented Program Testing Strategy. *IEEE Transactions on Software Engineering*, May 1983, pp. 347–354.

8. P. M. Herman. A Data Flow Analysis Approach to Program Testing. *Australian Computer Journal*, November 1976, pp. 92–96.

9. H. Ural. Test Sequence Selection Based on Static Data Flow Analysis. *Computer Communications*, October 1987, pp. 234–242.

10. S. C. Ntafos. A Comparison of Some Structural Testing Strategies. *IEEE Transactions on Software Engineering*, June 1988, pp. 868–874.

11. M. R. Woodward, D. Hedley, and M. A. Hennell. Experience with Path Analysis and Testing of Programs. *IEEE Transactions on Software Engineering*, May 1980, pp. 278–286.

12. L. A. Clarke, A. Podgurski, D. J. Richardson, and S. J. Zeil. A formal Evaluation of Data Flow Path Selection Criteria. *IEEE Transactions on Software Engineering*, November 1989, pp. 1318–1332.

13. L. S. Koh and M. T. Liu. Test Path Selection Based on Effective Domains. In *Proceedings of the International Conference on Network Protocols*, Boston, October 1994, IEEE Press, Piscataway, pp. 64–71.

14. B. Sarikaya, G. v. Bochmann, and E. Cerny. A Test Design Methodology for Protocol Testing. *IEEE Transactions on Software Engineering*, May 1987, pp. 518–531.

15. R. Doong and P. Frankl. The ASTOOT Approach to Testing Object-Oriented Programs. *ACM Transactions on Software Engineering and Methodology*, April 1994, pp. 101–130.

16. M. J. Harrold and G. Rothermel. Performing Data Flow Testing on Classes. In *Proceedings of ACM SIGSOFT Foundation of Software Engineering*, New Orleans, December 1994, ACM Press, New York pp. 154–163.

17. D. Kung, J. Gao, P. Hsia, Y. Toyoshima, C. Chen, K.-S. Kim, and Y.-K. Song. Developing an Object-Oriented Software Testing and Maintenance Environment. *Communications of the ACM*, October 1995, pp. 75–86.

18. A. S. Parrish, R. B. Borie, and D. W. Cordes. Automated Flow Graph-Based Testing of Object-Oriented Software Modules. *Journal of Systems and Software*, November 1993, pp. 95–109.

19. J. M. Barth. A Practical Interprocedural Data Flow Analysis Algorithm. *Communications of the ACM*, September 1978, pp. 724–736.

20. M. J. Harrold and M. L. Sofa. Efficient Computation of Interprocedural Definition-Use Chains. *ACM Transactions on Programming Languages and Systems*, March 1994, pp. 175–204.

21. H. Pande, W. Landi, and B. G. Ryder. Interprocedural Def-Use Associations in C Programs. *IEEE Transactions on Software Engineering*, May 1994, pp. 385–403.

22. O. A. L. Lemos, A. M. R. Vincenzi, J. C. Maldonado, and P. C. Masiero. Control and Data Flow Structural Testing Criteria for Aspect-Oriented Programs. *Journal of Systems and Software*, June 2007, pp. 862–882.

23. G. Kiczales, J. Lamping, A. Mendhekar, C. Maeda, C. V. Lopes, J.-M. Loingtier, and J. Irwin. Aspect-Oriented Programming. In *Proceedings of the European Conference on Object-Oriented Programming*, LNCS 1241, Finland, June 1997, pp. 220–242.

24. A. M. R. Vincenzi, J. C. Maldonado, W. E. Wong, and M. E. Delamaro. Coverage Testing of Java Programs and Components. *Science of Computer Programming*, April 2005, pp. 211–230.

25. J. Zhao. Data-Flow Based Unit Testing of Aspect-Oriented Programs. In *Proceedings of the 27th Annual International Computer Software and Applications Conference*, Dallas, Texas, IEEE Press, Piscataway, 2003, pp. 188–197.

26. B. Beizer. *Software Testing Techniques*, 2nd ed. Van Nostrand Reinhold, New York, 1990.

Exercises

1. Draw a data flow graph for the binsearch() function given in Figure 5.8.

2. Assuming that the input array $V[\ ]$ has at least one element in it, find an infeasible path in the data flow graph for the binsearch() function.

```
int binsearch(int X, int V[], int n){
    int low, high, mid;
    low = 0;
    high = n - 1;
    while (low <= high) {
      mid = (low + high)/2;
      if (X < V[mid])
          high = mid - 1;
      else if (X > V[mid])
            low = mid + 1;
      else
            return mid;
    }
    return -1;
}
```

Figure 5.8   Binary search routine.

```
int modifiedbinsearch(int X, int V[], int n){
  int low, high, mid;
  low = 0;
  high = n - 1;
  while (low <= high) {
    mid = (low + high)/2;
    if (X < V[mid]) {
        high = mid - 1;
        mid = mid - 1;
    }
    else if (X > V[mid])
        low = mid + 1;
    else
        return mid;
  }
  return -1;
}
```

Figure 5.9   Modified binary search routine.

3. Identify a data flow anomaly in the code given in Figure 5.9.

4. By referring to the data flow graph obtained in exercise 1, find a set of complete paths satisfying the all-defs selection criterion with respect to variable mid.

5. By referring to the data flow graph obtained in exercise 1, find a set of complete paths satisfying the all-defs selection criterion with respect to variable high.

6. Write a function in C such that the all-uses criterion produces more test cases than the all-branches criterion.

7. What is meant by the *gap* between all-branches testing and all-paths testing and how does data flow testing fill the gap?

8. Explain why the presence of data flow anomaly does not imply that execution of the program will definitely produce incorrect results.

9. Program anomaly has been defined by considering three operations, namely, define (d), reference (r), and undefine (u). The three sequences of operations identified to be program anomaly are dd, du, and ur. Explain why the rest of the two-operation sequences are not considered to be program anomaly.

10. Identify some difficulties in identifying data flow anomaly in programs.

CHAPTER 6

Domain Testing

> Even granting that the genius subjected to the test of critical inspection emerges
> free from all error, we should consider that everything he has discovered in a
> given domain is almost nothing in comparison with what is left to be discovered.
> — *Santiago Ramón y Cajal*

6.1 DOMAIN ERROR

Two fundamental elements of a computer program are *input domain* and *program paths*. The input domain of a program is the set of all input data to the program. A program path is a sequence of instructions from the start of the program to some point of *interest* in the program. For example, the end of the program is a point of interest. Another point of interest is when the program waits to receive another input from its environment so that it can continue its execution. In other words, a program path, or simply *path*, corresponds to some flow of control in the program. A path is said to be *feasible* if there exists an input data which causes the program to execute the path. Otherwise, the path is said to be *infeasible*.

Howden [1] identified two broad classes of errors, namely, *computation error* and *domain error*, by combining the concepts of *input data* and program path. The two kinds of errors have been explained in the following.

> *Computation Error*: A computation error occurs when a specific input data
> causes the program to execute the correct, i.e., desired path, but the output
> value is wrong. Note that the output value can be wrong even if the desired
> path has been executed. This can happen due to a wrong function being
> executed in an *assignment* statement. For example, consider a desired path
> containing the statement result = f(a, b), where *a* and *b* are input values.
> A computation error may occur if the statement is replaced by a faulty
> one, such as result = f(b, a). Therefore, the result of executing the path
> can be erroneous because of a fault in the assignment statement, and this
> can happen in spite of executing a correct path.

Domain Error: A domain error occurs when a specific input data causes the program to execute a *wrong*, that is, undesired, path in the program. An incorrect path can be selected by a program if there is a fault in one or more of the *conditional* statements in the program. Let us consider a conditional statement of the form *if (p) then f1() else f2()*. If there is a fault in the formulation of the predicate p, then the wrong function call is invoked, thereby causing an incorrect path to be executed.

The above two kinds of program errors lead us to view a computer program as performing an abstract mapping function as follows. Ideally, for each input value, the program assigns a program path to execute; the same program path can be exclusively assigned (i.e., executed) for a subset of the input values. Here, the subset of the input values causing the same path to be executed is referred to an input *domain* or *subdomain*. Thus, the program is said to map a domain to a path within itself. Since there are a large number of values in the input domain of the program and there are a large number of paths in a program, we can view a program as partitioning the input space into a finite number of subdomains and assigning a distinct program path to each of the input subdomains.

We further explain the concept of program domains using Figure 6.1. The set D is the entire input set of a program P (Figure 6.1a). We call D the domain of the entire program. Set D can be an infinite set, and P may not have different computation behavior for each element of D. Instead, P may perform the same computation for all the elements in a certain subset of D. For example, as shown in Figure 6.1b, P performs *five* different computations, one for each subset D_1, ..., D_5. It may be noted that the partition of D is not visible outside P. Instead, P has a conceptual, in-built mechanism, as illustrated in Figure 6.1c, to decide the computation method needed to choose a specific branch when P is invoked with a certain input. Such an input classifier may not exist in a program in a single, clearly identifiable form. The concept can exist as an entity as a cross-cutting concept; it is cross-cutting because portions of the input classifier can be found in different program modules. We show five different computations, *computation for D_1* through *computation for D_5*, for subsets D_1, ..., D_5, respectively (Figure 6.1c). The part of P that decides what computation to invoke for a given element of D is called an *input classifier*. We remind the reader that the structure of a program may not resemble the case we have shown inside the larger circle in Figure 6.1c. The figure simply denotes the fact that a program does different computations for different subsets of its input domain. Programs perform input classification through sequences of predicates, though an input classifier may not exist as a single module.

Therefore, a program will perform the wrong computation if there are faults in the input classification portion. With the above backdrop, we define the following two terms:

- A *domain* is a set of input values for which the program performs the same computation for every member of the set. We are interested in maximal domains such that the program performs different computations on *adjacent* domains.

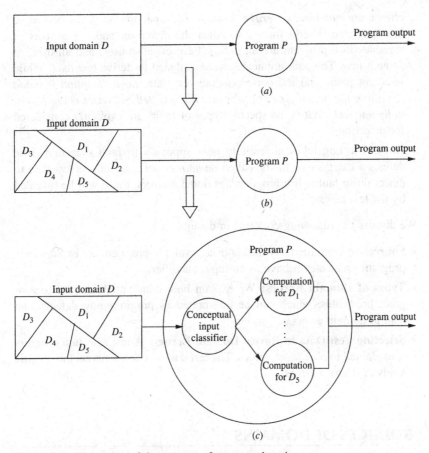

Figure 6.1   Illustration of the concept of program domains.

- A program is said to have a *domain error* if the program incorrectly performs input classification. Assuming that adjacent domains perform different computations, a domain error will cause the program to produce incorrect output.

6.2   TESTING FOR DOMAIN ERRORS

The idea of *domain testing* was first studied by White and Cohen in 1978 [2, 3]. There is a fundamental difference between flow graph–based testing techniques and domain testing. By flow graph we mean control flow graph and data flow graph. The difference is explained as follows:

- Select paths from a control flow graph or a data flow graph to satisfy certain *coverage criteria*. To remind the reader, the *control flow* coverage criteria are *statement coverage*, *branch coverage*, and *predicate coverage*. Similarly, the criteria studied to cover the *definition* and *use* aspects of variables in a program are all-defs, all-c-uses, all-p-uses, and all-uses, to name a few. The path predicates were analyzed to derive test data. While selecting paths and the corresponding test data, *no assumption is made regarding the actual type of faults that the selected test cases could potentially uncover*, that is, no specific types of faults are explicitly considered for detection.

- Domain testing takes an entirely new approach to fault detection. One defines a category of faults, called *domain errors*, and selects test data to detect those faults. If a program has domain errors, those will be revealed by the test cases.

We discuss the following concepts in detail:

- **Sources of Domains:** By means of an example program, we explain how program predicates behave as an input classifier.
- **Types of Domain Errors:** We explain how minor modifications to program predicates, which can be interpreted as programming defects, can lead to domain errors.
- **Selecting Test Data to Reveal Domain Errors:** A test selection criterion is explained to pick input values. The test data so chosen reveal the specific kinds of domain errors.

6.3 SOURCES OF DOMAINS

Domains can be identified from both specifications and programs. We explain a method to identify domains from source code using the following steps:

- Draw a control flow graph from the given source code.
- Find all possible interpretations of the predicates. In other words, express the predicates solely in terms of the input vector and, possibly, a vector of constants. The reader may note that a predicate in a program may have multiple interpretations, because control may arrive at a predicate node via different paths.
- Analyze the interpreted predicates to identify domains.

In the following, we explain the above procedure to identify domains. We show an example C function in Figure 6.2 to illustrate a procedure to identify domains.

The function accepts two inputs x and y and returns an integer. A control flow graph representation of codedomain() is shown in Figure 6.3. The two predicates in the two if() statements have been represented by nodes **3** and **6** in Figure 6.3. The predicate

$$P_1: \qquad c > 5$$

```
int codedomain(int x, int y){
  int c, d, k
  c = x + y;
  if (c > 5) d = c - x/2;
  else       d = c + x/2;
  if (d >= c + 2) k = x + d/2;
  else            k = y + d/4;
  return(k);
}
```

Figure 6.2   A function to explain program domains.

in the first if() statement has just one interpretation, namely,

$$P_1: \qquad x + y > 5$$

because program control reaches the if() statement via only one path from the initial node. However, predicate

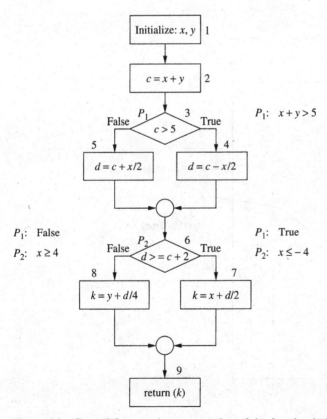

Figure 6.3   Control flow graph representation of the function in Figure 6.2.

$$P_2: \qquad d \geq c + 2$$

in the second if() statement gets two interpretations, because program control can reach the second if() statement along two paths: (i) when the first if() evaluates to true and (ii) when the first if() evaluates to false. These two interpretations are summarized in Table 6.1.

We explain a procedure to obtain domains from the interpretations of P_1 and P_2 (Figure 6.3). We show a two-dimensional grid labeled x and y in Figure 6.4. The grid size is large enough to show all the domains of the program under consideration. We consider the predicate nodes of the control flow graph one by one (Figure 6.3). Predicate P_1 divides the grid into two regions. The P_1 boundary is shown by a straight line represented by the equality $x + y = 5$. All the points above, but excluding this line, satisfy predicate P_1.

**TABLE 6.1 Two Interpretations of Second if()
Statement in Figure 6.2**

Evaluation of P_1	Interpretation of P_2
True	$x \leq -4$
False	$x \geq 4$

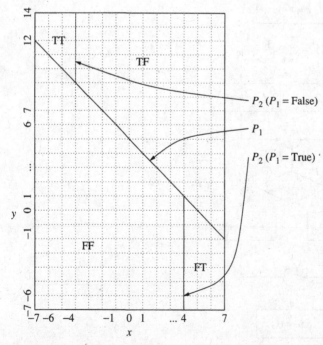

Figure 6.4   Domains obtained from interpreted predicates in Figure 6.3.

Next, we consider the two interpretations of predicate P_2. For $P_1 = $ True, P_2 has the following interpretation

$$P_2: \qquad x \leq -4$$

Therefore, P_2 further divides the area, or set of points, defined by $P_1 = $ True into two sets corresponding to its two truth values. The P_2 boundary, when P_1 evaluates to true, is represented by the straight line $x = -4$. The area to the left of the P_2 boundary and above the P_1 boundary corresponds to $P_1P_2 = $ TT, and the area to the right of the P_2 boundary and above the P_1 boundary corresponds to $P_1P_2 = $ TF.

For $P_1 = $ False, P_2 has the following interpretation:

$$P_2: \qquad x > 4$$

In other words, P_2 further divides the area, or set of points, defined by $P_1 = $ False into two sets corresponding to its two truth values. The P_2 boundary, when P_1 evaluates to false, is represented by the straight line $x = 4$. The area to the right of the P_2 boundary and below the P_1 boundary corresponds to $P_1P_2 = $ FT, and the area to the left of the P_2 boundary and below the P_1 boundary corresponds to $P_1P_2 = $ FF in Figure 6.4.

The reader may note that if a program contains k predicates in a sequence, the maximum number of domains obtained is 2^k. In practice, the number of domains obtained is much smaller than 2^k, because certain combinations of truth values of those k predicates may not hold simultaneously.

6.4 TYPES OF DOMAIN ERRORS

The reader may recall the following properties of a domain:

- A domain is a set of values for which the program performs identical computations.
- A domain can be represented by a set of predicates. Individual elements of the domain satisfy the predicates of the domain.

Example: The domain **TT** in Figure 6.4 is mathematically represented by the set of predicates shown in Figure 6.5.

A domain is defined, from a geometric perspective, by a set of constraints called *boundary inequalities*. Properties of a domain are discussed in terms of the properties of its *boundaries* as follows:

P1:	$x + y > 5$	$\equiv$ *True*
P2:	$x <= -4$	$\equiv$ *True*

Figure 6.5 Predicates defining the **TT** domain in Figure 6.4.

Closed Boundary: A boundary is said to be closed if the points on the boundary are included in the domain of interest.

Example: Consider the domain **TT** in Figure 6.4 and its boundary defined by the inequality

$$P_2: \quad x \leq -4$$

The above boundary is a closed boundary of the domain **TT**.

Open Boundary: A boundary is said to be open if the points on the boundary do not belong to the domain of interest.

Example: Consider the domain **TT** in Figure 6.4 and its boundary defined by the inequality

$$P_1: \quad x + y > 5$$

The above boundary is an open boundary of the domain **TT**. The reader may notice that it is the *equality symbol* (=) in a relational operator that determines whether or not a boundary is closed. If the relational operator in a boundary inequality has the equality symbol in it, then the boundary is a closed boundary; otherwise it is an open boundary.

Closed Domain: A domain is said to be closed if all of its boundaries are closed.

Open Domain: A domain is said to be open if some of its boundaries are open.

Extreme Point: An extreme point is a point where two or more boundaries cross.

Adjacent Domains: Two domains are said to be adjacent if they have a boundary inequality in common.

A program path will have a *domain error* if there is incorrect formulation of a path predicate. After an interpretation of an incorrect path predicate, the path predicate expression causes a boundary segment to

- be shifted from its correct position or
- have an incorrect relational operator.

A domain error can be caused by

- an incorrectly specified predicate or
- an incorrect assignment which affects a variable used in the predicate.

Now we discuss different types of domain errors:

Closure Error: A closure error occurs if a boundary is open when the intention is to have a closed boundary, or vice versa. Some examples of closure error are:

- The relational operator $\leq$ is implemented as $<$.
- The relational operator $<$ is implemented as $\leq$.

Shifted-Boundary Error: A shifted-boundary error occurs when the implemented boundary is parallel to the intended boundary. This happens when the *constant term* of the inequality defining the boundary takes up a value different from the intended value. In concrete terms, a shifted-boundary error occurs due to a change in the *magnitude* or the *sign* of the constant term of the inequality.

Example: Consider the boundary defined by the following predicate (Figure 6.4):

$$P_1 : \qquad x + y > 5$$

If the programmer's intention was to define a boundary represented by the predicate

$$P_1' : \qquad x + y > 4$$

then the boundary defined by P_1 is parallel, but not identical, to the boundary defined by P_1'.

Tilted-Boundary Error: If the constant coefficients of the variables in a predicate defining a boundary take up wrong values, then the tilted-boundary error occurs.

Example: Consider the boundary defined by the following predicate (Figure 6.4):

$$P_1 : \qquad x + y > 5$$

If the programmer's intention was to define a boundary represented by the predicate

$$P_1'' : \qquad x + 0.5y > 5$$

then the boundary defined by P_1 is tilted with respect to the boundary defined by P_1''.

The reader may recall that for all the data points in a domain the program performs identical computations. It is not difficult to notice that input data points fall in the wrong domain if there is a closure defect, a shifted boundary, or a tilted boundary. Assuming that domains are maximal in size in the sense that adjacent domains perform different computations, a program will produce a wrong outcome because of wrong computations performed on those input data points which fall in the wrong domains.

6.5   ON AND OFF POINTS

In domain testing a programmer targets domain errors where test cases are designed with the objective of revealing the domain errors as discussed in Section 6.4. Therefore, it is essential that we consider an important characteristic of domain errors, stated as follows: *Data points on or near a boundary are most sensitive to domain errors*. In this observation, by *sensitive* we mean data points falling in the wrong domains. Therefore, the objective is to identify the data points that are most sensitive to domain errors so that errors can be detected by executing the program with those input values. In the following, we define two kinds of data points *near* domain boundaries, namely, **ON** point and **OFF** point:

>   *ON Point*: Given a boundary, an **ON** point is a point *on* the boundary or "very close" to the boundary.
>   This definition suggests that we can choose an **ON** point in two ways. Therefore, one must know when to choose an **ON** point in which way:

>   - If a point can be chosen to lie exactly on the boundary, then choose such a point as an **ON** point. If the boundary inequality leads to an *exact* solution, choose such an exact solution as an **ON** point.

>   - If a boundary inequality leads to an *approximate* solution, choose a point very close to the boundary.

Example: Consider the following boundary inequality. This inequality is not related to our running example of Figure 6.4.

$$P_{ON1}: \qquad x + 7y \geq 6$$

For $x = -1$, the predicate P_{ON1} leads to an exact solution of $y = 1$. Therefore, the point $(-1, 1)$ lies on the boundary.

 However, if we choose $x = 0$, the predicate P_{ON1} leads to an approximate solution of y in the form of $y = 0.8571428 \ldots$. Since y does not have an exact solution, we either truncate it to 0.857 or round it off to 0.858. We notice that the point $(0, 0.857)$ does not satisfy the predicate P_{ON1}, whereas the point $(0, 0.858)$ does. Thus, $(0, 0.858)$ is an **ON** point which lies very close to the P_{ON1} boundary.

Example: Consider a domain with the following *open* boundary:

$$P_{ON2}: \qquad x + 7y < 6$$

Points lying exactly on the boundary defined by the predicate

$$P'_{ON2}: \qquad x + 7y = 6$$

are not a part of the domain under consideration. The point $(-1, 1)$ lies exactly on the boundary P'_{ON2} and is an ON point. Note that the point $(-1, 1)$ is *not* a part of the domain under consideration. Similarly, the point $(0, 0.858)$, which is almost on the boundary, that is, very close to the boundary, is an ON point and it lies outside the domain of interest.

OFF Point: An **OFF** point of a boundary lies *away* from the boundary. However, while choosing an **OFF** point, we must consider whether a boundary is *open* or *closed* with respect to a domain:

- If the domain is *open* with respect to the boundary, then an **OFF** point of that boundary is an *interior* point inside the domain within an ϵ-distance from the boundary.
- If the domain is *closed* with respect to the boundary, then an **OFF** point of that boundary is an *exterior* point outside the boundary within an ϵ-distance. The symbol ϵ denotes an arbitrarily small value.

Example: Consider a domain D_1 with a *closed* boundary as follows:

$$P_{\text{OFF1}}: \qquad x + 7y \geq 6$$

Since the boundary is closed, an OFF point lies outside the domain; this means that the boundary inequality is *not* satisfied. Note that the point $(-1, 1)$ lies exactly on the boundary and it belongs to the domain. Therefore, $(-1, 1)$ is *not* an OFF point. However, the point $(-1, 0.99)$ lies outside the domain, and it is not a part of the domain under consideration. This is easily verified by substituting $x = -1$ and $y = 0.99$ in the above P_{OFF1} inequality which produces a value of 5.93. Therefore, $(-1, 0.99)$ is an OFF point.

Example: Consider a domain D_2 which is adjacent to domain D_1 in the above example with an *open* boundary as follows:

$$P_{\text{OFF2}}: \qquad x + 7y < 6$$

It may be noted that we have obtained **POFF2** from **POFF1** by simply reversing the $\geq$ inequality. Since the P_{OFF2} boundary is open, an OFF point lies inside the domain. It can be easily verified that the point $(-1, 0.99)$ lies inside D_2, and hence it is an OFF point for domain D_2 with respect to boundary P_{OFF2}.

Summary The above ideas of ON and OFF points lead to the following conclusions:

- While testing a *closed* boundary, the ON points are in the domain under test, whereas the OFF points are in an adjacent domain.
- While testing an *open* boundary, the ON points are in an adjacent domain, whereas the OFF points are in the domain being tested.

The above ideas have been further explained in Figure 6.6, which shows two domains D_1 and D_2 defined by predicates $x < 4$ and $x \geq 4$, respectively. Therefore, the actual boundary is defined by the following predicate:

$$P_{\text{ON,OFF}}: \qquad x = 4$$

In the figure, we show two ON points A and B, where A lies exactly on the boundary and B lies "very close" to the boundary. Therefore, we have $A = 4$ and

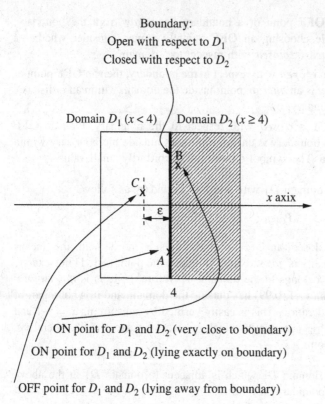

Figure 6.6   ON and OFF points.

$B = 4.00001$, for example. We show an OFF point C lying in D_1 away from the boundary. Point $C = 3.95$ lies inside domain D_1 and outside domain D_2.

6.6   TEST SELECTION CRITERION

In this section, we explain a criterion for test selection and show that test data so selected reveal the domain errors identified in Section 6.4. Before we explain the selection criterion, we state the assumptions made in domain testing as follows:

- A program performs different computations in adjacent domains. If this assumption does not hold, then data points falling in the wrong domains may not have any influence on program outcome, and therefore failures will not be observed.

- Boundary predicates are *linear functions* of input variables. This is not a strong assumption given that most of the predicates in real-life programs are linear. This is because programmers can easily visualize linear predicates and use them.

We present the following criterion for domain testing and show that test data selected using this criterion reveal domain errors:

> *Test Selection Criterion*: For each domain and for each boundary, select three points A, C, and B in an ON–OFF–ON sequence.

This criterion generates test data that reveal domain errors. Specifically, the following kinds of errors are considered:

1. Closed inequality boundary
   a. Boundary shift resulting in a reduced domain
   b. Boundary shift resulting in an enlarged domain
   c. Boundary tilt
   d. Closure error
2. Open inequality boundary
   a. Boundary shift resulting in a reduced domain
   b. Boundary shift resulting in an enlarged domain
   c. Boundary tilt
   d. Closure error
3. Equality boundary

In our analysis below, we consider two adjacent domains D_1 and D_2. We assume that the program computation associated with D_1 and D_2 are f_1 and f_2, respectively, and $f_1 \neq f_2$.

1a *(Closed Inequality) Boundary Shift Resulting in Reduced Domain:* The boundary between the two domains D_1 and D_2 has shifted by a certain amount (see Figure 6.7). The figure shows the actual boundary between the two domains and an arbitrary position of the expected boundary. One must remember that we do not know the exact position of the expected boundary. The expected boundary has been shown only to explain that the actual boundary has moved away from the expected boundary for conceptual understanding of boundary shift. The boundary between the two domains is closed with respect to domain D_1. Therefore, the two

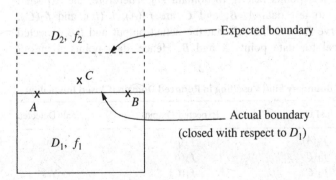

Figure 6.7   Boundary shift resulting in reduced domain (closed inequality).

ON points A and B belong to domain D_1, and the OFF point C belongs to domain D_2. Hence the actual output from the program corresponding to test data A, B, and C are $f_1(A)$, $f_1(B)$, and $f_2(C)$, respectively. It is obvious from Figure 6.7 that in the absence of any boundary shift all the test points belong to domain D_1. Therefore, the expected output corresponding to test data A, B, and C are $f_1(A)$, $f_1(B)$, and $f_1(C)$, respectively. These outputs are listed in Table 6.2. We observe, by comparing the second and the third columns of Table 6.2, that the actual output and the expected output are not identical for data point C. Hence, data point C reveals the shifted-boundary fault.

It is important to understand the following at this point:

- We do not need to know the exact position of the expected boundary. This is because what we actually need are the expected program outcomes in response to the three data points A, B, and C, which can be computed from the specification of a program without explicitly finding out the expected boundary.

- All three data points A, B, and C need not reveal the same fault. Our purpose is to show that test data selected according to the stated criterion reveal all domain errors. The purpose is satisfied if at least one data point reveals the fault. Different elements of the set $\{A, B, C\}$ reveal different kinds of domain errors.

- If point C is away from the boundary by a magnitude of ϵ, then a boundary shift of magnitude less than ϵ cannot be detected. This is because the expected output $f_2(C)$ is identical to the actual output $f_2(C)$.

1b *(Closed Inequality) Boundary Shift Resulting in Enlarged Domain:* To detect this fault, we use Figure 6.8, where the boundary between the two domains D_1 and D_2 has shifted from its expected position such that the size of the domain D_1 under consideration has enlarged. Once again, we do not know the exact position of the expected boundary. The boundary between the two domains is closed with respect to domain D_1. Therefore, the two ON points A and B belong to domain D_1, and the OFF point C belongs to domain D_2. Hence the actual outputs from the program corresponding to test data A, B, and C are $f_1(A)$, $f_1(B)$, and $f_2(C)$, respectively. From Figure 6.8 it is clear that, in the absence of any boundary shift, all the test points belong to domain D_2. Therefore, the expected outputs corresponding to test data A, B, and C are $f_2(A)$, $f_2(B)$, and $f_2(C)$, respectively. We observe from Table 6.3 that the actual output and the expected output are not identical for data points A and B. Hence, data points A and B

TABLE 6.2   Detection of Boundary Shift Resulting in Reduced Domain (Closed Inequality)

Test Data	Actual Output	Expected Output	Fault Detected
A	$f_1(A)$	$f_1(A)$	No
B	$f_1(B)$	$f_1(B)$	No
C	$f_2(C)$	$f_1(C)$	Yes

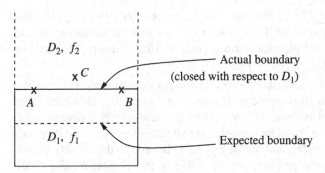

Figure 6.8   Boundary shift resulting in enlarged domain (closed inequality).

TABLE 6.3   Detection of Boundary Shift Resulting in Enlarged Domain (Closed Inequality)

Test Data	Actual Output	Expected Output	Fault Detected
A	$f_1(A)$	$f_2(A)$	Yes
B	$f_1(B)$	$f_2(B)$	Yes
C	$f_2(C)$	$f_2(C)$	No

reveal the shifted-boundary fault. If the magnitude of the shift is less than ϵ—the magnitude by which the OFF point is away from the boundary—the boundary shift cannot be detected by these test data.

1c *(Closed Inequality) Boundary Tilt:* In Figure 6.9 the boundary between the two domains D_1 and D_2 has tilted by an appreciable amount. The boundary between the two domains is closed with respect to domain D_1. Therefore, the two ON points A and B belong to domain D_1, and the OFF point C belongs to domain D_2. Hence the actual outputs from the program corresponding to test data A, B, and C are $f_1(A)$, $f_1(B)$, and $f_2(C)$, respectively. It is clear from Figure 6.9 that in the absence of any boundary tilt test point A falls in domain D_1 and test points B and C fall in domain D_2. Therefore, the expected outputs corresponding to test

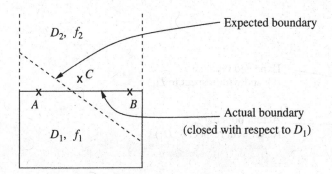

Figure 6.9   Tilted boundary (closed inequality).

data A, B, and C are $f_1(A)$, $f_2(B)$, and $f_2(C)$, respectively. By comparing the second and the third columns of Table 6.4 we observe that the actual output and the expected output are not identical for test point B. Hence, test point B reveals the tilted-boundary fault.

1d *(Closed Inequality) Closure Error:* The expected boundary between the two domains in Figure 6.10 is closed with respect to domain D_1. However, in an actual implementation, it is open with respect to D_1, resulting in a closure error. The boundary between the two domains belongs to domain D_2. The two ON points A and B belong to domain D_2, and the OFF point C belongs to domain D_1. Hence the actual outputs from the program corresponding to test data A, B, and C are $f_2(A), f_2(B)$, and $f_1(C)$, respectively. In the absence of any closure error all three test points A, B and C fall in domain D_1. These outputs are listed in Table 6.5. By comparing the second and the third columns of Table 6.5 we observe that the actual output and the expected output are not identical for data points A and B. Therefore, data points A and B reveal the closure boundary fault.

2a *(Open Inequality) Boundary Shift Resulting in Reduced Domain:* To explain the detection of this type of error, we use Figure 6.11, where the boundary between the two domains D_1 and D_2 has shifted by a certain amount. The boundary between the two domains is open with respect to domain D_1. Therefore, the two ON points A and B belong to domain D_2, and the OFF point C belongs to domain D_1. Hence the actual outputs from the program corresponding to test data A, B, and C are $f_2(A)$, $f_2(B)$, and $f_1(C)$, respectively. It is obvious from Figure 6.11 that, in the absence of any boundary shift, all the test points belong to domain D_1. Therefore, the expected outputs corresponding to test data A, B,

TABLE 6.4   Detection of Boundary Tilt (Closed Inequality)

Test Data	Actual Output	Expected Output	Fault Detected
A	$f_1(A)$	$f_1(A)$	No
B	$f_1(B)$	$f_2(B)$	Yes
C	$f_2(C)$	$f_2(C)$	No

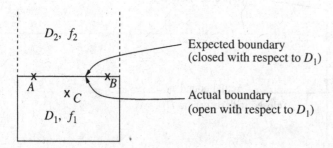

Figure 6.10   Closure error (closed inequality).

TABLE 6.5 Detection of Closure Error (Closed Inequality)

Test Data	Actual Output	Expected Output	Fault Detected
A	$f_2(A)$	$f_1(A)$	Yes
B	$f_2(B)$	$f_1(B)$	Yes
C	$f_1(C)$	$f_1(C)$	No

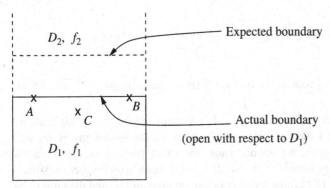

Figure 6.11   Boundary shift resulting in reduced domain (open inequality).

and C are $f_1(A)$, $f_1(B)$, and $f_1(C)$, respectively. By comparing the second and third columns of Table 6.6 we observe that the actual output and the expected output are not identical for the data point C. Therefore, data point C reveals the shifted-boundary fault.

2b *(Open Inequality) Boundary Shift Resulting in Enlarged Domain:* We use Figure 6.12 to explain the detection of this kind of errors. The boundary between the two domains D_1 and D_2 has shifted to enlarge the size of the domain D_1 under consideration. The boundary between the two domains is open with respect to domain D_1. Therefore, the two ON points A and B belong to domain D_2, and the OFF point C belongs to domain D_1. Hence the actual outputs from the program corresponding to test data A, B, and C are $f_2(A)$, $f_2(B)$, and $f_1(C)$, respectively. It follows from Figure 6.12 that, in the absence of any boundary shift, all the test points belong to domain D_2. Therefore, the expected outputs corresponding to test data A, B, and C are $f_2(A)$, $f_2(B)$, and $f_2(C)$, respectively. These outputs

TABLE 6.6 Detection of Boundary Shift Resulting in Reduced Domain (Open Inequality)

Test Data	Actual Output	Expected Output	Fault Detected
A	$f_2(A)$	$f_1(A)$	Yes
B	$f_2(B)$	$f_1(B)$	Yes
C	$f_1(C)$	$f_1(C)$	No

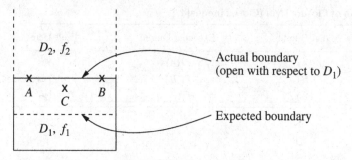

Figure 6.12   Boundary shift resulting in enlarged domain (open inequality).

are listed in Table 6.7. From Table 6.7 we observe that data point C reveals the shifted-boundary fault.

2c *(Open Inequality) Boundary Tilt:* We explain the boundary tilt fault by referring to Figure 6.13, where the boundary between the two domains D_1 and D_2 has tilted. Once again, we do not know the exact position of the expected boundary. The boundary between the two domains is open with respect to domain D_1. Therefore, the two ON points A and B belong to domain D_2, and the OFF point C belongs to domain D_1. Hence the actual outputs from the program corresponding to test data A, B, and C are $f_2(A), f_2(B)$, and $f_1(C)$, respectively. Figure 6.13 shows that in the absence of any boundary tilt test points A and C fall in domain D_1, and test point B falls in domain D_2. Therefore, the expected outputs corresponding to test data A, B, and C are $f_1(A)$, $f_2(B)$, and $f_1(C)$, respectively. We compare the second and third columns of Table 6.8 to observe that the actual output and the expected output are not identical for the test point A. Hence, the test point A reveals the tilted-boundary fault.

2d *(Open Inequality) Closure Error:* Detection of this kind of fault is explained by using the two domains of Figure 6.14, where the expected boundary between the two domains is open with respect to domain D_1. However, in an actual implementation it is closed with respect to D_1, resulting in a closure error. The two ON points A and B belong to domain D_1, and the OFF point C belongs to domain D_2. Hence the actual outputs from the program corresponding to test data A, B, and C are $f_1(A)$, $f_1(B)$, and $f_2(C)$, respectively. Figure 6.14 shows that, in the absence of any closure error, all three test points A, B and C fall in domain D_2. Table 6.9 shows the actual outputs and the expected outputs. By

TABLE 6.7   Detection of Boundary Shift Resulting in Enlarged Domain (Open Inequality)

Test Data	Actual Output	Expected Output	Fault Detected
A	$f_2(A)$	$f_2(A)$	No
B	$f_2(B)$	$f_2(B)$	No
C	$f_1(C)$	$f_2(C)$	Yes

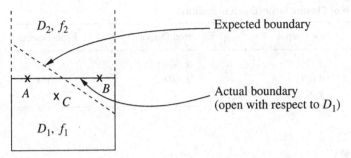

Figure 6.13   Tilted boundary (open inequality).

TABLE 6.8   Detection of Boundary Tilt (Open Inequality)

Test Data	Actual Output	Expected Output	Fault Detected
A	$f_2(A)$	$f_1(A)$	Yes
B	$f_2(B)$	$f_2(B)$	No
C	$f_1(C)$	$f_1(C)$	No

comparing the second and the third columns of Table 6.9 we observe that the actual output and the expected output are not identical for data points A and B. Therefore, data points A and B reveal the closure boundary fault.

3. *Equality Boundary:* Sometimes a domain may consist of an equality boundary sandwiched between two open domains, as shown in Figure 6.15, where D_1 and D_2 are two domains open with respect to their common equality boundary. In this case, to test the common boundary, we choose two ON points A and B on the boundary and two OFF points C and D—one in each open domain.

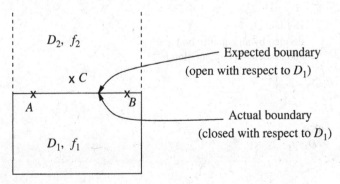

Figure 6.14   Closure error (open inequality).

TABLE 6.9 Detection of Closure Error (Open Inequality)

Test Data	Actual Output	Expected Output	Fault Detected
A	$f_1(A)$	$f_2(A)$	Yes
B	$f_1(B)$	$f_2(B)$	Yes
C	$f_2(C)$	$f_2(C)$	No

6.7 SUMMARY

Two kinds of program errors, namely *computation error* and *domain errors*, were identified. A computation error occurs when an input value causes the program to execute the correct path, but the program output is incorrect due to a fault in an assignment statement. A domain error occurs when an input value causes the program to execute the wrong path. A program executes a wrong path because of faults in conditional statements. A program can be viewed as an abstract classifier that partitions the input domain into a finite number of subdomains such that a separate program path executes for each input subdomain. Thus, a program is seen to be mapping the input subdomains to its execution paths. Program subdomains can be identified by considering individual paths in the program and evaluating path predicates. Each subdomain, also called domain, is defined by a set of boundaries. Often input data points would fall in a wrong domain if there are faults in defining domain boundaries, thereby executing the wrong paths. Input domains were characterized by means of a few properties, such as *closed boundary*, *open boundary*, *closed domain*, *open domain*, *extreme point*, and *adjacent domain*. Next, three kinds of boundary errors, namely, *closure error*, *shifted-boundary error*, and *tilted-boundary error*, were identified. Given a domain and its boundaries, the concept of **ON** and **OFF** points were explained. Finally, a test selection criterion was defined to choose test points to reveal domain errors. Specifically, the selection criterion is as follows: For each domain and for each boundary, select three points A, C, and B in an **ON–OFF–ON** sequence.

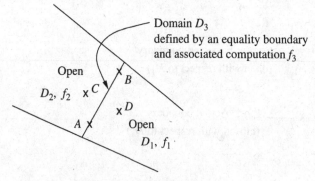

Figure 6.15 Equality border.

LITERATURE REVIEW

Since White and Cohen proposed the concept of domain testing in 1978, it has been analyzed and extended in several ways. In 1982, Clarke, Hassell, and Richardson [4] showed that some domain errors go undetected by the White and Cohen strategy. Next, they proposed a strategy, namely the $V \times V$ strategy, to improve domain testing. If a domain border under consideration contains V vertices, then the $V \times V$ strategy selects V **ON** points—one **ON** point as close as possible to each vertex—and V **OFF** points. The V **OFF** points are chosen at a uniform distance from the border. Zeil, Afifi, and White [5] introduced a domain testing strategy to detect linear errors in *nonlinear* predicate functions. A few other variants of domain testing have been proposed by White and Perera [6] and Onoma, Yamaura, and Kobayashi [7].

Zeil [8] considers domain errors that may be caused by faults in arithmetic and simple relational expressions. These expressions are restricted to floating-point or integer computations. Fault detection techniques, called perturbation techniques, are presented to reveal domain errors.

Koh and Liu [9] have presented an approach for generating paths that test both the control flow and the data flow in implementations of communication protocols. The protocols are assumed to be modeled as extended finite-state machines. The path selection approach consists of two steps: (i) select a set of paths to cover a data flow selection criterion and (ii) selectively augment the state transitions in the chosen set of paths with state check sequences so that control flow can be ensured and data flow coverage can be preserved. Augmentation of state transitions is performed by using the concept of *effective domains*.

Jeng and Weyuker [10] have proposed a simplified domain testing strategy that is applicable to arbitrary types of predicates and detects both linear and nonlinear errors for both continuous and discrete variable spaces. Moreover, the strategy requires a *constant* number of test points. That is, the number of test points is independent of the dimension or the type of border or the number of vertices on the border under consideration. Their simplified technique requires us to generate one **ON** point and one **OFF** point for an inequality (i.e., $\leq, <, \geq,$ or $>$) border. For an equality (i.e., $=$) or nonequality (i.e., $\neq$) border, one **ON** and two **OFF** test points are required. The test generation technique requires (i) an **ON** point to lie on the border, (ii) an **OFF** point to lie outside the border, and (iii) an **ON–OFF** pair to be as close to each other as possible. Hajnal and Forgacs [11] have given an algorithm to generate **ON–OFF** points that can be used by the simplified domain testing strategy.

In contrast, the test selection strategy of White and Cohen [3] requires the selection of N **ON** points in all cases, where N is the dimension of the input space, and the Clarke, Hassell, and Richardson [4] strategy requires the selection of V **ON** points, where V is the number of vertices on the border under consideration.

Zhao, Lyu, and Min [12] have studied an approach to generate **ON–OFF** test points for character string predicate borders associated with program paths. They use the idea of program slicing [13] to compute the current values of variables in the predicates. The same authors have shown in reference [14] that partition testing strategies are relatively ineffective in detecting faults related to small shifts in input domain boundary, and presented a different testing approach based on input domain analysis of specifications and programs.

An elaborate treatment of domain testing can be found in the book by Beizer [15]. Beizer explains how the idea of domains can be used in testing interfaces between program units.

REFERENCES

1. W. E. Howden. Reliability of the Path Analysis Testing Strategy. *IEEE Transactions on Software Engineering*, September 1976, pp. 208–215.
2. L. J. White and E. I. Cohen. A Domain Strategy for Computer Program Testing. Paper presented at the IEEE Workshop on Software Testing and Documentation, Fort Lauderdale, FL, 1978, pp. 335–346.
3. L. J. White and E. I. Cohen. A Domain Strategy for Computer Program Testing. *IEEE Transactions on Software Engineering*, May 1980, pp. 247–257.
4. L. Clarke, H. Hassell, and D. Richardson. A Close Look at Domain Testing. *IEEE Transactions on Software Engineering*, July 1982, pp. 380–392.
5. S. J. Zeil, F. H. Afifi, and L. J. White. Detection Linear Errors via Domain Testing. *ACM Transactions on Software Engineering and Methodology*, October 1992, pp. 422–451.
6. L. J. White and I. A. Perera. An Alternative Measure for Error Analysis of the DomainTesting Strategy. In *Proceedings of the ACM SIGSOFT/IEEE Workshop on Software Testing*, Banff, Canada, IEEE Press, New York, 1986, pp. 122–131.
7. A. K. Onoma, T. Yamaura, and Y. Kobayashi. Practical Approaches to Domain Testing: Improvements and Generalization. In *Proceedings of COMPSAC*, Tokyo, IEEE Computer Society Press, Piscataway, NJ, 1987, pp. 291–297.
8. S. J. Zeil. Perturbation Technique for Detecting Domain Errors. *IEEE Transactions on Software Engineering*, June 1989, pp. 737–746.
9. L. S. Koh and M. T. Liu. Test Path Selection Based on Effective Domains. In *Proceedings of the International Conference on Network Protocols*, Boston, IEEE Computer Society Press, Piscataway, NJ, October 1994, pp. 64–71.
10. B. Jeng and E. J. Weyuker. A Simplified Domain Testing Strategy. *ACM Transactions on Software Engineering and Methodology*, July 1994, pp. 254–270.
11. A. Hajnal and I. Forgacs. An Applicable Test Data Generation Algorithm for Domain Errors. In *Proceedings of the ACM SIGSOFT International Symposium on Software Testing and Analysis*, Clearwater Beach, FL, ACM Press, New York, March 1998, pp. 63–72.
12. R. Zhao, M. R. Lyu, and Y. Min. Domain Testing Based on Character String Predicate. Paper presented at the Asian Test Symposium, Xian, China, IEEE Computer Society Press, Piscataway, NJ, 2003, pp. 96–101.
13. F. Tip. A Survey of Program Slicing Techniques. *Journal of Programming Languages*, September 1995, pp. 121–189.
14. R. Zhao, M. R. Lyu, and Y. Min. A New Software Testing Approach Based on Domain Analysis of Specifications and Programs. In *Proceedings of 14th Symposium on Software Reliability Engineering*, Colorado, IEEE Computer Society Press, New York, 2003, pp. 60–70.
15. B. Beizer. *Software Testing Techniques*, 2nd ed. Van Nostrand Reinhold, New York, 1990.

Exercises

1. Explain what are *computation error* and *domain error*.

2. Give an example of code showing a domain error.

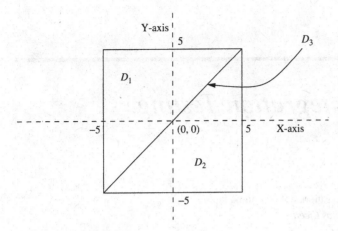

Figure 6.16   Domains D_1, D_2, and D_3.

3. Explain the difference between control flow–based testing and domain error–based testing.

4. Recall that the domain testing strategy requires us to select test points on and/or very close to domain boundaries. Why do we not select test points far from the boundaries?

5. Consider the three domains D_1, D_2, and D_3 shown in Figure 6.16. Domain D_3 consists of all those points lying on the indicated straight line. Assuming that the maximum X and Y span of all the three domains are $[-5, 5]$ and $[-5, 5]$, respectively, give concrete values of test points for domain D_3.

6. State four kinds of domain errors and explain how they occur.

7. Explain the following terms: *closed boundary*, *open boundary*, *closed domain*, *open domain*, *extreme point*, *adjacent domain*.

8. Explain the idea of **ON** points and **OFF** points.

9. Clearly explain the test selection criterion in domain-based testing and show the closed inequality error (boundary shift resulting in a reduced domain) is detected by the test points chosen by the selection criterion.

10. Identify some difficulties in applying the concept of domain testing to actual program testing.

CHAPTER 7

System Integration Testing

I criticize by creation, not by finding fault.
— *Marcus Tullius Cicero*

7.1 CONCEPT OF INTEGRATION TESTING

A software module, or component, is a self-contained element of a system. Modules have well-defined interfaces with other modules. A module can be a subroutine, function, procedure, class, or collection of those basic elements put together to deliver a higher level service. A system is a collection of modules interconnected in a certain way to accomplish a tangible objective. A subsystem is an interim system that is not fully integrated with all the modules. It is also known as a subassembly.

In moderate to large projects, from tens to hundreds of programmers implement their share of the code in the form of modules. Modules are individually tested, which is commonly known as *unit testing*, by their respective programmers using white-box testing techniques. At the unit testing level, the system exists in pieces under the control of the programmers. The next major task is to put the modules, that is, pieces, together to construct the complete system. Constructing a working system from the pieces is not a straightforward task, because of numerous interface errors. Even constructing a reasonably stable system from the components involves much testing. The path from tested components to constructing a deliverable system contains two major testing phases, namely, integration testing and system testing. The primary objective of integration testing is to assemble a reasonably stable system in a laboratory environment such that the integrated system can withstand the rigor of a full-blown system testing in the actual environment of the system. The importance of integration testing stems from three reasons as outlined below.

- Different modules are generally created by groups of different developers. The developers may be working at different sites. In spite of our best effort in system design and documentation, misinterpretation, mistakes, and

---

Software Testing and Quality Assurance: Theory and Practice, Edited by Kshirasagar Naik and Priyadarshi Tripathy
Copyright © 2008 John Wiley & Sons, Inc.

158

oversights do occur in reality. Interface errors between modules created by different programmers and even by the same programmers are rampant. We will discuss the sources of interface errors in Section 7.2.

- Unit testing of individual modules is carried out in a controlled environment by using test drivers and stubs. Stubs are dummy modules which merely return predefined values. If a module under unit test invokes several other modules, the effectiveness of unit testing is constrained by the programmer's ability to effectively test all the paths. Therefore, with the inherent limitations of unit testing, it is difficult to predict the behavior of a module in its actual environment after the unit testing is performed.

- Some modules are more error prone than other modules, because of their inherent complexity. It is essential to identify the ones causing most failures.

The objective of system integration is to build a "working" version of the system by (i) putting the modules together in an incremental manner and (ii) ensuring that the additional modules work as expected without disturbing the functionalities of the modules already put together. In other words, system integration testing is a systematic technique for assembling a software system while conducting tests to uncover errors associated with interfacing. We ensure that unit-tested modules operate correctly when they are combined together as dictated by the design. Integration testing usually proceeds from small subassemblies containing a few modules to larger ones containing more and more modules. Large, complex software products can go through several iterations of build-and-test cycles before they are fully integrated.

Integration testing is said to be complete when the system is fully integrated together, all the test cases have been executed, all the severe and moderate defects found have been fixed, and the system is retested.

7.2 DIFFERENT TYPES OF INTERFACES AND INTERFACE ERRORS

Modularization is an important principle in software design, and modules are interfaced with other modules to realize the system's functional requirements. An interface between two modules allows one module to access the service provided by the other. It implements a mechanism for passing control and data between modules. Three common paradigms for interfacing modules are as follows:

- **Procedure Call Interface:** A procedure in one module calls a procedure in another module. The caller passes on control to the called module. The caller can pass data to the called procedure, and the called procedure can pass data to the caller while returning control back to the caller.

- **Shared Memory Interface:** A block of memory is shared between two modules. The memory block may be allocated by one of the two modules or a third module. Data are written into the memory block by one module and are read from the block by the other.

- **Message Passing Interface:** One module prepares a message by initializing the fields of a data structure and sending the message to another module. This form of module interaction is common in client–server-based systems and web-based systems.

Programmers test modules to their satisfaction. The question is: If all the unit-tested modules work individually, why can these modules not work when put together? The problem arises when we "put them together" because of rampant interface errors. Interface errors are those that are associated with structures existing outside the local environment of a module but which the module uses [1]. Perry and Evangelist [2] reported in 1987 that interface errors accounted for up to a quarter of all errors in the systems they examined. They found that of all errors that required a fix within one module, more than half were caused by interface errors. Perry and Evangelist have categorized interface errors as follows:

1. *Construction*: Some programming languages, such as C, generally separate the interface specification from the implementation code. In a C program, programmers can write a statement #include header.h, where header.h contains an interface specification. Since the interface specification lies somewhere away from the actual code, programmers overlook the interface specification while writing code. Therefore, inappropriate use of #include statements cause construction errors.

2. *Inadequate Functionality*: These are errors caused by implicit assumptions in one part of a system that another part of the system would perform a function. However, in reality, the "other part" does not provide the expected functionality—intentionally or unintentionally by the programmer who coded the other part.

3. *Location of Functionality*: Disagreement on or misunderstanding about the location of a functional capability within the software leads to this sort of error. The problem arises due to the design methodology, since these disputes should not occur at the code level. It is also possible that inexperienced personnel contribute to the problem.

4. *Changes in Functionality*: Changing one module without correctly adjusting for that change in other related modules affects the functionality of the program.

5. *Added Functionality*: A completely new functional module, or capability, was added as a system modification. Any added functionality after the module is checked in to the version control system without a CR is considered to be an error.

6. *Misuse of Interface*: One module makes an error in using the interface of a called module. This is likely to occur in a procedure–call interface. Interface misuse can take the form of wrong parameter type, wrong parameter order, or wrong number of parameters passed.

7. *Misunderstanding of Interface*: A calling module may misunderstand the interface specification of a called module. The called module may assume that some parameters passed to it satisfy a certain condition, whereas the caller does not ensure that the condition holds. For example, assume that a called module is expected to return the index of an element in an array of integers. The called module may choose to implement binary search with an assumption that the calling module gives it a sorted array. If the caller fails to sort the array before invoking the second module, we will have an instance of interface misunderstanding.

8. *Data Structure Alteration*: These are similar in nature to the functionality problems discussed above, but they are likely to occur at the detailed design level. The problem arises when the size of a data structure is inadequate or it fails to contain a sufficient number of information fields. The problem has its genesis in the failure of the high-level design to fully specify the capability requirements of the data structure. Let us consider an example in which a module reads the data and keeps it in a record structure. Each record holds the person name followed by their employee number and salary. Now, if the data structure is defined for 1000 records, then as the number of record grows beyond 1000, the program is bound to fail. In addition, if management decides to award bonuses to a few outstanding employees, there may not be any storage space allocated for additional information.

9. *Inadequate Error Processing*: A called module may return an error code to the calling module. However, the calling module may fail to handle the error properly.

10. *Additions to Error Processing*: These errors are caused by changes to other modules which dictated changes in a module error handling. In this case either necessary functionality is missing from the current error processing that would help trace errors or current techniques of error processing require modification.

11. *Inadequate Postprocessing*: These errors are caused by a general failure to release resources no longer required, for example, failure to deallocate memory.

12. *Inadequate Interface Support*: The actual functionality supplied was inadequate to support the specified capabilities of the interface. For example, a module passes a temperature value in Celsius to a module which interprets the value in Fahrenheit.

13. *Initialization/Value Errors*: A failure to initialize, or assign, the appropriate value to a variable data structure leads to this kind of error. Problems of this kind are usually caused by simple oversight. For example, the value of a pointer can change; it might point to the first character in a string, then to the second character, after that to the third character, and so on. If the programmer forgets to reinitialize the pointer before using that function once again, the pointer may eventually point to code.

14. *Violation of Data Constraints*: A specified relationship among data items was not supported by the implementation. This can happen due to incomplete detailed design specifications.

15. *Timing/Performance Problems*: These errors were caused by inadequate synchronization among communicating processes. A race condition is an example of these kinds of error. In the classical race, there are two possible events event a and event b happening in communicating processes process A and process B, respectively. There is logical ground for expecting event a to precede event b. However, under an abnormal condition event b may occur before event a. The program will fail if the software developer did not anticipate the possibility of event b preceding event a and did not write any code to deal with the situation.

16. *Coordination of Changes*: These errors are caused by a failure to communicate changes to one software module to those responsible for other interrelated modules.

17. *Hardware/Software Interfaces*: These errors arise from inadequate software handling of hardware devices. For example, a program can send data at a high rate until the input buffer of the connected device is full. Then the program has to pause until the device frees up its input buffer. The program may not recognize the signal from the device that it is no longer ready to receive more data. Loss of data will occur due to a lack of synchronization between the program and the device.

Interface errors cannot be detected by performing unit testing on modules since unit testing causes computation to happen within a module, whereas interactions are required to happen between modules for interface errors to be detected. It is difficult to observe interface errors by performing system-level testing, because these errors tend to be buried in system internals. The major advantages of conducting system integration testing are as follows:

- Defects are detected early.
- It is easier to fix defects detected earlier.
- We get earlier feedback on the health and acceptability of the individual modules and on the overall system.
- Scheduling of defect fixes is flexible, and it can overlap with development.

System integration testing is performed by the system integration group, also known as a build engineering group. The integration test engineers need to know the details of the software modules. This means that the team of engineers who built the modules needs to be involved in system integration. The integration testers should be familiar with the interface mechanisms. The system architects should be involved in the integration testing of complex software systems because of the fact that they have the bigger picture of the system.

7.3   GRANULARITY OF SYSTEM INTEGRATION TESTING

System integration testing is performed at different levels of granularity. Integration testing includes both white- and black-box testing approaches. *Black-box* testing ignores the internal mechanisms of a system and focuses solely on the outputs generated in response to selected inputs and execution conditions. The code is considered to be a big black box by the tester who cannot examine the internal details of the system. The tester knows the input to the black box and observes the expected outcome of the execution. *White-box* testing uses information about the structure of the system to test its correctness. It takes into account the internal mechanisms of the system and the modules. In the following, we explain the ideas of *intrasystem* testing, *intersystem* testing, and *pairwise* testing.

1. *Intrasystem Testing:* This form of testing constitutes low-level integration testing with the objective of combining the modules together to build a cohesive system. The process of combining modules can progress in an incremental manner akin to constructing and testing successive builds, explained in Section 7.4.1. For example, in a client–server-based system both the client and the server are distinct entities running at different locations. Before the interactions of clients with a server are tested, it is essential to individually construct the client and the server systems from their respective sets of modules in an incremental fashion. The low-level design document, which details the specification of the modules within the architecture, is the source of test cases.

2. *Intersystem Testing:* Intersystem testing is a high-level testing phase which requires interfacing independently tested systems. In this phase, all the systems are connected together, and testing is conducted from end to end. The term *end to end* is used in communication protocol systems, and end-to-end testing means initiating a test between two access terminals interconnected by a network. The purpose in this case is to ensure that the interaction between the systems work together, but not to conduct a comprehensive test. Only one feature is tested at a time and on a limited basis. Later, at the time of system testing, a comprehensive test is conducted based on the requirements, and this includes functional, interoperability, stress, performance, and so on. Integrating a client–server system, after integrating the client module and the server module separately, is an example of intersystem testing. Integrating a call control system and a billing system in a telephone network is another example of intersystem testing. The test cases are derived from the high-level design document, which details the overall system architecture.

3. *Pairwise Testing:* There can be many intermediate levels of system integration testing between the above two extreme levels, namely intrasystem testing and intersystem testing. Pairwise testing is a kind of intermediate level of integration testing. In pairwise integration, only two interconnected systems in an overall system are tested at a time. The purpose of pairwise testing is to ensure that two systems under consideration can function together, assuming that the other systems

within the overall environment behave as expected. The whole network infrastructure needs to be in place to support the test of interactions of the two systems, but the rest of the systems are not subject to tests. The network test infrastructure must be simple and stable during pairwise testing. While pairwise testing may sound simple, several issues can complicate the testing process. The biggest issue is unintended side effects. For example, in testing communication between a network element (radio node) and the element management systems, if another device (radio node controller) within the 1xEV-DO wireless data network, discussed in Chapter 8, fails during the test, it may trigger a high volume of traps to the element management systems. Untangling this high volume of traps may be difficult.

7.4 SYSTEM INTEGRATION TECHNIQUES

One of the objectives of integration testing is to combine the software modules into a working system so that system-level tests can be performed on the complete system. Integration testing need not wait until all the modules of a system are coded and unit tested. Instead, it can begin as soon as the relevant modules are available. A module is said to be available for combining with other modules when the module's *check-in request form*, to be discussed in this section, is ready. Some common approaches to performing system integration are as follows:

- Incremental
- Top down
- Bottom up
- Sandwich
- Big bang

In the remainder of this section, we explain the above approaches.

7.4.1 Incremental

In this approach, integration testing is conducted in an incremental manner as a series of test cycles as suggested by Deutsch [3]. In each test cycle, a few more modules are integrated with an existing and tested build to generate a larger build. The idea is to complete one cycle of testing, let the developers fix all the errors found, and continue the next cycle of testing. The complete system is built incrementally, cycle by cycle, until the whole system is operational and ready for system-level testing.

The system is built as a succession of layers, beginning with some core modules. In each cycle, a new layer is added to the core and tested to form a new core. The new core is intended to be self-contained and stable. Here, "self-contained" means containing all the necessary code to support a set of functions, and "stable" means that the subsystem (i.e., the new, partial system) can stay up for 24 hours without any anomalies. The number of system integration test cycles and the total integration time are determined by the following parameters:

- Number of modules in the system
- Relative complexity of the modules (cyclomatic complexity)
- Relative complexity of the interfaces between the modules
- Number of modules needed to be clustered together in each test cycle
- Whether the modules to be integrated have been adequately tested before
- Turnaround time for each test–debug–fix cycle

Constructing a build is a process by which individual modules are integrated to form an interim software image. A *software image* is a compiled software binary. A *build* is an interim software image for internal testing within the organization. Eventually, the final build will be a candidate for system testing, and such a tested system is released to the customers. Constructing a software image involves the following activities:

- Gathering the latest unit tested, authorized versions of modules
- Compiling the source code of those modules
- Checking in the compiled code to the repository
- Linking the compiled modules into subassemblies
- Verifying that the subassemblies are correct
- Exercising version control

A simple build involves only a small number of modules being integrated with a previously tested build on a reliable and well-understood platform. No special tool or procedure needs to be developed and documented for a simple build. On the other hand, organized, well-documented procedures are applied for complex builds. A build process becomes complicated if a large number of modules are integrated together, and a significant number of those modules are new with complex interfaces. These interfaces can be between software modules and hardware devices, across platforms, and across networks. For complex builds, a version control tool is highly recommended for automating the build process and for fast turnaround of a test–debug–fix cycle.

Creating a daily build [4] is very popular in many organizations because it facilitates to a faster delivery of the system. It puts emphasis on small incremental testing, steadily increasing the number of test cases, and regression testing from build to build. The integrated system is tested using automated, reusable test cases. An effort is made to fix the defects that were found during the testing cycle. A new version of the system is constructed from the existing, revised, and newly developed modules and is made available for retesting. Prior versions of the build are retained for reference and rollback. If a defect is not found in a module of a build in which the module was introduced, the module will be carried forward from build to build until one is found. Having access to the version where the defective module was originally introduced is useful in debugging and fixing, limiting the side effects of the fixes, and performing a root cause analysis. During system development, integration, and testing, a typical practice is to retain the past 7–10 builds.

The software developer fills out a check-in request form before a new software module or a module with an error fix is integrated into a build. The form is reviewed by the build engineering group for giving approval. Once it is approved, the module can be considered for integration. The main portions of a check-in form are given in Table 7.1. The idea behind having a check-in request mechanism is fourfold:

1. All the files requiring an update must be identified and known to other team members.

2. The new code must have been reviewed prior to its integration.

3. The new code must have been unit tested.

4. The scope of the check-in is identified.

A release note containing the following information accompanies a build:

- What has changed since the last build?
- What outstanding defects have been fixed?
- What are the outstanding defects in the build?
- What new modules or features have been added?

TABLE 7.1 Check-in Request Form

Author	Name of the person requesting this check-in
Today's date	month, day, year
Check-in request date	month, day, year
Category (identify all that apply)	New Feature: (Y, N)
	Enhancement: (Y, N)
	Defect: (Y, N); if yes: defect numbers:
	Are any of these major defects: (Y, N)
	Are any of these moderate defects: (Y, N)
Short description of check-in	Describe in a short paragraph the feature, the enhancement, or the defect fixes to be checked in.
Number of files to be checked in	Give the number of files to be checked in. Include the file names, if possible.
Code reviewer names	Provide the names of the code reviewers.
Command line interface changes made	(Y, N); if yes, were they:
	Documented? (Y, N)
	Reviewed? (Y, N, pending)
Does this check-in involve changes to global header?	(Y, N); if yes, include the header file names.
Does this check-in involve changes in output logging?	(Y, N); if yes, were they documented? (Y, N)
Unit test description	Description of the unit tests conducted
Comments	Any other comments and issues

- What existing modules or features have been enhanced, modified, or deleted?
- Are there any areas where unknown changes may have occurred?

A test strategy is created for each new build based on the above information. The following issues are addressed while planning a test strategy:

- What test cases need to be selected from the system integration test plan, as discussed in Section 7.6, in order to test the changes? Will these test cases give feature coverage of the new and modified features? If necessary, add new test cases to the system integration test plan.
- What existing test cases can be reused without modification in order to test the modified system? What previously failed test cases should now be reexecuted in order to test the fixes in the new build?
- How should the scope of a partial regression test be determined? A full regression test may not be run on each build because of frequent turnaround of builds. At the least, any earlier test cases which pertain to areas that have been modified must be reexecuted.
- What are the estimated time, resource demand, and cost to test this build? Some builds may be skipped based on this estimate and the current activities, because the integration test engineers may choose to wait for a later build.

7.4.2 Top Down

Systems with hierarchical structures easily lend themselves to top-down and bottom-up approaches to integration. In a hierarchical system, there is a first, top-level module which is decomposed into a few second-level modules. Some of the second-level modules may be further decomposed into third-level modules, and so on. Some or all the modules at any level may be terminal modules, where a terminal module is one that is no more decomposed. An internal module, also known as a nonterminal module, performs some computations, invokes its subordinate modules, and returns control and results to its caller. In top-down and bottom-up approaches, a design document giving the module hierarchy is used as a reference for integrating modules. An example of a module hierarchy is shown in Figure 7.1, where module A is the topmost module; module A has been decomposed into modules B, C, and D. Modules B, D, E, F, and G are terminal modules, as these have not been further decomposed. The top-down approach is explained in the following:

Step 1: Let IM represent the set of modules that have already been integrated and the required stubs. Initially, IM contains the top-level module and stubs corresponding to all the subordinate modules of the top-level

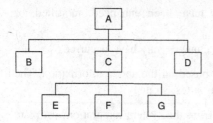

Figure 7.1 Module hierarchy with three levels and seven modules.

module. It is assumed that the top-level module has passed its entry criteria.

Step 2: Choose a stub member M′ in set IM. Let M be the actual module corresponding to stub M′. We obtain a new set CM from IM by replacing stub M′ with M and including in CM all stubs corresponding to the subordinate modules of M. We consider CM to be a union of four sets: {M}, CMs, CMi, CMr, where CMs is the set of stubs, CMi is the set of modules having direct interfaces with M, and CMr is the rest of the modules in CM.

Step 3: Now, test the combined behavior of CM. Testing CM means applying input to the top-level module of the system. It may be noted that though the integration team has access to the top module of the system, all kinds of tests cannot be performed. This is apparent from the fact that CM does not represent the full system. In this step, the integration team tests a subset of the system functions implemented by the actual modules in CM. The integration team performs two kinds of tests:

1. Run test cases to discover any interface defects between M and members of CMi.

2. Perform regression tests to ensure that integration of the modules in the two sets CMi and CMr is satisfactory in the presence of module M. One may note that in previous iterations the interfaces between modules in CMi and CMr were tested and the defects fixed. However, the said tests were executed with M′—a stub of M—and not M. The presence of M in the integrated system up to this moment allows us to test the interfaces between the modules in the combined set of CMi and CMr, because of the possibility of the system supporting more functionalities with M.

   The above two kinds of tests are continued until the integration team is satisfied that there is no known interface error. In case an interface error is discovered, the error must be fixed before moving on to the next step.

Step 4: If the set CMs is empty, then stop; otherwise, set IM = CM and go to step 2.

Now, let us consider an example of top-down integration using Figure 7.1. The integration of modules A and B by using stubs C′ and D′ (represented by grey boxes) is shown in Figure 7.2. Interactions between modules A and B is severely constrained by the dummy nature of C′ and D′. The interactions between A and B are concrete, and, as a consequence, more tests are performed after additional modules are integrated. Next, as shown in Figure 7.3, stub D′ has been replaced with its actual instance D. We perform two kinds of tests: first, test the interface between A and D; second, perform regression tests to look for interface defects between A and B in the presence of module D. Stub C′ has been replaced with the actual module C, and new stubs E′, F′, and G′ have been added to the integrated system (Figure 7.4). We perform tests as follows: First, test the interface between A and C; second, test the combined modules A, B, and D in the presence of C (Figure 7.4). The rest of the integration process is depicted in Figures 7.5 and 7.6 to obtain the final system of Figure 7.7.

The advantages of the top-down approach are as follows:

- System integration test (SIT) engineers continually observe system-level functions as the integration process continues. How soon such functions are observed depends upon their choice of the order in which modules are integrated. Early observation of system functions is important because it gives them better confidence.

- Isolation of interface errors becomes easier because of the incremental nature of top-down integration. However, it cannot be concluded that an interface error is due to a newly integrated module M. The interface error

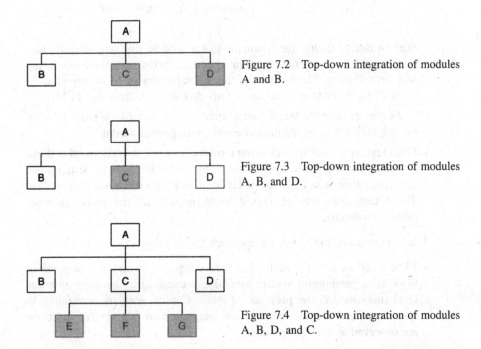

Figure 7.2   Top-down integration of modules A and B.

Figure 7.3   Top-down integration of modules A, B, and D.

Figure 7.4   Top-down integration of modules A, B, D, and C.

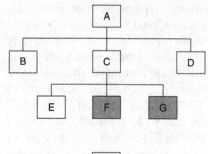

Figure 7.5 Top-down integration of modules A, B, C, D, and E.

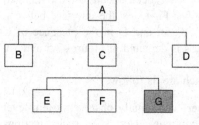

Figure 7.6 Top-down integration of modules A, B, C, D, E, and F.

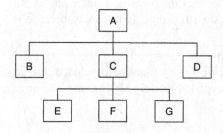

Figure 7.7 Top-down integration of modules A, B, C, D, E, F and G.

may be due to faulty implementation of a module that was already integrated much earlier. This is possible because earlier tests were conducted with or without a stub for M, and the full capability of M simply allowed the test engineers to conduct more tests that were possible due to M.

- Test cases designed to test the integration of a module M are reused during the regression tests performed after integrating other modules.

- Since test inputs are applied to the top-level module, it is natural that those test cases correspond to system functions, and it is easier to design those test cases than test cases designed to check internal system functions. Those test cases can be reused while performing the more rigorous, system-level tests.

The limitations of the top-down approach are as follows:

- Until a certain set of modules has been integrated, it may not be possible to observe meaningful system functions because of an absence of lower level modules and the presence of stubs. Careful analysis is required to identify an ordering of modules for integration so that system functions are observed as early as possible.

- Test case selection and stub design become increasingly difficult when stubs lie far away from the top-level module. This is because stubs support limited behavior, and any test run at the top level must be constrained to exercise the limited behavior of lower level stubs.

7.4.3   Bottom Up

In the bottom-up approach, system integration begins with the integration of lowest level modules. A module is said to be at the lowest level if it does not invoke another module. It is assumed that all the modules have been individually tested before. To integrate a set of lower level modules in this approach, we need to construct a test driver module that invokes the modules to be integrated. Once the integration of a desired group of lower level modules is found to be satisfactory, the driver is replaced with the actual module and one more test driver is used to integrate more modules with the set of modules already integrated. The process of bottom-up integration continues until all the modules have been integrated.

Now we give an example of bottom-up integration for the module hierarchy of Figure 7.1. The lowest level modules are E, F, and G. We design a test driver to integrate these three modules, as shown in Figure 7.8. It may be noted that modules E, F, and G have no direct interfaces among them. However, return values generated by one module is likely to be used in another module, thus having an indirect interface. The test driver in Figure 7.8 invokes modules E, F, and G in a way similar to their invocations by module C. The test driver mimics module C to integrate E, F, and G in a limited way, because it is much simpler in capability than module C. The test driver is replaced with the actual module—in this case C—and a new test driver is used after the testers are satisfied with the combined behavior of E, F, and G (Figure 7.9). At this moment, more modules, such as B and D, are integrated with the so-far integrated system. The test driver mimics the behavior of module A. We need to include modules B and D because those are invoked by A and the test driver mimics A (Figure 7.9). The test driver is replaced with module A (Figure 7.10), and further tests are performed after the testers are satisfied with the integrated system shown in Figure 7.9.

The advantages of the bottom-up approach are as follows. If the low-level modules and their combined functions are often invoked by other modules, then it is more useful to test them first so that meaningful effective integration of other modules can be done. In the absence of such a strategy, the testers write stubs to emulate the commonly invoked low-level modules, which will provide only a limited test capability of the interfaces.

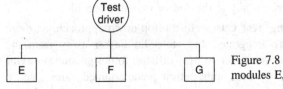

Figure 7.8   Bottom-up integration of modules E, F, and G.

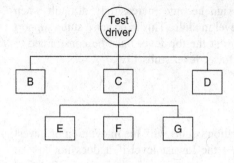

Figure 7.9   Bottom-up integration of modules B, C, and D with E, F, and G.

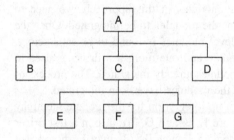

Figure 7.10   Bottom-up integration of module A with all others.

The disadvantages of the bottom-up approach are as follows:

- Test engineers cannot observe system-level functions from a partly integrated system. In fact, they cannot observe system-level functions until the top-level test driver is in place.

- Generally, major design decisions are embodied in top-level modules, whereas most of the low-level modules largely perform commonly known input–output functions. Discovery of major flaws in system design may not be possible until the top-level modules have been integrated.

Now we compare the top-down and bottom-up approaches in the following:

- **Validation of Major Design Decisions:** The top-level modules contain major design decisions. Faults in design decisions are detected early if integration is done in a top-down manner. In the bottom-up approach, those faults are detected toward the end of the integration process.

- **Observation of System-Level Functions:** One applies test inputs to the top-level module, which is akin to performing system-level tests in a very limited way in the top-down approach. This gives an opportunity to the SIT personnel and the development team to observe system-level functions early in the integration process. However, similar observations can be done in the bottom-up approach only at the end of system integration.

- **Difficulty in Designing Test Cases:** In the top-down approach, as more and more modules are integrated and stubs lie farther away from the top-level module, it becomes increasingly difficult to design stub behavior and test input. This is because stubs return predetermined values, and a test engineer must compute those values for a given test input at the top level. However, in the bottom-up approach, one designs the behavior of a test driver by simplifying the behavior of the actual module.

- **Reusability of Test Cases:** In the top-down approach, test cases designed to test the interface of a newly integrated module is reused in performing regression tests in the following iteration. Those test cases are reused as system-level test cases. However, in the bottom-up approach, all the test cases incorporated into test drivers, except for the top-level test driver, cannot be reused. The top-down approach saves resources in the form of time and money.

7.4.4   Sandwich and Big Bang

In the sandwich approach, a system is integrated by using a mix of the top-down and bottom-up approaches. A hierarchical system is viewed as consisting of three layers. The bottom layer contains all the modules that are often invoked. The bottom-up approach is applied to integrate the modules in the bottom layer. The top layer contains modules implementing major design decisions. These modules are integrated by using the top-down approach. The rest of the modules are put in the middle layer. We have the advantages of the top-down approach where writing stubs for the low-level module is not required. As a special case, the middle layer may not exist, in which case a module falls either in the top layer or in the bottom layer. On the other hand, if the middle layer exists, then this layer can be integrated by using the big-bang approach after the top and the bottom layers have been integrated.

In the big-bang approach, first all the modules are individually tested. Next, all those modules are put together to construct the entire system which is tested as a whole. Sometimes developers use the big-bang approach to integrate small systems. However, for large systems, this approach is not recommended for the following reasons:

- In a system with a large number of modules, there may be many interface defects. It is difficult to determine whether or not the cause of a failure is due to interface errors in a large and complex system.
- In large systems, the presence of a large number of interface errors is not an unlikely scenario in software development. Thus, it is not cost effective to be optimistic by putting the modules together and hoping it will work.

Solheim and Rowland [5] measured the relative efficacy of top-down, bottom-up, sandwich, and big-bang integration strategies for software systems. The empirical study indicated that top-down integration strategies are most effective in terms of defect correction. Top-down and big-bang strategies produced the most reliable systems. Bottom-up strategies are generally least effective at correcting defects and produce the least reliable systems. Systems integrated by the sandwich strategy are moderately reliable in comparison.

7.5 SOFTWARE AND HARDWARE INTEGRATION

A component is a fundamental part of a system, and it is largely independent of other components. Many products require development of both hardware and software components. These two kinds of components are integrated to form the complete product. In addition, a third kind of component, a product documentation, is developed in parallel with the first two components. A product documentation is an integration of different kinds of individual documentations. The overall goal is to reduce the time to market of the product by removing the sequential nature of product development processes.

On the hardware side, the individual hardware modules, or components, are diverse in nature, such as a chassis, a printed circuit board, a power supply, a fan tray for cooling, and a cabinet to hold the product. On the documentation side, the modules that are integrated together include an installation manual, a troubleshooting guide, and a user's manual in more than one natural language.

It is essential to test both the software and the hardware components individually as much as possible before integrating them. In many products, neither component can be completely tested without the other. Usually, the entry criteria for both the hardware and software components are establishedand satisfied before beginning to integrate those components. If the target hardware is not available at the time of system integration, then a hardware emulator is developed. The emulator replaces the hardware platform on which the software is tested until the real hardware is available. However, there is no guarantee that the software will work on the real hardware even if it worked on the emulator.

Integration of hardware and software components is often done in an iterative manner. A software image with a minimal number of core software modules is loaded on the prototype hardware. In each step, a small number of tests are performed to ensure that all the desired software modules are present in the build. Next, additional tests are run to verify the essential functionalities. The process of assembling the build, loading on the target hardware, and testing the build continues until the entire product has been integrated. If a problem is discovered early in the hardware/software integration and the problem can be resolved easily, then the problem is fixed without any delay. Otherwise, integration of software and hardware components may continue in a limited way until the root cause of the problem is found and analyzed. The integration is delayed until the fixes, based on the outcome of the root cause analysis, are applied.

7.5.1 Hardware Design Verification Tests

A hardware engineering process is viewed as consisting of four phases: (i) planning and specification, (ii) design, prototype implementation, and testing, (iii) integration with the software system, and (iv) manufacturing, distribution, and field service. Testing of a hardware module in the second phase of hardware development without software can be conducted to a limited degree. A hardware design verification test (DVT) plan is prepared and executed by the hardware group before integration with the software system. The main hardware tests are discussed below.

Diagnostic Test Diagnostic tests are the most fundamental hardware tests. Such tests are often imbedded in the basic input–output system (BIOS) component and are executed automatically whenever the system powers up. The BIOS component generally resides on the system's read-only memory (ROM). This test is performed as a kind of sanity test of the hardware module. A good diagnostic test covers all the modules in the system. A diagnostic test is the first test performed to isolate a faulty hardware module.

Electrostatic Discharge Test The concept of electrostatic discharge (ESD) testing is very old and it ensures that the system operation is not susceptible to ESD after having taken commonly accepted precautions. There are three common industry standards on ESD testing based on three different models: the human body model (HBM), the machine model (MM), and the charged device model (CDM). The HBM is the oldest one, and it is the most widely recognized ESD model. It was developed at a time when most ESD damages occurred as people touched hardware components without proper grounding. The capacitance and impedance of the human body vary widely, so the component values in the model were arbitrarily set to facilitate comparative testing. Devices damaged by the HBM generally have thermally damaged junctions, melted metal lines, or other types of damages caused by a high peak current and a high charge dissipated over several hundred nanoseconds. This model still applies whenever people handle devices so one should perform HBM testing on all new devices.

The MM is used primarily in Japan and Europe. This model was developed originally as a "worst-case" HBM to duplicate the type of failures caused by automated pick-and-place machines used to assemble printed circuit boards (PCBs). The model simulates a low-impedance machine that discharges a moderately high capacitance (e.g., 200 pF) through a device. A discharge produced using the MM can cause damage at relatively low voltages. Finally, the CDM reproduces realistic ESD damages that occur in small, plastic-packaged devices. As a packaged device slides on a surface, it accumulates charge due to triboelectric (friction) action between the plastic body and the surface. Thus, the device picks up a charge that produces a potential. In the HBM and the MM, something external to the device accumulates the charge. For small devices, the potential can be surprisingly high. Potentials of at least 650 V are needed to duplicate the observed damage.

Electromagnetic Emission Test Tests are conducted to ensure that the system does not emit excessive radiation to impact operation of adjacent equipments. Similarly, tests are conducted to ensure that the system does not receive excessive radiation to impact its own operation. The emissions of concern are as follows:

- Electric field radiated emissions
- Magnetic field radiated emissions
- Alternating-current (AC) power lead conducted emission (voltage)
- AC and direct-current (DC) power and signal lead conducted emission (current)
- Analog voice band lead conducted emission

Electrical Test A variety of electrical tests are performed on products with a hardware component. One such test is called "signal quality" testing in which different parts of the system are checked for any inappropriate voltages or potential current flows at the externally accessible ports and peripherals. Another type of electrical test is observing how the system behaves in response to various types of power conditions such as AC, DC, and batteries. In addition, tests are conducted to check the safety limits of the equipment when it is exposed to abnormal conditions. An abnormal condition can result from lightning surges or AC power faults.

Thermal Test Thermal tests are conducted to observe whether or not the system can stand the temperature and humidity conditions it will experience in both operating and nonoperating modes. The system is placed in a thermal chamber and run through a series of temperature and humidity cycles. The heat producing components, such as CPU and Ethernet cards, are instrumented with thermal sensors to verify whether the components exceed their maximum operating temperatures. A special kind of thermal test is thermal shock, where the temperature changes rapidly.

Environmental Test Environmental tests are designed to verify the response of the system to various types of strenuous conditions encountered in the real world. One such test involves shock and vibration from adjacent constructions and highways. Nearby heavy machinery, heavy construction, heavy industrial equipment, truck/train traffic, or standby generators can result in low-frequency vibration which can induce intermittent problems. It is important to know if such low-frequency vibration will cause long-term problems such as connectors becoming loose or short-term problems such as a disk drive crashing. Environmental tests also include other surprises the system is likely to encounter. For example, in a battlefield environment, the computers and the base transceiver stations are often subjected to smoke, sand, bullets, fire, and other extreme conditions.

Equipment Handling and Packaging Test These tests are intended to determine the robustness of the system to normal shipping and installation activities. Good pack and packaging design ensures that the shipping container will provide damage-free shipment of the system. Early involvement of these design skills will provide input on the positioning of handles and other system protrusions that can be the sources of failure. Selection of reasonable metal thickness and fasteners will provide adequate performance of systems to be installed into their final location.

Acoustic Test Acoustic noise limits are specified to ensure that personnel can work near the system without exceeding the safety limits prescribed by the local Occupational Safety and Health Administration (OSHA) agency or other negotiated levels. For example, noise levels of spinning hard disks, floppies, and other drives must be tested against their limits.

Safety Test   Safety tests are conducted to ensure that people using or working on or near the system are not exposed to hazards. For example, many portable computers contain rechargeable batteries which frequently include dangerous toxic substances such as cadmium and nickel. Adequate care must be taken to ensure that these devices do not leak the dangerous chemicals under any circumstances.

Reliability Test   Hardware modules tends to fail over time. It is assumed that (i) modules have constant failure rates during their useful operating life periods and (ii) module failure rates follow an exponential law of distribution. Failure rate is often measured in terms of the mean time between failures (MTBF), and it is expressed as MTBF = total time/number of failures. The probability that a module will work for some time T without failure is given by $R(T) = \exp(-T/\text{MTBF})$. The MTBF metric is a reliability measurement metric for hardware modules. It is usually given in units of hours, days, or months.

   The MTBF for a module or a system is derived from various sources: laboratory tests, actual field failure data, and prediction models. Another way of calculating the reliability and lifetime of a system is to conduct highly accelerated life tests (HALTs). The HALTs rely on the principle of *logarithmic time compression* to simulate a system's entire life in just a few days. This is done by applying a much higher level of stress than what exists in actual system use. A high level of stress forces failures to occur in significantly less time than under normal operating conditions. The HALTs generally include rapid temperature cycling, vibrating on all axes, operating voltage variations, and changing clock frequency until the system fails. The HALTs require only a few units of the product and a short testing period to identify the fundamental limits of the technologies in use. Generally, every weak point must be identified and fixed (i.e., redesigned) if it does not meet the system's specified limits. Understanding the concept of product reliability is important for any organization if the organization intends to offer warranty on the system for an extended period of time. One can predict with high accuracy the exact cost associated with the returns over a limited and an extended period of warranty. For example, for a system with an MTBF of 250,000 hours and an operating time of interest of five years (438,000 hours), we have $R(438,000) = \exp(-43,800/250,000) = 0.8392$, which says that there is a probability of 0.8932 that the product will operate for five years without a failure. Another interpretation of the quantity is that 83.9% of the units in the field will still be working at the end of five years. In other words, 16.1% of the units need to be replaced within the first five years.

7.5.2   Hardware and Software Compatibility Matrix

The hardware and software compatibility information is maintained in the form of a compatibility matrix. Such a matrix documents the compatibility between different revisions of the hardware and different versions of the software and is used for official release of the product. An engineering change order (ECO) is a formal document that describes a change to the hardware or software. An ECO document includes the hardware/software compatibility matrix and is distributed to

TABLE 7.2 Example Software/Hardware Compatibility Matrix

Software Release	RNC Hardware Version	RN Hardware Version	EMS Hardware Version	PDSN Hardware Version	Tested by SIT	Tested by ST
2.0	hv1.0	hv2.0	hv3.2	hv2.0.3	Yes	Yes
2.5	hv2.0 and hv1.0	hv2.0	hv4.0 and hv3.2	hv3.0 and hv2.0.3	Yes	Yes
3.0	hv3.0	hv3.0 and hv2.0	hv5.0	hv4.0 and hv3.0	Yes	Not yet
3.0	hv4.0 and hv3.0	hv3.0	hv5.0	hv4.5	Not yet	Not yet
Not yet decided	hv4.0 and hv3.0	hv3.0	hv6.0	hv5.0	Not yet	Not yet

the operation, customer support, and sales teams of the organization. An example compatibility matrix for a 1xEV-DO wireless data network, discussed in Chapter 8, is given in Table 7.2.

In the following, we provide the hardware and software ECO approval process in an organization. The first scenario describes the ECO process to incorporate a new hardware in the product. The second scenario describes the ECO process for a software revision.

Scenario 1 A hardware ECO process is shown in Figure 7.11. Assume that the hardware group needs to release a new revision of a hardware or has to recommend a new revision of an original equipment manufacturer (OEM) hardware to the operation/manufacturing group. The steps of the ECO process to incorporate the new hardware in the product are as follows:

1. The hardware group issues a design change notification for the new hardware revision. This notification includes identification of specific hardware changes likely to impact the software and incompatibilities between the revised hardware and other hardware. The software group reviews the notification with the hardware group to assess the impact of the hardware changes and to identify software changes that affect the hardware structure.

2. The hardware group creates an ECO and reviews it with the change control board (CCB) to ensure that all impacts of the ECO are understood and agreed upon and that the version numbering rules for software components are followed. The CCB constitutes a group of individuals from multiple departments responsible for reviewing and approving each ECO.

3. The ECO is released, and the hardware group updates the hardware/software compatibility matrix based on the information received from the review process.

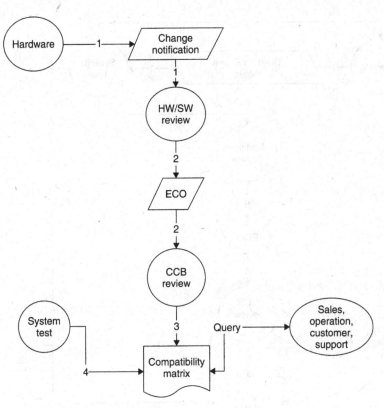

Figure 7.11   Hardware ECO process.

4. The system testing group updates the compatibility matrix after it has tested a given combination of released hardware and software versions.

Scenario 2   A software release ECO process is shown in Figure 7.12. Assume that the group needs to release a new version of software to the operation/manufacturing group. The steps of the ECO process to incorporate the new version of the software product are as follows:

1. The system integration group releases a build with a release note identifying the hardware compatibility information to the system test group.

2. The system test group tests the build and notifies the software group and other relevant groups in the organization of the results of the tests.

3. The system test group deems a particular build to be viable for customer release. The system test group calls a cross-functional readiness review meeting to ensure, by verifying the test results, that all divisions of the organization are prepared for an official release.

4. The software group writes an ECO to officially release the software build and reviews it with the CCB after the readiness review is completed.

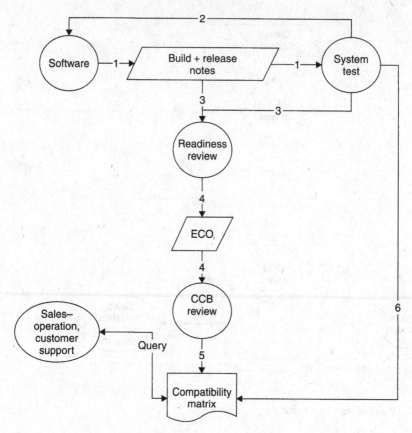

Figure 7.12   Software ECO process.

The build is considered to be released after the ECO is approved and documented.

5. The software group updates the hardware/software compatibility matrix with information about the new release.

6. The system test group updates the compatibility matrix after it has tested a given combination of released hardware and software versions.

7.6   TEST PLAN FOR SYSTEM INTEGRATION

System integration requires a controlled execution environment, much communication between the developers and the test engineers, judicious decision making along the way, and much time, on the order of months, in addition to the fundamental tasks of test design and test execution. Integrating a large system is a challenging task, which is handled with much planning in the form of developing a SIT plan. A useful framework for preparing an SIT plan is outlined in Table 7.3.

TABLE 7.3   Framework for SIT Plan

1. Scope of testing
2. Structure of integration levels
    a. Integration test phases
    b. Modules or subsystems to be integrated in each phase
    c. Building process and schedule in each phase
    d. Environment to be set up and resources required in each phase
3. Criteria for each integration test phase *n*
    a. Entry criteria
    b. Exit criteria
    c. Integration Techniques to be used
    d. Test configuration set-up
4. Test specification for each integration test phase
    a. Test case ID number
    b. Input data
    c. Initial condition
    d. Expected results
    e. Test procedure
       How to execute this test?
       How to capture and interpret the results?
5. Actual test results for each integration test phase
6. References
7. Appendix

In the scope of testing section, one summarizes the system architecture. Specifically, the focus is on the functional, internal, and performance characteristics to be tested. System integration methods and assumptions are included in this section.

The next section, structure of integration levels, contains four subsections. The first subsection explains the division of integration testing into different phases, such as functional, end-to-end, and endurance phases. The second subsection describes the modules to be integrated in each of the integration phases. The third subsection describes the build process to be followed: daily build, weekly build, biweekly build, or a combination thereof. A schedule for system integration is given in the third subsection. Specifically, one identifies the start and end dates for each phase of testing. Moreover, the availability windows for unit-tested modules are defined. In the fourth subsection, the test environment and the resources required are described for each integration phase. The hardware configuration, emulators, software simulators, special test tools, debuggers, overhead software (i.e., stubs and drivers), and testing techniques are discussed in the fourth subsection.

An important decision to be made for integration testing is establishing the start and stop dates of each phase of integration testing. The start date and stop date for a phase are specified in terms of *entry criteria* and *exit criteria*, respectively. These criteria are described in the third section of the plan. A framework for defining entry criteria to start system integration is given in Table 7.4. Similarly, the exit criteria for system integration are given in Table 7.5. Test configuration and integration techniques (e.g., top down or bottom up) to be used in each of these phases are described in this section.

The test specification section describes the test procedure to be followed in each integration phase. The detailed test cases, including the input and expected outcome for each case, are documented in the test specification section. The history of actual test results, problems, or peculiarities is recorded in the fifth section of the SIT plan. Finally, references and an appendix, if any, are included in the test plan.

System integration testing is performed in phases of increasing complexity for better efficiency and effectiveness. In the first phase interface integrity and functional validity within a system are tested. In the second phase end-to-end and pairwise tests are conducted. Finally, in the third phase, stress and endurance tests are performed. Each of the system integration phases identified in the SIT plan delineates a broad functionality category within the software structure, and it can be related to a specific domain of the system software structure. The categories

TABLE 7.4   Framework for Entry Criteria to Start System Integration

Softwave functional and design specifications must be writen, reviewed, and approved.
Code is reviewed and approved.
Unit test plan for each module is written, reviewed, and executed.
All of the unit tests passed.
The entire check-in request form must be completed, submitted, and approved.
Hardware design specification is written, reviewed, and approved.
Hardware design verification test is written, reviewed, and executed.
All of the design verification tests passed.
Hardware/software integration test plan is written, reviewed, and executed.
All of the hardware/software integrated tests passed.

TABLE 7.5   Framework for System Integration Exit Criteria

All code is completed and frozen and no more modules are to be integrated.
All of the system integration tests passed.
No major defect is outstanding.
All the moderate defects found in the SIT phase are fixed and retested.
Not more than 25 minor defects are outstanding.
Two weeks system uptime in system integration test environment without any anomalies, i.e., crashes.
System integration tests results are documented.

of system integration tests and the corresponding test cases discussed below are applicable for the different test phases.

Interface Integrity   Internal and external interfaces are tested as each module is integrated into the structure. When two modules are integrated, the communication between them is called internal, whereas when they communicate with the outside environment, it is called external. Tests that are required to be designed to reveal interface errors are discussed in Section 7.2. An important part of interface testing is to map an incoming message format to the expected message format of the receiving module and ensure that the two match. Tests are designed for each message passing through the interface between two modules. Essentially, tests must ensure that:

- The number of parameters sent in a message agree with the number of parameters expected to be received.
- The parameter order in the messages match the order expected.
- The field sizes and the data types match.
- The boundaries of each data field in a message match the expected boundaries.
- When a message is generated from stored data prior to being sent, the message truly reflects the stored data.
- When a received message is stored, data copying is consistent with the received message.

Functional Validity   Tests are designed to uncover functional errors in each module after it is integrated with the system. Errors associated with local or global data structures are uncovered with such tests. Selected unit tests that were designed for each module are reexecuted during system integration by replacing the stubs with their actual modules.

End-to-End Validity   Tests are performed to ensure that a completely integrated system works together from end to end. Interim checkpoints on an end-to-end flow provide a better understanding of internal mechanisms. This helps in locating the sources of failures.

Pairwise Validity   Tests are performed to ensure that any two systems work properly when connected together by a network. The difference between pairwise tests and end-to-end tests lies in the emphasis and type of test cases. For example, a toll-free call to an 800 number is an end-to-end test of a telephone system, whereas a connectivity test between a handset and local private branch exchange (PBX) is a pairwise test.

Interface Stress   Stress is applied at the module level during the integration of the modules to ensure that the interfaces can sustain the load. On the other hand, full-scale system stress testing is performed at the time of system-level testing. The following areas are of special interest during interface stress testing:

- **Error Handling:** Trigger errors that should be handled by the modules.
- **Event Handling:** Trigger events (e.g., messages, timeouts, callbacks) that should be handled by the modules.
- **Configuration:** Repeatedly add, modify, and delete managed objects.
- **Logging:** Turn on the logging mechanism during stress tests to ensure proper operation for boundary conditions.
- **Module Interactions:** Run tests repeatedly that stress the interactions of a module with other modules.
- **CPU Cycles:** Induce high CPU utilization by using a CPU overload tool; pay attention to any resulting queue overflows and other producer/consumer overrun conditions.
- **Memory/Disk Usage:** Artificially reduce the levels of heaps and/or memory buffers and disk space;
- **Starvation:** Ensure that the processes or tasks are not starved; otherwise eventually the input queues overflow for the starved processes.
- **Resource Sharing:** Ensure that resources, such as heap and CPU, are shared among processes without any contention and bottlenecks.
- **Congestion:** Run tests with a mechanism that randomly discards packets; test modules with congested links.
- **Capacity:** Run tests to ensure that modules can handle the maximum numbers of supporting requirements such as connections and routes.

System Endurance   A completely integrated system is expected to stay up continuously for weeks without any crashes. In the case of communication protocol systems, formal rules govern that two systems communicate with each other via an interface, that is, a communication channel. The idea here is to verify that the format and the message communication across the interface of the modules works for an extended period.

7.7 OFF-THE-SHELF COMPONENT INTEGRATION

Instead of developing a software component from scratch, organizations occasionally purchase off-the-shelf (OTS) components form third-party vendors and integrate them with their own components [6]. In this process, organizations create less expensive software systems. A major issue that can arise while integrating different components is mismatches among code pieces developed by different parties usually unaware of each other [7, 8].

Vigder and Dean [9] have presented elements of an architecture for integration and have defined rules that facilitate integration of components. They have identified a useful set of supporting components for integrating the actual, serving components. The supporting components are *wrappers*, *glue*, and *tailoring*.

A wrapper is a piece of code that one builds to isolate the underlying components from other components of the system. Here *isolate* means putting restrictions around the underlying component to constrain its capabilities. A glue component provides the functionality to combine different components. Component tailoring refers to the ability to enhance the functionality of a component. Tailoring is done by adding some elements to a component to enrich it with a functionality not provided by the vendor. Tailoring does not involve modifying the source code of the component. An example of tailoring is "scripting," where an application can be enhanced by executing a script upon the occurrence of some event. Rine et al. [10] have proposed the concept of adapters to integrate components. An adapter is associated with each component; the adapter runs an interaction protocol to manage communications among the components. Components request services from others through their associated adapters. An adapter is responsible for resolving any syntactic interface mismatch.

7.7.1   Off-the-Shelf Component Testing

Buyer organizations perform two types of testing on an OTS component before purchasing: (i) acceptance testing of the OTS component based on the criteria discussed in Chapter 14 and (ii) integration of the component with other components developed in-house or purchased from a third party. The most common cause of problems in the integration phase is inadequate acceptance testing of the OTS component. A lack of clear documentation of the system interface and less cooperation from the vendor may create an ordeal in integration testing, debugging, and fixing defects. Acceptance testing of an OTS component requires the development and execution of an acceptance test plan based on the acceptance criteria for the candidate component. All the issues are resolved before the system integration process begins. During integration testing, additional software components, such as a glue or a wrapper, can be developed to bind an OTS component with other components for proper functioning. These new software components are also tested during the integration phase. Integration of OTS components is a challenging task because of the following characteristics identified by Basili and Boehm [11]:

The buyer has no access to the source code.

The vendor controls its development.

The vendor has nontrivial installed base.

Voas [12] proposed three types of testing techniques to determine the suitability of an OTS component:

- **Black-Box Component Testing:** This is used to determine the quality of the component.

- **System-Level Fault Injection Testing:** This is used to determine how well a system will tolerate a failing component. System-level fault injection does not demonstrate the reliability of the system; instead, it can predict the behavior of the system if the OTS component fails.

- **Operational System Testing:** This kind of test is used to determine the tolerance of a software system when the OTS component is functioning correctly. Operational system testing is conducted to ensure that an OTS component is a good match for the system.

The OTS components produced by the vendor organizations are known as commercial off-the-shelf (COTS) components. A COTS component is defined by Szyperski et al. [13] (p. 34) as "a unit of composition with contractually specified interfaces and explicit context dependencies only. A software component can be deployed independently and is subject to composition by third parties." Interfaces are the access points of COTS components through which a client component can request a service declared in an interface of the service providing component. Weyuker [14] recommends that vendors building COTS components must try to envision many possible uses of the component and develop a comprehensive range of test scenarios. A component should be defect free because prudent buyers will perform significant amount of testing while integrating the component with their system. If potential buyers encounter a large number of defects in a COTS component, they may not accept the component. Therefore, it is in the best interest of the component builder to ensure that components are thoroughly tested. Several related artefacts should be archived and/or modified for each COTS component, because a potential buyer may demand these artifacts to be of high quality. The artefacts to be archived include the following:

- Individual requirements, including the pointers between the software functional specification and the corresponding implementations: This information makes it easy to track when either the code or the specification is modified, which implies that the specification remains up to date.
- The test suite, including the requirement traceability matrix: This will show which part of the functionality is tested inadequately or not at all. In addition, it identifies the test cases that (i) must be executed as regression tests or (ii) need to be updated when the component undergoes a change.
- The individual pass–fail result of each test case in the test suite: This indicates the quality of the COTS component.
- The details of individual test cases, including input and expected output: This facilitates regression testing of changes to a component.
- The system test report corresponding to the final release of the COTS component, which includes performance characteristics, scalability limitation, stability observations, and interoperability of the COTS component: This document is a useful resource for potential buyers before they begin acceptance testing of the COTS components.

7.7.2 Built-in Testing

A component reused in a new application environment requires real-time detection, diagnosis, and handling of software faults. Built-in test (BIT) methods for producing self-testable software components hold potential for detecting faults during run time. A software component can contain test cases or can possess facilities that are capable of generating test cases which can be accessed by a component user on demand [15]. The corresponding capabilities allowing this are called built-in testing capabilities of software components. In the BIT methodology, testability is incorporated into software components, so that testing and maintenance can be self-contained.

Wang et al. [16] have proposed a BIT model that can operate in two modes, namely, *normal* mode and *maintenance* mode. In the normal mode, the BIT capabilities are transparent to the component user, and the component does not differ from other non-BIT-enabled components. In the maintenance mode, however, the component user can test the component with the help of its BIT features. The component user can invoke the respective methods of the component, which execute the test, evaluate autonomously its results, and output the test summary. The authors describe a generic technical framework for enhancing BIT. One of their assumptions is that the component is implemented as a class. A benefit of such an implementation is that the methods for BIT can be passed to a subclass by inheritance.

Hörnstein and Edler [17] have proposed a *component + BIT* architecture comprising three types of components, namely, BIT, testers, and handlers. The BIT components are the BIT-enabled components. These components implement certain mandatory interfaces. Testers are components which access the BIT capabilities of BIT components through the corresponding interfaces and contain the test cases in a certain form. Finally, handlers are components that do not directly contribute to testing but provide recovery mechanisms in case of failures.

7.8 SUMMARY

This chapter began with the objective and a description of system integration testing. One creates a "working version of the system" by putting the modules together in an incremental manner while performing tests to uncover different types of errors associated with interfacing. Next, we explored various levels of granularities in system integration testing: intrasystem testing, intersystem testing, and pairwise testing.

We then examined five types of commonly used system integration techniques: topdown, bottomup, sandwich, bigbang, and incremental. We compared those techniques in detail. The incremental technique is widely used in the industry.

We described the integration of hardware and software components to form a complete product. This led to the discussion of the hardware engineering process and, specifically, of different types of hardware design verification tests: diagnostic, electrostatic discharge, electromagnetic emission, electrical, thermal, environmental, packaging and handling, acoustic, safety, and reliability. Finally, we described two scenarios of an engineering change order process. The two scenarios are used to keep track of the hardware/software compatibility matrix of a released product.

We provided a framework of an integration test plan. The following categories of tests, which are included in an integration test plan, were discussed in detail: interface integrity tests, functional validity tests, end-to-end validity tests, pairwise validity tests, interface stress tests, and endurance tests.

Finally, we described the integration of OTS components with other components. An organization, instead of developing a software component from scratch, may decide to purchase a COTS software from a third-party source and integrate it with its own software system. A COTS component seller must provide BITs along with the components, whereas a buyer organization must perform three types of testing to assess the COTS software: (i) acceptance testing of the OTS software component to determine the quality of the component, (ii) system-level fault injection testing, which is used to determine the tolerance of the software system to a failing OTS component, and (iii) operational system testing, which is used to determine the tolerance of the software system to a properly functioning OTS component.

LITERATURE REVIEW

For those actively involved in software testing or interested in knowing more about common software errors, appendix A of the book by C. Kaner, J. Falk, and H. Q. Nguyen (*Testing Computer Software*, Wiley, New York, 1999) is an excellent repository of real-life software errors. The appendix contains 12 categories of approximately 400 different types of errors with illustrations.

A good discussion of hardware test engineering, such as mechanical, electronics, and accelerated tests, can be found in Patrick O'Connor's book (*Test Engineering: A Concise Guide to Cost-effective Design, Development and Manufacture*, Wiley, New York, 2001). The author (i) describes a broad spectrum of modern methods and technologies in hardware test engineering, (ii) offers principles of cost-effective design, development, and manufacture of products and systems, and (iii) gives a breakdown of why product and systems fail and which methods would best prevent these failures.

Researchers are continuously working on topics related to certification of COTS components. The interested reader is recommended to read the following articles. Each of these articles helps in understanding the issues of software certification and why it is important:

> J. Voas, "Certification Reducing the Hidden Costs of Poor Quality," *IEEE Software*, Vol. 16, No. 4, July/August 1999, pp. 22–25.

> J. Voas, "Certifying Software for High-Assurance Environments," *IEEE Software*, Vol. 16, No. 4, July/August 1999, pp. 48–54.

> J. Voas, "Developing Usage-Based Software Certification Process," *IEEE Computer*, Vol. 16, No. 8, August 2000, pp. 32–37.

> S. Wakid, D. Kuhn, and D. Wallace, "Toward Credible IT Testing and Certification," *IEEE Software*, Vol. 16, No. 4, July/August 1999, pp. 39–47.

Readers actively involved in COTS component testing or interested in a more sophisticated treatment of the topic are recommended to read the book edited by S. Beydeda and V. Gruhn (*Testing Commercial-off-the-Shelf Components and Systems*, Springer, Bonn, 2005). The book contains 15 articles that discuss in great detail: (i) testing components context independently, (ii) testing components in the context of a system, and (iii) testing component–based systems. The book lists several excellent references on the subject in a bibliography.

REFERENCES

1. V. R. Basili and B. T. Perricone. Software Errors and Complexity: An Empirical Investigation. *Communications of the ACM*, January 1984, pp. 42–52.
2. D. E. Perry and W. M. Evangelist. An Empirical Study of Software Interface Faults—An Update. In *Proceedings of the Twentieth Annual Hawaii International Conference on Systems Sciences*, Hawaii Vol. II, IEEE Computer Society Press, Piscataway, NJ, January 1987, pp. 113–126.
3. M. S. Deutsch. *Software Verification and Validation: Realistic Project Approaches*. Prentice-Hall, Englewood Cliffs, NJ, 1982, pp. 95–101.
4. M. Cusumano and R. W. Selby. How Microsoft Builds Software. *Communications of the ACM*, June 1997, pp. 53–61.
5. J. A. Solheim and J. H. Rowland. An Empirical Study of Testing and Integration Strategies Using Artificial Software Systems. *IEEE Transactions on Software Engineering*, October 1993, pp. 941–949.
6. S. Mahmood, R. Lai, and Y. S. Kim. Survey of Component-Based Software Development. *IET Software*, April 2007, pp. 57–66.
7. G. T. Heineman and W. T. Councill. *Component-Based Software Engineering: Putting the Pieces Together*. Addison-Wesley, Reading, MA, 2001.
8. A. Cechich, M. Piattini, and A. Vallecillo. Assessing Component Based Systems. Component Based Software Quality. *Lecture Notes in Computer Science*, Vol. 2693, 2003, pp. 1–20.
9. M. R. Vigder and J. Dean. An Architectural Approach to Building Systems from COTS Software Components. In *Proceedings of the 22nd Annual Software Engineering Workshop*, NASA Goddard Space Flight Center, Greenbelt, MD, December 1997, pp. 99–113, NRC41610.
10. D. Rine, N. Nada, and K. Jaber. Using Adapters to Reduce Interaction Complexity in Reusable Component-Based Software Development. In *Proceedings of the 1999 Symposium on Software Reusability*, Los Angeles, CA, ACM Press, New York, May 1999, pp. 37–43.
11. V. R. Basili and B. Boehm. COTS-Based Systems Top 10 List. *IEEE Computer*, May 2001, pp. 91–93.
12. J. Voas. Certifying Off-the-Shelf Software Component. *IEEE Computer*, June 1998, pp. 53–59.
13. C. Szyperski, D. Gruntz, and S. Murer. *Component Software: Beyond Object-Oriented Programming*, 2nd ed. Addison-Wesley, Reading, MA, 2002.
14. E. J. Weyuker. Testing Component-Based Software: A Cautionary Tale. *IEEE Software*, September/October 1998, pp. 54–59.
15. S. Beydeda and V. Gruhn. Merging Components and Testing Tools: The Self-Testing COTS Components (STECC) Strategy. In *Proceedings of the 29th EUROMICRO Conference (EUROMICRO'03)*, Belek-Antalya, Turkey, IEEE Computer Society Press, Piscataway, September 2003, pp. 107–114.
16. Y. Wang, G. King, and H. Wickburg. A Method for Built-in Tests in Component-Based Software Maintenance. In *Proceedings of the IEEE International Conference on Software Maintenance and Reengineering (CSMR-99)*, University of Amsterdam, The Netherland, IEEE Computer Society Press, Piscataway, March 1999, pp. 186–189.

17. J. Höornstein and H. Edler. Test Reuse in CBSE Using Built-in Tests. In *Proceedings of the 9th IEEE Conference and Workshops on Engineering of Computer Based Systems*, Workshop on Component-Based Software Engineering, Lund University, Lund, Sweden, IEEE Computer Society Press, Piscataway, 2002.

Exercises

1. Describe the difference between black-box and white-box testing techniques?

2. If a program passes all the black-box tests, it means that the program should work properly. Then, in addition to black-box testing, why do you need to perform white-box testing?

3. Describe the difference between unit testing and integration testing?

4. Why should integration testing be performed? What types of errors can this phase of testing reveal?

5. Discuss the advantages and disadvantages of top-down and bottom-up approaches to integration testing.

6. Does automation of integration tests help the verification of the daily build process? Justify your answer.

7. Using the module hierarchy given in Figure 7.13, show the orders of module integration for the top-down and bottom-up integration approaches. Estimate the number of stubs and drivers needed for each approach. Specify the integration testing activities that can be done in parallel, assuming you have three SIT engineers. Based on the resource needs and the ability to carry out concurrent SIT activities, which approach would you select for this system and why?

8. Suppose that you plan to purchase COTS components and integrate them with your communication software project. What kind of acceptance criteria will you develop to conduct acceptance testing of the COTS components?

9. During integration testing of COTS components with a software system, it may be required to develop a wrapper software around the OTS component to limit what it can do. Discuss the general characteristics that a wrapping software

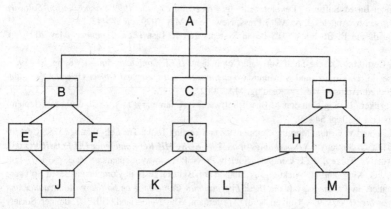

Figure 7.13   Module hierarchy of software system.

should have in order to be able to integrate COTS with the software system without any problem.

10. Describe the circumstances under which you would apply white-box testing, back-box testing, or both techniques to evaluate a COTS component.

11. For your current test project, develop an integration test plan.

12. Complete Section 5 (i.e., actual test results for each integration test phase) of the integration test plan after executing the integration test cases you developed in exercise 11.

CHAPTER 8

System Test Categories

As a rule, software systems do not work well until they have been used, and have failed repeatedly, in real applications.
— *Dave Parnas*

8.1 TAXONOMY OF SYSTEM TESTS

The objective of system-level testing, also called system testing, is to establish whether an implementation conforms to the requirements specified by the customers. It takes much effort to guarantee that customer requirements have been met and the system is acceptable. A variety of tests are run to meet a wide range of unspecified expectations as well. As integrated systems, consisting of both hardware and software components, are often used in reality, there is a need to have a much broader view of the behavior of the systems. For example, a telephone switching system not only is required to provide a connection between two users but also is expected to do so even if there are many ongoing connections below a certain upper limit. When the upper limit on the number of simultaneous connections is reached, the system is not expected to behave in an undesired manner. In this chapter, we identify different categories of tests in addition to the core functionality test. Identifying test categories brings us the following advantages:

- Test engineers can accurately focus on different aspects of a system, one at a time, while evaluating its quality.

- Test engineers can prioritize their tasks based on test categories. For example, it is more meaningful and useful to identify the limitations of a system only after ensuring that the system performs all basic functions to the test an engineer's satisfactions. Therefore, stress tests, which thrive to identify the limitations of a system, are executed after functionality tests.

- Planning the system testing phase based on test categorization lets a test engineer obtain a well-balanced test suite. Practical limitations make it difficult to be exhaustive, and economic considerations may restrict the

---

Software Testing and Quality Assurance: Theory and Practice, Edited by Kshirasagar Naik and Priyadarshi Tripathy
Copyright © 2008 John Wiley & Sons, Inc.

testing process from continuing any further. However, it is important to design a balanced test suite, rather than an unbalanced one with many test cases in one category and no tests in another.

In the following, first we present the taxonomy of system tests (Figure 8.1). Thereafter, we explain each category in detail.

- *Basic tests* provide an evidence that the system can be installed, configured, and brought to an operational state.
- *Functionality tests* provide comprehensive testing over the full range of the requirements within the capabilities of the system.
- *Robustness tests* determine how well the system recovers from various input errors and other failure situations.
- *Interoperability tests* determine whether the system can interoperate with other third-party products.
- *Performance tests* measure the performance characteristics of the system, for example, throughput and response time, under various conditions.
- *Scalability tests* determine the scaling limits of the system in terms of user scaling, geographic scaling, and resource scaling.
- *Stress tests* put a system under stress in order to determine the limitations of a system and, when it fails, to determine the manner in which the failure occurs.

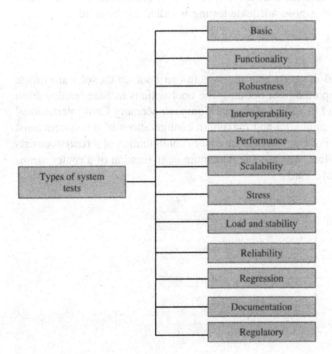

Figure 8.1   Types of system tests.

- *Load and stability tests* provide evidence that the system remains stable for a long period of time under full load.
- *Reliability tests* measure the ability of the system to keep operating for a long time without developing failures.
- *Regression tests* determine that the system remains stable as it cycles through the integration of other subsystems and through maintenance tasks.
- *Documentation tests* ensure that the system's user guides are accurate and usable.
- *Regulatory tests* ensure that the system meets the requirements of government regulatory bodies in the countries where it will be deployed.

8.2 BASIC TESTS

The basic tests (Figure 8.2) give a *prima facie* evidence that the system is ready for more rigorous tests. These tests provide limited testing of the system in relation to the main features in a requirement specification. The objective is to establish that there is sufficient evidence that a system can operate without trying to perform thorough testing. Basic tests are performed to ensure that commonly used functions, not all of which may directly relate to user-level functions, work to our satisfaction. We emphasize the fact that test engineers rely on the proper implementation of these functions to carry out tests for user-level functions. The following are the major categories of subsystems whose adequate testing is called the basic test.

8.2.1 Boot Tests

Boot tests are designed to verify that the system can boot up its software image (or build) from the supported boot options. The boot options include booting from ROM, FLASH card, and PCMCIA (Personal Computer Memory Card International Association) card. The minimum and maximum configurations of the system must be tried while booting. For example, the minimum configuration of a router consists of one line card in its slots, whereas the maximum configuration of a router means that all slots contains line cards.

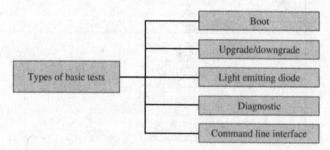

Figure 8.2   Types of basic tests.

8.2.2 Upgrade/Downgrade Tests

Upgrade/downgrade tests are designed to verify that the system software can be upgraded or downgraded (rollback) in a graceful manner from the previous version to the current version or vice versa. Suppose that the system is running the $(n-1)$th version of the software build and the new nth version of the software build is available. The question is how one upgrades the build from the $(n-1)$th version to the nth version. An upgradation process taking a system from the $(n-1)$th version to the nth version may not be successful, in which case the system is brought back to the $(n-1)$th version. Tests are designed in this subgroup to verify that the system successfully reverts back, that is, rolls back, to the $(n-1)$th version. An upgradation process may fail because of a number of different conditions: user-invoked abort (the user interrupts the upgrade process), in-process network disruption (the network environment goes down), in-process system reboot (there is a power glitch), or self-detection of upgrade failure (this is due to such things as insufficient disk space and version incompatibilities).

8.2.3 Light Emitting Diode Tests

The LED (light emitting diode) tests are designed to verify that the system LED status indicators function as desired. The LEDs are located on the front panels of the systems. These provide visual indication of the module operational status. For example, consider the status of a system chassis: Green indicates that the chassis is operational, off indicates that there is no power, and a blinking green may indicate that one or more of its submodules are faulty. The LED tests are designed to ensure that the visual operational status of the system and the submodules are correct. Examples of LED tests at the system and subsystem levels are as follows:

- System LED test: green = OK, blinking green = fault, off = no power.
- Ethernet link LED test: green = OK, blinking green = activity, off = fault.
- Cable link LED test: green = OK, blinking green = activity, off = fault.
- User defined T1 line card LED test: green = OK, blinking green = activity, red = fault, off = no power.

8.2.4 Diagnostic Tests

Diagnostic tests are designed to verify that the hardware components (or modules) of the system are functioning as desired. It is also known as the built-in self-test (BIST). Diagnostic tests monitor, isolate, and identify system problems without manual troubleshooting. Some examples of diagnostic tests are as follows:

- **Power-On Self-Test (POST):** This is a set of automatic diagnostic routines that are executed during the boot phase of each submodule in the system. The POSTs are intended to determine whether or not the hardware is in a proper state to execute the software image. It is not intended to be comprehensive in the analysis of the hardware; instead, it provides a high level of confidence that the hardware is operational. The POSTs execute on the following kinds of elements:

Memory

Address and data buses

Peripheral devices

- **Ethernet Loop-Back Test:** This test generates and sends out the desired number, which is a tunable parameter, of packets and expects to receive the same number of Ethernet packets through the loop-back interface—external or internal. If an error occurs (e.g., packet mismatch or timeout), an error message indicating the type of error, its probable cause(s), and recommended action(s) is displayed on the console. The data sent out are generated by a random-number generator and put into a data buffer. Each time a packet is sent, it is selected from a different starting point of the data buffer, so that any two consecutively transmitted packets are unlikely to be identical. These tests are executed to ensure that the Ethernet card is functioning as desired.

- **Bit Error Test (BERT):** The on-board BERT provides standard bit error patterns, which can be transmitted over a channel for diagnostic purpose. BERT involves transmitting a known bit pattern and then testing the trans-mitted pattern for errors. The ratio of the number of bits with errors to the total number of bits transmitted is called the bit error rate (BER). Tests are designed to configure all BERTs from the command line interface (CLI). These tests are executed to ensure that that the hardware is functioning as desired.

8.2.5 Command Line Interface Tests

The CLI tests are designed to verify that the system can be configured, or provi-sioned, in specific ways. This is to ensure that the CLI software module processes the user commands correctly as documented. This includes accessing the relevant information from the system using CLI. In addition to the above tests, test scenarios may be developed to verify the error messages displayed.

8.3   FUNCTIONALITY TESTS

Functionality tests (Figure 8.3) verify the system as thoroughly as possible over the full range of requirements specified in the requirements specification document. This category of tests is partitioned into different functionality subgroups as follows.

8.3.1   Communication Systems Tests

Communication systems tests are designed to verify the implementation of the communication systems as specified in the customer requirements specification.

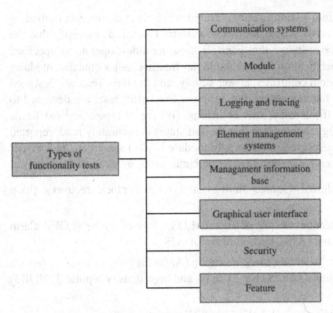

Figure 8.3   Types of functionality tests.

For example, one of the customer requirements can be to support Request for Comment (RFC) 791, which is the Internet Protocol (IP) specification. Tests are designed to ensure that an IP implementation conforms to the RFC791 standard. Four types of communication systems tests are recommended according to the extent to which they provide an indication of conformance [1]:

- *Basic interconnection tests* provide evidence that an implementation can establish a basic connection before thorough testing is performed.
- *Capability tests* check that an implementation provides the observable capabilities based on the static communication systems requirements. The static requirements describes the options, ranges of values for parameters, and timers.
- *Behavior tests* endeavor to verify the dynamic communication systems requirements of an implementation. These are the requirements and options that define the observable behavior of a protocol. A large part of behavior tests, which constitute the major portion of communication systems tests, can be generated from the protocol standards.
- *Systems resolution tests* probe to provide definite "yes" or "no" answers to specific requirements.

8.3.2   Module Tests

Module tests are designed to verify that all the modules function individually as desired within the systems. Mutual interactions among the modules glue these components together into a whole system. The idea here is to ensure that individual modules function correctly within the whole system. One needs to verify that the system, along with the software that controls these modules, operate as specified in the requirement specification. For example, an Internet router contains modules such as line cards, system controller, power supply, and fan tray. Tests are designed to verify each of the functionalities. For Ethernet line cards, tests are designed to verify (i) autosense, (ii) latency, (iii) collisions, (iv) frame types, and (v) frame lengths. Tests are designed to ensure that the fan status is accurately read, reported by the software, and displayed in the supply module LEDs (one green "in service" and one red "out of service"). For T1/E1 line cards, tests are designed to verify:

- **Clocking:** Internal (source timing) and receive clock recovery (loop timing).

- **Alarms:** Detection of loss of signal (LOS), loss of frame (LOF), alarm indication signal (AIS), and insertion of AIS.

- **Line Coding:** Alternate mark inversion (AMI) for both T1 and E1, bipolar 8 zero substitution (B8ZS) for T1 only, and high-density bipolar 3 (HDB3) for E1 only.

- **Framing:** Digital signal 1 (DS1) and E1 framing.

- **Channelization:** Ability to transfer user traffic across channels multiplexed from one or more contiguous or non contiguous time slots on a T1 or E1 link.

8.3.3 Logging and Tracing Tests

Logging and tracing tests are designed to verify the configurations and operations of logging and tracing. This also includes verification of "flight data recorder: non-volatile flash memory" logs when the system crashes. Tests may be designed to calculate the impact on system performance when all the logs are enabled.

8.3.4 Element Management Systems Tests

The EMS tests verify the main functions which are to manage, monitor, and upgrade the communication system network elements (NEs). Table 8.1 summarizes the functionalities of an EMS. An EMS communicates with its NEs by using, for example, the Simple Network Management Protocol (SNMP) [2] and a variety of proprietary protocols and mechanisms.

An EMS is a valuable component of a communication systems network. Not all EMSs will perform all of the tasks listed in Table 8.1. An EMS can support a subset of the tasks. A user working through the EMS graphical user interface (GUI) may accomplish some or all of the tasks. Remote access to an EMS allows the operators to access management and control information from any location. This facilitates the deployment of a distributed workforce that can rapidly respond to failure notifications. This means that thin client workstations can operate over the Internet and service provider intranets. In this subgroup, tests are designed to

TABLE 8.1 EMS Functionalities

Fault Management	Configuration Management	Accounting Management	Performance Management	Security Management
Alarm handling	System turn-up	Track service usage	Data collection	Control NE access
Trouble detection	Network provisioning	Bill for services	Report generation	Enable NE functions
Trouble correction	Autodiscovery		Data analysis	Access logs
Test and acceptance	Back-up and restore			
Network recovery	Database handling			

verify the five functionalities of an EMS (Table 8.1). This includes both the EMS client and the EMS server. Examples of EMS tests are given below.

- **Auto-Discovery:** EMS discovery software can be installed on the server to discover elements attached to the EMS through the IP network.
- **Polling and Synchronization:** An EMS server detects a system unreachable condition within a certain time duration. The EMS server synchronizes alarm status, configuration data, and global positioning system (GPS) time from the NE.
- **Audit Operations:** An audit mechanism is triggered whenever an out-of-service network element comes back. The mechanism synchronizes alarms between out-of-service NEs coming back online and the EMS.
- **Fault Manager:** Generation of critical events, such as reboot and reset, are converted to an alert and stored in the EMS database. The EMS can send an email/page to a configured address when an alarm is generated.
- **Performance Manager:** Data are pushed to the EMS server when the data buffer is full in the NE. Data in the server buffer are stored in the backup files once it is full.
- **Security Manager:** It supports authentication and authorization of EMS clients and NEs. The EMS server does the authorization based on user privileges.
- **Policies:** An EMS server supports schedulable log file transfer from the system. The EMS database is periodically backed up to a disk.
- **Logging:** An EMS server supports different logging levels for every major module to debug. An EMS server always logs errors and exceptions.
- **Administration and Maintenance:** This test configures the maximum number of simultaneous EMS clients. The EMS server backs up and restores database periodically.

- **Invoke Clients:** Several clients can be invoked to interact with the EMS server.

- **Live Data View:** A client can provide a live data viewer to monitor performance and show statistics of the system.

- **System Administration Task:** A client can shut down the server, configure logging levels, display server status, and enable auto-discovery.

- **File Transfer:** A client can check on-demand file transfer with a progress bar to indicate the progress and abort an on-demand file transfer operation.

SNMP Example The SNMP is an application layer protocol that facilitates the exchange of management information between network elements. The SNMP is a part of the Internet network management architecture consisting of three components: *network elements*, *agents*, and *network management stations* (NMSs). A NE is a network node that contains an SNMP agent and that resides on a managed network. Network elements collect and store management information and make this information available to the NMS over the SNMP protocol. Network elements can be routers, servers, radio nodes, bridges, hubs, computer hosts, printers, and modems. An agent is a network management software module that (i) resides on a NE, (ii) has the local knowledge of management information, and (iii) translates that information into a form compatible with the SNMP. An NMS, sometimes referred to as a console, executes management applications to monitor and control network elements. One or more NMSs exist on each managed networks. An EMS can act as an NMS.

A management information base (MIB) is an important component of a network management system. The MIB identifies the network elements (or managed objects) that are to be managed. Two types of managed objects exist:

- Scalar objects define a single object instance.
- Tabular objects define multiple related object instances that are grouped in MIB tables.

Essentially, a MIB is a virtual store providing a model of the managed information. For example, a MIB can contain information about the number of packets that have been sent and received across an interface. It contains statistics on the number of connections that exist on a Transmission Control Protocal (TCP) port as well as information that describes each user's ability to access elements of the MIB. The SNMP does not operate on the managed objects directly; instead, the protocol operates on a MIB. In turn, a MIB is the reflection of the managed objects, and its management mechanism is largely proprietary, perhaps through the EMS.

The important aspect of a MIB is that it defines (i) the elements that are managed, (ii) how a user accesses them, and (iii) how they can be reported. A MIB can be depicted as an abstract tree with an unnamed root; individual items are represented as leaves of the tree. An object identifier uniquely identifies a MIB object in the tree. The organization of object identifiers is similar to a telephone number hierarchy; they are organized hierarchically with specific digits assigned by different organizations. The Structure of Management Information (SMI) defines the rules for describing the management information. The SMI specifies that all managed objects have a name, a syntax, and an encoding mechanism. The name is used as the object identifier. The syntax defines the data type of the object. The SMI syntax uses a subset of the Abstract Syntax Notation One (ASN.1) definitions. The encoding mechanism describes how the information associated with the managed object is formatted as a series of data items for transmission on the network.

Network elements are monitored and controlled using four basic SNMP commands: *read*, *write*, *trap*, and traversal operations. The read command is used by an NMS to monitor NEs. An NMS examines different variables that are maintained by NEs. The write command is used by an NMS to control NEs. With the write command, an NMS changes the values of variables stored within NEs. The trap command is used by NEs to asynchronously report events to an NMS. When certain types of events occur, an NE sends a trap to an NMS. The traversal operations are used by the NMS to determine the variables an NE supports and to sequentially gather information in a variable table, such as a routing table.

The SNMP is a simple request/response protocol that can send multiple requests. Six SNMP operations are defined. The Get operation allows an NMS to retrieve an object instant from an agent. The GetNext operation allows an NMS to retrieve the next object instance from a table or list within an agent. The GetBulk operation allows an NMS to acquire large amounts of related information without repeatedly invoking the GetNext operation. The Set operation allows an NMS to set values for object instances within an agent. The Trap operation is used by an agent to asynchronously inform an NMS of some event. The Inform operation allows one NMS to send trap information to another.

The SNMP messages consist of two parts: a header and a protocol data unit (PDU). The message header contains two fields, namely, a version number and a community name. A PDU has the following fields: PDU type, request ID, error status, error index, and variable bindings. The following descriptions summarize the different fields:

- **Version Number:** The version number specifies the version of the SNMP being used.
- **Community Name:** This defines an access environment for a group of NMSs. NMSs within a community are said to exist within the same administrative domain. Community names serve as a weak form of authentication because devices that do not know the proper community name are precluded from SNMP operations.
- **PDU Type:** This specifies the type of PDU being transmitted.
- **Request ID:** A request ID is associated with the corresponding response.
- **Error Status:** This indicates an error and shows an error type. In GetBulk operations, this field becomes a nonrepeater field by defining the number of requested variables listed that should be retrieved no more than once from the beginning of the request. The field is used when some of the variables are scalar objects with one variable.

- **Error Index:** An error index associates the error with a particular object instance. In GetBulk operations, this field becomes a Max-repetitions field. This field defines the maximum number of times that other variables beyond those specified by the nonrepeater field should be retrieved.

- **Variable Bindings (varbinds):** This comprises the data of an SNMP PDU. Variables bindings associate particular object instances with their current values (with the exception of Get and GetNext requests, for which the value is ignored).

8.3.5 Management Information Base Tests

The MIB tests are designed to verify (i) standard MIBs including MIB II and (ii) enterprise MIBs specific to the system. Tests may include verification of the agent within the system that implements the objects it claims to. Every MIB object is tested with the following primitives: Get, GetNext, GetBulk, and Set. It should be verified that all the counters related to the MIBs are incremented correctly and that the agent is capable of generating (i) well known traps (e.g., coldstart, warmstart, linkdown, linkup) and (ii) application-specific traps (X.25 restart and X.25 reset).

8.3.6 Graphical User Interface Tests

In modern-day software applications, users access functionalities via GUIs. Users of the client-server technology find it convenient to use GUI based applications. The GUI tests are designed to verify the interface to the users of an application. These tests verify different components (objects) such as icons, menu bars, dialogue boxes, scroll bars, list boxes, and radio buttons. Ease of use (usability) of the GUI design and output reports from the viewpoint of actual system users should be checked. Usefulness of the online help, error messages, tutorials, and user manuals are verified. The GUI can be utilized to test the functionality behind the interface, such as accurate response to database queries. GUIs need to be compatible, as discussed in Section 8.5, and consistent across different operating systems, environments, and mouse-driven and keyboard-driven inputs.

Similar to GUI testing, another branch of testing, called *usability testing*, has been evolving over the past several years. The usability characteristics which can be tested include the following:

- **Accessibility:** Can users enter, navigate, and exit with relative ease?

- **Responsiveness:** Can users do what they want and when they want in a way that is clear? It includes ergonomic factors such as color, shape, sound, and font size.

- **Efficiency:** Can users do what they want with a minimum number of steps and time?

- **Comprehensibility:** Do users understand the product structure with a minimum amount of effort?

8.3.7 Security Tests

Security tests are designed to verify that the system meets the security requirements: *confidentiality*, *integrity*, and *availability*. Confidentiality is the requirement that data and the processes be protected from unauthorized disclosure. Integrity is the requirement that data and process be protected from unauthorized modification. Availability is the requirement that data and processes be protected from the denial of service to authorized users. The security requirements testing approach alone demonstrates whether the stated security requirements have been satisfied regardless of whether or not those requirements are adequate. Most software specifications do not include negative and constraint requirements. Security testing should include negative scenarios such as misuse and abuse of the software system. The objective of security testing is to demonstrate [3] the following:

- The software behaves securely and consistently under all conditions—both expected and unexpected.
- If the software fails, the failure does not leave the software, its data, or its resources to attack.
- Obscure areas of code and dormant functions cannot be compromised or exploited.
- Interfaces and interactions among components at the application, framework/middleware, and operating system levels are consistently secure.
- Exception and error handling mechanisms resolve all faults and errors in ways that do not leave the software, its resources, its data, or its environment vulnerable to unauthorized modification or denial-of-service attack.

The popularity of the Internet and wireless data communications technologies have created new types security threats, such as un-authorized access to the wireless data networks, eavesdropping on transmitted data traffic, and denial of service attack [4]. Even within an enterprise, wireless local area network intruders can operate inconspicuously because they do not need a physical connection to the network [5]. Several new techniques are being developed to combat these kinds of security threats. Tests are designed to ensure that these techniques work—and this is a challenging task. Useful types of security tests include the following:

- Verify that only authorized accesses to the system are permitted. This may include authentication of user ID and password and verification of expiry of a password.
- Verify the correctness of both encryption and decryption algorithms for systems where data/messages are encoded.
- Verify that illegal reading of files, to which the perpetrator is not authorized, is not allowed.
- Ensure that virus checkers prevent or curtail entry of viruses into the system.
- Ensure that the system is available to authorized users when a zero-day attack occurs.

- Try to identify any "backdoors" in the system usually left open by the software developers. Buffer overflows are the most commonly found vulnerability in code that can be exploited to compromise the system. Try to break into the system by exploiting the backdoors.

- Verify the different protocols used by authentication servers, such as Remote Authentication Dial-in User Services (RADIUS), Lightweight Directory Access Protocol (LDAP), and NT LAN Manager (NTLM).

- Verify the secure protocols for client–server communications, such as the Secure Sockets Layer (SSL). The SSL provides a secure channel between clients and servers that choose to use the protocol for web sessions. The protocol serves two functions: (i) authenticate the web servers and/or clients and (ii) encrypt the communication channel.

- Verify the IPSec protocol. Unlike the SSL, which provides services at layer 4 and secures the communications between two applications, IPSec works at layer 3 and secures communications happening on the network.

- Verify different wireless security protocols, such as the Extensible Authentication Protocol (EAP), the Transport Layer Security (TLS) Protocol, the Tunneled Transport Layer Security (TTLS) Protocol, and the Protected Extensible Authentication Protocol (PEAP).

8.3.8   Feature Tests

Feature tests are designed to verify any additional functionalities which are defined in the requirement specifications but not covered in the above categories. Examples of those tests are data conversion and cross-functionality tests. Data conversion testing is testing of programs or procedures that are used to convert data from an existing system to a replacement system. An example is testing of a migration tool that converts a Microsoft Access database to MySQL format. Cross-functionality testing provides additional tests of the interdependencies among functions. For example, the verification of the interactions between NEs and an element management system in a 1xEV-DO wireless data network, as illustrated later in Figure 8.5, is considered as cross-functionality testing.

8.4   ROBUSTNESS TESTS

Robustness means how sensitive a system is to erroneous input and changes in its operational environment. Tests in this category are designed to verify how gracefully the system behaves in error situations and in a changed operational environment. The purpose is to deliberately break the system, not as an end in itself, but as a means to find error. It is difficult to test for every combination of different operational states of the system or undesirable behavior of the environment. Hence, a reasonable number of tests are selected from each group illustrated in Figure 8.4 and discussed below.

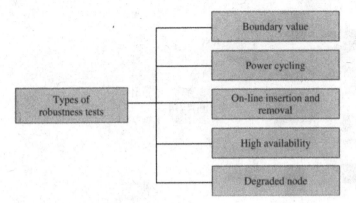

Figure 8.4   Types of robustness tests.

8.4.1 Boundary Value Tests

Boundary value tests are designed to cover boundary conditions, special values, and system defaults. The tests include providing invalid input data to the system and observing how the system reacts to the invalid input. The system should respond with an error message or initiate an error processing routine. It should be verified that the system handles boundary values (below or above the valid values) for a subset of configurable attributes. Examples of such tests for the SNMP protocol are as follows:

- Verify that an error response wrong_type is generated when the Set primitive is used to provision a variable whose type does not match the type defined in the MIB.
- Verify that an error response wrong_value is generated when the Set primitive is used to configure a varbind list with one of the varbinds set to an invalid value. For example, if the varbind can have values from set 0,1,2,3, then the input value can be − 1 to generate a wrong_value response.
- Verify that an error response too_big is generated when the Set primitive is used to configure a list of 33 varbinds. This is because the Set primitive accepts 32 varbinds at a time.
- Verify that an error response not_writable is generated when the Set primitive is used to configure a variable as defined in the MIB.
- Assuming that the SNMP protocol can support up to 1024 communities, verify that it is not possible to create the 1025th community.

Examples of robustness tests for the 1xEV-DO network, as shown in Figure 8.5, are as follows:

- Assuming that an EMS can support up to 300 NEs, verify that the EMS cannot support the 301st NE. Check the error message from the EMS when the user tries to configure the 301st network element.

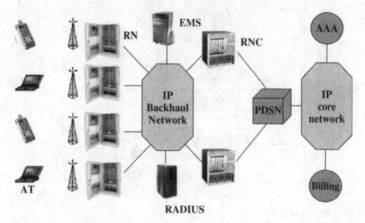

Figure 8.5   Typical 1xEV-DO radio access network. (Courtesy of Airvana, Inc.)

- Assuming that an RNC can support 160,000 simultaneous sessions, verify that the 160,001th session cannot be established on an RNC. Check the error message from the EMS when the user tries to establish the 160,001th session.
- Assuming that a base transceiver station (BTS) can support up to 93 simultaneous users, verify that the 94th user cannot be connected to a BTS.

8.4.2   Power Cycling Tests

Power cycling tests are executed to ensure that, when there is a power glitch in a deployment environment, the system can recover from the glitch to be back in normal operation after power is restored. As an example, verify that the boot test is successful every time it is executed during power cycling.

8.4.3   On-Line Insertion and Removal Tests

On-line insertion and removal (OIR) tests are designed to ensure that on-line insertion and removal of modules, incurred during both idle and heavy load operations, are gracefully handled and recovered. The system then returns to normal operation after the failure condition is removed. The primary objective is to ensure that the system recovers from an OIR event without rebooting or crashing any other components. OIR tests are conducted to ensure the fault-free operation of the system while a faulty module is replaced. As an example, while replacing an Ethernet card, the system should not crash.

8.4.4   High-Availability Tests

High-availability tests are designed to verify the redundancy of individual modules, including the software that controls these modules. The goal is to verify that the system gracefully and quickly recovers from hardware and software failures without adversely impacting the operation of the system. The concept of high availability is also known as fault tolerance. High availability is realized by means of proactive methods to maximize service up-time and to minimize the downtime. One module operates in the active mode while another module is in the standby mode to achieve $1 + 1$ redundancy. For this mode of operation, tests are designed to verify the following:

- A standby module generates an OIR event, that is, hot swapped, without affecting the normal operation of the system.
- The *recovery time* does not exceed a predefined limit while the system is operational. Recovery time is the time it takes for an operational module to become a standby module and the standby module to become operational.
- A server can automatically switch over from an active mode to a standby mode in case a fail-over event occurs. A fail-over is said to occur when a standby server takes over the workload of an active server.

Tests can be designed to verify that a fail-over does not happen without any *observable failure*. A fail-over without an observable failure is called *silent fail-over*. This can only be observed during the load and stability tests described in Section 8.9. Whenever a silent fail-over occurs, a causal analysis must be conducted to determine its cause.

8.4.5   Degraded Node Tests

Degraded node (also known as failure containment) tests verify the operation of a system after a portion of the system becomes nonoperational. It is a useful test for all mission-critical applications. Examples of degraded node tests are as follows:

- Cut one of the four T1 physical connections from one router to another router and verify that load balancing occurs among the rest of the three T1 physical connections. Confirm that packets are equally distributed among the three operational T1 connections.
- Disable the primary port of a router and verify that the message traffic passes through alternative ports with no discernible interruption of service to end users. Next, reactivate the primary port and verify that the router returns to normal operation.

Example of 1xEV-DO Wireless Data Networks The code division multiple-access (CDMA) 2000 1xEV-DO (one-time evolution, data only) is a standardized technology to deliver high data rate at the air interface between an access terminal (AT) and a base transceiver station (BTS), also known as a radio node (RN) [6–8]. The 1xEV-DO Revision 0 delivers a peak data rate of 2.54 Mbits/s on the forward link (from a BTS to an AT) using only 1.25 MHz of spectrum width and a peak data rate of 153.6 kbits/s on the reverse link. We show an architecture for connecting all the BTS with the Internet (IP core network) in Figure 8.5. In this architecture, a base station controller (BSC), also known as a radio network controller (RNC), need not be directly connected by dedicated, physical links with a set of BTSs. Instead, the BTSs are connected to the RNCs via an IP back-haul network. Such an interconnection results in flexible control of the BTSs by the RNCs. The RNCs are connected with the Internet (IP core network) via one or more packet data serving nodes (PDSNs). Finally, the EMS allows the operator to manage the 1xEV-DO network.

The ATs (laptop, PDA, mobile telephone) implement the end-user side of the 1xEV-DO and TCP/IP. The ATs communicate with the RNs over the 1xEV-DO airlink. The RNs are the components that terminate the airlink to/from the ATs. The functions performed by the RNs are (i) control and processing of the physical airlink, (ii) processing of the 1xEV-DO media access control (MAC) layer, and (iii) communication via a back-haul network to the RNC. In addition, RNs in conjunction with the RNCs perform the softer handoff mobility function of the 1xEV-DO protocol, where an AT is in communication with multiple sector antennas of the same RN.

An RNC is an entity that terminates the higher layer components of the 1xEV-DO protocol suite. An RNC has logical interfaces to RNs, the authentication, authorization, and accounting (AAA) servers, other RNCs, and the PDSN. An RNC terminates 1xEV-DO signaling interactions from the ATs and processes the user traffic to pass it on to the PDSN. It manages radio resources across all the RNs in its domain and performs mobility management in the form of softer and soft handoffs. The AAA servers are carrier-class computing devices running RADIUS protocol and having an interface to a database. These servers may be configured for two AAA functions, namely, access network AAA and core network AAA. The access network AAA is connected to the RNCs, which perform the terminal authentication function. The core network AAA is connected to the PDSN, which performs user authentication at the IP level. The PDSN is a specialized router implementing IP and mobile IP. The PDSN may be implemented as a single, highly available device or as multiple devices clustered together to form a high-availability device. The PDSN is the edge of the core IP network with respect to the AT, that is, the point where (i) the Point-to-Point Protocol (PPP) traffic of the AT is terminated, (ii) the user is authenticated, and (iii) the IP service options are determined. The core IP network is essentially a network of routers. The EMS server is a system that directly controls the NEs. It is responsible for fault handling, network configuration, and statistics management of the network interfaces. The EMS server interfaces with the NEs via TCP/IP. The EMS server is accessed via a client—and not directly—by the network management staff of a wireless operator. An EMS client is a workstation from which a network operator manages the radio access network.

8.5 INTEROPERABILITY TESTS

In this category, tests are designed to verify the ability of the system to interoperate with third-party products. An interoperability test typically combines different network elements in one test environment to ensure that they work together. In other words, tests are designed to ensure that the software can be connected with other systems and operated. In many cases, during interoperability tests, users may require the hardware devices to be interchangeable, removable, or reconfigurable. Often, a system will have a set of commands or menus that allow users to make the configuration changes. The reconfiguration activities during interoperability tests are known as *configuration testing* [9]. Another kind of interoperability test is called a *(backward) compatibility test*. Compatibility tests verify that the system works the same way across different platforms, operating systems, and database management systems. Backward compatibility tests verify that the current software build flawlessly works with older version of platforms. As an example, let us consider a 1xEV-DO radio access network as shown in Figure 8.5. In this scenario, tests are designed to ensure the interoperability of the RNCs with the following products from different vendors: (i) PDSN, (ii) PDA with 1xEV-DO card, (iii) AAA server, (iv) PC with 1xEV-DO card, (v) laptop with 1xEV-DO card, (vi) routers from different vendors, (vii) BTS or RNC, and (viii) switches.

8.6 PERFORMANCE TESTS

Performance tests are designed to determine the performance of the actual system compared to the expected one. The performance metrics needed to be measured vary from application to application. An example of expected performance is: The response time should be less than 1 millisecond 90% of the time in an application of the "push-to-talk" type. Another example of expected performance is: A transaction in an on-line system requires a response of less than 1 second 90% of the time. One of the goals of router performance testing is to determine the system resource utilization, for maximum aggregation throughput rate considering zero drop packets. In this category, tests are designed to verify response time, execution time, throughput, resource utilization, and traffic rate.

For performance tests, one needs to be clear about the specific data to be captured in order to evaluate performance metrics. For example, if the objective is to evaluate the response time, then one needs to capture (i) end-to-end response time (as seen by external user), (ii) CPU time, (iii) network connection time, (iv) database access time, (v) network connection time, and (vi) waiting time.

Some examples of performance test objectives for an EMS server are as follows:

- Record the CPU and memory usage of the EMS server when 5, 10, 15, 20, and 25 traps per second are generated by the NEs. This test will validate the ability of the EMS server to receive and process those number of traps per second.
- Record the CPU and memory usage of the EMS server when log files of different sizes, say, 100, 150, 200, 250 and 300 kb, are transferred from NEs to the EMS server once every 15 minutes.

Some examples of performance test objectives of SNMP primitives are as follows:

- Calculate the response time of the Get primitive for a single varbind from a standard MIB or an enterprise MIB.

- Calculate the response time of the GetNext primitive for a single varbind from a standard MIB or an enterprise MIB.
- Calculate the response time of the GetBulk primitive for a single varbind from a standard MIB or an enterprise MIB.
- Calculate the response time of the Set primitive for a single varbind from a standard MIB or an enterprise MIB.

Some examples of performance test objectives of a 1xEV-DO Revision 0 are as follows:

- Measure the maximum BTS forward-link throughput.
- Measure the maximum BTS reverse-link throughput.
- Simultaneously generate maximum-rate BTS forward- and reverse-link data capacities.
- Generate the maximum number of permissible session setups per hour.
- Measure the AT-initiated connection setup delay.
- Measure the maximum BTS forward-link throughput per sector carrier for 16 users in the 3-km/h mobility model.
- Measure the maximum BTS forward-link throughput per sector carrier for 16 users in the 30-km/h mobility model.

The results of performance are evaluated for their acceptability. If the performance metric is unsatisfactory, then actions are taken to improve it. The performance improvement can be achieved by rewriting the code, allocating more resources, and redesigning the system.

8.7   SCALABILITY TESTS

All man-made artifacts have engineering limits. For example, a car can move at a certain maximum speed in the best of road conditions, a telephone switch can handle a certain maximum number of calls at any given moment, a router has a certain maximum number of interfaces, and so on. In this group, tests are designed to verify that the system can scale up to its engineering limits. A system may work in a limited-use scenario but may not scale up. The run time of a system may grow exponentially with demand and may eventually fail after a certain limit. The idea is to test the limit of the system, that is, the magnitude of demand that can be placed on the system while continuing to meet latency and throughput requirements. A system which works acceptably at one level of demand may not scale up to another level. Scaling tests are conducted to ensure that the system response time remains the same or increases by a small amount as the number of users are increased. Systems may scale until they reach one or more engineering limits. There are three major causes of these limitations:

i. Data storage limitations—limits on counter field size and allocated buffer space

ii. Network bandwidth limitations—Ethernet speed 10 Mbps and T1 card line rate 1.544 Mbps

iii. Speed limit—CPU speed in megahertz

Extrapolation is often used to predict the limit of scalability. The system is tested on an increasingly larger series of platforms or networks or with an increasingly larger series of workloads. Memory and CPU utilizations are measured and plotted against the size of the network or the size of the load. The trend is extrapolated from the measurable and known to the large-scale operation. As an example, for a database transaction system calculate the system performance, that is, CPU utilization and memory utilization for 100, 200, 400, and 800 transactions per second, then draw graphs of number of transactions against CPU and memory utilization. Extrapolate the measured results to 20,0000 transactions. The drawback in this technique is that the trend line may not be accurate. The system behavior may not degrade gradually and gracefully as the parameters are scaled up. Examples of scalability tests for a 1xEV-DO network are as follows:

- Verify that the EMS server can support the maximum number of NEs, say, 300, without any degradation in EMS performance.
- Verify that the maximum number of BTS, say, 200, can be homed onto one BSC.
- Verify that the maximum number of EV-DO sessions, say, 16,000, can be established on one RNC.
- Verify that the maximum number of EV-DO connections, say, 18,400, can be established on one RNC.
- Verify that the maximum BTS capacity for the three-sector configuration is 93 users per BTS.
- Verify the maximum softer handoff rate with acceptable number of call drops per BTS. Repeat the process every hour for 24 hours.
- Verify the maximum soft handoff rate with no call drops per BTS. Repeat the process for every hour for 24 hours.

8.8 STRESS TESTS

The goal of stress testing is to evaluate and determine the behavior of a software component while the offered load is in excess of its designed capacity. The system is deliberately stressed by pushing it to and beyond its specified limits. Stress tests include deliberate contention for scarce resources and testing for incompatibilities. It ensures that the system can perform acceptably under worst-case conditions under an expected peak load. If the limit is exceeded and the system does fail, then the recovery mechanism should be invoked. Stress tests are targeted to bring out the problems associated with one or more of the following:

- Memory leak
- Buffer allocation and memory carving

One way to design a stress test is to impose the maximum limits on all system performance characteristics at the same time, such as the response time, availability, and throughput thresholds. This literally provides the set of worst-case conditions under which the system is still expected to operate acceptably.

The best way to identify system bottlenecks is to perform stress testing from different locations inside and outside the system. For example, individually test each component of the system, starting with the innermost components that go directly to the core of the system, progressively move outward, and finally test from remote locations far outside the system. Testing each link involves pushing it to its full-load capacity to determine the correct operation. After all the individual components are tested beyond their highest capacity, test the full system by simultaneously testing all links to the system at their highest capacity. The load can be deliberately and incrementally increased until the system eventually does fail; when the system fails, observe the causes and locations of failures. This information will be useful in designing later versions of the system; the usefulness lies in improving the robustness of the system or developing procedures for a disaster recovery plan. Some examples of stress tests of a 1xEV-DO network are as follows:

- Verify that repeated establishment and teardown of maximum telnet sessions to the BSC and BTS executed over 24 hours do not result in (i) leak in the number of buffers or amount of memory or (ii) significant increase in the degree of fragmentation of available memory. Tests should be done for both graceful and abrupt teardowns of the telnet session.

- Stress the two Ethernet interfaces of a BTS by sending Internet traffic for 24 hours and verify that no memory leak or crash occurs.

- Stress the four T1/E1 interfaces of a BTS by sending Internet traffic for 24 hours and verify that no memory leak or crash occurs.

- Verify that repeated establishment and teardown of AT connections through a BSC executed over 24 hours do not result in (i) leaks in the number of buffers or amount of memory and (ii) significant increase in the degree of fragmentation of available memory. The sessions remain established for the duration of the test.

- Verify that repeated soft and softer handoffs executed over 24 hours do not result in leaks in the number of buffers or amount of memory and do not significantly increase the degree of fragmentation of available memory.

- Verify that repeated execution of all CLI commands over 24 hours do not result in leaks in the number of buffers or amount of memory and do not significantly increase the degree of fragmentation of available memory.

Examples of stress tests of an SNMP agent are as follows:

- Verify that repeated walking of the MIBs via an SNMP executed over 24 hours do not result in leaks in number of buffers or amount of memory and do not significantly increase the degree of fragmentation of available memory

- Verify that an SNMP agent can successfully respond to a GetBulk request that generates a large PDU, preferably of the maximum size, which is 8 kbytes under the following CPU utilization: 0, 50, and 90%.

- Verify that an SNMP agent can simultaneously handle multiple GetNext and GetBulk requests over a 24-hour testing period under the following CPU utilizations: 0, 50, and 90%.

- Verify that an SNMP agent can handle multiple Get requests containing a large number of varbinds over a 24-hour testing period under the following CPU utilizations: 0, 50, and 90%.

- Verify that an SNMP agent can handle multiple Set requests containing a large number of varbinds over a 24-hour testing period under the following CPU utilizations: 0, 50, and 90%.

8.9 LOAD AND STABILITY TESTS

Load and stability tests are designed to ensure that the system remains stable for a long period of time under full load. A system might function flawlessly when tested by a few careful testers who exercise it in the intended manner. However, when a large number of users are introduced with incompatible systems and applications that run for months without restarting, a number of problems are likely to occur: (i) the system slows down, (ii) the system encounters functionality problems, (iii) the system silently fails over, and (iv) the system crashes altogether. Load and stability testing typically involves exercising the system with virtual users and measuring the performance to verify whether the system can support the anticipated load. This kind of testing helps one to understand the ways the system will fare in real-life situations. With such an understanding, one can anticipate and even prevent load-related problems. Often, operational profiles are used to guide load and stability testing [10]. The idea is to test the system the way it will be actually used in the field. The concept of *operation profile* is discussed in Chapter 15 on software reliability.

Examples of load and stability test objectives for an EMS server are as follows:

- Verify the EMS server performance during quick polling of the maximum number of nodes, say, 300. Document how long it takes to quick poll the 300 nodes. Monitor the CPU utilization during quick polling and verify that the results are within the acceptable range. The reader is reminded that quick polling is used to check whether or not a node is reachable by doing a ping on the node using the SNMP Get operation.

- Verify the EMS performance during full polling of the maximum number of nodes, say, 300. Document how long it takes to full poll the 300 nodes. Monitor the CPU utilization during full polling and verify that the results are within the acceptable range. Full polling is used to check the status and any configuration changes of the nodes that are managed by the server.

- Verify the EMS server behavior during an SNMP trap storm. Generate four traps per second from each of the 300 nodes. Monitor the CPU utilization during trap handling and verify that the results are within an acceptable range.
- Verify the EMS server's ability to perform software downloads to the maximum number of nodes, say, 300. Monitor CPU utilization during software download and verify that the results are within an acceptable range.
- Verify the EMS server's performance during log file transfers of the maximum number of nodes. Monitor the CPU utilization during log transfer and verify that the results are within an acceptable range.

In load and stability testing, the objective is to ensure that the system can operate on a large scale for several months, whereas, in stress testing, the objective is to break the system by overloading it to observe the locations and causes of failures.

8.10 RELIABILITY TESTS

Reliability tests are designed to measure the ability of the system to remain operational for long periods of time. The reliability of a system is typically expressed in terms of mean time to failure (MTTF). As we test the software and move through the system testing phase, we observe failures and try to remove the defects and continue testing. As this progresses, we record the time durations between successive failures. Let these successive time intervals be denoted by $t_1, t_2, \ldots, t_i$. The average of all the i time intervals is called the MTTF. After a failure is observed, the developers analyze and fix the defects, which consumes some time—let us call this interval the *repair* time. The average of all the repair times is known as the mean time to repair (MTTR). Now we can calculate a value called mean time between failures (MTBF) as MTBF = MTTF + MTTR. The random testing technique discussed in Chapter 9 is used for reliability measurement. Software reliability modeling and testing are discussed in Chapter 15 in detail.

8.11 REGRESSION TESTS

In this category, new tests are not designed. Instead, test cases are selected from the existing pool and executed to ensure that nothing is broken in the new version of the software. The main idea in regression testing is to verify that no defect has been introduced into the unchanged portion of a system due to changes made elsewhere in the system. During system testing, many defects are revealed and the code is modified to fix those defects. As a result of modifying the code, one of four different scenarios can occur for each fix [11]:

- The reported defect is fixed.
- The reported defect could not be fixed in spite of making an effort.

- The reported defect has been fixed, but something that used to work before has been failing.
- The reported defect could not be fixed in spite of an effort, and something that used to work before has been failing.

Given the above four possibilities, it appears straightforward to reexecute every test case from version $n - 1$ to version n before testing anything new. Such a full test of a system may be prohibitively expensive. Moreover, new software versions often feature many new functionalities in addition to the defect fixes. Therefore, regression tests would take time away from testing new code. Regression testing is an expensive task; a subset of the test cases is carefully selected from the existing test suite to (i) maximize the likelihood of uncovering new defects and (ii) reduce the cost of testing. Methods for test selection for regression testing are discussed in Chapter 13.

8.12 DOCUMENTATION TESTS

Documentation testing means verifying the technical accuracy and readability of the user manuals, including the tutorials and the on-line help. Documentation testing is performed at three levels as explained in the following:

Read Test: In this test a documentation is reviewed for clarity, organization, flow, and accuracy without executing the documented instructions on the system.

Hands-On Test: The on-line help is exercised and the error messages verified to evaluate their accuracy and usefulness.

Functional Test: The instructions embodied in the documentation are followed to verify that the system works as it has been documented.

The following concrete tests are recommended for documentation testing:

- Read all the documentations to verify (i) correct use of grammar, (ii) consistent use of the terminology, and (iii) appropriate use of graphics where possible.
- Verify that the glossary accompanying the documentation uses a standard, commonly accepted terminology and that the glossary correctly defines the terms.
- Verify that there exists an index for each of the documents and the index block is reasonably rich and complete. Verify that the index section points to the correct pages.
- Verify that there is no internal inconsistency within the documentation.
- Verify that the on-line and printed versions of the documentation are same.
- Verify the installation procedure by executing the steps described in the manual in a real environment.

- Verify the troubleshooting guide by inserting error and then using the guide to troubleshoot the error.

- Verify the software release notes to ensure that these accurately describe (i) the changes in features and functionalities between the current release and the previous ones and (ii) the set of known defects and their impact on the customer.

- Verify the on-line help for its (i) usability, (ii) integrity, (iii) usefulness of the hyperlinks and cross-references to related topics, (iv) effectiveness of table look-up, and (v) accuracy and usefulness of indices.

- Verify the configuration section of the user guide by configuring the system as described in the documentation.

- Finally, use the document while executing the system test cases. Walk through the planned or existing user work activities and procedures using the documentation to ensure that the documentation is consistent with the user work.

8.13 REGULATORY TESTS

In this category, the final system is shipped to the regulatory bodies in those countries where the product is expected to be marketed. The idea is to obtain compliance marks on the product from those bodies. The regulatory approval bodies of various countries have been shown in Table 8.2. Most of these regulatory bodies issue safety and EMC (electromagnetic compatibility)/EMI (electromagnetic interference) compliance certificates (emission and immunity). The regulatory agencies are interested in identifying flaws in software that have potential safety consequences. The safety requirements are primarily based on their own published standards. For example, the CSA (Canadian Standards Association) mark is one of the most recognized, accepted, and trusted symbols in the world. The CSA mark on a product means that the CSA has tested a representative sample of the product and determined that the product meets the CSA's requirements. Safety-conscious and concerned consumers look for the CSA mark on products they buy. Similarly, the CE (Conformité Européenne) mark on a product indicates conformity to the European Union directive with respect to safety, health, environment, and consumer protection. In order for a product to be sold in the United States, the product needs to pass certain regulatory requirements of the Federal Communications Commission (FCC).

Software safety is defined in terms of *hazards*. A hazard is a state of a system or a physical situation which when combined with certain environmental conditions could lead to an accident or mishap. An *accident* or *mishap* is an unintended event or series of events that results in death, injury, illness, damage or loss of property, or harm to the environment [12]. A hazard is a logical precondition to an accident. Whenever a hazard is present, the consequence can be an accident. The existence of a hazard state does not mean that an accident will happen eventually. The concept of safety is concerned with preventing hazards.

TABLE 8.2   Regulatory Approval Bodies of Different Countries

Country	Regulatory Certification Approval Body
Argentina	IRAM is a nonprofit private association and is the national certification body of Argentina for numerous product categories. The IRAM safety mark is rated based on compliance with the safety requirements of a national IRAM standard.
Australia and New Zealand	The Australian Communications Authority (ACA) and the Radio Spectrum Management Group (RSM) of New Zealand have agreed upon a harmonized scheme in producing the C-tick mark that regulates product EMC compliance.
Canada	Canadian Standards Association
Czech Republic	The Czech Republic is the first European country to adopt conformity assessment regulations based on the European Union CE mark without additional approval certification or testing.
European Union	Conformité Européenne
Japan	The VCCI mark (Voluntary Control Council for Interference by Information Technology Equipment) is administered by VCCI for information technology equipment (ITE) sold in Japan.
Korea	All products sold in Korea are required to be compliant and subject to the MIC (Ministry of Information and Communication) mark certification. EMC and safety testing are both requirements.
Mexico	The products must be tested in Mexico for the mandatory NOM (Normality of Mexico) mark.
Peoples Republic of China	The CCC (China Compulsory Certification) mark is required for a wide range of products sold in the Peoples Republic of China.
Poland	The Polish Safety B-mark (B for *bezpieczny*, which means "safe") must be shown on all hazardous domestic and imported products. Poland does not accept the CE mark of the European Union.
Russia	GOST-R certification. This certification system is administered by the Russian State Committee on Standardization, Metrology, and Certification (Gosstandart). Gosstandart oversees and develops industry mandatory and voluntary certification programs.
Singapore	The PSB mark is issued by the Singapore Productivity and Standards Board. The Safety Authority (PSB) is the statutory body appointed by the Ministry of Trade and Industry to administer the regulations.
South Africa	The safety scheme for electrical goods is operated by the South African Bureau of Standards (SABS) on behalf of the government. Compliance can be provided by the SABS based on the submission of the test report from any recognized laboratory.
Taiwan	Most products sold in Taiwan must be approved in accordance with the regulations as set forth by the BSMI (Bureau of Standards, Metrology and Inspection).
United States	Federal Communications Commission

A software in isolation cannot do physical damage. However, a software in the context of a system and an embedding environment could be vulnerable. For example, a software module in a database application is not hazardous by itself, but when it is embedded in a missile navigation system, it could be hazardous. If a missile takes a U-turn because of a software error in the navigation system and destroys the submarine that launched it, then it is not a safe software. Therefore, the manufacturers and the regulatory agencies strive to ensure that the software is safe the first time it is released.

The organizations developing safety-critical software systems should have a safety assurance (SA) program to eliminate hazards or reduce their associated risk to an acceptable level [13]. Two basic tasks are performed by an SA engineering team as follows:

- Provide methods for identifying, tracking, evaluating, and eliminating hazards associated with a system.

- Ensure that safety is embedded into the design and implementation in a timely and cost-effective manner such that the risk created by the user/operator error is minimized. As a consequence, the potential damage in the event of a mishap is minimized.

8.14 SUMMARY

In this chapter we presented a taxonomy of system tests with examples from various domains. We explained the following categories of system tests:

- *Basic tests* provide an evidence that the system can be installed, configured, and brought to an operational state. We described five types of basic tests: boot, upgrade/downgrade, light emitting diode, diagnostic, and command line interface tests.

- *Functionality tests* provide comprehensive testing over the full range of the requirements within the capabilities of the system. In this category, we described eight types of tests: communication systems, module, logging and tracing, element management systems, management information base, graphical user interface, security, and feature tests.

- *Robustness tests* determine the system recovery process from various error conditions or failure situations. In this category, we described five types of robustness tests: boundary value, power cycling, on-line insertion and removal, high availability, degraded node tests.

- *Interoperability tests* determine if the system can interoperate with other third-party products.

- *Performance tests* measure the performance characteristics of the system, for example, throughput and response time, under various conditions.

- *Scalability tests* determine the scaling limits of the system.

- *Stress tests* stress the system in order to determine the limitations of the system and determine the manner in which failures occur if the system fails.

- *Load and stability tests* provide evidence that, when the system is loaded with a large number of users to its maximum capacity, the system is stable for a long period of time under heavy traffic.

- *Reliability tests* measure the ability of the system to keep operating over long periods of time.

- *Regression tests* determine that the system remains stable as it cycles through the integration with other projects and through maintenance tasks.

- *Documentation tests* ensure that the system's user guides are accurate and usable.

- *Regulatory tests* ensure that the system meets the requirements of government regulatory bodies. Most of these regulatory bodies issue safety, emissions, and immunity compliance certificates.

LITERATURE REVIEW

A good discussion of software safety concepts, such as *mishap, hazard, hazard analysis, fault tree analysis, event tree analysis, failure modes and effects analysis, and firewall*, can be found in Chapter 5 of the book by Freidman and Voas [13]. The book presents useful examples and opinions concerning the relationship of these concepts to software reliability.

For those readers who are actively involved in usability testing or are interested in a more detailed treatment of the topic, Jeffrey Rubin's book (*Handbook of Usability Testing—How to Plan, Design, and Conduct Effective Tests*, Wiley, New York, 1994) provides an excellent guide. Rubin describes four types of usability tests in great detail: (i) exploratory, (ii) assessment, (iii) validation, and (iv) comparison. The book lists several excellent references on the subject in its bibliography section. Memon et al. have conducted innovative research on test adequacy criteria and automated test data generation algorithms that are specifically tailored for programs with graphical user interfaces. The interested readers are recommended to study the following articles:

A. M. Memon, "GUI Testing: Pitfalls and Process," *IEEE Computer*, Vol. 35, No. 8, 2002, pp. 90–91.

A. M. Memon, M. E. Pollock, and M. L. Soffa, "Hierarchical GUI Test Case Generation Using Automated Planning," *IEEE Transactions on Software Engineering*, Vol. 27, No. 2, 2001, pp. 144–155.

A. M. Memon, M. L. Soffa, and M. E. Pollock, "Coverage Criteria for GUI Testing," in *Proceedings of the 9th ACM SIGSOFT International Symposium on Foundation of Software Engineering*, ACM Press, New York 2001, pp. 256–267.

In the above-mentioned work, a GUI is represented as a series of operators that have preconditions and postconditions related to the state of the GUI. This representation classifies the GUI events into four categories: menu-open events, unrestricted-focused events, restricted-focus events, and system interaction events. Menu-open events are normally associated with the usage of the pull-down menus in a GUI. The unrestricted-focus events simply expand the interaction options available to a GUI user, whereas the restricted-focus events require the attention of the user before additional interactions can occur. Finally, system interaction events require the GUI to interact with the actual application.

An excellent collection of essays on the usability and security aspects of a system appears in the book edited by L. F. Cranor and S. Garfinkel (*Security and Usability*, O'Reilly, Sebastopol, CA, 2005). This book contains 34 groundbreaking articles that discuss case studies of usable secure system design. This book is useful for researchers, students, and practitioners in the fields of security and usability.

Mathematically rigorous treatments of performance analysis and concepts related to software performance engineering may be found in the following books:

R. Jain, *The Art of Computer Systems Performance Analysis*, John, New York, 1991.

C. U. Smith, *Performance Engineering of Software Systems*, Addison-Wesley, Reading, MA, 1990.

Each of these books provides a necessary theoretical foundation for our understanding of performance engineering.

REFERENCES

1. D. Rayner. OSI Conformance Testing. *Computer Networks and ISDN Systems*, Vol. **14**, 1987, pp. 79–98.
2. D. K. Udupa. *TMN: Telecommunications Management Network*. McGraw-Hill, New York, 1999.
3. J. Jarzombek and K. M. Goertzel. Security in the Software Cycle. *Crosstalk, Journal of Defense Software Engineering*, September 2006, pp. 4–9.
4. S. Northcutt, L. Zeltser, S. Winters, K. Kent, and R. W. Ritchey. *Inside Network Perimeter Security*, 2nd ed. Sams Publishing, Indianapolis, IN, 2005.
5. K. Sankar, S. Sundaralingam, A. Balinsky, and D. Miller. *Cisco Wireless LAN Security*. Cisco Press, Indianapolis, IN, 2004.
6. IOS for 1 × EV, IS-878, 3Gpp2, http://www.3gpp2.org, June 2001.
7. CDMA2000 IOS Standard, IS-2001, 3Gpp2, http://www.3gpp2.org, Nov. 2001.
8. CDMA2000 High Rate Packet Data Air Interface, IS-856–1, 3Gpp2, http://www.3gpp2.org, Dec. 2001.
9. B. Beizer. *Software Testing and Quality Assurance*. Von Nostrand Reinhold, New York, 1984.
10. A. Avritzer and E. J. Weyuker. The Automatic Generation of Load Test Suites and Assessment of the Resulting Software. *IEEE Transactions on Software Engineering*, September 1995, pp. 705–716.
11. J. A. Whittaker. What Is Software Testing? And Why Is It So Hard? *IEEE Software*, January/February 2000, pp. 70–79.
12. N. G. Leveson. Software Safety: Why, What, and How. *ACM Computing Surveys*, June 1986, pp. 125–163.
13. M. A. Friedman and J. M. Voas. *Software Assessment: Reliability, Safety, Testability*. Wiley, New York, 1995.

Exercises

1. What is an element management system (EMS)? How is it different from a network management station (NMS)?

2. What are the differences between configuration, compatibility, and interoperability testing?

3. What are the differences between performance, stress, and scalability testing? What are the differences between load testing and stress testing?

4. What is the difference between performance and speed?

5. Buffer overflow is the most commonly found vulnerability in network-aware code that can be exploited to compromise a system. Explain the reason.

6. What are zero-day attacks? Discuss its significance with respect to security testing.

7. Discuss the importance of regression testing when developing a new software release. What test cases from the test suite would be more useful in performing a regression test?

8. What are the differences between safety and reliability? What are the differences between safety testing and security testing?

9. What is the similarity between software safety and fault tolerance?

10. For each of the following situations, explain whether it is a hazard or a mishap:

    (a) Water in a swimming pool becomes electrified.

    (b) A room fills with carbon dioxide.

    (c) A car stops abruptly.

    (d) A long-distance telephone company suffers an outage.

    (e) A nuclear weapon is destroyed in an unplanned manner.

11. What are the similarities and differences between quality assurance (QA) and safety assurance (SA)?

12. For your current test project, develop a taxonomy of system tests that you plan to execute against the implementation.

CHAPTER 9

Functional Testing

The test of a first-rate intelligence is the ability to hold two opposed ideas in the mind at the same time, and still retain the ability to function.
— *F. Scott Fitzgerald*

9.1 FUNCTIONAL TESTING CONCEPTS OF HOWDEN

William E. Howden developed the idea of functional testing of programs while visiting the International Mathematics and Statistics Libraries (IMSL) in Houston in 1977–1978. IMSL is presently known as Visual Numerics (http://www.vni.com/). The IMSL libraries are a comprehensive set of mathematical and statistical functions that programmers can embed into their software applications. IMSL uses proven technology that has been thoroughly tested, well documented, and continuously maintained. Howden applied the idea of functional testing to programs from edition 5 of the IMSL package. The errors he discovered can be considered to be of some subtlety to have survived to edition 5 status [1].

A *function* in mathematics is defined to be a set of ordered pairs (X_i, Y_i), where X_i is a vector of input values and Y_i is a vector of output values. In functional testing, a program P is viewed as a *function* that transforms the input vector X_i into an output vector Y_i such that $Y_i = P(X_i)$.

Examples

1. Let $Y_1 = \sqrt{X_1}$. Here, P is a square-root computing function which calculates the squareroot Y_1 of nonnegative integer X_1. The result is assigned to Y_1.

2. Let $Y_2 = \text{C\_compiler}(X_2)$. The program P is viewed as a C_compiler function that produces object code from C program X_2. The object code is held in Y_2.

Software Testing and Quality Assurance: Theory and Practice, Edited by Kshirasagar Naik and Priyadarshi Tripathy
Copyright © 2008 John Wiley & Sons, Inc.

3. Let $Y_3 = $ TelephoneSwitch(X_3). A telephone switch program P produces a variety of tones and voice signals represented by the vector

$$Y_3 = \{\text{idle, dial, ring, fast busy, slow busy tone, voice}\}$$

by processing input data represented by the vector

$$X_3 = \{\text{off hook, on hook, phone number, voice}\}.$$

4. Let $Y_4 = $ sort(X_4). The program P in this example is an implementation of a sorting algorithm which produces a sorted array Y_4 from the input vector $X_4 = \{A, N\}$, where A is the array to be sorted and N is the number of elements in A.

The above four examples suggest that sometimes it is easy to view a program as a function in the mathematical sense and sometimes it is more difficult. It is easier to view a program as a function when the input values are algorithmically, or mathematically, transformed into output values, such as in the first and the fourth examples above. In the fourth example, Y_4 is a certain permutation of the input array A. It is more difficult to view a program as a function when the input values are not directly transformed into the output values. For instance, in the third example above, an *off-hook* input is not mathematically transformed into a *dial tone* output. In functional testing we are not concerned with the details of the mechanism by which an input vector is transformed into an output vector. Instead, a program is treated as a function in the general sense.

Three key elements of a function are its input, output, and expected transformation of input to output. Ignoring the details of the actual transformation of input to output, we analyze the domains of the input and the output variables of programs to generate test data. The four key concepts in functional testing [2] are as follows:

- Precisely identify the domain of each input and each output variable.
- Select values from the data domain of each variable having *important* properties.
- Consider combinations of special values from different input domains to design test cases.
- Consider input values such that the program under test produces special values from the domains of the output variables.

One can identify the domain of an input or an output variable by analyzing the requirements specification and the design documents. In the following sections, we discuss Howden's method for selecting test data from the domains of input and output variables.

9.1.1 Different Types of Variables

In this section, we consider numeric variables, arrays, substructures, and subroutine arguments and their *important* values. These types of variables are commonly used as input to and output from a large number of systems for numeric calculations. The MATLAB package and a number of tax filing software systems are examples of such systems.

Numeric Variable The domain of a numeric variable is specified in one of two ways as follows:

- **A set of discrete values:** An example of this type of domain is MODE = {23, 79} from the Bluetooth specification. The variable MODE is a numeric variable which takes one of the two values from the set {23, 79}. The MODE value is used in a modulo operation to determine the channel frequency for packet transmission.

- **A few contiguous segments of values:** As an example, the gross income input to a tax filing software for a person or company is specified as a value from the range {0, . . . , ∞}. Each contiguous segment is characterized by a *minimum (MIN)* value and a *maximum (MAX)* value.

Example: The inputs and the output variables of the frequency selection box (FSB) module of the Bluetooth wireless communication system are shown in Figure 9.1. Bluetooth communication technology uses a frequency hopping spread-spectrum technique for accessing the wireless medium. A piconet *channel* is viewed as a possibly infinite sequence of *slots*, where one slot is 625 μs long. The frequency on which a data packet will be transmitted during a given slot is computed by the FSB module illustrated in Figure 9.1. The FSB module accepts three input variables MODE, CLOCK, and ADDRESS and generates values of the output variable INDEX. All four are numeric variables. The domains of these variables are characterized as follows:

MODE: The domain of variable MODE is the discrete set {23, 79}.

CLOCK: The CLOCK variable is represented by a 28-bit unsigned number with MIN = 0x0000000 and MAX = 0xFFFFFFFF. The smallest increment

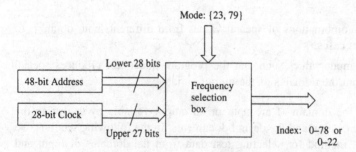

Figure 9.1 Frequency selection box of Bluetooth specification.

in CLOCK represents the elapse of 312.5 μs. The FSB module uses the *upper* 27 bits of the 28-bit CLOCK in frequency calculations.

ADDRESS: The ADDRESS variable is represented by a 48-bit unsigned number. The FSB module uses the *lower* 28 bits of the 48-bit ADDRESS. Therefore, the range of ADDRESS from the viewpoint of the FSB module is specified as follows:

- MIN = 0xyyyyy0000000, where yyyyy is a 20-bit arbitrary value.

- MAX = 0xzzzzzFFFFFFF, where zzzzz is a 20-bit arbitrary value.

INDEX: This variable assumes values in a given range as specified in the following:

- MIN = 0.

- MAX = 22 if MODE = 23.

- MAX = 78 if MODE = 79.

Having characterized the domain of a numeric variable as a discrete set of values or as a set of contiguous segments, test data are chosen by applying different *selection criteria* depending upon the use of those variables, namely, (i) input, (ii) output, (iii) dualuse, and (iv) multipletype. A dual-use variable is one that holds an input to the system under test at the beginning of system execution and receives an output value from the system at some point thereafter. A multiple-type variable is one that can hold input (or even output) values of different types, such as numeric and string, at different times. In this section we give an example of such a variable from a real-life system. Next, we explain the four selection criteria.

1. *Selection Criteria for Input Variables*: If the input domain is a discrete set of values, then tests involving each value are performed. The domain of the input variable MODE in Figure 9.1 consists of the set {23, 79}. The FSB module is tested at least once with MODE = 23 and at least once with MODE = 79. If the domain of a variable consists of one or more segments of values, then test data are selected as follows:

- Consider the minimum value of a segment.

- Consider the maximum value of a segment.

- Consider a typical representative value in a segment.

- Consider certain values which have special mathematical properties. These values include 0, 1, and real numbers with *small* absolute values.

- Consider, if possible, values lying outside a segment. Here the idea is to observe the behavior of the program in response to invalid input.

- In case the conceptual minimum (maximum) of a variable is $-\infty$ ($+\infty$), then a large negative (positive) value is chosen to represent $-\infty$ ($+\infty$).

2. *Selection Criteria for Output Variables*: If the domain of an output variable consists of a *small* set of discrete values, then the program is tested with input which results in the generation of each of the output values. The output variable of the frequency hopping box in Figure 9.1 has a

domain of two discrete sets $\{0, \ldots, 22\}$ and $\{0, \ldots, 78\}$ for MODE $= 23$ and MODE $= 79$, respectively. The frequency hopping box must be adequately tested so that it produces each of the output values as desired. For a *large* set of discrete values, the program is tested with many different inputs that cause the program to produce many different output values. If an output variable has a domain consisting of one or more segments of numbers, then the program is tested as follows:

- Test the program with different inputs so that it produces the *minimum* values of the segments.

- Test the program with different inputs so that it produces the *maximum* values of the segments.

- Test the program with different inputs so that it produces some *interior* values in each segment.

3. *Selection Criteria for Dual-Use Variables*: A variable often serves as an input to a program (or function) and holds the output from the program (or function) at the end of the desired computation. Such a variable is called a *dual-use* variable. Additional test cases are designed to meet the following selection criteria for dual-use variables:

- Consider a test case such that the program produces an output value which is *different* from the input value of the same dual-use variable. The idea behind this test is to avoid coincidental correctness of the output.

- Consider a test case such that the program produces an output value which is *identical* to the input value of the same dual-use variable.

4. *Selection Criteria for Multiple-Type Variables*: Sometimes an input variable can take on values of different types. For example, a variable may take on values of type *integer* in one program invocation and of type *string* in another invocation. It may be unlikely for a programmer to define a single storage space to hold values of different types. The program will read the input value into different locations (i.e., variables) depending upon the type of value provided by the user. This scenario requires us to test that the program correctly reads an input value depending upon its type and, subsequently, correctly processes the value. Such multiple-type variables may arise in real-life systems, and programs must take necessary actions to handle them. If an input or output variable can take on values of different types, then the following criteria are used:

- For an input variable of multipletype, the program is tested with input values of all the types.

- For an output variable of multipletype, the program is tested with different inputs so that the variable holds values of all different types.

Example: We show a part of the tax forms prepared by Canada Customs and Revenue Agency (CCRA) in Figure 9.2. By analyzing this specification we conclude that a taxpayer (user) inputs a *real number* or a *blank* in *line 2*. The

Enter your net income from line 236 of your return		1
Enter your spouse or common-law partner's net income from page 1 of your return	+	2
Add lines 1 and 2 **Income for Ontario credits**	=	3

Involuntary separation   6089

If, on December 31, 2001, you and your spouse or common-law
partner occupied separate principal residences for medical,
educational, or business reasons, **leave line 2 blank**
and enter his or her address in the area beside box 6089.

Figure 9.2   Part of form ON479 of T1 general—2001, published by the CCRA.

value input in line 2 is a real number representing the net income of the spouse or
common-law partner of the user if both of them occupied the same residence on
December 31, 2001. Otherwise, if they occupied separate principal residences for
the specified reasons, then line 2 must be left blank and the address of the spouse
or common-law partner must be provided in box 6089.

Clearly, line 2 is an input to a tax filing software system which must
be able to handle different *types* of values input in *line 2* —namely *real* values and
blank, and a blank is not the same as 0.0. This is because, if we equate a blank
with 0.0, then the software system may not know when and how to interpret the
information given in box 6089. Referring to line 2 input of Figure 9.2, a tax filing
program must be tested as follows:

1. Interpret line 2 as a *numeric* variable taking on values from an interval
   and apply selection criteria such as selecting the minimum value, the
   maximum value, and an interior value of the defined interval.

2. Interpret line 2 as a *string* variable taking on values from a discrete set
   of values, where the discrete set consists of just one member, namely a
   blank.

Arrays   An array holds values of the same type, such as integer and real. Individual elements of an array are accessed by using one or more indices. In some
programming languages, such as MATLAB, an array can hold values of both integer
and real types. An array has a more complex structure than an individual numeric
variable. This is because of the following three distinct properties of an array.
The three properties are individually and collectively considered while testing a
program.

- An array can have one or more dimensions. For example, $A[i][j]$ is the
  element at row i and column j of a two-dimensional array A. Array dimensions are considered in testing because their values are likely to be used in
  controlling *for* and *while* loops. Just as we select extremal—both minimum
  and maximum—values and an intermediate value of a numeric variable,
  we need to consider arrays of different configurations, such as an array of

minimum size, an array of maximum size, an array with a minimum value for the first dimension and a maximum value for the second dimension, and so on.

- Individual array elements are considered as distinct numeric variables. Each value of an array element can be characterized by its minimum value, maximum value, and special values, such as 0, 1, and ϵ. All these values need to appear in tests in order to observe the program behavior while processing the extremal and special values.

- A portion of an array can be collectively interpreted as a distinct substructure with specific application-dependent properties. For example, in the field of numerical analysis a matrix structure is a common representation of a set of linear equations. The diagonal elements of a matrix, the lower triangular matrix, and the upper triangular matrix are substructures with significance in numerical analysis.

    Just as we consider special values of a numeric variable, such as 0, 1, and a small value ϵ, there exist special values of substructures of an array. For example, some well-known substructures of a two-dimensional array are individual rows and columns, diagonal elements, a lower triangular matrix, and an upper triangular matrix. These substructures are interpreted as a whole.

The selection criteria for array dimensions is based on the following three intuitive steps:

1. **Completely specify the dimensions of an array variable.** In programming languages such as C and Java, the dimensions of an array are statically defined. On the other hand, in the programming language MATLAB, there is no such concept as static definition of an array dimension. Instead, an array can be dynamically built without any predefined limit.

2. **Construct different, special configurations of the array** by considering special values of individual array dimensions and their combinations. Consider an array with k dimensions, where each dimension is characterized by a minimum value, a maximum value, and an intermediate value. These selections can be combined to form 3^k different sets of dimensions for a k-dimensional array.

    Let us take a concrete example with a two-dimensional array, where $k = 2$. The two dimensions are commonly known as row and column dimensions. The minimum number of rows of an array for an application can be an arbitrary value, such as 1. Similarly, the maximum number of rows can be 20. An intermediate row number is 10. The minimum number of columns of the array can be 2, the maximum number of columns can be 15, and an intermediate column number can be 8. By considering the three row values and three column values, one can enumerate the $3^k = 3^2 = 9$ combinations of different array configurations. Some examples of those 9 different configurations of arrays are 1×2, 1×15, 20×2, 20×15, and so on.

3. Apply the selection criteria of Section 9.1.1 to individual elements of the selected array configurations.

Substructure In general, a structure means a data type that can hold multiple data elements. In the field of numerical analysis, a matrix structure is commonly used. For example, a set of n linear equations in n unknown quantities is represented by an $n \times (n + 1)$ matrix. The n rows and the first n columns of the matrix represent the coefficients of the n linear equations, whereas the $(n + 1)$th column represents the constants of the n equations. The n rows and the first n columns can be considered as one substructure, whereas the $(n + 1)$th column is another substructure. In addition, individual columns, rows, and elements of the matrix can be considered distinct substructures. In general, one can identify a variety of substructures of a given structure. Given the fact that there can be a large number of substructures of a structure, it is useful to find *functionally identifiable* substructures. In the above example of an $n \times (n + 1)$ matrix, the $(n + 1)$th column is one functionally identifiable substructure, whereas the rest of the matrix is another functionally identifiable substructure. Individual columns and individual rows are functionally identifiable substructures as well. For example, a row of identical values means that the coefficients of all the variables and the constant of an equation have identical values. Sometimes, pairs of columns can form substructures. For example, one may use a pair of columns to represent complex numbers—one column for the "real" part and another column for the "imaginary" part. It is useful to consider both the full structure and the substructures, such as rows, columns, and individual elements, in functional testing involving matrix structures. The following criteria are considered in identifying substructures:

- **Dimensions of Substructures:** Choose structure dimensions such that substructures can take on all possible dimension values. Examples of substructures taking on special values are as follows:(i) the number of elements in a row is 1 and (ii) the number of elements in a row is "large."

- **Values of Elements of Substructures:** Choose values of elements of structures such that substructures take on all possible special values. Examples of substructures taking on special values are as follows: (i) all elements of a row take on value 0, (ii) all elements take on value 1, and (iii) all elements take on value ϵ.

- **Combinations of Individual Elements with Array Dimensions:** Combine the *dimension* aspect with the *value* aspect. For example, one can select a *large* vector—a row or a column—of elements with identical special values, such as all 0's, all 1's, and so on.

Subroutine Arguments Some programs accept input variables whose values are the *names* of functions. Such programs are found in numerical analysis and statistical applications [1]. Functional testing requires that each value of such a variable be included in a test case. Consider a program P calling a function $f(g, \text{param\_list})$, where $f()$ accepts a list of parameters denoted by param_list and another parameter

g of enumerated type. When $f()$ is invoked, it invokes the function held in g. Let the values of g be represented by the set $\{g_1, g_2, g_3\}$. We design three test cases to execute $f(g_1, \text{list}_1)$, $f(g_2, \text{list}_2)$, and $f(g_3, \text{list}_3)$ such that, eventually, $g_1()$, $g_2()$, and $g_3()$ are executed.

9.1.2   Test Vector

A *test vector*, also called test data, is an instance of the input to a program. It is a certain configuration of the values of all the input variables. Values of individual input variables chosen in the preceding sections must be combined to obtain a test vector. If a program has n input variables $\text{var}_1, \text{var}_2, \ldots, \text{var}_n$ which can take on $k_1, k_2, \ldots, k_n$ special values, respectively, then there are $k_1 \times k_2 \times \cdots \times k_n$ possible combinations of test data.

Example: We show the number of special values of different input variables of the FSB module of Figure 9.1 in Table 9.1. Variable MODE takes on values from a discrete set of size 2 and both the values from the discrete set are considered. Variables CLOCK and MODE take on values from one interval each and *three* special values for each of them are considered. Therefore, one can generate $2 \times 3 \times 3 = 18$ test vectors from Table 9.1.

Some programs accept a large number of input variables. Tax filing software systems are examples of such programs. Consider all possible combinations of a few special values of a large number of input variables is a challenging task. If a program has n input variables, each of which can take on k special values, then there are k^n possible combinations of test vectors. We know that k is a *small* number, but n may be large. We have more than one million test vectors even for $k = 3$ and $n = 20$. Therefore, there is a need to identify a method for reducing the number of test vectors obtained by considering all possible combinations of all the sets of special values of input variables.

Howden suggested that there is no need of combining values of *all* input variables to design a test vector if the variables are not *functionally related*. To reduce the number of input combinations, Howden suggested [3, 4] that we produce all possible combinations of special values of variables falling in the same functionally related subset. In this way, the total number of combinations of special values of the input variables is reduced. It is difficult to give a formal definition

TABLE 9.1   Number of Special Values of Inputs to FBS Module of Figure 9.1

Variable	Number of Special Values (k)	Special Values
MODE	2	{23, 79}
CLOCK	3	{0x0000000, 0x000FF00, 0xFFFFFFF}
ADDRESS	3	{0xFFFFF0000000, 0xFFFFF00FFF00, 0xFFFFFFFFFFFF}

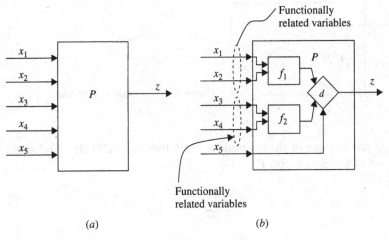

Figure 9.3   Functionally related variables.

of the idea of functionally related variables, but it is easy to identify them. Let us consider the following examples:

- Variables appearing in the same assignment statement are functionally related.
- Variables appearing in the same branch predicate—the condition part of an if statement, for example—are functionally related.

Example: The program P in Figure 9.3a has *five* input variables such that $x_1, \ldots, x_4$ take on *three* special values and x_5 is a Boolean variable. The total number of combinations of the special values of the five input variables is $3^4 \times 2 = 162$. Let us assume that program P has an internal structure as shown in Figure 9.3b, where variables x_1 and x_2 are functionally related and variables x_3 and x_4 are functionally related. Function f_1 uses the input variables x_1 and x_2. Similarly, function f_2 uses the input variables x_3 and x_4. Input variable x_5 is used to decide whether the output of f_1 or the output of f_2 will be the output of P. We consider $3^2 = 9$ different combination of x_1 and x_2 as input to f_1, 9 different combinations of x_3 and x_4 as input to f_2, and two different values of x_5 to the decision box d in P. We need 36 $[(9 + 9) \times 2]$ combinations of the five input variables $x_1, \ldots, x_5$, which is much smaller than 162.

9.1.3 Testing a Function in Context

Let us consider a program P and a function f in P as shown in Figure 9.4. The variable x is an input to P and input to f as well. Suppose that x can take on values in the range $[-\infty, +\infty]$ and that f is called only when the predicate $x \geq 20$

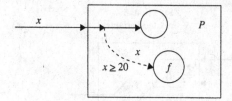

Figure 9.4   Function in context.

holds. If we are unaware of the predicate $x \geq 20$, then we are likely to select the following set of test data to test P:

$$x = +k,$$
$$x = -k,$$
$$x = 0.$$

Here, k is a number with a large magnitude.

The reader may note that the function f will be invoked just once for $x = +k$, assuming that $k \geq 20$, and it will not be invoked when P is run with the other two test data because of the conditional execution of f. Testing function f in isolation will require us to generate the same test data as above. It may be noted that the latter two data points are invalid data because they fall outside the range of x for f in P. The valid range of x for f is $[20, +\infty]$, and functional testing *in context* requires us to select the following values of x:

$$x = k \quad \text{where } k \gg 20$$
$$x = y \quad \text{where } 20 < y \ll k$$
$$x = 20$$

where the symbols $\ll$ and $\gg$ are read as "much larger" and "much smaller," respectively.

9.2   COMPLEXITY OF APPLYING FUNCTIONAL TESTING

In order to have an idea of the difficulty in applying the concept of functional testing, let us summarize the main points in functional testing in the following:

- *Identify* the input and the output variables of the program and their data domains.
- *Compute* the expected outcomes as illustrated in Figure 9.5a for selected input values.
- *Determine* the input values that will cause the program to produce selected outputs as illustrated in Figure 9.5b.

Input domains   Output domains

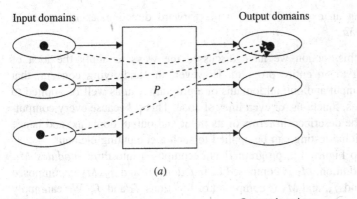

(a)

Input domains   Output domains

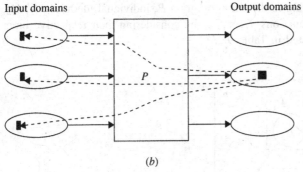

(b)

Figure 9.5   (a) Obtaining output values from an input vector and (b) obtaining an input vector from an output value in functional testing.

Generating test data by analyzing the *input domains* has the following two characteristics.

- The number of test cases obtained from an analysis of the input domains is likely to be *too many* because of the need to design test vectors representing different combinations of special values of the input variables.

- Generation of the expected output for a certain test vector is relatively simple. This is because a test designer computes an expected output from an understanding and analysis of the specification of the system.

On the other hand, generating test data by analyzing the *output domains* has the following characteristics:

- The number of test cases obtained from an analysis of the output domains is likely to be *fewer* compared to the same number of input variables because there is no need to consider different combinations of special values of the output variables.

- Generating an input vector required to produce a chosen output value will require us to analyze the specification in the *reverse* direction, as illustrated in Figure 9.5b. Such reverse analysis will be a more challenging task than computing an expected value in the forward direction, as illustrated in Figure 9.5a.

So far in this section we have discussed the ways to apply the idea of functional testing to an entire program. However, the underlying concept, that is, analyzing the input and output domains of a program, can as well be applied to individual modules, functions, or even lines of code. This is because every computing element can be described in terms of its input and output domains, and hence the idea of functional testing can be applied to such a computing element.

Referring to Figure 9.6, program P is decomposed into three *modules* M_1, M_2, and M_3. In addition, M_1 is composed of functions f_1 and f_5, M_2 is composed of functions f_2 and f_3, and M_3 is composed of functions f_4 and f_6. We can apply the idea of functional testing to the entire program P, individual modules M_1, M_2, and M_3, and individual functions $f_1, \ldots, f_6$ by considering their respective input and output domains as listed in Table 9.2.

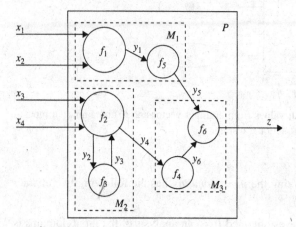

Figure 9.6   Functional testing in general.

TABLE 9.2   Input and Output Domains of Functions of *P* in Figure 9.6

Entity Name	Input Variables	Output Variables
P	$\{x_1, x_2, x_3, x_4\}$	$\{z\}$
M_1	$\{x_1, x_2\}$	$\{y_5\}$
M_2	$\{x_3, x_4\}$	$\{y_4\}$
M_3	$\{y_4, y_5\}$	$\{z\}$
f_1	$\{x_1, x_2\}$	$\{y_1\}$
f_2	$\{x_3, x_4, y_3\}$	$\{y_2, y_4\}$
f_3	$\{y_2\}$	$\{y_3\}$
f_4	$\{y_4\}$	$\{y_6\}$
f_5	$\{y_1\}$	$\{y_5\}$
f_6	$\{y_5, y_6\}$	$\{z\}$

Conceptually, one can apply functional testing at any level of abstraction, from a single line of code at the lowest level to the entire program at the highest level. As we consider individual modules, functions, and lines of code, the task of accurately identifying the input and output domains of the computing element under test becomes more difficult.

The methodology for developing functional test cases is an analytical process that decomposes specification of a program into different classes of behaviors. The functional test cases are designed for each class separately by identifying the input and output domains of the class. Identification of input and output domains help in classifying the specification into different classes. However, often, in practice, the total number of input and output combinations can be very large. Several well-known techniques are available to tackle this issue, which we discuss in the following sections.

9.3 PAIRWISE TESTING

Pairwise testing is a special case of all-combination testing of a system with n input variables. Let us consider n input variables denoted by $\{v_1, v_2, \ldots, v_i, \ldots, v_n\}$. For simplicity, assume that for each variable v_i, $1 \leq i \leq n$, we choose k values of interest. An all-combination testing means considering all the k^n different test vectors. On the other hand, pairwise testing means that each possible combination of values for every pair of input variables is covered by at least one test case. Pairwise testing requires a subset of test cases (vectors) covering all pairwise combinations of values instead of all possible combinations of values of a set of variables.

Pairwise testing is also referred to as all-pair/two-way testing. One can also generate three- four-way or 4-way tests to cover all combinations of values of three or four variables. As all combinations of values of more and more variables (e.g., 2, 3, 4, ...) are considered, the size of the test suite grows rapidly. Empirical results [5] for medical devices and distributed database systems show that two-way testing would detect more that 90% of the defects, whereas, four-way testing would detect 100% of the defects. Pairwise testing would detect approximately 70% of the defects, whereas six-way testing would detect 100% of defects for browser and server applications.

Consider the system S in Figure 9.7, which has three input variables $X, Y,$ and Z. Let the notation $D(w)$ denote the set of values for an arbitrary variable w. For the three given variables $X, Y,$ and Z, their value sets are as follows: $D(X) = \{$True, False$\}$, $D(Y) = \{0, 5\}$, and $D(Z) = \{Q, R\}$. The total number of

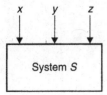

Figure 9.7   System S with three input variables.

TABLE 9.3 Pairwise Test Cases for System S

Test Case ID	Input X	Input Y	Input Z
TC_1	True	0	Q
TC_2	True	5	R
TC_3	False	0	Q
TC_4	False	5	R

all-combination test cases is $2 \times 2 \times 2 = 8$. However, a subset of four test cases, as shown in Table 9.3, covers all pairwise combinations. Different test generation strategies for pairwise testing have been reported in the literature [6]. In this section, two popular techniques, namely, orthogonal array (OA) [7] and in parameter order (IPO) [8], are discussed.

9.3.1 Orthogonal Array

Orthogonal arrays were originally studied as a kind of numerical curiosity by monks [9]. It was further studied by C. R. Rao, a statistician, in the late 1940s, [10]. Genichi Taguchi first used the idea of orthogonal arrays in his experimental design of total quality management (TQM) [11]. The method, known as the Taguchi method, has been used in experimental design in the manufacturing field and provides an efficient and systematic way to optimize designs for performance, quality, and cost. It has been used successfully in Japan and the United States in designing reliable, high-quality products at low cost in the automobile and consumer electronics industries. Mandl was the first to use the concept of orthogonal array in designing test cases for pairwise testing of compilers [12].

Let us consider the two-dimensional array of integers shown in Table 9.4. The array has an interesting property: Choose any two columns at random and find all pairs (1,1), (1,2), (2,1), and (2,2); however, not all the combinations of 1's and 2's appear in the table. For example, (2,2,2) is a valid combination, but it is not in the table. Only four of the eight combinations can be found in the table. This is an example of $L_4(2^3)$ orthogonal array. The 4 indicates that the array has four rows, also known as *runs*. The 2^3 part indicates that the array has three columns, known

TABLE 9.4 $L_4(2^3)$ Orthogonal Array

	Factors		
Runs	1	2	3
1	1	1	1
2	1	2	2
3	2	1	2
4	2	2	1

TABLE 9.5   Commonly Used Orthogonal Arrays

Orthogonal Array	Number of Runs	Maximum Number of Factors	Maximum Number of Columns at These Levels			
			2	3	4	5
L_4	4	3	3			
L_8	8	7	7			
L_9	9	4	—	4		
L_{12}	12	11	11			
L_{16}	16	15	15			
L'_{16}	16	5	—	—	5	
L_{18}	18	8	1	7		
L_{25}	25	6	—	—	—	6
L_{27}	27	13	—	13		
L_{32}	32	31	31			
L'_{32}	32	10	1	—	9	
L_{36}	36	23	11	12		
L'_{36}	36	16	3	13		
L_{50}	50	12	1	—	—	11
L_{54}	54	26	1	25		
L_{64}	64	63	63			
L'_{64}	64	21	—	—	21	
L_{81}	81	40	—	40		

as factors, and each cell in the array contains two different values, known as levels. *Levels* mean the maximum number of values that a single factor can take on. The maximum number of columns at levels 1 and 2 are 0 and 3, respectively. Orthogonal arrays are generally denoted by the pattern L_{Runs} (Levels^{Factors}). Commonly used orthogonal arrays are given in Table 9.5.

Let us consider our previous example of the system S, where S has three input variables X, Y, and Z. For the three given variables X, Y, and Z, their value sets are as follows: $D(X) = \{\text{True, False}\}$, $D(Y) = \{0, 5\}$, and $D(Z) = \{Q, R\}$. Let us map the variables to the factors and values to the levels onto the $L_4(2^3)$ orthogonal array (Table 9.4) with the resultant in Table 9.3. In the first column, let $1 = \text{True}$, $2 = \text{False}$. In the second column, let $1 = 0$, $2 = 5$. In the third column, let $1 = Q$, $2 = R$. Note that not all combinations of all variables have been selected; instead combinations of all pairs of input variables have been covered with four test cases. It is clear from the above example that orthogonal arrays provide a technique for selecting a subset of test cases with the following properties:

- The technique guarantees testing the pairwise combinations of all the selected variables.
- The technique generates fewer test cases than the all-combination approach.

- The technique generates a test suite that has an even distribution of all pairwise combinations.
- The technique can be automated.

In the following, the steps of a technique to generate orthogonal arrays are presented. The steps are further explained by means of a detailed example.

Step 1: Identify the maximum number of independent input variables with which a system will be tested. This will map to the *factors* of the array—each input variable maps to a different factor.

Step 2: Identify the maximum number of values that each independent variable will take. This will map to the levels of the array.

Step 3: Find a suitable orthogonal array with the smallest number of runs $L_{Runs}(X^Y)$, where X is the number of levels and Y is the number of factors [7, 13]. A suitable array is one that has at least as many factors as needed from step 1 and has at least as many levels for each of those factors as identified in step 2.

Step 4: Map the variables to the factors and values of each variable to the levels on the array.

Step 5: Check for any "left-over" levels in the array that have not been mapped. Choose arbitrary valid values for those left-over levels.

Step 6: Transcribe the runs into test cases.

Web Example.   Consider a website that is viewed on a number of browsers with various plug-ins and operating systems (OSs) and through different connections as shown in Table 9.6. The table shows the variables and their values that are used as elements of the orthogonal array. We need to test the system with different combinations of the input values.

Following the steps laid out previously, let us design an orthogonal array to create a set of test cases for pairwise testing:

Step 1: There are four independent variables, namely, Browser, Plug-in, OS, and Connection.

Step 2: Each variable can take at most three values.

TABLE 9.6   Various Values That Need to Be Tested in Combinations

Variables	Values
Browser	Netscape, Internet Explorer (IE), Mozilla
Plug-in	Realplayer, Mediaplayer
OS	Windows, Linux, Macintosh
Connection	LAN, PPP, ISDN

Note: LAN, local-area network; PPP, Point-to-Point Protocal; ISDN, Integrated Services Digital Network.

TABLE 9.7 $L_9(3^4)$ Orthogonal Array

Runs	Factors			
	1	2	3	4
1	1	1	1	1
2	1	2	2	2
3	1	3	3	3
4	2	1	2	3
5	2	2	3	1
6	2	3	1	2
7	3	1	3	2
8	3	2	1	3
9	3	3	2	1

Step 3: An orthogonal array $L_9(3^4)$ as shown in Table 9.7 is good enough for the purpose. The array has nine rows, three levels for the values, and four factors for the variables.

Step 4: Map the variables to the factors and values to the levels of the array: the factor 1 to Browser, the factor 2 to Plug-in, the factor 3 to OS, and the factor 4 to Connection. Let 1 = Netscape, 2 = IE, and 3 = Mozilla in the Browser column. In the Plug-in column, let 1 = Realplayer and 3 = Mediaplayer. Let 1 = Windows, 2 = Linux, and 3 = Macintosh in the OS column. Let 1 = LAN, 2 = PPP, and 3 = ISDN in the Connection column. The mapping of the variables and the values onto the orthogonal array is given in Table 9.8.

Step 5: There are left-over levels in the array that are not being mapped. The factor 2 has three levels specified in the original array, but there are only two possible values for this variable. This has caused a level (2) to be left

TABLE 9.8 $L_9(3^4)$ Orthogonal Array after Mapping Factors

Test Case ID	Browser	Plug-in	OS	Connection
TC_1	Netscape	Realplayer	Windows	LAN
TC_2	Netscape	2	Linux	PPP
TC_3	Netscape	Mediaplayer	Macintosh	ISDN
TC_4	IE	Realplayer	Linux	ISDN
TC_5	IE	2	Macintosh	LAN
TC_6	IE	Mediaplayer	Windows	PPP
TC_7	Mozilla	Realplayer	Macintosh	PPP
TC_8	Mozilla	2	Windows	ISDN
TC_9	Mozilla	Mediaplayer	Linux	LAN

TABLE 9.9   Generated Test Cases after Mapping Left-Over Levels

Test Case ID	Browser	Plug-in	OS	Connection
TC_1	Netscape	Realplayer	Windows	LAN
TC_2	Netscape	Realplayer	Linux	PPP
TC_3	Netscape	Mediaplayer	Macintosh	ISDN
TC_4	IE	Realplayer	Linux	ISDN
TC_5	IE	Mediaplayer	Macintosh	LAN
TC_6	IE	Mediaplayer	Windows	PPP
TC_7	Mozilla	Realplayer	Macintosh	PPP
TC_8	Mozilla	Realplayer	Windows	ISDN
TC_9	Mozilla	Mediaplayer	Linux	LAN

over for variable Plug-in after mapping the factors. One must provide a value in the cell. The choice of this value can be arbitrary, but to have a coverage, start at the top of the Plug-in column and cycle through the possible values when filling in the left-over levels. Table 9.9 shows the mapping after filling in the remaining levels using the cycling technique mentioned.

Step 6: We generate nine test cases taking the test case values from each run. Now let us examine the result:

- Each Browser is tested with every Plug-in, with every OS, and with every Connection.
- Each Plug-in is tested with every Browser, with every OS, and with every Connection.
- Each OS is tested with every Browser, with every Plug-in, and with every Connection.
- Each Connection is tested with every Browser, with every Plug-in, and with every OS.

9.3.2   In Parameter Order

Tai and Lei [8] have given an algorithm called in parameter order (IPO) to generate a test suite for pairwise coverage of input variables. The algorithm generates a test suite that satisfies pairwise coverage for the values of the first two parameters. Then the test suite is extended by the algorithm to satisfy pairwise coverage for the values of the third parameters and continues to do so for the values of each additional parameter until all parameters are included in the test suite.

The algorithm runs in three phases, namely, *initialization*, *horizontal growth*, and *vertical growth*, in that order. In the initialization phase, test cases are generated to cover two input variables. In the horizontal growth phase, the existing test cases are extended with the values of the other input variables. In the vertical growth phase, additional test cases are created such that the test suite satisfies pairwise coverage for the values of the new variables. In order to use the IPO test generation techniques, one can follow the steps described below. Assume that there are n number of variables denoted by $\{p_i | 1 \leq i \leq n\}$ and a dash denotes an unspecified value of a variable.

Algorithm: In Parameter Order

   Input: Parameter p_i and its domain $D(p_i) = \{v_1, v_2, \ldots, v_q\}$, where $i = 1, \ldots, n$.

   Output: A test suite T satisfying pairwise coverage.

Initialization Phase:

Step 1:   For the first two parameters p_1 and p_2, generate the test suite

$$T := \{(v_1, v_2) | v_1 \text{ and } v_2 \text{ are values of } p_1 \text{ and } p_2, \text{respectively}\}$$

Step 2:   If $i = 2$, stop. Otherwise, for $i = 3, 4, \ldots, n$ repeat **steps 3** and **4**.

Horizontal Growth Phase:

Step 3:   Let $D(p_i) = \{v_1, v_2, \ldots, v_q\}$. Create a set

$$\pi_i := \{\text{pairs between values of } p_i \text{ and all values of } p_1, p_2, \ldots, p_{i-1}\}$$

```
If |T| ≤ q, then
{ for 1 ≤ j ≤ |T|, extend the jth test in T by adding
    values vⱼ and remove from πᵢ pairs covered by the
    extended test}
else
{ for 1 ≤ j ≤ q, extend the jth test in T by adding
    value vⱼ and remove from πᵢ pairs covered by the
    extended test;
  for q < j ≤ |T|, extend the jth test in T by adding
    one value of pᵢ such that the resulting test covers
    the most numbers of pairs in πᵢ, and remove from
    πᵢ pairs covered by the extended test };
```

Vertical Growth Phase:

Step 4:   Let $T' := \Phi$ (empty set) and $|\pi_i| > 0$;

```
for each pair in πᵢ (let the pairs contain value w
    of pₖ, 1 ≤ k < i, and values u of pᵢ)
{
    if (T' contains a test with − as the value of pₖ and u
        as the value of pᵢ)
```

```
modify this test by replacing the − with w;
else
    add a new test to T' that has w as the value of p_k,
    u as the value of p_i, and − as the value of every
    other parameter;
};
T := T ∪ T';
```

The test cases may contain — values after the generation of test suite T. If p_i is the last parameter, each — value p_k, $1 \leq k \leq i$, is replaced with any value of p_k. Otherwise, these — values are replaced with parameter values in the horizontal growth phase for p_{i+1} as follows: Assuming that value v of p_{i+1} is chosen for the horizontal growth of a test that contains — as the value for p_k, $1 \leq k \leq i$. If there are uncovered pairs involving v and some values of p_k, the — for p_k is replaced with one of these values of p_k. Otherwise, the — for p_k is replaced with any value of p_k.

Example: Consider the system S in Figure 9.7 which has three input parameters X, Y, and Z. Assume that a set D, a set of input test data values, has been selected for each input variable such that $D(X) = \{\text{True, False}\}$, $D(Y) = \{0, 5\}$, and $D(Z) = \{P, Q, R\}$. The total number of possible test cases is $2 \times 2 \times 3 = 12$, but the IPO algorithm generates six test cases. Let us apply step 1 of the algorithm.

Step 1: Generate a test suite consisting of four test cases with pairwise coverage for the first two parameters X and Y:

$$T = \begin{bmatrix} (\text{True,} & 0) \\ (\text{True,} & 5) \\ (\text{False,} & 0) \\ (\text{False,} & 5) \end{bmatrix}$$

Step 2: $i = 3 > 2$; therefore, steps 2 and 3 must be executed.

Step 3: Now $D(Z) = \{P, Q, R\}$. Create a set $\pi_3 := \{$ pairs between values of Z and values of X, $Y\}$, which is

$$\pi_3 = \begin{bmatrix} (\text{True}, P), & (\text{True}, Q), & (\text{True}, R) \\ (\text{False}, P), & (\text{False}, Q), & (\text{False}, R) \\ (0, P), & (0, Q), & (0, R) \\ (5, P), & (5, Q), & (5, R) \end{bmatrix}$$

Since Z has three values, we have $q = 3$ and $|T| = 4 > q = 3$. We extended (True, 0), (True, 5), and (False, 0) by adding P, Q, and R, respectively. Next, we remove the pairs (True, P), (True, Q), (False, R), (0, P), (5, Q), and (0, R) from the set π_3 because these pairs are covered by the partially extended test suite. The extended test suite T and π_3 become

$$T = \begin{bmatrix} \text{(True,} & 0, & P) \\ \text{(True,} & 5, & Q) \\ \text{(False,} & 0, & R) \\ \text{(False,} & 5, &) \end{bmatrix}$$

$$\pi_3 = \begin{bmatrix} & & \text{(True, } R) \\ \text{(False, } P), & \text{(False, } Q) & \\ & (0, Q) & \\ (5, P), & (5, R) & \end{bmatrix}$$

Now we need to select one of P, Q, and R for (False, 5). If we add P to (False, 5), the extended test (False, 5, P) covers two missing pairs (False, P) and $(5, P)$. If we add Q to (False, 5), the extended test (False, 5, Q) covers only one missing pair (False, Q). If we add R to (False, 5), the extended test (False, 5, R) covers only one missing pair $(5, R)$. Therefore, the algorithm will choose (False, 5, P) as the fourth test case. Remove the pairs (False, P) and $(5, P)$ from the set π_3 because these pairs are covered by the partial extended test suite. Now the extended test suite T and π_3 become

$$T = \begin{bmatrix} \text{(True,} & 0, & P) \\ \text{(True,} & 5, & Q) \\ \text{(False,} & 0, & R) \\ \text{(False,} & 5, & P) \end{bmatrix} \qquad \pi_3 = \begin{bmatrix} \text{(True, } R) \\ \text{(False, } Q) \\ (0, Q) \\ (5, R) \end{bmatrix}$$

So far the tests in T have not yet covered the four tests in π_3, namely, (True, R), (False, Q), $(0, Q)$, and $(5, R)$.

Step 4: The algorithm will generate a set $T' = \{(\text{True}, —, R), (\text{False}, —, Q)\}$ from the first two pairs of π_3, that is, (True, R) and (False, Q). The algorithm changes the test case (False, —, Q) to (False, 0, Q) without adding a new test case to cover the next pair $(0, Q)$. The algorithm modifies the test case (True, —, R) to (True, 5, R) without adding any new test case to be able to cover the pair $(5, R)$. The union $T \cup T'$ generates the six pairwise test cases as follows:

$$T = \begin{bmatrix} \text{(True,} & 0, & P) \\ \text{(True,} & 5, & Q) \\ \text{(False,} & 0, & R) \\ \text{(False,} & 5, & P) \\ \text{(False,} & 0, & Q) \\ \text{(True,} & 5, & R) \end{bmatrix}$$

9.4   EQUIVALENCE CLASS PARTITIONING

An input domain may be too large for all its elements to be used as test input (Figure 9.8a). However, the input domain can be partitioned into a finite number of subdomains for selecting test inputs. Each subdomain is known as an equivalence class (EC), and it serves as a source of at least one test input (Figure 9.8b). The objective of equivalence partitioning is to divide the input domain of the system under test into classes, or groups, of inputs. All the inputs in the same class have a similar effect on the system under test [14, 15]. An EC is a set of inputs that the system treats identically when the system is tested. It represents certain conditions, or predicates, on the input domain. An input condition on the input domain is a predicate over the values of the input domain. A valid input to a system is an element of the input domain that is expected to return a nonerror value. An invalid input is an input that is expected to return an error value. Input conditions are used to partition the input domain into ECs for the purpose of selecting inputs.

Guidelines for EC Partitioning   Equivalence classes can be derived from an input domain by a heuristic technique. One can approximate the ECs by identifying classes for which different program behaviors are specified. Identification of ECs becomes easier with experience. Myers suggests the following guidelines to identify ECs [16].

1. *An input condition specifies a range [a, b]*: Identify one EC for $a \leq X \leq b$ and two other classes for $X < a$ and $X > b$ to test the system with invalid inputs.

2. *An input condition specifies a set of values*: Create one EC for each element of the set and one EC for an invalid member. For example, if the input is selected from a set of N items, then $N + 1$ ECs are created: (i) one EC for each element of the set $\{M_1\}, \{M_2\}, \dots, \{M_N\}$ and (ii) one EC for elements outside the set $\{M_1, M_2, \dots, M_N\}$.

3. *Input condition specifies for each individual value*: If the system handles each valid input differently, then create one EC for each valid input. For

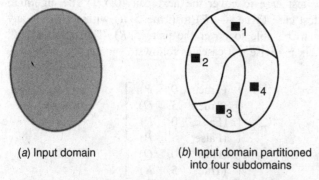

(*a*) Input domain   (*b*) Input domain partitioned
                                   into four subdomains

Figure 9.8   (a) Too many test inputs; (b) one input selected from each subdomain.

example, if the input is from a menu, then create one EC for each menu item.

4. *An input condition specifies the number of valid values (say N):* Create one EC for the correct number of inputs and two ECs for invalid inputs—one for zero values and one for more than N values. For example, if a program can accept 100 natural numbers for sorting, then three ECs are created: (i) one for 100 valid input of natural numbers, (ii) one for no input value, and (iii) one for more than 100 natural numbers.

5. *An input condition specifies a "must-be" value:* Create one EC for a must-be value and one EC for something that is not a must-be value. For example, if the first character of a password must be a numeric character, then we are required to generate two ECs: (i) one for valid values, {pswd | the first character of pswd has a numeric value}, and (ii) one for invalid values, {pswd | the first character of pswd is not numeric}.

6. *Splitting of EC:* If elements in a partitioned EC are handled differently by the system, then split the EC into smaller ECs.

Identification of Test Cases from ECs   Having identified the ECs of an input domain of a program, test cases for each EC can be identified by the following:

Step 1:   Assign a unique number to each EC.

Step 2:   For each EC with valid input that has not been covered by test cases yet, write a new test case covering as many uncovered ECs as possible.

Step 3:   For each EC with invalid input that has not been covered by test cases, write a new test case that covers one and only one of the uncovered ECs.

In summary, the advantages of EC partitioning are as follows:

- A small number of test cases are needed to adequately cover a large input domain.
- One gets a better idea about the input domain being covered with the selected test cases.
- The probability of uncovering defects with the selected test cases based on EC partitioning is higher than that with a randomly chosen test suite of the same size.
- The EC partitioning approach is not restricted to input conditions alone; the technique may also be used for output domains.

Example: Adjusted Gross Income.   Consider a software system that computes income tax based on adjusted gross income (AGI) according to the following rules:

If AGI is between $1 and $29,500, the tax due is 22% of AGI.

If AGI is between $29,501 and $58,500, the tax due is 27% of AGI.

If AGI is between $58,501 and $100 billion, the tax due is 36% of AGI.

TABLE 9.10 Generated Test Cases to Cover Each Equivalence Class

Test Case Number	Test Value	Expected Result	Equivalence Class Being Tested
TC$_1$	$22,000	$4,840	EC1
TC$_2$	$46,000	$12,420	EC3
TC$_3$	$68,000	$24,480	EC4
TC$_4$	$-20,000	Rejected with an error message	EC2
TC$_5$	$150 billion	Rejected with an error message	EC5

In this case, the input domain is from $1 to $100 billion. There are three input conditions in the example:

1. $1 $\leq$ AGI $\leq$ $29,500.
2. $29,501 $\leq$ AGI $\leq$ $58,500.
3. $58,501 $\leq$ AGI $\leq$ $100 billion.

First we consider condition 1, namely, $1 $\leq$ AGI $\leq$ $29,500, to derive two ECs:

EC1: $1 $\leq$ AGI $\leq$ $29,500; valid input.

EC2: AGI < 1; invalid input.

Then, we consider condition 2, namely, $29,501 $\leq$ AGI $\leq$ $58,500, to derive one EC:

EC3: $29,501 $\leq$ AGI $\leq$ $58,500; valid input.

Finally, we consider condition 3, namely, $58,501 $\leq$ AGI $\leq$ $100 billion, to derive two ECs:

EC4: $58,501 $\leq$ AGI $\leq$ $100 billion; valid input.

EC5: AGI > $100 billion; invalid input.

Note that each condition was considered separately in the derivation of ECs. Conditions are not combined to select ECs. Five test cases are generated to cover the five ECs, as shown in Table 9.10.

In the EC partition technique, a single test input is arbitrarily selected to cover a specific EC. We need to generate specific test input by considering the extremes, either inside or outside of the defined EC partitions. This leads us to the next technique, known as boundary value analysis, which focuses on the boundary of the ECs to identify test inputs.

9.5 BOUNDARY VALUE ANALYSIS

The central idea in boundary value analysis (BVA) is to select test data near the boundary of a data domain so that data both within and outside an EC are selected.

It produces test inputs near the boundaries to find failures caused by incorrect implementation of the boundaries. Boundary conditions are predicates that apply directly on and around the boundaries of input ECs and output ECs. In practice, designers and programmers tend to overlook boundary conditions. Consequently, defects tend to be concentrated near the boundaries between ECs. Therefore, test data are selected on or near a boundary. In that sense, the BVA technique is an extension and refinement of the EC partitioning technique [17]. In the BVA technique, the boundary conditions for each EC are analyzed in order to generate test cases.

Guidelines for BVA   As in the case of EC partitioning, the ability to develop high-quality effective test cases using BVA requires experience. The guidelines discussed below are applicable to both input conditions and output conditions. The conditions are useful in identifying high-quality test cases. By high-quality test cases we mean test cases that can reveal defects in a program.

1. *The EC specifies a range*: If an EC specifies a range of values, then construct test cases by considering the boundary points of the range and points just beyond the boundaries of the range. For example, let an EC specify the range of $-10.0 \leq X \leq 10.0$. This would result in test data $\{-9.9 - 10.0, -10.1\}$ and $\{9.9, 10.0, 10.1\}$.

2. *The EC specifies a number of values*: If an EC specifies a number of values, then construct test cases for the minimum and the maximum value of the number. In addition, select a value smaller than the minimum and a value larger than the maximum value. For example, let the EC specification of a student dormitory specify that a housing unit can be shared by one to four students; test cases that include 1, 4, 0, and 5 students would be developed.

3. *The EC specifies an ordered set*: If the EC specifies an ordered set, such as a linear list, table, or sequential file, then focus attention on the first and last elements of the set.

Example: Let us consider the five ECs identified in our previous example to compute income tax based on AGI. The BVA technique results in test as follows for each EC. The redundant data points may be eliminated.

EC1: $\$1 \leq$ AGI $\leq \$29,500$; This would result in values of $\$1, \$0, \$-1$, $\$1.50$ and $\$29,499.50, \$29,500, \$29,500.50$.

EC2: AGI < 1; This would result in values of $\$1, \$0, \$-1, \$-100$ billion.

EC3: $\$29,501 \leq$ AGI $\leq \$58,500$; This would result in values of $\$29,500$, $\$29,500.50, \$29,501, \$58,499, \$58,500, \$58,500.50, \$58,501$.

EC4: $\$58,501 \leq$ AGI $\leq \$100$ billion; This would result in values of $\$58,500$, $\$58,500.50, \$58,501, \$100$ billion, $\$101$ billion.

EC5: AGI > $100 billion; This would result in $100 billion, $101 billion, $10000 billion.

Remark. Should we test for an AGI value of $29,500.50 (i.e., between the partitions), and if so, what should be the result? Since we have not been told whether the decimal values are actually possible, the best decision to make is to test for this value and report the result.

9.6 DECISION TABLES

A major limitation of the EC-based testing is that it only considers each input separately. The technique does not consider combining conditions. Different combinations of equivalent classes can be tried by using a new technique based on the *decision table* to handle multiple inputs. Decision tables have been used for many years as a useful tool to model software requirements and design decisions. It is a simple, yet powerful notation to describe complex systems from library information management systems to embedded real-time systems [18].

The general structure of a decision table is shown in Table 9.11. It comprises a set of *conditions* (or *causes*) and a set of *effects* (or *results*) arranged in the form of a column on the left of the table. In the second column, next to each condition, we have its possible values: yes (Y), no (N), and don't care (dash). To the right of the values column, we have a set of *rules*. For each combination of the three conditions $\{C_1, C_2, C_3\}$, there exists a rule from the set $\{R_1, R_2, \cdots, R_8\}$. Each rule comprises a yes, no, or don't care response and contains associated list of effects $\{E_1, E_2, E_3\}$. Then, for each relevant effect, an *effect sequence number* specifies the order in which the effect should be carried out if the associated set of conditions are satisfied. For example, if C_1 and C_2 are true but C_3 is not true, then E_3 should be followed by E_1. The checksum is used for verification of the combinations the decision table represents.

TABLE 9.11 Decision Table Comprising Set of Conditions and Effects

Conditions	Values	Rules or Combinations							
		R_1	R_2	R_3	R_4	R_5	R_6	R_7	R_8
C_1	Y, N,—	Y	Y	Y	Y	N	N	N	N
C_2	Y, N,—	Y	Y	N	N	Y	Y	N	N
C_3	Y, N,—	Y	N	Y	N	Y	N	Y	N
Effects									
E_1		1		2	1				
E_2			2	1			2	1	
E_3		2	1	3		1	1		
Checksum	8	1	1	1	1	1	1	1	1

Test data are selected so that each rule in a table is exercised and the actual results are verified with the expected results. In other words, each rule of a decision table represents a test case. The steps in developing test cases using the decision table technique are as follows:

Step 1: The test designer needs to identify the conditions and the effects for each specification unit. A condition is a distinct input condition or an EC of input conditions. An effect is an output condition. Determine the logical relationship between the conditions and the effects.

Step 2: List all the conditions and effects in the form of a decision table. Write down the values the condition can take.

Step 3: Calculate the number of possible combinations. It is equal to the number of different values raised to the power of the number of conditions.

Step 4: Fill the columns with all possible combinations—each column corresponds to one combination of values. For each row (condition) do the following:

1. Determine the repeating factor (RF): divide the remaining number of combinations by the number of possible values for that condition.
2. Write RF times the first value, then RF times the next, and so forth until the row is full.

Step 5: Reduce combinations (rules). Find indifferent combinations—place a dash and join column where columns are identical. While doing this, ensure that effects are the same.

Step 6: Check covered combinations (rules). For each column calculate the combinations it represents. A dash represents as many combinations as the condition has. Multiply for each dash down the column. Add up total and compare with step 3. It should be the same.

Step 7: Add effects to the column of the decision table. Read column by column and determine the effects. If more than one effect can occur in a single combination, then assign a sequence number to the effects, thereby specifying the order in which the effects should be performed. Check the consistency of the decision table.

Step 8: The columns in the decision table are transformed into test cases.

Decision table–based testing is effective under certain conditions as follows:

- The requirements are easily mapped to a decision table.
- The resulting decision table should not be too large. One can break down a large decision table into multiple smaller tables.
- Each column in a decision table is independent of the other columns.

Example: Let us consider the following description of a payment procedure. Consultants working for more than 40 hours per week are paid at their hourly rate for the first 40 hours and at two times their hourly rate for subsequent hours. Consultants working for less than 40 hours per week are paid for the hours worked at their hourly rates and an absence report is produced. Permanent workers working for less than 40 hours a week are paid their salary and an absence report is produced. Permanent workers working for more than 40 hours a week are paid their salary. We need to describe the above payment procedure using a decision table and generate test cases from the table.

Step 1: From the above description, the conditions and effects are identified as follows:

C_1: Permanent workers

C_2: Worked < 40 hours

C_3: Worked exactly 40 hours

C_4: Worked > 40 hours

E_1: Pay salary

E_2: Produce an absence report

E_3: Pay hourly rate

E_4: Pay 2 × hourly rate

Step 2: The decision table with all the conditions and the effects are shown in Table 9.12.

Step 3: The total number of combinations is $2^4 = 16$.

Step 4: The RFs for row 1, row 2, row 3, and row 4 are $\frac{16}{2} = 8$, $\frac{8}{2} = 4$, $\frac{4}{2} = 2$, and $\frac{2}{2} = 1$, respectively. Therefore, the first row is filled with eight Y followed by eight N. The second row is filled with four Y, followed by four N, and so on.

Step 5: If condition C_1: Permanent workers is yes and condition C_2: Worked < 40 hours is yes, then conditions C_3: Worked exactly 40 hours and C_4: worked > 40 hours do not matter. Therefore, rules 1, 2, 3, and 4 can be reduced to a single rule without impacting the effects.

TABLE 9.12   Pay Calculation Decision Table with Values for Each Rule

Conditions	Values	Rules or Combinations															
		1	2	3	4	5	6	7	8	9	10	11	12	13	14	15	16
C_1	Y, N	Y	Y	Y	Y	Y	Y	Y	Y	N	N	N	N	N	N	N	N
C_2	Y, N	Y	Y	Y	Y	N	N	N	N	Y	Y	Y	Y	N	N	N	N
C_3	Y, N	Y	Y	N	N	Y	Y	N	N	Y	Y	N	N	Y	Y	N	N
C_4	Y, N	Y	N	Y	N	Y	N	Y	N	Y	N	Y	N	Y	N	Y	N
Effects																	
E_1																	
E_2																	
E_4																	
E_4																	

If condition C_1: Permanent workers is yes and condition C_2: Worked < 40 hours is no, then conditions C_3: Worked exactly 40 hours and C_4: worked > 40 hours do not matter. Therefore, rules 5, 6, 7, and 8 can be reduced to a single rule—permanent workers get paid regardless.

If condition C_1: Permanent workers is no and condition C_2: Worked < 40 hours is yes, then conditions C_3: Worked exactly 40 hours and C_4: worked > 40 hours are immaterial. Therefore, rules 9, 10, 11, and 12 can be reduced to a single rule without impacting the effects.

If conditions C_1: Permanent workers and C_2: Worked < 40 hours are no but condition C_3: Worked exactly 40 hours is yes, then rules 13 and 14 can be reduced to a single rule.

Rules 15 and 16 stand as they are. In summary, 16 rules can be reduced to a total of 6 rules, which are shown in Table 9.13.

Step 6: The checksum for columns 1, 2, 3, 4, 5, and 6 are 4, 4, 4, 2, 1, and 1, respectively, as shown in Table 9.14. The total checksum is 16, which is the same as calculated in step 3.

Step 7: In this step, the effects are included for each column (rule). For the first column, if the conditions C_1: Permanent workers and C_2: Worked < 40 hours are satisfied, then the employee must be paid and an absence report must be generated; therefore, E_1: Pay salary and E_2: Produce an absence report are marked as 1 and 2 in the decision table, respectively—the 1 and 2 indicating the order in which the effects are expected. The final decision table with effects are shown in Table 9.14. Note that for column 6 no effects are marked.

Step 8: A test case purpose can be generated from column 1 which can be described as follows: If an employee is a permanent worker and worked less than 40 hours per week, then the system should pay his or her salary and generate an absence report. Similarly, other test cases can be generated from the rest of the columns.

TABLE 9.13 Pay Calculation Decision Table after Column Reduction

Conditions	Values	Rules or Combinations					
		1	2	3	4	5	6
C_1	Y, N	Y	Y	N	N	N	N
C_2	Y, N	Y	N	Y	N	N	N
C_3	Y, N	—	—	—	Y	N	N
C_4	Y, N	—	—	—	—	Y	N
Effects							
E_1							
E_2							
E_4							
E_4							

TABLE 9.14 Decision Table for Payment Calculation

Conditions	Values	Rules or Combinations					
		1	2	3	4	5	6
C_1	Y, N	Y	Y	N	N	N	N
C_2	Y, N	Y	N	Y	N	N	N
C_3	Y, N	—	—	—	Y	N	N
C_4	Y, N	—	—	—	—	Y	N
Effects							
E_1							
E_1		1	1				
E_2		2		2			
E_4					1	1	1
E_4							2
Checksum	16	4	4	4	2	1	1

9.7 RANDOM TESTING

In the random testing approach, test inputs are selected randomly from the input domain of the system. We explain the idea of random testing with a simple example of computing $\sqrt{X}$, where X is an integer. Suppose that the system will be used in an environment where the input X takes on all values from the interval $[1, 10^8]$ with equal likelihood and that the result must be accurate to within 2×10^{-4}. In order to test this program, one can generate uniformly distributed pseudorandom integers within the interval $[1, 10^8]$. Then we execute the program on each of these inputs t and obtain the output z_t. For each t, we compute z_t and z_t^2 and compare z_t^2 with t. If any of the outputs fails to be within 2×10^{-4} of the desired results, the program must be fixed and the test repeated. Based on the above example, random testing can be summarized as a four-step procedure [19]:

Step 1: The input domain is identified.

Step 2: Test inputs are selected independently from the domain.

Step 3: The system under test is executed on these inputs. The inputs constitute a random test set.

Step 4: The results are compared to the system specification. The test is a failure if any input leads to incorrect results; otherwise it is a success.

Random testing corresponds to simple random sampling from the input domain [20]. If the distribution of the selected inputs (step 2) is the same as the distribution of inputs in the expected-use scenario (the operational profile), then statistical estimates for the reliability of the program can be obtained from test outcomes. Random testing gives us an advantage of easily estimating software reliability from test outcomes. Test inputs are randomly generated according to an operational profile, and failure times are recorded. The data obtained from random testing can then be used to estimate reliability. Other testing methods cannot be used in this way to estimate software reliability.

A large number of test inputs are typically required to get meaningful statistical results. Consequently, some kind of automation is required to generate a large number of inputs for random testing. For effective generation of a large set of inputs for statistical estimation, one needs to know the operational profile of the system. On the other hand, the expected results (step 4) are usually not obvious. Computing expected outcomes becomes difficult if the inputs are randomly chosen. Therefore, the technique requires good test oracles to ensure the adequate evaluation of test results. A test oracle is a mechanism that verifies the correctness of program outputs. The term *test oracle* was coined by William E. Howden [21]. An oracle provides a method to (i) generate expected results for the test inputs and (ii) compare the expected results with the actual results of execution of the implementation under test (IUT). In other words, it consists of two parts: a result generator to obtain expected results and a comparator. Four common types of oracles are as follows [22]:

- **Perfect Oracle:** In this scheme, the system (IUT) is tested in parallel with a trusted system that accepts every input specified for the IUT and always produces the correct result. A trusted system is a defect-free version of the IUT.
- **Gold Standard Oracle:** A previous versions of an existing application system is used to generate expected results, as shown in Figure 9.9.
- **Parametric Oracle:** An algorithm is used to extract some parameters from the actual outputs and compare them with the expected parameter values, as shown in Figure 9.10.
- **Statistical Oracle:** It is a special case of a parametric oracle. In a statistical oracle, statistical characteristics of the actual test results are verified.

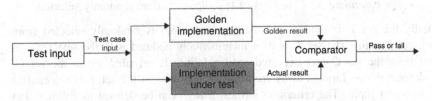

Figure 9.9   Gold standard oracle.

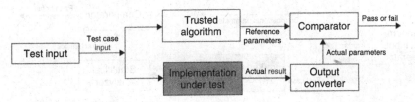

Figure 9.10   Parametric oracle.

Moreover, the actual test results are random in the case of randomized software and random testing. Therefore, it is not possible to give an exact expected value. In this scheme, the expected statistical characteristic is compared with the actual test results. A statistical oracle does not check the actual output but only some characteristics of it. Therefore, a statistical oracle cannot decide whether or not a single test case passes. If a failure occurs, identification of the failure cannot be attributed to the success of a single test case; rather, the entire group of test cases is credited with the success. The decision of a statistical oracle is not always correct. In other words, at best the probability for a correct decision can be given. Figure 9.11 shows the structure of a statistical oracle [23]. It consists of a statistical analyzer and a comparator. The statistical analyzer computes various characteristics that may be modeled as random variables and delivers it to the comparator. The comparator computes the empirical sample mean and the empirical sample variance of its inputs. Furthermore, expected values and properties of the characteristics are computed by the comparator based on the distributional parameters of the random test input.

Adaptive Random Testing In adaptive random testing the test inputs are selected from the randomly generated set in such a way that these are evenly spread over the entire input domain. The goal is to select a small number of test inputs to detect the first failure. A number of random test inputs are generated, then the "best" one among them is selected. We need to make sure the selected new test input is not too close to any of the previously selected ones. That is, the selected test inputs should be distributed as spaced out as possible.

An adaptive random testing technique proposed by Chen et al. [24] keeps two sets, namely, T and C, as follows:

- *The executed set* T is the set of distinct test inputs that have been selected and executed without revealing any failure.

- *The candidate set* C is a set of test inputs that are randomly selected.

Initially the set T is empty, and the first test input is randomly selected from the input domain. The set T is then incrementally updated with the selected element from the set C and executed until a failure is revealed. From the set C, an element that is farthest away from all the elements in the set T is selected as the next test input. The criterion "farthest away" can be defined as follows. Let

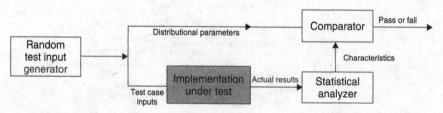

Figure 9.11 Statistical oracle.

$T = \{t_1, t_2, \ldots, t_n\}$ be the executed set and $C = \{c_1, c_2, \ldots, c_k\}$ be the candidate set such that $C \cap T = \phi$. The criterion is to select the element c_h such that, for all $j \in \{1, 2, \ldots, k\}$ and $j \neq h$,

$$\min_{i=1}^{n} \text{dist}(c_h, t_i) \geq \min_{i=1}^{n} \text{dist}(c_j, t_i)$$

where dist is defined as the Euclidean distance. In an m-dimensional input domain, for inputs $a = (a_1, a_2, \ldots, a_m)$ and $b = (b_1, b_2, \ldots, b_m)$, $\text{dist}(a, b) = \sqrt{\sum_{i=1}^{m}(a_i - b_i)^2}$. The rationale of this criterion is to evenly spread the test input by maximizing the minimum distance between the next test input and the already executed test cases.

It should be noted that there are various ways to construct the candidate set C giving rise to various versions of adaptive random testing. For example, a new candidate set can be constructed of size 10 each time a test input is selected. Empirical study shows that adaptive random testing does outperform ordinary random testing by 50% [24]. In the above comparison the performance metric is the size of the test suite used to detect the first failure.

9.8 ERROR GUESSING

Error guessing is a test case design technique where a test engineer uses experience to (i) guess the types and probable locations of defects and (ii) design tests specifically to reveal the defects. For example, if memory is allocated dynamically, then a good place to look for error is the portion of the code after the allocated memory is used—there is a possibility that unused memory is not deallocated. An experienced test engineer can ask the question: Are all the allocated memory blocks correctly deallocated?

Though experience is of much use in guessing errors, it is useful to add some structure to the technique. It is good to prepare a list of types of errors that can be uncovered. The error list can aid us in guessing where errors may occur. Such a list should be maintained from experience gained from earlier test projects. The following are the critical areas of the code where defects are most likely to be found:

- Different portions of the code have different complexity. One can measure code complexity by means of cyclomatic complexity. Portions of the code with a high cyclomatic complexity are likely to have defects. Therefore, it is productive to concentrate more efforts on those portions of code.

- The code that has been recently added or modified can potentially contain defects. The probability of inadvertently introducing defects with addition and modification of code is high.

- Portions of code with prior defect history are likely to be prone to errors. Such code blocks are likely to be defective, because of clustering tendency of the defects, despite the efforts to remove the defects by rewriting the code.

- Parts of a system where new, unproven technology has been used is likely to contain defects. For example, if the code has been automatically generated from a formal specification of the system, then there is higher possibility of defects imbedded into the code.

- Portions of the code for which the functional specification has been loosely defined can be more defective.

- Code blocks that have been produced by novice developers can be defective. If some developers have not been careful during coding in the past, then any code written by these developers should be examined in greater detail.

- Code segments for which a developer may have a low confidence level should receive more attention. The developers know the internal details of the system better than anyone else. Therefore, they should be quizzed on their comfort levels and more test effort be put on those areas where a developer feels less confident about their work.

- Areas where the quality practices have been poor should receive additional attention. An example of poor quality practice is not adequately testing a module at the unit level. Another example of poor quality practice is not performing code review for a critical part of a module.

- A module that involved many developers should receive more test effort. If several developers worked on a particular part of the code, there is a possibility of misunderstanding among different developers and, therefore, there is a good possibility of errors in these parts of the code.

9.9 CATEGORY PARTITION

The category partition method (CPM) is a generalization and formalization of a classical functional testing approach. The reader is reminded of the two steps of the classical functional testing approach: (i) partition the input domain of the functional unit to be tested into equivalence classes and (ii) select test data from each EC of the partition. The CPM [25] is a systematic, specification-based methodology that uses an informal functional specification to produce formal test specification. The test designer's key job is to develop *categories*, which are defined to be the major characteristics of the input domain of the function under test. Each category is partitioned into ECs of inputs called *choices*. The choices in each category must be disjoint, and together the choices in each category must cover the input domain. In a later paper [26], Grochtmann and Grimm extend this approach by capturing the constraints using a tree structure to reduce the number of impossible test cases.

The main advantage of this approach is the creation of a formal test specification written in languages such as test specification language (TSL) [27], Z [28], [29], or testing and test control notation (TTCN) [30] to represent an informal or natural language formal specification. The formal test specification gives the test engineer a logical way to control test generation and is easily modified to accommodate changes or mistakes in the functional specification. The use of Z allows more flexibility in the specification of constraints and more formalities in the representation.

The category partition testing method is comprised of the following steps:

Step 1: **Analyze the Specification** The method begins with the decomposition of a functional specification into functional units that can be separately tested. For each functional unit, identify the following:

- Parameters of the functional unit
- Characteristics of each parameter, that is, the elementary characteristics of the parameters that affect the execution of the unit
- Objects in the environment whose state might affect the operation of the functional unit
- Characteristics of each environment object

Parameters are the explicit input to a functional unit, and environment conditions are the state characteristics of the system at the time of execution of a functional specification.

Step 2: **Identify Categories** A category is a classification of the major properties (or characteristics) of a parameter or an environmental condition. Consider, for instance, a program P_{SORT} that reads an input file F containing a variable-length array of values of arbitrary type. The expected output is a permutation of input with values sorted according to some total ordering criterion. The environmental condition for P_{SORT} is status of F, which can be classified into three categories, namely Status of F = Does Not Exist, Status of F = Exists But Empty, and Status of F = Exists and Nonempty. The properties of the input parameter categories for the P_{SORT} are as follows: the array size, the type of elements, the minimum element value, the maximum element value, and the positions in the array of the maximum and minimum values. Categories can be derived directly from the functional specification, implicit design information, or intuition of the test engineer. Often categories are derived from preconditions and type information about the input parameters and system state components.

Step 3: **Partition Categories into Choices** Partition each category into distinct choices that include all the different kinds of values that are possible for the category. Each choice is an equivalent class of values assumed to have identical properties as far as testing and error detection capability are concerned. The choices must be disjoint and cover all the categories. While the categories are derived from a functional specification, the choices can be based on specification and the test engineer's past experience of designing effective test cases, such as error guessing.

In the sorting program P_{SORT} example, one possible way to partition the category *array size* is size = 0, size = 1, $2 \Leftarrow$ size $\Leftarrow 100$, and size > 100. These choices are based primarily on experience with likely errors. The selection of a single choice from each category determines a *test frame*, which is the basis for constructing the actual test cases. A test frame consists of a set of choices from the specification, with each category contributing either zero or one choice. Since the choices in different categories frequently interact with each other in ways that affect the resulting test cases, the choices can be annotated with *constraints* (see next step) to indicate these relations. In the absence of constraints the number of potential test frames is the product of the number of choices in each category—and this is likely to be very large.

Step 4: **Determine Constraints among Choices** Constraints are restrictions among the choices within different categories that can interact with one another. A typical constraint specifies that a choice from one category cannot occur together in a test frame with certain choices from another category. Choices and constraints are derived from the natural language functional specifications but can often be specified by formal methods, thus making their analysis easier to automate. With a careful specification of constraints, the number of potential test frames can be reduced to a manageable number.

Step 5: **Formalize and Evaluate Test Specification** Specify the categories, choices, and constraints using a specification technique that is compatible with the test generation tool, such as TSL, Z, or TTCN, that produces test frames. Most test generation tools also provide automated techniques for evaluating the internal consistency of the formal specification. This evaluation often discovers errors or inconsistencies in the specification of constraints and sometimes leads to discovery of errors in the source functional specification.

Step 6: **Generate and Validate Test Cases** The final step in the test production process is to transform the generated test frames into executable test cases. If the test specification includes postconditions that must be satisfied, then the tool verifies the postconditions. In case a reference implementation is available, the test cases can be validated by executing them and checking their results against the reference implementation. The validation of test cases is a labor-intensive process in the absence of a reference implementation [31].

9.10 SUMMARY

This chapter began with an introduction to the concept of functional testing, which consists of (i) precise identification of the domain of each input and each output variable, (ii) selection of values from a data domain having important properties, and (iii) combination of values of different variables. Next, we examined four different types of variables, namely, numeric, arrays, substructures, and strings. Only functionally related subsets of input variables are considered to be combined to reduce the total number of input combinations [3, 4]. In this way, the total number of combinations of special values of the variables is reduced. Then, we discussed the scope and complexity of functional testing. Next, we introduced seven testing techniques as summarized in the following:

- **Pairwise Testing:** Pairwise testing requires that for a given numbers of input parameters to the system each possible combination of values for any pair of parameters be covered by at least one test case. It is a special case of combinatorial testing that requires n-way combinations be tested, $n = 1, 2, \ldots, N$, where N is the total number of parameters in the system. We presented two popular pairwise test selection techniques, namely, OA and IPO.

- **Equivalence Class Partitioning:** The aim of EC partitioning is to divide the input domain of the system under test into classes (or groups) of test cases that have a similar effect on the system. Equivalence partitioning is a systematic method for identifying sets of interesting classes of input conditions to be tested. We provided guidelines to identify (i) ECs and (ii) test data from the ECs that need to be executed.

- **Boundary Value Analysis:** The boundary conditions for each EC are analyzed in order to generate test cases. Boundary conditions are predicates that apply directly on, above, and beneath the boundaries of input ECs and output ECs. We explained useful guidelines which are applicable to the input and the output conditions of the identified EC. These are useful in identifying quality test cases.

- **Decision Tables:** This is a simple but powerful technique to describe a complex system. A decision table comprises a set of conditions placed above a set of effects (or results) to perform in a matrix form. There exists a rule for each combination of conditions. Each rule comprises a Y (yes), N (no), or—(don't care) response and contains an associated list of effects. Thus, each rule of the decision table represents a test case.

- **Random Testing:** The random testing technique can be summarized as a four-step procedure:

  1. The input domain is identified.

  2. The test inputs are independently selected from this domain.

  3. The system under test is executed on a random set of inputs.

  4. The results are compared with the system specification.

  The test is a failure if any input leads to incorrect results; otherwise it is a success.
  The procedure requires a test oracle to ensure adequate evaluation of the test results. A test oracle tells us whether a test case passes or not. We discussed four standard types of oracles, namely, perfect, gold, parametric, and statistical. We also examined the concept of adaptive random testing in which test inputs are selected from a randomly generated set. These test

inputs are evenly spread over the entire input domain in order to achieve a small number of test inputs to detect the first failure.

- **Error Guessing:** This is a test case design technique where the experience of the testers is used to (i) guess the type and location of errors and (ii) design tests specifically to expose those errors. Error guessing is an ad hoc approach in designing test cases.

- **Category Partition:** The category partition methodology requires a test engineer to divide the functional specification into independent functional units that can be tested separately. This method identifies the input parameters and the environmental conditions, known as categories, by relying upon the guidance of the test engineer. Next, the test engineer decomposes each identified category into mutually exclusive choices that are used to describe the partition of the input within the category. Then the categories, choices, and constraints are specified using a formal specification language such as TSL. The specification is then processed to produce a set of *test frames* for the functional unit. The test engineer examines the test frames and determines if any changes to the test specification are necessary. Finally, the test frames are converted to executable test cases.

LITERATURE REVIEW

The IPO algorithm discussed in this chapter has been implemented in a tool called PairTest [8] which provides a graphical interface to make the tool easy to use. A test tool called automatic efficient test generator (AETG) was created at Telcordia and published in the following two articles:

D. M. Cohen, S. R. Dalal, M. L. Fredman, and G. C. Patton, "The AETG System: An Approach to Testing Based on Combinatorial Design," *IEEE Transactions on Software Engineering*, Vol. 23, No. 7, July 1997, pp.437–444.

D. M. Cohen, S. R. Dalal, J. Parelius, and G. C. Patton, "The Combinatorial Design Approach to Automatic Test Generation," *IEEE Software*, Vol. 13, No. 5, September 1996, pp.83–89.

The strategy used in this tool starts with an empty test suite and adds one test case at a time. The tool produces a number of candidate test cases according to a greedy algorithm and then selects one that covers the most uncovered pairs.

Few topics related to software testing techniques seem to be more controversial than the question of whether it is efficient to use randomly generated test input data. The relative effectiveness of random testing (i.e., random selection of test inputs from the entire input domain) versus partition testing (i.e., dividing the input domain into nonoverlapping subdomains and selecting one test input from each subdomain) has been the subject of many research papers. The interested reader is referred to the following papers for some of these discussions:

T. Chen and Y. Yu, "On the Expected Number of Failures Detected by Subdomain Testing and Random Testing," *IEEE Transactions on Software Engineering*, Vol. 22, 1996, pp.109–119.

J .W. Duran and S. C. Ntafos, "An Evaluation of Random Testing," *IEEE Transactions on Software Engineering*, Vol. 10, July 1984, pp.438–444.

R. Hamlet and R. Taylor, "Partition Testing Does Not Inspire Confidence," *IEEE Transactions on Software Engineering*, Vol. 16, 1990, pp.1402–1411.

W. Gutjahr, "Partition Testing versus Random Testing: The Influence of Uncertainty," *IEEE Transactions on Software Engineering*, Vol. 25, 1999, pp.661–674.

E. J. Weyuker and B. Jeng, "Analyzing Partition Testing Strategies," *IEEE Transactions on Software Engineering*, Vol. 17, 1991, pp.703–711.

The boundary value analysis technique produces test inputs near the boundaries to find failures caused by incorrect implementation of the boundaries. However, boundary value analysis can be adversely affected by coincidental correctness, that is, the system produces the the expected output, but for the wrong reason. The article by Rob M. Hierons ("Avoiding Coincidental Correctness in Boundary Value Analysis," *ACM Transactions on Software Engineering and Methodology*, Vol. 15, No. 3, July 2006, pp. 227–241) describes boundary value analysis that can be adapted in order to reduce the likelihood of coincidental correctness. The work described by the author can be seen as a formalization and generalization of work suggested by Lori A. Clarke, Johnette Hassell, and Debra J. Richardson ("A Close Look at Domain Testing," *IEEE Transactions on Software Engineering*, Vol. 8, No. 4, July 1982, pp. 380–390).

REFERENCES

1. W. E. Howden. Functional Program Testing. *IEEE Transactions on Software Engineering*, March 1980, pp. 162–169.
2. W. E. Howden. *Functional Program Testing and Analysis*. McGraw-Hill, New York, 1987.
3. W. E. Howden. Applicability of Software Validation Techniques to Scientific Programs. *ACM Transactions on Software Engineering and Methodology*, July 1980, pp. 307–320.
4. W. E. Howden. A Functional Approach to Program Testing and Analysis. *IEEE Transactions on Software Engineering*, October 1986, pp. 997–1005.
5. D. R. Kuhn, D. R. Wallace, and A. M. Gallo, Jr. Software Fault Interactions and Implications for Software Testing. *IEEE Transactions on Software Engineering*, June 2004, pp. 418–421.
6. M. Grindal, J. Offutt, and S. F. Andler. Combination Testing Strategies: A Survey. *Journal of Software Testing, Verification, and Reliability*, September 2005, pp. 97–133.
7. M. S. Phadke. *Quality Engineering Using Robust Design*. Prentice-Hall, Englewood Cliffs, NJ, 1989.
8. K. C. Tai and Y. Lei. A Test Generation Strategy for Pairwise Testing. *IEEE Transactions on Software Engineering*, January 1992, pp. 109–111.
9. L. Copeland. Object-Oriented Testing. *Software Quality Engineering*, STAR East, Orlando, FL, May 2001.
10. A. S. Hedayat, N. J. A. Sloane, and J. Stufken. *Orthogonal Arrays: Theory and Applications*, Springer Series in Statistics, Springer-Verlag, New York, 1999.

11. R. K. Roy. *Design of Experiments Using the Taguchi Approach: 16 Steps to Product and Process Improvement*. Wiley, New York, 2001.

12. B. Mandl. Orthogonal Latin Square: An Application of Experiment Design to Compiler Testing. *Communications of the ACM*, October 1985, pp. 1054–1058.

13. N. J. A. Sloane. *A Library of Orthogonnal Arrays*. Information Sciences Research Center, AT&T Shannon Labs, 2001. Available at http://www.research.att.com/~njas/oadir/.

14. B. Beizer. *Software Testing Techniques*, 2nd ed. Van Nostrand Reinhold, New York, 1990.

15. D. Richardson and L. Clarke. A Partition Analysis Method to Increase Program Reliablity. In *Proceedings of the 5th International Conference Software Engineering*, San Diego, CA, IEEE Computer Society Press, Piscataway, March 1981, pp. 244–253.

16. G. Myers. *The Art of Software Testing*, 2nd ed. Wiley, New York, 2004.

17. B. Beizer. *Black Box Testing*. Wiley, New York, 1995.

18. D. Thomas. Agile Programming: Design to Accommodate Change. *IEEE Software*, May/June 2005, pp. 14–16.

19. R. Hamlet. Random Testing. *In Encyclopedia of Software Engineering*, J. Marciniak, Ed. Wiley, New York, 1994, pp. 970–978.

20. W. Cochran. *Sampling Techniques*. Wiley, New York, 1977.

21. W. E. Howden. A Survey of Dynamic Analysis Methods. In *Software Testing and Validation Techniques*, 2nd ed., E. Miller and W. E. Howden, Eds. IEEE Computer Society Press, Los Alamito, CA, 1981.

22. R. V. Binder. *Testing Object-Oriented Systems: Models, Patterns, and Tools*. Addison-Wesley, Reading, MA, 2000.

23. J. Mayer and R. Guderlei. *Test Oracles Using Statistical Methods*. SOQUA/TECOS, Erfurt, Germany, 2004, pp. 179–189.

24. T. Y. Chen, H. Leung, and I. K. Mak. Adaptive Random Testing. *Advances in Computer Science—ASIAN 2004, Higher-Level Decision Making*, 9th Asian Computing Science Conference, Dedicated to Jean-Louis Lassez on the Occasion of His 5th Cycle Birthday, Chiang Mai, Thailand, December 8–10, 2004, M. J. Maher, Ed., *Lecture Notes in Computer Science*, Vol. 3321, Springer, Berlin/Heidelberg, 2004, pp. 320–329.

25. T. J. Ostrand and M. J. Balcer. The Category-Partition Method for Specifying and Generating Functional Tests. *Communications of the ACM*, June 1988, pp. 676–686.

26. M. Grochtmann and K. Grimm. Classification Trees for Partition Testing. *Journal of Testing, Verification, and Reliability*, June 1993, pp. 63–82.

27. M. Balcer, W. Halsing, and T. J. Ostrand. Automatic Generation of Test Scripts from Formal Test Specification. In *Proceeding of the Third Symposium on Software Testing, Analysis, and Verification*, Key West, FL, ACM Press, New York, December 1989, pp. 210–218.

28. G. Laycock. Formal Specification and Testing: A Case Study. *Journal of Testing, Verification, and Reliability*, March 1992, pp. 7–23.

29. P. Ammann and J. Offutt. Using Formal Methods to Derive Test Frames in Category-Partition Testing. Paper presented at the Ninth Annual Conference on Computer Assurance, Gaithersburg, MD, June 1994, pp. 69–80.

30. C. Willcock, T. Deiss, S. Tobies, S. Keil, F. Engler, and S. Schulz. *An Introduction to TTCN-3*. Wiley, New York, 2005.

31. K. Naik and B. Sarikaya. Test Case Verification by Model Checking. *Formal Methods in Systems Design*, June 1993, pp. 277–321.

Exercises

1. (a) What is the central idea in Howden's theory of functional testing?

   (b) What is a *functionally identifiable* substructure?

   (c) All combinations of special values of input variables can lead to a large number of test cases being selected. What technique can be used to reduce the number of combinations of test cases?

2. Consider the system S in Figure 9.7, which has three input parameters X, Y, and Z. Assume that set D, a set of input test data values, has been selected for each of the input variables such that $D(X) = \{$True, False$\}$, $D(Y) = \{0, 5\}$, and $D(Z) = \{P, Q, R\}$. Using the orthogonal array method discussed in this chapter, generate pairwise test cases for this system. Compare the results with the test suite generated using the IPO algorithm.

3. Discuss the drawback of the orthogonal array methodology compared to the IPO algorithm.

4. Consider the system S which can take n input parameters and each parameter can take on m values. For this system answer the following questions:

   (a) What is the maximum number of pairs a single test case for this system can cover?

   (b) In the best case, how many test cases can provide full pairwise coverage?

   (c) Calculate the total number of pairs the test suite must cover.

   (d) Suppose that $n = 13$ and $m = 3$. What is the minimum number of test cases to be selected to achieve pairwise coverage?

5. Consider the following triangle classification system, originally used by Myers [16]: The system reads in three positive values from the standard input. The three values A, B, and C are interpreted as representing the lengths of the sides of a triangle. The system then prints a message on the standard output saying whether the triangle is scalene, isosceles, equilateral, or right angled if a triangle can be formed. Answer the following questions for the above program:

   (a) What is the input domain of the system?

   (b) What are the input conditions?

   (c) Identify the equivalence classes for the system?

   (d) Identify test cases to cover the identified ECs?

6. Consider again the triangle classification program with a slightly different specification: The program reads floating values from the standard input. The three values A, B, and C are interpreted as representing the lengths of the sides of a triangle. The program then prints a message to the standard output that states whether the triangle, if it can be formed, is scalene, isosceles, equilateral, or right angled. Determine the following for the above program:

   (a) For the boundary condition $A + B > C$ case (scalene triangle), identify test cases to verify the boundary.

   (b) For the boundary condition $A = C$ case (isosceles triangle), identify test cases to verify the boundary.

   (c) For the boundary condition $A = B = C$ case (equilateral triangle), identify test cases to verify the boundary.

   (d) For the boundary condition $A^2 + B^2 = C^2$ case (right-angle triangle), identify test cases to verify the boundary.

(e) For the nontriangle case, identify test cases to explore the boundary.

(f) For nonpositive input, identify test points.

7. Consider the triangle classification specification. The system reads in three positive values from the standard input. The three values A, B, and C are interpreted as representing the lengths of the sides of a triangle. The system then prints a message to the standard output saying whether the triangle, if it can be formed, is scalene, isosceles, equilateral, or not a triangle. Develop a decision table to generate test cases for this specification.

8. What are the advantages and disadvantages of random testing?

9. What is a test oracle? What are the differences between a parametric oracle and a statistical oracle?

10. Discuss the similarity between the decision table–based and category partition–based testing methodology.

CHAPTER 10

Test Generation from FSM Models

The sciences do not try to explain, they hardly even try to interpret, they mainly make models. By a model is meant a mathematical construct which, with the addition of certain verbal interpretations describes observed phenomena. The justification of such a mathematical construct is solely and precisely that it is expected to work.
— *John von Neumann*

10.1   STATE-ORIENTED MODEL

Software systems can be broadly classified into two groups, namely, *stateless* and *state-oriented* systems. The actions of a stateless system do not depend on the previous inputs to the system. A compiler is an example of a stateless system because the result of compiling a program does not depend on the programs that had been previously compiled. The response of the system to the present input depends on the past inputs to the system in a state-oriented system. A state-oriented system memorizes the sequence of inputs it has received so far in the form of a *state*. A telephone switching system is an example of a state-oriented system. The interpretation of digits by a telephone switch depends on the previous inputs, such as a phone going off the hook, the sequence of digits dialed, and other the keys pressed.

A state-oriented system can be viewed as having a *control portion* and a *data portion*. The control portion specifies the sequences of interactions with its environment, and the data portion specifies the data to be processed and saved. Depending on the characteristics of systems, a system can be predominantly data oriented, be predominantly control oriented, or have a balanced mix of both data and control, as illustrated in Figure 10.1.

In a data dominating system, the system spends most of its time processing user requests, and the interaction sequences with the user are very simple. Therefore, the control portion is simpler compared to the data processing, which is more complex. This situation is depicted in Figure 10.2.

Software Testing and Quality Assurance: Theory and Practice, Edited by Kshirasagar Naik and Priyadarshi Tripathy
Copyright © 2008 John Wiley & Sons, Inc.

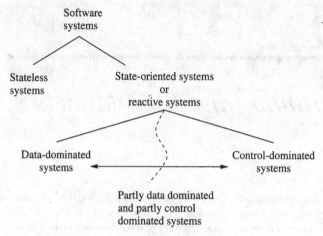

Figure 10.1   Spectrum of software systems.

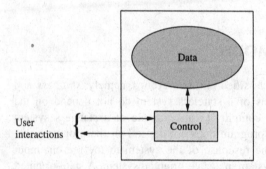

Figure 10.2   Data-dominated systems.

Example. A *web browsing* application is an example of data dominating systems. The system spends a significant amount of time in accessing remote data by making http requests and formatting it for display. The system responds to each command input from the user, and there is not much state information that the system must remember. A need for having state information is to perform the **Back** operation. Moreover, web browsing is not a time-dependent application, except for its dependence on the underlying Transmission Control Protocol/Internet Protocol (TCP/IP) operations.

In a control dominating system, the system performs complex (i.e., many time-dependent and long-sequence) interactions with its user, while the amount of data being processed is relatively small. Therefore, the control portion is a large one, whereas the data processing functionality is very small. This situation is depicted in Figure 10.3.

Example. A telephone switching system is an example of a control dominating system. The amount of user data processed is rather minimal. The data involved are

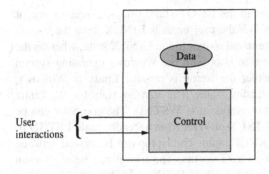

Figure 10.3 Control-dominated systems.

User interactions

Control

Data

a mapping of phone numbers to equipment details, off- and on-hook events generated by a user, phone number dialed, and possibly some other events represented by the push of other keys on a telephone.

The control portion of a software system can often be modeled as a finite-state machine, (FSM), that is, the interactions between the system and its user or environment (Figures 10.2 and 10.3).

We have modeled the interactions of a user with a dual-boot laptop computer (Figure 10.4). Initially, the laptop is in the **OFF** state. When a user presses the

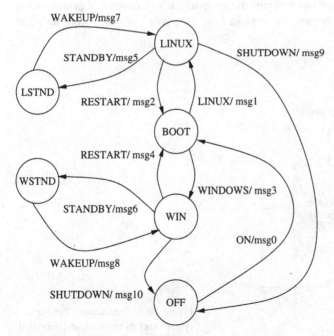

Figure 10.4   FSM model of a dual-boot laptop computer.

power **ON** button, the system moves to the **BOOT** state, where it receives one of two inputs **LINUX** and **WINDOWS**. If the user input is **LINUX**, then the system boots with the Linux operating system and moves to the **LINUX** state, whereas the **WINDOWS** input causes the system to boot with the Windows operating system and moves to the **WIN** state. Whether the laptop is running Linux or Windows, the user can put the machine in standby states. The standby state for the Linux mode is **LSTND** and for the Windows mode it is **WSTND**. The computer can be brought back to its operating state **LINUX** or **WIN** from a standby state **LSTND** or **WSTND**, respectively, with a **WAKEUP** input. The laptop can be moved between **LINUX** and **WIN** states using **RESTART** inputs. The laptop can be shut down using the **SHUTDOWN** input while it is in the **LINUX** or **WIN** state. The laptop can also be brought to the **OFF** state by using the power button, but we have not shown these transitions in Figure 10.4.

The reader may note that for the purpose of generating test cases we do not consider the *internal* behavior of a system; instead we assume that the external behavior of the system has been modeled as an FSM. To be more precise, the interactions of a system with its environment is modeled as an FSM, as illustrated in Figure 10.5.

Now we can make a correspondence between Figures 10.5 and 10.4. The **software system** block in Figure 10.5 can be viewed as the boot software running on a laptop, and the **environment** block in Figure 10.5 can be viewed as a user. The FSM shown in Figure 10.4 models the interactions shown by the bidirectional arrows in Figure 10.5.

An FSM model of the external behavior of a system describes the sequences of input to and expected output from the system. Such a model is a prime source of test cases. In this chapter, we explain how to derive test cases from an FSM model.

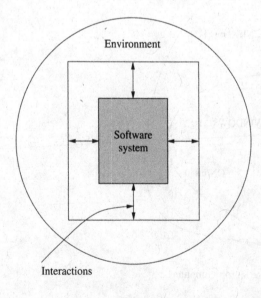

Figure 10.5 Interactions between system and its environment modeled as FSM.

10.2 POINTS OF CONTROL AND OBSERVATION

A *point of control and observation* (PCO) is a well-designated point of interaction between a system and its *users*. We use the term *users* in a broad sense to include all entities, including human users and other software and hardware systems, lying outside but interacting with the system under consideration. PCOs have the following characteristics:

- A PCO represents a point where a system receives input from its users and/or produces output for the users.
- There may be multiple PCOs between a system and its users.
- Even if a system under test (SUT) is a software system, for a human user a PCO may be "nearer" to the user than to the software under test. For example, a user may interact with a system via a push button, a touch screen, and so on. We want to emphasize that even if we have a software SUT, we may not have a keyboard and a monitor for interacting with the system.
- In case a PCO is a *physical entity*, such as a push button, a keyboard, or a speaker, there is a need to find their computer representations so that test cases can be automatically executed.

Example. Assume that we have a software system controlling a telephone switch PBX to provide connections between users. The SUT and the users interact via the different subsystems of a telephone. We show the user–interface details of a basic telephone to explain the concept of a PCO (Figure 10.6) and summarize those details in Table 10.1.

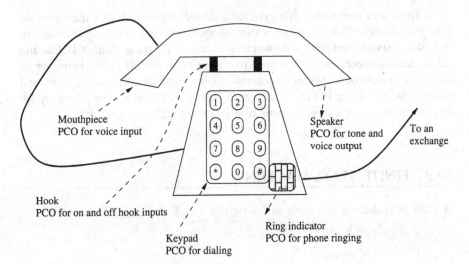

Figure 10.6   PCOs on a telephone.

TABLE 10.1   PCOs for Testing Telephone PBX

PCO	In/Out View of System	Description
Hook	In	The system receives off-hook and on-hook events.
Keypad	In	The caller dials a number and provides other control input.
Ring indicator	Out	The callee receives ring indication.
Speaker	Out	The caller receives tones (dial, fast busy, slow busy, etc.) and voice.
Mouthpiece	In	The caller produces voice input.

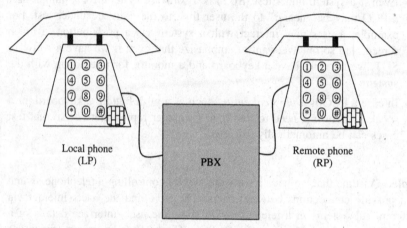

Figure 10.7   FSM model of a PBX.

The reader may notice that even for a simple device such as a telephone we have *five* distinct PCOs via which a user interacts with the switching software. In real life, users interact with the switching software via these distinct PCOs, and automated test execution systems must recognize those distinct PCOs. However, to make our discussion of test case generation from FSM models simple, clear, and concise, we use fewer PCOs. We designate all the PCOs on a *local phone* by LP and all the PCOs on a *remote phone* by RP (Figure 10.7).

10.3   FINITE-STATE MACHINE

A FSM M is defined as a tuple as follows: $M = <S, I, O, s_0, \delta, \lambda>$, where

S is a set of states,

I is a set of inputs,

O is a set of outputs,

s_0 is the initial state,

$\delta : S \times I \rightarrow S$ is a next-state function, and

$\lambda : S \times I \rightarrow O$ is an output function.

Note the following points related to inputs and outputs because of the importance of the concept of *observation* in testing a system:

- Identify the inputs and the outputs which are observed by explicitly specifying a set of PCOs. For each state transition, specify the PCO at which the input occurs and the output is observed.

- There may be many outputs occurring at different PCOs for a single input in a state.

An FSM specification of the interactions between a user and a PBX system is shown in Figure 10.8. The FSM has nine distinct states as explained in Table 10.2.

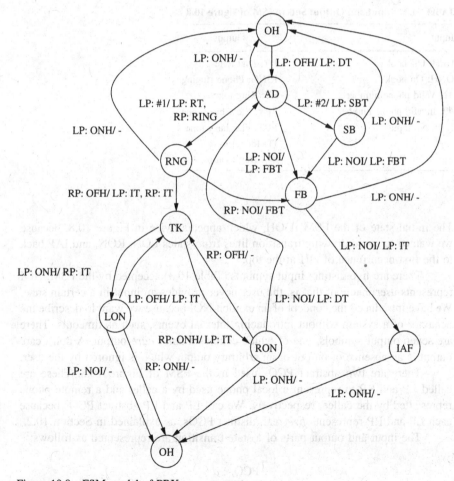

Figure 10.8   FSM model of PBX.

TABLE 10.2   Set of States in FSM of Figure 10.8

Abbreviation	Expanded Form	Meaning
OH	On hook	A phone is on hook.
AD	Add digit	The user is dialing a number.
SB	Slow busy	The system has produced a slow busy tone.
FB	Slow busy	The system has produced a fast busy tone.
RNG	Ring	The remote phone is ringing.
TK	Talk	A connection is established.
LON	Local on hook	The local phone is on hook.
RON	Remote on hook	The remote phone is on hook.
IAF	Idle after Fast busy	The local phone is idle after a fast busy.

TABLE 10.3   Input and Output Sets in FSM of Figure 10.8

Input	Output
OFH: Off hook	DT: Dial tone
ONH: On hook	RING: Phone ringing
#1: Valid phone number	RT: Ring tone
#2: Invalid phone number	SBT: Slow busy tone
NOI: No input	FBT: Fast busy tone
	IT: Idle tone
	—: Don't care

The initial state of the FSM is OH, which appears twice in Figure 10.8, because we wanted to avoid drawing transition lines from states LON, RON, and IAF back to the first occurrence of OH at the top.

There are five distinct input symbols (Table 10.3) accepted by the FSM. NOI represents user inaction; that is, the user never provides an input in a certain state. We have introduced the concept of an explicit NOI because we want to describe the behavior of a system without introducing internal events, such as timeouts. There are seven output symbols, one of which denotes a *don't care* output. A don't care output is an absence of output or an arbitrary output which is ignored by the user.

There are two abstract PCOs used in the FSM of Figure 10.8. These are called LP and RP to represent a local phone used by a caller and a remote phone represented by the callee, respectively. We call LP and RP abstract PCOs because each LP and RP represents *five* real, distinct PCOs, as explained in Section 10.2.

The input and output parts of a state transition are represented as follows:

$$\frac{\text{PCO}_i : a}{\text{PCO}_j : b}$$

where input a occurs at PCO_i and output b occurs at PCO_j. If a state transition produces multiple outputs, we use the notation

$$\frac{PCO_i : a}{\{PCO_j : b, PCO_k : c\}}$$

where input a occurs at PCO_i, output b occurs at PCO_j, and output c occurs at PCO_k. We will represent a complete transition using the following syntax:

<present state, input, output, next state> or <present state, input/output, next state>

The state transition <OH, LP: OFH, LP: DT, AD> means that if the FSM is in state OH and receives input OFH (off hook) at port (PCO) LP, it produces output DT (dial tone) at the same port LP and moves to state AD (Figure 10.8).

10.4 TEST GENERATION FROM AN FSM

Given an FSM model M of the requirements of a system and an implementation I_M of M, the immediate testing task is to confirm that the implementation I_M behaves as prescribed by M. The testing process that verifies that an implementation conforms to its specification is called *conformance testing*. The basic idea in conformance testing is summarized as follows:

- Obtain sequences of state transitions from M.
- Turn each sequence of a state transition into a test sequence.
- Test I_M with a set of test sequences and observe whether or not I_M possesses the corresponding sequences of state transitions.
- The conformance of I_M with M can be verified by carefully choosing enough state transition sequences from M.

In the following sections, first, we explain the ways to turn a state transition sequence into a test sequence. Next, we explain the process of selecting different state transition sequences.

10.5 TRANSITION TOUR METHOD

In this section, we discuss a process to generate a *test sequence* or *test case* T_c from a *state transition sequence* S_t of a given FSM M. Specifically, we consider *transition tours*, where a transition tour is a sequence of state transitions beginning and ending at the initial state. Naito and Tsunoyama [1] introduced the transition tour method for generating test cases from FSM specifications of sequential circuits. Sarikaya and Bochmann [2] were the first to observe that the transition tour method can be applied to protocol testing. An example of a transition tour obtained from

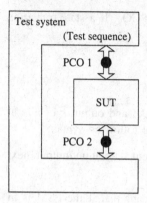

Figure 10.9   Interaction of test sequence with SUT.

Figure 10.8 is as follows: <OH, LP: OFH, LP: DT, AD>, <AD, LP: ONH, LP: —, OH>. One can easily identify the *state*, *input*, and *expected output* components in the sequence of Figure 10.8. However, it may be noted that a test case is not merely a sequence of pairs of <input, expected output>, but rather a complete test case must contain additional behavior such that it can be executed autonomously even if the SUT contains faults. A *test system* interacting with a SUT is shown in Figure 10.9. A test system consists of a set of *test cases* and a test case *scheduler*. The scheduler decides the test case to be executed next depending on the *test case dependency* constraints specified by a test designer. A test case in execution produces inputs for the SUT and receives outputs from the SUT. It is obvious that a faulty SUT may produce an output which is different from the expected output, and sometimes it may not produce any output at all. Therefore, the test system must be able to handle these exceptional cases in addition to the normal cases. This idea leads us to the following formalization of a process for designing a complete test case:

- A test case contains a sequence of input and expected output data. This information is derived from the FSM specification of the SUT.

- A test case must be prepared to receive *unexpected* outputs from the SUT.

- A test case must not wait indefinitely to receive an output—expected or unexpected.

Example: Transition Tour.   Let us derive a test case from the state transition sequence <OH, LP: OFH, LP: DT, AD>, <AD, LP: ONH, LP: —, OH>. It is useful to refer to a PCO of Figure 10.9, which explains an input–output relationship between the test system and a SUT. A sequence of inputs to the SUT can be obtained from its FSM model. For instance, the state transition sequence contains the input sequence {OFH, ONH}. Therefore, the test system must produce an output sequence {OFH, ONH} for the SUT. Therefore, an input in a state transition sequence of an FSM is an output of the test system at the same PCO. An output is represented by prefixing an *exclamation* mark ('!') to an event (or message)

```
1      LP !OFH
2        START(TIMER1, d1)
3          LP ?DT                    PASS
4            CANCEL(TIMER1)
5              LP !ONH
6          LP ?OTHERWISE             FAIL
7            CANCEL(TIMER1)
8              LP !ONH
9          ?TIMER1                   FAIL
10           CANCEL(TIMER1)
11             LP !ONH
```

Figure 10.10   Derived test case from transition tour.

in Figure 10.10. In line 1 of Figure 10.10, LP !OFH means that the test system outputs an event OFH at PCO LP.

An output produced in a state transition of an FMS M is interpreted as an *expected* output of an implementation I_M. Sometimes a faulty implementation may produce unexpected outputs. An output of an SUT becomes an input to the test system. Therefore, an output in a state transition sequence of an FSM is an input to the test system at the same PCO. In Figure 10.10, an input is represented by prefixing a *question* mark ('?') to an event (or message). Therefore, in line 3 of Figure 10.10, LP ?DT means that the test system is ready to receive the input DT at PCO LP.

Here the test system expects to receive an input DT at PCO LP, which has been specified as LP ?DT. However, a faulty SUT may produce an unexpected output instead of the expected output DT at PCO LP. In line 6, the test system is ready to receive any event *other* than a DT at PCO LP. The reader may notice that LP ?DT in line 3 and LP ?OTHERWISE in line 6 appear at the same level of indentation and both lines have the same immediate predecessor action START(TIMER1, d1) in line 2.

If an SUT fails to produce any output—expected or unexpected—then the test system and the SUT will be deadlocked, which is prevented by including a timeout mechanism in the test system. Before a test system starts to wait for an input, it starts a timer of certain duration as shown in line 2. The name of the timer is TIMER1 in line 2, and its timeout duration is d1. If the SUT fails to produce the expected output DT or any other output within an interval of d1 after receiving input OFH at PCO LP, the test system will produce an internal timeout event called TIMER1, which will be received in line 9. One of the events specified in lines 3, 6, and 9 eventually occurs. This means that the test system is not deadlocked in the presence of a faulty SUT.

Coverage Metrics for Selecting Transition Tours.   One can design one test case from one transition tour. One transition tour may not be sufficient to cover an entire FSM, unless it is a long one. Considering the imperative to simplify test design and to test just a small portion of an implementation with one test case, there is a need to design many test cases. A perpetual question is: How many test cases should one design? Therefore, there is a need to identify several transition tours from an FSM. The concept of *coverage metrics* is used in selecting a set of transition tours. In order to test FSM-based implementations, two commonly used coverage metrics are:

- State coverage
- Transition coverage

Transition Tours for State Coverage. We select a set of transition tours so that every state of an FSM is visited at least once to achieve this coverage criterion. We have identified three transition tours, as shown in Table 10.4, to cover all the states of the FSM shown in Figure 10.8. One can easily obtain test sequences from the three transition tours in Table 10.4 following the design principles explained in Section 10.5 to transform a transition tour into a test sequence. State coverage is the weakest among all the selection criteria used to generate test sequences from FSMs. The three transition tours shown in Table 10.4 cover every state of the FSM shown in Figure 10.8 at least once. However, of the 21 state transitions, only 11 are covered by the three transition tours. The 10 state transitions which have not been covered by those three transition tours are listed in Table 10.5. We next consider a stronger form of coverage criterion, namely, *transition coverage*.

Transition Tours for Transition Coverage. We select a set of transition tours so that every state transition of an FSM is visited at least once to achieve this coverage criterion. We have identified nine transition tours, as shown in Table 10.6, to cover all the state transitions of the FSM shown in Figure 10.8. One can easily obtain test sequences from the nine transition tours in Table 10.6 following the design principles explained in Section 10.5 to transform a transition tour into a test sequence.

TABLE 10.4   Transition Tours Covering All States in Figure 10.8

Serial Number	Transition Tours	States Visited
1	<OH, LP:OFH/LP:DT, AD>; <AD, LP:#2/LP:SBT, SB>; <SB, LP:NOI/LP:FBT, FB>; <FB, LP:NOI/LP:IT, IAF>; <IAF, LP:ONH/—, OH>	OH, AD, SB, FB, IAF
2	<OH, LP:OFH/LP:DT, AD>; <AD, LP:#1/{LP:RT, RP:RING}, RNG>; <RNG, RP:OFH/{LP:IT, RP:IT}, TK>; <TK, LP:ONH/RP:IT, LON>; <LON, LP:NOI/—, OH>	OH, AD, RNG, TK, LON
3	<OH, LP:OFH/LP:DT, AD>; <AD, LP:#1/{LP:RT, RP:RING}, RNG>; <RNG, RP:OFH/{LP:IT, RP:IT}, TK>; <TK, RP:ONH/LP:IT, RON>; <RON, LP:ONH/—, OH>	OH, AD, RNG, TK, RON

TABLE 10.5   State Transitions Not Covered by Transition Tours of Table 10.4

Serial Number	State Transitions
1	<AD, LP:ONH/—, OH>
2	<AD, LP:NOI/LP:FBT, FB>
3	<SB, LP:ONH/—, OH>
4	<FB, LP:ONH/—, OH>
5	<LON, LP:OFH/LP:IT, TK>
6	<LON, RP:ONH/—, OH>
7	<RON, RP:OFH/—, TK>
8	<RON, LP:NOI/LP:DT, AD>
9	<RNG, LP:ONH/—, OH>
10	<RNG, RP:NOI/FBT, FB>

TABLE 10.6   Transition Tours Covering All State Transitions in Figure 10.8

Serial Number	Transition Tours
1	<OH, LP:OFH/LP:DT, AD>; <AD, LP:#2/LP:SBT, SB>; <SB, LP:NOI/LP:FBT, FB>; <FB, LP:NOI/LP:IT, IAF>; <IAF, LP:ONH/—, OH>
2	<OH, LP:OFH/LP:DT, AD>; <AD, LP:#1/\{LP:RT, RP:RING\}, RNG>; <RNG, RP:OFH/{LP:IT, RP:IT}, TK>; <TK, LP:ONH/RP:IT, LON>; <LON, LP:NOI/—, OH>
3	<OH, LP:OFH/LP:DT, AD>; <AD, LP:#1/{LP:RT, RP:RING}, RNG>; <RNG, RP:OFH/{LP:IT, RP:IT}, TK>; <TK, RP:ONH/LP:IT, RON>; <RON, LP:ONH/—, OH>
4	<OH, LP:OFH/LP:DT, AD>; <AD, LP:#2/LP:SBT, SB>; <SB, LP:ONH/—, OH>;
5	<OH, LP:OFH/LP:DT, AD>; <AD, LP:NOI/LP:FBT, FB>; <FB, LP:ONH/—, OH>
6	<OH, LP:OFH/LP:DT, AD>; <AD, LP:#1/{LP:RT, RP:RING}, RNG>; <RNG, RP:OFH/{LP:IT, RP:IT}, TK>; <TK, LP:ONH/RP:IT, LON>; <LON, LP:OFH/LP:IT, TK>; <TK, RP:ONH/LP:IT, RON>; <RON, RP:OFH/—, TK>; <TK, LP:ONH/RP:IT, LON>; <LON, LP:NOI/—, OH>
7	<OH, LP:OFH/LP:DT, AD>; <AD, LP:#1/{LP:RT, RP:RING}, RNG>; <RNG, RP:OFH/{LP:IT, RP:IT}, TK>; <TK, RP:ONH/LP:IT, RON>; <RON, LP:NOI/LP:DT, AD>; <AD, LP:ONH/LP:DT, OH>
8	<OH, LP:OFH/LP:DT, AD>; <AD, LP:#1/{LP:RT, RP:RING}, RNG>; <RNG, LP:ONH/—, OH>
9	<OH, LP:OFH/LP:DT, AD>; <AD, LP:#1/{LP:RT, RP:RING}, RNG>; <RNG, RP:NOI/FBT, FB>; <FB, LP:ONH/—, OH>

10.6   TESTING WITH STATE VERIFICATION

There are two *functions* associated with a state transition, namely, an *output* function (λ) and a *next-state* function (δ). Test cases generated using the transition tour method discussed in Section 10.5 focused on the outputs. Now we discuss a method

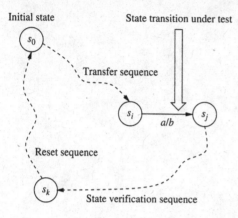

Figure 10.11 Conceptual model of test case with state verification.

for generating test cases by putting emphasis on both the output and the next state of every state transition of an FSM. It is easy to verify outputs since they appear at PCOs, which are external to a system under test. However, verification of the next state of a state transition is not an easy task because the concept of *state* is purely internal to a SUT. The next state of a state transition is verified by applying further inputs to an SUT and observing its response at the PCOs. A conceptual model of a method to generate test cases from an FSM with both output and state verifications is illustrated in Figure 10.11. The five steps of the method are explained in the following. The method is explained from the standpoint of testing a state transition from state s_i to s_j with input a.

Methodology for Testing with State Verification

Step 1: Assuming that the FSM is in its initial state, move the FSM from the initial state s_0 to state s_i by applying a sequence of inputs called a *transfer sequence* denoted by $T(s_i)$. It may be noted that different states will have different transfer sequences, that is, $T(s_i) \neq T(s_j)$ for $i \neq j$. For state s_i, $T(s_i)$ can be obtained from the FSM. At the end of this step, the FSM is in state s_i.

Step 2: In this step we apply input a to the SUT and observe its actual output, which is compared with the expected output b of the FSM. At the end of this step, a correctly implemented state transition takes the SUT to its new state s_j. However, a faulty implementation can potentially take it to a state different from s_j. The new state of the SUT is verified in the following step.

Step 3: Apply a verification sequence VER_j to the SUT and observe the corresponding output sequence. An important property of VER_j is that $\lambda(s_j, VER_j) \neq \lambda(s_\ell, VER_j) \; \forall s_\ell$ and $s_\ell \neq s_j$. At the end of this step, the SUT is in state s_k.

Step 4: Move the SUT back to the initial state s_0 by applying a *reset* sequence RI. It is assumed that an SUT has correctly implemented a reset mechanism.

Step 5: Repeat steps 1–4 for all state transitions in the given FSM.

For a selected transition from state s_i to state s_j with input a, the above four steps induce a transition tour defined by the *input sequence* $T(s_i)@a@\text{VER}_j@\text{RI}$ applied to the system in its initial state s_0. The symbol '@' represents *concatenation* of two sequences. Applying the test design principles discussed in Section 10.5, one can derive a test case from such transition tours. Identifying a transfer sequence $T(s_i)$ out of the input sequence $T(s_i)@a@\text{VER}_j@\text{RI}$ for state s_i is a straightforward task. However, it is not trivial to verify the next state of an implementation. There are three kinds of commonly used input sequences to verify the next state of a SUT. These input sequences are as follows:

- Unique input–output sequence
- Distinguishing sequence
- Characterizing sequence

In the following sections, we explain the meanings of the three kinds of input sequences and the ways to generate those kinds of sequences.

10.7   UNIQUE INPUT–OUTPUT SEQUENCE

We define a *unique input–output* (UIO) sequence and explain an algorithm to compute UIO sequences from an FSM $M = <S, I, O, s_0, \delta, \lambda>$, where $S, I, O,$ $s_0, \delta,$ and λ have been explained in Section 10.3. First, we extend the semantics of δ and λ as follows:

- We extend the domain of λ and δ to include strings of input symbols. For instance, for state s_0 and input sequence $x = a_1, \ldots, a_k$, the corresponding output sequence is denoted by $\lambda(s_0, x) = b_1, \ldots, b_k$, where $b_i = \lambda(s_{i-1}, a_i)$ and $s_i = \delta(s_{i-1}, a_i)$ for $i = 1, \ldots, k$ and the final state is $\delta(s_0, x) = s_k$.

- Similarly, we extend the domain and range of the transition and output functions to include sets of states. For example, if Q is a set of states and x is an input *sequence*, then $\delta(Q, x) = \{\delta(s, x) | s \in Q\}$.

- If x and y are two input strings, the notation $x@y$ denotes *concatenation* of the two strings in that order.

Next, we define four properties of FSMs in the following. These properties are essential to the computation of UIO sequences.

Completely Specified: An FSM M is said to be *completely specified* if for each input $a \in I$ there is a state transition defined at each state of M.

Deterministic: An FSM M is said to be *deterministic* if (i) for each input $a \in I$ there is at most one state transition defined at each state of M and (ii) there is no *internal* event causing state transitions in the FSM. A timeout is an example of internal events that can cause a state transition.

Reduced: An FSM M is said to be *reduced* if for any pair of states s_i and s_j, $i \neq j$, there is an input sequence y such that $\lambda(s_i, y) \neq \lambda(s_j, y)$.

Intuitively, an FSM is reduced if no two states are equivalent, that is, there exists an input sequence that distinguishes one state from the other.

Strongly Connected: An FSM M is said to be *strongly connected* if any state is reachable from any other state.

An input–output sequence $y/\lambda(s_i, y)$ is said to be a UIO sequence for state s_i if and only if $y/\lambda(s_i, y) \neq y/\lambda(s_j, y)$, $i \neq j$, $\forall s_j$ in M. Hsieh [3] introduced the concept of simple input–output sequence in 1971 to identify FSMs. Sabnani and Dahbura [4] were the first to coin the term UIO sequences and applied the concept to testing communication protocols. In the following, an efficient algorithm to compute UIO sequences is explained [5].

Given an FSM M, a *path vector* is a collection of state pairs $(s_1/s_1', \ldots, s_i/s_i', \ldots, s_k/s_k')$ with the following two properties: (i) s_i and s_i' denote the head and tail states, respectively, of a path, where a path is a sequence of state transitions; (ii) an identical input–output sequence is associated with all the paths in the path vector. Given a path vector $\text{PV} = (s_1/s_1', \ldots, s_i/s_i', \ldots, s_k/s_k')$, the *initial vector* (IV) is an ordered collection of head states of PV, that is, $\text{IV(PV)} = (s_1, \ldots, s_i, \ldots, s_k)$. Similarly, the *current vector* (CV) is the ordered collection of tail states of PV, that is, $\text{CV(PV)} = (s_1', \ldots, s_i', \ldots, s_k')$. A path vector is said to be a *singleton* vector if it contains exactly one state pair. A path vector is said to be a *homogeneous* vector if all members of CV(PV) are identical. It may be noted that a singleton vector is also a homogeneous vector. For an n-state FSM, we define a unique *initial* path vector $(s_1/s_1, \ldots, s_i/s_i, \ldots, s_n/s_n)$ such that a *null* path is associated with all state pairs.

Given a path vector and the input–output label a/b of a transition, *vector perturbation* means computing a new path vector PV′ from PV and a/b. Given $\text{PV} = (s_1/s_1', \ldots, s_i/s_i', \ldots, s_k/s_k')$ and a transition label a/b, *perturbation* of PV with respect to edge label a/b, denoted by $\text{PV}' = \text{pert(PV}, a/b)$, is defined as $\text{PV}' = \{s_i/s_i'' | s_i'' = \delta(s_i', a) \wedge \lambda(s_i', a) = b \wedge s_i/s_i' \in \text{PV}\}$. We can infinitely perturb all the path vectors for all transition labels given a reduced FSM and its initial path vector. One can imagine the perturbation function $\text{PV}' = \text{pert(PV}, a/b)$ as an edge from a node PV to a new node PV′ with edge label a/b. In addition, given PV and a set of transition labels L, we can arrange the new $|L|$ nodes $\{\text{pert(PV}, a/b) \ \forall a/b \in L\}$ on one level. That is, all the path vectors of a given FSM can be arranged in the form of a tree with successive levels $1, 2, \ldots, \infty$. Such a tree is called a *UIO tree*. It may be noted that graphically a path vector is represented by two rows of states—the top row denotes IV(PV) and the bottom row denotes CV(PV). Theoretically, a UIO tree is a tree with infinite levels. However, we need to prune the tree based on some conditions, called *pruning* conditions. After each perturbation $\text{PV}' = \text{pert(PV}, a/b)$, we check the following conditions:

C1: CV(PV′) is a homogeneous vector or a singleton vector.

C2: On the path from the initial vector to PV, there exists PV″ such that $\text{PV}' \subseteq \text{PV}''$.

While constructing a UIO tree, if one of the pruning conditions is satisfied, we declare PV′ to be a *terminal* path vector. Given a UIO tree and a state s_i of an FSM, s_i has a UIO sequence if and only if the UIO tree obtained from M has a singleton path vector ψ such that $v_i = IV(\psi)$, that is, v_i is the initial vector of the singleton ψ. The input–output sequence associated with the edges of the path from the initial path vector to a singleton path vector is a UIO sequence of the state found in the initial vector of the singleton. In the following, we present an algorithm to compute a finite UIO tree from an FSM.

Algorithm. Generation of UIO Tree

> *Input*: $M = <S, I, O, \delta, \lambda>$ and L.
>
> *Output*: UIO tree.
>
> *Method*: Execute the following steps:
>
> > **Step 1:** Let Ψ be the set of path vectors in the UIO tree. Initially, Ψ contains the initial vector marked as *nonterminal*.
> >
> > **Step 2:** Find a nonterminal member $\psi \in \Psi$ which has not been perturbed. If no such member exists, then the algorithm terminates.
> >
> > **Step 3:** Compute $\psi' = \text{pert}(\psi, a_i/b_i)$ and add ψ' to $\Psi \ \forall a_i/b_i \in L$. Mark ψ to be perturbed and update the UIO tree.
> >
> > **Step 4:** If $\text{pert}(\psi, a_i/b_i)$, computed in **step 3**, satisfies termination condition **C1** or **C2**, then mark ψ' as a terminal node.
> >
> > **Step 5:** Go to **step 2**.

Example. Consider the FSM $G_1 = <S, I, O, A, \delta, \lambda>$ of Figure 10.12, where $S = \{A, B, C, D\}$ is the set of states, $I = \{0, 1\}$ is the set of inputs, $O = \{0, 1\}$ is the set of outputs, A is the initial state, $\delta : S \times I \to S$ is the next-state function, and $\lambda : S \times I \to O$ is the output function. The set of distinct transition labels is given by $L = \{0/0, 0/1, 1/0\}$. The initial path vector is given by

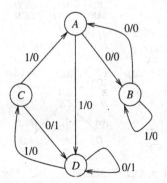

Figure 10.12 Finite-state machine G_1 (From ref. 5. © 1997 IEEE.)

$\psi_1 = (A/A, B/B, C/C, D/D)$ and is perturbed by using all members of L as follows:

$$(A/B, B/A) = \text{pert}(\psi_1, 0/0)$$
$$(C/D, D/D) = \text{pert}(\psi_1, 0/1)$$
$$(A/D, B/B, C/A, D/C) = \text{pert}(\psi_1, 1/0)$$

Now, we represent the UIO tree in graphical form. We put three edges from the initial path vector $\psi_1 = (A/A, B/B, C/C, D/D)$ to path vectors $(A/B, B/A)$, $(C/D, D/D)$, and $(A/D, B/B, C/A, D/C)$ with transition labels 0/0, 0/1, and 1/0, respectively, as shown in Figure 10.13. The reader may recall that the new

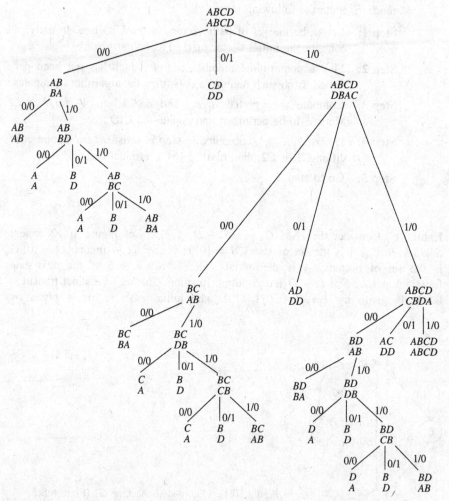

Figure 10.13   UIO tree for G_1 in Figure 10.12. (From ref. 5. © 1997 IEEE.)

path vector $(C/D, D/D)$ is a terminal node because its current vector (D, D) is a homogeneous vector. Therefore, path vector $(C/D, D/D)$ is no more perturbed, whereas the other two path vectors $(A/B, B/A)$ and $(A/D, B/B, C/A, D/C)$ are further perturbed, as shown in Figure 10.13. A complete UIO tree is shown in Figure 10.13.

Figure 10.13 is redrawn in the form of Figure 10.14 by highlighting a UIO sequence of minimal length for each state. We have identified four singleton path vectors, namely, (A/A), (B/D), (C/A), and (D/A), and highlighted the corresponding paths leading up to them from the initial path vector. We show the UIO sequences of the four states in Table 10.7.

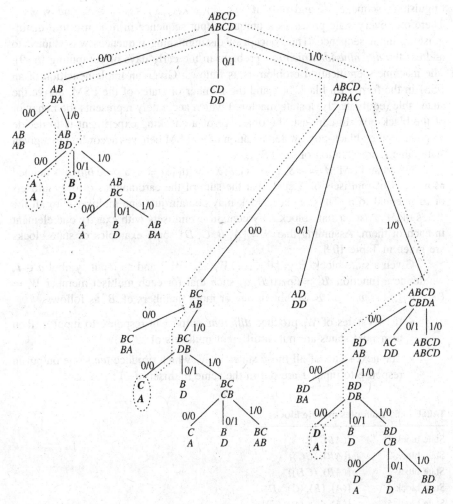

Figure 10.14   Identification of UIO sequences on UIO tree of Figure 10.13.

TABLE 10.7 UIO Sequences of Minimal Lengths Obtained from Figure 10.14

State	Input Sequence	Output Sequence
A	010	000
B	010	001
C	1010	0000
D	11010	00000

10.8 DISTINGUISHING SEQUENCE

Given an FSM $M = <S, I, O, s_0, \delta, \lambda>$, an input sequence x is said to be a distinguishing sequence if and only if $\lambda(s_i, x) \neq \lambda(s_j, x)$ $\forall s_i, s_j \in S$, and $s_i \neq s_j$. Therefore, every state produces a unique output sequence in response to a distinguishing input sequence. The concept of distinguishing sequences was studied to address the *machine identification* problem in the early days of computing [6–9]. The machine identification problem is as follows: Given an implementation of an FSM in the form of a black box and the number of states of the FSM, derive the state table (equivalently, a state machine) which accurately represents the behavior of the black box. In contrast, the objective of a checking experiment is to decide whether a given black-box implementation of an FSM behaves according to a given state table representation of the FSM.

Given an FSM $M = <S, I, O, s_0, \delta, \lambda>$ with $|S| = n$, a *state block* is defined as a set $\mathcal{B}$ of multisets of S such that the sum of the cardinalities of the multisets of $\mathcal{B}$ is equal to n. Thus, a state block may contain just one multiset with all the states of M. Also, a state block may contain n multisets with exactly one element in each of them. Assuming that $S = \{A, B, C, D\}$ some examples of state blocks are given in Table 10.8.

Given a state block $\mathcal{B} = \{W_1, \ldots, W_i, \ldots, W_m\}$ and an input symbol $a \in I$, we define a function $\mathcal{B}' = \text{dpert}(\mathcal{B}, a)$ such that for each multiset member $W_i = (w_{i1}, w_{i2}, \ldots, w_{ik})$ of $\mathcal{B}$ we obtain one or more members of $\mathcal{B}'$ as follows:

- If two states of W_i produce *different* outputs in response to input a, then their next states are put in different multisets of $\mathcal{B}'$.

- The next states of all those states in W_i which produce the same output in response to input a are put in the same multiset of $\mathcal{B}'$.

TABLE 10.8 Examples of State Blocks

State block 1	$\{(ABCD)\}$
State block 2	$\{(AB), (CC)\}$
State block 3	$\{(AB), (CD)\}$
State block 4	$\{(A), (B), (C), (D)\}$
State block 5	$\{(A), (A), (B), (C)\}$

Given a reduced FSM, the initial state block consists of just one element containing the set of states of the FSM. Next, we can infinitely perturb all the state blocks for all the input symbols using the dpert() function. One can view the perturbation function $\mathcal{B}' = \text{dpert}(\mathcal{B}, a)$ as an edge from a node $\mathcal{B}$ to a new node $\mathcal{B}'$ with edge label a. Given a state block and the set of inputs I, we can arrange the new $|I|$ nodes $\{\text{dpert}(\mathcal{B}, a), \forall a \in I\}$ at the same level. All the state blocks of a given FSM can be arranged in the form of a tree with successive levels $1, 2, \ldots, \infty$. Such a tree is called a *DS tree*. Theoretically, a distinguishing sequence (DS) tree is a tree with infinite levels. However, a finite-level tree would serve our purpose. A finite-level tree is obtained by pruning the tree based on some conditions, called *pruning conditions*, defined using the following terms:

D1: A state block $\mathcal{B}$ is a homogeneous state block if at least one multiset member W_i of $\mathcal{B}$ has repeated states.

D2: A state block $\mathcal{B}$ is a singleton state block if all elements of $\mathcal{B}$ have exactly one state member.

D3: On the path from the initial state block to the current state block $\mathcal{B}$, there exists a state block $\mathcal{B}$.

While constructing a DS tree, if one of the above three pruning conditions is satisfied, we declare state block $\mathcal{B}$ to be a terminal state block. Given a DS tree of an FSM M, M has a distinguishing sequence if and only if there exists a singleton state block in the DS tree. The sequence of inputs from the initial state block to a singleton state block is a DS of machine M. In the following, we present an algorithm to compute a finite DS tree from an FSM.

Algorithm.   Generation of DS Tree

Input: $M = <S, I, O, s_0, \delta, \lambda>$.

Output: DS tree.

Method: Execute the following steps:

Step 1:   Let Ψ be the set of state blocks in the DS tree. Initially, Ψ contains the initial state block marked as nonterminal.

Step 2:   Find a nonterminal member $\psi \in \Psi$ which has not been perturbed. If no such member exists, then the algorithm terminates.

Step 3:   Compute $\psi' = \text{dpert}(\psi, a)$ and add ψ' to $\Psi \, \forall a \in I$. Mark ψ to be perturbed and update the DS tree.

Step 4:   If $\text{dpert}(\psi, a)$, computed in **step 3**, satisfies the termination condition **D1**, **D2**, or **D3**, then mark ψ' as a terminal node.

Step 5:   Go to **step 2**.

Example.   Let us consider an FSM $G_2 = <S, I, O, A, \delta, \lambda>$, shown in Figure 10.15, where $S = \{A, B, C, D\}$ is the set of states, $I = \{0, 1\}$ is the set of inputs, $O = \{0, 1\}$ is the set of outputs, A is the initial state, $\delta : S \times I \rightarrow S$

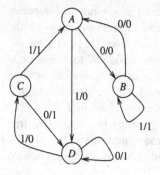

Figure 10.15   Finite-state machine G_2.

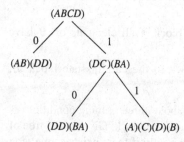

Figure 10.16   Distinguishing sequence tree for G_2 in Figure 10.15.

is the next-state function, and $\lambda : S \times I \to O$ is the output function. The DS tree for G_2 is shown in Figure 10.16. The initial state block contains just one multiset $\{A, B, C, D\}$, which has been represented as the initial node $(ABCD)$. We have perturbed the initial node $(ABCD)$ with the members of the input set $I = \{0, 1\}$. Perturbation of the initial state block with input 0 produces the state block $(AB)(DD)$ because of the following reasons:

- States A and B produce the same output 0 with input 0 and move the machine to states B and A, respectively.
- States C and D produce the same output 1 with input 0 and move the FSM to the same state D.

Since $(AB)(DD)$ is a homogeneous state block, it is a terminal node in the DS tree, and, thus, it is no more perturbed. Perturbation of the initial state block with input 1 produces the state block $(DC)(BA)$ because of the following reasons:

- States A and D produce the same output 0 with input 1 and move the machine to states D and C, respectively.
- States B and C produce the same output 1 with input 1 and move the machine to states B and A, respectively.

We obtain a homogeneous state block $(DD)(BA)$ by perturbing the state block $(DC)(BA)$ with input 0 and we obtain a singleton state block $(A)(C)(D)(B)$ by perturbing state block $(DC)(BA)$ with input 1. The complete DS tree is shown

TABLE 10.9   Outputs of FSM G_2 in Response to Input Sequence 11 in Different States

Present State	Output Sequence
A	00
B	11
C	10
D	01

in Figure 10.16. Therefore, the input sequence 11 that takes the DS tree from its initial state block to its only singleton state block is a DS for FSM G_2. The output sequences of FSM G_2 in Figure 10.15 in response to the distinguishing input sequence 11 in all the four different states are shown in Table 10.9.

10.9   CHARACTERIZING SEQUENCE

It is still possible to determine uniquely the state of an FSM for FSMs which do not possess a DS. The FSM shown in Figure 10.17 does not have a DS because there is no singleton state block in the DS tree, as shown in Figure 10.18. The *W-method* was introduced for FSMs that do not possess a DS [9, 10]. A *characterizing set* of a state s_i is a set of input sequences such that, when each sequence is applied to the implementation at state s_i, the set of output sequences generated by the implementation uniquely identifies state s_i. Each sequence of the characterizing set of state s_i distinguishes state s_i from a group of states. Therefore, applying all of the sequences in the characterizing set distinguishes state s_i from all other state. For an FSM-based specification, a set that consists of characterizing sets of every state is called the W-set $= \{W_1, W_2, \ldots, W_p\}$ of the FSM. The members of the W-set are called *characterizing sequences* of the given FSM.

The basic test procedure for testing a state transition $(s_i, s_j, a/b)$ using the W-method follows.

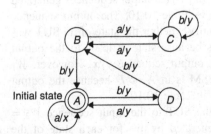

Figure 10.17   FSM that does not possess distinguishing sequence. (From ref. 11. © 1994 IEEE.)

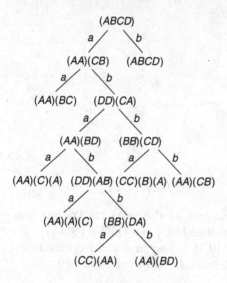

Figure 10.18   DS tree for FSM (Figure 10.17).

Testing Transition (s_i, s_j, a/b) Using W-Method   Repeat the following steps for each input sequence of the W-set:

Step 1:   Assuming that the SUT is in its initial state, bring the SUT from its initial state s_0 to state s_i by applying a transfer sequence $T(s_i)$ as shown in Figure 10.11.

Step 2:   Apply the input a and verify that the SUT generates the output b.

Step 3:   Apply a verification sequence from the W-set to the SUT and verify that the corresponding output sequence is as expected. Assume that the SUT is in state s_k at the end of this step.

Step 4:   Move the SUT back to the initial state s_0 by applying a *reset* sequence RI in state s_k.

Example: Characterizing Sequences.   Consider the FSM specification $M = <S, I, O, A, \delta, \lambda>$, shown in Figure 10.17, where $S = \{A, B, C, D\}$ is the set of states, $I = \{a, b\}$ is the set of inputs, $O = \{x, y\}$ is the set of outputs, A is the initial state, $\delta : \times I \to S$ is the next-state function, and $\lambda : S \times I \to O$ is the output function. Kohavi [9] used *multiple experiments* to construct the W-set for this FSM. Consider the input sequence $W_1 = aba$. The output sequences generated by W_1 for each state of the FSM are shown in Table 10.10. The output sequence generated by the input sequence W_1 can identify whether the state of an SUT was either B or C before W_1 is applied. This is because state B leads to the output sequence yyy, whereas state C leads to the output sequence yyx. However, W_1 cannot identify the state of an SUT if the FSM is in A or D because the output sequences are xyx for both states, as shown in Table 10.10.

Now let us examine the response of the SUT to the input sequence $W_2 = ba$ for each state. The output sequences generated by W_2 for each state of the

TABLE 10.10   Output Sequences Generated by FSM of Figure 10.17 as Response to W_1

Starting States	Output Generated by $W_1 = aba$
A	xyx
B	yyy
C	yyx
D	xyx

TABLE 10.11   Output Sequences Generated by FSM of Figure 10.17 as Response to W_2

Starting States	Output Generated by $W_2 = ba$
A	yx
B	yx
C	yy
D	yy

FSM are shown in Table 10.11. The FSM implementation generates distinct output sequences as a response to W_2 if an SUT was at A or D, as shown in Table 10.11. This is because states A and D lead to distinct output sequences yx and yy, respectively. Therefore, the W-set for the FSM consists of two input sequences: W-set $= \{W_1, W_2\}$, where $W_1 = aba$ and $W_2 = ba$. The transfer sequences for all the states are $T(B) = bb$, $T(C) = ba$, and $T(D) = b$. The reset input sequence is RI $= bababa$. The input sequence for testing the state transition $(D, A, a/x)$ is given in Table 10.12. In Table 10.12, the columns labeled "message to SUT" and "message from SUT" represent the input message sent to the SUT and the expected output message generated by the SUT, respectively. The current state and the expected next state of the SUT are shown in the columns labeled "current state" and "next state," respectively. During testing, the inputs are applied to the SUT in the order denoted by the column "step." In the first step a transfer sequence is applied to bring the SUT to state D. In step 2, the transition is tested. Then $W_1 = aba$ is applied to verify the state (steps 3, 4, and 5). At this point, the state transition is only partially tested, since W_1 is not enough to identify the state of an implementation. The reset sequence RI $= bababa$ (steps 6–11) is applied followed by the transfer sequence of $T(D) = b$ (step 12) to bring the SUT into the initial state and into state D, respectively. The test is repeated for the same transition by using $W_2 = ba$ (steps 13–21). If all the outputs received from the SUT are defined by the FSM, the state transition test is completed successfully. If the output of the SUT is not the expected response at any step, an error is detected in the SUT.

TABLE 10.12   Test Sequences for State Transition (D, A, a/x) of FSM in Figure 10.17

Step	Current State	Next State	Message to SUT	Message from SUT
Apply $T(D)$				
1	A	D	b	y
Test Transition (D, A, a/x)				
2	D	A	a	x
Apply W_1				
3	A	A	a	x
4	A	D	b	y
5	D	A	a	x
Apply RI				
6	A	D	b	y
7	D	A	a	x
8	A	D	b	y
9	D	A	a	x
10	A	D	b	y
11	D	A	a	x
Apply $T(D)$				
12	A	D	b	y
Test Transition (D, A, a/x)				
13	D	A	a	x
Apply W_2				
14	A	D	b	y
15	D	A	a	x
Apply RI				
16	A	D	b	y
17	D	A	a	x
18	A	D	b	y
19	D	A	a	x
20	A	D	b	y
21	D	A	a	x

Source: From ref. 11.

Four major methods—*transition tours, distinguishing sequences, characterizing sequences, and unique input–output sequences*—are discussed for the generation of tests from an FSM. A question that naturally comes to mind is the effectiveness of these techniques, that is, the types of discrepancies detected by each of these methods. Sidhu and Leung [12] present a fault model based on the Monte Carlo simulation technique for estimating the fault coverage of the above four test generation methods. The authors introduced 10 different *classes* of randomly faulty specification, each obtained by random altering a given specification. For example, *class I* faults consist of randomly altering an output operation in a given specification. The authors conclude that all four methods, except for the transition tour method, can detect all single faults as opposed to several faults introduced in a given specification. In addition, it is also shown that distinguishing, characterizing, and UIO sequences have the same fault detection capability. Another study, similar to the one by Sidhu and Leung, is reported by Dahbura and Sabnani for the UIO sequence method [13].

10.10   TEST ARCHITECTURES

An overview of four abstract test architectures developed by the ISO is presented in this section. The ISO documents [14–16] and Linn [17] and Rayner [18] provide more detail about the test architectures. The ISO test architectures are based on the Open System Interconnection (OSI) reference architecture, which consists of a hierarchical layer structure of entities. The purpose of an entity at layer N is to provide certain services, called N-services, to its upper layer entity. It uses the service provided by the $N - 1$ layer while isolating the implementation details of the lower layer entities from the upper layers. Peer N entities communicate with each other through an $N - 1$ service provider by exchanging N-protocol data units [(N)-PDUs], as shown in Figure 10.19. Interactions of an N-entity with its upper and lower entities are defined by N and $N - 1$ abstract service primitives (ASPs).

The abstract test architectures are described in terms of the inputs to the IUT that can be given in a controlled manner and the corresponding outputs from the IUT are observed. Specifically, an abstract test architecture is described by identifying the points closest to the IUT where controls and observations are specifed. The abstract test architectures are classified into two major categories: *local* and *external*. The local test architectures are characterized by observation and control being specified in terms of events occurring within the SUT at the layer boundaries immediately below and above the IUT, as shown in Figure 10.20. On the other

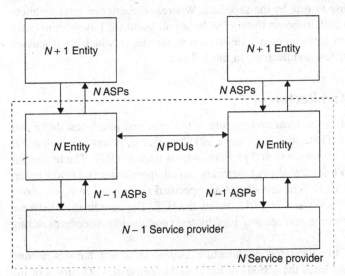

Figure 10.19   Abstraction of N entity in OSI reference architecture.

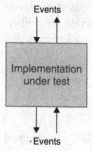

Figure 10.20 Abstract local test architecture.

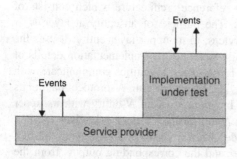

Figure 10.21 Abstract external test architecture.

hand, external test architectures are characterized by the observation and control of the events taking place externally from the SUT, on the other side of the underlying service provider from the IUT, as shown in Figure 10.21. The system in which an IUT resides is a SUT. The external architectures assume that an underlying communications service is used in testing. The local test architectures are only applicable to in-house testing by the suppliers. Whereas the external tests architectures are applied to both in-house testing by the supplier and the buyers/third-party test centers. There are three types of external test architectures, which are discussed along with the local test architecture, in the following.

10.10.1 Local Architecture

A basic assumption in the local architecture is that exposed interfaces above and below the IUT exist. These interfaces serve as PCOs, that is, points at which a real test system can provide inputs to and observe outputs from the IUT. The test architecture includes two logically distinct elements, called upper tester and lower tester, as shown in Figure 10.22. The test events are specified in terms of N ASPs above the IUT, and $N - 1$ ASPs and N PDUs below the IUT. The coordination between the upper and the lower testers are provided by test coordination procedures during the testing.

In summary, the local test architecture comprises a test harness around the IUT, which coordinates the actions of lower and upper testers. The roles of the upper and lower testers are to stimulate the IUT by exchanging test events at the

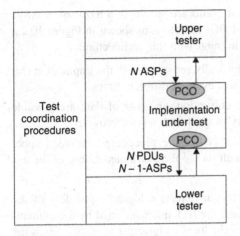

Figure 10.22   Local architecture.

top and bottom interfaces of the IUT. The local architecture implicitly provides the capability to synchronize and control the upper and lower testers because both of them are elements of the same test harness.

10.10.2   Distributed Architecture

The distributed architecture is illustrated in Figure 10.23. This architecture is one of three external architectures and makes no assumptions about the existence of a PCO below the IUT. This test architecture defines the PCOs as being at the service boundaries above the IUT and at the opposite side of the $N - 1$ service provider from the IUT.

Note that the lower tester and the IUT reside in two different systems. The lower tester and the IUT are connected by an underlying service which offers an $N - 1$ service using lower layer protocol and the physical media connecting the two systems. The lower tester is obviously a peer entity of the IUT in Figure 10.23. The arrows between the IUT and the $N - 1$ service provider are not real interfaces, just

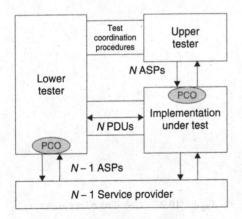

Figure 10.23   Distributed architecture.

the conceptual flow of N PDUs. The test events are specified in terms of N ASPs above the IUT and $N-1$ ASPs and N PDUs remotely, as shown in Figure 10.23. Three important points should be kept in mind with this architecture:

- The lower tester and IUT are physically separated with the implication that they perhaps observe the same test event at different times.
- Delivery out of sequence, data corruption, and loss of data are possible because of the unreliable quality of the lower service provider.
- Synchronization and control (test coordinate procedures) between upper and lower testers are more difficult due to the distributed nature of the test system.

In summary, the distributed test architecture is a logical equivalent of the local architecture with the lower tester and the IUT interconnected by a communication service. However, the structure of the local architecture implicitly gives the capability to synchronize and control the upper and lower testers because they are elements of the same test harness. Thus, distributed architecture is not a functional equivalent to the local architecture.

10.10.3 Coordinated Architecture

The coordinated architecture is an enhancement of the distributed architecture. Control and observation of N ASPs are performed by a Test Management Protocol (TMP). There is just one PCO at the opposite side of the $N-1$ service provider from the IUT, as shown in Figure 10.24. Note that, even though a PCO appears between the upper tester and the IUT, it is optional; as a choice made by the implementer, the upper tester is perhaps integrated as part of the IUT. Two features that distinguish the coordinated architecture are as follows:

- No interface is exposed to the upper tester of an IUT (although this is not precluded).
- A standard TMP and TMP data units (TMPDUs) are used to communicate between the upper tester and the lower tester.

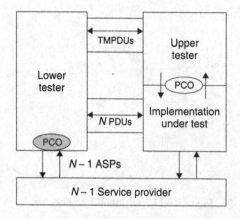

Figure 10.24 Coordinated architecture.

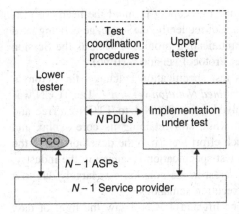

Figure 10.25   Remote architecture.

The lower tester is considered to be the master of the upper tester. The actions of the upper tester are controlled by the lower tester through a TMP. Test events are specified in terms of $N - 1$ ASPs, N PDUs, and TMPDUs, as illustrated in Figure 10.24.

10.10.4   Remote Architecture

The remote architecture is applicable to IUTs that do not have an exposed upper interface. In the absence of an upper tester, the test architecture identifies a PCO away from the IUT, on the opposite side of the $N - 1$ service provider. The test events are specified in terms of the $N - 1$ ASPs and N PDUs, as shown in Figure 10.25. There are two major features of this architecture:

- No interface at the top of the IUT is assumed.
- No explicit test coordination procedure is used. The coordination between upper and lower testers is manual (e.g., talking over the telephone). The coordination is implicit in the PDUs initiated by the lower tester or provided by the actions taken by an upper layer entity to stimulate the IUT.

The architecture relies on the protocol being tested for synchronization between the lower tester and the IUT. Verdicts must be formulated based on the stimulus provided by the lower tester and the responses of the IUT as observed by the lower tester.

10.11   TESTING AND TEST CONTROL NOTATION VERSION 3 (TTCN-3)

As the name suggests, TTCN-3 is a language for specifying test cases [19]. The language is increasingly being accepted in the industry as a test specification language after it was standardized by the ETSI (European Telecommunication Standards

Institute). The language has been designed by keeping in mind the needs of testing complex telecommunication systems. Consequently, the language is being used to write test cases to test complex communication protocols, such as the Session Initiation Protocol (SIP) and the Internet Protocol version 6 (IPv6).

In the early efforts to develop a test specification language, the acronym TTCN-1 stood for *Tree and Tabular Combined Notation version 1*. The TCCN was developed in the mid-1980s and it evolved from TTCN-1 to TTCN-2 (Tree and Tabular Combined Notation version 2) while still retaining its core syntax and semantics to a large extent. Though much effort went into the development of the TCCN, it was not widely accepted as a test specification language in the industry. The reason for an absence of a broad interest in the notation was largely due to a wide gap between the syntax and the execution semantics.

In 2001, TTCN-2 got a major face lift and TTCN-3 saw the light of day. Though TTCN-3 still retains the basic characteristics of TTCN-2, the syntax of TTCN-3 was designed in line with a procedural programming language. Programmers and test designers can write test cases the way they write programs, thereby reducing the gap between syntax and execution semantics. The programming language look and feel of TTCN-3 makes it more acceptable. TTCN-3 has seen much improvement since 2001, and the user and support bases are ever expanding. There is increasing tool support and an active team maintaining the language.

In this section, we give a brief introduction to TTCN-3. We focus on the core features of TTCN-3, such as *module*, *data types*, *templates*, *ports*, *components*, and *test cases*.

10.11.1 Module

A module is a fundamental unit for specifying test cases. In terms of programming, a test case comprises some data declarations and some execution behavior, which are specified in the form of one or more modules. The execution behavior of a test case is referred to as the *control* part. The structure of a module is shown in Figure 10.26.

10.11.2 Data Declarations

TTCN-3 allows the declarations of constants and variables. A constant is denoted by the const keyword, and the value of the constant is assigned at the point of declaration. The value of a constant cannot be changed afterward.

TTCN-3 has its own scoping rules for all data definitions. All declarations made at the "top" level, that is, module level, are accessible throughout the module. Here, top level means before the control part. The concept of a "code block," enclosed by a matching pair of curly braces, helps us understand scoping rules. Definitions made within a specific code block are only accessible within that code block, and identifiers are not reused in nested code blocks. In other words, there do not exist two data items with the same name but different scopes. No *variable* can be defined at the module level, and, therefore, all module-level declarations are constants. Absence of module-level variables means absence of global variables.

```
/* One can document a module by writing comments in this way. */
// Additional comments can be included here.
module ExampleTestModule1 { // A module can be empty.
    // First, define some data to be used in the control part
    const integer MaxCount := 15;
    constant integer UnitPacket = 256;
    // More data can be defined here ...

    // Second, specify the control part to execute
    control { // The control part is optional
        var integer counter := 0;
        var integer loopcount := MaxCount;
        const integer PacketSize := UnitPacket * 4;

        // Specify more execution behavior here ...

    } // End of the control part
} // end of module TestCase1
```

Figure 10.26   Structure of module in TTCN-3.

Since a test case can have distributed components, it is difficult to guarantee the semantics of global variable across distributed test components.

TTCN-3 supports a powerful set of built-in types, such as integer, float, Boolean (universal), charstring, verdicttype, bitstring, hexstring, octetstring, objid, and default. Such a rich set of built-in types is essential to protocol testing. TTCN-3 also allows the definitions of structured types and list types from existing types. Constructs to define structured types are enumerated, record, set, and union. Similarly, constructs to define list types are array, set of, and record of.

TTCN-3 allows programmers to use the concept of data subtyping. Subtyping means restricting the values of a type to a subset of all values allowed by the original type. For example, given the set of all integers, one can create a subtype of all unsigned numbers that can be represented with 16 bits. Such a subtype is useful in representing port numbers while testing using TCP. Two examples of subtyping are shown in Figure 10.27, where TCPPort is a new user-defined type. A variable of type TCPPort can take on values in the range $0, \ldots, 65535$. Similarly, IPUserProtocol is a subtype of charstring. A variable of type IPUserProtocol can take on values from the given set and not outside the set.

A PDU in a communication protocol can be defined using a record type. In some protocols, their PDUs are simply called *messages*. TTCN-3 allows one to

```
type integer TCPPort ( 0 .. 65535 ); // a 16 bit unsigned number
type charstring IPUserProtocol ( ``TCP'', ``UDP'', ``OSPF'',
                                 ``RIP'' );
```

Figure 10.27   Definitions of two subtypes.

define a PDU field of arbitrary bit length. For example, one can define PDU fields of 1 bit, 4 bits, and 6 bits which are found in the packet header of IPv4 (Internet Protocol version 4). Often protocols put a limit on the length of some of the PDU fields. Such limits are easily expressed using the length attribute of variables.

One creates instances of those types by using concrete values after defining a PDU or a message type. Such concrete instances have two applications: (i) send messages to a remote protocol entity and (ii) receive messages having the desired values. Concrete instances of message types are called *templates* in TTCN-3. TTCN-3 allows parameterization of templates for easily creating messages. An example of a template is shown in Figure 10.28, where MyMessage is a message type and SFCRequest is an instance of MyMessage. The MyMessage type consists of four fields. The response field can be *omitted* while creating an instance of the template.

An example definition of a response message of type MyMessage is shown in Figure 10.29. One can specify what message is expected to be received from a SUT by defining a response message. The identification field can be used to associate a response message with a request message. A "?" value of the input field in the SFCResponse tells us that the field can contain any value, which is ignored. The response field in the received SFCResponse carries the actual value expected to be received from the SUT.

10.11.3   Ports and Components

A test infrastructure may consist of one or more test components, where a test component is an entity that can send and/or receive messages (templates). There is

```
template MyMessage SFCRequest( Identification id, Input Ival) := {
    identification := id,
    msgtype        := Request,
    input          := Ival,
    response       := omit // ``omit'' is a keyword
}
```

Figure 10.28   Parameterized template for constructing message to be sent.

```
template MyMessage
    SFCResponse( Identification id, Response Rval) := {
    identification := id,
    msgtype        := Response,
    input          := ?, // This means the field can contain any
                          value
    response       := Rval
}
```

Figure 10.29   Parameterized template for constructing message to be received.

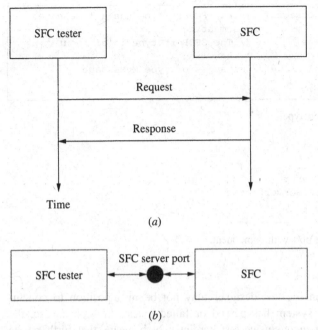

Figure 10.30   Testing (a) square-root function (SRF) calculator and (b) port between tester and SRF calculator.

a need for communication between test components and between the SUT and the test components. The points at which communication takes place are called ports in TTCN-3. A port is modeled as an infinite FIFO (first in–first out) queue from the viewpoint of a receiver. Two kinds of communication semantics are associated with a port: *message* semantics and *procedure call* semantics. One can specify the kinds of messages or calls a port handles and the *input–output* direction of the port. A port can be an *in* (input) port, an *out* (output) port, or *in–out* (both input and output) port. We explain the testing of a square-root function calculator (SFC) in terms of a test component and the SFC component, as shown in Figure 10.30a. A port between the two components is shown in Figure 10.30b. The declaration of an in–out port type that handles messages of type MyMessage is shown in Figure 10.31. Figure 10.32 illustrates the attachment of test component SFCTester with the SFCServerPort. The SFC component is assumed to be running on a port called SFCServerPort.

10.11.4   Test Case Verdicts

A test designer wants to conclude something after having executed a test case. For example, two simple conclusions are whether the SUT has *passed* or *failed* the test. If a SUT behaves as expected, then it is natural to say that it has passed the test; otherwise the test has failed. Thus, pass and fail are two obvious test

```
type port SFCPort message { // The SFCPort type has a ''message''
                            // semantics
     inout MyMessage        // The SFCPort type is of inout type
                            // handling
                            // messages of type MyMessage
}
```

Figure 10.31   Defining port type.

```
type component SFCTester {
     port SFCPort SFCServerPort
}
```

Figure 10.32   Associating port with component.

verdicts. However, often the test designer may not be in a position to conclusively say whether the system has passed or failed a test. In such a case, the test designer assigns an *inconclusive* test verdict, which means that further tests need to be conducted to refine the inconclusive verdict into either a pass or a fail verdict.

TTCN-3 provides a mechanism to record test verdicts. Associated with each test component there is an implicitly defined variable of type verdicttype. The initial, default value of the implicitly defined test verdict variable is *none*. A test designer can assign new values to the test verdict variable by calling the operation setverdict. For example, the calls setverdict(Pass), setverdict(Fail), and setverdict(Inconc) assign verdicts pass, fail, and inconclusive, respectively. There is a fourth test verdict, namely, *error*, which is assigned by the run time system. The run time assigns the test verdict error to the test verdict variable when a run time error occurs. For example, dividing a numeric value by zero leads to a run time error. TTCN-3 does not allow a test designer to explicitly set the value of the verdict variable to error, that is, the operation setverdict(error) is not allowed in TTCN-3. The value of the verdict assigned so far in a test component can be retrieved with the operation getverdict.

10.11.5   Test Case

A simple test case running on the SFCTester component is shown in Figure 10.33. We assume a message passing semantic of communication between the test component SFCTester and the SUT, namely, SFC. SFCTester sends a request message to the SFC and waits for a response message from SFC. Since a faulty SFC may not generate a response message, SFCTester must exit from a possible infinite wait. Therefore, we define a timer, namely, responseTimer, by using the keyword *timer*. Next, the test case sends a message, namely, SFCMessage, and starts a timer with

```
// A test case description with alternative behavior
testcase  SFCtestcase1() runs on SFCTester {
    timer responseTimer; // Define a timer
    SFCPort. send (SFCRequest(7, 625));
    responseTimer.start(5.0);

    alt { // Now handle three alternative cases ...
          // Case 1: The expected result of computation
          // is received.
          [] SFCPort.receive(SFCResponse(7, 25)) {
              setverdict(pass);
              responseTimer.stop;
          }

          // Case 2: An unexpected result of computation
          // is received.
          [] SFCPort.receive {
              setverdict(fail);
              responseTimer.stop;
          }
          // Case 3: No result is received within a reasonable
          // time.
          [] responseTimer.timeout {
              setverdict(fail);
          }
    }
    stop;
} // End of test case
```

Figure 10.33   Test case for testing SRF calculator.

a duration of 5.0 s. SFCMessage contains two important fields, namely, identifier and input. We are interested in calculating the square root of input, which has been given the value of 625. In the given example, the identifier takes on an arbitrary, but known, value of 7.

After sending a request to the SFC component and starting a timer, the test component waits for the expected message to arrive from the SFC component. At this point, three different situations can arise. First, the SFC component can correctly respond with the expected result of 25 in a message having an identifier value of 7. Second, the SFC component responds with an incorrect value; for example, the identifier field can have an incorrect value or the response field can have a value *not* equal to 25. Third, the SFC component may fail to produce a response.

In the first case, SFCTester records a pass test verdict. In the second case, the test component records a fail test verdict. In the third case, the test component comes out of an infinite wait and records a fail test verdict. If one of the first two alternatives occur, the test component naturally stops the timer, whereas in the third alternative the test component gets a timeout. The alternative behaviors have been

```
module ExampleTestModule2 {
      // Define variables and constants to be used ...
      // Define templates to be used ...
      // Define ports to be used ...
      // Associate test components with ports ...
      // Define test cases, such as SFCtestcase1 ...

    control {
         execute( SFCtestcase1() );
    }
}
```

Figure 10.34   Executing test case.

expressed by using the *alt* construct, and individual alternative behaviors have been explicitly represented by using the [ ] symbol.

Finally, the test case SFCtestcase1 can be executed by having an *execute* statement in the **control** portion of a test module, as shown in Figure 10.34.

10.12   EXTENDED FSMS

Two conceptual components of a software system are *flow of control* and *manipulation of data*. A FSM model is useful at describing the former but has no provision for specifying the latter. Though there are many systems which can be conveniently and accurately modeled as FSMs, many systems in the real world require us to specify the associated computations while a system makes transitions from state to state. The associated computations can take on the following forms:

- Manipulate local variables.
- Start and stop timers.
- Create instances of processes.
- Compare values and make control flow decisions.
- Access databases.

In this section we will frequently refer to the FSM model of a telephone PBX shown in Figure 10.8. There is a need to record the start time of a call, and this can be done by noting the time when the FSM moves to the talk state. Constructs to start and stop timers are essential to the specification of real-time systems. Manipulation of local variables and conditional jumps are central to repeatedly executing a sequence of state transitions for a certain number of times. Accessing a database is essential to logging values of local variables for business purposes, such as billing and maintenance.

Therefore, there is a need to augment the basic structure of a state transition with capability to perform additional computations, such as updating values of variables, manipulating timers, and making decisions. Such an *extension* of an FSM results in an *extended finite-state machine* (EFSM). Processes in the Specification and Description Language (SDL) [20, 21] are EFSMs. SDL processes are built around the following basic concepts:

- *System*, which is described hierarchically by elements called systems, blocks, channels, processes, services, signals, and signal routes
- *Behavior*, which is described using am extension of the FSM concept
- *Data*, which are described using the concept of abstract data types with the addition of a notion of program variable and data structure
- *Communication*, which is asynchronous via channels that are infinite queues

An SDL specification can be written in two different forms: *SDL/GR* and *SDL/PR*. SDL/GR is a graphical syntax which shows most of the language constructs in flow-chart-like graphical form. Data definitions can only be textually represented. On the other hand, SDL/PR is written in textual form for machine processing. The "PR" in SDL/PR stands for *processing*. A one-to-one mapping is defined between the two forms. We show the structure of a state transition in an FSM in Figure 10.35a. This state transition specifies that if the FSM—the complete one has not been shown here—receives input *a* in state *A*, the machine produces an output *b* and moves to state *B*. The SDL/GR representation of the same transition is shown in Figure 10.35b. This example shows that one can easily represent an FSM as an SDL process. The state transition of Figure 10.35b has been extended in Figure 10.35c by including a *task* block that starts a timer. We show two state transitions—one from state *A* to state *B* and the other from

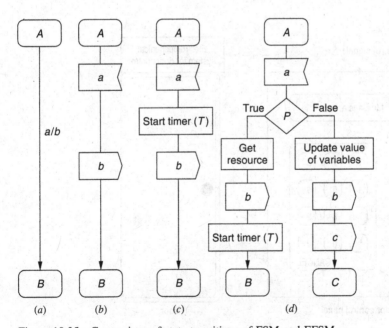

Figure 10.35   Comparison of state transitions of FSM and EFSM.

state A to state C—that include *task* blocks and a *decision* box (Figure 10.35*d*). To summarize the discussion of an EFSM, an EFSM is similar to an FSM with *computations* associated with every state transition. In the following, we give an EFSM model of a real-life system.

Example: Door Control System. Let us consider a *door control* system, as illustrated in Figure 10.36. A door is equipped with an electromechanical unit so that it can be opened and closed by sending electrical signals to the unit from a control panel. The user keys in a four-digit number to access a door. The door control unit compares the user-supplied number with a programmed number. If the two numbers match, then the control system turns the green light on, sends a signal to the electromechanical unit to open the door, and starts a timer called DoorOpen. If the two numbers do not match, then the red light goes on for 5 seconds followed by a welcome message to enter the PIN.

The door unit detects whether or not someone has passed through the door. If someone passes through the door, the door unit sends a Passed signal to the control unit. If no one passes through the door, the door unit sends a NotPassed signal to the control unit. If the control unit receives neither a Passed nor a NotPassed signal, it will eventually receive a timeout from the DoorOpen timer. The door unit must produce an appropriate signal irrespective of whether a user passes through the door or not. If the door unit fails to produce these signals, then the control unit assumes that the door unit is faulty, makes the yellow light turn on, displays a message saying that users are not welcome, and waits in the idle state for the necessary repair work to be done.

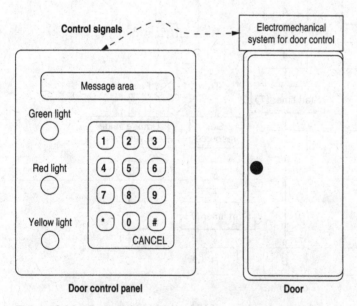

Figure 10.36 Controlled access to a door.

If the control unit receives a Passed or a NotPassed signal while the green light is on, the DoorOpen timer is stopped, the green light is switched off, a signal is sent to the door to close, and, finally, the system readies itself to handle another user request. A user could change his or her mind while entering the PIN by pressing the cancel button. Moreover, the same effect of cancellation can be achieved by abandoning the PIN entry process which is detected by a timer.

The above description of a door control system has been specified in SDL in Figures 10.37, 10.38, and 10.39. The system-level diagrams are found in Figure 10.37, and the behavior of the door control system can be found in the process diagrams of Figures 10.38 and 10.39. The reader may be reminded that we have specified the behavior of the door control system as an EFSM in the form of an SDL process shown in Figures 10.38 and 10.39.

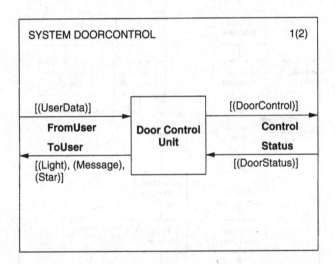

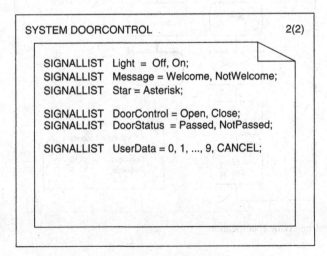

Figure 10.37   SDL/GR door control system.

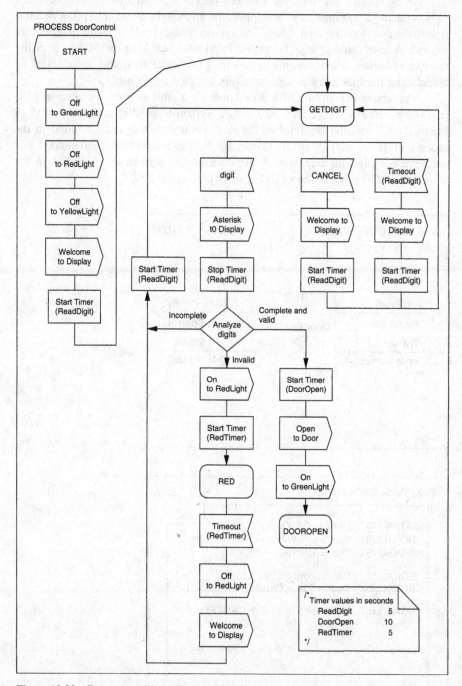

Figure 10.38   Door control behavior specification.

PROCESS DoorControl

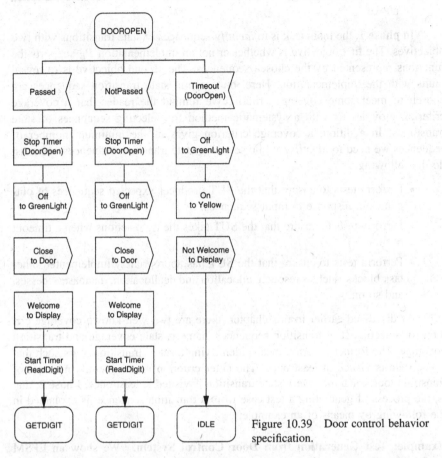

Figure 10.39 Door control behavior specification.

10.13 TEST GENERATION FROM EFSM MODELS

This section explains the mechanisms to generate test cases from an EFSM model of a system. Specifically, we generate test cases from an SDL process. Assume that we have an EFSM model E and a program P_E that correctly implements E. Our task is to generate test cases from E to test program P_E. Ideally, we want to generate a test suite T_E from E so that by testing P_E with T_E, we verify whether P_E implements the functions specified in E. Theoretically, in general, it is impossible to design such a test suite which, when applied to P_E, can reveal all the faults with P_E. In practice, however, we want to design T_E with the goal of verifying that P_E *behaves as expected for the commonly used input sequences*. This goal is achieved by designing T_E in two phases:

> *Phase 1*: Identify a set of state transition sequences such that each sequence of state transitions represents a common *use sequence*.

Phase 2: Design a test case from each state transition sequence identified above.

In **phase 1**, the main task is to *identify* sequences of state transitions with two objectives. The first objective is whether or not an implementation P_E supports the functions represented by the chosen sequences. The second objective is to reveal faults with the implementation. Here, once again, state transition sequences are chosen to meet some coverage criteria. We remind the reader that a coverage criterion provides us with a systematic method for selecting sequences of state transitions. In addition, a coverage criterion gives us the minimum number of sequences we need to identify. While selecting state transition sequences, we must do the following:

- Perform tests to ensure that the SUT produces expected sequences of outcomes in response to input sequences.

- Perform tests to ensure that the SUT takes the right actions when a timeout occurs.

- Perform tests to ensure that the SUT has appropriately implemented other task blocks, such as resource allocation and deallocation, database accesses, and so on.

As discussed earlier in this chapter, there are two well-known coverage criteria for selecting state transition sequences, namely, state coverage and transition coverage. The former criterion means identifying a set of transition tours such that every state is visited at least once. The latter criterion means identifying a set of transition tours such that every state transition is visited at least once. **Phase 2**, that is, the process of generating a test case from a transition sequence, is explained in the following by means of an example.

Example: Test Generation from Door Control System.   We show an EFSM model of a door control system in Figures 10.38 and 10.39. The control system has four states, namely, GETDIGIT, RED, DOOROPEN, and IDLE. After a sequence of initialization steps, the EFSM moves to its initial state GETDIGIT. Normal behavior of the system is restricted to the state transitions among the three states GETDIGIT, RED, and DOOROPEN. If the electromechanical door unit fails to respond to signals from the door control system, the EFSM moves from the DOOROPEN state to the IDLE state. The IDLE state can be thought of as an error state. Once faults with the door unit are fixed and the control unit is reset, the system moves back from the IDLE state to the GETDIGIT state. Therefore, by adding a sequence of tasks from the IDLE state to the START of the EFSM, we can make the EFSM strongly connected.

Assuming that the SDL process of Figures 10.38 and 10.39 is in state GETDIGIT, we design a test case that covers the transition tour shown in Figure 10.40. This transition tour executes the loop induced by digit inputs in state GETDIGIT while the read digits are incomplete. We assume that a user keys in an acceptable sequence of digits; that is, *analysis* of the digits in the decision box is *complete* and *valid*.

GETDIGIT ⇒ ... GETDIGIT ⇒ ... GETDIGIT ⇒ DOOROPEN ⇒ GETDIGIT.

Figure 10.40   Transition tour from door control system of Figures 10.38 and 10.39.

The reader may notice that control can flow from the DOOROPEN state to the GETDIGIT state in two ways, namely, by receiving Passed and NotPassed inputs, corresponding to someone passing through the door and not passing through the door, respectively. While generating a test case to cover the above transition tour, we assume that the Passed input occurs. In the following, we generate a test case using the three test design principles discussed in Section 10.5:

Step 1:   We transform the inputs and outputs in a transition tour into outputs and expected inputs, respectively, to derive the core behavior of a test case. We obtain the ports, namely, DISPLAY, KEYPAD, GREENLIGHT, and DOOR, as shown in Figure 10.41 by analyzing the transition tour of Figure 10.40. The sequence of *inputs* and *outputs* found in Figures 10.38 and 10.39, corresponding to the transition tour shown in Figure 10.40, have been transformed into outputs and inputs, respectively, in the TTCN-3 notation of Figure 10.42. The reader may note that the test behavior shown in Figure 10.42 is in terms of the four ports identified in Figure 10.41.

If the test system observes that the SUT behaves as specified in Figure 10.42, then it assigns a Pass test verdict. We informally express a condition such that a test case outputs a number of digits in line 3 of Figure 10.42. We have obtained the test behavior shown in Figure 10.43 from Figure 10.42 by refining the if statement in line 3 of Figure 10.42 as follows. We initialize a counter count with value 0 in line 1 of

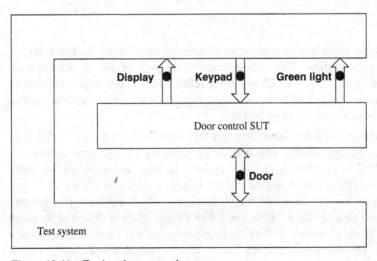

Figure 10.41   Testing door control system.

```
1.    label label1  KEYPAD.send(digit);
2.      DISPLAY.receive(Asterisk);
3.        if (NOT enough number of digits) goto label1;
                // Not in TTCN-3 form yet.
4.          DOOR.receive(Open);
5.            GREENLIGHT.receive(On);
6.              DOOR.send(Passed);
7.                GREENLIGHT.receive(Off);
8.                  DOOR.receive(Close);
9.                    DISPLAY.receive(Welcome);
10.                     setverdict(Pass);
```

Figure 10.42   Output and input behavior obtained from transition tour of Figure 10.40.

```
1.    count := 0; // Count is of type integer.
2.    label label1 KEYPAD.send( digit );
3.        DISPLAY.receive( Asterisk );
4.          count := count + 1;
5.            if (count < 4) goto label1;
6.          else {
7.              DOOR.receive( Open );
8.                GREENLIGHT.receive( On );
9.                  DOOR.send( Passed );
10.                   GREENLIGHT.receive( Off );
11.                     DOOR.receive (Close);
12.                       DISPLAY.receive(Welcome);
13.                         setverdict(Pass);
14.            };
```

Figure 10.43   Test behavior obtained by refining if part in Figure 10.42.

Figure 10.43 and increment the counter in line 4 after the test behavior outputs a digit. The informal condition part of the if statement in line 7 of Figure 10.42 has been refined into a concrete condition in Figure 10.43 (line 5) by assuming that the door control system accepts a sequence of digits of length 4.

Step 2: We augment a test behavior to prepare itself to receive events *other* than the expected events. This is done by including an *any* event, denoted by a "?," as an alternative event to each expected event. When we apply this transformation step to the test behavior shown in Figure 10.43, we obtain the test behavior shown in Figure 10.44. For example, the any event denoted by a "?" in line 20 of Figure 10.44 is designed to match with any event which does not match the expected event specified in line 18. The any events in lines 23, 26, 29, 32, and 36 are alternative events to the expected events in lines 16, 14, 11, 9, and 4, respectively.

```
1.    count := 0; // Count is of type integer.
2.    label label1 KEYPAD.send( digit );
3.    alt {
4.        [] DISPLAY.receive( Asterisk );
5.            count := count + 1;
6.            if (count < 4) goto label1;
7.            else {
8.                   alt {
9.                       [] DOOR.receive( Open );
10.                        alt {
11.                            [] GREENLIGHT.receive( On );
12.                                DOOR.send( Passed );
13.                                alt {
14.                                    [] GREENLIGHT.receive( Off );
15.                                        alt {
16.                                            [] DOOR.receive (Close);
17.                                                alt {
18.                                                    [] DISPLAY.receive(Welcome);
19.                                                        setverdict(Pass);
20.                                                    [] DISPLAY.receive(?);
21.                                                        setverdict(Fail);
22.                                                }
23.                                            [] DOOR.receive(?);
24.                                                setverdict(Fail);
25.                                        }
26.                                    [] GREENLIGHT.receive(?);
27.                                        setverdict(Fail);
28.                                }
29.                            [] GREENLIGHT.receive(?);
30.                                setverdict(Fail);
31.                        }
32.                    [] DOOR.receive(?);
33.                        setverdict(Fail);
34.                }
35.            } // end of else
36.        [] DISPLAY.receive(?);
37.            setverdict(Fail);
38.    }
```

Figure 10.44   Test behavior that can receive unexpected events (derived from Figure 10.43).

Step 3:   We augment a test behavior with timers so that a test system does not enter into a deadlock in case the SUT produces no output, that is, before waiting to receive an expected event, the test behavior starts a timer. The corresponding timeout input event is specified as an alternative to the expected input and the any event explained before. When we apply this transformation step to the test behavior shown in Figure 10.44, we obtain the test behavior shown in Figure 10.45. Finally, the test behavior is augmented with test verdicts. A Pass verdict is assigned if the system under test behaves as expected, and this is shown in line 10 of Figure 10.42. The Pass verdict in line 10 of Figure 10.42 can be found in line 13 in Figure 10.43, line 19 in Figure 10.44, and line 27 in Figure 10.45, as we

```
1.    count := 0; // Count is of type integer.
2.    label label1 KEYPAD.send( digit );
3.    Timer1.start(d1);
4.    alt {
5         [] DISPLAY.receive( Asterisk );
6.            Timer1.stop;
7.            count := count + 1;
8.            if (count < 4) goto label1;
9.            else {
10.                 Timer2.start(d2);
11.                 alt {
12.                     [] DOOR.receive( Open );
13.                         Timer2.stop; Timer3.start(d3);
14.                         alt {
15.                             [] GREENLIGHT.receive( On );
16.                                 Timer3.stop;
17.                                 DOOR.send( Passed );
18.                                 Timer4.start( d4 );
19.                                 alt {
20.                                     [] GREENLIGHT.receive( Off );
21.                                         Timer4.stop; Timer5.start( d5 );
22.                                         alt {
23.                                             [] DOOR.receive (Close);
24.                                                 Timer5.stop; Timer6.start( d6 );
25.                                                 alt {
26.                                                     [] DISPLAY.receive(Welcome);
27.                                                         Timer6.stop; setverdict(Pass);
28.                                                     [] DISPLAY.receive(?);
29.                                                         Timer6.stop; setverdict(Fail);
30.                                                     [] Timer6.timeout;
31.                                                         setverdict(Inconc);
32.                                                 }
33.                                             [] DOOR.receive(?);
34.                                                 Timer5.stop; setverdict(Fail);
35.                                             [] Timer5.timeout;
36.                                                 setverdict(Inconc);
37.                                         }
38.                                     [] GREENLIGHT.receive(?);
39.                                         Timer4.stop; setverdict(Fail);
40.                                     [] Timer4.timeout;
41.                                         setverdict(Inconc);
42.                                 }
43.                             [] GREENLIGHT.receive(?);
44.                                 Timer3.stop; setverdict(Fail);
45.                             [] Timer3.timeout;
46.                                 setverdict(Inconc);
47.                         }
48.                     [] DOOR.receive(?);
49.                         Timer2.stop; setverdict(Fail);
50.                     [] Timer2.timeout;
51.                         setverdict(Inconc);
52.                 }
53.             }
54.         [] DISPLAY.receive(?);
55.             Timer1.stop; setverdict(Fail);
56.         [] Timer1.timeout;
57.             setverdict(Inconc);
58.    }}
```

Figure 10.45 Core behavior of test case for testing door control system (derived from Figure 10.44.)

go on making the test case more and more complete. We assign a Fail verdict when the test system receives an unexpected event in the form of any events and an Inconclusive verdict when a timeout occurs.

10.14 ADDITIONAL COVERAGE CRITERIA FOR SYSTEM TESTING

We discussed two coverage criteria, namely, state coverage and state transition coverage, to select test cases from FSM and EFSM models of software systems in Sections 10.5 and 10.13. Those two criteria focused on sequences of events, possibly including internal events, occurring at PCOs. In this section, we explain some more coverage criteria in line with the concepts of functional testing.

The reader may recall from Chapter 9 on functional testing that we identify the domains of input and output variables and select test data based on special values from those domains. For example, if an output variable takes on a small number of discrete values, then test cases are designed to make the SUT produce all those output values. If an output variable takes on values from a contiguous range, test data are selected such that the SUT produces the external points and an interior point in the specified range.

In line with the above concept of functional testing, in the following, we explain some coverage criteria for *event-driven* systems modeled as FSMs or EFSMs. First, we identify the PCOs, also referred to as ports—points where a SUT interacts with the external world. Next, we apply the following coverage criteria to select test cases:

PCO Coverage: Select test cases such that the SUT receives an event at each input PCO and produces an event at each output PCO.

Sequences of Events at PCOs: Select test cases such that *common* sequences of inputs and outputs occur at the PCOs. By a common sequence we mean sequences commonly found in the uses of the system.

Events Occurring in Different Contexts: In many applications, a user produces an event for the system by pressing a button, for example. Here, a button represents an input PCO, and pressing the button represents an event. However, the semantics of pressing a button, that is, interpretations of events at a PCO, depend on *data contexts* used by the system. For a given context, test data are selected such that all events, both desired and undesired, occur in the context.

Inopportune Events: A system is expected to discard invalid, or erroneous, events. On the other hand, inopportune events are normal events which occur at an inappropriate time.

Example: Automated Teller Machine. Let us consider the user interface of an ATM system as shown in Figure 10.46. A user selects one of the transaction options and specifies a transaction amount using buttons B1 through B6. The meaning of a

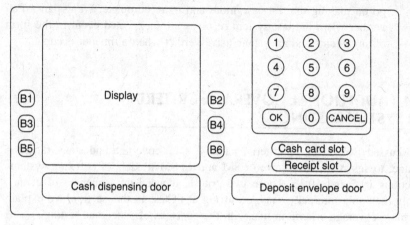

Figure 10.46 User interface of ATM.

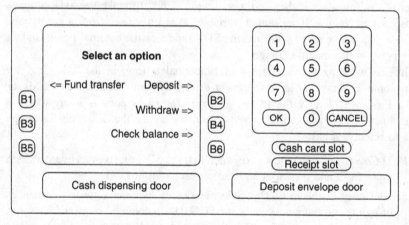

Figure 10.47 Binding of buttons with user options.

button changes as the message in the display area changes. For example, a user can choose a transaction option, such as Deposit or Withdraw, by pressing buttons B2 or B4, respectively, as shown in Figure 10.47. However, as shown in Figure 10.48, when it comes to selecting an amount, buttons B2 and B4 represent options $40 and $100, respectively. Moreover, all the buttons for the *amount* context shown in Figure 10.48 do not represent the same *type* of data. For example, buttons B1 through B5 represent discrete, integer values, whereas button B6 gives the user an option to specify other values. In the context shown in Figure 10.47, buttons B3 and B5 are undefined, and, thus, those are potential sources of undesirable (erroneous) events. Test cases must be selected to observe how the system responds to undefined events. The OK button produces a normal event while the user is entering a PIN after inserting the cash card. The OK event essentially tells the system that the user

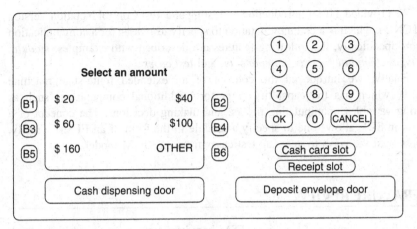

Figure 10.48   Binding of buttons with cash amount.

has completely entered a PIN. However, it may not be meaningful to press OK in the context shown in Figure 10.48. Therefore, pressing the OK button produces an inopportune event for the system to handle. Test cases need to be selected to consider inopportune events in addition to normal (valid) and abnormal (invalid or erroneous) events.

10.15   SUMMARY

This chapter began with the classification of software systems in terms of *stateless* and *state-oriented* systems. A stateless system does not memorize the previous inputs, and, therefore, its response to a new input does not depend on the previous inputs. On the other hand, a state-oriented system memorizes the sequence of inputs it has received so far in the form of a *state*. Next, we examined the concept of *ports* in the context of software testing. State-oriented systems were modeled as FSMs.

We explained two broad methods for generating test sequences from an implementation of an FSM—one *without* state verification and one *with* state verification. One can design weak test sequences in the form of transition tours without using state verification. On the other hand, one can design stronger test sequences by performing state verification with one of three kinds of sequences, namely, *unique input–output sequences*, *distinguishing sequences*, and *characterizing sequences*.

We examined four test architectures: *local*, *distributed*, *coordinated*, and *remote* with the test generation methods in place. These abstract test architectures are described in terms of controllable inputs given to an IUT and observable outputs from the IUT. The concept of *points of control and observation* (PCOs) is introduced. A PCO is a point of interaction called a port, which is accessible to a test entity, between the test entity and an IUT.

We provided a brief introduction to Testing and Test Control Notation Version 3 (TTCN-3), which is a common notation to specify test cases for a communication system. Specifically, the following features are described with examples: *module*, *data types*, *templates*, *ports*, *components*, and *test cases*.

Finally, we introduced the concept of an extended finite-state machine (EFSM), which has the capability to perform additional computations such as updating variables, manipulating timers, and making decisions. The concept of a *process* in SDL allows one to specify a module in the form of an EFSM. Finally, we presented the ways to generate test cases from an EFSM model.

LITERATURE REVIEW

An excellent collection of papers on FSM-based testing can be found in the book edited by Richard J. Linn and M. Umit Uyar [11]. Many articles referenced in this chapter have been reprinted in the book.

Those interested in knowing more about EFSM-based testing may refer to the excellent book by B. Sarikaya (*Principles of Protocol Engineering and Conformance Testing*, Ellis Horwood, Hemel Hempstead, Hertfordshire, 1993). Sarikaya explained formal specification languages Estelle, SDL, LOTOS, TTCN (the original Tree and Tabular Combined Notation), and Abstract Syntax Notation One (ASN.1) in the first part of his book. In the second part of the book, he explains the generation of transition tours from an unified model of Estelle, SDL, and LOTOS using the concepts of *control flow* and *data flow*.

In the past decade, researchers have proposed several techniques for generating test cases from nondeterministic FSMs. In the following we list the commonly referenced ones:

A. Alur, C. Couroubetis, and M. Yannakakis, "Distinguishing Tests for Nondeterministic and Probabilistic Machines," in *Proceedings of the 27th Annals of the ACM Symposium on Theory of Computing*, Las Vegas, Nevada, ACM Press, New York, 1995, pp. 363–372.

R. M. Hierons, "Applying Adaptive Test Cases to Nondeterministic Implementations," *Information Processing Letters*, Vol. 98, No. 2, April 2006, pp. 56–60.

R. M. Hierons and H. Ural, "Reducing the Cost of Applying Adaptive Test Cases," *Computer Networks: The International Journal of Computer and Telecommunications Networking*, Vol. 51, No. 1, January 2007, pp. 224–238.

G. Luo, G. v. Bochmann, and A. Petrenko, "Test Selection Based on Communicating Nondeterministic Finite-State Machines Using a Generalized Wp-Method," *IEEE Transactions on Software Engineering*, Vol. 20, No. 2, February 1994, pp. 149–162.

P. Tripathy and K. Naik, "Generation of Adaptive Test Cases from Nondeterministic Finite State Models," in *Proceeding of the Fifth International*

Workshop on Protocol Test Systems, G. v. Bochmann, R. Dssouli, and A. Das, Eds., Montreal, North-Holland, Amsterdam, 1992, pp. 309–320.

F. Zhang and T. Cheung, "Optimal Transfer Trees and Distinguishing Trees for Testing Observable Nondeterministic Finite-State Machines," *IEEE Transactions on Software Engineering*, Vol. 29, No. 1, January 2003, pp. 1–14.

REFERENCES

1. S. Naito and M. Tsunoyama. Fault Detection for Sequential Machine by Transition Tours. In *Proceedings of the 11th IEEE Fault Tolerant Computer Symposium*, Los Alamitos, CA, IEEE Computer Society Press, 1981, pp. 238–243.
2. B. Sarikaya and G. v. Bochmann. Some Experience with Test Sequence Generation. In *Proceedings of Second International Workshop on Protocol Specification, Testing, and Verification*, North Holland, Amsterdam, The Netherlands, 1982, pp. 555–567.
3. E. P. Hsieh. Checking Experiments for Sequential Machines. *IEEE Transactions on Computers*, October 1971, pp. 1152–1166.
4. K. K. Sabnani and A. T. Dahbura. A Protocol Testing Procedure. *Computer Networks and ISDN System*, Vol. 15, 1988, pp. 285–297.
5. K. Naik. Efficient Computation of Unique Input/Output Sequences in Finite-State Machines. *IEEE/ACM Transactions on Networking*, August 1997, pp. 585–599.
6. G. Gonenc. A Method for the Design of Fault Detection Experiments. *IEEE Transactions on Computers*, June 1970, pp. 551–558.
7. F. C. Hennie. Fault-Detecting Experiments for Sequential Circuits. In *Proceedings of the 5th Annual Symposium on Switching Circuit Theory and Logical Design*, Princeton University, Princeton, IEEE Press, New York, Lenox Hill Station, November 1964, pp. 95–110.
8. A. Gill. State-Identification Experiments in Finite Automata. *Information and Control*, Vol. 4, 1961, pp. 132–154.
9. Z. Kohavi. *Switching and Finite Automata Theory*. McGraw-Hill, New York, 1978.
10. T. S. Chow. Testing Software Designs Modeled by Finite State Machines. *IEEE Transactions on Software Engineering*, May 1978, pp. 178–187.
11. R. J. Linn and M. U. Uyar, Ed. *Conformance Testing Methodologies and Architectures for OSI Protocols*. IEEE Computer Society Press, Los Alamitos, CA, 1994.
12. D. Sidhu and T. Leung. Fault Coverage of Protocol Test Methods. In *Proceeding of the IEEE INFOCOM*, IEEE Press, New Orleans, LA, March 1988, pp. 80–85.
13. A. T. Dahbura and K. K. Sabnani. An Experience in the Fault Coverage of a Protocol Test. In *Proceeding of the IEEE INFOCOM*, IEEE Press, New Orleans, LA, March 1988, pp. 71–79.
14. Information Processing Systems. *OSI Conformance Testing Methodology and Framework*. ISO/IEC JCT 1/SC 21 DIS 9646, Part 3, February 1989. International Organization for Standardization, available at http://www.standardsinfo.net/.
15. Information Processing Systems. *OSI Conformance Testing Methodology and Framework*. ISO/IEC JCT 1/SC 21 DIS 9646, Parts 4–5, March 1989. International Organization for Standardization, available at http://www.standardsinfo.net/.
16. Information Processing Systems. *OSI Conformance Testing Methodology and Framework*. ISO/IEC JCT 1/SC 21 DIS 9646, Parts 1–2, November 1988. International Organization for Standardization, available at http://www.standardsinfo.net/.
17. R. J. Linn, Jr. Conformance Testing for OSI Protocols. *Computer Networks and ISDN Systems*, Vol. 18, 1989/1990, pp. 203–219.
18. D. Rayner. OSI Conformance Testing. *Computer Networks and ISDN Systems*, Vol. 14, 1987, pp. 79–98.
19. C. Willcock, T. Deiss, S. Tobies, S. Keil, F. Engler, and S. Schulz. *An Introduction to TTCN-3*. Wiley, New York, 2005.

20. F. Belina, D. Hogrefe, and A. Sarma. *SDL—With Application from Protocol Specification*. Prentice-Hall, Upper Saddle River, NJ, 1991.

21. CCITT. *Specification and Description Language*, Recommendation z.100, CCITT SG X, ITU, Geneva, Switzerland, 1992.

Exercises

1. Considering the FSM of Figure 10.17 discussed in this chapter, provide a test sequence table, similar to Table 10.12, for the state transition $(D, B, b/y)$.

2. What are the fundamental differences between UIO sequence and distinguishing sequence methods of state verification?

3. Consider the FSM $G = <S, I, O, A, \delta, \lambda>$, shown in Figure 10.49, where $S = \{A, B, C\}$ is the set of states, $I = \{a, b, c\}$ is the set of inputs, $O = \{e, f\}$ is the set of outputs, A is the initial state, $\delta : S \times I \rightarrow S$ is the next-state function, and $\lambda : S \times I \rightarrow O$ is the output function.

   (a) Generate a distinguishing sequence for the FSM, if it exists.

   (b) Generate characterizing sequences for the FSM.

   (c) Generate UIO sequence(s) for each state of the FSM, if those exist.

   (d) Compare the distinguishing sequence with the UIO sequences generated from the FSM. Are there any similarities and/or differences between the two kinds of sequences?

4. Consider the FSM $H = <S, I, O, A, \delta, \lambda>$ of Figure 10.50, where $S = \{A, B, C, D, E, F, G\}$ is the set of states, $I = \{ri, a, c, x, z\}$ is the set

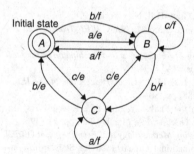

Figure 10.49   FSM G.

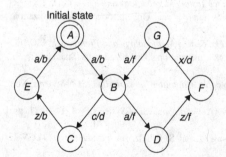

Figure 10.50   FSM H.

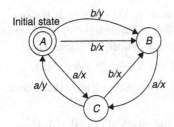

Figure 10.51 FSM K.

of inputs, $O = \{null, b, f, d\}$ is the set of outputs, A is the initial state, $\delta : S \times I \to S$ is the next-state function, and $\lambda : S \times I \to O$ is the output function.

(a) Generate UIO sequence(s) for each state of the FSM, if those exist.

(b) Generate test sequences for each transition of the FSM using UIO sequences for state verification. Assume that a reset input ri will always bring the FSM back to its initial state A. The FSM produces a null output in response to the ri input.

(c) Represent the following two test cases in TTCN-3 form with verdicts: $(B, C, c/d)$ and $(A, B, a/b)$.

5. Consider the FSM $K = <S, I, O, A, \delta, \lambda>$ of Figure 10.51, where $S = \{A, B, C\}$ is the set of states, $I = \{a, b\}$ is the set of inputs, $O = \{x, y\}$ is the set of outputs, A is the initial state, $\delta : S \times I \to S$ is the next-state function, and $\lambda : S \times I \to O$ is the output function.

(a) Show that the FSM K does not possess a distinguishing sequence.

(b) Can you generate a UIO sequence for each state of this FSM? Justify your answer.

(c) Generate characterizing sequences for the FSM.

6. Consider the nondeterministic FSM NFSM $= <S, I, O, A, \delta, \lambda>$ of Figure 10.52, where $S = \{A, B, C, D, E, F, G\}$ is the set of states, $I = \{ri, a, c, x, z\}$ is the set of inputs, $O = \{null, b, f, d\}$ is the set of outputs, A is the initial

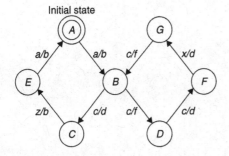

Figure 10.52 Nondeterministic FSM.

state, $\delta : S \times I \to S$ is the next-state function, and $\lambda : S \times I \to O$ is the output function. NFSM is nondeterministic means that for some input $a_k \in I$ there are more than one transitions with different outputs defined for some state.

(a) Generate UIO sequence(s) for each state of the NFSM, if those exist.

(b) Do you think the generated UIO sequences can uniquely identify the states? Justify your answer.

(c) Devise a methodology to uniquely identify the states of the NFSM. (*Hint:* The tree structure will identify the state of the NFSM uniquely.) Using your methodology, generate UIO trees for each state of the NFSM.

(d) Generate test cases for the following transitions: (a) $(F, G, x/d)$, (b) $(B, C, c/d)$, and (c) $(A, B, a/b)$.

(e) Represent the following two test cases in TTCN-3 form with verdicts: $(B, C, c/d)$ and $(A, B, a/b)$.

7. Discuss the effectiveness of the error detection capabilities among the abstract test architectures presented in this chapter.

8. Design a test component to test the system, represented in Figure 10.8, from the standpoint of a local phone alone. In your test component, consider the partial transition tour OH–AD–RNG–TK.

9. Assuming that a called (remote) phone is far away from the calling (local) phone, explain the difficulty you will encounter while designing a test case in TTCN-3 from the following transition tour in Figure 10.8: OH–AD–RNG–TK–LON–TK–RON–AD–OH.

10. Explain the concept of test case verdicts.

CHAPTER 11

System Test Design

Many things difficult to design prove easy to perform.
— *Samuel Johnson*

11.1 TEST DESIGN FACTORS

The central activity in test design is to identify inputs to and the expected outcomes from a system to verify whether the system possesses certain features. A feature is a set of related requirements. The test design activities must be performed in a planned manner in order to meet some technical criteria, such as effectiveness, and economic criteria, such as productivity. Therefore, we consider the following factors during test design: (i) coverage metrics, (ii) effectiveness, (iii) productivity, (iii) validation, (iv) maintenance, and (v) user skill. In the following, we give motivations for considering these factors.

Coverage metrics concern the extent to which the DUT is examined by a test suite designed to meet certain criteria. Coverage metrics lend us two advantages. First, these allow us to quantify the extent to which a test suite covers certain aspects, such as functional, structural, and interface of a system. Second, these allow us to measure the progress of system testing. The criteria may be path testing, branch testing, or a feature identified from a requirement specification.

Each test case is given an identifier(s) to be associated with a set of requirements. This association is done by using the idea of a coverage matrix. A coverage matrix $[A_{ij}]$ is generated for the above idea of coverage [1]. The general structure of the coverage matrix $[A_{ij}]$ is represented as shown in Table 11.1, where T_i stands for the ith test case and N_j stands for the jth requirement to be covered; $[A_{ij}]$ stands for coverage of the test case T_i over the tested element N_j. The complete set of test cases, that is, a test suite, and the complete set of tested elements of the coverage matrix are identified as $T_c = \{T_1, T_2, .., T_q\}$ and $N_c = \{N_1, N_2, .., N_p\}$, respectively.

A structured test case development methodology must be used as much as possible to generate a test suite. A structured development methodology also minimizes maintenance work and improves productivity. Careful design of test cases

TABLE 11.1   Coverage Matrix [A_{ij}]

Test Case	Requirement Identifier			
Identifier	N_1	N_2	...	N_p
T_1	A_{11}	A_{12}	...	A_{1p}
T_2	A_{21}	A_{22}	...	A_{2p}
T_3	A_{31}	A_{32}	...	A_{3p}
⋮	⋮	⋮	⋮	⋮
T_q	A_{q1}	A_{q2}	...	A_{qp}

in the early stages of test suite development ensures their maintainability as new requirements emerge. The correctness of the requirements is very critical in order to develop effective test cases to reveal defects. Therefore, emphasis must be put on identification and analysis of the requirements from which test objectives are derived. Test cases are created based on the test objectives. Another aspect of test case production is validation of the test cases to ensure that those are reliable. It is natural to expect that an executable test case meets its specification before it is used to examine another system. This includes ensuring that test cases have adequate error handling procedures and precise pass–fail criteria. We need to develop a methodology to assist the production, execution, and maintenance of the test suite. Another factor to be aware of is the potential users of the test suite. The test suite should be developed with these users in mind; the test suite must be easy to deploy and execute in other environments, and the procedures for doing so need to be properly documented. Our test suite production life cycle considers all six factors discussed above.

11.2   REQUIREMENT IDENTIFICATION

Statistical evidence gathered by Vinter [2] demonstrates the importance of requirements captured in the development of embedded real-time system projects. Vinter analyzed 1000 defects during his studies, out of which 23.9% of the defect reports stemmed from requirement issues, functionality 24.3%, component structure (the code) 20.9%, data 9.6%, implementation 4.3%, integration 5.2%, architecture 0.9%, testing 6.9%, and other 4.3%. Within those defect reports that were associated with requirements problems, Vinter argued that 48% could be classified as "misunderstanding." Typically, disagreement existed over the precise interpretation of a particular requirement. Missing constraints constitute 19% of the defect reports that stemmed from requirements problem while changed requirements account for 27%. A further 6% were classified as "other" issues. These statistical studies have inspired practitioners to advocate a new vision of requirements identification.

Requirements are a description of the needs or desires of users that a system is supposed to implement. There are two main challenges in defining requirements. First is to ensure that the right requirements are captured, which is essential for meeting the expectations of the users. Requirements must be expressed in such a form that the users and their surrogates can easily review and confirm their correctness. Therefore, the "form" of a requirement is crucial to the communication between users (and their surrogates) and the representatives of a software development organization. Second is to ensure that the requirements are communicated unambiguously to the developers and testers so that there are no surprises when the system is delivered. A software development team may not be in charge of collecting the requirements from the users. For example, a team of marketing people may collect the requirements. In such a case, there may not be a direct link between the ultimate users and the technical teams, such as development team, system integration team, and system test team. It is undesirable for the teams to interpret the requirements in their own ways. There are two severe consequences of different teams interpreting a requirement in different ways. First, the development team and the system test team may have conflicting arguments about the quality of the product while analyzing the requirements before delivery. Second, the product may fail to meet the expectations of the users. Therefore, it is essential to have an unambiguous representation of the requirements and have it made available in a centralized place so that all the stakeholders have the same interpretation of the requirements [3].

We describe a formal model to capture the requirements for review and analysis within an organization in order to achieve the above two goals. Figure 11.1 shows a state diagram of a simplified requirement life cycle starting from the submit state to the closed state. This transition model provides different phases of a requirement, where each phase is represented by a state. This model represents the life of a requirement from its inception to completion through the following states: submit, open, review, assign, commit, implement, verification, and finally closed. At each of these states certain actions are taken by the owner, and the requirement is moved to the next state after the actions are completed. A requirement may be moved to the decline state from any of the states open, review, assign, implement, and verification for several reasons. For example, a marketing manager may decide

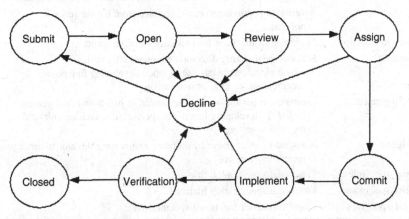

Figure 11.1 State transition diagram of requirement.

that the implementation of a particular requirement may not generate revenue. Therefore, the marketing manager may decline a requirement and terminate the development process.

The state transition diagram showing the life cycle of an individual requirement can be easily implemented using a database system with a graphical user interface (GUI). One can customize any existing open-source tracking system to implement the requirement model described here [4]. The idea behind implementing the state transition diagram is to be able to track the requirements as these flow through the organization [5, 6]. A requirement schema is designed with different tabbed panes using commonly used GUI and database. Subsequently, requirements can be stored and queries generated for tracking and reporting the status of the requirements. A list of fields of the schema is given in Table 11.2. It is necessary to implement a secure access system for different users of the database. Customers

TABLE 11.2   Requirement Schema Field Summary

Field Name	Description
requirement_id	A unique identifier associated with the requirement
title	Title of the requirement; one-line summary of the requirement
description	Description of the requirement
state	Current state of the requirement; can take a value from the set {Submit, Open, Review, Assign, Commit, Implement, Verification, Closed, Decline}
product	Product name
customer	Name of customer who requested this requirement
note	Submitter's note; any additional information the submitter wants to provide that will be useful to marketing manager or director of software engineering
software_release	Assigned to a software release; software release number in which the requirement is desired to be available for end customer
committed_release	Software release number in which requirement will be available
priority	Priority of requirement; can take value from the set {high, normal}
severity	Severity of requirement; can take value from the set {critical, normal}
marketing_justification	Marketing justification for existence of requirement
eng_comment	Software engineering director's comment after review of requirement; comments useful when developing functional specification, coding, or unit testing
time_to_implement	Estimated in person-week; time needed to implement requirement, including developing functional specification, coding, unit, and integration testing
eng_assigned	Assigned to an engineer by software engineering director in order to review requirement
functional_spec_title	Functional specification title
functional_spec_name	Functional specification filename
functional_spec_version	Latest version of functional specification

TABLE 11.2   (Continued)

Field Name	Description
decline_note	Explanation of why requirement is declined
ec_number	Engineering change (EC) document number
attachment	Attachment (if any)
tc_id	Test case identifier; multiple test case identifiers can be entered; these values may be obtained automatically from test factory database
tc_results	Test case result; can take value from the set {Untested, Passed, Failed, Blocked, Invalid}; can be automatically obtained from test factory database
verification_method	Verification method; T—by testing; A—by analysis; D—by demonstration; I—by inspection
verification_status	Verification state (passed, failed, incomplete) of requirement.
compliance	Compliance; can take value from the set {compliance, partial compliance, noncompliance}
testing_note	Notes from test engineer; may contain explanation of analysis, inspection, or demonstration given to end customer by test engineer
defect_id	Defect identifier; value can be extracted from test factory database along with test results. If the tc_results field takes the value "failed," then the defect identifier is associated with the failed test case to indicate the defect that causes the failure.

may be given restricted access to the database, so that they can see the status of their requirements within the organization. Customers can generate a traceability matrix from the requirement database system, which gives them confidence about test coverage [7]. A traceability matrix allows one to find a two-way mapping between requirements and test cases as follows [8]:

- From a requirement to a functional specification to specific tests which exercise the requirements
- From each test case back to the requirement and functional specifications

A traceability matrix finds two applications: (i) identify and track the functional coverage of a test and (ii) identify which test cases must be exercised or updated when a system evolves [9]. It is difficult to determine the extent of coverage achieved by a test suite without a traceability matrix. The test suite can contain a sizable number of tests for the features of a system, but without the cross-referencing provided by a traceability matrix it is difficult to discern whether a particular requirement has been adequately covered. The following definition by Gotel and Finkelstein [10] sums up the general view of requirements traceability (p. 97):

> The requirements traceability is the ability to describe and follow the life of a requirement, in both forward and backward direction, i.e., from its origins, through its development and specification, to its subsequent deployment and use, and through periods of ongoing refinement and iteration in any of these phases.

Submit State   A new requirement is put in the submit state to make it available to others. The owner of this state is the submitter. A new requirement may come from different sources: customer, marketing manager, and program manager. A program manager oversees a software release starting from its inception to its completion and is responsible for delivering it to the customer. A software release is the release of a software image providing new features. For example, one can release an OS to customers every eight months by adding new features and using an appropriate numbering scheme, such as OS release 2.0, OS release 2.1, and so on. Usually, the requirements are generated from the customers and marketing managers.

A defect filed by a test engineer may become a requirement in a future release because it may become apparent that the reported defect is not really a true defect and should be treated as an enhancement request. In case of a dispute between the test engineers and the developers, the program manager may make a final decision in consultation with relevant people. The program manager can submit a new requirement based on the issue raised in the defect if he or she decides that the disputed defect is, in fact, an enhancement request. The following fields of the schema given in Table 11.2 are filled out when a requirement is submitted:

requirement_id: A unique identifier associated with the requirement.

priority: A priority level of the requirement—high or normal.

title: A title for the requirement.

submitter: The submitter's name.

description: A short description of the requirement.

note: Some notes on this requirement, if there are any.

product: Name of the product in which the requirement is desired.

customer: Name of the customer who requested this requirement.

The priority level is an indication of the order in which requirements need to be implemented. Requirements prioritization [11] is an important aspect in a market-driven requirements engineering process [12, 13]. All the high-priority requirements should be considered for implementation before the normal priority requirements. The submitter can assign a priority level to a requirement that defines the requirement's level of importance. The marketing manager can move the state from submit to open by assigning the ownership to himself.

Open State   In this state, the marketing manager is in charge of the requirement and coordinates the following activities.

- Reviews the requirement to find duplicate entries. The marketing manager can move the duplicate requirement from the open state to the decline state with an explanation and a pointer to the existing requirement. Also, he or she may ensure that there are no ambiguities in the requirement and, if there is any ambiguity, consult with the submitter and update the description and the note fields of the requirement.

- Reevaluates the priority of the requirement assigned by the submitter and either accepts it or modifies it.

- Determines the severity of the requirement. There are two levels of severity defined for each requirement: normal and critical. The severity option provides a tag for the upper management, such as the director of software engineer, in order to review the requirement. If the severity level is critical, then it is a flag to the director to complete the review as soon as possible. Assignment of a severity level is made independent of the priority level.
- Suggests a preferred software release for the requirement.
- Attaches a marketing justification to the requirement.
- Moves the requirement from the open state to the review state by assigning the ownership to the director of software engineering.
- The marketing manager may decline a requirement in the open state and terminate the development process, thereby moving the requirement to the decline state with a proper explanation.

The following fields may be updated by the marketing manager, who is the owner of the requirement in the open state:

priority: Reevaluate the priority—high or normal—of this requirement.

severity: Assign a severity level—normal or critical—to the requirement.

decline_note: Give an explanation of the requirement if declined.

software_release: Suggest a preferred software release for the requirement.

marketing_justification: Provide a marketing justification for the requirement.

description: Describe the requirement, if there is any ambiguity.

note: Make any useful comments, if there is a need.

Review State   The director of software engineering is the owner of the requirement in the review state. A requirement stays in the review state until it passes through the engineering process as explained in the following. The software engineering director reviews the requirement to understand it and estimate the time required to implement this. The director thus prepares a preliminary version of the functional specification for this requirement. This scheme provides a framework to map the requirement to the functional specification which is to be implemented. The director of software engineering can move the requirement from the review state to the assign state by changing the ownership to the marketing manager. Moreover, the director may decline this requirement if it is not possible to implement. The following fields may be updated by the director:

eng_comment: Comments generated during the review are noted in this field. The comments are useful in developing a functional specification, generating code, or performing unit-level testing.

time_to_implement: This field holds the estimated time in person-weeks to implement the requirement.

attachment: An analysis document, if there is any, including figures and descriptions that are likely to be useful in the future development of functional specifications.

functional_spec_title: The name of the functional specification that will be written for this requirement.

functional_spec_name: The functional specification filename.

functional_spec_version: The latest version number of the functional specification.

eng_assigned: Name of the engineer assigned by the director to review the requirement.

Assign State   The marketing manager is the owner of the requirement in the assign state. A marketing manager assigns the requirement to a particular software release and moves the requirement to the commit state by changing the ownership to the program manager, who owns that particular software release. The marketing manager may decline the requirement and terminate the development process, thereby moving the requirement to the decline state. The following fields are updated by the marketing manager: decline_note and software_release. The former holds an explanation for declining, if it is moved to the decline state. On the other hand, if the requirement is moved to the commit state, the marketing manager updates the latter field to specify the software release in which the requirement will be available.

Commit State   The program manager is the owner of the requirement in the commit state. The requirement stays in this state until it is committed to a software release. The program manager reviews all the requirements that are suggested to be in a particular release which is owned by him. The program manger may reassign a particular requirement to a different software release by consulting with the marketing manager, the software engineering director, and the customer. The requirement may be moved to the implement state by the program manager after it is committed to a particular software release. All the functional specifications should be frozen after a requirement is committed, that is, exited from the commit state. It is important to stabilize and freeze the functional specification for test design and development. The test engineers must complete the review of the requirement and the relevant functional specification from a testability point of view. Next, the test engineers can start designing and writing test cases for this requirement, as discussed in Section 11.6. The only field to be updated by the program manager, who is the owner of the requirement in the commit state, is committed_release. The field holds the release number for this requirement.

Implement State   The director of software engineering is the owner of the requirement in the implement state. This state implies that the software engineering group is currently coding and unit testing the requirement. The director of software engineering may move the requirement from the implement state to the verification

TABLE 11.3   Engineering Change Document Information

EC number	A unique number
Requirement(s) affected	Requirement ID(s) and titles
Problem/issue description	Brief description of issue
Description of change required	Description of changes needed to original requirement description
Secondary technical impact	Description of impact EC will have on system
Customer impacts	Description of impact EC will have on end customer
Change recommended by	Name of the engineer(s)
Change approved by	Name of the approver(s)

state after the implementation is complete and the software is released for system testing, The director can assign an EC number and explain that the requirement is not doable in its current definition. The EC document is attached to the requirement definition. An outline of an EC document is given in Table 11.3. The director can also decline the requirement, if it is technically not possible to implement it, and move the requirement to the decline state. The following fields may be updated by the director, since he or she is the owner of a requirement in the implement state:

> *decline_note*: An explanation of the reasons the requirement is declined if it is moved to the decline state.
>
> *ec_number*: The EC document number.
>
> *attachment*: The EC document.

Verification State   The test manager is the owner of the requirement in the verification state. The test manager verifies the requirement and identifies one or more methods for assigning a test verdict: (i) testing, (ii) inspection, (iii) analysis, and (iv) demonstration. If testing is a method for verifying a requirement, then the test case identifiers and their results are provided. This information is extracted from the test factory discussed in Section 11.6. Inspection means review of the code. Analysis means mathematical and/or statistical analysis. Demonstration means observing the system in a live operation. A verdict is assigned to the requirement by providing the degree of compliance information: full compliance, partial compliance, or noncompliance. A testing note is included if a method other than testing is used for verification. The notes may contain an explanation of the analysis, inspection, or demonstration given to the customer.

The requirement may get an EC number from the test manager as a testing note. The EC document specifies any deficiency in the implementation of the requirement. A deviation or an error discovered at this stage can rarely be corrected. It is often necessary to negotiate with the customer through an EC document to the requirement. The program manager coordinates this negotiation activity with the customer. The test manager may decline the implementation with an EC number, explaining that the implementation is not conforming to the requirement, and move to the decline state. The test manager may move the requirement to the closed state after it has been verified and the value of the verification_status field set to "passed." The following fields are updated by the test manager since he or she is the owner of the requirement at the verification state:

decline_note: The reasons to decline this requirement.

ec_number: An EC document number.

attachment: The EC document.

verification_method: Can take one of the four values from the set {Testing, Analysis, Demonstration, Inspection}.

verification_status: Can take one of the three values from the set {Passed, Failed, Incomplete}, indicating the final verification status of the requirement.

compliance: Can take one of the three values from the set {compliance, partial compliance, noncompliance}, which indicate the extent to which the software image complies with the requirements.

tc_id: The test case identifiers that cover this requirement.

tc_results: The test case results for the above tests. It can take on one of the five values from the set {Untested, Passed, Failed, Blocked, Invalid}. These values are extracted from the test factory database, which is discussed in Section 11.7.

defect_id: A defect identifier. If the tc_results field takes the value "failed," then the defect identifier is associated with the failed test case to indicate the defect that causes the failure. This value is extracted from test factory database.

testing_note: May hold an explanation of the analysis, inspection, or demonstration given to the end customer by the test engineer.

Closed State The requirement is moved to the closed state from the verification state by the test manager after it is verified.

Decline State In this state, the marketing department is the owner of the requirement. A requirement comes to this state because of some of the following reasons:

- The marketing department rejected the requirement.
- It is technically not possible to implement this requirement and, possibly, there is an associated EC number.
- The test manager declines the implementation with an EC number.

The marketing group may move the requirement to the submit state after reviewing it with the customer. The marketing manager may reduce the scope of the requirement after discussing it with the customer based on the EC information and resubmit the requirement by moving it to the submit state.

11.3   CHARACTERISTICS OF TESTABLE REQUIREMENTS

System-level tests are designed based on the requirements to be verified. A test engineer analyzes the requirement, the relevant functional specifications, and the standards to determine the testability of the requirement. The above task is performed in the commit state. Testability analysis means assessing the static behavioral characteristics of the requirement to reveal test objectives. One way to determine the requirement description is testable is as follows:

- Take the following requirement description: The system must perform X.
- Then encapsulate the requirement description to create a test objective: Verify that the system performs X correctly.
- Review this test objective by asking the question: Is it workable? In other words, find out if it is possible to execute it assuming that the system and the test environment are available.
- If the answer to the above question is yes, then the requirement description is clear and detailed for testing purpose. Otherwise, more work needs to be done to revise or supplement the requirement description.

As an example, let us consider the following requirement: The software image must be easy to upgrade/downgrade as the network grows. This requirement is too broad and vague to determine the objective of a test case. In other words, it is a poorly crafted requirement. One can restate the previous requirement as: The software image must be easy to upgrade/downgrade for 100 network elements. Then one can easily create a test objective: Verify that the software image can be upgraded/downgraded for 100 network elements. It takes time, clear thinking, and courage to change things.

In addition to the testability of the requirements, the following items must be analyzed by the system test engineers during the review:

- **Safety:** Have the safety-critical requirements [14] been identified? The safety-critical requirements specify what the system shall *not* do, including means for eliminating and controlling hazards and for limiting any damage in the case that a mishap occurs.
- **Security:** Have the security requirements [15], such as confidentiality, integrity, and availability, been identified?
- **Completeness:** Have all the essential items been completed? Have all possible situations been addressed by the requirements? Have all the irrelevant items been omitted?
- **Correctness:** Are the requirements understandable and have they been stated without error? Are there any incorrect items?
- **Consistency:** Are there any conflicting requirements?
- **Clarity:** Are the requirement materials and the statements in the document clear, useful, and relevant? Are the diagrams, graphs, and illustrations

clear? Have those been expressed using proper notation to be effective? Do those appear in proper places? Is the writing style clear?

- **Relevance:** Are the requirements pertinent to the subject? Are the requirements unnecessarily restrictive?

- **Feasibility:** Are the requirements implementable?

- **Verifiable:** Can tests be written to demonstrate conclusively and objectively that the requirements have been met? Can the functionality of the system be measured in some way that will assess the degree to which the requirements are met?

- **Traceable:** Can each requirement be traced to the functions and data related to it so that changes in a requirements can lead to easy reevaluation?

Functional Specification   A functional specification provides:

i. A precise description of the major functions the system must fulfill the requirements, description of the implementation of the functions, and explanation of the technological risks involved

ii. External interfaces with other software modules

iii. Data flow such as flowcharts, transaction sequence diagrams, and FSMs describing the sequence of activities

iv. Fault handling, memory utilization and performance estimates

v. Any engineering limitation, that is, inferred requirements that will not be supported

vi. The command line interface or element management system to provision/configure the feature in order to invoke the software implementation related to this feature

Once again, the functional specification must be reviewed from the point of view of testability. The characteristics of testable functional specifications are outlined in Table 11.4. The functional specifications are more likely to be testable if they satisfy all the items in the Table 11.4. Common problems with functional specifications include lack of clarity, ambiguity, and inconsistency. The following are the objectives that are kept in mind while reviewing a functional specification [16]:

- **Achieving Requirements:** It is essential that the functional specification identifies the formal requirements to be achieved. One determines, by means of review, whether requirements have been addressed by the functional specification.

- **Correctness:** Whenever possible, the specification parts should be compared directly to an external reference for correctness.

- **Extensible:** The specification is designed to easily accommodate future extensions that can be clearly envisioned at the time of review.

- **Comprehensible:** The specification must be easily comprehensible. By the end of the review process, if the reviewers do not understand how the system works, the specification or its documentation is likely to be flawed.

TABLE 11.4 Characteristics of Testable Functional Specifications

Purpose, goals, and exception are clearly stated. Address the right objectives.

Contain the requirements and standards with which this document complies.

Clearly stated operating environment. For what hardware, OS, and software release the feature is targeted. Minimum hardware configuration that supports this application.

Clearly list the major functions which the system must perform.

Clearly define the success criteria which the system must fulfill to be effective.

Provide an understandable, organized, and maintainable model of the processes, and or data or objects, using a standard structured method and the principle of functional decomposition.

Use standard and clearly defined terminology (key words, glossary, syntax and semantics).

Display a heavy use of model and graphics (e.g., SDL-GR, finite-state model), not primarily English narrative.

Document the assumptions.

The document should have a natural structure/flow and with each atomic feature labeled with an identifier for easy cross-referring to specific test cases.

Should have standard exception handling procedure, consistent error messages, and on-line help functions.

External interfaces, such as CLI, MIBs, EMS, and Web interface are defined clearly.

Clearly stated possible trade-offs between speed, time, cost, and portability.

Performance requirements are defined, usually in terms of packets per second, transactions per second, recovery time, response time, or other such metrics.

Scaling limits and resource utilization (CPU utilization, memory utilization) are stated precisely.

Documentation of unit tests.

Note: SDL-GR, Specification and Description Language Graphical Representation

Such specifications and documentations need to be reworked to make them more comprehensible.

- **Necessity:** Each item in the document should be necessary.

- **Sufficiency:** The specification should be examined for missing or incomplete items. All functions must be described as well as important properties of input and output data such as volume and magnitude.

- **Implementable:** It is desirable to have a functional specification that is implementable within the given resource constraints that are available in the target environment such as hardware, processing power, memory, and network bandwidth. One should be able to implement a specification in a short period of time without a technological breakthrough.

- **Efficient:** The functional specification must optimize those parts of the solution that contribute most to the performance (or lack thereof) of the system. The reviewers have the discretion of rejecting the specification on the ground of ineffectiveness in specifying efficiency requirements.

- **Simplicity:** In general, it is easier to achieve and verify requirements stated in the form of simple functional specifications.

- **Reusable Components:** The specification should reuse existing components as much as possible and be modular enough that the common components can be extracted to be reused.

- **Consistency with Existing Components:** The general structure of the specification should be consistent with the choices made in the rest of the system. It should not require the design paradigm of a system to be changed for no compelling reason.

- **Limitations:** The limitations should be realistic and consistent with the requirements.

11.4 TEST OBJECTIVE IDENTIFICATION

The question "What do I test?" must be answered with another question: "What do I expect the system to do?" We cannot test the system comprehensively if we do not understand it. Therefore, the first step in identifying the test objective is to read, understand, and analyze the functional specification. It is essential to have a background familiarity with the subject area, the goals of the system, business processes, and system users for a successful analysis.

Let us consider our previously revised requirement: The software image must be easy to upgrade/ downgrade for 100 network elements. The test engineer needs to ask one question: What do I need to know to develop a comprehensive set of test objectives for the above requirement? An inquisitive test engineer may also ask the following questions:

- Do we have to upgrade the software image sequentially on each of the network elements or at the same time on all the 100 elements? Or, do we proceed in a batch of 20 elements at a time?

- What is the source of the upgrade? Will the source be on an element management server?

- What does "easy" mean here? Does it refer to the length of time, say, 200 seconds, taken by the upgrade process?

- Can we have a mix of old and new software images on different network elements on the same network? In other words, is a new software image compatible with the old image?

- If we support old and new software images on different network elements on the same network, then the EMS should be capable of managing two versions of a software installed on the same network. Is it possible for an EMS to manage network elements running different software versions?

- To what release will the software be downgraded? Suppose the software image is upgraded to the nth release from the $(n-1)$th release. Now, if the software image is to be downgraded, to what release should it be downgraded—$(n-1)$th or $(n-2)$th release?

- While a system is being upgraded, do we need to observe the CPU utilization of the network elements and the EMS server? What is the expected CPU utilization?

We critically analyze requirements to extract the inferred requirements that are embedded in the requirements. An inferred requirement is one that a system is expected to support but is not explicitly stated. Inferred requirements need to be tested just like the explicitly stated requirements. As an example, let us consider the requirement that the system must be able to sort a list of items into a desired order. One obvious test objective is: Verify that the system can sort an unsorted list of items. However, there are several unstated requirements not being verified by the above test objective. Many more test objectives can be identified for the requirement:

- Verify that the system produces the sorted list of items when an already sorted list of items is given as input.
- Verify that the system produces the sorted list of items when a list of items with varying length is given as input.
- Verify that the number of output items is equal to the number of input items.
- Verify that the contents of the sorted output records are the same as the input record contents.
- Verify that the system produces an empty list of items when an empty list of items is given as input.
- Check the system behavior and the output list by giving an input list containing one or more empty (null) records.
- Verify that the system can sort a list containing a very large number of unsorted items.

The test objectives are put together to form a test group or a subgroup after they have been identified. A set of (sub)groups of test cases are logically combined to form a larger group. A hierarchical structure of test groups as shown in Figure 11.2 is called a test suite. It is necessary to identify the test groups based on test categories and refine the test groups into sets of test objectives. Individual test cases are created for each test objective within the subgroups; this is explained in the next section with an example. Test groups may be nested to an arbitrary depth. They may be used to aid system test planning and execution, which are discussed in Chapters 13 and 13, respectively.

11.5 EXAMPLE

The Frame Relay Forum (FRF) defines two kinds of frame relay (FR)/asynchronous transfer mode (ATM) interworking scenarios: network interworking [17] and service interworking [18]. These two interworking functions provide a means by which two technologies, namely ATM and FR, can interoperate. Simply stated, network

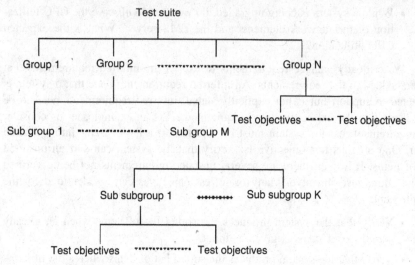

Figure 11.2   Test suite structure.

Interworking provides a transport between two FR devices (or entities). Service interworking enables an ATM user to transparently interwork with an FR user, and neither knows that the other end uses a different technology.

Suppose that one of the requirements is to support service interworking as described in FRF.8 [18] on a switch. The director of software engineering develops a functional specification after the requirements are approved by the marketing manager. The test group develops a test category based on the requirements and the functional specification. Since the actual functional specification is not available, we assume the following for simplicity:

- The term *FrAtm* refers to the software component that provides the FR-ATM permanent virtual connection (PVC) service interworking functionality.

- FrAtm supports a variety of ATM cell-based physical interfaces on the ATM side: OC3, E3, DS3, E1, and DS1.

- FrAtm supports a variety of frame-based physical interfaces on the FR side: V.11, V.35, DS1, E1, DS3, and E3.

- The subcomponents of FrAtm are as follows: local management interface (LMI) and data-link connection identifier (DLCI).

- FrAtm software components are being implemented on an FR and ATM switch. In other words, both FR and ATM functionality is available on the same switch.

Let us briefly analyze the service interworking functionality before we develop different categories of tests. Figure 11.3 illustrates the service interworking between FR and ATM. Service interworking applies when (i) an FR service user

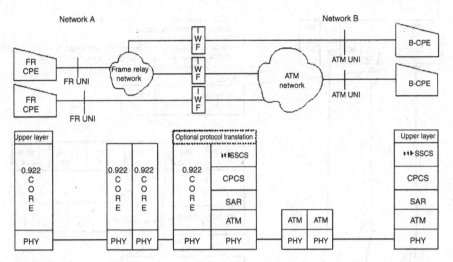

Figure 11.3   Service interworking between FR and ATM services.

interworks with an ATM service user, (ii) the ATM service user performs no frame relaying specific functions, and (iii) the frame relaying service user performs no ATM service-specific functions. Broadband-customer premise equipment (B-CPE) has no knowledge that a distant device is attached to an FR network. As shown in Figure 11.3, an FR user sends traffic on a PVC through the FR network to an interworking function (IWF), which then maps it to an ATM PVC. The FR PVC address–ATM PVC address mapping and other options are configured by the network management system associated with the IWF. Again, the IWF can be extended to the networks as shown, but it is more likely to be integrated into the ATM network switch or FR switch. Note that there is always one ATM PVC per FR PVC in the case of service internetworking. The IWF can be explained using a protocol stack model described in Figure 11.3. This protocol stack uses a "null" service-specific convergence sublayer (SSCS) for describing the IWF. This SSCS provides interfaces using standard primitives to Q.922 DL core on one side and to AAL5 (ATM adaptation layer) CPCS (common part convergence sublayer) on the other side within the IWF. Figure 11.4 shows the transformation of FR to ATM cells.

Frame Formatting and Delimiting

- **FR to ATM:** The FR frame is mapped into AAL5 PDU; the frame flags, inserted zero bits, and CRC-16 are stripped. The Q922 frame header is removed and some of the fields of the header are mapped into the ATM cell header fields.

- **ATM to FR:** The message delineation provided by AAL5 is used to identify frame boundaries; insert zero bits, CRC-16, and flags. Protocol fields and functions of the ATM AAL5 PDU are translated into the protocol fields and function of the FR frame.

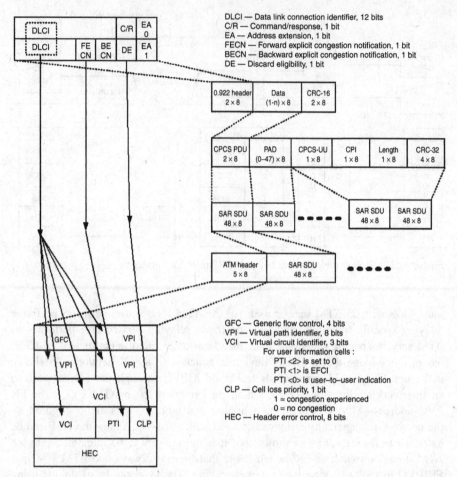

Figure 11.4 Transformation of FR to ATM cell.

Discard Eligibility and Cell Loss Priority Mapping

- **FR to ATM:** Mode 1 or mode 2 may be selected per PVC at subscription time; the default is mode 1 operation:

    Mode 1: The discard eligibility (DE) field in the Q.922 core frame shall be mapped to the ATM CLP field of every cell generated by the segmentation process of the AAL5 PDU containing the information of that frame.

    Mode 2: The ATM CLP of every cell generated by the segmentation process of the AAL5 PDU containing the information of that frame shall be set to a constant value (either 0 or 1) configured at the service subscription time.

- ATM to FR: Mode 1 or 2 may be selected per PVC at subscription time; the default is mode 1 operation:

  Mode 1: If one or more cells of a frame have their CLP fields set, the IWF shall set the DE field of the Q.922 core frame.

  Mode 2: The DE field of the Q.922 core frame shall be set to a constant value (either 0 or 1) configured at service subscription time.

Forward Congestion Indication Mapping

- FR to ATM: Mode 1 or 2 may be selected per PVC at subscription time; the default is mode 1 operation:

  Mode 1: The FECN (Forward Explicit Congestion Notification) field in the Q.922 core frame shall be mapped to the ATM EFCI (Explicit Forward Congestion Indication) field of every cell generated by the segmentation process of the AAL5 PDU containing the information of that frame.

  Mode 2: The FECN field in the Q.922 core frame shall not be mapped to the ATM EFCI field of cells generated by the segmentation process of the AAL5 PDU containing the information of that frame. The EFCI field is always set to "congestion not experienced."

- ATM to FR: If the EFCI field in the last cell of a segmented frame received is set to "congestion experienced," the IWF will set the FECN core frame to "congestion experienced."

Backward Congestion Indication Mapping

- FR to ATM: BECN (Backward Explicit Congestion Notification) is ignored.
- ATM to FR: BECN of the Q.922 core frame is set to 0.

Command/Response Field Mapping

- FR to ATM: The C/R bit of the Q.922 core frame is mapped to the least significant bit in the common part convergence sublayer user-to-user (CPCS_UU) field of the CPCS PDU.
- ATM to FR: The least significant bit in the CPCS_UU field of the CPCS PDU is mapped to the C/R bit of the Q.922 core frame.

DLCI Field Mapping There is a one-to-one mapping between the Q.922 DLCI and the VPI/VCI (Virtual Path Identifier/Virtual Circuit Identifier) field in the ATM cells. The mapping is defined when the PVC is established. The association may be arbitrary or systematic.

Traffic Management Frame relay quality-of-service (QoS) parameters (CIR, B_c, B_e) will be mapped to ATM QoS parameters (PCR, SCR, MBS) using method 1, one-to-one mapping of the ATM Forum B-ICI (BISDN-Inter Carrier Interface) specification, which is given in Table 11.5. The value of the frame size variable used in the calculations is configurable per PVC. Also configurable per PVC will be CDVT.

TABLE 11.5 Mapping of FR QoS Parameters to ATM QoS Parameters

$PCR_{0+1} = AR/8 \times [OHA(n)]$

$SCR_0 = CIR/8 \times [OHB(n)]$

$MBS_0 = [B_c/8 \times (1/(1 - CIR/AR)) + 1] \times [OHB(n)]$

$SCR_1 = EIR/8 \times [OHB(n)]$

$MBS_1 = [B_e/8 \times (1/(1 - EIR/AR)) + 1] \times [OHB(n)]$

$CDVT = 1/PCR_{0+1}$

where n - number of user information octets in frame

AR - access line rate

CIR - committed information rate, B_c/T (bits/s)

EIR - excess information rate, B_e/T (bits/s), $CIR + EIR < AR$

B_c - committed burst size (bits)

B_e - excess burst size (bits)

T - measurement interval

PCR - peak cell rate (cells/s)

SCR - sustained cell rate (cells/s)

MBS - maximum burst size (number of cells)

CDVT - cell delay variation tolerance

$|X|$ - smallest integer greater than or equal to X

$OHA(n) = |(n + h_1 + h_2)/48|/(n + h_1 + h_2)$, overhead factor for access rate (cells/byte)

h_1 = FR header size (octets), 2-, 3:, or 4-octet headers

h_2 = FR HDLC overhead size of CRC-16 and flags (4 octets)

$OHB(n) = |(n + h_1 + h_2)/48|/n$, overhead factor for committed/excess rate (cells/byte) and subscript $0+1$, 0, or 1 applied to PCR, SCR, or MBS implies the parameter values for $CLP = 0 + 1$ cell stream, $CLP = 0$ cell stream, and $CLP = 1$ cell stream, respectively

Note: This method characterizes FR traffic using three generic cell rate algorithms (GCRAs) described in Appendix B of the ATM Forum UNI specification, 1993. Frames are with n user interface bytes.

PVC Mapping

- FR to ATM: When the IWF is notified that an FR PVC changes state from active to inactive, it will begin sending AIS (Alarm Indication Signal) F5 OAM (Operation, Administration, and Management) cells on the corresponding ATM PVC. An AIS F5 OAM cell is sent once per second until the state of the PVC changes from inactive to active.

- ATM to FR: When the IWF is notified that an ATM PVC changes state from active to inactive, it will set the FR PVC status bit to inactive. *Note:* An ATM PVC is considered inactive if (i) AIS or RDI (Remote Defect Indication) OAM cells are received or (ii) the ILMI (Interim Local Management Interface) MIB variable atmVccOperStatus is either localDown or end2endDown or (iii) the ATM interface is down. ATM responds to received AIS cells by sending RDI cells.

Upper Layer User Protocol Encapsulation   The network provider can configure one of the following two modes of operation for each pair of interoperable FR and ATM PVCs regarding upper protocol encapsulations:

- Mode 1—transparent mode: The upper layer encapsulation methods will not be mapped between ATM and FR standards.

- Mode 2—translation mode: Encapsulation methods for carrying multiple upper layer user protocols (e.g., LAN to LAN) over FR PVC and an ATM PVC conform to the standard RFC 1490 [19] and RFC 1483 [20], respectively. The IWF shall perform mapping between the two encapsulations due to the incompatibilities of the two methods. This mode supports the interworking of the internetworking (routed and/or bridged) protocol.

Fragmentation and Reassembly

- FR to ATM: When fragmented packets are received on an FR PVC by the IWF, reassembly should be performed while forwarding the assembled frame to the ATM PVC.

- ATM to FR: Fragmentation should be performed on the received CPCS PDU before forwarding them to the FR PVC if the CPCS PDU is greater than the maximum frame size supported on the FR PVC.

FR–ATM PVC Service Interworking Test Category   The FR–ATM PVC service interworking requirement is divided into six main categories: (i) functionality, (ii) robustness, (iii) performance, (iv) stress, (v) load and stability, and (vi) regression. The complete structure of the test categories is given in Figure 11.5.

Functionality Tests   Functionality tests are designed to verify the FrAtm software as thoroughly as possible over all the requirements specified in the FRF.8 document. This category has been further subdivided into six different functional subgroups. For each identified functional subgroup, test objectives are formed that adequately exercise the function. Within each subgroup test objectives are designed to cover the valid values. The following major functionalities of the FrAtm feature must be tested adequately: (1) configuration and monitoring tests, (2) traffic management tests, (3) congestion tests, (4) service interworking function (SIWF) translation mode mapping tests, (5) alarm tests, and (6) interface tests:

1. Configuration and Monitoring Tests: Tests are designed to verify all the configurable attributes of the FrAtm component using the CLI command. These configurable attributes are implementation dependent and should be defined in the functional specification. Configuration tests configure the FrAtm using CLI. Monitoring tests verify the ability to use the CLI to determine the status and functioning of FrAtm. Statistics counters are validated for accuracy by using known amounts of traffic.

2. Traffic Management Tests: Tests are designed to verify mapping between ATM traffic parameters PCR_{0+1}, SCR_{0+1}, and MBS and FR rate enforcement parameters CIR, B_c, and B_e. Mapping between these parameters is subject to engineering consideration and is largely dependent on the balance between acceptable loss probabilities and network costs.

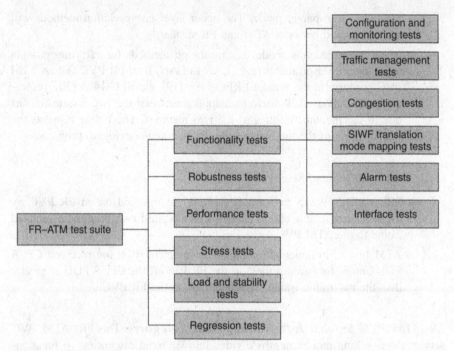

Figure 11.5 FrAtm test suite structure.

3. **Congestion Tests:** Various tests are designed to verify the extent of the FrAtm congestion control mechanism. The test objectives of each test are as follows:

   - Verify that the long-term maximum rate for the committed burst is CIR.
   - Verify that the long-term maximum rate for the excess burst is EIR.
   - Verify that DE = 0 and DE = 1 frames are counted toward the committed burst and excess burst, respectively.
   - Verify that FrAtm sets the BECN bit on the FrAtm to signal local congestion to the FR user.

4. **Service Interworking Function Translation Mode Mapping Tests:** Tests are designed to verify the SIWF translation mode mapping from FR to ATM and vice versa with the following objectives:

   - Verify that for frames from FR to ATM the IWF replaces the RFC 1490 encapsulation with the RFC 1483 encapsulation header.
   - Verify that for frames from ATM to FR the IWF replaces the RFC 1483 encapsulation with the RFC 1490 encapsulation header.
   - In the FR-to-ATM direction, verify that the FECN bit on a given frame maps directly into the EFCI bit of every cell that constitutes a frame if the EFCI attribute is configured as "preserve"; otherwise, the EFCI bit of every cell generated is set to zero.

- In the ATM-to-FR direction, verify that the EFCI bit of the last cell constituting a given frame is mapped directly into the FECN bit of that frame.

- In the FR-to-ATM direction, verify that the DE bit of a given frame maps directly into the CLP bit of every cell that constitutes that frame if so configured.

- In the ATM-to-FR direction, verify that the CLP-to-DE mapping can be configured with values "preserve," "always 0," and "always 1."

- In the FR-to-ATM direction, verify that the command/response (C/R) bit of the FR frame is mapped directly to the least significant bit of UU data in the CPCS of AAL5 encapsulation.

- In the ATM-to-FR direction, verify that the least significant bit of the UU data in the CPCS is mapped directly to the C/R bit of the constituting FR frame.

- In the FR-to-ATM direction, verify that the IWF will send AIS F5 OAM cells on the ATM PVC when the FR PVC changes state from active to inactive. Also, verify that the OAM cells are sent once per second until the state of the PVC changes from inactive to active.

- In the ATM-to-FR direction, verify that the IWF will set the FR PVC status bit to inactive when the ATM PVC changes state from active to inactive. Verify that RDI cells are sent corresponding to the received AIS cells.

- In the FR-to-ATM direction, verify that the IWF reassembles the fragmented packets received on a FR PVC and forwards it to the ATM PVC.

- In the ATM-to-FR direction, verify that the fragmentation ID is performed by the IWF on the received CPCS PDU before forwarding them to the FR PVC. Ensure that the CPCS PDU size is greater than the maximum frame size supported on the FR PVC.

5. Alarm Tests: Tests are designed to make sure that various alarms are generated for the FR–ATM service. The test objectives of each test are as follows:

  - Verify that FrAtm generates appropriate alarms per PVC for individual DLCI.

  - Verify that FrAtm generates state change notification (SCN) alarms when the operational state changes. The state change can occur when the link comes up or goes down. The state change can also occur by locking and unlocking FrAtm.

  - Verify that FrAtm generates alarms to indicate the receipt of unexpected messages.

  - Verify that alarms are generated to indicate the failure to allocate storage to create the service or to create subcomponents such as DLCIs.

6. Interface Tests: Verify that FrAtm supports V.11, V35, DS1, E1, DS3, and E3 on the FR side and OC3, E3, and DS3 interfaces on the ATM side.

Robustness Tests   One verifies the robustness of the FrAtm implementations to error situations:

FrAtm Tests: Verify that (i) the FrAtm software component can handle continuous lock/unlock without any crash, (ii) the DLCI software component can handle multiple lock/unlock commands generated at high rate, and (iii) the DLCI software component can handle lock/unlock while traffic is going through the switch without any crash.

Boundary Value Tests: Verify that FrAtm handles boundary values and values below and values above the valid boundary for a subset of configurable attributes. For example, if the maximum number of DLCI configurable is 1024, then try to configure 1025 DLCI subcomponents and verify that the 1025th DLCI subcomponent is not created.

Performance Tests   Tests are designed to measure data delay and throughput across different interfaces on both the FR and the ATM sides. Tests are conducted to measure the delay and throughput over a full range of ATM interface cards and FR interface cards for frame sizes 64, 128, 256, 512, 1024, 2048, and 4096 bytes.

Stress Tests   Tests are designed to observe and capture the behavior of the FR–ATM services under various types of load profiles. The test objectives of each test are as follows:

- Verify that FrAtm works without any hiccups when it is stressed for 48 hours or more while lock/unlock activities and data transfer activity are going on.
- Verify that FrAtm works without any hiccups when the maximum number of DLCIs on the FR side using one FR card and the maximum number of ATM VCCs (Virtual Channel Connection) are configured.

Load and Stability Tests   Tests are designed to simulate a real customer configuration by sending real data traffic. For these tests, setting up the customer environment in the laboratory is challenging and expensive. An example of this test is to verify that a user file can be transferred correctly from an FR network to an ATM network by using the FR–ATM PVC service interworking feature.

Regression Tests   New test cases are not designed; rather, tests are selected from the groups explained before. In our opinion, a subset of test cases from each subgroup may be selected as regression tests. In addition, test cases from FR and ATM must be selected and executed to ensure that the previously supported functionality works with the new software component FrAtm.

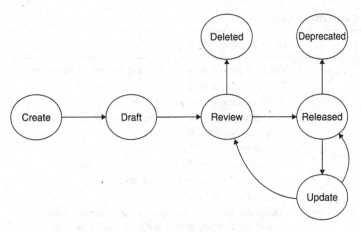

Figure 11.6   State transition diagram of a test case.

11.6   MODELING A TEST DESIGN PROCESS

Test objectives are identified from a requirement specification, and one test case is created for each test objective. Each test case is designed as a combination of modular components called test steps. Test cases are clearly specified so that testers can quickly understand, borrow, and reuse the test cases.

Figure 11.6 illustrates the life-cycle model of a test case in the form of a state transition diagram. The state transition model shows the different phases, or states, in the life cycle of a test case from its inception to its completion through the following states: create, draft, review, deleted, released, update, and deprecated. Certain actions are taken by the "owner" of the state, and the test case moves to a next state after the actions are completed. In the following, the states are explained one by one. One can easily implement a database of test cases using the test case schema shown in Table 11.6. We refer to such a database of test cases as a test factory.

Create State   A test case is put in this initial state by its creator, called the owner or creator, who initiates the design of the test case. The creator initializes the following mandatory fields associated with the test case: requirement_ids, tc_id, tc_title, originator_group, creator, and test_category. The test case is expected to verify the requirements referred to in the requirement_ids field. The originator_-group is the group who found a need for the test. The creator may assign the test case to a specific test engineer, including himself, by filling out the eng_assigned field, and move the test case from the create to the draft state.

Draft State   The owner of this state is the test group, that is, the system test team. In this state, the assigned test engineer enters the following information: tc_author, objective, setup, test_steps, cleanup, pf_criteria, candidate_for_automation, automation_priority. After completion of all the mandatory fields, the test engineer may reassign the test case to the creator to go through the test case. The

TABLE 11.6   Test Case Schema Summary

Field	Description
tc_id	Test case identifier assigned by test author (80 characters)
tc_title	Title of test case (120 characters)
creator	Name of person who created test case
status	Current state of the record: create, draft, review, released, update, deleted, and deprecated
owner	Current owner of test case
eng_assigned	Test engineer assigned to write test procedure
objective	Objective of test case (multiline string)
tc_author	Name of test case author (user name)
originator_group	Group that originates test (performance testing group, functional testing group, scaling testing group, etc.)
test_category	Test category name (performance, stress, interoperability, functionality, etc.)
setup	List of steps to perform prior to test
test_steps	List of test steps
cleanup	List of posttest activities
pf_criteria	List of pass/fail criteria
requirement_ids	List of references to requirements ID from requirement database
candidate_for_automation	If test can be/should be automated
automation_priority	Automation priority.
review_action	Action items from review meeting minutes
approver_names	List of approver names

test case stays in this state until it is walked through by the creator. After that, the creator may move the state from the draft state to the review state by entering all the approvers' names in the approver_names field.

Review and Deleted States   The owner of the review state is the creator of the test case. The owner invites test engineers and developers to review and validate the test case. They ensure that the test case is executable, and the pass–fail criteria are clearly specified. Action items are created for the test case if any field needs a modification. Action items from a review meeting are entered in the review_actions field, and the action items are executed by the owner to effect changes to the test case. The test case moves to the released state after all the reviewers approve the changes. If the reviewers decide that this is not a valid test case or it is not executable, then the test case is moved to the deleted state. A review action item must tell to delete this test case for a test case to be deleted.

Released and Update States   A test case in the released state is ready for execution, and it becomes a part of a test suite. On the other hand, a test case in the update state implies that it is in the process of being modified to enhance its reusability, being fine tuned with respect to its pass–fail criteria, and/or having the detailed test procedure fixed. For example, a reusable test case should be parameterized rather than hard coded with data values. Moreover, a test case should be updated to adapt it to changes in system functionality or the environment. One can improve the repeatability of the test case so that others can quickly understand, borrow, and reuse it by moving a test case in the released–update loop a small number of times. Also, this provides the foundation and justification for the test case to be automated. A test case should be platform independent. If an update involves a small change, the test engineer may move the test case back to the released state after the fix. Otherwise, the test case is subject to a further review, which is achieved by moving it to the review state. A test case may be revised once every time it is executed.

Deprecated State   An obsolete test case may be moved to a deprecated state. Ideally, if it has not been executed for a year, then the test case should be reviewed for its continued existence. A test case may become obsolete over time because of the following reasons. First, the functionality of the system being tested has much changed, and due to a lack of test case maintenance, a test case becomes obsolete. Second, as an old test case is updated, some of the requirements of the original test case may no longer be fulfilled. Third, reusability of test cases tend to degrade over time as the situation changes. This is especially true of test cases which are not designed with adequate attention to possible reuse. Finally, test cases may be carried forward carelessly long after their original justifications have disappeared. Nobody may know the original justification for a particular test case, so it continues to be used.

11.7   MODELING TEST RESULTS

A test suite schema can be used by a test manager to design a test suite after a test factory is created. A test suite schema, as shown in Table 11.7, is used to group test cases for testing a particular release. The schema requires a test suite ID, a title, an objective, and a list of test cases to be managed by the test suite. One also identifies the individual test cases to be executed (test cycles 1, 2, 3 and/or regression) and the requirements that the test cases satisfy. The idea here is to gather a selected number of released test cases and repackage them to form a test suite for a new project.

Test engineers concurrently execute test cases from a selected test suite on different test beds. The results of executing those test cases are recorded in the test factory database for gathering and analyzing test metrics. In a large, complex system with many defects, there are several possibilities of the result of a test execution, not merely passed or failed. Therefore, we model the results of test execution by using a state transition diagram as shown in Figure 11.7, and the corresponding schema is given in Table 11.8. Figure 11.7 illustrates a state diagram of a test case result starting from the untested state to four different states: passed, failed, blocked, and invalid.

TABLE 11.7 Test Suite Schema Summary

Field	Description
test_suite_id	Unique identifier assigned by originator
test_suite_title	Test suite title, one-line title for test suite
test_suite_objective	Objective of test suite, short description.
tests	Reference list of test case identifiers
test_id	Test case ID, selected
test_title	Test case title, read only, filled in when test case is created
test_category	Category name (performance, stress, interoperability, functionality, etc.)
tester	Engineer responsible for testing
sw_dev	Software developer responsible for this test case who will assists test engineer in execution of test case
priority	Priority of test case
requirement_ids	Requirement identifier, read only, filled in when test case is created
cycle 1–3	Check box to indicate test is cycle 1, 2, or 3 test case
regression	Check box to indicate test is regression test case

TABLE 11.8 Test Result Schema Summary

Field	Description
tc_id	Reference to test case identifier record
test_title	Test case title, read only, filled in when result is created
test_category	Test category name (performance, stress, interoperability, functionality, etc.)
status	State of test case result: passed, failed, blocked, invalid or untested; initially status of test case is "untested"
run date	Date test case was run
time	Time spent in executing test case
tester	Name of person who ran test
release	Software release (03.00.00)
build	Software integration number (1–100).
defect_ids	List of defects which cause test to fail; value can come from bug tracking database
test_suite	Test suite this results pertains to

The execution status of a test case is put in its initial state of untested after designing or selecting a test case. If the test case is not valid for the current software release, the test case result is moved to the invalid state. In the untested state, the test suite identifier is noted in a field called test_suite_id. The state of the test result, after execution of a test case is started, may change to one of the following states:

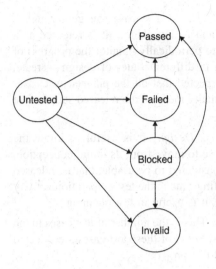

Figure 11.7 State transition diagram of test case result.

passed, failed, invalid, or blocked. A test engineer may move the test case result to the passed state from the untested state if the test case execution is complete and satisfies the pass criteria.

If the test execution is complete and satisfied the fail criteria, a test engineer moves the test result to the failed state from the untested state and associates the defect with the test case by initializing the defect_ids field. The test case must be reexecuted when a new build containing a fix for the defect is received. If the reexecution is complete and satisfies the pass criteria, the test result is moved to the passed state.

The test case result is moved to a blocked state if it is not possible to completely execute it. If known, the defect number that blocks the execution of the test case is recorded in the defect_ids field. The test case may be reexecuted when a new build addressing a blocked test case is received. If the execution is complete and satisfies the pass criteria, the test result is moved to the passed state. On the other hand, if it satisfies the fail criteria, the test result is moved to the failed state. If the execution is unsuccessful due to a new blocking defect, the test result remains in the blocked state and the new defect that blocked the test case is listed in the defect_ids field.

11.8 TEST DESIGN PREPAREDNESS METRICS

Management may be interested to know the progress, coverage, and productivity aspects of the test case preparation work being done by a team of test engineers. Such information lets them (i) know if a test project is progressing according to schedule and if more resources are required and (ii) plan their next project more accurately. The following metrics can be used to represent the level of preparedness of test design.

Preparation Status of Test Cases (PST):   A test case can go through a number of phases, or states, such as draft and review, before it is released as a valid and useful test case. Thus, it is useful to periodically monitor the progress of test design by counting the test cases lying in different states of design—create, draft, review, released, and deleted. It is expected that all the planned test cases that are created for a particular project eventually move to the released state before the start of test execution.

Average Time Spent (ATS) in Test Case Design: It is useful to know the amount of time it takes for a test case to move from its initial conception, that is, create state, to when it is considered to be usable, that is, released state. This metric is useful in allocating time to the test preparation activity in a subsequent test project. Hence, it is useful in test planning.

Number of Available Test (NAT) Cases: This is the number of test cases in the released state from existing projects. Some of these test cases are selected for regression testing in the current test project.

Number of Planned Test (NPT) Cases: This is the number of test cases that are in a test suite and ready for execution at the start of system testing. This metric is useful in scheduling test execution. As testing continues, new, unplanned test cases may be required to be designed. A large number of new test cases compared to NPT suggest that initial planning was not accurate.

Coverage of a Test Suite (CTS): This metric gives the fraction of all requirements covered by a selected number of test cases or a complete test suite. The CTS is a measure of the number of test cases needed to be selected or designed to have good coverage of system requirements.

11.9   TEST CASE DESIGN EFFECTIVENESS

The objectives of the test case design effectiveness metric is to (i) measure the "defect revealing ability" of the test suite and (ii) use the metric to improve the test design process. During system-level testing, defects are revealed due to the execution of planned test cases. In addition to these defects, new defects are found during testing for which no test cases had been planned. For these new defects, new test cases are designed, which are called test case escaped (TCE). Test escapes occur because of deficiencies in the test design process. This happens because the test engineers get new ideas while executing the planned test cases. A metric commonly used in the industry to measure test case design effectiveness is the test case design yield (TCDY), defined as

$$\text{TCDY} = \frac{\text{NPT}}{\text{NPT} + \text{number of TCE}} \times 100\%$$

.The TCDY is also used to measure the effectiveness of a particular testing phase. For example, the system integration manager may want to know the TCDY value for his or her system integration testing.

11.10 SUMMARY

This chapter began with an introduction to six factors that are taken into consideration during the design of test cases: coverage metrics, effectiveness, productivity, validation, maintenance, and user skill. Then we discussed the reasons to consider these factors in designing system tests.

Next, we discussed the requirement identification process. We provided a state transition model to track the individual requirements as they flow through the organization. At each state of the transition model, certain actions are taken by the owner. The requirement is moved to a new state after the actions are completed. We presented a requirement schema that can be used to generate a traceability matrix. A traceability matrix finds two applications: (i) identifying and tracking the functional coverage of a test suite and (ii) identifying which test cases must be exercised or updated when a system undergoes a change. A traceability matrix allows one to find a mapping between requirements and test cases as follows:

- From a requirement to a functional specification to specific tests which exercise them
- From each test case back to the requirements and functional specifications

Next, we examined the characteristics of testable requirements and functional specification. We provided techniques to identify test objectives from the requirements and functional specifications. A requirement must be analyzed to extract the inferred requirements that are embedded in the requirement. An inferred requirement is anything that a system is expected to do but not explicitly stated. Finally, we showed the ways to create a hierarchical structure of test groups, called a test suite. As an example, we illustrated in detail the design of a system test suite for the FR–ATM serviceinterworking protocol.

Next, we provided a state transition model of a test case from its inception to completion. At each state of the transition model, certain actions are taken by the owner. The test case is moved to a new state after the actions are completed. We presented a test case schema to create a test factory that can be used to design a test suite and monitor the test case preparedness metrics.

Finally, we provided a metric used in the industry to measure test case design effectiveness, known as the test case design yield. The objectives of the test case effectiveness metric are to (i) measure the "defect revealing ability" of the test suite and (ii) use the metric to improve the test design process.

11.11 LITERATURE REVIEW

A good discussion of testing requirements is presented in the article by Suzanne Robertson, entitled "An Early Start to Testing: How to Test Requirements," which is reprinted in Appendix A of the book by E. Dustin, J. Rashka, and J. Paul (*Automated Software Testing: Introduction, Management, and Performance*, Addison-Wesley,

Reading, MA, 1999). The author describes a set of requirement tests that cover relevance, coherency, traceability, completeness, and other qualities that successful requirements must have.

The requirements traceability reference models described in the article by B. Ramesh and M. Jarke ("Towards Reference Models for Requirements Traceability," *IEEE Transactions on Software Engineering*, Vol.27, No.1, January 2001, pp. 58–93) is based on several empirical studies. Data collection for the work spanned a period of over three years. The main study comprised 30 focus group discussions in 26 organizations conducted in a wide variety of industries, including defense, aerospace, pharmaceuticals, electronics, and telecommunications. The participants had an average of 15.5 years of experience in several key areas of systems development, including software engineering, requirements management, software testing, system integration, systems analysis, maintenance, and software implementation. The participants are categorized into two distinct groups with respect to their traceability practices. These groups are referred to as low-end and high-end traceability users. Separate reference models for these two groups are discussed in the article.

The IEEE standard 829-1983 (*IEEE Standard for Software Test Documentation: IEEE/ANSI Standard*) provides templates for test case specifications and test procedure specifications. A test case specification consists of the following components: test case specification identifier, test items, input specification, output specification, special environment needs, special procedural requirements, and test case dependencies. A test procedure specification consists of the following components: test procedure specification identifier, purpose, specific requirements, and procedure steps.

Another approach to measuring test case effectiveness has been proposed by Yuri Chernak ("Validating and Improving Test-Case Effectiveness," *IEEE Software*, Vol. 18, No. 1, January/February 2001, pp. 81–86). The effectiveness metric called test case escaped is defined as

$$\text{TCE} = \frac{\text{number of defects found by test cases}}{\text{total number of defects}} \times 100\%$$

The total number of defects in the above equation is the sum of the defects found by the test cases and the defects found by chance, which the author calls "side effects." Chernak illustrates his methodology with a client–server application using a baseline TCE value (< 75 for this case) to evaluate test case effectiveness and make test process improvements. Incomplete test design and incomplete functional specifications were found to be the main causes of test escapes.

Formal verification of test cases is presented in the article by K. Naik and B. Sarikaya, "Test Case Verification by Model Checking," *Formal Methods in Systems Design*, Vol. 2, June 1993, pp. 277–321. The authors identified four classes of safety properties and one liveness property and expressed them as formulas in branching time temporal logic. They presented a model checking algorithm to verify those properties.

REFERENCES

1. H. S. Wang, S. R. Hsu, and J. C. Lin. A generalized optimal path-selection model for the structure program testing. *Journal of Systems and Software*, July, 1989, pp. 55–62.
2. O. Vinter. *From Problem Reports to Better Products*. In *Improving Software Organizations: From Principles to Practice*, L. Mathiassen, J. Pries-Heje, and O. Ngwenyama, Eds. Addison-Wesley, Reading, MA, 2002, Chapter 8.
3. M. Glinz and R. J. Wieringa. Stakeholders in Requirements Engineering. *IEEE Software*, March/April 2007, pp. 18–20.
4. N. Serrano and I. Ciordia. Bugzilla, ITtracker, and Other Bug Trackers. *IEEE Software*, March/April 2005, pp. 11–13.
5. D. Jacobs. Requirements Engineering So Things Don't Get Ugly. *Crosstalk, the Journal of Defense Software Engineering*, October 2004, pp. 19–25.
6. P. Carlshamre and B. Regnell. Requirements Lifecycle Management and Release Planning in Market-Driven Requirements Engineering Process. In *Proceedings of the 11th International Workshop on Database and Expert System Applications*, Greenwich, UK, IEEE Computer Society Press, Piscataway, NJ, September 2000, pp. 961–966.
7. J. Bach. Risk and Requirements-Based Testing. *IEEE Computer*, June 1999, pp. 113–114.
8. B. J. Brown. Assurance of Quality Software. SEI Curriculum Module, SEI-CM-7-1.1, July 1987.
9. M. Lehman and J. Ramil. Software Evolution—Background, Theory, Practice. *Information Processing Letters*, October 2003, pp. 33–44.
10. O. C. Z. Gotel and A. C. W. Finkelstein. An Analysis of the Requirements Traceability Problem. In *Proceedings of First International Conference on Requirements Engineering*, Colorado Spring, IEEE Computer Society Press, Piscataway, NJ, 1994, pp. 94–101.
11. J. Karlsson and K. Ryan. A Cost-Value Approach for Prioritizing Requirements. *IEEE Software*, September/October 1997, pp. 67–74.
12. E. Carmel and S. Becker. A Process Model for Packaged Software Development. *IEEE Transactions on Engineering Management*, February 1995, pp. 50–61.
13. P. Soffer, L. Goldin, and T. Kuflik. A Unified RE Approach for Software Product Evolution. In *Proceedings of SREP'05*, Paris, Printed in Ireland by the University of Limerick, August 2005, pp. 200–210.
14. C. W. Johnson and C. M. Holloway. Questioning the Role of Requirements Engineering in the Causes of Safety-Critical Software Failures. In *Proceedings of the IET 1st International Conference on System Safety*, IEEE Computer Society Press, Piscataway, NJ, London, June 2006.
15. S. L. Pfleeger. A Framework for Security Requirements. *Computers & Security*, October 1991, pp. 515–523.
16. W. E. Howden. Validation of Scientific Programs. *ACM Computing Surveys*, June 1982, pp. 193–227.
17. Frame Relay/ATM PVC Network Inter-Working-Implementation Agreement, FRF.5. Frame Relay Forum, December 1994. Available at http://www.ipmplsforum.org/Approved/FRF.5/FRF5.TOC.shtml.
18. Frame Relay/ATM PVC Service Inter-Working-Implementation Agreement, FRF.8. Frame Relay Forum, April 1995. Available at http://www.ipmplsforum.org/Approved/FRF.8/FRF8.TOC.shtml.
19. Internet Engineering Task Force (IETF). Multiprotocol Interconnect over Frame Relay, RFC 1490. IETF, July 1993. Available at http://www.apps.ietf.org/rfc/rfc1490.html.
20. Internet Engineering Task Force (IETF). Multiprotocol Encapsulation over AAL, RFC 1483. IETF, July 1993. Available at http://www.apps.ietf.org/rfc/rfc1483.html.

Exercises

1. Explain the difference between coverage metrics and traceability matrix.
2. Explain the difference between requirement testability and software testability.

3. Justify the statement that software testability and fault tolerant are opposites to each other, and attaining both at the same time for the same piece of software is not feasible. When do you want high testability and when don't you during the life cycle of a critical software system? Justify your answer.

4. What are the differences between software testability and reliability? What is more important in a software: high testability or high reliability? Justify your answer.

5. In a software test project, the number of unit-, integration-, and system-level test cases specified are 250, 175, and 235, respectively. The number of test cases added during the unit, integration, and system testing phases are 75, 60, and 35, respectively. Calculate the TCDY for unit, integration, and system testing phases.

6. Prepare a checklist of items that will serve as the focal point for reviewing test cases.

7. Under what circumstances can the execution result of a test case be declared as blocked?

8. Implement the requirement model discussed in this chapter.

9. Implement the test factory model discussed in this chapter.

10. For your current test project, develop the test suite hierarchy and identify a test objective for each test case within each test (sub)group.

11. Develop detailed test cases using the schema defined in Table 11.6 as a template for the test objectives you identified in the previous exercise.

System Test Planning and Automation

> When planning for a year, plant corn. When planning for a decade, plant trees. When planning for life, train and educate people.
>
> — *Chinese proverb*

12.1 STRUCTURE OF A SYSTEM TEST PLAN

A good plan for performing system testing is the cornerstone of a successful software project. In the absence of a good plan it is highly unlikely that the desired level of system testing is performed within the stipulated time and without overusing resources such as manpower and money. Moreover, in the absence of a good plan, it is highly likely that a low-quality product is delivered even at a higher cost and later than the expected date.

The purpose of system test planning, or simply test planning, is to get ready and organized for test execution. Starting a system test in an ad hoc way, after all the modules are checked in to the version control system, is ineffective. Working under deadline pressure, people, that is, test engineers, have a tendency to take shortcuts and to "just get the job done," which leads to the shipment of a highly defective product. Consequently, the customer support group of the organization has to spend a lot of time in dealing with unsatisfied customers and be forced to release several patches to demanding customers. Test planning is essential in order to complete system testing and ship quality product to the market on schedule. Planning for system testing is part of overall planning for a software project. It provides the framework, scope, resources, schedule, and budget for the system testing part of the project.

Test efficiency can be monitored and improved, and unnecessary delay can be avoided with a good test plan. The purpose of a system test plan is summarized as follows:

Software Testing and Quality Assurance: Theory and Practice, Edited by Kshirasagar Naik and Priyadarshi Tripathy
Copyright © 2008 John Wiley & Sons, Inc.

TABLE 12.1 Outline of System Test Plan

1. Introduction
2. Feature description
3. Assumptions
4. Test approach
5. Test suite structure
6. Test environment
7. Test execution strategy
8. Test effort estimation
9. Scheduling and milestones

- It provides guidance for the executive management to support the test project, thereby allowing them to release the necessary resources to perform the test activity.
- It establishes the foundation of the system testing part of the overall software project.
- It provides assurance of test coverage by creating a requirement traceability matrix.
- It outlines an orderly schedule of events and test milestones that are tracked.
- It specifies the personnel, financial, equipment, and facility resources required to support the system testing part of a software project.

The activity of planning for system testing combines two tasks: *research* and *estimation*. Research allows us to define the scope of the test effort and resources already available in-house. Each major functional test suite consisting of test objectives can be described in a bounded fashion using the system requirements and functional specification as references. The reader may refer to Chapter 11 for a discussion of the test suites described in a bounded fashion.

A system test plan is outlined in Table 12.1. We explain the ways one can create a test plan. The test plan is released for review and approval after the author, that is, the leader of the system test group, completes it with all the pertinent details. The review team must include software and hardware development staff, customer support group members, system test team members, and the project manager responsible for the project. The author(s) should solicit reviews of the test plan and ask for comments prior to the meeting. The comments can then be addressed at the review meeting. The system test plan must be completed before the software project is committed.

12.2 INTRODUCTION AND FEATURE DESCRIPTION

The introduction section of the system test plan describes the structure and the objective of the test plan. This section includes (i) test project name, (ii) revision history, (iii) terminology and definitions, (iv) names of the approvers and the date of approval, (v) references, and (vi) summary of the rest of the test plan.

The feature description section summarizes the system features that will be tested during the execution of this test plan. In other words, a high-level description of the functionalities of the system is presented in this section. The feature description for the FR/ATM service interworking example is discussed in Chapter 11.

12.3 ASSUMPTIONS

The assumptions section describes the areas for which test cases will not be designed in this plan due to several seasons. First, the necessary equipment to carry out scalability testing may not be available. Second, it may not be possible to procure third-party equipment in time to conduct interoperability testing. Finally, it may not be possible to conduct compliance tests for regulatory bodies and environment tests in the laboratory. These assumptions must be considered while reviewing a system test plan.

12.4 TEST APPROACH

The overall test approach is an important aspect of a testing project which consists of the following:

- Lessons learned from past test projects are useful in focusing on problematic areas in the testing process. Issues discovered by customers that were not caught during system testing in past projects are discussed. For example, if a customer encountered a memory leak in the system in the past project, action must be taken to flush out any memory leak early in system test execution. An appropriate response may be needed to develop effective test cases by using sophisticated software tools such as memory leak detectors from the market.

- If there are any outstanding issues that need to be tested differently, for example, requiring specific hardware and software configuration, then these issues need to be discussed here.

- A test automation strategy for writing scripts is a topic of discussion.

- Test cases should be identified in the test factory that can be reused in this test plan.

- Outline should be prepared of the tools, formats, and organizing scheme, such as a traceability matrix, that will be used and followed during the test project.

- Finally, the first level of test categories, which are likely to apply to the present situation and as discussed in Chapter 8, are identified.

12.5 TEST SUITE STRUCTURE

Detail test groups and subgroups are outlined in the test suite structure section based on the test categories identified in the test approach section. Test objectives are created for each test group and subgroup based on the system requirements and functional specification discussed in Chapter 11. A traceability matrix is generated to make an association between requirements and test objectives to provide the highest degree of confidence. Note that at this stage only test suites along with the test objectives are identified but not the detail test cases. Identification of test objectives provides a clue to the total number of new test cases that need to be developed for this project. If some existing test cases, automated or manual, need to be run as regression tests, those test cases must be included in the test suite. This information is useful in estimating the time required to create the test cases and to execute the test suite, as discussed in Section 12.8. The test suite structure for the FR/ATM service interworking example is discussed in Chapter 11.

12.6 TEST ENVIRONMENT

It is necessary to plan for and design the test environment, also called a *test bed* or a *test laboratory*, to make the execution of system-level test cases effective. It is a challenge to design test environments which contain only a small proportion of the equipment and facilities used in actual operation because of budget limitations. The central idea in using a small proportion of equipment and facilities is *to do more with less*. The objective here is to achieve effective testing whereby most of the defects in the system are revealed by utilizing a limited quantity of resources. One has to be innovative in designing a test bed such that the test objectives are fulfilled by executing the test cases on the test bed. One must consider alternatives, or, at least, a scaled-down version of the deployment environment from the standpoint of cost-effectiveness. Efforts must be made to create a deployment environment by using simulators, emulators, and third-party traffic generation tools. Such tools are found to be useful in conducting scalability, performance, load, and stress testing. An emulator may not be an ideal substitute for real equipment, but as long as it satisfies the purpose, it is worth investing in. We explained in Chapter 8 that there are different categories of test cases designed at the system level. Therefore, multiple test environments are constructed in practice for the following reasons:

- To run scalability tests, we need more resources than needed to run functional tests.
- Multiple test beds are required to reduce the length of system testing time.

Preparing for a test environment is a great challenge in test planning. This is especially true in testing distributed systems and computer networks where a variety of equipment are connected through communication protocols. For example, such equipment includes user computers, servers, routers, base stations in a wireless network, authentication servers, and billing servers. It may take several months to set up an effective test bed for large, complex systems. It requires careful planning, procurement of test equipment, and installation of the equipment in a test facility different from the software development facilities so that system testing is performed effectively. Developers have their own test environments to perform unit tests and integration tests. However, a separate, dedicated system test laboratory, different from the ones used in unit and integration testing, is essential for the following reasons:

- Test engineers need to have the ability to reconfigure a test environment.
- Test activities need not interfere with development activities or live operations.
- Increased productivity is achieved by having a dedicated test laboratory.

A central issue concerning setting up of a system test laboratory is the justification to procure the equipment. Note that there is a need to justify each item to be procured. A good justification for procuring the equipment can be made by answering the following questions:

- Why do we need this equipment?
- What will be the impact of not having this equipment?
- Is there an alternative to procuring this equipment?

The technical leader of the system test engineering group should gather some facts and perform some preparation activities in order to get answers to these questions. The following items are part of a good fact gathering process:

- Reviews the system requirements and the functional specification
- Participates in the review processes to better understand the system and raise potential concerns related to the migration of the system from the development environment to the deployment environment
- Documents his or her findings

The following preparation activities are conducted to support the development of a system test bed:

- Obtain information about the customer deployment architecture, including hardware, software, and their manufacturers. For example, the real deployment network diagram along with the software configuration is useful in designing a scaled-down version of the system in the laboratory. The manufacturer names will be handy in procuring the exact equipment for interoperability and compatibility testing.
- Obtain a list of third-party products to be integrated with the SUT. Identification of the external products is important because of the need for performing interoperability testing.
- List third-party test tools to be used to monitor, simulate, and/or generate real traffic. This traffic will be used as input to the SUT.

- Identify the third-party software tools to be used under licenses.
- Identify the hardware equipment necessary to support special features specified in the requirement/test objectives, such as high availability and backup/recovery exercises within the test environment.
- List the number of hardware copies to carry out system testing if the project involves new hardware.
- Analyze the functional, performance, stress, load, and scalability test objectives to identify elements of the test environment that will be required to support those tests.
- Identify the security requirements for the test environment. Ensure that the security test cases can be executed using the test environment and an intruder cannot disrupt the stress and stability tests that may be running overnight or over the weekends.
- List the small, but necessary networking gears that may be required to set up the test laboratory, such as switches, terminal servers, hubs, attenuators, splitters, personal computers, servers, and different kinds and sizes of cables to interconnect these gears.
- List any other accessories required to facilitate system testing, such as racks, vehicles, and special shielding to prevent radiation.

After the above fact gathering and researching activities, the team leader develops a schematic diagram of one or more test beds in terms of the following two items:

- High-level graphic layout of test architectures
- Table of types of equipment, their quantities, and their descriptions to support the test architecture

The equipment list should be reviewed to determine the equipment available in-house and those that need to be procured. The list of equipment to be procured constitutes a test equipment purchase list. The list needs to include quantities required, unit price information, including maintenance cost, and justification, as outlined in the template shown in Table 12.2. The team leader must specify, for each item in the justification column, the justification for the item and the impact it will have on system testing in terms of quality and a time-to-market schedule. The team leader may obtain a quote from the suppliers to get an accurate unit price. The test team leader needs to keep track of the equipment received and their installation after the budget is

TABLE 12.2 Equipment Needed to be Procured

Equipment to Procure	Quantity	Unit Price	Maintenance Cost	Justification

approved and the orders are placed. The leader needs to ensure that these activities are on track to meet the overall software project schedule.

12.7   TEST EXECUTION STRATEGY

It is important to have a proper game plan ready before the system test group receives a software system for the first time for performing system testing.

The game plan is in the form of a system test execution strategy to carry out the task [1]. We address the following concerns by putting a game plan in place before initiating system testing:

- How many times are the test cases executed and when?

- What does one do with the failed test cases?

- What happens when too many test cases fail?

- In what order are the test cases executed?

- Which test cases are to be run just before ending the system testing phase?

In the absence of a good system test execution strategy, it is highly unlikely that the desired system-level test is performed within the given time and without overusing resources.

Let us consider a simple execution strategy. Assume that a system test team has designed a test suite T for a system S. Due to the detection and removal of defects and the possibility of causing more defects, S is an evolving system that can be characterized by a sequence of builds $B_0, B_1, B_2, \ldots, B_k$, where each build is expected to have fewer defects than its immediate predecessor. A simple strategy to perform system testing is as follows: Run the test set T on B_0 to detect a set of defects D_0; let B_1 be a build obtained from B_0 by fixing defects D_0; run T on B_1 to detect a set of defects D_1; let B_2 be a build obtained from B_1 by fixing defects D_1; and this process can continue until the quality level of the system is at least the desired quality level. One can adopt such a simple execution strategy if all the test cases in T can be independently executed, that is, no test case is blocked due to a defect in the system. If all the reported defects are immediately fixed and no new defects are introduced, then system testing can be considered to be over by running T just twice: once on B_0 to detect D_0 and a second time on B_1 for confirmation. In the above discussion, we refer to running T, or a subset thereof, on a new build of a software SUT as a system test cycle.

However, the processes of test execution, defect detection, and fixing defects are intricately intertwined. The key characteristics of those processes are as follows:

- Some test cases cannot be executed unless certain defects are detected and fixed.

- A programmer may introduce new defects while fixing one defect, which may not be successful.

- The development team releases a new build for system testing by working on a subset of the reported defects, rather than all the defects.

- It is a waste of resources to run the entire test set T on a build if too many test cases fail.

- As the number of reported defects significantly reduces over a few iterations of testing, it is not necessary to run the entire test set T for regression testing—a carefully chosen subset of T is expected to be adequate.

Therefore, the simple test execution strategy explained above is not practical. An effective and efficient execution strategy must take into account those characteristics of test execution, defect detection, and defect removal.

We present a process model for a metric-based, multicycle test execution strategy which clearly defines an entry criterion to start system testing, how to prioritize execution of test cases, when to move from one test cycle to the next, when to rerun failed test cases, when to suspend a test cycle and initiate root cause analysis, and how to choose a subset of test cases in the final test cycle for regression testing. We characterize each test cycle by a set of six parameters: goals, assumptions, test execution, revert and extension criteria, action, and exit criteria. The idea behind a parameterized test cycle is twofold: (i) the quality level of a system is raised in a measurable, controlled, and incremental manner possibly from the initial low level to the final high level and (ii) the process of system testing is broken down into a sequence of repeatable steps. The parameter values in each test cycle allow the system test leader to effectively control the progress of system testing so that the system moves one step closer to the desired, final quality level.

12.7.1 Multicycle System Test Strategy

The idea of a multicycle test execution strategy with three cycles, for example, is illustrated in Figure 12.1a. Figure 12.1b shows how the quality of a product increases from test cycle to test cycle. In one test cycle, all the test cases in the entire test suite T, or a carefully chosen subset of T, are executed at least once. It is expected that a number of defects are fixed within the life-span of a test cycle so that the quality level of the system is raised by a certain amount, as illustrated in Figure 12.1b. The need for two root cause analyses, one by the development team and one by the system test team, is explained later in this section. The total number of test cycles to be used in individual test projects is a matter of a management decision based on the level of the delivered quality one wants to achieve, the extent to which a test suite covers the requirements of the system, and the effectiveness of defect fixes.

12.7.2 Characterization of Test Cycles

Each test cycle is characterized by a set of six parameters: goals, assumptions, test execution, actions, revert and extension criteria, and exit criteria. Appropriate values must be assigned to these parameters while preparing a concrete test execution strategy. In Section 12.7.6, we give real-life, representative instances of these parameters for three test cycles, where the third test cycle is the final one.

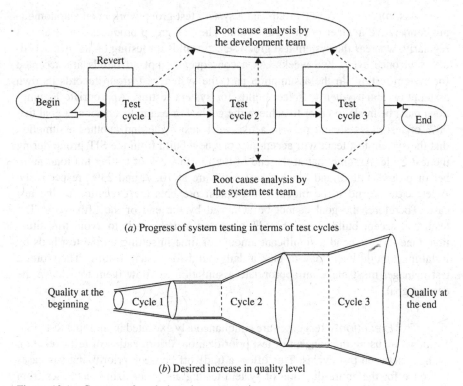

(a) Progress of system testing in terms of test cycles

(b) Desired increase in quality level

Figure 12.1   Concept of cycle-based test execution strategy.

Goals   A system test team sets its own goals to be achieved in each test cycle. These goals are *ideal* in the sense that these are very high standard goals, and consequently, may not be achievable in a given test cycle. The motivation for setting ideal goals is that it is not known what weaker goal is desirable and achievable. Setting a weaker goal has the danger of discouraging the development and test teams from achieving stronger goals. Therefore, we aim to achieve ideal goals in each test cycle, but we are ready to exit from a test cycle even if the goals are not fully achieved. An exit criterion specifies the termination of a test cycle. Goals are specified in terms of the number of test cases to pass within a test cycle. Though goals can also be specified in terms of the number of defects remaining in the software product at the end of each system test cycle [2], predicting the remaining number of defects is a very difficult task [3].

Remark 1.   The goal of a test cycle may be changed due to unforeseen circumstances. For example, a testing cycle is terminated prematurely because of the poor quality of the software. However, the system test group may proceed to complete the system testing cycle to gain hands-on experience and to be able to identify needs for additional test cases. In this situation, the specified goal of the test cycle can be changed to understanding and improving the effectiveness of the test cases.

Assumptions   A SIT group and a system test group work in an autonomous but cooperative manner in an organization. The SIT group produces builds almost regularly, whereas the system test group selects builds for testing on its own schedule, say, once every two weeks. As a consequence, not all builds are accepted for system testing. In the assumption part, the system test group records its own assumption about when to select builds for system testing. Appropriate assumptions must be made in order to achieve the goals. For example, consider a goal that 90% of test cases should pass in a five-week test cycle and another assumption that the system test team will accept just one new build from the SIT group during the test cycle. Assume that at the end of the fourth week of testing the total number of passed, failed, and blocked test cases are at 70, 7, and 23%, respectively. A test case is said to be blocked if a defect prevents the execution of the test case. Therefore, the goal cannot be achieved by the end of the fifth week. The team can accept builds from the SIT group on a daily basis to avoid this situation. One has to spend a significant amount of time in setting up the test beds by installing a build every day to pick a daily build for system testing. Therefore, a test manager must make an appropriate assumption to allow them to achieve the desired goal.

Test Execution   Test cases are simultaneously executed in multiple test environments by using the concept of test prioritization. Prioritization of test execution changes between test cycles. This offers a trade-off between prioritizing test cases just once for the entire duration of system testing and prioritizing test cases from build to build. Some basic ideas in test prioritization are as follows: (i) test cases that exercise basic functionalities have higher priority than the rest in the first test cycle; (ii) test cases that have failed in one test cycle have a higher priority in the following test cycle; and (iii) test cases in certain test groups have higher priority than the others. There are three differences between test prioritization studied in the past [4–6] and a new approach presented in this book, which are as follows:

1. Test prioritization has been considered largely for regression testing. In our test strategy, test cases are prioritized for development testing as well. Test cases are prioritized during system testing in order to exercise the likely vulnerable part of the code early so that developers will have more time to debug and fix the defects, if there are any. For example, if the defects are revealed toward the end of a test cycle, the developers may not have enough time to fix the defects; moreover, the system test team may not be able to validate the fixes in a very short time. Srivastava and Thiagarajan [7] present a test prioritization technique for regression testing during development. Their test prioritization algorithm is based on block-level differences between the compiled binary code of the previous version of a system and its current version to be tested. The prioritization algorithm tries to pick a test from the remaining tests that will cover the maximum number of the remaining impacted, that is, new or modified, blocks.

2. Test prioritization produces a single sequence of ordered test cases, while the need and opportunity for producing smaller, concurrent test execution sequences have been ignored. In our approach, simultaneity of test executions and *importance* of test cases have been factored into test prioritization. Multiple, concurrent test environments allow us to shorten the length of system testing. Kapfhammer [8] proposes the idea of running regression tests on multiple communicating machines.

3. It is highly unlikely that tens of engineers working on a test project have identical interest and expertise in all aspects of a system. For example, one person might be an expert in performance evaluation, whereas another person may be useful in user-interface testing. Test cases falling in their respective categories are separately prioritized.

Revert and Extension Criteria   Each test cycle must be completed within a stipulated time. However, the duration of a test cycle may be extended under certain circumstances, and in the worst case, the test cycle must be restarted from the beginning. The conditions for prematurely terminating a test cycle and for extending a test cycle must be precisely stated. Essentially, the concept of a revert criterion is used to ensure that system testing contributes to the overall quality of the product at reduced cost. It may not be useful to continue a test cycle if it is found that the software is of too poor quality. On the other hand, a test cycle can be extended due to various reasons, such as (i) a need to reexecute all the test cases in a particular test group because a large fraction of the test cases within the group failed or (ii) a significantly large number of new test cases were added while test execution was in progress. The idea of a revert criterion discussed above is similar to the idea of stopping rules for testing [9].

Actions   Two unexpected events may occur while a test cycle is in progress: (i) too many test cases fail and (ii) the system test team has to design a large number of new test cases during the test cycle. On the one hand, the development team tries to understand what went wrong during development when too many test cases fail. On the other hand, when too many new test cases have to be designed, the system test team tries to understand what went wrong in the test planning phase. The two kinds of events require different kinds of responses from the development team and the system test team, as explained below.

It is useful to alert the development team once the number of failed test cases reaches a predefined level. Consequently, the developers take an action in the form of root cause analysis (RCA). In this analysis, the developers study the software components to identify whether a defect was in new, old, rewritten, or refixed code, which is discussed in Chapter 13. Next, the following question is asked: Would it have been possible to detect the defect during an earlier phase in the development cycle, such as design review, code review, unit testing, or integration testing? If the answer is yes, then corrective actions are taken by updating the design specification, reviewing the code, and adding new test cases for unit testing and integration testing to improve the quality of these error-prone software components. The detailed defect analysis is discussed in the system test execution Chapter 13.

Test engineers may find the need to design new test cases as test executions reveal defects and those defects are fixed. The total number of test cases keep increasing as testing continues. A significant increase in the number of test cases implies that the initial planning for test design was not very accurate, and this may adversely affect the test execution schedule. In addition, management may want to know the reason for the initial number of test cases being low. The system test team initiates an RCA when the total number of newly designed test cases crosses a certain threshold. The test team studies all the new test cases and categorizes them into different groups based on the functional requirements. Next, the functional specification and/or any other relevant documents are studied to understand why the test team was unable to identify the objectives of these new test cases in the first place.

Exit Criteria We know when a test cycle has completed by applying an exit criterion. Mere execution of all the test cases in a test suite, or a subset thereof, does not mean that a cycle has completed. There is a need to monitor some quality metrics associated with the test cycle. Examples of these metrics are explained in detail for three test cycles. Determining the exit criteria of the final test cycle is a complex issue. It involves the nature of products (e.g., shrink-wrap application versus an operating system), business strategy related to the product, marketing opportunities and timing, and customer requirements, to name just a few [10]. The exit criteria considered here takes the view that quality is an important attribute and that time-to-market with desirable qualities is a major goal.

12.7.3 Preparing for First Test Cycle

It is desirable to understand the following concepts in order to get ready for the first test cycle: (i) the different states of a known defect in the form of a life cycle from the new state to the closed state, (ii) assignment of test cases to test engineers, and (iii) an entry criterion telling us when to start the first test cycle. These concepts are explained below.

Life Cycle of a Defect The idea behind giving a life-cycle model to defects is to be able to track them from the time they are detected to the time they are closed. The life cycle of a defect is represented by a state transition diagram with five states: new, assigned, open, resolved, and closed. The states of defects are used in the description of individual test cycles. A defect is put in the new state by a test engineer, called a submitter, as soon as it is revealed by a failed test case. After a defect in the new state is reviewed and presumed to be a true defect, it is moved to the assigned state, which means that the defect has been assigned to a software developer. The software developer moves the defect from the assigned state to the open state as soon as he or she starts working on the defect. Once the developer is satisfied by means of unit testing that the defect has been fixed, the defect is moved to the resolved state. The submitter verifies the fix by executing the associated failed test cases against the new build prepared by the development team after a defect moves to the resolved state. If the submitter is satisfied by means of system testing that a defect in the resolved state has been truly fixed, the defect is moved to the closed state, and the associated test cases are declared as passed. Otherwise, the defect is moved back to the open state, and the associated test cases are still considered to have failed. A detailed model of a defect life-cycle is discussed in Chapter 13.

Assignment of Test Cases   Since no single engineer is going to execute all the test cases all by themselves, it is desirable to assign test cases to appropriate test engineers by considering their expertise and interest. Assignment of test cases to test engineers may be changed from test cycle to test cycle for three reasons: (i) when a test case is assigned to a different engineer, the test case is likely to be executed from a different perspective; (ii) an opportunity to learn something new makes a positive impact on employee morale; and (iii) knowledge about test cases is distributed throughout the test group, so if a test engineer is temporarily unavailable for the task, it is easy to find a competent replacement.

Entry Criteria for First Test Cycle   The entry criteria for the first test cycle, given in Table 12.3, tell us when we should start executing system tests. The criteria consist of five groups which depend on five cross-functional groups: marketing, hardware, software, technical publication, and system testing. Each group has one or more condition items to be satisfied. System testing should not start until all the groups of the entry criteria are satisfied. Otherwise, a revert criterion may be triggered sooner during system test execution.

The first group of the entry criteria concerns the completion of the project plan. The marketing team provides a business justification for the proposed product and its requirements. The engineering team defines a development approach, an execution environment, a schedule of the milestones, and the possible risks involved, identifying the dependencies of the product on other elements. The software project plan must be reviewed and approved by the software, hardware, marketing, and technical publication groups before system testing is initiated.

System testing may include new hardware, and, therefore, the second group of the entry criteria is about adequate testing of any new hardware system or subsystem used by the software system. The pass-and-fail results obtained from executing test cases cannot be considered to be dependable without a stable hardware base. It is important to ensure that the hardware has gone through the following three phases: (i) planning and specification; (ii) design, prototype implementation, and testing; and (iii) integration with the software system.

The third group of the entry criteria is about completion of the development and testing work by the software development group. It consists of seven criteria, which provides evidence that the system is sufficiently stable to withstand the rigor of system testing. The stability of a system should be based on metrics and evidence, rather than statements from software managers to start system testing. For example, documentation of weekly passed-and-failed status of all the unit and integration test cases should be available for review. The unit test and system

TABLE 12.3 Entry Criteria for First System Test Cycle

Group	Criteria
1. Marketing	1. Project plan and/or system requirements document is complete and updated.
2. Hardware	2. All approved hardware versions for field deployment are available in-house. A list of these hardware versions should be provided.
	3. Hardware version control process is in place and documented.
	4. Hardware DVT plan is completed and results are available.
3. Software	5. All functional specifications (FSs) are complete and have been updated to be in sync with the implementation. A list of individual FSs, including version number and status, must be provided.
	6. All design specifications (DSs) are complete and have been updated to be in sync with the implementation. A list of DSs, including version number and status, must be provided.
	7. All code complete and frozen; code changes allowed for only defect fixing but not features.
	8. A software version control is in place.
	9. 100% unit tests are executed and passed.
	10. 100% system integration tests are executed and passed.
	11. Not more than two unique crashes have been observed during the last two weeks of integration testing.
4. Technical publication	12. A draft version of the user guide is available.
5. System testing	13. The system test plan is in place (reviewed and approved).
	14. Test execution working document is in place and complete.

integration test reports must be thoroughly reviewed by the system test team before the start of the first test cycle.

The fourth group of the entry criteria concerns the readiness of the user guides written by technical writers. Unless the user guides are ready, the system test engineers will not be able to verify the accuracy and usability.

The fifth group of the entry criteria relates to a system test plan. Detailed test cases are included in the test plan. One can estimate the quality of the software early in the system testing phase [11] by documenting the test cases. The system test plan must be reviewed and approved by the software, hardware, marketing, and technical publication groups before the start of system testing.

Cross-functional review meetings must be conducted to track the status of the readiness criteria, outlined in Table 12.3, at least four weeks prior to the start of the first test cycle. Representatives from the five groups must attend the cross-functional review meeting to provide the status in their respective areas. Any exceptions to these criteria must be documented, discussed, and agreed upon at the final cross-functional status review meeting.

12.7.4   Selecting Test Cases for Final Test Cycle

Though it is desirable to reexecute all the test cases in the final test cycle, a lack of time and additional cost may not allow the system test team to do so. The concept of regression testing is applied only in the final test cycle. In our approach, test cases are selected based on (i) the results of their prior execution; (ii) their membership in certain test groups: basic, functionality, robustness, interoperability, stress, scalability, performance, and load and stability; and (iii) their association with software components that have been modified.

Test cases are selected in three steps: In the first step, the test suite is partitioned into four different bins—red, yellow, green, and white—based on certain criteria which are described in the selection procedure given below. The red bin is used to hold the test cases that must be executed. The yellow bin is used to hold the test cases that are useful to execute. The green bin is used to hold the test cases that will not add any value to regression testing and thus can be skipped. The rest of the test cases are included in the white bin. In other words, the test cases for which no concrete decision can be made in the first step are put in the white bin. In the second step, test cases from the white bin are moved to the other bins by considering the software components that were modified during system testing and the test cases that are associated with those components. Finally, in the third step, the red and yellow bins are selected for regression testing. In the following, we present the test selection procedure:

Step 1:   The test suite is partitioned into red, yellow, green, and white bins as follows:

- **Red:** The red bin holds the following kinds of test cases that *must* be executed:

  Test cases that failed at least once in the previous test cycles.

  Test cases from those test groups for which RCA was conducted by the development team in the previous test cycles.

  Test cases from the stress, scalability, and load and stability test groups. These test cases are more likely to reveal system crash defects. They are selected to ensure that the final build is stable and the probability of the system crashing at the customer site is extremely low.

  Test cases from the performance test category. The performance characteristic must be measured against the final build that is going to be released to the customers.

- **Yellow:** The yellow bin holds the test cases that are *useful* to execute. This bin includes those test cases whose objectives are similar to the objectives of the test cases in the red bin. For example, let a test case with the following objective be in the red bin: While software up-gradation is in progress, the CPU utilization should not exceed 60%. Then, a test case with the following objective is put in the yellow bin: Verify that software image can be upgraded to the nth release from the $(n-1)$th release in less than 300 seconds. The condition, that is, less than 60% CPU utilization, tells us when to execute the upgradation test.

- **Green:** The green bin holds the test cases that will not add any value to regression testing and thus can be skipped. This bin includes those test cases whose objectives are implicitly covered by the execution of the test cases in the red and yellow bins. For example, if a test case with the objective "Verify that a software image can be upgraded to the nth release from the $(n-1)$th release in less than 300 seconds" is in the yellow bin, then a basic test case with the objective "The software can be upgraded to the nth release from the $(n-1)$th release" is included in the green bin.

- **White:** The test cases for which no concrete decision can be made in the first step are put in the white bin. This includes the rest of the test cases not falling in the red, yellow, or green bin.

Step 2: Test cases from the white bin are moved to the other bins by considering the software components that were modified during the system testing and the test cases that are associated with those components. The software developers identify all the software components that have been modified after the start of the first test cycle. Each test case from the white bin is mapped to the identified software components. This mapping is done by analyzing the objective of the test case and then checking whether the modified code of the identified software components is exercised by executing the test cases. The test cases that are mapped to more than one, one, or zero software components are moved to the red, yellow, or green bin, respectively.

Step 3: Test cases from the red and yellow bins are selected for regression testing as follows:

- All the test cases from the red bin are selected for the final test cycle.

- Depending on the schedule, time to market, and customer demand, test cases from the yellow bin are selected for the final test cycle.

Remark 2. It is useful to understand the selection strategy explained above. The red bin holds the test cases that must be selected in the final test cycle. The test cases falling in the "must execute" category are (i) the test cases which had failed in the previous test cycles; (ii) the test cases from the groups for which RCA was performed in the previous test cycles; (iii) test cases from the stress, scalability, and load and stability test groups; and (iv) the test cases which concern modified software components. We remind the reader that RCA for a test group is performed if too many test cases had failed from that group. We put emphasis on a test group by selecting its test cases in the final test cycle. Test cases from the stress, scalability, and load and stability groups are also included in the final test cycle by default, even though those test cases may not concern the modified components. The rationale for their inclusion is that one must run a final check on the stress, scalability, load, and stability aspects of software systems—such as servers, Internet routers, and base stations in wireless communication—which are likely to serve thousands of simultaneous end users.

12.7.5 Prioritization of Test Cases

Prioritization of test cases means ordering the execution of test cases according to certain test objectives. Formulating test objectives for prioritization of individual test cases is an extremely difficult task. Here, we discuss test prioritization in terms of groups of test cases with common properties. An example of a test objective for prioritization is: Execute the maximum number of test cases without being blocked. Furthermore, a major concern from software developers is that test engineers report critical defects (e.g., defects related to system crash) toward the end of test cycles. This does not give them enough time to fix those defects. In addition, blocking defects need to be fixed earlier in the test cycles in order to execute the blocked test cases. Therefore, we need to prioritize the execution of tests to detect critical defects early in the test cycles. In a multicycle-based test execution strategy, it is desirable to have different test objectives for prioritization in different test cycles for three reasons: (i) initially the quality level of the system under test is not very high, (ii) the quality of the system keeps improving from test cycle to test cycle, and (iii) a variety of defects are detected as testing progresses. Below we explain test prioritization in individual test cycles.

Test Prioritization in Test Cycle 1

Principle.   Prioritize the test cases to allow the maximum number of test cases to completely execute without being blocked.

Test engineers execute their assigned test cases in different test environments. Each engineer prioritizes the execution of their subset of test cases as follows:

- A high priority is assigned to the test cases in the basic and functionality test groups.
- A medium priority is assigned to the robustness and interoperability test groups.
- A low priority is assigned to the test cases in the following groups: documentation, performance, stress, scalability, and load and stability tests.

The basic tests give *prima facie* evidence that the system is ready for more rigorous tests. The functionality tests provide a comprehensive testing over the full range of the requirements within the capabilities of the system. Both of these test groups are given high priority in the first test cycle to ensure that any functionality defects are fixed first. Functionality defects can block the execution of other test group. Stress, performance, scalability, load, and stability tests need complex configurations across different platforms, operating systems, and database management systems. Execution of these tests depends on the outcome of the interoperability and robustness tests. Therefore, interoperability and robustness test cases are executed next to flush out any issues that may block the execution of stress, performance, scalability, load, and stability tests.

Test Prioritization in Test Cycle 2

Principle. Test cases which failed in the previous test cycle are executed early in the test cycle.

In the second test cycle, the test cases are reassigned to the test engineers based on their interest and expertise. The process described in Section 12.7.4 is used to distribute all the test cases into three different bins: red, yellow, and green. In this step, we are not selecting a subset of the test suite. Instead, the idea of partitioning a test suite is further used in prioritizing test cases. Each test engineer prioritizes the execution of test cases in their subset as follows:

- A high priority is assigned to the test cases in the red bin.
- A medium priority is assigned to the test cases in the yellow bin.
- A low priority is assigned to the test cases in the green bin.

Test Prioritization in Test Cycle 3

Principle. Test prioritization is similar to that in the second test cycle, but it is applied to a selected subset of the test cases chosen for regression testing.

Once again, the test cases are reassigned based on interest and expertise among the test engineers. Then each test engineer prioritizes the execution of test cases in their assigned subset as follows:

- A high priority is assigned to the test cases in the red bin.
- A low priority is assigned to the test cases in the yellow bin.

The reader may recall from the discussion of Section 12.7.4 that the test cases in the green bin are not executed in the final test cycle.

12.7.6 Details of Three Test Cycles

As we move from test cycle to test cycle, new test cases may be included, and the revert criteria and the exit criteria are made more stringent so that the quality of a system improves, rather than deteriorates, as testing progresses. Note that we have given values of the parameters in a test cycle. The concrete values used in the test cycles are customizable according to the testing capabilities and needs of an organization. The values used in the paper are actual values used in real test projects. We have used concrete values in the description of test cycles to make the descriptions meaningful and to be able to observe improvement in quality from test cycle to test cycle.

Test Cycle 1   In this cycle, we try to detect most of the defects by executing all the test cases. The six characteristic parameters of the first test cycle are described in the following.

Goals   We intend to execute all the test cases from the test suite and maximize the number of passed test cases. The goal is to ensure that 98% of the test cases have passed.

Assumptions   The system test group accepts a software image once every week for the first four weeks and once every two weeks afterward. The possibility of some test cases being blocked is more in the first four weeks of the test cycle because of more priority 1 ("critical") defects being reported earlier in the test cycle due to the execution of higher priority test cases. Unless these defects are resolved quickly, the test execution rate may slow down. Therefore, it is useful to accept new software images every week. We have observed that software images become more stable after four weeks, and test execution is not blocked. Subsequently, the system test team may accept software images once every two weeks.

Test Execution   Test cases are executed according to the prioritization strategy for this test cycle explained in Section 12.7.5.

Revert and Extension Criteria   Essentially, if the number of failed test cases reaches 20% of the total number of test cases to be executed, the system test team abandons this test cycle. The test cycle is restarted when the development team claims that the defects have been fixed. Assume that there are 1000 test cases to be executed. If the system test team observes that 200 test cases, which is 20% of 1000, out of the first, say, 700 test cases have failed, there is no point in continuing with the test cycle. This is because the quality of the product is too low, and any further testing before the defects are fixed is a waste of testing resources. If more than two unique crashes are observed during the test cycle, the system test team runs regression tests after the crash defects are fixed. If the number of failed test cases for any group of test cases, such as functionality, performance, and scalability, reaches 20% of the number of test cases in the group during the test cycle, the system test team reexecutes all the test cases in that group in this cycle after the defects are presumed to be fixed. Consequently, the duration of the test cycle is extended. Similarly, if the number of new test cases increases by 10% of the system test cases, the test cycle is extended to document the additional test cases.

Action   The software development group initiates an RCA during the test cycle if the total number of failed test cases reaches some preset values as shown in Table 12.4. For example, if 25% of all test cases executed fail in a single week from a single group, then the development team performs an RCA. The system test group initiates an RCA if the number of new test cases increases by 10% of the total number of test cases designed before the test cycle was started.

TABLE 12.4 Test Case Failure Counts to Initiate RCA in Test Cycle 1

	Test Case Failure Count (%)	
	Single Week	Cumulative Weeks
Single test group	25	20
All test groups	20	15

Exit Criteria The test cycle is considered to have completed when the following predicates hold: (i) new test cases are designed and documented for those defects that were not detected by the existing test case, referred to as *test case escapes*; (ii) all test cases are executed at least once; (iii) 95% of test cases pass; and (iv) all the known defects are in the closed state.

Remark 3. Test case escapes occur because of deficiencies in the test design process. They are identified when test engineers find defects or when they encounter conditions that are not described in the plan. This happens by accident or when a new test scenario occurs to test engineers while executing the planned test cases. As test engineers learn more about the product, they develop innovative ways to test the product and find new defects. These test cases had escaped from the test case design effort, which is also known as side effects [12].

Remark 4. A software development group may take more time to fix defects that cause the failure of 5% of test cases. In that case there is no point in waiting for the fix and indefinitely delaying the completion of the first test cycle until an additional 3% of test cases pass in order to achieve the stated goal of 98% passed test cases set out for the first test cycle. It is indeed the case that some defects take much more time to be fixed, and some are deferred until the next software release. It is advisable to exit from the first test cycle to start the second cycle for effective and efficient utilization of resources. In any case, our strategy in the second test cycle is to execute all the test cases, which includes those failed 5% of test cases as well.

Test Cycle 2 The fixes for the defects found in the first test cycle are verified in the second test cycle. One of the four possibilities occurs for each modification while fixing a defect: (i) the defect is fixed without introducing a new defect; (ii) the defect is fixed, but something working is broken; (iii) neither the defect is fixed nor new defects are introduced; and (iv) the defect is not fixed, but something else is broken. Moreover, all the entry criteria may not be satisfied before the start of the first test cycle, which may be resolved by cross-functionality groups during the execution of the first test cycle. Sometimes, a demanding customer may cause a last-minute feature check-in before the start of the second test cycle; otherwise, the customer will not deploy the product. It is desirable to reexecute every test case during the second test cycle to ensure that those changes did not adversely impact the quality of the software due to those uncertainties. The six characteristic parameters of the second test cycle are described below.

Goals All test cases are executed once again to ensure that there is no collateral damage due to the fixes applied in the first test cycle. The number of passed test cases are maximized, ensuring that 99% of the test cases have passed at the end of the second test cycle.

Assumption The system test group accepts software images every two weeks. This is because the system is relatively stable after having gone through the first test cycle.

Test Execution Test cases are executed according to the prioritization strategy for this test cycle explained in Section 12.7.5.

Revert and Extension Criteria At any instant in the test cycle, if the total number of failed test cases reaches 10% of the total number of test cases to be executed, the system test team stops testing. The test cycle is restarted from the beginning after the development team claims that the defects have been fixed. If more than one unique crash is observed during this test cycle, the system test team runs regression tests after the crash defects are fixed. This means that the duration of the test cycle is extended. If the number of failed test cases reaches 10% of the total number of tests in a group during the test cycle, the system test team reexecutes all the test cases from that group in this test cycle after the defects are claimed to be fixed. Therefore, the duration of the test cycle needs to be extended. The test cycle is extended to document the additional test cases if the number of new test cases increases by 5% of the total number of test cases.

Action The software development group initiates an RCA during the test cycle if the counts of failed test cases reach some preset values as shown in Table 12.5. For example, if 15% of all test cases executed in a single week from a single group fail, then the development team performs an RCA.

The system test group initiates an RCA if the number of new test cases is increased by 5% of the total number of test cases before the start of the second test cycle. A specific explanation is given if new test cases are added during the first test cycle and also new test cases are added during the second test cycle.

TABLE 12.5 Test Case Failure Counts to Initiate RCA in Test Cycle 2

	Test Case Failure Count (%)	
	Single Week	Cumulative Weeks
Single test group	15	10
All test groups	10	5

Exit Criteria The test cycle is considered to have completed when the following hold: (i) new test cases are designed and documented for those defects that were not detected by the existing test case, (ii) all test cases are executed at least once, (iii) 98% of test cases pass, and (iv) all the known defects are in the closed state.

Remark 5. One of the exit criteria is that 98% of test cases must pass, which is higher than the first test cycle. Once again, there is no point for test engineers to wait for the fixes and indefinitely postpone the completion of the second test cycle until another 1% of the failed test cases are passed in order to achieve the 99% pass goal set before the start of the second test cycle.

Test Cycle 3 In the third and final test cycle, a selected subset of test cases of the original test suite is reexecuted to ensure that the software is stable before it is released to the customer. The objective of this test cycle is to execute all the selected test cases against a single software image.

Goals A selected subset of test cases from the test suite are reexecuted. The process of selecting test cases for this test cycle has been explained in Section 12.7.4. At the end of the cycle, the software is released to the customer. Therefore, 100% of the selected test cases should pass.

Assumption The system test group accepts just one software image at the beginning of the test cycle. In exceptional circumstances, the system test group may accept a second image during this cycle, but it should not be less than three weeks before the end of the test cycle.

Test Execution Test cases are executed according to the prioritization strategy for this test cycle explained in Section 12.7.5.

Revert and Extension Criteria At any instant during the test cycle, if the total number of failed test cases exceeds 5% of the total number of test cases to be executed, the system test team stops testing. Testing is also stopped if a single crash is observed. The test cycle restarts from the beginning after the development team claims that the defects have been fixed, since this is the final test cycle before the release. All the selected test cases need to be reexecuted to ensure that there is no collateral damage due to the fix. Therefore this test cycle can be terminated and restarted again, but not extended.

Exit Criteria The final test cycle is considered to have completed if all of these predicates hold: (i) all the selected test cases are executed; (ii) the results of all the tests are available; (iii) 98% of test cases pass; (iv) the 2% failed test cases should not be from stress, performance, scalability, and load and stability test groups; (v) the system does not crash in the final three weeks of testing; and (vi) the test report is completed and approved. The test report summarizes the test results of all the three test cycles, performance characteristics, scaling limitations (if any), stability observations, and interoperability of the system.

Remark 6.   One of the exit criteria is that 98% of test cases must pass in the third test cycle. One can ask: Why is it not 100%? This was the goal set before the start of the third test cycle. It must be noted that the exit criteria of the final test cycle are influenced by a trade-off among time, cost and quality. As Yourdon [13] has argued, sometimes less than perfect is good enough. Only business goals and priority determine how much less than perfect is acceptable. Ultimately, the exit criteria must be related to the business goals of the organization. Exit criteria are generally not based solely on quality; rather, they take into consideration the innovation and timeliness of the product to be released to the market. Of course, for any mission-critical application, the pass rate of system test cases must be 100%.

Our experience told us that fewer than three test cycles is not good enough to give us much confidence in a large software system unless everything works to perfection as planned—which is a rare case. By "perfection" we mean that (i) the product does not change apart from the defect fixes, (iii) the fixes work as intended, and (iii) the test engineers do not add any new test cases. Rarely are these three conditions satisfied. More than three test cycles can be scheduled with appropriate exit criteria in terms of increasing percentage of test cases passing in successive test cycles. However, more than three test cycles incurs a much higher cost, while delaying the launch of a product "just in time" to the market. Management does not want to delay the launch of a product unless it is a mission-critical project, where the goal is to have a zero-defect product. It is better to plan for three-cycle-based system testing but skip the third test cycle if there is no need. On the other hand, it is not desirable to budget for two test cycles and fall behind when the software is of low quality.

12.8   TEST EFFORT ESTIMATION

The system test group needs to estimate testing effort to produce a schedule of test execution. Intuitively, testing effort defines the amount of work that needs to be done. In concrete terms, this work has two major components:

- The number of test cases created by one person in one day
- The number of test case executed by one person in one day

The above components are also referred to as test productivity. Unfortunately, there is no mathematical formula to compute the test productivity numbers. Rather, the test effort data are gathered by measuring the test creation and execution time in real projects by taking a microscopic view of real testing processes. If productivity data are collected for many test projects, an average test productivity measure can be estimated. Our experience on this issue is discussed in this section.

In the planning stage it is natural to estimate the cost of the test and the time to complete the test. Together the two parameters *cost* and *time* are called *test effort*.

In most cases, estimation of the system test effort is combined with estimation of the entire software project. However, it is useful to separate the test effort estimate from the estimate of the entire project so that enough time is allocated to plan for the system testing from the beginning and conduct it as soon as the entry criteria are satisfied. The three key factors in estimating test effort are as follows:

1. Number of test cases to be designed for the software project
2. Effort required to create a detailed test case
3. Effort required to execute a test case and analyze the result of execution

Some other factors affecting the test effort are as follows:

- Effort needed to create test environments
- Effort needed to train test engineers on the details of the project
- Availability of test engineers for system testing as they are needed

We now discuss the ways to estimate the key factors affecting test effort. Test planners rely on their past experience in testing similar projects and a thorough knowledge of the current project to provide accurate estimation of the above three key items.

12.8.1 Number of Test Cases

It is useful to understand the commonly used term "test case" before it is used for estimation. The *granularity* of test cases has a significant impact on the estimation of the number of test cases needed. For example, one person may use the term test case to mean one atomic test step, which is just a single input–output interaction between the tester and the SUT. Another person may use the same term test case to mean hundreds of test steps. Our definition of test case is independent of the number of test steps needed to construct a test case. The granularity of a test case is tightly coupled with the test objective, or purpose. A simple test case typically contains 7–10 test steps, while a complex test case can easily contain 10–50 test steps. The test steps are atomic building blocks which are combined to form a test case satisfying a well-defined objective. We discuss several ways to estimate the number of test cases.

Estimation Based on Test Group Category   It is straightforward to estimate the number of test cases after the test suite structure and the test objectives are created, as discussed in Section 12.5, by simply counting the number of test objectives. However, this will give an underestimation of the total number of test cases designed by the end of the system test execution cycle. This is because as system testing progresses with the initially estimated and designed test cases, test engineers want to observe additional behavior of the system due to their observations of some unforeseen failures of the system. The number of test cases used by the end of the system testing phase is more than its initial estimation. A more accurate estimation of the number of test cases for each group is obtained by adding a "fudge factor" of 10–15% to the total number of test objectives identified for the group. On the one hand, underestimation of the number of test cases causes reduced allocation of resources to system testing at its beginning. However, it demands more resources when the need is felt, causing uncontrollable project delay. On the other hand, overestimation of the number of test cases leads to their inefficient utilization. For pragmatic reasons, for any moderate-size, moderate-risk testing project, a reasonable factor of safety, in the form of a fudge factor, needs to be included in the estimate in order to provide a contingency for uncertainties.

The test team leader can generate a table consisting of test (sub)groups and for each (sub)group the estimated number of test cases. An additional column may be included for time required to create and time required to execute the test cases, which are discussed later in Sections 12.8.2 and 12.8.3, respectively.

Example: FR–ATM PVC Service Interworking. Let us consider the FR–ATM PVC service interworking example discussed in Chapter 11. A test effort estimation is given in Table 12.6 based on the test categories and FrAtm structure discussed in Chapter 11. The first column is estimated based on the number of test objectives identified for the system. The procedure to obtain the estimations is given below. The estimation of the next two columns of Table 12.6 are discussed in Sections 12.8.2 and 12.8.3, respectively.

One test case is required to test the attribute for each configurable attribute of the FrAtm component. Therefore, we estimate that 40 test cases will be required to test the configuration functionality with our assumption of 40 configuration attributes. Similarly, 30 test cases need to be created in order to test the monitoring feature with our assumption that 30 monitoring attributes are available in the implementation of an FrAtm component. The configuration and monitoring attributes information should be available in the functional specification of the

TABLE 12.6 Test Effort Estimation for FR–ATM PVC Service Interworking

Test (Sub)Groups	Estimated Number of Test Cases	Person-Day to Create	Person-Day to Execute
Configuration	40	4	6
Monitoring	30	4	4
Traffic Management	3	2	3
Congestion	4	2	4
SIWF Translation Mode Mapping	12	4	4
Alarm	4	1	1
Interface	9	5	3
Robustness	44(4 + 40)	4	6
Performance	18	6	10
Stress	2	1.5	2
Load and stability	2	1.5	2
Regression	150(60 + 90)	0	15
Total	**318**	**35**	**60**

FrAtm component. The traffic management test cases are estimated based on the number of QoS parameters to be mapped from FR to ATM, which is approximately 3. The number of interface tests is estimated based on the number of RF and ATM cards supported by the FrAtm component, which is 9. One test case needs to be created for each interface card. Therefore, 9 test cases are estimated for the interface test group. Forty-four test cases are estimated for robustness group, 4 for the FrAtm subgroup and 40 for boundary value tests. One boundary value test case needs to be designed for each configuration attribute. Therefore, we estimated 40 test cases for boundary value functionality testing. Performance test cases are estimated based on the following assumptions:

- Delay measurement for FrAtm with 3 types of ATM cards. This requires us to design 3 test cases.
- Delay measurement for FrAtm with 6 types of FR cards. Therefore, we need to design 6 test cases.
- Throughput measurement using one FR card one at a time. There are 6 types of FR cards, and thus we need 6 test cases.
- Throughput measurement using one ATM card at a time. There are 3 types of ATM cards, and thus we need 3 test cases.

The estimated number of test cases for performance testing may change if the combinations of cards are considered with different objectives. Finally, a number of test cases for regression testing are selected from the existing FR and ATM test suites. For simplicity, we assume that 60 and 90 test cases are selected from the existing FR and ATM test suites, respectively.

Estimation Based on Function Points   The concept of *function points* is used to estimate resources by analyzing a requirements document. This methodology was first proposed by A. J. Albrecht in 1979 [14, 15]. The function point method is becoming more popular in the industry, though it is felt that it is still in an experimental state. The central idea in the function point method is as follows: *Given a functional view of a system in the form of the number of user inputs, the number of user outputs, the number of user on-line queries, the number of logical files, and the number of external interfaces, one can estimate the project size in number of lines of code required to implement the system and the number of test cases required to test the system.*

Albrecht [14] has shown that it is useful to measure a software system in terms of the number of "functions" it performs and gave a method to "count" the number of those functions. The count of those functions is referred to as function points. The function point of a system is a weighted sum of the numbers of inputs, outputs, master files, and inquiries produced to or generated by the software. The four steps of computing the function point of a system are described below:

Step 1:   Identify the following five types of components, also known as "user function types," in a software system and count them by analyzing the requirements document:

- Number of external input types (NI): This is the distinct number of user data or user control input entering the boundary of a system.

- Number of external output types (NO): This is the distinct number of user data or control output type that leaves the external boundary of the system.

- Number of external inquiry types (NQ): This is the distinct number of unique input–output combinations, where an input causes and generates an immediate output. Each distinct input–output pair is considered as an inquiry type.

- Number of logical internal file types (NF): This is the distinct number of major logical groups of user data or control information in the system. Each logical group is treated as a logical file. These groups of data are generated, used, and maintained by the system.

- Number of external interface file types (NE): This is the distinct number of files passed or shared between systems. Each major group of data or control that leaves the system boundary is counted as an external interface file type.

Step 2: Analyze the complexity of each of the above five types of user functions and classify those to three levels of complexity, namely simple, average, or complex. For example, the external input types are simple, the logical internal file types have average complexity, and the number of external interface file types are complex in nature.

A weighting factor is associated with each level of complexity for each type of user function. Two types of user functions with the same level of complexity need not have the same weighting factor. For example, simple external inputs may have a weighting factor of 3, whereas simple external inquiry types may have a weighting factor of 4. Let WFNI denote the weighting factor of external input types, WFNO denote the weighting factor of external output types, and so on. Now, the unadjusted, or crude, function point, denoted by UFP, is computed as

$$UFP = WFNI \times NI + WFNO \times NO + WFNQ \times NQ$$
$$+ WFNL \times NL + WFNE \times NE$$

Compute the unadjusted function point by using the form shown in Table 12.7.

Step 3: Albrecht [14] has identified 14 factors that affect the required development effort for a project. A grade—between 0 and 5—is assigned to each of the 14 factors for a certain project, where 0 = not present or no influence if present, 1 = insignificant influence, 2 = moderate influence, 3 = average influence, 4 = significant influence, and 5 = strong influence. The sum of these 14 grades is known as the processing complexity adjustment (PCA) factor. The 14 factors are listed in Table 12.8.

TABLE 12.7 Form for Computing Unadjusted Function Point

No.	Identifier	Complexity (Use One Item in Each Row)			Total
		Simple	Average	Complex	
1	NI	— × 3 = —	— × 4 = —	— × 6 = —	
2	NO	— × 4 = —	— × 5 = —	— × 7 = —	
3	NQ	— × 7 = —	— × 10 = —	— × 15 = —	
4	NF	— × 5 = —	— × 7 = —	— × 10 = —	
5	NE	— × 3 = —	— × 4 = —	— × 6 = —	
				Total(UFP)	

TABLE 12.8 Factors Affecting Development Effort

1. Requirement for reliable backup and recovery
2. Requirement for data communication
3. Extent of distributed processing
4. Performance requirements
5. Expected operational environment
6. Extent of on-line data entries
7. Extent of multiscreen or multioperation data input
8. Extent of on-line updating of master files
9. Extent of complex inputs, outputs, on-line queries, and files
10. Extent of complex data processing
11. Extent that currently developed code can be designed for reuse
12. Extent of conversion and installation included in the design
13. Extent of multiple installations in an organization and variety of customer organizations
14. Extent of change and focus on ease of use

Step 4: Now, we compute the function point (FP) of a system using the following empirical expression:

$$FP = UFP \times (0.65 + 0.01 \times PCA)$$

By multiplying the unadjusted function point, denoted by UFP, by the expression $0.65 + 0.01 \times PCA$, we get an opportunity to adjust the function point by $\pm 35\%$. This adjustment is explained as follows. Let us analyze the two extreme values of PCA, namely 0 and 70 ($= 14 \times 5$):

$$PCA = 0: \quad FP = 0.65 \times UFP$$
$$PCA = 70: \quad FP = UFP \times (0.65 + 0.01 \times 70) = 1.35 \times UFP$$

Therefore, the value of FP can range from $0.65 \times UFP$ to $1.35 \times UFP$. Hence, we adjust the value of FP within a range of $\pm 35\%$ by using intermediate values of PCA.

The function point metric can be utilized to estimate the number of test cases in the following ways:

- **Indirect Method:** Estimate the code size from the function points and then estimate the number of test cases from the code size.

- **Direct Method:** Estimate the number of test cases directly from function points.

Indirect Method   The function points of a software system are computed by examining the details of the requirements of the system from the requirement database. At the time of such a computation, the programming language in which the system will be implemented may not be known. Implementation of the system in different programming languages will produce different measures of line of code (LOC). Therefore, the choice of a programming language has a direct impact on the LOC metric. Capers Jones [16] gave a relationship between function points and the code size of a software system. Specifically, he gave the number of LOC per function point for a number of programming languages as shown in Table 12.9.

Given the total number of function points for a system, one can predict the number of LOC for a software system by making an assumption of a programming language in implementing the system. At this point, there is a need to utilize one's experience in estimating the number of test cases to be designed for system testing. This estimation practice varies among organizations and even within the same organization for different categories of software systems.

The 30 year empirical study of Hitachi Software [11] gives a standard of one test case per 10–15 LOC. A system with 100 function points and implemented in C will produce a code size of $100 \times 128 = 12{,}800$ lines. Test cases numbering between 850 and 1280 are designed for system-level testing of the software system under consideration. It must be remembered that these test cases do not include those test cases needed for unit testing and integration testing. This is because the test engineers in the system test group must be unbiased and never reuse the test cases of the programmers. Instead, the system testing team designs the test cases from the scratch.

TABLE 12.9   Empirical Relationship between Function Points and LOC

Programming Language	Average LOC/FP
Assembly language	320
C	128
COBOL	106
FORTRAN	106
C++	64
Visual Basic	32

Direct Method Capers Jones [16] gave a direct relationship between function points and the total number of test cases created as

$$\text{Total number of test cases} = (\text{function points})^{1.2}$$

The number of test cases estimated above encompasses all forms of testing done on a software system, such as unit testing, integration testing, and system testing. It does not distinguish system test size from total testing effort.

Now it is useful to compare the test estimation method used by Hitachi Software [11] and the Caper Jones method [16]. The method used by Hitachi Software estimates the number of test cases by considering code size in number of LOC, whereas Caper Jones estimates the number of test cases by considering function points. We start with a certain number of function points and estimate the code size therefrom for a meaningful comparison. For example, we have considered 100 function points in the two preceding examples. Next, we derive the LOC information by assuming a certain programming language to be able to apply to the Hitachi Software method. Assuming that our target language is C, the estimated number of LOC to be produced in C is $100 \times 128 = 12,800$ LOC. The method adopted by Hitachi Software produces 850–1280 test cases to test a system with 12,800 LOC, whereas the Caper Jones method estimates 251 test cases. Note that there is a four- to five-fold difference between the number of test cases estimated by the two methods. The difference is interpreted as follows: The Japanese software industry (e.g., Hitachi Software) uses the term *test point* rather than *test case*, and a test point is similar to a *test step*. A test case normally contains between 1 and 10 test steps. The number of test cases estimated by using the Hitachi Software method represents the number of test steps (or test points). Now, if we assume that a test case contains an average of five test steps, the number of test cases estimated by the Hitachi Software method is between 170 and 256, and this range is closer to 251—the number estimated by the Caper Jones method.

12.8.2 Test Case Creation Effort

It is necessary to allocate time to create test cases after the test suite structure and the test objectives are identified. On average, the productivity of the manual test case creation is summarized in Table 12.10. The time represents the duration from the entry to the create state to the entry to the released state of the state transition diagram of a test case discussed in Chapter 11.

TABLE 12.10 Guidelines for Manual Test Case Creation Effort

Size of Test Case	Average Number of Test Cases per Person-Day
Small, simple test case (1–10 atomic test steps)	7–15
Large, complex test case (10–50 atomic test steps)	1.5–3

The activities involved in creating test cases have been discussed in detail in Chapter 11 and are summarized here:

- Reading and understanding the system requirements and functional specifications documents
- Creating the test cases
- Entering all the mandatory fields, including test steps, and pass–fail criteria
- Reviewing and updating the test case

The skill and effectiveness of a test engineer are significant factors that influence the estimation of test case creation. We assume in our guideline provided in Table 12.10 that a test engineer is skilled in developing test cases, that is, he or she has four to six years of prior experience in developing test cases in the relevant area of expertise. Caper Jones [17] estimated that test cases are created at a rate of 30–300 per person-month. In other words 1.5–15 test cases can be created by one person in one day. Our estimation of creating test cases for each group of FR–ATM service interworking is given in the third column of Table 12.6 based on the guidelines provided in Table 12.10.

12.8.3   Test Case Execution Effort

The time required to execute a test case depends on the complexity of the test case and the expertise of the executer on the subject matter of the system. Arguably, the test cases in the telecommunications area are the most complex ones and require understanding configuration of switches, routers, and different protocols. In any case, one must consider the following factors in order to estimate the work effort for manual test execution:

- Understanding the test cases if the test cases have not been created by the executer
- Configuring the test beds
- Executing the test steps and evaluating the test steps
- Determining the execution status (pass–fail) of the test case
- Logging of test results in the test factory database
- Collecting and analyzing the data if performance and stress–load test cases are being executed
- Updating the test case in the test factory, as discussed in Chapter 11
- In the event of a failure, performing the following tasks:

    Trying to reproduce the failure

    Executing different scenarios related to the failure observed

    Collecting details of the configuration, logs, and hardware configuration

    Filing a defect report in the defect tracking system

- If the software developers cannot reproduce a failure, following up with them in debugging and localizing the problem

Intuitively—and it can also be observed—the test execution rate is linearly proportional to the pass rate of test cases. In other words, if the test case failure rate is high, it slows down the test case execution rate. This is because a test engineer needs to help the developers in replicating the problem and in identifying the root cause of the problem by trial and error, which takes away a lot of time from execution of test cases.

We have summarized, based on our experience, the execution rate of test cases for both new and regression tests in Tables 12.11 and 12.12, respectively. The execution time for newly created test cases is different than the time for the regression test. The difference is due to the fact that the regression test cases were run before, and their test steps and pass–fail criteria were validated earlier. However, if a test engineer has not executed a particular group of regression tests before, he may have to spend more time in understanding the tests and in setting up the test bed in order to execute the assigned regression tests. As a consequence, the execution time for the regression test is almost the same as that of the newly created test case for an inexperienced engineer. Therefore, test automation must be considered for regression tests, which is discussed in a later section of this chapter.

Our estimation of test case execution for each group of FR–ATM service interworking is given in the fourth column of Table 12.6 based on the guidelines provided in Tables 12.11 and 12.12. It may be noted that if automated regression tests are available, the total execution time could have been reduced.

TABLE 12.11 Guidelines for Manual Test Case Execution Effort

Size of Test Case	Average Number of Test Cases per Person-Day
Small, simple test case (1–10 atomic test steps)	7–15
Large, complex test case (10–50 atomic test steps)	1.5–2.5

TABLE 12.12 Guidelines for Estimation of Effort to Manually Execute Regression Test Cases

Size of Test Case	Average Number of Regression Test Cases per Person-Day	
	Did Not Execute Test Cases Earlier	Test Cases Executed Earlier
Small, simple test case (1–10 atomic test steps)	10–15	10–20
Large, complex test case (10–50 atomic test steps)	1–2.5	2.5–5

12.9   SCHEDULING AND TEST MILESTONES

For reasons of economy and to meet contractual deadlines, it is important to outline a schedule and the milestones for the test project. Organizations are constrained to release products within the time frame recommended by their marketing and sales departments because of today's high competitiveness in the market. The system test group is constrained to distribute its testing effort to accommodate the marketing requirement to release the product within a prescribed time frame. One must consider different avenues to complete the system testing phase on time without much delay in product delivery and without compromising the quality of a product. In scheduling the activities in system testing, the leader of the system test group attempts to coordinate the available resources to achieve the projected productivity. The leader considers any interdependency among tasks and schedules the tasks in parallel whenever possible. The milestones, reviews, and test deliverables are specified in the test schedule to accurately reflect the progress of the test project.

Scheduling system testing is a portion of the overall scheduling of a software development project. It is merged with the overall software project plan after a schedule for system testing is produced. It is essential to understand and consider the following steps in order to schedule a test project effectively:

- Develop a detailed list of tasks, such as:

    Procurement of equipment to set up the test environments

    Setting up the test environments

    Creation of detail test cases for each group and subgroup in the test factory

    Creation of a test suite in the test factory

    Execution of test cases during the system test cycles

    Writing the final test report after completion of system testing

- List all the major milestones needed to be achieved during the test project, such as:

    Review of the test plan with cross-functional team members

    Completion of the approved version of the test plan

    Review of the newly created test cases and the chosen test cases for regression testing

    Completion of test cases; all test cases are in their released states so that those can be a part of a test suite, as discussed in Chapter 11

    Creation of the test suite to be executed, as discussed in Chapter 11

    Preparation of test environments

    Date of entry criteria readiness review meeting

    Official release of the software image to system test team

    Start of first system test cycle

End of first system test cycle

Start of second system test cycle

End of second system test cycle

Start of final system test cycle

End of final system test cycle

Final test report delivery date

- Identify the interdependencies among the test tasks and any software milestones that may influence the flow of work, such as official release of the software image to the system test group. In addition, identify the tasks that can be performed concurrently. Some examples of concurrent implementations of test tasks are as follows:

  Test beds can be set up concurrently with the creation of test cases.

  Creation of test cases in different groups can be done concurrently.

  Test cases from different groups can be concurrently executed on different test beds.

- Identify the different kinds of resources and expertise needed to fulfill each task on the list.

- Estimate the quantity of resources needed for each task, such as equipment and human resources, as discussed earlier in this chapter.

- Identify the types and quantities of resources available for this testing project, such as:

  Human resources: persons available and their dates of availability, part- or full-time availability of each individual human resource, and area of expertise of each individual human resource

  Hardware/ software resources: availability of all the hardware/software to build the test environment as discussed in Section 12.6

- Assume that the rest of the resources will be available by certain dates.

- Allocate the resources to each task. This allocation is done task by task in sequence, starting backward from the end date of the test project.

- Schedule the start and end dates of each task. For example, the test execution task can be based on the estimates discussed in Section 12.8.3. Allow delays for unforeseen events, such as illness, vacation, training, and meetings.

- At this point insert the rest of the milestones into the overall schedule. You may have to adjust the resource allocation and the schedule dates.

- Determine the earliest and the latest possible start date and end date for each task by taking into account any interdependency between tasks identified earlier.

- Review the schedule for reasonableness of the assumptions. At this stage, it is a good idea to ask "what if" questions. Analyze and change the schedule through iterations as the assumptions change.

- Identify the conditions required to be satisfied for the schedule. In addition, identify the contingency plan to be prepared for a possibility that those conditions are not met. For example, if it is not possible to hire a full-time test engineer by a certain date, one should go for a contractor or move in other test engineers from a different project.

- Document the assumptions, such as (i) new test engineer must be hired by a certain date, (ii) new equipment must be available by a certain date, and (iii) space availability to set up the test environment.

- Review the schedule with the test team and get their feedback. The schedule may not be met without their active participation.

The test effort estimate and schedule need to go through a few rounds of iterations in order to make them reliable. A good software tool available in the market is valuable to juggle the test schedule. A major problem the test team leader may encounter from management is how to shorten the test case execution time. Some tasks might be completely eliminated by reducing the scope and depth of testing. If not possible, one may include skilled test professionals with high proficiency, ask people to work overtime, and add more people and test beds. Another way to reduce the execution time is to automate all the test cases upfront so that execution time is reduced drastically.

Gantt Chart   A Gantt chart is often used to represent a project schedule that includes the duration of individual tasks, their dependencies, and their ordering. A typical Gantt chart graphically displays the start and end points of each task—the total duration needed to complete each task. As the project progresses, it displays the percentage of completion of each task. It allows the planner to assess the duration of a project, identify the resources needed, and lay out the order in which tasks need to be carried out. It is useful in managing the dependencies between tasks. It is widely used for project planning and scheduling in order to:

- Assess the time characteristics of a project
- Show the task order
- Show the link between scheduled tasks
- Define resources involved
- Monitor project completion

In a Gantt chart, each task takes one row. Dates run along the top in increments of days, weeks, or months, depending on the length of the project. The expected time for each task is represented by a horizontal rectangle or line. Tasks may overlap or run in sequence or in parallel. Often the project has important events, and one would want to show those events on the project timeline. For example, we may wish to highlight when a prototype is completed or the date of a test plan review. One can enter these on a Gantt chart as milestone events and mark them with a special symbol, often a diamond. The tasks should be kept to a manageable number (no more than 15 or 20) during the construction of a Gantt chart so that the chart fits on a single page. More complex projects may require subordinate charts which detail the timing of all the subtasks of the main tasks. It often helps to have an additional column containing numbers or initials which identify the team member responsible for the task for team projects.

Remark. The idea of a Gantt chart was originally proposed in 1917 by the American engineer Henry L. Gantt. He developed the first Gantt chart to be used in production flow planning. Accepted as a commonplace project management tool today, it was an innovation of worldwide importance in the 1920s. Gantt charts have been successfully used in large construction projects such as the Hoover Dam project started in 1931 and the interstate highway network started in 1956.

Example: FR–ATM PVC Service Interworking. Let us consider the FR–ATM PVC service interworking example discussed in Chapter 11. A high-level test schedule for this test project is shown in Figure 12.2 using the Gantt chart. We made the following assumptions in planning the test schedule:

- Four test engineers: Alex, Rohan, Inu, and Lucy are available for this project from day 1, and Alex is the test team leader for this project.

- All four engineers are well trained to generate test cases in the test factory.

- All of them are knowledgeable in the area of FR and ATM protocol.

- It took five days for Alex to develop the test plan for this project.

ID	Task Name	Duration	Start	Finish	December	January	February	March	April
1	Development of the test plan	5 days	Jan 3	Jan 7		Alex			
2	Review the test plan	0 days	Jan 7	Jan 7		1/7			
3	Update the test plan	1 day	Jan 10	Jan 10		Alex			
4	Test plan approved	0 days	Jan 10	Jan 10		1/10			
5	Procurement of equipment	7 days	Jan 11	Jan 19		Lucy			
6	Set up the test environment	10 days	Jan 20	Feb 2			Lucy		
7	Creation of test cases in test factory	18 days	Jan 11	Feb 3			Alex,Inu,Rohan		
8	Review the test cases	0 days	Feb 3	Feb 3			2/3		
9	Update the test cases in test factory	4 days	Feb 4	Feb 9			Alex,Rohan,Inu,		
10	Test cases are in released state	0 days	Feb 9	Feb 9			2/9		
11	Creation of test suite in test factory	1 day	Feb 10	Feb 10			Rohan,Lucy,Inu,		
12	Entrance criteria readiness meeting	1 day	Feb 11	Feb 11			Alex		
13	Official release of S/W to system test	0 days	Feb 14	Feb 14			2/14		
14	Start of first test cycle	0 days	Feb 14	Feb 14			2/14		
15	First test cycle	15 days	Feb 14	Mar 4	Alex,Rohan,Lucy,Inu				
16	End of first test cycle	0 days	Mar 4	Mar 4				3/4	
17	Start of second test cycle	0 days	Mar 4	Mar 4				3/4	
18	Second test cycle	15 days	Mar 7	Mar 25	Alex,Rohan,Inu,Lucy				
19	End of second test cycle	0 days	Mar 25	Mar 25					3/25
20	Beta release criteria review meeting	0 days	Mar 25	Mar 25					3/25
21	Release the software to beta customer	1 days	Mar 28	Mar 28					Alex
22	Start of third test cycle	0 days	Mar 28	Mar 28					3/28
23	Third test cycle	5 days	Mar 29	Apr 4	Alex,Rohan,Inu,Lucy				
24	End of third test cycle	0 days	Apr 4	Apr 4					4/4
25	Test report preparation	4 days	Apr 5	Apr 8				Alex,Rohan	
26	Release criteria review meeting	0 days	Apr 8	Apr 8					4/8
27	Release the software to the customer	1 day	Apr 13	Apr 13				Alex	

Figure 12.2   Gantt chart for FR–ATM service interworking test project.

- No one has any plans to take a vacation during the system testing period.
- Test equipment is available for this test project.

The test environment setup and the creation of test cases are done concurrently. Lucy is assigned to set up the test beds whereas the rest of the engineers are assigned to design test cases. We have estimated approximately 35 person-days to create 168 test cases, excluding the regression test case as given in Table 12.6. Therefore, we have allocated 18 days to design the test cases distributed among three test engineers, Alex, Inu, and Rohan, with a combined 54 person-days. This includes training and understanding of the FR–ATM service internetworking protocol. The first test cycle is started after the entry criteria are verified at the readiness review meeting. According to our estimation, it will take 60 person-days to execute all the selected 318 test cases, including the regression tests. Therefore, we have allocated 15 days to execute all the test cases by four test engineers, Alex, Inu, Rohan, and Lucy, with a combined resource of 60 person-days. After the second test cycle, the software is scheduled to be released to beta customers. A subset of the test cases is selected for regression testing in the final test cycle. Therefore, only one week is allocated for this task. The software is released to the customers after the final test report is created and reviewed.

12.10   SYSTEM TEST AUTOMATION

It is absolutely necessary for any testing organization to move forward to become more efficient, in particular in the direction of test automation. The reasons for automating test cases are given in Table 12.13. It is important to think about automation as a strategic business activity. A strategic activity requires senior management support; otherwise it will most likely fail due to lack of funding. It should be aligned with the business mission and goals and a desire to speed up delivery of the system to the market without compromising quality. However, automation is a long-term investment; it is an on-going process. It cannot be achieved overnight; expectation need to be managed to ensure that it is realistically achievable within a certain time period.

TABLE 12.13   Benefits of Automated Testing

1. Test engineer productivity
2. Coverage of regression testing
3. Reusability of test cases
4. Consistency in testing
5. Test interval reduction
6. Reduced software maintenance cost
7. Increased test effectiveness

The organization must assess and address a number of considerations before test automation can proceed. The following prerequisites need to be considered for an assessment of whether or not the organization is ready for test automation:

- The system is stable and its functionalities are well defined.
- The test cases to be automated are unambiguous.
- The test tools and infrastructure are in place.
- The test automation professionals have prior successful experience with automation.
- Adequate budget has been allocated for the procurement of software tools.

The system must be stable enough for automation to be meaningful. If the system is constantly changing or frequently crashing, the maintenance cost of the automated test suite will be rather high to keep the test cases up to date with the system. Test automation will not succeed unless detailed test procedures are in place. It is very difficult to automate a test case which is not well defined to be manually executed. If the tests are executed in an ad hoc manner without developing the test objectives, detailed test procedure, and pass–fail criteria, then they are not ready for automation. If the test cases are designed as discussed in Chapter 11, then automation is likely to be more successful.

The test engineers should have significant programming experience. It is not possible to automate tests without using programming languages, such as Tcl (Tool command language), C, Perl, Python, Java, and Expect. It takes months to learn a programming language. The development of an automation process will fail if the testers do not have the necessary programming skills or are reluctant to develop it. Adding temporary contractors to the test team in order to automate test cases may not work. The contractors may assist in developing test libraries but will not be able to maintain an automated test suite on an on-going basis.

Adequate budget should be available to purchase and maintain new software and hardware tools to be used in test automation. The organization should keep aside funds to train the staff with new software and hardware tools. Skilled professionals with good automation background may need to be added to the test team in order to carry out the test automation project. Therefore, additional head count should be budgeted by the senior executive of the organization.

12.11 EVALUATION AND SELECTION OF TEST AUTOMATION TOOLS

A test automation tool is a software application that assists in the automation of test cases that would otherwise be run manually. Some tools are commercially available in the market, but for testing complex, imbedded, real-time systems, very few commercial test tools are available in the market. Therefore, most organizations build their own test automation frameworks using programming languages such as C and Tcl. It is essential to combine both hardware and software for real-time testing tools. This is due to the fact that special kinds of interface cards are required to be connected to the SUT. The computing power of personal computers with network interface cards may not be good enough to send traffic to the SUT.

Test professionals generally build their own test tools in high-technology fields, such as telecommunication equipment and application based on IP. Commercial third-party test tools are usually not available during the system testing phase. For example, there were no commercially available test tools during the testing of the 1xEv-DO system described in Chapter 8. The second author of this book developed in-house software tools to simulate access terminals using their own products. However, we advocate that testers should build their own test automation tools only if they have no alternative. Building and maintaining one's own test automation tool from scratch are time-consuming tasks and an expensive undertaking. The test tool evaluation criteria are formulated for the selection of the right kind of software tool. There may be no tool that fulfills all the criteria. Therefore, we should be a bit flexible during the evaluation of off-the-self automation tools available in the market. The broad criteria for evaluating test automation tools have been classified into the following eight categories as shown in Figure 12.3.

1. *Test Development Criteria:* An automation test tool should provide a high-level, preferably nonproprietary, easy-to-use test scripting language such as Tcl. It should have the ability to interface and drive modules that can be easily written in, for example, C, Tcl, Perl, or Visual Basic. The tool must provide facility to directly access, read, modify, and control the internals of the automated test scripts. The input test data should be stored separately from the test script but easily cross-referenced to the corresponding test scripts, if necessary. The tool should have built-in templates of test scripts, test cases, tutorials, and demo application examples to show how to develop automated test cases. Finally, no changes should be made to the SUT in order to use the tool. The vendor's

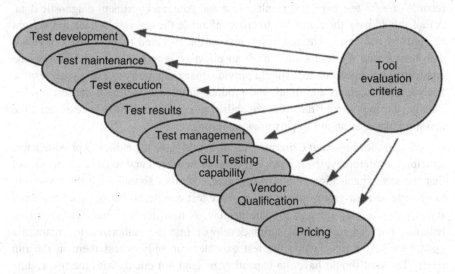

Figure 12.3   Broad criteria of test automation tool evaluation.

recommended environment should match the real test laboratory execution environment.

2. *Test Maintenance Criteria:* The tool should possess a rich set of features, such as version control capability on test cases, test data, and migration of test cases across different platforms. The tool must provide powerful, easy-to-use facilities to browse, navigate, modify, and reuse the test suites. The tool should have the ability to select a subset of test cases to form a group for a particular test run based on one or more distinguishing characteristics. A tool needs to have features to allow modification and replication of test cases, easy addition of new test cases, and import from another. The tool should have the capability to add multiple tags to a test case and modify those tags so that the test case can be easily selected in a subgroup of test cases sharing a common characteristic.

3. *Test Execution Criteria:* An automation tool should allow test cases to be executed individually, as a group, or in a predefined sequence. The user should have the ability to check the interim results during the execution of a group of tests and exercise other options for the remainder of the tests based on the interim results. The user should have the option to pause and resume the execution of a test suite. The tool should have the facility to execute the test suite over the Internet. The tool should allow simultaneous execution of several test suites that can be distributed across multiple machines for parallel execution. This substantially reduces the time needed for testing if multiple test machines are available. The test tool should have a capability for monitoring, measuring, and diagnosing performance characteristics of the SUT. Finally, the tool should have the capability to be integrated with other software tools which are either in use or expected to be used.

4. *Test Results Criteria:* The test tool must provide a flexible, comprehensive logging process during execution of the test suite, which may include detailed records of each test case, test results, time and date, and pertinent diagnostic data. A tool should have the capability to cross-reference the test results back to the right versions of test cases. The test result log can be archived in an industry standard data format and the tool should have an effective way to access and browse the archived test results. The tool should provide query capability to extract test results, analyze the test status and trend, and produce graphical reports of the test results. Finally, the tool should have the capability to collect and analyze response time and throughput as an aid to performance testing.

5. *Test Management Criteria:* A tool should have the ability to provide a test structure, or hierarchy, that allows test cases to be stored and retrieved in a manner that the test organization wants to organize. The tool should have the capability to allocate tests or groups of tests to specific test engineers and compare the work status with the plan through graphic display. A tool needs to have authorization features. For example, a test script developer may be authorized to create and update the test scripts, while the test executer can only access them in the run mode. The tool should have the capability to send out emails with the test results after completion of test suite execution.

6. *GUI Testing Capability Criteria:* An automated GUI test tool should include a record/playback feature which allows the test engineers to create, modify, and run automated tests across many environments. These tools should have a capability to recognize and deal with all types of GUI objects, such as list boxes, radio buttons, icons, joysticks, hot keys, and bit-map images with changes in color shades and presentation fonts. The recording activity of the tool capturing the keystrokes entered by the test engineer can be represented as scripts in a high-level programming language and saved for future replay. The tools must allow test engineers to modify test scripts to create reusable test procedures to be played back on a new software image for comparison. The performance of a GUI test tool needs to be evaluated. One may consider the question: How fast can the tool record and playback a complex test scenario or a group of test scenarios?

7. *Vendor Qualification Criteria:* Many questions need to be asked about the vendor's financial stability, age of the vendor company, and its capability to support the tool. The vendor must be willing to fix problems that arise with the tool. A future roadmap must exist for the product. Finally, the maturity and market share of the product must be evaluated.

8. *Pricing Criteria:* Pricing is an important aspect of the product evaluation criteria. One can ask a number of questions: Is the price competitive? Is it within the estimated price range for an initial tool purchase? For a large number of licenses, a pricing discount can be negotiated with the vendor. Finally, the license must explicitly cap the maintenance cost of the test tool from year to year.

Tool vendors may guarantee the functionality of the test tool; however, experience shows that often test automation tools do not work as expected within the particular test environment. Therefore, it is recommended to evaluate the test tool by using it before making the decision to purchase it. The test team leader needs to contact the tool vendor to request a demonstration. After a demonstration of the tool, if the test team believes that the tool holds potential, then the test team leader may ask for a temporary license of the tool for evaluation. At this point enough resources are allocated to evaluate the test tool. The evaluator should have a clear understanding of the tool requirements and should make a test evaluation plan based on the criteria outlined previously. The goal here is to ensure that the test tool performs as advertised by the vendor and that the tool is the best product for the requirement. Following the hands-on evaluation process, an evaluation report is prepared. The report documents the hands-on experience with the tool. This report should contain background information, a tool summary, technical findings, and a conclusion. This document is designed to address the management concerns because eventually it has to be approved by executive management.

12.12 TEST SELECTION GUIDELINES FOR AUTOMATION

Test cases should be automated only if there is a clear economic benefit over manual execution. Some test cases are easy to automate while others are more cumbersome.

The general guideline shown in Figure 12.4 may be used in evaluating the suitability of test cases to be automated as follows:

Less Volatile: A test case is stable and is unlikely to change over time. The test case should have been executed manually before. It is expected that the test steps and the pass–fail criteria are not likely to change any more.

Repeatability: Test cases that are going to be executed several times should be automated. However, one-time test cases should not be considered for automation. Poorly designed test cases which tend to be difficult to reuse are not economical for automation.

High Risk: High-risk test cases are those that are routinely rerun after every new software build. The objectives of these test cases are so important that one cannot afford to not reexecute them. In some cases the propensity of the test cases to break is very high. These test cases are likely to be fruitful in the long run and are the right candidates for automation.

Easy to Automate: Test cases that are easy to automate using automation tools should be automated. Some features of the system are easier to test than other features, based on the characteristics of a particular tool. Custom objects with graphic and sound features are likely to be more expensive to automate.

Manually Difficult: Test cases that are very hard to execute manually should be automated. Manual test executions are a big problem, for example, causing eye strain from having to look at too many screens for too long in a GUI test. It is strenuous to look at transient results in real-time applications. These nasty, unpleasant test cases are good candidates for automation.

Boring and Time Consuming: Test cases that are repetitive in nature and need to be executed for longer periods of time should be automated. The tester's time should be utilized in the development of more creative and effective test cases.

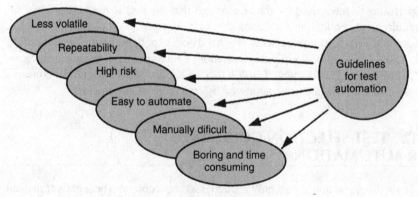

Figure 12.4   Test selection guideline for automation.

12.13   CHARACTERISTICS OF AUTOMATED TEST CASES

The largest component of test case automation is programming. Unless test cases are designed and coded properly, their execution and maintenance may not be effective. The design characteristics of effective test cases were discussed in Chapter 11. A formal model of a standard test case schema was also provided in Chapter 11. In this section, we include some key points which are pertinent to the coding of test cases. The characteristics of good automated test cases are given in Figure 12.5 and explained in the following.

1. *Simple:* The test case should have a single objective. Multiobjective test cases are difficult to understand and design. There should not be more than 10–15 test steps per test case, excluding the setup and cleanup steps. Multipurpose test cases are likely to break or give misleading results. If the execution of a complex test leads to a system failure, it is difficult to isolate the cause of the failure.

2. *Modular:* Each test case should have a setup and cleanup phase before and after the execution test steps, respectively. The setup phase ensures that the initial conditions are met before the start of the test steps. Similarly, the cleanup phase puts the system back in the initial state, that is, the state prior to setup. Each test step should be small and precise. One input stimulus should be provided to the system at a time and the response verified (if applicable) with an interim verdict. The test steps are building blocks from reusable libraries that are put together to form multistep test cases.

3. *Robust and Reliable:* A test case verdict (pass–fail) should be assigned in such a way that it should be unambiguous and understandable. Robust test cases can ignore trivial failures such as one-pixel mismatch in a graphical display. Care should be taken so that false test results are minimized. The test cases must have built-in mechanisms to detect and recover from errors. For example, a test case

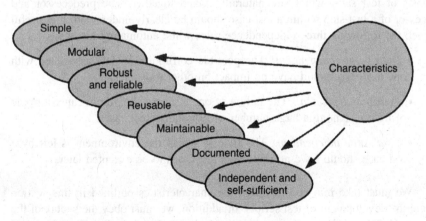

Figure 12.5   Characteristics of automated test cases.

need not wait indefinitely if the SUT has crashed. Rather, it can wait for a while and terminate an indefinite wait by using a timer mechanism.

4. *Reusable:* The test steps are built to be configurable, that is, variables should not be hard coded. They can take values from a single configurable file. Attention should be given while coding test steps to ensure that a single global variable is used, instead of multiple, decentralized, hard-coded variables. Test steps are made as independent of test environments as possible. The automated test cases are categorized into different groups so that subsets of test steps and test cases can be extracted to be reused for other platforms and/or configurations. Finally, in GUI automation hard-coded screen locations must be avoided.

5. *Maintainable:* Any changes to the SUT will have an impact on the automated test cases and may require necessary changes to be done to the affected test cases. Therefore, it is required to conduct an assessment of the test cases that need to be modified before an approval of the project to change the system. The test suite should be organized and categorized in such a way that the affected test cases are easily identified. If a particular test case is data driven, it is recommended that the input test data be stored separately from the test case and accessed by the test procedure as needed. The test cases must comply with coding standard formats. Finally, all the test cases should be controlled with a version control system.

6. *Documented:* The test cases and the test steps must be well documented. Each test case gets a unique identifier, and the test purpose is clear and understandable. Creator name, date of creation, and the last time it was modified must be documented. There should be traceability to the features and requirements being checked by the test case. The situation under which the test case cannot be used is clearly described. The environment requirements are clearly stated with the source of input test data (if applicable). Finally, the result, that is, pass or fail, evaluation criteria are clearly described.

7. *Independent and Self-Sufficient:* Each test case is designed as a cohesive entity, and test cases should be largely independent of each other. Each test case consists of test steps which are naturally linked together. The predecessor and successor of a test step within a test case should be clearly understood. It is useful to keep the following three independence rules while automating test cases:

- *Data value independent:* The possible corruption of data associated with one test case should have no impact on other test cases.

- *Failure independent:* The failure of one test case should not cause a ripple of failures among a large number of subsequent test cases.

- *Final state independent:* The state in which the environment is left by a test case should have no impact on test cases to be executed later.

We must take into consideration the characteristics outlined in this section during the development of test scripts. In addition, we must obey the syntax of the test case defined in the next section while implementing a test case.

12.14   STRUCTURE OF AN AUTOMATED TEST CASE

An automated test case mimics the actions of a human tester in terms of creating initial conditions to execute the test, entering the input data to drive the test, capturing the output, evaluating the result, and finally restoring the system back to its original state. The six major steps in an automated test case are shown in Figure 12.6. Error handling routines are incorporated in each step to increase the maintainability and stability of test cases.

Setup: The setup includes steps to check the hardware, network environment, software configuration, and that the SUT is running. In addition, all the parameters of the SUT that are specific to the test case are configured. Other variables pertinent to the test case are initialized.

Drive the Test: The test is driven by providing input data to the SUT. It can be a single step or multiple steps. The input data should be generated in such a way that the SUT can read, understand, and respond.

Capture the Response: The response from the SUT is captured and saved. Manipulation of the output data from the system may be required to extract the information that is relevant to the objective of the test case.

Determine the Verdict: The actual outcome is compared with the expected outcome. Predetermined decision rules are applied to evaluate any discrepancies between the actual outcome against the expected outcome and decide whether the test result is a pass or a fail. If a fail verdict is assigned to the test case, additional diagnostic information is needed. One must be careful in designing the rules for assigning a passed/failed verdict to a test case. A failed test procedure does not necessarily indicate a problem with the SUT—the problem could be a *false positive*. Similarly, a passed test procedure does not necessarily indicate that there is no problem with the SUT—the problem could be due to a *false negative*. The problems of false negative and false positive can occur due to several reasons,

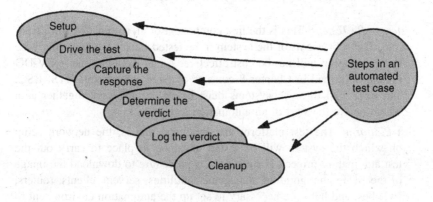

Figure 12.6   Six major steps in automated test case.

such as setup errors, test procedure errors, test script logic errors, or user errors [18].

Log the Verdict: A detailed record of the results are written in a log file. If the test case failed, additional diagnostic information is needed, such as environment information at the time of failure, which may be useful in reproducing the problem later.

Cleanup: A cleanup action includes steps to restore the SUT to its original state so that the next test case can be executed. The setup and cleanup steps within the test case need to be efficient in order to reduce the overhead of test execution.

12.15   TEST AUTOMATION INFRASTRUCTURE

A test automation infrastructure, or framework, consists of test tools, equipment, test scripts, procedures, and people needed to make test automation efficient and effective. The creation and maintenance of a test automation framework are key to the success of any test automation project within an organization. The implementation of an automation framework generally requires an automation test group, as discussed in Chapter 16. The six components of a test automation framework are shown in Figure 12.7. The idea behind an automation infrastructure is to ensure the following:

- Different test tools and equipment are coordinated to work together.
- The library of the existing test case scripts can be reused for different test projects, thus minimizing the duplication of development effort.
- Nobody creates test scripts in their own ways.
- Consistency is maintained across test scripts.
- The test suite automation process is coordinated such that it is available just in time for regression testing.
- People understand their responsibilities in automated testing.

System to Be Tested: This is the first component of an automation infrastructure. The subsystems of the system to be tested must be stable; otherwise test automation will not be cost effective. As an example, the 1xEV-DO system described in Chapter 8 consists of three subsystems, BTS, BSC, and EMS. All three subsystems must be stable and work together as a whole before the start of an automation test project.

Test Platform: The test platform and facilities, that is, the network setup on which the system will be tested, must be in place to carry out the test automation project. For example, a procedure to download the image of the SUT, configuration management utilities, servers, clients, routers, switches, and hubs are necessary to set up the automation environment to execute the test scripts.

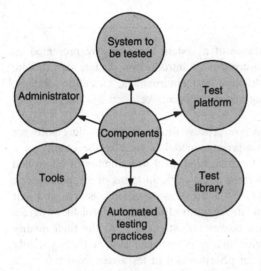

Figure 12.7   Components of automation infrastructure.

Test Case Library: It is useful to compile libraries of reusable test steps of basic utilities to be used as the building blocks of automated test scripts. Each utility typically performs a distinct task to assist the automation of test cases. Examples of such utilities are *ssh* (secure shell) from client to server, *exit* from client to server, response capture, information extraction, rules for verdicts, verdict logging, error logging, cleanup, and setup.

Automated Testing Practices: The procedures describing how to automate test cases using test tools and test case libraries must be documented. A template of an automated test case is useful in order to have consistency across all the automated test cases developed by different engineers. A list of all the utilities and guidelines for using them will enable us to have better efficiency in test automation. In addition, the maintenance procedure for the library must be documented.

Tools: Different types of tools are required for the development of test scripts. Examples of such tools are test automation tool, traffic generation tool, traffic monitoring tool, and support tool. The support tools include test factory, requirement analysis, defect tracking, and configuration management tools. Integration of test automation and support tools, such as defect tracking, is crucial for the automatic reporting of defects for failed test cases. Similarly, the test factory tool can generate automated test execution trends and result patterns.

Administrator: The automation framework administrator (i) manages test case libraries, test platforms, and test tools; (ii) maintains the inventory of templates; (iii) provides tutorials; and (iv) helps test engineers in writing test scripts using the test case libraries. In addition, the administrator provides tutorial assistance to the users of test tools and maintains a liaison with the tool vendors and the users.

12.16 SUMMARY

This chapter focused on the importance of a system test plan. We presented an outline of a system test plan which consists of introduction, feature description, assumptions, approach, test suite structure, test environment, execution strategy, test effort estimation, and scheduling and milestones. We discussed the processes to create such a plan.

The chapter presented an effective process model for performing software system testing. The key idea in this process model is to raise the quality of a system from its initial low level to the final high level in a number of controlled steps called test cycles. We characterized a test cycle in terms of six parameters: goals, assumptions, test execution, revert and extension criteria, action, and exit criteria. These parameters allow test managers to effectively control the progress of system testing so that the system moves one step closer to the final quality level. We explained an entry criterion that tells us when system testing should start. We presented new techniques for prioritization of test cases from test cycle to test cycle and selection of test cases for regression testing in the final test cycle. Typical values of the parameters were given for three-cycle-based test projects.

We discussed techniques, such as function points, to estimate the number of test cases for a test project with concrete examples. Guidelines to estimate the time required to create and execute system-level test cases were proposed. We presented ways of using a Gantt chart to create a system test schedule and milestones for the test project.

Next, we outlined the benefits of test automation: (i) test engineer productivity, (ii) coverage of regression testing, (iii) reusability of test cases, (iv) consistency in testing, (v) test interval reduction, (vi) reduction of software maintenance cost, and (vii) increased test effectiveness. The following five prerequisites must be considered while assessing whether or not a test organization is ready for test automation:

- The system is stable and the functionalities are well defined.
- The test cases that need to be automated are well defined.
- The test tools and infrastructure are in place.
- The test automation professionals have prior successful experience with automation.
- Adequate budget was allocated for the procurement of software tools.

We presented a process to evaluate and select third-party test tools available in the market. The test tool evaluation criteria are classified into eight categories: (i) test development, (ii) test maintenance, (iii) test execution, (iv) test results, (v) test management, (vi) GUI testing capability, (vii) vendor qualification and (viii) pricing. These criteria are formulated in order to select the right kind of software test tool. We advocated that test engineers should build their own test automation tools only if they have no alternative. Building and maintaining one's own test automation tool from scratch are time consuming and an expensive undertaking. There is no point in reinventing the wheel if off-the-shelf test tools satisfying the criteria are readily available.

We provided general guidelines to be used in the selection of test cases that can be automated. The characteristics of automatable test cases are as follows: less volatile, repeatability, high risk, easy to automate, manually difficult to execute, and boring and time consuming. We discussed the characteristics of automated test cases: simple, modular, reusable, maintainable, documented, robustness, reliable, and independent and self-sufficient.

Finally, we described the structure of an automated test case, which consists of setup, driving the test, capturing the response, determining the verdict, logging the verdict, and cleanup. We explained the need of a test automation infrastructure. We provided six components of a test automation framework: (i) the system to be tested, (ii) the test platform, (iii) the test case library, (iv) the automated testing practices, (v) the tools, and (vi) the administrator.

LITERATURE REVIEW

A generic test plan template has been described in the IEEE standard 829-1983 (*IEEE Standard for Software Test Documentation: IEEE/ANSI Standard*). Other topics described in the standard are test design specifications, test case specifications, test procedure specifications, test item transmittal report, and test result reports. The following are the sections of a test plan as defined in the standard:

- **Test Plan Identifier:** A unique identifier, useful if all the documents are stored in a database.
- **Introduction:** Overall description of the test project. This includes references to all the relevant documents.
- **Items to be Tested:** List of entities (function, module, systems, and subsystems) to be tested. The list includes references to specifications and manuals.
- **Features to be Tested:** Identification of the features to be tested. Cross-reference them to the test design specifications.
- **Features Not to be Tested:** Which ones and why not.
- **Approach:** Description of the overall approach to testing. The standard also says that this section—and not the schedule section—is the place to identify constraints, including deadlines and availability of resources (human and equipment).
- **Pass/Fail Criteria:** A set of criteria to decide the test case has been passed or failed upon execution.
- **Suspension and Resumption Criteria:** List of anything that would cause testing to stop until it is fixed. What would have to be done to resume testing? What tests should be reexecuted at this point?

- **Test Deliverables:** List of all testing documents that will be written for this project.

- **Testing Tasks:** List of all tasks necessary to prepare and conduct testing. Show dependency between tasks, special skills needed to do them, who does each task, how much effort is involved, and when each will be done.

- **Test Environment:** Description of the hardware, software, testing tool, and lab facilities required to conduct the testing.

- **Responsibilities:** Name of the engineers (or groups) responsible for managing, designing, preparing, and executing the tests.

- **Staffing and Training Needs:** How many people are required? What training they need?

- **Scheduling:** List of all the milestones with dates and when all the resources will be needed.

- **Risks and Contingencies:** What are the highest risk assumptions in the test plan? What can go sufficiently wrong to delay the schedule, and what can be done about it?

- **Approvals:** Who has to approve this plan? Provide space for their signatures.

Cangussu et al. [2] have studied a general testing process by using a state-variable-based model. By mathematically quantifying the effects of parameter variations on the behavior of a system test process, the system test manager can estimate the impact of parameter variation on the test schedule.

Several regression test selection techniques have been proposed by researchers to reduce software maintenance costs. The test selection techniques proposed for regression testing can be broadly classified into two categories based on the kinds of information they utilize to perform the task: *specification* based and *code* based. The following articles discuss the selection of regression tests utilizing information from specification and code.

J. Bible, G. Rothermel, and D. S. Rosenblum "A Comparative Study of Coarse- and Fine-Grained Safe Regression Test-Selection Techniques," *ACM Transactions on Software Engineering and Methodology (TOSEM)*, Vol. 10, No. 2, 2001, pp. 149–183.

D. Binkley, "Semantics Guided Regression Test Cost Reduction," *IEEE Transactions on Software Engineering*, Vol. 23, No. 8, August 1997, pp. 498–516.

T. L. Graves, M. J. Harrold, J. M. Kim, A. Porter, and G. Rothermel, "An Empirical Study of Regression Test Selection Techniques," *ACM Transactions on Software Engineering and Methodology (TOSEM)*, Vol. 10, No. 2, 2001, pp. 184–208.

G. Rothermel, S. Elbaum, A. G. Malishevsky, P. Kallakuri, and X. Qui, "On Test Suite Composition and Cost-Effective Regression Testing," *ACM Transactions on Software Engineering and Methodology (TOSEM)*, Vol. 13, No. 3, 2004, pp. 277–331.

G. Rothermel and M. J. Harrold, "Analyzing Regression Test Selection Techniques," *IEEE Transactions on Software Engineering*, Vol. 22, No. 8, August 1996, pp. 529–551.

G. Rothermel and M. J. Harrold, "Empirical Studies of a Safe Regression Test Selection Technique," *IEEE Transactions on Software Engineering*, Vol. 24, No. 6, June 1998, pp. 401–419.

In addition, several *code*-based techniques have been proposed by Rothermel, et al. [4] to prioritize regression tests by using information gathered from previous execution of test cases. Those techniques are fine grained in the sense that prioritization is done at the level of source code statements. Elbaum, et al. [5] have proposed 12 coarse-grained techniques for test prioritization at the function level for regression testing. They suggest that it may be desirable to change the priority of test cases from version to version. Test case prioritization and selection algorithms for regression testing with the goal of achieving modified condition/decision coverage have been studied by Jones and Harrold [6].

Computer-aided software engineering (CASE) tools are continuously evolving. Tool evaluation processes continue to evolve as the tools continue to mature and the technology advances. The following two articles give managers and tool evaluators a reliable way to identify tools that best fit their needs:

V. Mosley, "How to Assess Tools Efficiently and Quantitatively," *IEEE Software*, May 1992, pp. 29–32.

R. M. Poston and M. P. Sexton, "Evaluating and Selecting Testing Tools," *IEEE Software*, May 1992, pp. 33–42.

A voluminous survey of test automation tools can be found in Appendix B of the book by Dustin, et al. [18]. The book also outlines a number of excellent test automation tools to improve a testing process.

REFERENCES

1. P. Tripathy and K. Naik. A Multi-Cycle Based Execution Strategy for Software System Testing, TR:2007-L086. NEC Laboratories America Electronic TR/TN Distribution, Princeton, NJ, June 2007, pp. 1–45.
2. J. W. Cangussu, R. A. Decarlo, and A. P. Mathur. Using Sensitivity Analysis to Validate a State Variable Model of the Software Test Process. *IEEE Transactions on Software Engineering*, June 2003, pp. 430–443.
3. N. E. Fenton and M. Neil. A Critique of Software Defect Prediction Models. *IEEE Transactions on Software Engineering*, September/October 1999, pp. 675–689.
4. G. Rothermel, R. H. Untch, C. Chu, and M. J. Harrold. Prioritizing Test Cases for Regression Testing. *IEEE Transactions on Software Engineering*, October 2001, pp. 929–948.
5. S. Elbaum, A. G. Malishevsky, and G. Rothermel. Test Case Prioritization: A Family of Empirical Studies. *IEEE Transactions on Software Engineering*, February 2002, pp. 159–182.
6. J. A. Jones and M. J. Harrold. Test-Suite Reduction and Prioritization for Modified Condition/Decision Coverage. *IEEE Transactions on Software Engineering*, March 2003, pp. 195–209.

7. A. Srivastava and J. Thiagarajan. Effectively Prioritizing Tests in Development Environment. Paper presented at the International Symposium on Software Testing and Analysis (ISSTA), Roma, Italy, ACM Press, New York, 2002, pp. 97–106.

8. G. M. Kapfhammer. Automatically and Transparently Distributing the Execution of Regression Test Suites. Paper presented at the 18th International Conference on Testing Computer Software, 2001, pp. 1–16.

9. B. Littlewood and D. Wright. Some Conservative Stopping Rules for the Operational Testing of Safety-Critical Software. *IEEE Transactions on Software Engineering*, November 1997, pp. 673–683.

10. S. H. Kan, J. Parrish, and D. Manlove. In-Process Metrics for Software Testing. *IBM Systems Journal*, January 2001, pp. 220–241.

11. T. Yamaura. How to Design Practical Test Cases. *IEEE Software*, November/December 1998, pp. 30–36.

12. Y. Chernak. Validating and Improving Test-Case Effectiveness. *IEEE Software*, January/February 2001, pp. 81–86.

13. E. Yourdon. When Good Enough Software Is Best. *IEEE Software*, May 1995, pp. 79–81.

14. A. J. Albrecht. Measuring Application Development Productivity. Paper presented at the Process Joint SHARE/GUIDE/IBM Application Development Symposium, October 1979, pp. 34–43.

15. A. J. Albrecht and J. E Gaffney. Software Functions Source Lines Code and Development Efforts Prediction: A Software Science Validation. *IEEE Transactions on Software Engineering*, November 1983, pp. 639–648.

16. C. Jones. *Estimating Software Costs*. McGraw-Hill, New York, 1998.

17. C. Jones. *Applied Software Measurement*. McGraw-Hill, New York, 1996.

18. E. Dustin, J. Rashka, and J. Paul. *Automated Software Testing: Introduction, Management, and Performance*. Addison-Wesley, Reading, MA, 1999.

Exercises

1. What is the purpose of having a system test plan ready before the start of system test cycles?

2. What are some essential items a tester should include in a system test plan?

3. What are the advantages and disadvantages of having separate unit, integration, and system test plans as opposed to an inclusive test plan containing all three in the same document?

4. Study the test plan proposed in the IEEE standard 829 standard described in the literature review section of this chapter. What are the essential items not addressed in this test plan?

5. Why are multiple test environments set up for the execution of system-level test cases? Why should these test environments not be shared for software development activities?

6. What are the parameters of the multicycle system test execution strategy? What is the idea behind the parameterized system test cycle?

7. Why must the entry criteria be satisfied before the start of the first system test cycle?

8. What are the objectives of the first, second, and the third system test cycles?

9. If the test case failure rate is high, why does it slow down the test execution rate?

10. Develop a system test plan for your current test project.

11. What are the advantages and disadvantages of early test automation, that is, for the first release of a product?

12. What are the advantages and disadvantages of late test automation, that is, after the first release of the product?

13. Develop evaluation criteria for the selection of a defect tracking tool.

14. Evaluate the ClearQuest defect tracking system by getting a trial copy of the tool from IBM using the criteria developed for exercise 13.

15. What are the components of a test automation infrastructure? What is the role of a test automation framework administrator?

CHAPTER 13

System Test Execution

Execute every act of thy life as though it were thy last.
— *Marcus Aurelius*

13.1 BASIC IDEAS

Preparing for and executing system-level tests are a critical phase in a software development process because of the following: (i) There is pressure to meet a tight schedule close to the delivery date; (ii) there is a need to discover most of the defects before delivering the product; and (iii) it is essential to verify that defect fixes are working and have not resulted in new defects. It is important to monitor the processes of test execution and defect fixing. To be able to monitor those test processes, we identify two key categories of metrics: (i) *system test execution status* and (ii) *defects status*. We provide a detailed *defect schema*, which includes a general FSM model of defects for ease of collecting those metrics. Analyzing defects is a crucial activity performed by the software development team while fixing defects. Therefore, in this chapter, we describe three types of defect analysis techniques: *causal, orthogonal*, and *Pareto methodology*. In addition, we provide three metrics, namely, *defect removal efficiency, spoilage*, and *fault seeding*, to measure test effectiveness. The objective of a test effectiveness metric is to evaluate the effectiveness of a system testing effort in the development of a product in terms of the number of defects escaped from the system testing effort.

The product is ready for beta testing at the customer site during the system testing. We provide a framework for beta testing and discuss how beta testing is conducted at the customer's site. Moreover, we provide a detailed structure of the system test execution report, which is generated before a product's *general availability* is declared.

Software Testing and Quality Assurance: Theory and Practice, Edited by Kshirasagar Naik and Priyadarshi Tripathy
Copyright © 2008 John Wiley & Sons, Inc.

13.2 MODELING DEFECTS

The key to a successful defect tracking system lies in properly modeling defects to capture the viewpoints of their many stakeholders, called cross-functionality groups. The cross-functionality groups in an organization are those groups that have different stakes in a product. For example, a marketing group, a customer support group, a development group, a system test group, and a product sustaining group are collectively referred to as cross-functionality groups in an organization. It is not enough to merely report a defect from the viewpoint of software development and product management and seek to understand it by means of reproduction before fixing it. In reality, a reported defect is an evolving entity that can be appropriately represented by giving it a life-cycle model in the form of a state transition diagram, as shown in Figure 13.1. The states used in Figure 13.1 are briefly explained in Table 13.1.

The state transition model allows us to represent each phase in the life cycle of a defect by a distinct state. The model represents the life cycle of a defect from its initial reporting to its final closing through the following states: new, assigned, open, resolved, wait, FAD, hold, duplicate, shelved, irreproducible, postponed, and closed. When a defect moves to a new state, certain actions are taken by the owner of the state. By "owner" of a state of a defect we mean the person or group of people who are responsible for taking the required actions in that state. Once the associated actions are taken in a state, the defect is moved to a new state.

Two key concepts involved in modeling defects are the levels of *priority* and *severity*. On one hand, a priority level is a measure of how soon the defect needs to be fixed, that is, urgency. On the other hand, a severity level is a measure of the extent of the detrimental effect of the defect on the operation of the product. Therefore, priority and severity assignments are separately done. In the following, four levels of defect priority are explained:

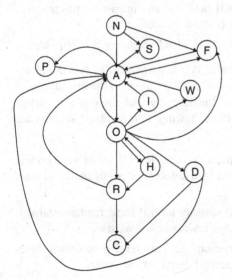

Figure 13.1 State transition diagram representation of life cycle of defect.

TABLE 13.1 States of Defect Modeled in Figure 13.1

State	Semantic	Description
N	New	A problem report with a severity level and a priority level is filed.
A	Assigned	The problem is assigned to an appropriate person.
O	Open	The assigned person is actively working on the problem to resolve it.
R	Resolved	The assigned person has resolved the problem and is waiting for the submitter to verify and close it.
C	Closed	The submitter has verified the resolution of the problem.
W	Watt	The assigned person is waiting for additional information from the submitter.
F	FAD	The reported defect is not a true defect. Rather, it is a function as designed.
H	Hold	The problem is on hold because this problem cannot be resolved until another problem is resolved.
S	Shelved	There is a problem in the system, but a conscious decision is taken that this will not be resolved in the near future. Only the development manager can move a defect to this state.
D	Duplicate	The problem reported is a duplicate of a problem that has already been reported.
I	Irreproducible	The problem reported cannot be reproduced by the assigned person.
P	Postponed	The problem will be resolved in a later release.

1. *Critical*: Defects at this level must be resolved as soon as possible. Testing should not progress until a known critical defect is fixed.

2. *High*: Defects at this level must be resolved with high priority. A subset of the system functionalities cannot be tested unless this level of defect is resolved.

3. *Medium*: Defects at this level will not have any impact on the progress of testing. Medium-priority defects stand by themselves.

4. *Low*: Defects at this level should be resolved whenever it is possible.

Intuitively, a critical-priority defect affects a large number of functionalities of a system, a high-priority defect affects a smaller subset of functionalities, a medium-priority defect affects an individual functionality, and a low-priority defect is considered to be a minor irritation. In the following, four levels of severity are explained:

1. *Critical*: A defect receives a "critical" severity level if one or more critical system functionalities are impaired by a defect with is impaired and there is no workaround.

2. *High*: A defect receives a "high" severity level if some fundamental system functionalities are impaired but a workaround exists.

3. *Medium*: A defect receives a "medium" severity level if no critical functionality is impaired and a workaround exists for the defect.

4. *Low*: A defect receives a "low" severity level if the problem involves a cosmetic feature of the system.

Intuitively, defects with high severity should receive a high priority in the resolution phase, but a situation may arise where a high-severity defect may be given a low priority. For example, let a system crash when the system date is set to December 32. Though a crash defect has severe consequences, an occurrence of December 32 as the system date is unlikely in normal circumstances. The said defect receives a critical severity but a low priority. In other words, if a critically severe defect occurs with an extremely low probability, then it may not be fixed immediately, that is, it may be treated with low priority.

Someone reporting a defect makes a preliminary assessment of the severity and priority levels of the defect. If there is a dispute among the different cross-functional groups concerning the priority and severity levels of a defect, an agreement can be reached in a regular review meeting. Note that the severity of a defect remains the same throughout its life cycle, whereas the priority level may change as the software product approaches its release date. A defect may be assigned a low priority at the beginning of system testing if it may not have any impact on the progress of testing, but it must be fixed before the software is released. For example, a spelling mistake in the GUI may be a low-priority defect at the beginning of system testing but its priority becomes high as the release date approaches.

In the following, we describe the states of a defect modeled as a state transition diagram, as shown in Figure 13.1, and explain how a defect moves from state to state. When a new defect is found, it is recorded in a defect tracking system, and the defect is put in its initial state new. The owner of this state is the software development manager. In this state, the following fields, explained as parts of a schema given in Table 13.2, are initialized: defect_id, submit_date, product, submitter, group, owner, headline, keywords, severity, priority, reproducible, category, software_version, build, description, h/w_configuration, s/w_configuration, attachments, notes, and number_tc_fail, tc_id.

The software development manger, who is the owner of the new state, moves the defect from the new state to the assigned state by changing the ownership either to a software developer or to himself. The software development manager may reject this defect by explaining why it is not a true defect and move the defect to the FAD state with a change in ownership back to the submitter. The development manager may change the state to the shelved state, which means that it is a true defect and a conscious decision has been made to the effect that this defect will not be fixed in the near future. All the relevant parties, especially the customer support group of the organization, must agree to shelve the defect before a defect is moved to the shelved state. There are several reasons to move a defect to the shelved state. For example, a defect may not have much impact on system operation in the customer's operational environment, and it may consume a lot of resources to fix it. In practice, very few defects land in the shelved state.

The assigned state means that someone has been assigned to fix the defect but the actual work required to fix the defect has not begun. The software development

TABLE 13.2 Defect Schema Summary Fields

Field Name	Description
defect_id	A unique, internally generated identifier for the defect
state	Current state of the defect; takes a value from the set {New, Assigned, Open, Resolved, Information, FAD, Hold, Duplicate, Shelved, Irreproducible, Postponed, Closed}
headline	One-line summary of defect
severity	Severity level of defect; takes a value from the set {critical, high, medium, low}
priority	Priority level of defect; takes a value from the set {critical, high, medium low}
submitter	Name of the person who submits the defect
group	Group affiliation of submitter; takes a value from the set {ST, SIT, software, hardware, customer support}
owner	Current owner of defect
reproducible	Says, in terms of yes or no, whether or not defect can be reproduced
crash	Says, in terms of yes or no, whether or not defect causes system to crash
keywords	Some common words that can be associated with this defect for searching purpose
product	Name of product in which defect was found
category	Test category name that revealed defect
software_version	Software version number in which defect was observed
build	Build number in which defect was observed
submit_date	Date of submission of defect
description	Brief description of defect
h/w_configuration	Description of hardware configuration of test bed
s/w_configuration	Description of software configuration of test bed
attachments	Attachments, in the form of log files, configuration files, etc., useful in understanding the defect
notes	Additional notes or comments, if there are any
number_tc_fail	Number of test cases failed or blocked because of defect
tc_id	List of test case identifiers of those test cases, from test factory database, which will fail because of defect
forecast_fix_version	Software version in which fix for defect will be available
forecast_build_number	Build number in which fix for defect will be available
actual_fix_version	Software version in which fix is actually available
actual_build_number	Build number in which fix is actually available
fix_description	Brief description of fix for defect
fix_date	Date when fix was checked in to code
duplicate_defect_id	Present defect considered to be duplicate of duplicate defect_id
requirement_id	Requirement identifier from requirement database that is generated as result of agreement that defect be turned into requirement

manager, or a developer, is the owner of the defect in the assigned state. The ownership may change to a different software developer who will fix the defect. The assigned software developer may move the defect from the assigned state to the open state as soon as the process of defect fixing begins. Note that only the software development manager moves a defect from the assigned state to one the following states: shelved, postponed, and FAD. The ownership is changed to the submitter when a defect is moved to the FAD state.

A software developer, the owner of the defect, is actively working to fix the defect in the open state. The developer initializes the forecast_fix_version and forecast_build_number fields of the defect schema given in Table 13.2 so that the submitter can plan and schedule a retest of the fix. A defect may lie in the open state for several weeks. The software developer moves the defect from this state to five possible next states—irreproducible, resolved, wait, hold, and duplicate—which are explained in Table 13.3 along with the actions that need to be taken when the state is changed.

If a software developer working on a defect is satisfied that the defect has been fixed, he or she moves the defect to a resolved state and changes the ownership

TABLE 13.3   State Transitions to Five Possible Next States from Open State

Possible *Next* State	Actions
Irreproducible	If the owner, i.e., a developer, cannot reproduce a defect, the defect is moved to irreproducible state with the ownership changed back to the submitter.
Wait	If the amount of information given by the submitter is not enough to understand and/or reproduce the defect, then the owner asks for more information on the defect from the submitter. Essentially, the developer is asking for more information about the defect in the notes field. The ownership field is changed back to the submitter.
Resolved	1. The ownership field is changed back to the submitter.
	2. The following fields need to be filled out:
	3. Actual_fix_version: Software version where the fix is available
	4. Actual_build_number: Build number where the fix is available.
	5. Fixed_description: Brief description of the fix. The developer must list all the files that are modified and what has been changed in the files in order to fix the problem.
	6. Fixed_date: Date the defect was fixed on and moved to the resolved state.
Hold	It has to be explained in the notes field why the defect was moved to this state. The hold state means that no firm decision has been made regarding the defect because the problem depends on some other issues, such as a software defect in a third-party product. Unless the other issues are resolved, the problem described in the defect report cannot be resolved.
Duplicate	If this defect is identical to, i.e., a duplicate of another defect, then the identifier of the original defect is recorded in the duplicate_defect_id field.

of the defect back to the submitter. A defect in the resolved state merely implies that the defect has been fixed to the satisfaction of the developer, and the associated tests need to be executed to further verify the claim in a wider context. The submitter moves the defect from the resolved state to the closed state by initializing the following fields of the defect schema after it is verified that the defect has been fixed: verifier, closed_in_version, closed_in_build, closed_date, and verification_description. Essentially, verification_description describes the details of the verification procedure. The closed state signifies that the defect has been resolved and verified. On the other hand, if the verifier is convinced that the defect has not been actually or completely fixed, the fix is rejected by moving the defect back to the assigned state, and the ownership of the defect is changed back to the responsible software developer. The verifier provides the following information while rejecting a fix:

- Explanation for rejection of fix
- Any new observation and/or problem encountered

A defect is moved to the FAD state by the development team if the team concludes that it is not a true defect and the system behaves as expected. The submitter, the owner of the defect in the FAD state, may involve the development team, the customer support group, the product management, and the project leadear to review defects in this state. There are three possible alternative outcomes of a defect review meeting:

- The reporting of the defect was due to a procedural error on the part of the submitter. The defect remains in the FAD state for this outcome. The idea behind keeping the defect in the FAD state, and not in the closed state, is to record the fact that the submitter had designated it as a defect.
- The reported defect is a true defect. The defect is moved to the assigned state with a note for the software development manager saying that this is a defect agreed to by all the parties.
- A suggestion is made that a new feature enhancement request be made to accommodate the system behavior perceived to be a "defect" at this moment. The submitter moves the defect to the assigned state with a note for the development manager saying that the defect may be resolved by creating a new requirement and submitting the requirement identifier in the requirement_id field of the defect schema.

If a defect cannot be fixed in a particular release, it is moved to the postponed state, where the development manager is the owner of the defect. Fixing a defect is postponed due to lack of time to fix it for a certain release. The defect is moved, after the release for its fix is known, to the assigned state, where the following fields of the defect schema are initialized: (i) forecast_build_number—the build in which a fix will be available for testing—and (ii) forecast_fix_version—the version in which a fix will be available.

All the outstanding defects that are still open are moved to the postponed state after the product is released to the customer, so that the defects can be scheduled to be fixed in future software releases. The defects are moved to the assigned state after it is finalized in which release these defects will be fixed. The postponed state is useful in tracking and scheduling all the outstanding defects in the system that must be fixed in future releases.

If a developer finds that the information provided by the submitter is not adequate to fix a defect, the developer asks for additional information from the submitter by moving the defect from the open state to the wait state. In the wait state, the submitter is the owner of the defect. The submitter provides the information asked for by the developer by initializing the notes field of the defect schema, moves the defect to the assigned state, and changes the ownership back to the software developer.

The developer may try to reproduce the symptom to understand the defect. If the developer cannot reproduce the reported symptom, the defect is moved to the irreproducible state with the ownership changed back to the submitter. The submitter makes an effort to reproduce the defect, collect all the relevant information into the defect report, and move the defect to the assigned state if the defect is reproduced. If the submitter cannot reproduce the defect, the defect stays in the irreproducible state.

It may be observed that the defect is caused by an extraneous factor, such as a defect in a third-party product which is being used. The reported defect cannot be fixed unless the defect in the outside component is resolved. In such a case, the defect is put on hold by moving it to the hold state, where the software development manager is the owner of the defect. The software development manager moves the defect to either the resolved state or the open state depending on if the primary defect in the outside component has been resolved or is being fixed, respectively.

A defect in the duplicate state, where the submitter is the owner, means that the problem is a duplicate of a defect reported earlier. The original defect identifier is used to initialize the schema field duplicate_defect_id. Once the duplicate defect is in the closed state, the submitter must verify this defect. If the verification is successful, the submitter moves the defect to the closed state. On the other hand, if the verification fails, the submitter rejects the duplicity claim by moving the defect back to the assigned state, where the software developer is the owner of the defect. The verifier must give a reason for rejecting a defect as a duplicate defect. This information contains any observation and/or problem encountered while verifying the defect.

13.3   PREPAREDNESS TO START SYSTEM TESTING

The status of the entry criteria outlined in Chapter 13 must be tracked at least four weeks before the start of the first system test cycle. Any exceptions to these criteria must be noted and discussed at the weekly project status review meeting. We discuss the last item of the entry criteria, namely that the test execution working document is in place and complete. A framework of such a document is outlined in Table 13.4 and is explained subsequently. This working document is created, controlled, and tracked by the test team leader.

TABLE 13.4 Outline of Test Execution Working Document

1. Test engineers
2. Test cases allocation
3. Test beds allocation
4. Automation progress
5. Projected test execution rate
6. Execution of failed test cases
7. Development of new test cases
8. Trial of system image
9. Schedule of defect review meeting

The test engineers section contains the names of the test engineers assigned to this project as well as their availability and expertise in the specific areas of the project. The training requirement for each team members that may be necessary to successfully execute the test project is noted in detail. The action plan and training progress for each team member are tracked in this section. Any issue related to human resource availability or training is referred to the software project lead.

The test cases are allocated among test engineers based on their expertise and interest after the test suite is created in the test factory. The software development engineers and system test engineers are identified and included in the sw_dev and tester fields of the test cases, respectively. The idea here is to give the ownership of the test case execution to the individual test engineers. A test engineer reviews the test cases allocated to him or her to understand them and prioritize them in consultation with the software developers. Priority of a test case is set to one of the values from the set {high, medium, low}. If necessary, a test engineer may update the test cases to fine tune the test procedures and the pass–fail criteria as discussed in Section 11.6. The activities of prioritization and allocation of test cases among engineers and software developers are tracked in the test case allocation section, and this must be completed before the start of the system test cycle. This is achieved by calling several meetings with the team members of the software project.

The test beds allocation section of the document states the availability of the number and kinds of test beds and the ways these test beds are distributed so that the test cases are executed concurrently. A mapping is established between the available test beds and the subgroups of test cases from the test suite. The mapping is based on the configuration requirements to execute the groups of test cases. The test engineer responsible for executing a subgroup of test cases is then assigned to that test bed. The test engineer owns that particular test bed and must ensure that the test bed is up and ready to go before the start of system test cycles. Precaution must be taken to ensure that each test engineer is allocated the same test bed throughout the entire test execution cycle. The idea here is to maximize the execution efficiency of the engineer. If necessary, new test beds are created, or allocated from other projects, so that the idle time is minimized.

In the automation progress section of the document, a table is created to track the progress of the automation of the test cases and the availability of those automated test cases for execution. This is of particular interest in the case of regression test cases that were developed earlier and executed manually, but their automation is in progress. The test team leader interacts with the responsible test automation engineers to gather the information on the test automation progress. In case the automated test cases are available on time, that is, before the start of the test cycle, then the scheduled manual execution of these test cases may be skipped. Instead, the automated test cases can be executed.

In the projected test execution rate section of the document, a table is created to show the number of test cases that are anticipated to be executed on a weekly basis during a test cycle. The projected number of test cases is tracked against the actual execution of test cases during the test cycle. As an example, let us consider a test project name, Bazooka, for which the total number of test cases selected is 1592. The projected execution of 1592 test cases on a weekly basis for a 14-week test cycle is shown in Table 13.2 in the form of a cumulative chart. The execution of the 1592 test cases is expected to take 14 weeks; 25 test cases will be executed in the first week; 75 test cases will be executed in the second week; thus, 100 test cases will executed by the end of the second week. As the execution proceeds, the second row of Figure 13.2, namely, actually executed test cases, is updated. This gives the test group an idea of the progress of the testing. If the number of actually executed test cases falls far behind the projected number for several weeks, the test manager will know that the project is going to be delayed.

A strategy for the execution of failed test cases and verification of defect fixes is outlined in the execution of failed test cases section of the document. There are two possibilities here: (i) The failed test cases are executed in the next test cycle and (ii) the failed test cases are executed in the current cycle as soon

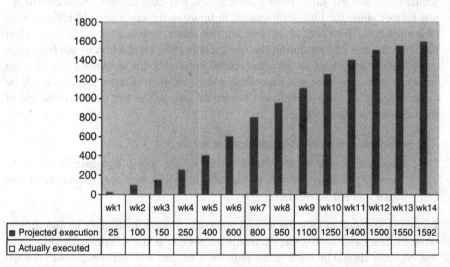

	wk1	wk2	wk3	wk4	wk5	wk6	wk7	wk8	wk9	wk10	wk11	wk12	wk13	wk14
■ Projected execution	25	100	150	250	400	600	800	950	1100	1250	1400	1500	1550	1592
□ Actually executed														

Figure 13.2   Projected execution of test cases on weekly basis in cumulative chart form.

as the corresponding fixes are available. In the first case, all the fixes, which are already integrated into the system, are subject to a regression test. No fixes are inserted into the system midway through a test cycle which are available at the beginning of a test cycle. In the second scenario, the fixes are checked in to the version control system, and a new build is created. The build is then sanity tested by the system integration group, and then it is released to the system testing group to be retested by running the test cases which failed earlier. If a test case now passes, then the fix has been verified to have resolved the defect. However, any collateral damage may not have been detected. A fix causing collateral damage is called a "bad fix," A handful of passed test cases around the fix may be reexecuted after a previously failed test case is observed to have passed irrespective of a fix that has caused collateral damage. The idea is to identify the high-impact region of the fix, select a set of previously passed test cases in consultation with the software developer who fixed the defect, and then execute those tests as a regression test. The following information is collected and analyzed in selecting the regression test cases:

- Parts of the software modules that were modified in order to incorporate the fix
- Functionality areas that are closely related to the fix and susceptible to defects
- Kinds of defects likely to be introduced because of the fix

Based on the above information, existing or new test cases are selected that are most likely to uncover any possible new defects that might have been introduced.

The test engineers learn more about the system and are in a better position to develop additional test cases during the first test cycle of testing. This is in particular important when a repeatable problem is observed and there are no test scenarios in the test suite. In this case, a new test case needs to be added to the test factory since the long-term goal is to improve the coverage and effectiveness of the test suite. However, a decision must be made regarding the addition of a test case into the test factory during the test cycle or after completion of the test cycle.

The development of new test cases section of the document clarifies the strategy for writing new test cases during the execution of test cases. It should be communicated to the test engineers before the start of the test cycle so that one of the following actions is taken:

- Develop new test cases during the test cycle.
- Include a note in the defect report saying that a test case needs to be developed later for this defect and continue with the execution of test cases as per schedule.

It is recommended to take the second approach, since it is difficult to find time to write the test cases during test execution unless it is in the schedule. Therefore, the test engineer should go back to the individual defects and add test cases to the test factory based on the defect report after completion of the test cycle.

Quite often the test engineers download a software image from the system integration group to their allocated test beds at least two or three weeks prior to the official start of the first test cycle. This allows the test engineer to be familiar with the software image and to ensure that the test bed is fully operational. This activity is tracked for each system test engineer in the trial of system image section of the working document, even though the build is not officially released to start system testing. There are several advantages of using the trial software image before the official start date of the system test cycle:

- The test engineers are trained to become familiar with the system so that test execution productivity is higher during the system test cycle.
- To ensure that the test bed is operational without any downtime at the beginning of the system test cycle.
- The basic test cases can be executed earlier to validate the test steps.

A schedule of the defect review meeting must be in place before the start of the system test cycle. The schedule is established for the entire test cycle duration before the start of the system test. The test leader may use a Gantt chart to represent a schedule and include it in the schedule the defect review meeting section of the test execution working document. The cross-functional team members from software development, hardware development, and the customer support groups are invited to this meeting.

13.4 METRICS FOR TRACKING SYSTEM TEST

The system test execution brings forth (three) different facets of software development. The developers would like to know the degree to which the system meets the explicit as well as implicit requirements. The delivery date cannot be precisely predicted due to the uncertainty in fixing the problems. The customer is excited to take the delivery of the product. It is therefore a highly visible and exciting activity. At this stage, it is desirable to monitor certain metrics which truly represent the progress of system testing and reveal the quality level of the system. Based on those metrics, the management can trigger actions for corrective and preventive measures. By putting a small but critical set of metrics in place executive management is in a position to know whether they are on the right track [1]. We make a difference between *statistics* and *in-process* metrics: Statistics are used for postproject analysis to gather experience and use it in future projects, whereas in-process metrics let us monitor the progress of the project while we still have an opportunity to steer the course of the project. By considering three large, real-life test projects, we categorize execution metrics into two classes:

- For monitoring test execution
- For monitoring defects

The first class of metrics concerns the process of executing test cases, whereas the second class concerns the defects found as a result of test execution. These metrics need to be tracked and analyzed on a periodic basis, say, daily or weekly. It is important to gather valid and accurate information about the project for the leader of a system test group to effectively control a test project. One example of effective control of a test project is to precisely determine the time to trigger the revert criteria for a test cycle and initiate root cause analysis of the problems before more tests are performed. A test manager can effectively utilize the time of test engineers by triggering such a revert criterion, and possibly money, by suspending a test cycle on a product with too many defects to carry out a meaningful system test. Therefore, our objective is to identify and monitor the metrics while system testing is in progress so that the nimble decisions can be taken by the management team [2].

13.4.1 Metrics for Monitoring Test Execution

It is desirable to monitor the execution of system test cases of a large project involving tens of test engineers and taking several months. The system test execution for large projects is monitored weekly in the beginning and daily toward the finish. It is strongly recommended to use automated tools, such as a test factory, for monitoring and reporting the test case execution status. Different kinds of queries can be generated to obtain the *in-process* metrics after a database is in place. The following metrics are useful in successfully tracking test projects:

- **Test Case Escapes (TCE):** The test engineers may find the need to design new test cases during the testing, called test case escapes, as testing continues. The number of test case escapes is monitored as it rises. A significant increase in the number of test case escapes implies the deficiencies in the test design process, and this may adversely affect the project schedule.

- **Planned versus Actual Execution (PAE) Rate:** The actual number of test cases executed every week is compared with the planned number of test cases [3]. This metric is useful in representing the productivity of the test team in executing test cases. If the actual rate of execution falls far short of the planned rate, managers may have to take preventive measures so that the time required for system testing does not adversely affect the project schedule.

- **Execution Status of Test (EST) Cases:** It is useful to periodically monitor the number of test cases lying in different states—failed, passed, blocked, invalid, and untested—after their execution. It is also useful to further subdivide those numbers by test categories, such as basic, functionality, and robustness.

13.4.2 Test Execution Metric Examples

We give examples of test case execution metrics from a real-life test project called Bazooka. A total of 1592 test cases were designed to be executed. The projected execution of the 1592 test cases on a weekly basis for a 14-week test cycle is shown

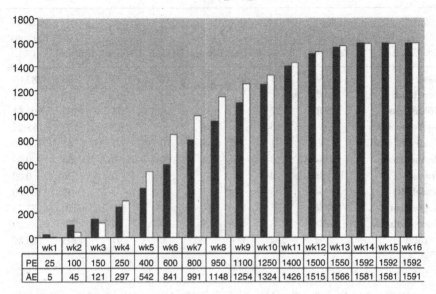

	wk1	wk2	wk3	wk4	wk5	wk6	wk7	wk8	wk9	wk10	wk11	wk12	wk13	wk14	wk15	wk16
PE	25	100	150	250	400	600	800	950	1100	1250	1400	1500	1550	1592	1592	1592
AE	5	45	121	297	542	841	991	1148	1254	1324	1426	1515	1566	1581	1581	1591

Figure 13.3   PAE metric of Bazooka (PE: projected execution; AE: actually executed) project.

in Figure 13.3 in the form of a cumulative bar chart for the PAE metric. Twenty-five test cases are planned to be executed in the first week, 75 in the second week. A total of 100 test cases are planned to be executed by the end of first 2 weeks. The second row at the bottom of Figure 13.3, those actually executed, is updated. One should monitor the numbers of projected and actually executed test cases on a weekly basis during the execution cycles. If there is a large difference between the two, immediate action can be taken to understand its root cause and improve the execution rate before it is too late. The test execution rate was lower than the planned rate, as shown in the table, for the first 3 weeks. It took approximately 3 weeks for the test engineers to understand the whole system and come up to speed. The test project took 16 weeks, instead of the planned 14, to complete one execution cycle for all the test cases, including reexecution of all the failed ones. Initially, the test engineers did not run the test cases for the stress, load, and stability categories because some of the fixes concerning memory leak were checked in only at the end of week 13. Therefore, the test cycle was extended for 2 more weeks to ensure that the system could stay up without any memory leaks for an extended period of time.

Let us consider our previous example, the Bazooka test project, for which we had selected 1592 test cases. The EST metric that we monitor on a weekly basis for each test group concerns the number of test cases in the following states: passed, failed, invalid, blocked, and untested. As an example, the test execution status of week 4 is shown in Table 13.5.

TABLE 13.5   EST Metric in Week 4 of Bazooka Project

Test Groups	Total Number of Test Cases	Passed	Failed	Blocked	Invalid	Executed	Untested	Passed/ Executed (%)
Basic	156	64	9	0	0	73	83	87.67
Functionality	480	56	7	0	0	63	417	88.89
Robustness	230	22	1	0	0	23	207	95.65
Interoperability	149	15	2	0	0	17	132	88.24
Load and stability	43	1	0	0	0	1	42	100.00
Performance	54	0	0	0	0	0	54	0.00
Stress	36	0	0	0	0	0	36	0.00
Scalability	54	5	0	0	0	5	49	100.00
Regression	356	93	13	0	0	106	250	87.74
Documentation	34	8	1	0	0	9	25	88.89
Total	1592	264	33	0	0	297	1295	88.89

We explain how the Bazooka team controlled the progress of system testing. A revert criterion for a test cycle is a predicate on the quality level of a product in terms of percentage of executed test cases that have passed. If such a criterion holds, the test cycle is suspended. An example of a revert criteria is: *At any instant during the test cycle, if the cumulative failure rate reaches 20%, the cycle will restart all over after the reported defects are claimed to have been fixed*. We show the percentage of executed test cases that have passed in the rightmost column of Table 13.6. The pass rate was 71.11% at the end of the second week of Bazooka, which implies that the failed rate was 28.89%. Considering the example revert criteria given above, the test cycle should have been abandoned. However, as a special case, the Bazooka project management team made a decision not to abandon the test cycle for the following reasons:

- Only 45 out of 1592 test cases had been executed.
- Some of the test cases were considered to have failed due to procedural errors on the part of test engineers; these test cases were eventually considered to have passed.

A unanimous decision was made by the Bazooka team to wait for one more week and to monitor the test results on a daily basis. The pass rate went up to 89.26% by the end of the third week, as shown in Table 13.6. Since the failure rate was well below the 20% threshold for the revert criteria to be activated, the test cycle was continued until its completion.

The above example tells us that it is important to analyze the test metrics, rather than take decisions based on the raw data. It is interesting to note that the highest cumulative failure rate of 19.5% was observed in week 6, and 841 test cases—or 52% of the total number of test cases to be executed—were already executed. The system test cycle would have been abandoned with an increase of

TABLE 13.6   EST Metric in Bazooka Monitored on Weekly Basis

Week	Executed	Passed	Failed	Executed/ Total (%)	Passed/ Total (%)	Passed/ Executed (%)
1	5	5	0	0.31	0.31	100.00
2	45	32	13	2.83	2.01	71.11
3	121	108	13	7.60	6.78	89.26
4	297	264	33	18.66	16.58	88.89
5	542	451	91	34.05	28.33	83.21
6	841	677	164	52.83	42.53	80.50
7	991	835	156	62.25	52.45	84.26
8	1148	1009	139	72.11	63.38	87.89
9	1254	1096	158	78.77	68.84	87.40
10	1324	1214	110	83.17	76.26	91.69
11	1426	1342	84	89.57	84.30	94.11
12	1515	1450	65	95.16	91.08	95.71
13	1566	1519	47	98.37	95.41	97.00
14	1581	1567	14	99.31	98.43	99.11
15	1581	1570	11	99.31	98.62	99.30
16	1591	1580	11	99.94	99.25	99.31

Note: Total valid test cases 1592.

just 0.5% in the failure rate. Test cases concerning the most vulnerable areas of the system were executed on a priority basis in the beginning of the cycle. Therefore, a maximum number of 164 test cases failed within the first 6 weeks of testing. New images with fixes were released for system testing after the week 6. The failed test cases were reexecuted, and the system passed those tests, thus improving the pass rate, as shown in the rightmost column of Table 13.6. Only one test case from the stress group was still in the untested state by the end of week 16.

13.4.3   Metrics for Monitoring Defect Reports

Queries can be developed to obtain various kinds of information from the database after a defect tracking system is put in place. As the system test engineers submit defects, the defects are further analyzed. Useful data can be gathered from the analysis process to quantify the quality level of the product in the form of the following metrics:

- **Function as Designed (FAD) Count:** Often test engineers report defects which are not really true defects because of a misunderstanding of the system, called FADs. If the number of defects in the FAD state exceeds, say, 10% of the submitted defects, we infer that the test engineers have an inadequate understanding of the system. The lower the FAD count, the higher the level of system understanding of the test engineers.

- **Irreproducible Defects (IRD) Count:** One must be able to reproduce the corresponding failure after a defect is reported so that developers can understand the failure to be able to fix it. If a defect cannot be reproduced, then the developers may not be able to gain useful insight into the cause of the failure. Irreproducibility of a defect does not mean that the defect can be overlooked. It simply means that the defect is an intricate one and it is very difficult to fix it. The number of defects in the irreproducible state, or hidden-defect count, is a measure of the unreliability of the system.

- **Defects Arrival Rate (DAR) Count:** Defect reports arrive from different sources during system testing: system testing group (ST), software development group (SW), SIT group, and others with their own objectives in mind. The "others" group includes customer support, marketing, and documentation groups. Defects reported by all these groups are gathered and the percentage of defects reported by each group on a weekly basis computed. This is called the rate of defects reported by each group.

- **Defects Rejected Rate (DRR) Count:** The software development team makes an attempt to fix the reported defects by modifying the existing code and/or writing more code. A new software image is available for further system testing after these defects are fixed. The system testing group verifies that the defects have been actually fixed by rerunning the appropriate tests. At this stage the system testing team may observe that some of the supposedly fixed defects have not actually been fixed. Such defects are used to produce the DRR count. The DRR count represents the extent to which the development team has been successful in fixing defects. It also tells us about the productivity of the software development team in fixing defects. A high DRR count for a number of weeks should raise an alert because of the high possibility of the project slipping out of schedule.

- **Defects Closed Rate (DCR) Count:** The system testing group verifies the resolution by further testing after a defect is claimed to be resolved. The DCR metric represents the efficiency of verifying the claims of defect fixes.

- **Outstanding Defects (OD) Count:** A reported defect is said to be an outstanding defect if the defect continues to exist. This metric reflects the prevailing quality level of the system as system testing continues. A diminishing OD count over individual test cycles is an evidence of the increasingly higher level of quality achieved during the system testing of a product.

- **Crash Defects (CD) Count:** The defects causing a system to crash must be recognized as an important category of defects because a system crash is a serious event leading to complete unavailability of the system and possibly loss of data [4]. This metric, generally known as a stability metric, is very useful in determining whether to release the system with its current level of stability.

- **Arrival and Resolution of Defects (ARD) Count:** It is useful to compare the rate of defects found with the rate of their resolution [5]. Defect resolution involves rework cost which should be minimized by doing the first time development work in a better way. Hence, this metric is useful for the development team and helps them to estimate the time it may take to fix all the defects. Actions are taken to expedite the defect resolution process based on this information.

13.4.4 Defect Report Metric Examples

We give examples for most of the above metrics by using data from a second test project called Stinger. The weekly DAR from each group of the organization performing system-level testing in the second test cycle of execution for 16 weeks is shown in Table 13.7. The total remaining open defects from the first test cycle are given in the first row of the table as week 0. The average number of defects filed per week by ST, SW, SIT, and others are 57, 15, 10, and 18, respectively. Here, the term "others" includes members from customer support, marketing, and documentation groups. The arrival rates of the defects in the first 6 weeks are much higher than the rest of the test cycle. This is due to the fact that early in the test cycle test cases are prioritized to flush out defects in the more vulnerable portions of the system.

The DRR count for the Stinger project is shown in Table 13.8. The average rate of defect rejection was 5.24%. The rejected rate was almost 6% during the

TABLE 13.7 DAR Metric for Stinger Project

Week	ST Number of Defects	ST Percentage	SW Number of Defects	SW Percentage	SIT Number of Defects	SIT Percentage	Others Number of Defects	Others Percentage	Total Number of Defects
0	663	69.21	172	17.95	88	9.19	35	3.65	958
1	120	79.47	28	18.54	2	1.32	1	0.66	151
2	99	55.00	44	24.44	31	17.22	6	3.33	180
3	108	53.73	54	26.87	31	15.42	8	3.98	201
4	101	65.16	16	10.32	22	14.19	16	10.32	155
5	107	57.22	21	11.23	26	13.90	33	17.65	187
6	108	56.25	16	8.33	35	18.23	33	17.19	192
7	59	57.84	0	0.00	1	0.98	42	41.18	102
8	15	31.91	9	19.15	3	6.38	20	42.55	47
9	28	59.57	0	0.00	1	2.13	18	38.30	47
10	14	50.00	4	14.29	0	0.00	10	35.71	28
11	12	48.00	1	4.00	0	0.00	12	48.00	25
12	59	53.64	5	4.55	9	8.18	37	33.64	110
13	28	54.90	5	9.80	0	0.00	18	35.29	51
14	23	51.11	0	0.00	0	0.00	22	48.89	45
15	12	31.58	21	55.26	3	7.89	2	5.26	38
16	24	38.71	23	37.10	0	0.00	15	24.19	62
Sum	917		247		164		293		1,621
Avearge	57	56.57	15	15.24	10	10.12	18	18.08	

TABLE 13.8 Weekly DRR Status for Stinger Test Project

Week	Number of Defects Verified	Number of Defects Closed	Number of Defects Rejected	Defects Rejected (%)
1	283	269	14	4.95
2	231	216	15	6.49
3	266	251	15	5.64
4	304	284	20	6.58
5	194	183	11	5.67
6	165	156	9	5.45
7	145	136	9	6.21
8	131	122	9	6.87
9	276	262	14	5.07
10	160	152	8	5.00
11	52	49	3	5.77
12	80	74	6	7.50
13	71	71	0	0.00
14	60	58	2	3.33
15	121	119	2	1.65
16	97	96	1	1.03
Sum	2636	2498	138	
Avearge	165	156	9	5.24

first 8 weeks, and for the next 4 weeks it was about 5%. For the remainder of the test cycle, the rejection rate dropped near 1.5%.

The OD counts are given in Table 13.9. Critical-, high-, medium-, and low-priority defects are denoted by P1, P2, P3, and P4, respectively. The *priority* level is a measure of how soon the defects are to be fixed. The outstanding defect counts carried forward from the first test cycle into the second cycle are given in the first row of the table as week 0 statistics. It is evident from this metric that the total number of outstanding defects gradually diminished from 958 to 81 within 16 weeks.

The number of crashes observed by different groups during the final 8 weeks of testing is shown in Table 13.10. It is evident from the table that the total number of crashes gradually diminished from 20 per week to 1 per week. One has to give these crashes a closer look to determine the root cause of each of the individual crashes. The development team must investigate these crashes individually.

Finally, we give an example of the ARD metric by considering a third test project called Bayonet. The projected number of defects submitted, resolved, and remaining open in the first four weeks of a test cycle are given in the upper half of Table 13.11. The projected numbers were derived from an earlier test project [6] that had very similar characteristics to Bayonet. At the start of the test cycle, the total number of open defects is 184. Out of these 184 defects, 50 defects are either of P1 or of P2 priority level, 63 defects are of level P3, and 71 defects are of

TABLE 13.9   Weekly OD on Priority Basis for Stinger Test Project

	P1		P1		P3		P4		Total
Week	Number of Defects	Percentage	Number of Defects	Percentage	Number of Defects	Percentage	Number of Defects	Percentage	Number of Defects
0	14	1.46	215	22.44	399	41.65	330	34.45	958
1	19	2.26	164	19.52	280	33.33	377	44.88	840
2	17	2.11	138	17.16	236	29.35	413	51.37	804
3	11	1.46	108	14.32	181	24.01	454	60.21	754
4	7	1.12	44	7.04	123	19.68	451	72.16	625
5	5	0.79	28	4.45	123	19.55	473	75.20	629
6	10	1.50	33	4.96	123	18.50	499	75.04	665
7	11	1.74	83	13.15	52	8.24	485	76.86	631
8	5	0.90	34	6.12	32	5.76	485	87.23	556
9	8	2.35	21	6.16	39	11.44	273	80.06	341
10	4	1.84	21	9.68	36	16.59	156	71.89	217
11	4	2.07	26	13.47	38	19.69	125	64.77	193
12	3	1.31	28	12.23	84	36.68	114	49.78	229
13	3	1.44	40	19.14	84	40.19	82	39.23	209
14	10	5.10	42	21.43	68	34.69	76	38.78	196
15	2	1.74	34	29.57	38	33.04	41	35.65	115
16	3	3.70	25	30.86	24	29.63	29	35.80	81

TABLE 13.10   Weekly CD Observed by Different Groups for Stinger Test Project

	S/W		ST		SIT		Others		Total
Week	Number of Defects	Percentage	Number of Defects	Percentage	Number of Defects	Percentage	Number of Defects	Percentage	Number of Crashes
9	6	30.00	8	40.00	6	30.00	0	0.00	20
10	5	31.25	6	37.50	3	18.75	2	12.50	16
11	4	25.00	9	56.25	0	0.00	3	18.75	16
12	3	33.33	4	44.44	0	0.00	2	22.22	9
13	2	22.22	6	66.67	0	0.00	1	11.11	9
14	1	14.29	2	28.57	1	14.29	3	42.86	7
15	0	0.00	2	66.67	1	33.33	0	0.00	3
16	0	0.00	1	100.00	0	0.00	0	0.00	1
Sum	21		38		11		11		81
Average	3	25.93	5	46.91	1	13.58	1	13.58	10

level P4. The actual numbers of submitted and resolved defects are shown in the lower half of the same table. The actual numbers of open defects are slightly lower than the projected numbers after the completion of the first week. However, the actual number of resolved defects is much lower than the projected number in the second week. This suggests that the software developers were slower in resolving the defects. The total number of open defects at the end of the second week is higher than the estimated number. At this stage the software development manager must take actions to improve the defect resolution rate by either increasing the working hours or moving software developers from another project to Bayonet. In

TABLE 13.11 ARD Metric for *Bayonet*

		Submitted				Resolved				Open			
Week	Build	Total	P1+P2	P3	P4	Total	P1+P2	P3	P4	Total	P1+P2	P3	P4
						Projected							
										184	50	63	71
1	build10	75	24	36	15	118	38	60	20	141	36	39	66
2	build11	75	24	36	15	118	38	60	20	98	22	15	61
3	build12	75	24	36	15	95	38	37	20	78	8	14	56
4	build13	14	5	7	2	20	10	5	5	72	3	16	53
						Actual							
1	build10	67	23	27	17	119	37	49	33	132	36	41	55
2	build11	77	26	36	15	89	37	37	15	120	25	40	55
3	build12	62	18	32	12	100	36	52	12	82	7	20	55
4	build13	27	11	12	4	33	15	8	10	76	3	24	49

this case, the manager moved an experienced software developer to this project to expedite the resolution of outstanding defects. It is advisable to have the upper portion of the table in place before the start of a test cycle. The second half of the table evolves as the test cycle progresses so that everyone in the development team becomes aware of the progress of defect resolution.

13.5 ORTHOGONAL DEFECT CLASSIFICATION

Orthogonal defect classification (ODC) [7] is a methodology for rapid capturing of the semantics of each software defect. The ODC methodology provides both a classification scheme for software defects and a set of concepts that provide guidance in the analysis of the classified aggregate defect data. Here, orthogonality refers to the nonredundant nature of the information captured by the defect attributes and their values that are used to classify defects. The classification of defects occurs at two different points in time during the life cycle of a defect. First, a defect is put in its initial new state when it is discovered, where the circumstances leading up to the exposure of the defect and the likely impact are typically known. Second, a defect is moved to the resolved state, where the exact nature of the defect and the scope of the fix are known. ODC categories capture the semantics of a defect from these two perspectives. In the new state, the submitter needs to fill out the following ODC attributes, or fields:

- **Activity:** This is the actual activity that was being performed at the time the defect was discovered. For example, the developer might decide to do a code review of a particular procedure during the system testing phase. In this case, the term would be "system testing," whereas the activity is "code review."

- **Trigger:** The environment or condition that had to exist for the defect to surface. Triggers describe the requirements to reproduce the defect.
- **Impact:** This refers to the effect the defect would have on the customer if the defect had escaped to the field.

The owner of the defect moves the defect to the resolved state when the defect has been fixed and needs to fill out the following ODC attributes, or fields:

- **Target:** The target represents the high-level identity, such as design, code, or documentation, of the entity that was fixed.
- **Defect Type:** The defect type represents the actual correction that was made.
- **Qualifier:** The qualifier specifies whether the fix was made due to missing, incorrect, or extraneous code.
- **Source:** The source indicates whether the defect was found in code developed in-house, reused from a library, ported from one platform to another, or provided by a vendor.
- **Age:** The history of the design or code that had the problem. The age specifies whether the defect was found in new, old (base), rewritten, or refixed code:
    1. **New:** The defect is in a new function which was created by and for the current project.
    2. **Base:** The defect is in a part of the product which has not been modified by the current project and is not part of a standard reuse library. The defect was not injected by the current project, and therefore it was a latent defect.
    3. **Rewritten:** The defect was introduced as a direct result of redesigning and/or rewriting an old function in an attempt to improve its design or quality.
    4. **Refixed:** The defect was introduced by the solution provided to fix a previous defect.

The ODC attributes can be collected by modifying an existing defect tracking tool that is being used for modeling defects. As the data are collected, those must be *validated* and *assessed* on a regular basis. The individually classified defects are reviewed to ensure the consistency and correctness of the classification. The data are ready for assessment after those have been validated. The assessment is not done against each individual defect; rather trends and patterns in the aggregate data are studied. Data assessment of ODC classified data is based on the relationships of the ODC attributes to one another and to non-ODC attributes, such as category, severity, and defect submit date [8]. For example, the relationships among the attributes of defect type, qualifier, category, submit date, and severity of defects need to be considered to evaluate the product stability.

The ODC assessment must be performed by an analyst who is familiar with the project and has an interest in data analysis. A good user-friendly tool for visualizing data is needed. The ODC analyst must provide regular feedback, say, on a weekly basis, to the software development team so that appropriate actions can be taken. Once the feedback is given to the software development team, they can then identify and prioritize actions to be implemented to prevent defects from recurring.

The ODC along with application of the Pareto analysis technique [9, 10] gives a good indication of the parts of the system that are error prone and, therefore, require more testing. Juran [9] stated the Pareto principle very simply as "concentrate on the vital few and not the trivial many." An alternative expression of the principle is to state that 80% of the problems can be fixed with 20% of the effort, which is generally called the 80–20 rule. This principle guides us in efficiently utilizing the effort and resources. As an example, suppose that we have data on test *category* and the frequency of occurrence of defects for a hypothetical Chainsaw system test project as shown in Table 13.12. The data plotted on a Pareto diagram, shown in Figure 13.4, which is a bar graph showing the frequency of occurrence of defects with the most frequent ones appearing first. Note that the *functionality* and the *basic* groups have high concentration of defects. This information helps system test engineers to focus on the functionality and the basic category parts of the Chainsaw test project. The general guideline for applying Pareto analysis is as follows:

- Collect ODC and non-ODC data relevant to problem areas.
- Develop a Pareto diagram.
- Use the diagram to identify the vital few as issues that should be dealt with on an individual basis.
- Use the diagram to identify the trivial many as issues that should be dealt with as classes.

TABLE 13.12 Sample Test Data of Chainsaw Test Project

Category	Number of Defect Occurrences
1. Basic	25
2. Functionality	48
3. Robustness	16
4. Interoperability	4
5. Load and stability	6
6. Performance	12
7. Stress	6
8. Scalability	7
9. Regression	3
10. Documentation	2

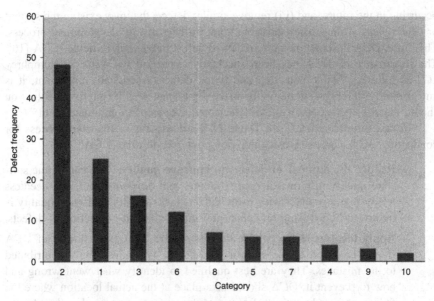

Figure 13.4   Pareto diagram for defect distribution shown in Table 13.12.

Remark. Vilfredo Federico Damaso Pareto was a French–Italian sociologist, economist, and philosopher. He made several important contributions, especially in the study of income distribution and in the analysis of individuals' choices. In 1906 he made the famous observation that 20% of the population owned 80% of the property in Italy, later generalized by Joseph M. Juran and others into the so-called Pareto principle (also termed the 80–20 rule) and generalized further to the concept of a Pareto distribution.

13.6   DEFECT CAUSAL ANALYSIS

The idea of defect causal analysis (DCA) in software development is effectively used to raise the quality level of products at a lower cost. Causal analysis can be traced back to the quality control literature [11] as one of the quality circle activities in the manufacturing sector. The quality circle concept is discussed in Section 1.1. The causes of manufacturing defects are analyzed by using the idea of a quality circle, which uses *cause–effect* diagrams and Pareto diagrams. A cause–effect diagram is also called an *Ishikawa* diagram or a *fishbone* diagram. Philip Crosby [12] described a case study of an organization called "HPA Appliance" involving the use of causal analysis to prevent defects on manufacturing lines. Causal analysis of software defects is practiced in a number of Japanese companies, usually in the context of quality circle activities [13, 14].

The idea of DCA was developed at IBM [15]. Defects are analyzed to (i) determine the cause of an error, (ii) take actions to prevent similar errors from occurring in the future, and (iii) remove similar defects that may exist in the system or detect them at the earliest possible point in the software development process. Therefore, DCA is sometimes referred to as defect prevention or defect RCA [16]. The importance of DCA has been succinctly expressed by Watts S. Humphrey [17] as follows: "While detecting and fixing defects is critically important, it is an inherently defensive strategy. To make significant quality improvements, you should identify the causes of these defects and take steps to eliminate them."

In his tutorial article [18], David N. Card explains a five-step process for conducting DCA. Card suggests three key principles to drive DCA:

- **Reduce the number of defects to improve quality:** One can define software quality in terms of *quality factors* and *attributes*, but it is needless to say that a product with many defects lacks quality. Software quality is improved by focusing on defect prevention and early detection of defects.

- **Apply local expertise where defects occur:** The responsibility of DCA should be given to the software developers who unwittingly contributed to the mistakes. They are best qualified to identify what went wrong and how to prevent it. DCA should take place at the actual location where the failure occurred, instead of in a remote conference room. In other words, DCA should be performed at the source.

- **Focus on systematic errors:** Intuitively, an error is said to be a systematic error if the same error or similar errors occur on many occasions. Systematic errors account for a significant portion of the defects found in software projects. Identifying and preventing systematic errors do have a huge impact on the quality of the product.

As the term suggests, DCA focuses on understanding the cause–effect relationship [19]. Three conditions are established to demonstrate a causal relationship between a cause and a symptom in the form of a failure:

- There must be a correlation between the hypothesized cause and the effect.
- The hypothesized cause must precede the effect in time.
- The mechanism linking the cause to the effect must be identified.

The first condition indicates that the effect is likely to be observed when a cause occurs. The second condition is obvious. The third condition requires investigation, which consists of five steps to select systematic errors associated with common failures and tracing them back to their original cause:

(i) *When was the failure detected and the corresponding fault injected?* Note the development phase, that is, code review, unit testing, integration testing, or system testing, where the failure is observed. Next, determine the phase of development in which the corresponding fault was injected. Developers identify the more problematic areas by considering the above information.

(ii) *What scheme is used to classify errors?* We identify the classes of important errors in this step. Grouping errors together helps us in identifying clusters in which common problems are likely to be found. One can use Pareto diagrams to identify problem clusters. Unlike the ODC scheme, DCA does not use a predefined set of error categories. The objective of DCA is not to analyze percentages of errors in each categories, but rather to analyze each error to understand the reason the error occurred and take preventive measures. Categorization of errors is based on the nature of the work performed, the opportunities for making mistakes, and the current dynamics of the project. Suppose that during our analysis we notice that there are many errors related to the program interface. Then we have two levels of error classification: (i) a coarse-grain classification called interface errors and (ii) many fine-grained subcategories, such as construction, misuse of interface, and initialization, as discussed in Section 7.2.

(iii) *What is the common problem (systematic error)?* The set of problem reports comprising a cluster of errors, identified in the second step above, gives an indication of a systematic error. In general, systematic errors are associated with the specific functionality of a product. Ignore the effects of individual errors in seeking out systematic errors during the identification process.

(iv) *What is the principal cause of the errors?* We endeavor to trace the error back to its cause and understand the root cause associated with many errors in the cluster. Finding the causes of errors requires (i) thorough understanding of the process and the product and (ii) experience and judgment. In order to achieve this goal, we may need to draw a cause–effect diagram as shown in Figure 13.5. First, the problem being analyzed must be stated and then the main branch of the diagram connected to the problem statement is drawn. Second, the generic causes to be used in the diagram are added. The generic causes usually fall into four categories as Ishikawa has identified [11]:

- **Tools:** The tools used in developing the system may be clumsy, unreliable, or defective.

- **Input:** It may be incomplete, ambiguous, or defective.

- **Methods:** The methods may be incomplete, ambiguous, wrong, or unenforced.

- **People:** They may lack adequate training or understanding.

We need to brainstorm to collect specific causes and attach the specific causes to the appropriate generic causes. The significance of the causes identified is discussed after all the ideas have been explored, focusing on the principal causes contributing to the systematic errors. Often this is found in the denser cluster of causes in the diagram. The cause–effect diagram provides a focused way to address the problem.

(v) *How could the error be prevented in the future?* Actions, which are preventive, corrective, or mitigating, are taken after the principal cause of a systematic error has been identified:

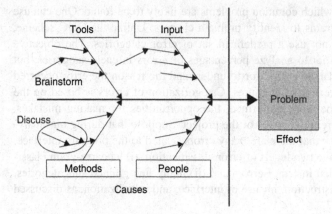

Figure 13.5 Cause–effect diagram for DCA.

- **Preventive:** A preventive action reduces the chances of similar problems occurring in the future. The idea is to detect a problem earlier and fix it.

- **Corrective:** A corrective action means fixing the problems. Attacking the cause itself may not be cost-effecive in all situations.

- **Mitigating:** A mitigating action tries to counter the adverse consequences of problems. Mitigating actions are a part of a risk management activity [20].

A combination of preventive, corrective, and mitigating actions may be applied, depending on the cost of taking actions and the magnitude of the symptoms observed. A comprehensive action plan is created to promote either prevention or detection of systematic errors at the earliest possible time in the software development process. The following are typical questions to ask at this point to elicit recommendations:

- What is the earliest a defect could have been recognized?
- What symptoms suggest that the defect may occur again?
- What did we need to know to avoid the defect?
- How could we have done things differently?

The recommended actions need to be specific and precise for others to be able to follow. Some common examples of preventive and corrective actions are as follows:

- **Training:** This allows people to improve their knowledge about the product. Training may include concrete actions such as organizing a seminar series on the components of the product, preparing a technical write-up on a complex aspect of the product, and writing an article about repetitive errors.

- **Improvement in Communication:** These are actions that improve communication procedures within the product organizations. One can think of notifying programmers and testers via email when the interface specification changes. Holding weekly team meetings helps in clarifying and disseminating useful information.

- **Using Tools:** Actions are taken to develop new tools or enhance existing tools that support the processes. One can develop or buy a tool to check memory utilization or add a new coverage metric to the module coverage tool.

- **Process Improvements:** These are actions that improve existing processes and define new processes. Such actions might modify the design change process or add new items to a common error list.

13.7 BETA TESTING

Beta testing is conducted by the potential buyers prior to the official release of the product. The purpose of beta testing is not to find defects but to obtain feedback from the field about the usability of the product. There are three kinds of beta tests performed based on the relationships between the potential buyers and the sellers:

- **Marketing Beta:** The purpose here is to build early awareness and interest in the product among potential buyers.

- **Technical Beta:** The goal here is to obtain feedback about the usability of the product in a real environment with different configurations from a small number of friendly customers. The idea is to obtain feedback from a limited number of customers who commit a considerable amount of time and thought to their evaluation.

- **Acceptance Beta:** The idea of this test is to ensure that the product meets its acceptance criteria. It is the fulfillment of the contract between a buyer and a seller. The system is released to a specific buyer, who has a contractual original equipment manufacturer (OEM) agreement with the supplier. Acceptance beta includes the objective of technical beta as well. Acceptance testing is discussed in Chapter 14.

The defects and the progress of test execution provide useful information about the quality of the system. The quality of the system under development is a moving target during test execution. A decision about when to release the system to the beta customers is made by software project team members. The consequences of early and delayed releases are as follows:

- If it is released too early, too many defects in the system may have a negative impact on the prospective customers, and it may generate bad publicity for both the product and the company.

- If the release is delayed, other competitors may capture the market.

The beta release criteria are established by the project team, and the criteria are less stringent than the final system test cycle criteria given in Chapter 13. A framework for writing beta release criteria is given in Table 13.13. All the beta release criteria in Table 13.13 are self-explanatory, except the last item, namely, that all the identified beta blocker defects are in the closed state. The beta blocker defects are the set of defects that must be in the closed state before the software is considered for beta testing. Three weeks before the beta release, the beta blocker defects are identified at the cross-functional project meeting. These defects are tracked on a daily basis to ensure that the defects are resolved and closed before the beta release. In the meantime, as new defects are submitted, these defects are evaluated to determine whether or not these are beta blockers. If it is concluded that a new defect is a beta blocker, then the defect is included on the list of beta blockers and all the defects are tracked for closure.

The system test cycle continues concurrently with beta testing. Weekly meetings are conducted with beta customers by the beta support team, which consists of cross-functional team members of the project. The weekly test status reports from the beta customers are analyzed, and actions are taken to resolve the issues by either fixing the defects or providing them a workaround of the issues raised by the beta customers. If a beta customer decides to deploy the system, an agreement can be reached to provide patch releases by fixing any outstanding deficiency in the system by a certain time frame. A final test cycle with a scaled-down number of test cases is executed as a regression test suite after an agreement is reached, and the product is prepared for first customer shipment (FCS).

TABLE 13.13 Framework for Beta Release Criteria

1. Ninety-eight percent all the test cases have passed.
2. The system has not crashed in the last week of all testing.
3. All the *resolved* defects must be in the closed state.
4. A release note with all the defects that are still in the open state along with workaround must be available. If the workaround does not exist, then an explanation of the impact on the customer must be incorporated in the release note.
5. No defect with "critical" severity is in the open state.
6. No defect with "high" severity has a probability of hitting at a customer site of more than 0.1.
7. The product does not have more than a certain *number* of defects with severity "medium." The number may be determined by the software project team members.
8. All the test cases for performance testing must have been executed, and the results must be available to the beta test customer.
9. A beta test plan must be available from all potential beta customers. A beta test plan is nothing but a user acceptance test plan.
10. A draft of the user guide must be available.
11. The training materials on the system are available for field engineers.
12. The beta support team must be available for weekly meetings with each beta customer.
13. All the identified beta blocker defects are in the closed state.

13.8   FIRST CUSTOMER SHIPMENT

The exit criterion of the final test cycle must be satisfied before the FCS which is established in the test execution strategy section of Chapter 13. An FCS readiness review meeting is called to ensure that the product meets the shipment criteria. The shipment criteria are more than just the exit criteria of the final test cycle. This review should include representatives from the key function groups responsible for delivery and support of the product, such as engineering, operation, quality, customer support, and product marketing. A set of generic FCS readiness criteria is as follows:

- All the test cases from the test suite should have been executed. If any of the test cases is unexecuted, then an explanation for not executing the test case should have been provided in the test factory database.
- Test case results are updated in the test factory database with passed, failed, blocked, or invalid status. Usually, this is done during the system test cycles.
- The requirement database is updated by moving each requirement from the verification state to either the closed or the decline state, as discussed in Chapter 11, so that compliance statistics can be generated from the database. All the issues related to the EC must be resolved with the development group.
- The pass rate of test cases is very high, say, 98%.
- No crash in the past two weeks of testing has been observed.
- No known defect with *critical* or *high* severity exists in the product.
- Not more than a certain number of known defects with *medium* and *low* levels of severity exist in the product. The threshold number may be determined by the software project team members.
- All the identified FCS blocker defects are in the closed state.
- All the resolved defects must be in the closed state.
- All the outstanding defects that are still in either the open or assigned state are included in the release note along with the workaround, if there is one.
- The user guides are in place.
- A troubleshooting guide is available.
- The test report is completed and approved. Details of a test report are explained in the following section.

Once again, three weeks before the FCS, the FCS blocker defects are identified at the cross-functional project meeting. These defects are tracked on a daily basis to ensure that the defects are resolved and closed before the FCS. In the meantime, as new defects are submitted, these are evaluated to determine whether these are FCS blockers. If it is concluded that a defect is a blocker, then the defect is included in the blocker list and tracked along with the other defects in the list for its closure.

13.9 SYSTEM TEST REPORT

During the test execution cycles test reports are generated and distributed as discussed in Sections 13.4.2 and 13.4.4. A final summary report is created after completion of all the test cycles. The structure of the final report is outlined in Table 13.14.

The introduction to the test project section of the test report summarizes the purpose of the report according to the test plan. This section includes the following information:

- Name of the project
- Name of the software image
- Revision history of this document
- Terminology and definitions
- Testing staff
- Scope of the document
- References

The summary of test results section summarizes the test results for each test category identified in the test plan. In each test cycle, the test results are summarized in the form of the numbers of test cases passed, failed, invalid, blocked, and untested and the reasons for not executing some test cases. A test case may not be tested because of several reasons, such as unavailability of equipment and difficulty in creating the test scenario using the available test bed setup. The latter may only be possible at a real beta testing site. For each test cycle, the following data are given in this section:

- Start and completion dates
- Number of defects filed
- Number of defects in different states, such as irreproducible, FAD, closed, shelved, duplicate, postponed, assigned, and open

TABLE 13.14 Structure of Final System Test Report

1. Introduction to the test project
2. Summary of test results
3. Performance characteristics
4. Scaling limitations
5. Stability observations
6. Interoperability of the system
7. Hardware/software compatible matrix
8. Compliance requirement status

Problems still remaining in the system, including any shortcoming or likelihood of failure, are summarized in this section in terms of their levels of severity and their potential impact on the customers. For example, if the password is case insensitive, then it should be stated so. As another example, if an operating system puts a limit of 20 on the number of windows that can be simultaneously opened, then it should be stated that the user should not open more than 20 windows simultaneously; exceeding the limit may cause the system to crash.

In the performance characteristics section of the document, the system response time, throughput, resource utilization, and delay measurement results are described along with the test environments and tools used in the measurement process.

The limits of the system are stated in the scaling limitation section of the document based on the findings of scalability testing. Once again the facilities and tools that are used in scaling testing are described here.

The stability observations section states the following information:

- Uptime in number of hours of the system
- Number of crashes observed by different groups, such as software developer, ST, and SIT, in each week of the test cycles
- Descriptions of symptoms of the defects causing system crash that are in the irreproducible state

We state in the interoperability section of the document those third-party software and hardware systems against which the system interoperability tests were conducted. The list may include software and hardware against which the system will not interoperate.

A table shows what software versions are compatible with what hardware revisions in the hardware/software compatible matrix section. Generation of this table is based on the different kinds of hardware systems and different versions of the software used during system test cycles.

Finally, in the compliance requirement status section of the document compliance statistics are summarized by generating them from the requirements database. The following reports are generated by creating appropriate queries on the database:

- Requirements that are in compliance, partial compliance, or noncompliance with the software image
- Requirements that are verified by testing, analysis, demonstration, and inspection
- Requirements that are covered by each test case of the test suite along with the status of the test case

13.10   PRODUCT SUSTAINING

Once a product is shipped to one of the paying customers and if there is no major issue reported by the customer within a time frame of, say, three weeks, then the product's general availability (GA) is declared. After that the software project is moved to a new phase called the sustaining phase. The goal of this phase is to maintain the software quality throughout the product's market life. Software maintenance activities occur because software testing cannot uncover all the defects in a large software system. The following three software maintenance activities were coined by Swanson [21]:

- **Corrective:** The process that includes isolation and correction of one or more defects in the software.
- **Adaptive:** The process that modifies the software to properly interface with a changing environment such as a new version of hardware or third-party software.
- **Perfective:** The process that improves the software by the addition of new functionalities, enhancements, and/or modifications to the existing functions.

The first major task is to determine the type of maintenance task to be conducted when a defect report comes in from a user through the customer support group. The sustaining team, which includes developers and testers, is assigned immediately to work on the defect if the defect reported by the customer is considered as *corrective* in nature. The status of the progress is updated to the customer within 24 hours. The group continues to work until a patch with the fix is released to the customer. If the defect reported is considered as either *adaptive* or *perfective* in nature, then it is entered in the requirement database, and it goes though the usual software development phases.

The sustaining test engineers are different from the system test engineers. Therefore, before a product transition occurs, the sustaining engineers are provided with enough training about the product to carry out sustaining test activities. In reality, the test engineers are rotated back and forth between the system test group and the sustaining group. The major tasks of sustaining test engineers are as follows:

- Interact with customers to understand their real environment
- Reproduce the issues observed by the customer in the laboratory environment
- Once the root cause of the problem is known, develop new test cases to verify it
- Develop upgrade/downgrade test cases from the old image to the new patch image
- Participate in the code review process
- Select a subset of regression tests from the existing pool of test cases to ensure that there is no side effect because of the fix
- Execute the selected test cases
- Review the release notes for correctness
- Conduct experiments to evaluate test effectiveness

13.11 MEASURING TEST EFFECTIVENESS

It is useful to evaluate the effectiveness of the testing effort in the development of a product. After a product is deployed in the customer environment, a common measure of test effectives is the number of defects found by the customers that were not found by the test engineers prior to the release of the product. These defects had escaped from our testing effort. A metric commonly used in the industry to measure test effectiveness is the defect removal efficiency (DRE) [22], defined as

$$\text{DRE} = \frac{\text{number of defects found in testing}}{\text{number of defects found in testing} + \text{number of defects not found}}$$

We obtain the number of defects found in testing from the defect tracking system. However, calculating the number of defects not found during testing is a difficult task. One way to approximate this number is to count the defects found by the customers within the first six months of its operation. There are several issues that must be understood to interpret the DRE measure in an useful way:

- Due to the inherent limitations of real test environments in a laboratory, certain defects are very difficult to find during system testing no matter how thorough we are in our approach. One should include these defects in the calculation if the goal is to measure the effectiveness of the testing effort including the limitations of the test environments. Otherwise, these kinds of defects may be eliminated from the calculation.

- The defects submitted by customers that need *corrective* maintenance are taken into consideration in this measurement. The defects submitted that need either *adaptive* or *perfective* maintenance are not real issues in the software; rather they are requests for new feature enhancements. Therefore, defects that need adaptive and perfective maintenance may be removed from the calculation.

- There must be a clear understanding of the duration for which the defects are counted, such as starting from unit testing or system integration testing to the end of system testing. One must be consistent for all test projects.

- This measurement is not for one project; instead it should be a part of the long-term trend in the test effectiveness of the organization.

Much work has been done on the *fault seeding* approach [23] to estimate the number of escaped defects. In this approach the effectiveness of testing is determined by estimating the number of actual defects using an extrapolation technique. The approach is to inject a small number of representative defects into the system and measure the percentage of defects that are uncovered by the sustaining test engineers. Since the sustaining test team remains unaware of the seeding, the extent to which the product reveals the known defects allows us to extrapolate the extent to which it found unknown defects. Suppose that the product contains N defects and K defects are seeded. At the end of the test experiments, the sustaining test team has found n unseeded and k seeded defects. The fault seeding theory asserts the following:

$$\frac{k}{K} = \frac{n}{N} \implies N = n\left(\frac{K}{k}\right)$$

For example, consider a situation where 25 known defects have been deliberately seeded in a system. Let us assume that the sustaining testers detect 20 (80%) of these seeded defects and uncovers 400 additional defects. Then, the total number of estimated defects in the system is 500. Therefore, the product still has $500 - 400 = 100$ defects waiting to be discovered plus 5 seed defects that still exist in the code. Using the results from the seeding experiment, it would be possible to obtain the total number of escaped defects from the system testing phase. This estimation is based on the assumption that the ratio of the number of defects found to the total number of defects is 0.80—the same ratio as for the seeded defects. In other words, we assume that the 400 defects constitute 80% of all the defects found by the sustaining test engineers in the system. The estimated remaining number of defects are still hidden in the system. However, the accuracy of the measure is dependent on the way the defects are injected. Usually, artificially injected defects are manually planted, but it has been proved difficult to implement defect seeding in practice. It is not easy to introduce artificial defects that can have the same impact as the actual defects in terms of difficulty of detection. Generally, artificial defects are much easier to find than actual defects.

Spoilage Metric Defects are injected and removed at different phases of a software development cycle [24]. Defects get introduced during requirements analysis, high-level design, detailed design, and coding phases, whereas these defects are removed during unit testing, integration testing, system testing, and acceptance testing phases. The cost of each defect injected in phase X and removed in phase Y is not uniformly distributed; instead the cost increases with the increase in the distance between X and Y. The delay in finding the dormant defects cause greater harms, and it costs more to fix because the dormant defects may trigger the injection of other related defects, which need to be fixed in addition to the original dormant defects. Therefore, an effective testing method would find defects earlier than a less effective testing method would. Hence an useful measure of test effectiveness is defect age, known as *PhAge*. As an example, let us consider Table 13.15, which shows a scale for measuring age. In this example, a requirement defect discovered during high-level design review would be assigned a PhAge of 1, whereas a requirement defect discovered at the acceptance testing phase would be assigned a PhAge of 7. One can modify the table to accommodate different phases of the software development life cycle followed within an organization, including the PhAge numbers.

If the information about a defect introduction phase can be determined, it can be used to create a matrix with rows corresponding to the defect injected in each phase and columns corresponding to defects discovered in each phase This is often called a *defect dynamic model*. Table 13.16 shows a defect injected–v discovered matrix from an imaginary test project called Boomerang. In this example, there were

TABLE 13.15   Scale for Defect Age

Phase Injected	Phase Discovered							
	Requirements	High-Level Design	Detailed Design	Coding	Unit Testing	Integration Testing	System Testing	Acceptance Testing
Requiremants	0	1	2	3	4	5	6	7
High-level design		0	1	2	3	4	5	6
Detailed design			0	1	2	3	4	5
Coding				0	1	2	3	4

TABLE 13.16   Defect Injection versus Discovery on Project Boomerang

Phase Injected	Phase Discovered								Total Defects
	Requirements	High-Level Design	Detailed Design	Coding	Unit Testing	Integration Testing	System Testing	Acceptance Testing	
Requiremants	0	7	3	1	0	0	2	4	17
High-level design		0	8	4	1	2	6	1	22
Detailed design			0	13	3	4	5	0	25
Coding				0	63	24	37	12	136
Summary	0	7	11	18	67	30	50	17	200

seven requirement defects found in high-level design, three in detailed design, one in coding, two in system testing, and four in acceptance testing phases.

Now a new metric called *spoilage* [25, 26] is defined to measure the defect removal activities by using the defect age and defect dynamic model. The spoilage metric is calculated as

$$\text{Spoilage} = \frac{\sum(\text{number of defects} \times \text{discovered PhAge})}{\text{total number of defects}}$$

Table 13.17 shows the spoilage values for the Boomerang test project based on the number of defects found (Table 13.15) weighted by defect age (Table 13.16). During acceptance testing, for example, 17 defects were discovered, out of which 4 were attributed to defects injected during the requirements phase of the Boomerang project. Since the defects that were found during acceptance testing could have been found in any of the seven previous phases, the requirement defects that were dormant until the acceptance testing were given a PhAge of 7. The weighted number of requirement defects revealed during acceptance testing is 28, that is, $7 \times 4 = 28$. The spoilage values for requirements, high-level design, detail design, and coding phases are 3.2, 2.8, 2.0, and 1.98, respectively. The spoilage value for the Boomerang test project is 2.2. A spoilage value close to 1 is an indication of

TABLE 13.17   Number of Defects Weighted by Defect Age on Project Boomerang

Phase Injected	Phase Discovered								Weight	Total Defects	Spoilage as Weight/Total Defects
	Requirements	High-Level Design	Detailed Design	Coding	Unit Testing	Integration Testing	System Testing	Acceptance Testing			
Requiremants	0	7	6	3	0	0	12	28	56	17	3.294117647
High-level design		0	8	8	3	8	30	6	63	22	2.863636364
Detailed design			0	13	6	12	20	0	51	25	2.04
Coding				0	63	48	111	48	270	136	1.985294118
Summary	0	7	14	24	72	68	173	82	440	200	2.2

a more effective defect discovery process. As an absolute value, the spoilage metric has little meaning. This metric is useful in measuring the long-term trend of test effectiveness in an organization.

13.12   SUMMARY

This chapter began with a state transition model which allows us to represent each phase in the life cycle of a defect by a state. At each state of the transition model, certain actions are taken by the owner; the defect is moved to a new state after the actions are completed. We presented a defect schema that can be used to monitor various defect metrics. Two key concepts involved in modeling defects are priority and severity. On the one hand, a priority level is a measure of how soon a defect needs to be fixed, that is, urgency. On the other hand, a severity level is a measure of the extent of the detrimental effect of the defect on the operation of the product.

Then we explored the idea of test preparedness to start system-level testing. We discussed the idea of a test execution working document that needs to be maintained before the start of the system test execution in order to ensure that system test engineers are ready to start the execution of system tests. We recommend two types of metrics to be monitored during the execution of system-level test cases:

- Metrics for monitoring test execution
- Metrics for monitoring defects

The first kind of metric concerns the process of executing test cases, whereas the second kind concerns the defects found as a result of test execution. We provided examples of test case execution and defect report metrics from different real-life test projects.

Next, we examined three kinds of defect analysis techniques: ODC, causal, and the Pareto methodology. Causal analysis is conducted to identify the root cause of the defects and to take actions to eliminate the sources of defects; this is done at the time of fixing defects. In the ODC method, assessment is not done against individual defects; rather, trends and patterns in the aggregate data are studied. The Pareto principle is based on the postulate that 80% of the problems can be fixed with 20% of the effort. We showed that ODC along with the application of Pareto analysis can give a good indication of which parts of the system are error prone and may require more testing.

We provided frameworks for beta releases and discussed the process of beta testing as is conducted at the customer's site. We classified three types of beta testing: marketing beta, technical beta, and acceptance beta. The purpose of marketing beta is to build early awareness and interest in the product among potential buyers. A technical beta test is performed to obtain feedback about the usability of the product in a real environment with different configurations. The idea is to obtain feedback from a limited number of users who commit a considerable amount of time and thought to their evaluation. An acceptance beta test is performed to ensure that the product is acceptable, that is, the product meets its acceptance criteria. Acceptance testing is the fulfillment of the contract between a buyer and a seller.

Next, we provided a detailed structure of the system test report, which must be generated before the product's general availability is declared. Once the product is declared as generally available, the software project is moved to a new phase called the sustaining phase for maintenance. During this phase sustaining test engineers are responsible for carrying out sustaining test activities. We explained the tasks of sustaining test engineers in this chapter.

Finally, we provided two metrics used to measure test effectiveness: defect removal efficiency and spoilage. The objective of a test effectiveness metric is to evaluate the effectiveness of the system testing effort in the development of a product, that is, the number of defects that had escaped from our testing effort. We presented the fault seeding approach in order to estimate the number of escaped defects.

LITERATURE REVIEW

In reference [4] a set of in-process metrics for testing phases of the software development process are described. For each metric the authors describe its purpose, data, interpretation, and use and present graphical examples with real-life data. These metrics are applicable to most software projects and are an integral part of system-level testing.

In reference [8] three case studies are presented to measure test effectiveness using ODC. All three case studies highlight how technical teams can use ODC data for objective feedback on their development processes and the evolution of their product. The case studies include background information on the products, how their ODC process was implemented, and the details of the assessments, including actions that resulted.

Several excellent examples of defect RCA efforts in software engineering have been published. Interested readers are recommended to go through the following articles for more information:

M. Leszak, D. E. Perry, and D. Stoll, "Classification and Evaluation of Defects in a Retrospective," *Journal of Systems and Software*, Vol. 61, April 2002, pp. 173–187.

W. D. Yu, "A Software Prevention Approach in Coding and Root Cause Analysis," *Bell Labs Technical Journal*, Vol. 3, April 1998, pp. 3–21.

The article by Leszak et al. describes a retrospective process with defect RCA, process metric analysis, and software complexity analysis of a network element as a part of an optical transmission network at Lucent Technologies (now Alcatel-Lucent). The article by Yu discusses the guidelines developed by the team to conduct defect RCA at various Lucent switching development organizations.

Mills's seminal article on *fault seeding* is reprinted in *Software Productivity* (H. D. Mills, Little, Brown and Company, Boston, 1983). The book consists of articles on the subject of software process written by the author over many years.

REFERENCES

1. D. Lemont. *CEO Discussion—From Start-up to Market Leader—Breakthrough Milestones*. Ernst and Young Milestones, Boston, May 2004, pp. 9–11.
2. G. Stark, R. C. Durst, and C. W. Vowell. Using Metrics in Management Decision Making. *IEEE Computer*, September 1994, pp. 42–48.
3. S. H. Kan. *Metrics and Models in Software Quality Engineering*, 2nd ed. Addison-Wesley, Reading, MA, 2002.
4. S. H. Kan, J. Parrish, and D. Manlove. In-Process Metrics for Software Testing. *IBM Systems Journal*, January 2001, pp. 220–241.
5. R. Black. *Managing Testing Process*, 2nd ed. Wiley, New York, 2002.
6. E. F. Weller. Using Metrics to Manage Software Projects. *IEEE Computer*, September 1994, pp. 27–33.
7. R. Chillarege, I. S. Bhandari, J. K. Chaar, M. J. Halliday, D. S. Moebus, B. K. Ray, and M. Y. Wong. Orthogonal Defect Classification—A Concept for In-Process Measurement. *IEEE Transactions on Software Engineering*, November 1992, pp. 943–956.
8. M. Butcher, H. Munro, and T. Kratschmer. Improving Software Testing via ODC: Three Case Studies. *IBM Systems Journal*, January 2002, pp. 31–44.
9. J. Juran, M. Gryna, M. Frank, Jr., and R. Bingham, Jr. *Quality Control Handbook*, 3rd ed. McGraw-Hill, New York, 1979.
10. T. McCabe and G. Schulmeyer. The Pareto Principle Applied to Software Quality Assurance. In *Handbook of Software Quality Assurance*, 2nd ed., G. Schulmeyer and J. McManus, Eds. Van Nostrand Reinhold, New York, 1992.
11. K. Ishikawa. *What Is Total Quality Control*. Prentice-Hall, Englewood Cliffs, NJ, 1985.
12. P. Crosby. *Quality Is Free*. New American Library, New York, 1979.
13. K. Hino. Analysis and Prevention of Software Errors as a Quality Circle Activity. *Engineers* (Japanese), January 1985, pp. 6–10.
14. H. Sugaya. Analysis of the Causes of Software Bugs. *Nikkei Computer* (Japanese), August 1985, pp. 167–176.
15. R. G. Mays, C. L. Jones, G. J. Holloway, and D. P. Studinski. Experiences with Defect Prevention. *IBM System Journal*, Vol. **29**, No. 1, 1990, pp. 4–32.
16. M. Pezzé and M. Young. *Software Testing and Analysis: Process, Principles, and Techniques*. Wiley, Hoboken, NJ, 2007.
17. W. S. Humphrey. *A Discipline for Software Engineering*. Addison-Wesley, Reading, MA, 1995.
18. D. N. Card. Learning from Our Mistakes with Defect Causal Analysis. *IEEE Software*, January-February 1998, pp. 56–63.
19. D. N. Card. Understanding Causal Systems. *Crosstalk, the Journal of Defense Software Engineering*, October 2004, pp. 15–18.
20. N. Crockford. *An Introduction to Risk Management*, 2nd ed. Woodhead-Faulkner, Cambridge, U.K. 1986.
21. E. B. Swanson. The Dimensions of Maintenance. In *Proceeding of the Second International Conference on Software Engineering*, October 1976, pp. 492–497.
22. C. Jones. *Applied Software Measurement*. McGraw-Hill, New York, 1991.
23. H. Zhu, P. A. V. Hall, and J. H. R. May. Software Unit Test Coverage and Adequacy. *ACM Computing Survays*, December 1997, pp. 366–427.
24. A. A. Frost and M. J. Campo. Advancing Defect Containment to Quantitative Defect Management. *Crosstalk, the Journal of Defense Software Engineering*, December 2007, pp. 24–28.
25. R. D. Craig and S. P. Jaskiel. *Systematic Software Testing*. Artech House, Norwood, MA, 2002.

26. R. B. Grady and D. L. Caswell. *Software Metrics: Establishing a Company-Wide Program*. Prentice-Hall, Upper Saddle River, NJ, 1998.

Exercises

1. Why is it important to assign both severity and priority levels to a defect?

2. Implement the schema and the defect model discussed in this chapter using a commercially available defect tracking tool (viz., ClearQuest of IBM).

3. Why do in-process metrics need to be tracked on daily or weekly basis during system testing?

4. What is the difference between causal analysis, statistical analysis, and Pareto analysis? The ODC method belongs to which category?

5. Modify the schema shown in Table 13.2, including values of the fields and the state transition diagram in Figure 13.1, to model ODC.

6. The projected number of defects submitted, resolved, and remaining open in the first four weeks of a test project are given in the upper half of Table 13.18. The actual numbers of submitted and resolved defects are shown in the lower half of the table. Calculate the actual number of open defects.

7. For your current system testing project, select a set of in-process metrics discussed in this chapter and track it during the system test execution phase.

8. Develop a set of beta release criteria for your current test project.

9. Write a system test report after the completion of your current test project.

10. In a test project, the number of defects found in different phases of testing are as follows: unit testing, 163 defects; integration testing, 186 defects; system testing, 271 defects. The number of defects found by sustaining test engineers by conducting fault seeding experimentation is 57. What is the value of DRE? Calculate the value of the system test DRE?

TABLE 13.18 ARD Metric for Test Project

Week	Build	Submitted Total	P1+P2	P3	P4	Resolved Total	P1+P2	P3	P4	Open Total	P1+P2	P3	P4
						Projected							
										184	50	63	71
1	build10	75	24	36	15	118	38	60	20	141	36	39	66
2	build11	75	24	36	15	118	38	60	20	98	22	15	61
3	build12	75	24	36	15	95	38	37	20	78	8	14	56
4	build13	14	5	7	2	20	10	5	5	72	3	16	53
						Actual							
1	build10	60	26	16	18	105	35	40	30				
2	build11	77	28	34	15	89	37	37	15				
3	build12	62	20	32	10	78	24	42	12				
4	build13	24	15	15	10	72	20	25	27				

TABLE 13.19   Scale for PhAge

Phase Injected	Phase Discovered							
	Requirements	High-Level Design	Detailed Design	Coding	Unit Testing	Integration Testing	System Testing	Acceptance Testing
Requiremants	0	1	2	4	6	8	10	14
High-level design		0	1	2	4	6	8	12
Detailed design			0	1	2	4	6	10
Coding				0	1	2	4	8

11. Modify the schema shown in Table 13.2, including values of the fields to capture in the defect dynamic model.

12. Use the defect age (PhAge) given in Table 13.19 to recalculate the spoilage metric for the Boomerang test project.

CHAPTER **14**

Acceptance Testing

Acceptance of others, their looks, their behaviors, their beliefs, bring you an inner peace and tranquility—instead of anger and resentment.
— *Anonymous*

14.1 TYPES OF ACCEPTANCE TESTING

A product is ready to be delivered to the customer after the system test group is satisfied with the product by performing system-level tests. Customers execute acceptance tests based on their expectations from the product. The services offered by a software product may be used by millions of users. For example, the service provider of a cellular phone network is a customer of the software systems running the phone network, whereas the general public forms the user base by subscribing to the phone services. It is not uncommon for someone to have a dual role as a customer and a user. The service provider needs to ensure that the product meets certain criteria before the provider makes the services available to the general public. Acceptance testing is a formal testing conducted to determine whether a system satisfies its acceptance criteria—the criteria the system must satisfy to be accepted by the customer. It helps the customer to determine whether or not to accept the system [1]. The customer generally reserves the right to refuse to take delivery of the product if the acceptance test cases do not pass. There are two categories of acceptance testing:

- User acceptance testing.
- Business acceptance testing.

The UAT is conducted by the customer to ensure that system satisfies the contractual acceptance criteria before being signed off as meeting user needs. Actual planning and execution of the acceptance tests do not have to be undertaken directly by the customer. Often third-party consulting firms offer their services to do this task. However, the customer must specify the acceptance criteria for the third party to seek in the product. The BAT is undertaken within the development organization

---

Software Testing and Quality Assurance: Theory and Practice, Edited by Kshirasagar Naik and Priyadarshi Tripathy
Copyright © 2008 John Wiley & Sons, Inc.

450

of the supplier to ensure that the system will eventually pass the UAT. It is a rehearsal of UAT at the premises of the supplier. The development organization of the supplier derives and executes test cases from the client's contract, which include the acceptance criteria.

The acceptance criteria must be defined and agreed upon between the supplier and the customer to avoid any kind of protracted arguments. Either party or a third-party consulting firm may design the acceptance test plan. The acceptance criteria document is a part of the contract in the case of an outsourced development under the OEM agreement. If some hardware is an integral part of the system, then the hardware acceptance criteria are included in the contractual agreement. In general, the marketing organization of the buyer defines the acceptance criteria. However, it is important that the software quality assurance team of the buyer's organization initiate a dialogue with the seller and provide a set of "straw man" acceptance criteria for the marketing department to review and react to. The users, the system engineers, customer support engineers, and the software quality assurance group of the buyer's organization do the actual planning and execution of the acceptance tests after the criteria are agreed upon. The personnel developing an acceptance test plan must have a thorough understanding of the acceptance criteria that have been agreed upon. It is unlikely that the system passes all the acceptance criteria in one go for large, complex systems. It is useful to focus on the following three major objectives of acceptance testing for pragmatic reasons:

- Confirm that the system meets the agreed-upon criteria. The broad categories of criteria are explained in Section 14.2.
- Identify and resolve discrepancies, if there are any. The sources of discrepancies and mechanisms for resolving them have been explained in Section 14.5.
- Determine the readiness of the system for cut-over to live operations. The final acceptance of a system for deployment is conditioned upon the outcome of the acceptance testing. The acceptance test team produces an acceptance test report which outlines the acceptance conditions. The details of an acceptance test report have been explained in Section 14.6.

Acceptance testing is only one aspect of the contractual fulfillment of the agreement between a supplier and a buyer. A contractual agreement may require the seller to provide other materials, such as the design solution document that addresses the requirement document of the buyer. The acceptance test team may evaluate the acceptability of the system design in terms of graphical user interface, error handling, and access control.

14.2 ACCEPTANCE CRITERIA

At the core of any contractual agreement is a set of acceptance criteria. A key question is what criteria must the system meet in order to be acceptable? The acceptance criteria must be measurable and, preferably, quantifiable. The basic principle of designing the acceptance criteria is to ensure that the quality of the system is acceptable. One must understand the meaning of the quality of a system, which is a complex concept. It means different things to different people, and it is highly context dependent [2].

Even though different persons may have a different view about quality, it is the customer's opinion that prevails. The concept of quality is, in fact, complex and multifaceted [3]. Five views of quality, namely, *transcendental view*, *user view*, *manufacturing view*, *product view*, and *value-based view*, have been explained in Chapter 17. The five views were originally presented by Garvin [3] in the context of production and manufacturing in general and subsequently explained by Kitchenham and Pfleeger [2] in a software development context. The five views are presented below in a concise form:

1. The transcendental view sees quality as something that can be recognized but is difficult to describe or define.

2. The user view sees quality as satisfying the purpose.

3. The manufacturing view sees quality as conforming to the specification.

4. The product view ties quality with the inherent characteristics of the product.

5. The value-based view puts a cost figure on quality—the amount a customer is willing to pay for it.

Acceptance criteria are defined on the basis of these multiple facets of quality attributes. These attributes determine the presence or absence of quality in a system. Buyers, or Customers, should think through the relevance and relative importance of these attributes in their unique situation at the time of formulating the acceptance criteria. The attributes of quality are discussed below and examples of acceptance criteria for each quality attribute are given.

Functional Correctness and Completeness One can ask the question: Does the system do what we want it to do? All the features which are described in the requirements specification must be present in the delivered system. It is important to show that the system works correctly under at least two to three conditions for each feature as a part of acceptance.

One can show the functional correctness of a system by using the requirements database, as discussed in Chapter 11. The database is used in generating a requirement traceability matrix during system-level testing. Basically a traceability matrix tells us the test cases that are used to verify a requirement and all the requirements that are partially verified by a test case. Such a traceability matrix is a powerful tool in showing the customer about the functional correctness of the system. It is important to obtain an early feedback from the customer on the requirements traceability matrix. The idea behind the feedback is to reach an agreement on the validation method to be employed for each requirement. The decision is especially significant because some validation methods are easier to implement and less time intensive than other methods. For example, the demonstration method is less time intensive than the testing method.

In reality, rigorous functional correctness testing is conducted during the system testing phase, rather than during acceptance testing. However, the buyer may ask for the requirement traceability matrix before the start of acceptance testing to ensure that the system does function according to the requirement specification.

Accuracy   The question is: Does the system provide correct results? Accuracy measures the extent to which a computed value stays close to the expected value. Accuracy is generally defined in terms of the magnitude of the error. A small gap—also called an error in numerical analysis, for example—between the actual value computed by a system and the expected value is generally tolerated in a continuous space. The accuracy problem is different in discrete space, leading to false-positive and false-negative results. False positives and false negatives are serious drawbacks in any diagnostic and monitoring software tools.

Data Integrity   Data integrity refers to the preservation of the data while it is transmitted or stored such that the value of data remains unchanged when the corresponding receive or retrieve operations are executed at a later time. Thus, data must not be compromised by performing update, restore, retrieve, transmit, and receive operations. The requirement of data integrity is included in the acceptance test criteria to uncover design flaws that may result in data corruption. In communication systems, an intruder can change the data without the sender and receiver detecting the change. If integrity check mechanisms are in place, the data may be changed, but the mechanism will detect the tampering. Data integrity mechanisms detect changes in a data set. The concepts of message digest and digital signature are used in preserving data integrity [4].

Remark.   A *message digest* algorithm takes in an input message of arbitrary length and produces a fixed-length code. The fixed-length code is called a *digest* of the original message. The commonly used message digest algorithms are the Message Digest 5 (MD5) and the Secure Hash Algorithm 1 and 2 (SHA-1 and SHA-2).

Remark.   A *digital signature* is an encrypted message digest that is appended to a document to be stored or transmitted. A message digest is obtained by using, for example, the MD5, SHA-1, or SHA-2 algorithm. The message digest is encrypted with the private key of the party that stores or transmits the message.

Data Conversion   Data conversion is the conversion of one form of computer data to another. For example, conversion of a file from one version of Microsoft Word to an earlier version for the sake of those who do not have the latest version of Word installed. Data conversion testing is testing of programs or procedures that are used to convert data from existing systems for use in replacement systems. Data may be converted into an invalid format that cannot be processed by the new system if this is not performed properly; thus the data will have no value.

In addition, data may be omitted from the conversion process resulting in gaps or system errors in the new system. Inability to process backup or archive files results in the inability to restore or interrogate old data.

An acceptance criterion for data conversion measures and reports the capability of the software to convert existing application data to new formats. The following questions must be answered in specifying the data conversion acceptance criteria:

- How can we undo a conversion and roll back to the earlier database version(s) if necessary?
- How much human involvement is needed to validate the conversion results?
- How are the current data being used and how will the converted data be used?
- Will the data conversion software conduct integrity checking as well?

Backup and Recovery   Backup and recovery of data are default functionalities of large, complex systems. This is because, though systems are not expected to crash, in reality, a system crash is not uncommon. The backup and recovery acceptance criteria specify the durability and recoverability levels of the software in each hardware platform. The aim of the recovery acceptance test criteria is to outline the extent to which data can be recovered after a system crash. The following questions must be answered in specifying the recoverability acceptance criteria:

- How much data can be recovered after a crash and how?
- Is the recovered data expected to be consistent?

Generally, a system cannot recover from a crash unless the data have been previously backed up. The backup process includes taking periodic snapshots of a state of the system and saving them in stable storage to be retrieved later [5]. The following questions must be answered in specifying the backup acceptance criteria:

- How frequently is the backup process initiated?
- How long does the backup process take?
- Is the backup expected to work on-line or off-line with normal operation suspended during backup?
- Does the backup process check if sufficient storage space is available to accommodate all the data?
- Is the backup process fully automated?

Competitive Edge   The system must provide a distinct advantage over existing methods and competing products through innovative features. An analysis of the competitiveness of the product is provided to the buyer. This document contains a comparative study of the system with products available in the market from other vendors. A competitive analysis is conducted by the systems engineering group of the marketing organization. The following questions need to be answered in specifying the competitive analysis report acceptance criteria:

- What are the nearest direct competitors of the product?
- What are the indirect competitors of the product?
- Who are the potential competitors?
- Is the business in the product area steady, growing, or declining?
- What can be learned from product operations or from advertisements of competitors?
- What are the strengths and weaknesses of competitors?
- How do their products differ from the product being developed?

Usability The question is: How easy it is to use the system and how easy it is to learn? The goal of usability acceptance criteria is to ensure that the system is flexible, it is easy to configure and customize the system, on-line help is available, work-around is available, and userinterface is friendly. The following questions need to be addressed in specifying the usability acceptance criteria:

- How will the system help the user in the day-to-day job?
- Will the productivity, customer satisfaction, reliability, and quality of work life of the user improve by using the system?
- Are the menus, commands, screens, and on-line help clear to a typical user?
- Are the user procedures simple, logical, and clear to the typical user?
- Is the user guide clear, easy to access, and understandable for a typical user?
- Will the methods of error and exception handling utilized by the system increase reliability and productivity?
- Are the reports generated by the system in order, consistent, and clear?
- Is the system easy to install?

Performance The desired performance characteristics of the system must be defined for the measured data to be useful. The following questions relate to specification of the performance acceptance criteria:

- What types of performance characteristics of the system need to be measured?
- What is the acceptable value for each performance parameter?
- With what external data source or system does the application interact?
- What kind of workload should be used while running the performance tests? The workload should be a representative of the likely real-world operating condition in terms of low load, average load, and peak load.

- Is it required to perform a before-and-after comparison of the performance results with the prior version of the system?

Start-Up Time The system start-up time reflects the time taken to boot up to become operational. The following questions address the start-up acceptance criteria:

- How is the start-up time defined?
- Does the start-up time include the power-on self-test of all the system hardware?
- · • What is the longest acceptable start-up time?

Stress The system should be capable of handling extremely high or stressful load. It is necessary to identify the system limitations and then stress the system to find the results when the system is pushed to the border and beyond. The system limitation must be identified in the acceptance criteria. The following questions must be addressed in specifying the stress acceptance criteria:

- What are the design limits of the system?
- What is the expected and acceptable behavior of the recovery mechanism?
- What test environment, close to customer deployment architecture, is needed in order to force the system to be stressed?

Reliability and Availability Software reliability is defined as the probability that the software executes without failure for a specified amount of time in a specified environment. The longer a system runs without failure, the more reliable it is. A large number of reliability models are available to predict the reliability of software. A software reliability model provides a family of growth curves that describe the decline of failure rate as defects are submitted and closed during the system testing phase. The failure rate is often calculated in terms of MTBF. A growth model can answer the following questions, which can be part of the reliability acceptance criteria:

- What is the current failure rate of the software?
- What will be the failure rate if the customer continues acceptance testing for a long time?
- How many defects are likely to be in the software?
- How much testing has to be performed to reach a particular failure rate?

The failure rate goal that is acceptable must be set separately for each level of problem severity—from *critical* to *low*. A customer may be willing to tolerate tens of low-severity issues per day but not more than one critical problem in a year.

System availability consists of proactive methods for maximizing service uptime, for minimizing the downtime, and for minimizing the time needed to recover from an outage. Downtime is measured in terms of MTTR. The creation of a customer environment is facilitated by gathering an *operational profile* from the customer. An operational profile describes the ways the system is to be used. One can uncover several deficiencies in the system while tuning the parameters of the system; parameter tuning will improve system availability level. Customers must be willing to share the operational profile of their computing environment to improve the target availability level, which may be proprietary information.

Maintainability and Serviceability   The maintainability of a system is its ability to undergo repair and evolution. One way to characterize maintainability is to measure the MTTR, which reflects the time it takes to analyze a *corrective* defect, design a modification, implement the change, test it, and distribute it. The important factors, from a customer's perspective, is the responsiveness of the service rather than the internal technical maintainability of the system. The following are useful acceptance criteria from a customer's perspective:

- The customer is the final arbiter of setting the severity of a system problem. If the customer calls a problem critical, it must be fixed immediately.

- If a system problem is assessed as critical by the customer, then staff must be assigned to work on resolving the problem immediately with utmost priority.

- If the severity of a system problem is assessed as high by the customer, then staff must be assigned to work on resolving the problem during normal business hours until it is resolved or until a work-around has been delivered as an interim solution. The staff responsible for resolving the problem must ensure that there is significant effort made toward resolving the problem. However, they may spend time on other activities as priorities dictate.

- If a system problem is assessed as low by the customer, then staff must be assigned to work on resolving the problem during normal business hours as time permits. If the problem solution involves a software change, it will normally wait until the next software release has been implemented to provide the resolution.

- All the critical- and high-severity fixes must work 100% when installed.

Serviceability is closely related to maintainability of the system, which are designed to ensure the correctness of the tools that are used to diagnose and service the system. For example, the software may need to be serviced remotely via an Internet connection. Diagnostic utilities are used to monitor the operation and the cause of any malfunction. The following questions must be addressed in specifying the serviceability acceptance criteria:

- What kind of tools will be available for servicing the system?
- How should these tools be used?

Robustness The robustness of a system is defined as its ability to recover from errors, continue to operate under worst conditions, and operate reliably for an extended period of time. The following questions must be addressed in specifying the robustness acceptance criteria:

- What are the types of errors from which the system is expected to recover?
- What are the causes, or sources, of the errors so that these can be simulated in a test environment?
- How are the errors initiated, or triggered, in the real world?
- What types of corrective and recovery actions are required for each type of error?
- What kinds of disasters can strike? What are those scenarios?
- What is an acceptable response to each of these identified scenarios?
- What is the recovery mechanism for each of the scenarios? Is it workable, understood, and accepted?
- How can disaster be simulated in order to test recovery?

Timeliness Time to market is an important aspect of any contractual agreement. The supplier must be able to deliver the system to the buyer within the time frame agreed upon. Rewards and penalties are associated with the timeliness acceptance criteria as follows:

- If coding is completed on time, the buyer will reward 5% extra money on top of the contractual agreement.
- If system-level testing is completed on time, the buyer will reward 10% extra money on top of the contractual agreement.
- For every week of delay in completing the system tests, the supplier has to pay 2% penalty on top of the contractual agreement, with a maximum of 20% penalty.

Confidentiality and Availability The confidentiality acceptance criteria refer to the requirement that the data must be protected from unauthorized disclosure and the availability acceptance criteria to the requirement that the data must be protected from a denial of service (DoS) to authorized users. Different types of possible confidentiality and availability acceptance criteria are as follows:

- No unauthorized access to the system is permitted, that is, user authentication is performed.
- Files and other data are protected from unauthorized access.
- The system is protected against virus, worm, and bot attacks.
- Tools are available for detecting attacks.
- There is support against DoS attack.
- Privacy in communication is achieved by using encryption.

- All the customer data must be stored in a secure place in accordance with the policies of customer right, such as confidentiality.

Remark. A worm is defined as a software component that is capable of, under its own means, infecting a computer system in an automated fashion. On the other hand, a virus spreads rapidly to a large number of computers. However, it cannot do so with its own capability; it spreads using the assistance of another program.

Remark. A bot is a software agent. A bot interacts with other network services intended for people as if it were a person. One typical use of bots is to gather information. Another more malicious use for bots is the coordination and operation of an automated attack on networked computers, such as a distributed DoS attack.

Compatibility and Interoperability   The compatibility of a system is defined as the ability to operate in the same way across different platforms and network configurations and in the *presence* of different mixes of other applications. On the other hand, the interoperability of a system is defined as the ability to *interface* with other network elements and work correctly as expected. The major challenge is in determining the platforms, configurations, and other applications with which the system is compatible. The following questions must be addressed in specifying the compatibility and interoperability acceptance criteria:

- What are the platforms, or configurations, on which the system must operate?
- Does the system have to work exactly the same way across different configurations? If not, what are the acceptable variations?
- What are the applications that must coexist with the system?
- With what network elements must the system interoperate?

Compliance   The system should comply with the relevant technical standards, such as the IEEE standards, operating system interface standards, and the IP standards. In addition, the system should comply with regulatory requirements as established by external agencies. The following questions must be addressed in specifying the acceptance criteria for compliance:

- With what technical standards should the system comply? Are there any exceptions to these standards? If yes, specify the exceptions.
- Identify the regulatory bodies that must certify the system?

Installability and Upgradability   The purpose of system installability and upgradability is to ensure that the system can be correctly installed and upgraded in the customer environment. If for some reason the customer wants to uninstall or downgrade the system software, it is required to be done smoothly. Installation and upgradation of a system is planned by identifying the major milestones and contingency steps. The system installation and upgradation process document must be available with specific steps. The acceptance criteria of system installation and upgradation are as follows:

- The document must identify the person to install the system, for example, the end user or a trained technician from the supplier side.
- Over what range of platforms, configurations, and versions of support software is the installation or upgradation process expected to work? The hardware and software requirements must be clearly explained in the document.
- Can the installation or upgradation process change the user's existing environment? If yes, the risks of this change should be clearly documented.
- The installation or upgradation process should include diagnostic and corrective steps to be used in the event of the process not progressing as expected.
- The installation or upgradation process should contain a workable uninstall, downgrade, or backoff process in case a specific installation does not proceed as expected.
- The installation or upgradation process should correctly work from all of the various delivery media, such as download via File Transfer Protocol (FTP), CD-ROM, and DVD.
- If the system includes a licensing and registration process, it should work smoothly and should be documented.
- The installation or upgradation instructions should be complete, correct, and usable.
- The installation or upgradation process should be verified during system testing.
- There should be zero defects outstanding against a system installation or upgradation process.

Scalability The scalability of a system is defined as its ability to effectively provide acceptable performance as the following quantities increase: (i) geographic area of coverage of a system, (ii) system size in terms of the number of elements in the system, (iii) number of users, and (iv) volume of workload per unit time. A system may work as expected in limited-use scenarios but may not scale up very well. The following questions must be addressed in specifying the scalability acceptance criteria:

- How many concurrent users is the system expected to handle?
- How many transactions per unit time is the system expected to process?
- How many database records is the system expected to support?
- How many elements, or objects, must be managed in live operation?
- What is the largest geographic area the system can cover?

Documentation The quality of the system user's guide must be high. The documentation acceptance criteria are formulated as follows:

- All the user documents should be reviewed and approved by the software quality assurance group for correctness, accuracy, readability, and usefulness.
- The on-line help should be reviewed and signed off by the software quality assurance group.

14.3 SELECTION OF ACCEPTANCE CRITERIA

The acceptance criteria discussed above provide a broad idea about customer needs and expectations, but those are too many and very general. The customer needs to select a subset of the quality attributes and prioritize them to suit their specific situation. Next, the customer identifies the acceptance criteria for each of the selected quality attributes. When the customer and the software vendor reach an agreement on the acceptance criteria, both parties must keep in mind that satisfaction of the acceptance criteria is a trade-off between time, cost, and quality. As Ed Yourdon opined, sometimes less than perfect is good enough [6]. Only business goals and priority can determine the degree of "less than perfect" that is acceptable to both the parties. Ultimately, the acceptance criteria must be related to the business goals of the customer's organization.

Many organizations associated with different application domains have selected and customized existing quality attributes to define quality for themselves, taking into consideration their specific business and market situation. For example, IBM used the quality attribute list CUPRIMDS—capability, usability, performance, reliability, installation, maintenance, documentation, and service—for its products [7]. Similarly, for web-based applications [8], a set of quality attributes are identified in decreasing order of priority: reliability, usability, security, availability, scalability, maintainability, and time to market. Such a prioritization scheme is often used in specific application domains. For example, usability and maintainability take precedence over performance and reliability for a word processor software. On the other hand, it might be the other way around for a real-time operating system or telecommunication software.

14.4 ACCEPTANCE TEST PLAN

Planning for acceptance testing begins as soon as the acceptance criteria are known. Early development of an acceptance test plan (ATP) gives us a good picture of the final product. The purpose of an ATP is to develop a detailed outline of the process to test the system prior to making a transition to the actual business use of the system. Often, the ATP is delivered by the vendor as a contractual agreement, so that the business acceptance testing can be undertaken within the vendor's development organization to ensure that the system eventually passes the acceptance test.

In developing an ATP, emphasis is put on demonstrating that the system works according to the customer's expectation, rather than passing a set of comprehensive tests. In any case, the system is expected to have already passed a set of comprehensive tests during system-level testing. The ATP must be kept very simple because the audience of this plan may include people from diverse backgrounds, such as marketing and business managers. Some people argue that the ATP is redundant and unnecessary if a comprehensive system test plan is developed. We believe that even if a system test plan is adequate, acceptance tests usually uncover additional significant problems. Moreover, user's concerns are not addressed during system-level testing.

An ATP needs to be written and executed by the customer's special user group. The user group consists of people from different backgrounds, such as software quality assurance engineers, business associates, and customer support engineers. In addition, the acceptance test cases are executed at the user's operational environment, whereas the system-level test cases are executed in a laboratory environment. An overall test plan for acceptance testing and description of specific tests are documented in the ATP. The structure of a typical ATP is outlined in Table 14.1.

The introduction section of the ATP describes the structure of the test plan and what we intend to accomplish with this test plan. This section typically includes (i) test project name, (ii) revision history, (iii) terminology and definitions, (iv) names of the approvers and the date of approval, (v) an overview of the plan, and (vi) references.

For each quality category from the acceptance criteria signed-off document two subsections are created: operational environment and test case specification. The operational environment deals with discussion on site preparation for the execution of the acceptance test cases. Test cases are specified for each acceptance criteria within the quality category.

An outline of the timeline of execution of acceptance tests is provided in the schedule section of the ATP. Acceptance test execution is not intended to be exhaustive, and therefore it does not continue for long. The acceptance test

TABLE 14.1 Outline of ATP

1. Introduction
2. Acceptance test category. For each category of acceptance criteria:
   (a) Operational environment
   (b) Test case specification
      (i) Test case ID number
      (ii) Test title
      (iii) Test objective
      (iv) Test procedure
3. Schedule
4. Human resources

may take up to six weeks for a large system. The point here is that comprehensive acceptance testing, to the same extent and depth as targeted by system-level testing, is not required to demonstrate that the acceptance criteria are satisfied by the system.

The human resources section of the ATP deals with (i) the identification of the acceptance testers that form the client organization and (ii) their specific roles in the execution of acceptance test cases. The section includes acceptance test site preparation, overseeing installation of new hardware, upgrading the software, and setting up of the networks. These are the people who are knowledgeable in the operational environment and business operations. In addition, the human resources requirement from the supplier organization during the acceptance testing is included in this section. These engineers are usually from the supplier's system test group, who participated in testing the system.

The ATP is reviewed and approved by the relevant groups, such as the marketing, customer support, and software quality assurance groups. It can be shared with the system supplier organization.

14.5   ACCEPTANCE TEST EXECUTION

The acceptance test cases are divided into two subgroups. The first subgroup consists of basic test cases, and the second consists of test cases that are more complex to execute. The acceptance tests are executed in two phases. In the first phase, the test cases from the basic test group are executed. If the test results are satisfactory, then the second phase, in which the complex test cases are executed, is taken up. In addition to the basic test cases, a subset of the system-level test cases are executed by the acceptance test engineers to independently confirm the test results. Obviously, a key question is: Which subset of the system-level test cases are selected? It is recommended to randomly select 5–10 test cases from each test category. If a very large fraction, say more than 0.95, of the basic test cases pass, then the second phase can proceed. It may be counterproductive to carry out the execution of the more complex tests if a significant fraction of the basic tests fail.

Acceptance test execution is an important activity performed by the customer with much support from the developers. The activity includes the following detailed actions:

- The developers train the customer on the usage of the system.
- The developers and the customer coordinate the fixing of any problem discovered during acceptance testing.
- The developers and the customer resolve the issues arising out of any acceptance criteria discrepancy.

System-level test personnel from the development organization travel to the customer location where the acceptance tests are to be conducted. They assist the

TABLE 14.2 ACC Document Information

1. ACC number	A unique number
2. Acceptance criteria affected	Existing acceptance criteria
3. Problem/issue description	Brief description of issue
4. Description of change required	Description of changes needed to be done to original acceptance criterion
5. Secondary technical impacts	Description of impact it will have on system
6. Customer impacts	Impact it will have on end user
7. Change recommended by	Name of acceptance test engineer(s)
8. Change approved by	Name of approver(s) from both parties

customer in preparing a test site and train the acceptance test engineers on how to use the system. They provide the earlier system-level test results to the customer's test engineers in order to make informal decisions about the direction and focus of the acceptance testing effort. In addition, the on-site system test engineers answer the customer's questions about the system and assist the acceptance test engineers in executing the acceptance tests.

Any defect encountered during acceptance testing are reported to the software development organization through the on-site system test engineers. The defects are submitted through the defect tracking system. The software build is retested by the supplier and a satisfactory software image is made available to the customer for continuation of acceptance testing when the defects are fixed. The failed tests are repeated after the system is upgraded with a new software image. An agreement must be reached between the on-site system test engineers and the acceptance test engineers when to accept a new software image for acceptance testing. The number of times the system can be upgraded to a new software image during acceptance testing is negotiated between the customer and the supplier. Multiple failures of a system during acceptance testing are an indication of poor system quality.

It is possible that an acceptance test engineer may encounter issues related to acceptance criteria during the execution of acceptance test cases. The system may not provide services to the users as described in the acceptance criteria. Any deviation from the acceptance criteria discovered at this stage may not be fixed immediately. The acceptance test engineer may create an acceptance criteria change (ACC) document to communicate the deficiency in the acceptance criteria to the supplier. A representative format of an ACC document is shown in Table 14.2. An ACC report is generally given to the supplier's marketing department through the on-site system test engineers.

14.6 ACCEPTANCE TEST REPORT

Acceptance test activities are designed to reach one of three conclusions: Accept the system as delivered, accept the system after the requested modifications have been made, or do not accept the system. Usually some useful intermediate decisions are made before making the final decision:

- A decision is made about the continuation of acceptance testing if the results of the first phase of acceptance testing are not promising. One may recall that the basic tests are executed in the first phase.
- If the test results are unsatisfactory, changes will be made to the system before acceptance testing can proceed to the next phase.

The intermediate decisions are made based on evaluation of the results of the first phase of testing. Moreover, during the execution of acceptance tests, the status of testing is reviewed at the end of every working day by the leader of the acceptance test team, on-site system test engineers, and project managers of the customer and the supplier. The acceptance team prepares a test report which forms the basis of discussion at the review meeting before they meet for a review. A template of the test report is given in Table 14.3.

The test report is reviewed on a daily basis to understand the status and progress of acceptance testing. If serious problems are encountered during acceptance testing, the project manager flags the issues to the senior management.

At the end of the first and the second phases of acceptance testing an acceptance test report is generated by the test team leader. A template for a test report is outlined in Table 14.4. Most of the information from the test status report can be used in the acceptance test summary report.

The report identifier uniquely identifies the report. It is used to keep track of the document under version control.

The summary section summarizes what acceptance testing activities took place, including the test phases, releases of the software used, and the test environment. This section normally includes references to the ATP, acceptance criteria, and requirements specification.

The variances section describes any difference between the testing that was planned and the actual testing carried out. It provides an insight into a process for improving acceptance test planning in the future.

TABLE 14.3 Structure of Acceptance Test Status Report

1. Date	Acceptance report date
2. Test case execution status	Number of test cases executed today
	Number of test cases passing
	Number of test cases failing
3. Defect identifier	Submitted defect number
	Brief description of issue
4. ACC number(s)	Acceptance criteria change document number(s), if any
5. Cumulative test execution status	Total number of test cases executed
	Total number of test cases passing
	Total number of test cases failing
	Total number of test cases not executed yet

TABLE 14.4   Structure of Acceptance Test Summary Report

1. Report identifier
2. Summary
3. Variances
4. Summary of results
5. Evaluation
6. Recommendations
7. Summary of activities
8. Approval

In the summary of results section of the document test results are summarized. The section gives the total number of test cases executed, the number of passing test cases, and the number of failing test cases; identifies all the defects; and summarizes the acceptance criteria to be changed.

The evaluation section provides an overall assessment of each category of the quality attributes identified in the acceptance criteria document, including their limitations. This evaluation is based on the test results from each category of the test plan. The deviations of the acceptance criteria that are captured in the ACC during the acceptance testing are discussed.

The recommendations section includes the acceptance test team's overall recommendation: (i) unconditionally accept the system, (ii) accept the system subject to certain conditions being met, or (iii) reject the system. However, the ultimate decision is made by the business experts of the supplier and the buyer organization.

The summary of activities section summarizes the testing activities and the major events. This section includes information about the resources consumed by the various activities. For example, the total manpower involved in and the time spent for each of the major testing activities are given. This section is useful to management for accurately estimating future acceptance testing efforts.

Finally, the names and titles of all the people that will approve this report are listed in the approvals section. Ideally, the approvers of this report should be the same people who approved the corresponding ATP because the summary report describes all the activities outlined in the ATP. If some of the reviewers have minor disagreements, they may note their views before signing off on the document.

14.7   ACCEPTANCE TESTING IN eXtreme PROGRAMMING

In the XP[9] framework user stories are used as acceptance criteria. The user stories are used to derive time estimates for each development iteration in release planning (time-to-market acceptance criteria) and acceptance tests. The user stories are written by the customer as things that the system needs to do for them. The stories are usually about two to three sentences of text written using the customer's terminology. Several acceptance tests are created to verify that the user story has been correctly implemented. Acceptance tests are specified in a format that is clear enough that the customer can understand and specific enough that it can be executed.

The customer is responsible for verifying the correctness of the acceptance tests and reviewing the test results [10]. The acceptance test results are reviewed by the customer to decide what failed tests are of highest priority that must pass during the next iteration. A story is incomplete until it passes its associated acceptance tests.

Acceptance tests are executed by an acceptance test group, which is a part of the development team. Ideally, acceptance tests should be automated using either the unit testing framework or a separate acceptance testing framework before coding. Acceptance test engineers and customers can run the tests multiple times per day as a regression acceptance test suite after the acceptance tests are automated. An automated acceptance test suite does not lose its value even after the customer has approved the successful implementation of the user story in a development iteration. The acceptance tests take on the role of regression tests to ensure that subsequent changes to the system do not affect the unaltered functionality.

14.8 SUMMARY

This chapter began with an introduction to two types of acceptance testing: user acceptance testing and business acceptance testing. Next, the chapter described acceptance criteria in terms of quality attributes. Formulation of acceptances criteria is governed by the business goals of the customer's organization.

We presented an outline of an acceptance test plan and described in detail how to create such a plan. Emphasis must be put on the notion that the system works according to the customer's expectations in developing an acceptance test plan, rather than just passing comprehensive testing. Less emphasis is put on a system passing a comprehensive set of tests because rigorous testing is assumed to have already occurred during the system testing phase.

Next, we discussed the execution of acceptance tests, which is an important activity performed by the customer with much needed support from the developers. Three major activities were identified and discussed: (i) providing training to the customer's test engineers, (ii) fixing problems during acceptance testing, and (iii) resolving issues concerning any discrepancy related to acceptance criteria. After that, we described the generation of an acceptance test report, which must be completed at the end of acceptance testing.

Finally, we explained how user stories are used in XP as acceptance criteria and acceptance test cases are created. These tests are reviewed, automated, and executed multiple times per day as a regression acceptance test suite in the presence of on-site customers.

LITERATURE REVIEW

A thorough treatment of software quality standard can be found in ISO/IEC 9126-1:2001, "Software Engineering—Product Quality—Part-I: Quality Model." The standards group has recommended a hierarchical framework for software quality characteristics and subcharacteristics. Six top-level software quality characteristics are *functionality, reliability, usability, efficiency, maintainability,* and *portability*.

An excellent taxonomy in the field of the *dependability* quality attribute is presented in the article by Algirdas Avižienis, Jean-Claude Laprie, Brian Randell, and Carl Landwehr, "Basic Concepts and Taxonomy of Dependable and Secure Computing," *IEEE Transactions on Dependable and Secure Computing,* Vol. 1, No. 1, January–March 2004, pp. 11–33. In this article, the relationship between dependability and *security* quality attributes is discussed in great detail. Dependability is defined as an integrating concept that encompasses the following attributes: availability, reliability, safety, integrity, and maintainability. On the other hand, security brings in concerns for confidentiality in addition to availability and integrity. The article addresses the concept of threats to dependability and security (faults, errors, failures), their attributes, and the means for their achievement, such as fault prevention, fault tolerance, fault removal, and fault forecasting.

An interesting view of software quality characteristics is presented in C. K. Prahalad and M. S. Krishnan, "The New Meaning of Quality in the Information Age," *Harvard Business Review,* September 1999, pp. 109–118. The authors provide a framework for measuring the performance of software in a company's information technology portfolio based on three basic attributes: conformance, adaptability, and innovation. To judge software quality properly, the authors argue that managers must measure applications against all the three attributes.

The students are encouraged to read the article by P. Hsia, D. Kung, and C. Sell, "Software Requirements and Acceptance Testing," *Annals of Software Engineering,* Vol. 3, No. 0, January 1997, pp. 291–317. The authors present a systematic approach to scenario analysis and its application to acceptance testing. Based on the model, different acceptance test criteria are defined, and various types of acceptance testing are discussed.

The book entitled *Testing Extreme Programming* (L. Crispin and T. House, Addison-Wesley, Boston, MA, 2003) gives an excellent exposition of unit and acceptance testing in XP. The book is divided into three parts: the XP tester role, test drive through an XP project, and road hazard survival kit. The book lists several excellent books on the subject in its bibliography.

REFERENCES

1. Institute of Electrical and Electronics Engineers (IEEE). *IEEE Standard Glossary of Software Engineering Terminology.* IEEE standard 610.12-1990. IEEE, New York, 1990.
2. B. Kitchenham and S. L. Pfleeger. Software Quality: The Elusive Target. *IEEE Software,* January 1996, pp. 12–21.

3. D. A. Garvin. What Does Product Quality Really Mean? *Sloan Management Review*, Fall 1984, pp. 25–45.

4. K. Sankar, S. Sundaralingam, A. Balinsky, and D. Miller. *Cisco Wireless LAN Security*. Cisco Press, Indianapolis, IN, 2005.

5. U. Troppens, R. Erkens, and W. Müller. In *Storage Networks Explained (Chapter 7: Network Back-up)*. Wiley, Hoboken, NJ, 2004.

6. E. Yourdon. When Good Enough Software Is Best. *IEEE Software*, May 1995, pp. 79–81.

7. S. H. Kan. *Metrics and Models in Software Quality Engineering*, 2nd ed. Addison-Wesley, Reading, MA, 2002.

8. J. Offutt. Quality Attributes of Web Application. *IEEE Software*, February 2002, pp. 25–32.

9. K. Beck and C. Andres. *Extreme Programming Explained: Embrace Change*, 2nd ed. Addison-Wesley, Reading, MA, 2004.

10. R. Mugridge. Managing Agile Project Requirements with Storytest-Driven Development. *IEEE Software*, January 2008, pp. 68–75.

Exercises

1. What are the objectives of acceptance testing?

2. What are the differences between UAT and BAT?

3. Discuss the advantages and disadvantages of customer involvement in testing.

4. What is software quality?

5. Who should define the acceptance quality attribute criteria of a test project. Justify your answer?

6. What other quality attributes not mentioned in this book can you think of?

7. What is meant by DoS attack? Explain its importance in acceptance testing.

8. The security quality attribute is not explicitly discussed in this book. However, it can be a combination of subattributes, which are discussed in this book. What are those quality subattributes?

9. In the following series of application examples, provide four most important quality attributes discussed in this book that you think are critical to the applications. Why are the quality attributes chosen by you critical ones?

    (a) Telecommunication software

    (b) Video game software

    (c) Intrusion detection system (IDS) software

    (d) Medical diagnostic software for assisting doctors

    (e) Highly popular music download website

    (f) Operating system on deep space mission probe

    (g) Pension payment calculation system

    (h) E-mail system

    (i) Aircraft system software

    (j) Semiautomated telephone service to help answer questions about immigration and citizenship laws

10. Why are acceptance test cases executed in two phases?

11. Why are system test engineers required to be present at the ATP execution site?

12. For the current software project you are working on, answer the following questions:

    (a) List the quality attributes most important to your project. In order to focus on the business acceptance tests, select no more than six quality attributes from this list as the most critical acceptance criteria for your system.

    (b) Why are the selected acceptance criteria the most critical ones for your system?

    (c) Are there any other acceptance criteria which apply to your system but not listed in this book?

13. Based on the six selected acceptance criteria you identified for your software project in the previous questions:

    (a) Develop a business ATP.

    (b) Execute the business ATP against the system.

    (c) Generate an ACC document if you observed any deviation from the acceptance criteria during the execution of the ATP.

    (d) Create an acceptance test summary report.

CHAPTER 15

Software Reliability

Failure is only postponed success as long as courage "coaches" ambition. The habit of persistence is the habit of victory.

— *Herbert Kaufman*

15.1 WHAT IS RELIABILITY?

The concept of *reliability* is very broad, and it can be applied whenever someone expects something or someone else to "behave" in a certain way. For example, a lighting switch is expected to stay in one of two states—on and off—as set by its user. If a lighting switch causes a lamp to flicker even when the power supply is stable and the connecting cables are fault free, we say that the switch has turned unreliable. As a customer, we expect a new switch not to cause any flicker. We say that the switch is faulty if it causes a lamp to flicker. Moreover, a new switch may operate in a fault-free manner for several years before it starts causing the lamp to flicker. In that case we say that wear and tear have caused the switch to malfunction, and thus the switch has become unreliable. Therefore, the concept of fault is intertwined with the concept of reliability.

An initially fault-free hardware system behaves in a reliable manner simply because it operates as expected due to absence of faults in its design and manufacturing. Once the new hardware system starts functioning, wear and tear can cause it to develop faults, thereby causing the system to behave in an unexpected, or unreliable, manner. The sources of failures in software systems are design and implementation faults. Software failures usually occur when a program is executed in an environment that it was not developed for or tested for.

Reliability is one of the metrics used to measure the quality of a software system. It is arguably the most important quality factor sought in a product. Reliability is a user-oriented quality factor relating to system *operation*, and it takes into account the frequency of system failure. Intuitively, if the users of a system rarely experience system failure, then the system is considered to be more reliable than one that fails more often. The more and more failures of a system are observed by

---

Software Testing and Quality Assurance: Theory and Practice, Edited by Kshirasagar Naik and Priyadarshi Tripathy
Copyright © 2008 John Wiley & Sons, Inc.

users, the less and less the system is perceived to be reliable. Ideally, if there are no faults in a software system, users will never experience system failure, thereby considering the system to be highly reliable. Constructing a "correct" system, that is, a fault-free system, is a difficult task by itself given that real-life systems are inherently complex. The problem of constructing a fault-free system becomes more difficult when real-life factors are considered. For example, developing software systems is largely an economic activity, and companies may rarely have all the time and money needed to produce a highly reliable system even when they have a team of highly qualified and experienced personnel in the best case. The concept of *market window* may not allow a company to make an effort at producing a "correct" system. A market window is considered to be a time interval available for the introduction of a product before the product is surpassed in capability or cost by another from a competing vendor. Economic considerations may drive companies to trade off reliability in favor of cutting cost and meeting delivery schedule.

Given that there are an unknown number of faults in a delivered system and users can tolerate some failures, system reliability is best represented as a continuous variable rather than a Boolean variable. More efforts put into the development phase generally lead to a higher degree of reliability. Conversely, less effort produces systems with lower reliability. Thus, the concept of reliability can be used in examining the significance of trends, in setting goals, and in predicting when those goals will be achieved. For example, developers may be interested in knowing how a certain development process, how the length of system testing, or how a design review technique impacts software reliability. Developers may be interested in knowing the rate of system failure in a certain operational environment so as to be able to decide when to release the product.

Software maintenance involves making different kinds of changes to the system, namely, changes to requirements, changes to the design, changes to source code, and changes to test cases. While making those changes, the software goes through a phase of instability. The instability is in the form of reduced reliability of the system. The reliability level of a system decreases during system maintenance because additional defects may be introduced while making all those kinds of changes to the system. Intuitively, the smaller the amount of changes made to a system, the lesser the degradation in the current reliability level of the system. On the other hand, too many changes being simultaneously made to the system may significantly degrade the reliability level. Thus, the amount of changes that should be made to a product at a given time is dependent upon how much reliability one is ready to sacrifice for the moment.

15.1.1 Fault and Failure

The notions of *fault, failure*, and *time* are central to our understanding of reliability. In general, if a user never observes failures, the system is considered to be very reliable. On the other hand, a frequently failing system is considered to be highly unreliable. Therefore, we revisit the terms fault and failure in this section. A failure is said to occur if the *observable* outcome of a program execution is different from the expected outcome. The concept of observable outcome is very broad, and it encompasses a variety of things, such as values produced, values communicated, performance demonstrated, and so on. The expected outcomes of program executions are specified as system requirements. System requirements are generally stated in explicit form in a requirements document. Sometimes, due to the complex nature of software systems, it is extremely difficult to explicitly state all the desired requirements. Where it is not possible to state all the requirements in an explicit manner, we still expect a system to behave in certain ways. Thus, while considering what is an expected outcome of program execution, one must take into account both the explicitly stated and the implicitly expected system requirements. Two characteristics of failures are as follows: (i) failures are associated with actual program executions and (ii) failures are observable concepts.

The adjudged cause of a failure is called a fault. While constructing a software system, a designer may mistakenly introduce a fault into the system. A fault can be introduced by having a defective block of code, a missing block of code for an unforeseen execution scenario, and so on. The mere presence of faults in a system does not cause failure. Rather, one or more defective portions of a system must execute for a fault to manifest itself as a system failure. One fault can cause more than one failure depending upon how the system executes the faulty code [1].

15.1.2 Time

Time plays a key role in modeling software reliability metrics. Let us go back to the concept of reliability of a lighting switch. Assume that a switch causes a lamp to flicker for a couple seconds, and let the average time gap between two successive flickers be six months. Here, flickering of the lamp can be considered as an observable failure of the switch. Though users may be irritated by such flickers, some may still consider the switch to be reliable because of the long time gap between two flickers. A time gap of six months can be considered to be long because a user may not remember when the lamp flickered last. However, if the lamp flickers a few times everyday, the switch appears less reliable and becomes a candidate for replacement. Thus, the notion of time is important in understanding the concept of reliability.

There are two commonly considered time models in the study of software reliability:

- Execution time (τ)
- Calendar time (t)

The *execution time* for a software system is the actual time spent by a processor in executing the instructions of the software system. Sometimes a processor may execute code from different software systems, and therefore, their individual execution times must be considered separately. On the one hand, there are many software systems which are expected to run continuously for months and years without developing failure. Examples of such systems are telephone switching software, air-traffic control software, and software for monitoring power plants. On the other hand, there are software systems which run for a while and terminate upon completion of their tasks. For example, a compiler terminates after compiling a program. Though the concept of software reliability can be applied to all kinds of software systems, the ones running continuously draw more attention.

Calendar time is the time more commonly understood and followed in everyday life by all, including software engineers and project managers. Since observation of failures, fixing the corresponding faults, and replacing an old version of a software with a new one are intertwined in the life cycle of software systems, calendar time is useful for pragmatic reasons such as engineers leaving a company, engineers going on leave, and so on.

A third time model occasionally referred to is the *clock time* of a software system. Clock time refers to the elapsed time between the start and the end of program execution. Clock time includes the wait time of the software system and execution times of other software systems. Clock time does not include system shutdown.

In order to have a better understanding of the reliability of a software, one can ask the following questions in terms of failure and time:

- What is the time interval between two successive failures?
- How many failures have been observed within a certain time interval, for example, in the past one month or one year?
- What is the total number of failures observed so far?

The answers to the above questions give an indication of the quality level of a software. One can ask the above questions at any instant after code is developed. By asking the above questions during development, a test manager can monitor how the quality of the software is improving. On the other hand, by answering the questions during the operation of the system, one can know the delivered quality of the product.

15.1.3 Time Interval between Failures

One can infer several characteristics of a software system by monitoring the time interval between successive failures as follows:

- A small time interval between successive failures tells us that the software system is failing frequently, and hence the reliability level is too low. This can happen during system testing or even while the system is in operation. If the time interval between successive failures is long, the reliability is perceived to be high, in spite of the occasional system failure. The concepts of "short" and "long" time intervals between successive failures is a matter of user perception that is largely defined by the consequences of the failures. For example, if the operating system of a personal computer crashes about once in a year, the users can still consider the system to be reliable. On the other hand, if an air-traffic control software installed in a major international airport crashes once in a year, the system will be considered to be highly unreliable.

  In the hardware industry, a number of reliability metrics have been identified by considering the instants when failures occur and the instants when the corresponding faults are repaired. The three commonly used metrics based on time intervals are the mean time to failure (MTTF), the mean time to repair (MTTR), and the mean time between failure (MTBF). When a failure occurs, it takes a certain amount of time to repair the system. The mean of all the repair times is the MTTR. We assume that a system is not in operation while it is being repaired. Thus, the mean of all the time intervals between the completion of a repair task and the occurrence of the next failure is the MTTF. The mean of the time intervals between successive failures is the (MTBF). The terms MTTR, MTTF, and MTBF are illustrated in Figure 15.1. A useful relationship between the three metrics can be stated as MTBF = MTTF + MTTR. It is easy to verify the relationship by considering the time intervals in Figure 15.1.

- At the beginning of system-level testing, usually a large number of failures are observed with small time intervals between successive failures. As system testing continues and faults are actually fixed, the time interval between successive failures increases, thereby giving an evidence that the reliability of the product is increasing. By monitoring the time interval between successive failures, one gets an idea about the reliability of the software system.

15.1.4   Counting Failures in Periodic Intervals

Useful information can be gathered by monitoring the cumulative failure count on a periodic basis. For example, we record the cumulative failure count every

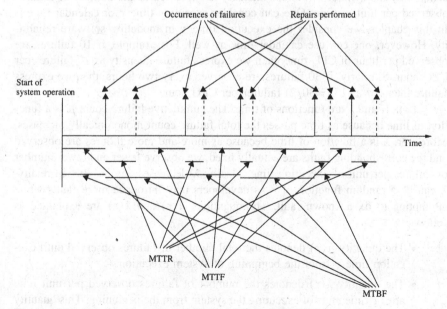

Figure 15.1   Relationship between MTTR, MTTF, and MTBF.

month, plot it as a bar chart, and observe the pattern. Such monitoring can be done during system testing as well as while a system is in operation. During system testing, monitoring can be done at a fast pace, such as once per week, because of the large number of failures observed during testing. Development engineers and managers would like to observe the improvement in the reliability of the system under development. For a system already in operation, monitoring can be done once or twice per year. One can observe a number of system failures during its operation because of two reasons. First, there is a residual number of faults in most systems and systems might not have been tested in their real execution environments. Second, additional faults might be inadvertently introduced into a system during system maintenance.

15.1.5 Failure Intensity

By counting the total number of failures observed so far and plotting the data as a function of time, one can observe the change in the reliability of the system. This information is useful while a software is undergoing system-level testing as well as while a system is in operation. Ideally, the reliability level should reach a stable value after a while. A rising graph of the cumulative number of failures tells us that there are more faults in the system, and hence the system is perceived to be unreliable. The rate of rising of the graph is the rate at which failures are being observed. If the rate of rising is very small, we know that failures are infrequently being observed.

Two failure-related quantities that are generally used in defining software reliability are *cumulative failure*, denoted by the symbol μ, and *failure intensity*, denoted by the symbol λ. Failure intensity is expressed as the number of failures observed per unit of time. One can consider execution time τ or calendar time t. In this chapter, we consider the execution time τ in modeling software reliability. However, one can use calendar time as well. For example, if 10 failures are observed per hour of CPU time, then we express failure intensity as 10 failures per CPU hour. Similarly, if 30 failures are observed every two hours, then we express failure intensity as 15 ($=30/2$) failures per CPU hour.

Both μ and λ are functions of time. The cumulative failure count μ is a function of time because as time passes the total failure count monotonically increases. Moreover, λ is a function of time because as more and more failures are observed and the corresponding faults are actually fixed, we observe fewer and fewer number of failures per unit of execution time. Ideally, λ decreases with τ. But, in reality, λ can be a random function of τ as developers may introduce more faults while attempting to fix a known fault. The quantities $\mu(\tau)$ and $\lambda(\tau)$ are explained as follows:

- The quantity $\mu(\tau)$ denotes the total number of failures observed until execution time τ from the beginning of system execution.
- The quantity $\lambda(\tau)$ denotes the number of failures observed per unit time after τ time units of executing the system from the beginning. This quantity is also called the failure intensity observed at time τ.

Given these definitions, it is not difficult to establish the following relationship between $\mu(\tau)$ and $\lambda(\tau)$:

$$\lambda(\tau) = \frac{d\mu(\tau)}{d\tau}$$

Conversely, if we know the *failure intensity function*, we obtain the *mean value function* [2]:

$$\mu(\tau) = \int_0^\tau \lambda(x) \, dx$$

15.2 DEFINITIONS OF SOFTWARE RELIABILITY

There are two commonly used software reliability metrics, namely, the *probability of failure-free operation* and the *failure intensity*. The concept of failure is common to both definitions. One metric is probabilistic in nature, whereas the other is an absolute one. The two definitions are not contradictory. Rather, both can be simultaneously applied to the same software system without any inconsistency between them. User expectations from different systems may be different, and therefore it is more useful to apply one of the two to a given system. In the following, first the two metrics are defined, followed by examples of their applications to different systems.

15.2.1 First Definition of Software Reliability

Definition. Software reliability is defined as the probability of failure-free operation of a software system for a specified time in a specified environment.

The key elements of the above definition of reliability are as follows:

- Probability of failure-free operation
- Length of time of failure-free operation
- A given execution environment

Software reliability is expressed as a continuous random variable due to the fact that most large software systems do have some unknown number of faults, and they can fail anytime depending upon their execution pattern. Therefore, it is useful to represent software reliability as a probabilistic quantity. Though software systems do fail from time to time, the users are interested in completing their tasks most of the time. The need for failure-free operation for a certain length of time is important due to the fact that a user intends to complete a task that demands some length of execution time. For example, consider an inventory management software system used by a large store. Assume that the store opens from 8 AM to 8 PM, and they shut down the system after store hours. The store owner expects the inventory system to be up and running for at least 12 hours without developing any failure.

One can specify the reliability of a software system running on a personal computer (PC) as follows. Assume that an office secretary turns on his or her PC every morning at 8.30 AM and turns it off at 4:30 PM before leaving for home. The secretary expects that the PC will run for eight hours without developing any failure. If he or she comes to the office for 200 days in a year and observes that the PC crashes five times on different days in a year for a few years, we can say that the probability of failure-free operation of the PC for eight hours was 0.975 [=(200 − 5)/200].

The third element in the definition of software reliability is an *execution environment*. An execution environment refers to how a user operates a software system. Not all users operate a software system in the same way. As an example, let us consider the case of a word processor. One group of users may be processing documents of small size, say 50 pages. A second group of users may be processing documents of large size, say, 1000 pages. Clearly, the two groups of users offer two different execution environments to the word processor. For example, to process documents of large size, the software is likely to invoke a part of its code for managing memory space which may not be needed to process a document of small size. The idea of how users operate a system gives rise to the concept of execution environment.

The concept of execution environment is an essential part of the definition of software reliability. Consider that a software system supports 10 different functions $f_1, \ldots, f_{10}$ and there are two groups of users. One group of users use only functions $f_1, \ldots, f_7$, and the second group uses all the functions. Let functions $f_1, \ldots, f_7$ be fault free, but there are faults in functions f_8, f_9, and f_{10}. Consequently, the first group of users will never observe any failure simply because their operations of the software system do not involve the faulty components of the software. From the viewpoint of the first group of users, the probability of failure-free operation of the software is 1.0. On the other hand, the second group of users will observe failure from time to time depending upon how frequently they use functions f_8, f_9, and f_{10}. Consequently, the level of reliability perceived by the second group of users is lower than that perceived by the first group of users. Therefore, the concept of execution environment is crucial to the definition of software reliability. In a later part of this chapter, the concept of operational profile will be discussed to describe execution environment.

15.2.2   Second Definition of Software Reliability

Definition.   Failure intensity is a measure of the reliability of a software system operating in a given environment.

According to the second definition, the lower the failure intensity of a software system, the higher is its reliability. To represent the current reliability level of a software system, one simply states the failure intensity of the system. For example, let a software system be in its system testing phase where test engineers are observing failures at the rate of 2 failures per eight hours of system execution.

Then, one can state the current level of the reliability of the system as 0.25 failure per hour. The figure 0.25 failure per hour is obtained by dividing 2 failures by eight hours.

15.2.3   Comparing the Definitions of Software Reliability

The first definition of software reliability emphasizes the importance of a software system operating without failure for a certain minimum length of time to complete a transaction. Here, reliability is a measure of what fraction of the total number of transactions a system is able to complete successfully. Let us assume that an autonomous robot is sent out to explore the underwater sea bed, and it takes three days to complete each round of exploration. In this case, we expect that the on-board software system resident in the robot is expected to run for at least three days continuously so that a round of exploration is successfully completed. If a robot system has successfully completed 99% of all the exploration rounds, we say that the software system's reliability is 0.99.

The second definition of reliability simply requires that there be as few failures as possible. Such an expectation takes the view that the risk of failure at any instant of time is of significant importance. This is very much the case in the operation of an air-traffic control system in an airport. This case is also applicable to the operation of telephone switches. In this definition, it does not matter for how long the system has been operating without failure. Rather, the very occurrence of a failure is of much significance. For example, the failing of a traffic control system in an airport can lead to a major catastrophe.

15.3   FACTORS INFLUENCING SOFTWARE RELIABILITY

A user's perception of the reliability of a software system depends upon two categories of information, namely, (i) the number of faults present in the software and (ii) the ways users operate the system. The second category of information is known as the *operational profile* of the system. The number of faults introduced in a system and the developers' inability to detect many of those faults depend upon several factors as explained below:

- **Size and Complexity of Code:** The number of LOC in a software system is a measure of its size. Large software systems with hundreds of thousands of LOC tend to have more faults than smaller systems. The likelihood of faults in a large system, because of more module interfaces, is higher. The more number of conditional statements the code contains, the more complex the system is considered to be. Due to the economic considerations in software development, one may not have much time to completely understand a large system. Consequently, faults are introduced into the system in all its development phases. Similarly, while removing faults from a large system, new faults may be introduced.

- **Characteristics of Development Process:** Much progress has been made in the past few decades in the field of software engineering. New techniques and tools have been developed to capture system requirements, to design software systems, to implement designs, and to test systems. For example, formal methods, such as SDL (Specification and Description Language) and UML (Unified Modeling Language), are used to specify the requirements of complex, real-time systems. Code review techniques have been developed to detect design and implementation faults. Test tools are available to assist programmers in their unit-level and system-level testing. By developing a system under a larger quality control umbrella in the form of embracing the above software engineering techniques and tools, the number of remaining faults in software systems can be reduced.

- **Education, Experience, and Training of Personnel:** The information technology industry has seen tremendous growth in the past 20 years or so. However, education of software engineering as a separate discipline of study at the undergraduate level is only emerging now on a large scale. It is not unusual to find many personnel with little training to be writing, modifying, and testing code in large projects. Lack of desired skills in personnel can cause a system to have a larger number of faults.

- **Operational Environment:** Detection of faults remaining in a software system depends upon a test engineer's ability to execute the system in its actual operational environment. If a test engineer fails to operate a system in the same manner the users will do, it is very likely that faults will go undetected. Therefore, test engineers must understand the ways the users will operate a system. Because of a lack of sufficient time and lack of experience on the part of development and test engineers, faults can be introduced into a system, and those faults can go undetected during testing.

Therefore, software reliability is determined by a complex combination of a number of factors with wide-ranging characteristics. Ideally, from the viewpoint of modeling, it is useful to have a mathematical model that takes in the influencing parameters and gives us a concrete value of the level of reliability of a software system. However, such an ideal model has not been devised because of the sheer complex nature of the problem. In reality, the reliability models studied in the literature consider a small number of influencing parameters. Despite the limited scope of those models, we gain much insight into the complex concept of software reliability. For example, the more the test engineers execute a system during system-level testing, the more is the likelihood of observing failures. By identifying and fixing the faults causing those failures, development engineers can improve the reliability level of the system. Thus, the amount of testing time directly influences the level of software reliability. Consequently, a reliability model can be developed where *system testing time*, or simply *time*, is the independent variable and level of reliability is the dependent variable in the reliability model. By using such a model, one can predict the length of system testing time required to achieve a given level of software reliability [3].

15.4 APPLICATIONS OF SOFTWARE RELIABILITY

Reliability is a quantitative measure of the failure-related quality aspect of a software system. A number of factors, as explained in Section 15.3, influence the reliability level of software systems. It is natural to evaluate the effectiveness of the influencing factors.

15.4.1 Comparison of Software Engineering Technologies

To develop higher quality software systems in a cost-effective manner, a number of technologies have been introduced. For example, there are numerous software development processes, such as the *waterfall* model [4], the *spiral* model [5], the *prototyping* model [6], the *eXtreme Programming* model [7], and the *Scrum* model [8, 9]. In terms of introduction of testing tools, many techniques have been studied to generate test cases. Several techniques have been introduced to capture customer requirements, such as entity relationship diagrams, data flow diagrams, and the UML [10, 11]. When a new technology is developed, it is necessary to evaluate its effectiveness before fully embracing it. Three useful criteria for evaluating a technology from the management viewpoint are as follows:

- What is the cost of adopting the technology?
- How does the new technology affect development schedule?
- What is the return from the new technology in terms of software quality?

The concept of software reliability can be used to evaluate a new technology in terms of its usefulness in allowing software developers to produce higher quality software. For example, consider two technologies M_1 and M_2. If an application is developed using technology M_1 to generate a system S_1, and technology M_2 is used to generate another system S_2 to implement the same application, it is useful to observe the difference in the reliability levels of S_1 and S_2. By monitoring the reliability levels of the two systems S_1 and S_2 for the same application, managers can observe what technology is more effective in producing software systems of higher reliability.

15.4.2 Measuring the Progress of System Testing

Measuring the progress of software development is central to managing a project. An important question in project management is: *How much has been completed?* An answer to the question lets us know if progress is being made as planned. It is important to monitor the progress of system testing, because it consumes a significant portion of money and time. Two useful metrics to monitor the progress of system-level testing are as follows:

- Percentage of test cases executed,
- Percentage of successful execution of high-priority functional tests

The concept of software reliability can be used to measure the progress of system testing. For example, one can monitor the failure intensity of the SUT to know where on the reliability scale the system lies at this moment. If the current failure intensity is much larger than a tolerable failure intensity at the time of its release, we know that much work remains to be done. On the other hand, if the difference between the current failure intensity and the desired failure intensity is very small, we realize that we are close to reaching the goal. Thus, the concept of software reliability can be used in an objective manner to measure how much progress has been made in system-level testing [12, 13].

15.4.3   Controlling the System in Operation

The reliability of a system usually reduces as a result of maintenance works. The larger the amount of change made to a system, the larger is the reduction in the reliability level of the system. For example, assume that a system has k number of faults per 1000 lines of code at the beginning of system testing. The value of k can be obtained from statistical measures. By adding N lines of code to the system as a part of a maintenance activity, statistically, $Nk/1000$ faults are introduced into the system. Introduction of the new faults will decrease the reliability of the system, and it will require prolonged system testing to detect the faults and raise system reliability by fixing those faults. A project manager may put a limit on the amount of change in system reliability for each kind of maintenance activity. Therefore, the size of a maintenance work can be determined by the amount of system reliability that can be sacrificed for a while.

15.4.4   Better Insight into Software Development Process

The concept of reliability allows us to quantify the failure-related quality aspect of a software system. Quantification of the quality aspect of software systems gives developers and managers a better insight into the process of software development. For example, by observing the failure intensity at the beginning of system testing, a test manager may be able to make an informed decision regarding how long system testing may take to bring down the failure intensity to an acceptable level. In other words, managers will be capable of making informed decisions.

15.5   OPERATIONAL PROFILES

The notion of *operational profiles*, or *usage profiles*, was developed at AT&T Bell Laboratories [14] and IBM [15, 16] independently. As the name suggests, an operational profile describes how actual users operate a system. An operational profile is a quantitative characterization of how a system will be used. However, for accurate estimation of the reliability of a system one must test it by considering how it will actually be used in the field.

15.5.1 Operation

An *operation* is a major system-level logical task of short duration which returns control to the initiator when the operation is complete and whose processing is substantially different from other operations. In the following, the key characteristics of an operation are explained:

- *Major* means that an operation is related to a functional requirement or feature of a software system.
- An operation is a *logical* concept in the sense that it involves software, hardware, and user actions. Different actions may exist as different segments of processing. The different processing time segments can be contiguous, noncontiguous, sequential, or concurrent.
- *Short duration* means that a software system is handling hundreds of operations per hour.
- *Substantially different processing* means that an operation is considered to be an entity in the form of some lines of source code, and there is a high probability that such an entity contains a fault not found in another entity.

15.5.2 Representation of Operational Profile

The operational profile of a system is the set of operations supported by the system and their probabilities of occurrence. For example, there are three operations, namely, A, B, and C, supported by a system, and they occur 50, 30, and 2% of the time. Then the operational profile is represented by the set $\{(A, 0.5), (B, 0.3), (C, 0.2)\}$. Operational profiles are represented in two alternative ways:

- *Tabular* representation
- *Graphical* representation

Tabular Representation of Operational Profile   An operational profile can be represented in a tabular form with three columns as shown in Table 15.1. The example is about a library information system. The first column lists the names of the operations, the second column gives the frequency of using the operations, and the final column shows the probability of using the operations. We list two kinds of book returned operations: books returned in time and books returned late. The two operations involve some separate processing because a book returned late may incur some penalty. The book renewed operation is a combination of one of the two book returned operations and a book checked out operation.

Graphical Representation of Operational Profile   An operational profile can also be represented in graphical form as shown in Figure 15.2. In a graphical form, an operational profile is represented as a tree structure consisting of nodes and branches. Nodes represent attributes of operations, and branches represent values of attributes with the associated probability of occurrence. In Figure 15.2, four

TABLE 15.1 Example of Operational Profile of Library Information System

Operation	Operations per Hour	Probability
Book checked out	450	0.45
Book returned in time	324	0.324
Book renewed	81	0.081
Book returned late	36	0.036
Book reported lost	9	0.009
⋮	⋮	⋮
Total	1000	1.0

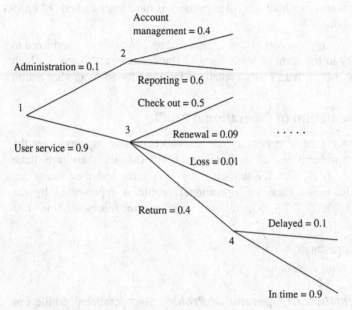

Figure 15.2   Graphical representation of operational profile of library information system.

nodes, namely 1, 2, 3, and 4 are shown. Node 1 represents the scope attribute of operations with two values, administration and user service. The scope of an operation refers to whether an operation is for the administration of the information system or for providing services to users. The probability of occurrence of the administration value of the scope attribute of an operation is 0.1, and the probability of occurrence of the user service value is 0.9. Node 2 represents an administration operation, whereas node 3 represents a user operation. There are two attributes of the administration operation, namely, account management and reporting, and the associated probabilities of occurrence are 0.4 and 0.6, respectively. There are four attributes of the user operations, namely, check out, renewal, loss, and return, with their associated probabilities of occurrence being 0.5, 0.09,

0.01, and 0.4, respectively. Node 4 represents a return operation with two attribute values, namely delayed and in-time, with their probabilities of occurrence being 0.1 and 0.9, respectively.

It is useful to note that a tabular form of an operational profile can be easily generated from a graphical form by considering all possible paths in the graphical form and multiplying the probabilities appearing on each path. For example, the probability of the book returned late operation (0.036) in Table 15.1 can be obtained from the graphical form shown in Figure 15.2 by multiplying the probabilities associated with user service (0.9), return (0.4), and delayed (0.1).

Choosing Tabular Form or Graphical Form   The tabular form of an operational profile can be easily obtained from the graphical form. It is easy to specify the operational profile in a tabular form if a system involves only a small number of operations. However, the graphical form is preferred if a system involves a large number of operations. Operations that can be easily described as sequences of smaller processing steps are better suited for the graphical form. Moreover, it is easy to identify missing operations in a graphical form.

Using Operational Profile During System Testing   The notion of operational profiles was created to guide test engineers in selecting test cases. Ideally, at least one test case should be selected to test an operation, and all the operations should be covered during testing. Since software reliability is very much tied with the concept of failure intensity, a software system with better reliability can be produced within a given amount of time by testing the more frequently used operations first. In reality, projects overrun their schedules, and there may be a tendency to deliver products without adequate testing. An operational profile can be used in making a decision concerning how much to test and what portions of a software system should receive more attention. The ways test engineers select test cases to operate a system may significantly differ from the ways actual users operate a system. However, for accurate estimation of the reliability of a system, test the system in the same way it will actually be used in the field.

Other Uses of Operational Profiles   The operational profile of a system can be used in a number of ways throughout the life-cycle model of a software system as follows:

- As a guiding document in designing user interface. The more frequently used operations should be easy to learn and easy to use.
- In developing a version of a system for early release. The early-release version can contain the more frequently used operations.
- To determine where to put more resources for system development. For example, more resources can be allocated to the development of those operations which are used more frequently.
- As a guiding document for organizing user manuals. For example, the more frequently used operations are described earlier than the rest.

15.6 RELIABILITY MODELS

The reliability models are developed based on the following assumptions:

- Faults in the program are independent.
- Execution time between failures is large with respect to instruction execution time.
- Potential *test space* covers its *use space*.
- The set of inputs per test run is randomly selected.
- All failures are observed.
- The fault causing a failure is immediately fixed or else its reoccurrence is not counted again.

To understand the idea of fault independence in the first assumption, we can consider a mapping between the set of faults in a system and the set of failures caused by the faults. Faults are said to be independent if there is a one-to-one or one-to-many relationship between faults and failures. Thus, if faults are independent and a fault is fixed, then the corresponding single or multiple failures are no longer observed. In a many-to-one relationship, fixing one fault will not eliminate the corresponding failure; all the faults need to be fixed to eliminate the failure.

The second assumption concerning the length of execution time between failures tells us that the system does not fail too often. A reasonably stable system is a prerequisite for the reliability models to be valid. No meaningful prediction can be done if a system fails too often.

The third assumption, concerning test space and use space, implies that a system be tested by keeping in mind how it will be used. For example, consider a telephone system comprising three features: (i) call processing, (ii) billing, and (iii) administrative operation. Assume that there are 15 basic operations to support each feature. Even though there are a total of 45 operations, actual operation of the system can produce a large number of execution scenarios. Call establishment between two phones is a basic operation in the call processing group, and updating a customer profile is a basic operation in the administrative group. Those two operations can be tested separately. However, there may be a need to update a customer's profile while the customer is in the middle of a call. Testing such an operational situation is different from individually testing the two basic operations. The usefulness of a reliability model depends on whether or not a system is tested by considering the use space of the system that can be characterized by an operational profile.

The fourth assumption emphasizes the need to select test input randomly. For example, referring to the telephone system in the explanation of the third assumption, to test the call establishment function, we randomly select the destination number. Randomness in the selection process reduces any bias in favor of certain groups of test data.

The fifth assumption concerning failures simply tells us to consider only the final discrepancies between actual system behavior and expected system behavior.

Even if a system is in an erroneous state, there may not be a system failure if the system has been designed to tolerate faults. Therefore, only the observed failures are taken into consideration, rather than the possibility of failures.

The sixth assumption tells us how to count failures. When a failure is observed, it is assumed that the corresponding fault is detected and fixed. Because of the first assumption that faults are independent, the same failure is not observed due to another, unknown fault. Thus, we count a failure once whether or not the corresponding fault is immediately fixed.

The details of the development of two mathematical models of reliability are presented. In these two models failure intensity as a measure of reliability is expressed as a function of execution time. That is, an expression for $\lambda(\tau)$ is developed. The models are developed based on the following intuitive idea: *As we observe another system failure and the corresponding fault is fixed, there will be a fewer number of faults remaining in the system and the failure intensity of the system will be smaller with each fault fixed. In other words, as the cumulative failure count increases, the failure intensity decreases.*

In the above intuitive idea, an important concept is the characterization of the *decrement* in failure intensity as a function of cumulative failure count. In this chapter, two reliability models are developed by considering two decrement processes as follows:

Decrement Process 1: The decrease in failure intensity after observing a failure and fixing the corresponding fault is constant. The reliability model developed using this model of failure intensity decrement is called the basic model.

Decrement Process 2: The decrease in failure intensity after observing a failure and fixing the corresponding fault is smaller than the previous decrease. In other words, fixing a fault leading to an earlier failure causes the failure intensity to be reduced by a larger amount than fixing a fault causing a later failure. Therefore, failure intensity is exponential in the number of failures observed. The reliability model developed using this model of failure intensity decrement is called the logarithmic model.

In the development of the two reliability models, the following notation is used:

- μ denotes the mean number of failures observed.
- λ denotes the mean failure intensity.
- λ_0 denotes the *initial* failure intensity observed at the beginning of system-level testing.
- ν_0 denotes the total number of system failures that we expect to observe over infinite time starting from the beginning of system-level testing.
- θ denotes the decrease in failure intensity in the logarithmic model. This term will be further explained in the discussion of logarithmic model below.

Basic Model   The constant decrement in failure intensity per failure observed is illustrated in Figure 15.3, where the straight line represents the failure decrement

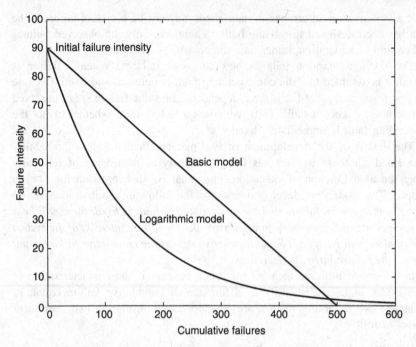

Figure 15.3 Failure intensity λ as function of cumulative failure μ ($\lambda_0 = 9$ failures per unit time, $\nu_0 = 500$ failures, $\theta = 0.0075$).

process in the basic model. Initially, the observed failure intensity is 9 failures per unit time. The total number of failures to be observed over infinite time is assumed to be 500. When all the 500 failures have been observed and the corresponding faults have been fixed, no more system failure will be observed. Therefore, the failure intensity becomes zero at the point we have observed the final failure. The rate of decrement in failure intensity is represented by the slope of the straight line and is equal to $-\lambda_0/\nu_0 = -9/500$ per unit time. The straight line in Figure 15.3 can be expressed as follows:

$$\lambda(\mu) = \lambda_0 \left(1 - \frac{\mu}{\nu_0} \right)$$

Since both λ and μ are functions of τ and $\lambda(\tau)$ is the derivative of $\mu(\tau)$, we have

$$\frac{d\mu(\tau)}{d\tau} = \lambda_0 \left(1 - \frac{\mu(\tau)}{\nu_0} \right)$$

By solving the above differential equation, we have

$$\mu(\tau) = \nu_0 (1 - e^{-\lambda_0 \tau/\nu_0})$$

and

$$\lambda(\tau) = \lambda_0 e^{-\lambda_0 \tau/\nu_0}$$

Logarithmic Model The curved line in Figure 15.3 illustrates the process of decrement in failure intensity per failure observed in the logarithmic model. Whichever reliability model chosen, the observed failure intensity remains the same. Therefore, in Figure 15.3, the initially observed failure intensity is shown to be the same, that is, 9 failures per unit time, as in the basic model. The total number of failures to be observed over infinite time is infinite. Therefore, the failure intensity never reaches zero. The relationship between failure intensity and cumulative failure count shows that faults fixed in the beginning cause a larger decrement in failure intensity than faults fixed at a later stage. This view of decrement in failure intensity is consistent with real-life systems. For example, those faults which cause a system to fail in many ways are likely to manifest in earlier failures than those faults which manifest themselves in fewer failures. Therefore, by fixing a fault early, one observes a larger drop in failure intensity than caused by fixing a fault at a later stage.

The nonlinear drop in failure intensity in the logarithmic model is captured by a decay parameter θ associated with a negative exponential function as shown in the following relationship between λ and μ:

$$\lambda(\mu) = \lambda_0 e^{-\theta\mu}$$

Since both λ and μ are functions of τ and $\lambda(\tau)$ is the derivative of $\mu(\tau)$, we can write

$$\frac{d\mu(\tau)}{d\tau} = \lambda_0 e^{-\theta\mu(\tau)}$$

By solving the above differential equation, we obtain

$$\mu(\tau) = \frac{\ln(\lambda_0\theta\tau + 1)}{\theta} \qquad \lambda(\tau) = \frac{\lambda_0}{(\lambda_0\theta\tau + 1)}$$

Comparison of Reliability Models In Figure 15.4, we have plotted the expressions for $\lambda(\tau)$ in both the models and in Figure 15.5 the expressions for $\mu(\tau)$. We have assumed that the initial failure intensities are $\lambda_0 = 9$ failures per unit time in both models, the total number of failures to be observed over infinite time in the basic model is $\nu_0 = 500$ failures, and the failure intensity decay parameter $\theta = 0.0075$ in the logarithmic model.

Therefore, if we choose one of the two models to apply to a real-life software system, the next task is to estimate the model's parameters. This can be done by noting the time instants $\tau_1, \ldots, \tau_k$ at which the first k failures $\mu(\tau_1), \ldots, \mu(\tau_k)$, respectively, occur. This gives us k data points $(\tau_1, \mu(\tau_1)), \ldots, (\tau_k, \mu(\tau_k))$. We may then determine the chosen model's parameters so that the resulting plot fits the set of actually observed points. We can use a least squares technique, for example, for this purpose.

Example Assume that a software system is undergoing system-level testing. The initial failure intensity of the system was 25 failures per CPU hour, and the current

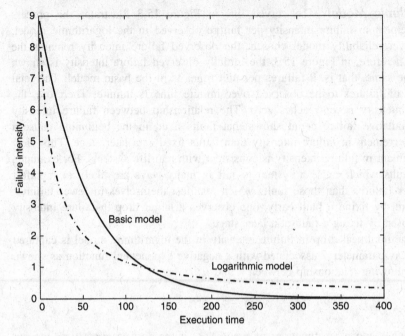

Figure 15.4 Failure intensity λ as function of execution time τ ($\lambda_0 = 9$ failures per unit time, $\nu_0 = 500$ failures, $\theta = 0.0075$).

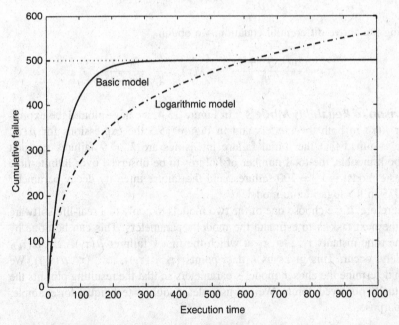

Figure 15.5 Cumulative failure μ as function of execution time τ ($\lambda_0 = 9$ failures per unit time, $\nu_0 = 500$ failures, $\theta = 0.0075$).

failure intensity is 5 failures per CPU hour. It has been decided by the project manager that the system will be released only after the system reaches a reliability level of at most 0.001 failure per CPU hour. From experience the management team estimates that the system will experience a total of 1200 failures over infinite time. Calculate the additional length of system testing required before the system can be released.

First, an appropriate reliability model for the software system is chosen. Because of the assumption that the system will experience a total of 1200 failures over infinite time, we use the basic model.

Let us denote the current failure intensity and the desired failure intensity at the time of release as λ_c and λ_r, respectively. Assume that the current failure intensity has been achieved after executing the system for τ_c hours. Let the release time failure intensity λ_r be achieved after testing the system for a total of τ_r hours. We can write λ_c and λ_r as

$$\lambda_c = \lambda_0 e^{-\lambda_0 \tau_c / \nu_0} \qquad \lambda_r = \lambda_0 e^{-\lambda_0 \tau_r / \nu_0}$$

The quantity $\lambda_r - \lambda_c$ denotes the additional amount of system testing time needed to achieve reliability λ_r at the time of release. The quantity $\lambda_r - \lambda_c$ can be represented as follows:

$$\frac{\lambda_c}{\lambda_r} = \begin{cases} \dfrac{\lambda_0 e^{-\lambda_0 \tau_c / \nu_0}}{\lambda_0 e^{-\lambda_0 \tau_r / \nu_0}} \\[2mm] e^{(-\lambda_0 \tau_c / \nu_0) + (\lambda_0 \tau_r / \nu_0)} \\[2mm] e^{(\tau_r - \tau_c) \lambda_0 / \nu_0} \end{cases}$$

or

$$\ln\left(\frac{\lambda_c}{\lambda_r}\right) = \frac{(\tau_r - \tau_c)\lambda_0}{\nu_0}$$

or

$$\tau_r - \tau_c = \begin{cases} \left(\dfrac{\nu_0}{\lambda_0}\right) \ln\left(\dfrac{\lambda_c}{\lambda_r}\right) \\[3mm] \left(\dfrac{1200}{25}\right) \ln\left(\dfrac{5}{0.001}\right) \\[3mm] 408.825 \text{ hours} \end{cases}$$

Therefore, it is required to test the system for more time so that the CPU runs for another 408.825 hours to achieve the reliability level of 0.001 failure per hour.

15.7 SUMMARY

This chapter began with an introduction to the following concepts: (i) fault and failure, (ii) execution and calendar time, (iii) time interval between failures, (iv) failures in periodic intervals, and (v) failure intensity. With these concepts in place, software reliability was defined in two ways: (i) the probability of failure-free operation of a software system for a specified time in a specified environment and (ii) failure intensity as a measure of software reliability.

Next, we discussed user's perception of software reliability, which depends upon two factors: (i) the number of faults present in the software and (ii) how the user operates the system, that is, operational profile of the system. The number of faults introduced into the system and the developer's inability to detect many of those faults are discussed, which include (i) size and complexity of code, (ii) characteristics of development process, (iii) education, experience, and training of personnel, and (iii) operational environment. In summary, software reliability is determined by a complex combination of a number of factors with wide-ranging characteristics. After that, we explained various applications of software reliability.

Then we presented the notion of operational profiles developed by Musa at Bell Laboratories. An operational profile is a quantitative characterization of how actual users operate a system. Operational profiles are represented in two alternative ways: tabular form and graphical form. Operational profiles can be used to guide the design of a user interface, the determination of where to put more resources for system development, the selection of test cases, and the development of user manuals.

Finally, two mathematical models of reliability were explained: the basic model and the logarithmic model. In these two models, failure intensity as a measure of reliability is expressed as a function of executed time.

LITERATURE REVIEW

Measuring the reliability of large software systems presents both technical and management challenges. Large software systems involve a large number of simultaneous users, say, several thousands, and most of them may be located in different geographic locations. Some examples of large software systems are software controlling the operation of cellular phone networks, on-line purchase systems, and banking systems, to name just a few. The books by Musa, Iannino, and Okumoto [7] and Musa [8] address a number of issues concerning software reliability: The technical issues addressed by Musa, Iannino, and Okumoto are as follows:

- **Parameter Determination:** Five methods of parameter determination, namely *prediction*, *estimation*, *identification*, *formula and/or experience*, and *data*, have been discussed.

- **Project-Specific Techniques:** Techniques for dealing with different special problems have been discussed. For example, they explain ways to estimate the execution time of occurrence of a failure. Another project-specific technique concerns measuring failure times in multiple installations.

The concept of operational profile has been presented in great detail by Musa (*Software Reliability Engineering*, McGraw-Hill, New York, 1999). Specifically, the main activities related to preparing an operational profile have been discussed. Moreover, the handling of the evolution of the definition of operation during system development has been discussed.

The management aspects of software reliability have been discussed in the books by both Musa, Iannino, and Okumoto [7] and Musa [8]. How to plan for implementing a reliability program has been discussed by Musa, Iannino, and Okumoto [7]. Specifically, the following activities have been explained to run a reliability program:

- **Data Collection:** Data collection for reliability analysis involves activities such as what data to gather, how to motivate data takers, how to make data collection easy, collecting data in real time, feeding results back, and recordkeeping.

- **Use of Consultants:** Consultants play an important role in technology transfer concerning reliability engineering. A consultant can be a professional external consultant or an individual inside the organization. By virtue of their expertise, consultants have a valuable impact throughout an organization.

Musa, Iannino, and Okumoto [17] present a few more models, such as Poisson-type models and binomial-type models. Lyu [19] presents several other reliability models and actual failure data from field operations of large software systems.

Another prominent method similar to reliability testing is known as *statistical testing*, which uses a formal experimental paradigm for random testing according to a usage model of the software. In statistical testing, a model is developed to characterize the population of uses of the software, and the model is used to generate a statistical correct sample of all possible uses of the software. Performance on the sample is used as a basis for conclusions about general operational reliability. Interested readers are referred to the following book and articles for discussion on this topic:

N. Baskiotis, M. Sebag, M.-C. Gaudel, and S. Gouraud, "A Machine Learning Approach for Statistical Software Testing," in *Proceedings, International Conference on Artificial Intelligence*, Hyderabad, India, Morgan Kaufman, San Francisco, January 6–12, 2007, pp. 2274–2278.

S. Prowell, C. Trammell, R. Linger, and J. Poore, *Cleanroom Software Engineering*, Addison-Wesley, Reading, MA, 1999.

G. H. Walton, J. H. Poore, and C. J. Trammell, "Statistical Testing of Software Based on a Usage Model," *Software Practice and Experience*, Vol. 25, No. 1, January 1995, pp. 97–108.

J. A. Whittaker and M. G. Thomason, "A Markov Chain Model for Statistical Software Testing," *IEEE Transactions on Software Engineering*, Vol. 20, No. 10, October 1994, pp. 812–824.

REFERENCES

1. W. K. Ehrlich, A. Iannino, B. S. Prasanna, J. P. Stampfel, and J. R. Wu. How Faults Cause Software Failures: Implications for Software Reliability Engineering. In *Proceedings of the International Symposium on Software Reliability Engineering*, Austin, TX, May 1991, IEEE Computer Society Press, Piscataway, New Jersey, 1991, pp. 233–241.
2. K. Trivedi. *Probability and Statistics with Relaibility, Queuing, and Computer Science Applications*. Wiley, Hoboken, NJ, 2002.
3. H. Pham. *System Software Reliability*. Springer, 2006.
4. W. W. Royce. Managing the Development of Large Software Systems: Concepts and Techniques. In *Proceedings of WESCON*, August 1970, pp. 1-9. Republished in ICSE, Monterey, CA, 1987, pp. 328-338.
5. B. W. Boehm. A Spiral Model for Software Development and Enhancement. *IEEE Computer*, May 1988, pp. 61–72.
6. I. Sommerville. *Software Engineering*. Addison-Wesley, Reading, MA, 2006.
7. K. Beck and C. Andres. *Extreme Programming Explained: Embrace Change*, 2nd ed. Addison-Wesley, Reading, MA, 2004.
8. K. Schwaber. *Agile Project Management with Scrum*. Microsoft Press, Redmond, WA, 2004.
9. H. Takeuchi and I. Nonaka. The New Product Development Game. *Harvard Business Review*, Harvard Business School Publishing, Boston, MA, January-February 1986, pp. 1-11.
10. M. Fowler. *UML Distilled: A Brief Guide to the Standard Object Modeling Language*. Addison-Wesley, Reading, MA, 2003.
11. I. Jacobson, G. Booch, and J. Rumbaugh. *The Unified Software Development Process*. Addison-Wesley Longman, Reading, MA, 1998.
12. S. Dalal and C. Mallows. When Should One Stop Testing Software. *Journal of the American Statistical Associations*, Vol. 81, 1988, pp. 872–879.
13. M. C. K. Yang and A. Chao. Reliability-Estimation and Stopping-Rules for Software Testing, Based on Repeated Appearances of Bugs. *IEEE Transactions on Reliability*, June 1995, pp. 315–321.
14. J. D. Musa. Software Reliability Engineering. *IEEE Software*, March 1993, pp. 14–32.
15. R. Cobb and H. D. Mills. Engineering Software-under Statistical Quality Control. *IEEE Software*, November 1990, pp. 44–54.
16. H. D. Mills, M. Dyer, and R. C. Linger. Cleanroom Software Engineering. *IEEE Software*, September 1987, pp. 19–24.
17. J. D. Musa, A. Iannino, and K. Okumoto. *Software Reliability*. McGraw-Hill, New York, 1987.
18. J. D. Musa. *Software Reliability Engineering*. McGraw-Hill, New York, 1999.
19. M. R. Lyu. *Handbook of Software Reliability Engineering*. McGraw-Hill, New York, 1995.

Exercises

1. What definition of software reliability is best suited for each of the following kinds of software systems? Justify your answers.
   (a) Operating system of computer for personal use
   (b) Operating system of computer used to control electric power plant
   (c) Spell checking system
   (d) Embedded software controlling washing machine
   (e) Video game software
   (f) Communication software system running on cellular phone
   (g) Communication software system controlling base stations of cellular phone system

2. Assume that a software system will experience 150 failures in infinite time. The system has now experienced 60 failures so far. The initial failure intensity at the beginning of system testing was 15 failures per CPU hour. What is the current failure intensity?

3. Assume that a software system is undergoing system-level tests and the initial failure intensity is 15 failures per CPU hour. The failure intensity decay parameter has been found to be 0.025 per failure. So far the test engineers have observed 60 failures. What is the current failure intensity?

4. Explain the consequence of not satisfying the assumption that potential *test space* covers its *use space* in developing the two reliability models.

5. Explain how the parameters of the basic model and the logarithmic model can be determined.

6. Explain how the operational profile concept can be applied to regression tests.

7. Explain how the idea of software reliability can uncover missing requirements.

8. Explain the relationship between the *correctness* and the *reliability* quality attributes of a software system.

9. Can an incorrect, that is, faulty, software system be considered to be reliable? Justify your answer.

10. Explain why it may not be possible to satisfy some of the assumptions used in the two models of software reliability.

CHAPTER 16

Test Team Organization

In the end, all business operations can be reduced to three words: people, product, and profits. Unless you've got a good team, you can't do much with the other two.
— *Lee Iacocca*

16.1 TEST GROUPS

There are many ways in which test teams can be organized. There are no right or wrong ways to organize test teams. The structure one chooses will affect productivity, quality, customer satisfaction, employee morale, and budget. As we know, testing is a distributed activity, distributed in time and space, conducted in different phases of a software development life cycle. The different, broad kinds of testing are unit testing, integration testing, system testing, and acceptance testing. It is logical to have different testing groups in an organization for each testing phase of a software development life cycle. However, it is recommended that the unit tests be developed and executed by the software developers themselves, rather than an independent group of unit test engineers. The programmer who develops a software unit should take the ownership of producing good-quality software to his or her satisfaction. Therefore, instead of forming a unit test group, software developers should be given the responsibilities of testing their own code. The acceptance test group is formed on a demand basis consisting of people from different backgrounds, such as integration test engineers, system test engineers, customer support engineers, and marketing engineers. The test group is dismantled after the project is completed. In any organization, it is recommended to have at least two test groups: integration test group and system test group. In the following sections, their details are discussed.

16.1.1 Integration Test Group

System integration testing, or simply, integration testing, is performed by an integration test group. Integration testing requires a thorough knowledge of the modules

---

and their interfaces. Since large systems are integrated in an incremental manner, possibly by using the concept of incremental builds, the integration test personnel must be very conversant with the idea of builds. Thus, it natural that software developers, who together built the modules, must be involved in performing integration testing. In practice, the developers themselves may integrate the system. The system architects are also involved in integration testing for complex systems because of their thorough understanding of the larger picture of the system. The mandate of this group is to ensure that unit-tested modules operate correctly when they are combined. The modules are combined by following the software structure identified during system design. System integration is performed as a part of the larger concept of system development. The leader of the integration test group reports to the software development manager. In addition to integrating the system, the test group may perform other duties, such as code inspection, configuration management, release management, and management of development laboratory. The activities pertaining to this group are described in Chapter 7.

16.1.2 System Test Group

A system test group is a team whose primary job is to perform testing without any bias and fear. The system test group is truly an independent group, and it usually has a separate head count and budget. Separate head count means that people are specifically hired and retained to perform testing. The reader may recall that some development engineers take up the role of an integration test engineer. However, to eliminate the possibility of any bias in system-level testing, the task is performed by a separate group, and not by some members of the development group. The manager of this group does not report to hardware or software development managers. Rather, they are all peers at the organizational level. The mandate of this group is to ensure that the system requirements have been satisfied and that the system is acceptable. The system test group conducts different categories of tests as discussed in Chapter 8. To facilitate the system to be eventually accepted by the customer, the group executes *business acceptance tests* identified in the user acceptance test plan.

The system test group can be further divided into several focused subgroups as the size of an organization becomes large: *development test group*, *performance test group*, *scalability test group*, *automation test group*, and *sustaining test group*, as shown in Figure 16.1. Each of the groups may be headed by a line manager, who in turn reports to the senior-level manager in charge of the system test group. The system test group structure must be regularly reviewed and adjusted to meet shifting internal and external needs. Note that the structure of the system test group is organized on a functional basis, and not on a project basis. A long-lasting organization of a test group will lead to better development of its member skills.

In order to form a test group, a crucial thing is the *size* of the system test group. This essentially tells us the number of people should be performing system-level testing. The size of the system test group impacts the delivered quality of the product, the development cost of the product, and the time to deliver the product. The *tester–developer* ratio is a matter of considerable debate. In practice, $\frac{1}{2}$, $\frac{2}{3}$, and $\frac{1}{4}$ are common values of the tester–developer ratio [1]. An appropriate

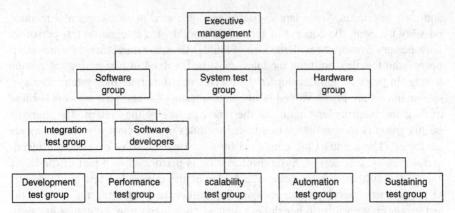

Figure 16.1   Structure of test groups.

value of the ratio depends upon the nature of the software under development. A value of the ratio is estimated during the development of a test planning document, and it has been discussed in Chapter 12.

Development Test Group   The focus of this group is on the testing of new features in a particular release. This includes *basic tests, functionality tests, robustness tests, interoperability tests, stress tests, load and stability tests, regression tests, documentation tests*, and *business acceptance tests*.

Performance Test Group   This group puts emphasis on system performance. Tests are conducted to identify system bottlenecks and recommendations are made to the developers for improving system performance. The group uses test, measurement, and analysis tools to carry out its tasks. This group may take up additional responsibilities such as reliability testing.

Scalability Test Group   The focus of this group is on determining whether or not the system can scale up to its engineering limits. For example, a cellular phone network might have been designed with certain engineering limits in mind, such as the maximum number of base stations it can support, the maximum number of simultaneous calls it can handle, and so on. The group tests whether the designed system can reach those limits. This group may take up additional responsibilities such as load and stability testing.

Automation Test Group   The responsibility of this group is to develop test automation infrastructure, test libraries, and tests tools. This group assists other groups in the development of automated test suites.

Sustaining Test Group   This group maintains the software quality throughout the product's market life. This team is responsible for maintaining the *corrective* aspect of software maintenance. The group works very closely with customers and conducts regression testing of patch software.

16.2   SOFTWARE QUALITY ASSURANCE GROUP

Software testing is a part of the larger concept of software quality assurance. Testing encompasses the processes of finding defects and fixing them. Defects can be found through a combination of code inspection and actual execution of test cases. On the other hand, software quality assurance deals not only with the location of the defects but also with mechanisms to prevent defects. In the IEEE standard 610-12-1990 [2] quality assurance is defined as follows:

1. A planned and systematic pattern of all actions necessary to provide adequate confidence that an item or product conforms to established technical requirements

2. A set of activities designed to evaluate the process by which products are developed or manufactured

The first item above deals with testing which contributes to the quality of a product. The second item is procedural in nature; it includes actively ensuring the continuous improvement of product quality. This implies that a software quality assurance group has a larger role in ensuring *conformance to the best development practices* throughout the organization. Such a role is well beyond the scope of a test group. The software quality assurance group should have sufficient authority, power, and standing to work with the entire organization in defining processes and dictating peers to follow the processes [3]. The software quality assurance team should have sufficient members to do a thorough and professional job at system testing as well as quality management work. It is recommended to have a separate group for quality management work, as shown in Figure 16.2, rather than assign quality management task to system test engineers.

Quality Management Group   This group works on customizing software development processes and ensuring that processes are adhered to. The group is responsible for creating and implementing a quality management program plan for the entire organization by following a standard framework, such as the ISO9000:2000 quality model. The group proactively works to drive process improvement initiatives across the organization. The group makes an effort to understand the best practices followed around the world through systematic benchmarking and to amalgamate those practices with the one existing within the organization. The team can take up additional responsibilities to implement

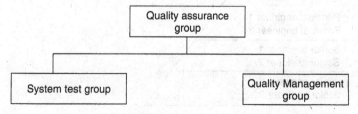

Figure 16.2   Structure of software quality assurance group.

automated collection, tracking, and reporting of metrics relevant to product development, testing, and project management.

Quality control is another term that is often used in the literature. Quality control is defined in the IEEE standard 610 [2] as *a set of activities designed to evaluate the quality of developed or manufactured products*. The term is used in a production or hardware manufacturing environment, where a large number of physical items are produced and shipped. Each of the items has to go through a testing process to ensure that the quality of the product is good enough for shipment; otherwise, the item is rejected. The quality check is conducted by the quality control group within the manufacturing organization, and the person who conducts the testing is called a quality controller.

16.3 SYSTEM TEST TEAM HIERARCHY

Five kinds of subgroups within the system test group of an organization have been identified in Section 16.1.2. Each subgroup is organized in a hierarchical fashion headed by a test manager. The size of a test subgroup can grow to a maximum of 12 test engineers. A subgroup with more than 12 members may be divided into two subgroups for better management. Members of a subgroup include *technical leaders, principal engineers, senior engineers*, and *junior engineers* as depicted in Figure 16.3.

The duties of the team members are different from subgroup to subgroup. The role and responsibilities of each team member must be clearly defined. In the following, we give a brief description of the role and responsibilities for each kind of team member that are common to most organizations:

- **Test Managers:** The manager of a test subgroup is a key person in charge of all aspects of the assigned testing task. The manager leads the group by working with other test subgroups to perform testing functions to ensure that high-quality products are released. The administrative responsibilities

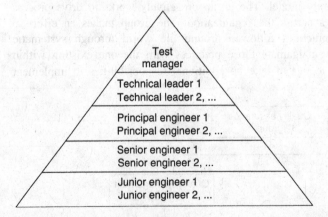

Figure 16.3 System test team hierarchy.

of a manager include managing the budget, hiring personnel, assigning tasks, training personnel, developing their career, and reviewing their performance. The technical responsibilities of a test manager include (i) developing a test plan, executing a test plan, and handling crises; (ii) developing, following, and improving test processes; and (iii) defining, collecting, and analyzing metrics. The manager is proactive in improving people, productivity, and processes. The manager is expected to be able to work with other test groups within the company as well as the customer test organization. A particular test group may be located in different places and even different countries. The test manager acts as a nodal point between upper management, project management, quality management, and the marketing people.

- **Junior Engineers:** New, inexperienced test engineers are put at a junior level. They gain experience by assisting the senior and principal engineers in charge of test execution, setting up of test beds, and developing scripts for test automation. They may also be asked to test the user manual, the on-line help feature, and the graphical user interface.

- **Senior Engineers:** The senior engineers design, develop, and execute test cases. They design and set up test laboratories and environments. Senior engineers assist software developers in reproducing known defects. They participate in test plan review meetings and support maintenance of test laboratories, automated test suites, and test tools. Test tools include a defect tracking system and a test factory.

- **Principal Engineers:** The principal engineers are test specialists responsible for test planning, test automation, test environment planning, test tool development, procurement of test equipment, performance modeling, reliability engineering, and business acceptance testing. In addition, the principal engineers execute test cases and mentor junior engineers within the group.

- **Technical Leaders:** A technical leader often needs to coordinate the tasks of many engineers working on complex projects. At this level the engineer should have technical testing skills of a principal engineer as well as negotiation skills, process and project management skills, and communication skills. The technical leader provides the strategic direction for software testing, assists test managers in collecting test metrics, coordinates test plan review meetings, attends entry/exit criteria review meetings, and participates in cross-functional review meetings such as for requirements review, functional specification review, and entry/exit criteria selection.

16.4 EFFECTIVE STAFFING OF TEST ENGINEERS

Designing test cases to reveal defects in a complex system is a challenging task. One may not get as much satisfaction from designing test cases as from designing a system. However, designing test cases to reveal defects in a system is definitely an ingenuous task. Top-notch test engineering talent is not only desirable but also essential to making high-quality products. A poor-quality test engineer can do much damage in terms of reporting false positives and false negatives. A hiring process should focus on never letting in a bad fit, even if that means accidentally rejecting some good fits. One must remember the saying, *you can only be as good as your people*. A leader must set a personal standard to staff the team with the best test engineers, developing them fully, and letting them take advantage of opportunities.

A team leader must have a clear picture of the experience and skills required for a test position. It is useful to keep in mind the following five-C characteristics identified by Bill Hetzel [4] that a good test engineer must possess.

1. *Controlled*: A test engineer must be organized, disciplined, and method-ical in his or her work.

2. *Comprehensive*: A test engineer must be very attentive to the details [5].

3. *Considerate*: A test engineer must have good interpersonal skills such as the ability to handle aggressive behavior, not to be easily offended, to be malleable, and, finally, to bring situations to a win–win closure.

4. *Critical*: A test engineer must be very good in analysis and assertive-ness. Assertiveness typically consists of being persistent, using multiple methods of reflective listening to determine exactly what is being com-municated.

5. *Competent*: A test engineer must be aware of test techniques, tools, tech-nology, and domain knowledge that can be used in order to carry out the job efficiently.

In addition to the five-C characteristics, test engineers are expected to have the following skills [6] as a part of their competence to become successful test spe-cialists:

- Have credibility with software developers
- Understand developers' terminologies
- Know when the code is ready for testing
- Be able to evaluate the impact of a problem on the customers
- Assist software developers in expediting defect resolution
- Reduce false-positive and false-negative results in testing
- Develop expertise in test automation
- Mentor the junior test engineers

A successful test team is made up of members whose strengths are comple-mentary. An effort must be made to avoid hiring test engineers who are mirror images of existing staff or yourself. Otherwise, the team will be constrained with limited skills and perspectives. The team should be well balanced with people who have a variety of skills. There should be a good cross section of experience and technical abilities. Therefore, it is advisable to have people on the test team with diverse background and experience, such as developers, integration testers, information technology administrators, technical support personnel, technical writers, quality management personnel, experienced test engineers, and recent graduates. The roles of people with such diverse backgrounds are explained in the following.

- **Developers:** A developer's expertise in system design, coding, and unit testing is very useful in becoming an effective test engineers. To effectively communicate with software developers, test engineers must use their vocabulary, such as object, class, inheritance, polymorphism, variables, pointers, structures, and so on, to have credibility with the software development group. Code development experience is useful when a test engineer participates in code review. Another reason for test engineers to have development experience is to be able to automate the tests without much problem. A key criterion in hiring is to develop competency and effectiveness in the long term, anticipating the staffing needs and challenges one will face in the future. In the long term, automation of tests is a key process activity for a test organization to be successful. Therefore, it is better to staff a test team with personnel having much coding experience.

- **Integration Testers:** Experienced integration test engineers are an asset in the system test group. When an integration test engineer experiences a defect, he or she is in a better position to identify the area where the problem may exist and assist developers in expediting defect resolution. It saves the developers much time because they do not have to attempt to reproduce the problem(s). Test engineers with integration testing experience are in a better position to know when the code is ready for system-level testing.

- **Information Technology Administrators:** Information technology (IT) administrators are very knowledgeable in configuring; setting up routers, servers, and firewalls; and troubleshooting. In addition, they know about different kinds of tools available in the market. Test engineers with IT experience can easily set up the test environments and maintain test laboratories.

- **Technical Support Personnel:** Customer support engineers are often good testers, especially in performing high level-tests such as acceptance tests. They are in a position to evaluate the impact of a defect on the customers. Their knowledge of business functions and interaction with many different customers make them invaluable to a test group.

- **Technical Writers:** One of the tasks of a system test engineer is to go through all the manuals, user guides, troubleshooting guides, and release notes. Therefore, it is useful to have technical writers in a test group to execute documentation tests. The idea in performing documentation tests is to ensure that all the user documentations are accurate and usable. Moreover, they can be useful in performing usability and graphical user interface testing.

- **System Test Engineers:** It is effective and efficient to hire test specialists who are already trained, say, by another company, in test techniques, tools, technology, and domain knowledge. An experienced test engineer knows the various testing strategies and techniques used to find more defects with less effort, including thorough understanding of system architectures and their functionalities, programming languages, code structures, and implementations. This is also a good way to acquire expertise in specific testing tools and domain knowledge.

- **Recent Graduates:** One can hire recent engineering graduates as junior test engineers and train them the way one wants them to be. They are much eager, enthusiastic, and willing to learn more about testing. They are good at developing test tools and automating test cases. New graduates need mentoring from a senior test engineer to be productive.

16.5 RECRUITING TEST ENGINEERS

Interviewing is the primary way of evaluating applicants in the recruiting process. One must possess good skills at identifying the strengths and weaknesses of an applicant. However, interviewing is a skill that improves with practice. The following characteristics make an excellent interviewer:

- The interviewer should be prepared in advance.
- The interviewer must be a good listener.
- The interviewer must be focused in questioning and probing.
- The interviewer needs to accurately document his or her assessment of the candidate during the interview.
- It is effective to give the candidate an opportunity to ask questions.
- It is effective to be focused on specific requirements of the job to be filled and not on the resume.
- It is fruitful to evaluate an applicant based on facts and data, rather than one's "gut feeling."

A recruiting process must be in place in order to be effective in hiring excellent test engineers. Six simple phases are recommended to be followed in staffing the system test team, as illustrated in Figure 16.4.

16.5.1 Job Requisition

The first step in hiring is to get an approval from executive management, which is sometimes referred to as having a "requisition number." A requisition number means that the position has been approved by the chief financial officer (CFO) of the organization. The requisition application form, which is usually available from the human resources department, is filled out and submitted to executive

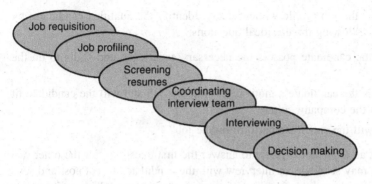

Figure 16.4   Six phases of effective recruiting process.

management for approval. The following information is provided on the application form: *title of the position*, *salary range*, and *justification*. The hiring manager needs to justify why and for which test project this position is being created and explain the impact if this position is not filled. Salary may vary depending on the test position, experience, and education sought in an applicant. Therefore, it is recommended to put a range, rather than an exact figure. Of course, the salary range should be based on the recommended guidelines provided by the human resources department. It is recommended to have a requisition number for the test position from human resources before proceeding to the next step in the hiring process.

16.5.2   Job Profiling

During or after the requisition phase one determines the specific requirements, also called a *job profile*, of the job to be filled. At this point it is useful to keep in mind the principle: *if you don't know what you are looking for, you're not likely to find it*. The job profile serves two purposes: (i) for job posting by recruiters at various places such as career portals, job fairs, newspapers, and state department of employment and (ii) as a formal definition of the role and responsibilities of the new hiree that can be used when the applicant is interviewed. A job profile contains the following information:

- Position
- Essential duties and responsibilities
- Skills and competence
- Experience
- Education, training, certificate, security clearances (if required)

16.5.3   Screening Resumes

Resumes come from different sources, including employee referrals, advertisements, job fairs, career portals, college job boards, and agencies. Evaluate the resumes against the job profile without delay. Identify the qualified candidates by addressing the following three critical questions:

- Does the candidate possess the necessary experience and skills to do the job?
- What is the candidate's motivation to do the job and will the candidate fit within the company culture?
- How will the candidate perform on the job?

The resume of an applicant is likely to answer the first question. For the other two questions, one may schedule an interview with the candidate. To cut cost and save time, the idea of a phone interview is gaining much ground. The telephone interview should continue uninterrupted for 30 minutes and be documented. One can ask open-ended questions about candidates' past actions to explore their behavior and the motivation behind them. An example of an open-ended question is: Tell me about one or two defects you reported and how you verified the fixes. Another open-ended question is: What is your motivation for doing this kind of work?

At this point it is useful to recall the five-C characteristics. An example question that explores the *controlled* characteristic is: Can you tell me about a specific project where you had a million details? A question that explores the probing ability of an applicant is: What method do you use to keep track of all the defects you need to verify? At the end of the telephone screening, the candidate should be allowed to ask questions. Hiring is a two-way street, meaning the hiring test manager and the candidate need to develop mutual respect. By the end of the telephone screening, one should have answers to all three questions. If an answer to any of the three questions is not positive, the resume should be put aside and the interview terminated. Otherwise, an on-site interview with the candidate should be scheduled.

16.5.4   Coordinating an Interview Team

The method of using multiple interviewers helps reduce the individual bias, makes efficient use of individual interviewer time, and permits the collection of in-depth information about the candidate. The following guidelines can help make the team interview process effective:

1. One person coordinates the team interview process.
2. The team size may vary from three to six, and at least one member must be from another group, such as software development or customer support. Other managers may be included in the team to interview principal engineers, technical leads, or management candidates.
3. Give each interviewer a copy of the job profile and the candidate's resume. This will ensure that the interviewers know about the candidate's background before the meeting and what to look for when they interview.
4. Assign each interviewer a different dimension of the job so that each can focus on a specific area. For example, one person could obtain information

on technical skills, another on professional skills, and a third about the candidate's behavior. Some overlap in their assigned areas will give more than one perspective on each skill area.

5. Have each interviewer use a standard outline containing questions that focus on the candidate's past behavior and accomplishments in the area being evaluated. Decide which interviewer will tell the applicant about various aspects of the job and the test organization so the interviewers do not repeat or contradict one another. Schedule that interviewer as the first to meet the candidate.

6. After the interview, have each interviewer rate the candidate on the dimension he or she was assigned.

16.5.5 Interviewing

One must remember that interviewing is a process for gathering information about the candidate. The gathered information is used to evaluate the candidate immediately after the interview. Questioning and probing are two important aspects of an interview. After asking the right question, the interviewer should remain silent to allow the candidate to formulate a response and should listen carefully. A follow-up question will help to understand and assess the depth of the candidate's experience. Providing examples and time to think will help the candidate come up with an answer. It is the interviewer's responsibility to provide a memorable environment. In order to improve the effectiveness of an interview, the interviewes may follow these steps:

1. Introduce yourself and your position to give the interview a gentle start.

2. If you are the first interviewer, then explain the various aspects of the job and the test organization.

3. Ask the first question based on the specific assigned area that needs to be explored. Take notes by paraphrasing what was said. Probe until you get an accurate understanding.

4. Ask the next question and probe until you get a good understanding. Similarly, ask more questions.

5. Invite the candidate to ask a few questions.

6. Close the interview and introduce the applicant to the next interviewer.

7. Complete the evaluation immediately after the interview.

During the interview aim for an 80/20 ratio of talk of the applicant to the interviewer. Display energy and show enthusiasm for the job for which the candidate is being interviewed. Be precise with the language, and interrupt the candidate with "I understand," "I agree," or "I appreciate" phrases. Formulating questions is a critical aspect of a successful interview. Therefore, be prepared with a questionnaire before the interview. In the following, we provide some sample questions in each dimension of the five-C characteristics.

Meticulous and thorough:

- Can you tell me about a specific test project where you had a large number of details? (Probe) How did you organize them?

Systematized and tidy:

- What do you do to keep yourself on track for your commitments and priorities?
- What method do you have for keeping track of what you have agreed to with clients or colleagues?

Dependable and trustworthy:

- Tell me about a team project you worked on. (Probe) What was the project and how were responsibilities assigned and managed? (Probe) How did you manage your responsibilities?

Precise and scrupulous:

- How do you approach completing testing tasks?
- Give me an example of a test project that demanded precision and thoroughness.
- Walk me through your solution to one of the most difficult testing problems you have faced.

Written communication:

- What rules, or standards, do you personally follow when writing a test plan document? Describe a time when you had to compose an acceptance test plan document to be viewed by people with diverse backgrounds.
- How do you write a defect report?

Accomplish and Carrythrough:

- Describe a time when you worked hard on a test project only to end without completing it? (Probe) Why did it not get finished?
- Tell me about a test project that you led? (Probe) What did the project accomplish and what did you do?

Adjustable and malleable:

- Have you ever had to shift gears in the middle of a test project? (Probe) What happened and what did you do?

Synergetic and team player:

- Do you prefer working on your own or in a team?
- People who work on test projects often find that priorities vary or last-minute things occur that cause you to have to change what you are doing or pinch-hit for someone else. Has that ever happened to you? (Probe) What did you do?
- Tell me about a recent test project that was a success. (Probe) What made the project so successful?

Verbal communication:

- In your last job who did you have to communicate with on a regular basis? (Probe) How did you communicate with them? How would you describe yourself as a communicator?
- Tell me about the manner and the tone you used to discuss a defect report with other members in a project team meeting.

Tactful and relationship building:

- Tell me about your best business relationships.
- Describe a situation where you had to build a relationship with someone (developers) you did not like.
- What makes a good working relationship?
- With what type of people do you like to work?

Determined and tenacious:

- Tell me about a time when you really had to persist to get the outcome you wanted.
- Tell me about a controversial defect for which you advocated.

Results driven and goal oriented:

- Do you consider yourself goal driven or task driven? (Probe) Can you give me an example?
- Can you explain the strategy you followed in your last testing project? (Probe) What was your tactics to execute the strategy?
- What personal goals have you set for the next year or so?
- Describe the career you see for yourself in testing?

Fast learner and quick study:

- Describe a situation where you had to learn new testing skills quickly before you could start? (Probe) How did you handle the fast-paced learning?

Innovative and visionary:

- Give me some specific examples of creative solutions of which are proud? (Probe) What did others think about them?

Apart from evaluating the candidate's technical and interpersonnel skills, other kinds of assessments are conducted to ensure that the candidate can and will do the job. These assessments are explained in the following.

- Assess the candidate's listening skills by observing whether or not the candidate frequently interrupts the interviewer.
- Assess how well the candidate answers the questions. Observe whether or not the answers are well articulated and brief.
- Assess the kinds of questions the candidate asks and whether or not the candidate takes the initiative to know more about the position and the company.

- Assess the response to know whether the candidate will do the job whatever it takes.
- Take note of the attitude of the candidate toward the testing profession.
- Take note of the candidate's attitude toward supervisors and colleagues in past workplaces.
- If the resume indicates excessive job changes, observe how the candidate explains it. Frequent job changes may indicate that the candidate may not be a stable person, may easily get bored, or cannot get along with colleagues.
- Do not hire an engineer who did not get a job as a software developer. A bad software developer is not likely to make a good software tester.

It is important to select good, incisive questions. At the same time, it is counterproductive to ask ineffective questions. Some examples of types of ineffective questions are as follows:

- A question that produces a "yes" or "no" answer is ineffective unless the candidate is asked to justify the answer.
- It is not useful to provide a lead in a question. For example, "You must have had to work over the weekend to get everything done on time?" can be adapted to "What did you do to handle the situation?" to elicit a more meaningful response.
- It is not conducive to ask a threatening question. The question, "Why didn't you work over the weekend?" may be perceived as threatening. Such a question may put candidates on the defensive and may inhibit their responses during the rest of the interview.
- Avoid multiple-choice questions. These questions may create confusion in the mind of the candidate.
- Completely avoid questions about philosophy, beliefs, and opinion. An example is "In your opinion, what qualities are essential to be an effective test engineer?" Candidates tend to answer what the interviewer wants to hear.
- Avoid illegal questions. A question can be considered illegal if it can be used to discriminate against the candidate on a basis that is not critical to the job. Avoid questions that may probe for a possible *disability*, *personal characteristics*, or *personal situation*. Examples of such questions are as follows:

  What is your date of birth?

  Is your wife expecting a child?

  How will your spouse feel about you traveling?

  What does your spouse do?

  Do you have any handicaps that might prevent you from performing this job?

  By the way, where did you say you are from?

Show me your green card?

I have a little kid, how many do you have?

Are your kids in daycare?

It is more effective to perform an evaluation of the candidate right after the interview. This is because the general impression about the candidate is still fresh in the mind of the interviewer. The evaluation should contain the following information:

- Basic information: State the position, the candidate's name, the interviewer's name, and the date.
- Professional skill: Rank on a scale of 1 (poor) to 10 (excellent).
- Behaviors: Rank on a scale of 1 (poor) to 10 (excellent).
- Organizational fit: Rank on a scale of 1 (poor) to 10 (excellent).
- Strengths: Summarize the candidate's strengths for this position.
- Weakness: Summarize the candidate's weaknesses for this position.
- General comments: State any other information that may be useful.

16.5.6   Making a Decision

It is recommended to have a debriefing meeting of all the interviewers at the end of the interview to compare their individual ratings. If there is a discrepancy among the ratings, a consensus is sought. A reference check needs to be done for a candidate about to be hired. Such checks provide additional and valuable information about the candidate which may not be possible to obtain during an interview process. Attention must be given to the words the references use during the conversation, hence the underlying message. The hiring manager should make a decision as quickly as possible because good candidates do not stay in the market for long.

16.6   RETAINING TEST ENGINEERS

Retaining testers is a big challenge, especially in today's market. Test engineers must know they have support from various levels of management. Managers should be encouraged to recognize testing efforts at par with development efforts. Management should treat its test engineers as professionals and as a part of the overall team that delivers a quality product. The following are key factors that positively impact the ability of an organization to retain good system test engineers.

16.6.1   Career Path

It is desirable to have a clear career path within the system testing group to be able to attract and retain qualified staff test engineers. Each organization needs to establish its own career path and responsibility levels for test engineers. This can be similar to the test team hierarchy described in Section 16.3. An organization can establish performance- and experience-based criteria to move from one role to another. To deliver high-quality products, testing must not be a dead-end career path. There must be ample opportunities within an organization for test engineers to move into other areas, such as development, system engineering, customer support, and project management. A test manager must work with team members for their career advancement—this is true for any division of an organization, and it is no different for system test engineers.

16.6.2 Training

Testing technology is changing almost as fast as development. Training is necessary to continually improve testing knowledge, business knowledge, interpersonal skill, leadership capability, communication skills, and process issues related to testing. For example, testing tools are changing with the technology. It is no longer cost-effective to build in-house automation tools when there are corporations focusing on just that effort. Testing tools should be continuously evaluated to know what they can and cannot do and test engineers should be trained in new tools. If test engineers have not done any test automation, they should be encouraged to attend some introductory lectures on test automation. They are likely to become very good in the development of automated test cases with some training. There are several options available to train the staff [7]:

- **On-Site Commercial Training:** An individual contractor from another company is invited to train a group of system test engineers. Training materials are customized to meet the unique needs of the group. The trainer provides hands-on training on test tools for automation, code review process, and design of test cases using examples from the domain of interest.

- **Public Forum Training:** Individual test engineers are sent to a public training class. This is useful if the group size is small. Here, the instructor cannot customize the material for a couple of students because the students may be from different companies with diverse backgrounds.

- **In-House Training:** Some companies run in-house training programs for new employees in development and quality assurance processes, such as the ISO certification process. The drawbacks of this approach are the unavailability of good trainers and lack of good training materials.

- **Specialty Training:** There are many special training programs available, such as web-enabled training and distance learning. There are product-based training programs, such as Microsoft's certified systems engineer (MCSE) and Cisco's certified internetwork expert (CCIE). It is important for a network system test engineer to have a thorough understanding of how a network system works, rather than just if it works.

- **Mentoring:** This is a process where a new employee works with a senior, experienced system test engineer called a mentor. The mentor's job is to train and promote the career of a newly hired test engineer. A mentor's responsibility begins the day the new person arrives for work. A mentor owns the following minimal responsibilities:

Showing how to fill out corporate paperwork to get things done

Handling questions the person may have regarding normal everyday operations

Training the person in the methodology being used

Having discussions on how to test, what are good tests, when, how, and why tools should be used, and so on

16.6.3 Reward System

Rewards are a great way to encourage people to continue improving and stay within the test organization. Salary increment based on merit, pay range adjustment, stock option, and office environment are all the things that can make a difference. Pay is not everything, but it is definitely an issue that must be addressed. It is recommended to have test engineers' pay scales above developers'. The key idea is to attract developers in to the testing group and then train them to be system testers. Another way to appreciate the good work of test engineers is to institute a formal awards program with certificates, plaques, and other awards, such as gift certificates from a very nice restaurant, to honor teams for their special effort.

16.7 TEAM BUILDING

It is important that the test engineers in a group work together with solidarity to maximize the ultimate success of the group. Building a team attitude means managing the engineers in a way that fosters teamwork instead of individual gains. It involves ongoing effort and practice among all the team members, including the team manager. The essential ingredients of a good work environment for test engineers are explained in the following.

16.7.1 Expectations

All test engineers should know what their assignments are and the expectations that come with the assignments. They should also know the larger consequences of not being able to meet the expectations. The role and responsibilities of a test engineer need to be clearly defined. Team members need to have opportunities to clarify and, if possible, negotiate their roles and relationships with one another. Team members may be empowered to work out responsibilities and roles among themselves and report their recommendations to the test manager. A test manager should schedule a weekly one-on-one meeting with each test engineer to talk about how things are going and to know the engineers and their interests beyond the official work. A manager needs to listen to their concerns and show empathy, understanding, and encouragement. Informal discussions and sharing of thoughts can go a long way in understanding their needs, and a manager can help them to improve their self-esteem.

16.7.2   Consistency

Consistency is typically something system test engineers look for in their testing. Having it in the testing process is just as beneficial. The process should not be a fluid one—it should be changing all the time. For example, when filing a defect, the severity of the defect must be assigned based on the defined criteria, and it should not be changed from time to time. It should be used consistently throughout the organization. Stability is essential for successful testing of software, and the same holds for the processes people are expected to follow. It is important to be consistent with the entry and exit criteria for testing. If and when inconsistency is accepted, it is necessary to tell the reasons to everyone and indicate the need to correct the direction.

16.7.3   Information Sharing

Sharing information is key to being successful. An atmosphere for timely, smooth flow of high-value information between self and system test engineers should be created and open expression of ideas and opinions encouraged. Methods for expressing ideas and opinions include e-mail, white boards, discussions, presentations, centralized documentation repositories, and short and regular meetings. Test engineers should be kept up-to-date with useful information, such as company policy change, upcoming test projects, and organizational events. It is important to ensure that there are no *surprises* for the team members. Team members should be encouraged to share beneficial information by talking. Direct and open communication with others fosters trust, enhances information flow, and builds stronger relationship. Brainstorming is also an efficient method for information sharing. A manger needs to take notes during the brainstorming sessions to distribute the minutes. At these sessions, all ideas are welcome, but no analysis is performed during the meetings. Brainstorming sessions are generally fun and educational. Sometimes the most ridiculous sounding idea becomes the *concept* in the future.

16.7.4   Standardization

It is imperative to have a standard vocabulary of terms so everyone understands what is being said. For instance, in a defect review meeting of eight people, if a test manager asks the question "What is the difference between priority and severity of a defect?" one will hear many different answers. Standardization of terminology will not only help the team, but if it is shared with others in the organization, the terms will begin showing up in requirements and other documents. Eventually, everyone will understand what is being said.

16.7.5   Test Environments

It would be reasonable to ask "What do test environments have to do with team building?" Having test environments that can be shared will greatly enhance testing efforts. However, if one has a single test environment, teamwork is critical to being responsive. Having good test environments leads to better team cohesiveness. A test environment should provide test engineers with access to the defect tracking database, test factory database, system configuration database, and other information resources to execute the test cases and report results efficiently. It is recommended to have a separate test laboratory, where the test environments can be set up by test engineers to execute test cases. To help the test organization to maximize productivity and efficiency through their test laboratory, the following ideas should be considered: (i) creating more than one test environment, (ii) purchasing new tools and equipment, (iii) updating existing equipment, (iv) replacing old equipment, (v) keeping the test environments clean, and (vi) keeping an inventory of all the equipment in the laboratory.

16.7.6 Recognitions

It is productive and cost-effective to value the work every test engineer performs. Verbal recognitions for engineer's contributions should be given. Acknowledging and celebrating the group accomplishment are a powerful way to recognize the team efforts and to keep the motivation and momentum afloat. The test team should be told that its efforts make a difference to the quality of the product through a personal memo. Special get-togethers, such as team lunches and breakfasts, should be organized upon successful completion of a test project.

16.8 SUMMARY

This chapter dealt with the organization of test groups in terms of functionality, management, and staffing. The recommendation is to have at least two test groups: integration test group and system test group. Unit testing must be performed by the programmers during coding so that there is no need for a separate test group for unit-level testing. A integration test group largely consists of developers. A system test group can be further divided into a number of subgroups, each handling a specialized task, as an organization grows. The need for differentiating between the quality assurance group and the system testing group was explained. The mandate of a quality assurance group is much broader than a system testing group. A quality assurance group has a larger role in ensuring conformance to best development practices throughout the organization, which is beyond the scope of a system test group.

Next, details of effectively staffing junior, senior, and principal test engineers were presented. Six simple phases of recruiting test engineers were discussed: job requisition, job profiling, screening resume, coordinating an interview team, interviewing, and decision making. The chapter explained some details of how to retain test engineers by means of training, rewarding, and establishing a clear career path for them within the test organization.

Finally, the chapter explained the ways to build and manage a test team with solidarity in a way that fosters team spirit instead of individual gain. Six ingredients were discussed to maximize the effectiveness of a test team: expectations, consistency, information sharing, standardization, testing environment, and recognition.

LITERATURE REVIEW

A good discussion of test team organization, staffing test engineers, and management of test teams can be found in Chapters 8 and 9 of the books by Black [3] and Craig and Jaskiel [7], respectively. Each chapter presents useful examples and opinions concerning hiring, test organizations, motivating testers, and managing test team. In addition, the book by Craig and Jaskiel presents an excellent chapter, namely Chapter 10, on what makes a good test manager. A good tutorial on test team management can be found in Chapter 5 of the book by Dustin, Rashka, and Paul [1]. The chapter contains sections on the organizational structure of a test team, test effort sizing, test engineer recruiting, and roles and responsibilities of a test manager and a test engineer.

A description of career paths for test engineers can be found in E. Weyuker, T. Ostrand, J. Brophy, and R. Prasad, "Clearing a Career Path for Software Tester," *IEEE Software*, Vol. 17, No. 2, March/April 2000, pp. 76–82. The authors describe five phases, namely apprenticeship, mastery, specialization, leadership, and top-level tester, in a test engineer career path at AT&T. The researchers have identified a group of general engineering skills that a test engineer needs to have. The general skill set includes knowledge about computers, system architecture, software development methods, information systems, and operating and database systems.

Successful Manager's Handbook (B. Davis, C. Skube, L. Hellervik, S. Gebelein, and J. Sheard, Personnel Decisions International, Minneapolis, 1996) is a comprehensive book on improving managerial skills. The book contains a thorough discussion of how to become an effective manager by practicing nine dimensions/factors: administrative factor, leadership factor, interpersonal factor, communication factor, motivation factor, self-management factor, organizational knowledge factor, organizational strategy factor, and thinking factor. This is a highly recommended book to become a successful test manager.

REFERENCES

1. E. Dustin, J. Rashka, and J. Paul. *Automated Software Testing: Introduction, Management, and Performance*. Addison-Wesley, Reading, MA, 1999.
2. Institute of Electrical and Electronics Engineers (IEEE). *IEEE Standard Glossary of Software Engineering Terminology*, IEEE standard 610. 12–1990. IEEE, New York, 1990.
3. R. Black. *Managing Testing Process*, 2nd ed. Wiley, New York, 2002.
4. B. Hetzel. *The Complete Guide to Software Testing*. Wiley, New York, 1988.
5. J. J. Cappel, V. R. Prybutok, and B. Varghese. A Closer Look At: Attention to Detail. *Communications of the ACM*, July 2005, pp. 87-92.
6. J. Cook. Building a Responsive Testing Team. Paper presented at the International Conference on Software Testing, Analysis and Review, Orlando, FL, May 1999.

7. R. D. Craig and S. P. Jaskiel. *Systematic Software Testing*. Artech House, Norwood, MA, 2002.

Exercises

1. Why does the integration test group function within the development group?

2. Unit-level tests are designed and executed by individual developers. Why don't we form a unit test group within a development group similar to an integration test group?

3. Discuss the advantages and disadvantages of having an independent system test group that is separated from the software development group with its own reporting structure.

4. What are the roles and responsibilities of a test manager and a (software) quality assurance manager?

5. Assume that you are a system test manager for a startup software development organization. Your company develops software in the network security domain. You want to hire a new test engineer for your team. Prepare a job profile for the test engineer that you could use for job posting and for screening the applicants.

6. For the organization described in exercise 5, prepare a job profile for hiring a quality assurance manager to lead the quality management group.

7. Do you think you can ask the following questions during an interview. Justify your answers.

    (a) Do you smoke? We maintain a smoke-free work environment. Can you work without smoking on the job?

    (b) Have you ever been convicted of a felony?

    (c) Have you ever been arrested?

    (d) Have you ever tested positive for the AIDS virus?

    (e) Are you gay?

    (f) What kind of name is Sagar?

    (g) Is it an Indian name?

8. Write some of your interview questions to assess test engineers in the following areas:

    (a) Time management

    (b) Problem solving

    (c) Decision making

    (d) Multitasking

    (e) Leadership

    (f) Motivation

    (g) Sincerity

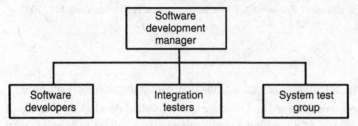

Figure 16.5   System test organization as part of development.

(h) Work environment

(i) Quickness and promptness

9. In small startup organizations, the system test group is a part of the development group, as shown in Figure 16.5. Do you think it is a good idea to have this structure? Justify your answer.

10. What role does a test manager play in building a system test team?

CHAPTER 17

Software Quality

Quality is never an accident; it is always the result of intelligent effort.
— *John Ruskin*

17.1 FIVE VIEWS OF SOFTWARE QUALITY

In the early days of computers, software developers mainly focused on product functionalities, and most of the end users were highly qualified professionals, such as mathematicians, scientists, and engineers. Development of personal computers and advances in computer networks, the World Wide Web, and graphical user interface made computer software highly accessible to all kinds of users. These days there is widespread computerization of many processes that used to be done by hand. For example, until the late 1990s taxpayers used to file returns on paper, but these days there are numerous web-based tax filing systems. There has been increasing customer expectations in terms of better quality in software products, and developers are under tremendous pressure to deliver high-quality products at a lower cost. Even though competing products deliver the same functionalities, it is the lower cost products with better quality attributes that survive in the competitive market. Therefore, all stakeholders—users, customers, developers, testers, and managers—in a product must have a broad understanding of the overall concept of software quality.

A number of factors influence the making and buying of software products. These factors are user's needs and expectations, the manufacturer's considerations, the inherent characteristics of a product, and the perceived value of a product. To be able to capture the quality concept, it is important to study quality from a broader perspective. This is because the concept of quality predates software development. In a much cited paper published in the *Sloan Management Review* [1], Garvin has analyzed how quality is perceived in different manners in different domains, namely, philosophy, economics, marketing, and management:

> *Transcendental View*: In the transcendental view quality is something that can be recognized through experience but is not defined in some tractable

Software Testing and Quality Assurance: Theory and Practice, Edited by Kshirasagar Naik and Priyadarshi Tripathy
Copyright © 2008 John Wiley & Sons, Inc.

form. Quality is viewed to be something ideal, which is too complex to lend itself to be precisely defined. However, a good-quality object stands out, and it is easily recognized. Because of the philosophical nature of the transcendental view, no effort is made to express it using concrete measures.

User View: The user view concerns the extent to which a product meets user needs and expectations. Quality is not just viewed in terms of what a product can deliver, but it is also influenced by the service provisions in the sales contract. In this view, a user is concerned with whether or not a product is fit for use. This view is highly personalized in nature. The idea of *operational profile*, discussed in Chapter 15, plays an important role in this view. Because of the personalized nature of the product view, a product is considered to be of good quality if it satisfies the needs of a large number of customers. It is useful to identify what product attributes users consider to be important. The reader may note that the user view can encompass many subjective elements apart from the expected functionalities central to user satisfaction. Examples of subjective elements are *usability*, *reliability*, *testability*, and *efficiency*.

Manufacturing View: The manufacturing view has its genesis in the manufacturing sectors, such as the automobile and electronics sectors. In this view, quality is seen as conforming to requirements. Any deviation from the stated requirements is seen as reducing the quality of the product. The concept of *process* plays a key role in the manufacturing view. Products are to be manufactured "right the first time" so that development cost and maintenance cost are reduced. However, there is no guarantee that conforming to process standards will lead to good products. Some criticize this view with an argument that conformance to a process can only lead to *uniformity* in the products, and, therefore, it is possible to manufacture bad-quality products in a consistent manner. However, product quality can be incrementally enhanced by continuously improving the process. Development of the *capability maturity model* (CMM) [2] and ISO 9001 [3] are based on the manufacturing view.

Product View: The central hypothesis in the product view is this: *If a product is manufactured with good internal properties, then it will have good external qualities*. The product view is attractive because it gives rise to an opportunity to explore causal relationships between *internal properties* and *external qualities* of a product. In this view, the current quality level of a product indicates the presence or absence of measurable product properties. The product view of quality can be assessed in an objective manner. An example of the product view of software quality is that high degree of modularity, which is an internal property, makes a software testable and maintainable.

Value-Based View: The value-based view represents a merger of two independent concepts: *excellence* and *worth*. Quality is a measure of excellence, and value is a measure of worth. The central idea in the value-based view is how much a customer is willing to pay for a certain level of quality. The reality is that quality is meaningless if a product does not make economic sense. Essentially, the value-based view represents a trade-off between cost and quality.

Measuring Quality   The five viewpoints help us in understanding different aspects of the quality concept. On the other hand, measurement allows us to have a quantitative view of the quality concept. In the following, we explain the reasons for developing a quantitative view of a software system [4]:

- Measurement allows us to establish baselines for qualities. Developers must know the minimum level of quality they must deliver for a product to be acceptable.

- Organizations make continuous improvements in their process models—and an improvement has a cost associated with it. Organizations need to know how much improvement in quality is achieved at a certain cost incurred due to process improvement. This causal relationship is useful in making management decisions concerning process improvement. Sometimes it may be worth investing more in process improvement, whereas some other time the return may not be significant.

- The present level of quality of a product needs to be evaluated so the need for improvements can be investigated.

Measurement of User's View   The user's view encompasses a number of quality factors, such as functionality, reliability, and usability. It is easy to measure how much of the functionalities a software product delivers by designing at least one test case for each functionality. A product may require multiple test cases for the same functionality if the functionality is to be performed in different execution environments. Then, the ratio of the number of passed test cases to the total number of test cases designed to verify the functionalities is a measure of the functionalities delivered by the product. Among the qualities that reflect the user's view, the concept of *reliability* has drawn the most attention of researchers.

In the ISO 9126 quality model, *usability* has been broken down into three subcharacteristics, namely, *learnability*, *understandability*, and *operability*. Learnability can be specified as the average elapsed time for a typical user to gain a certain level of competence in using the product. Similarly, understandability can be quantified as the average time needed by a typical user to gain a certain level of understanding of the product. One can quantify operability in a similar manner. The basic idea of breaking down usability into learnability, understandability, and operability can be seen in light of Gilb's technique [5]: *The quality concept is broken down into component parts until each can be stated in terms of directly measurable attributes*. Gilb's technique is a general one to be applicable to a wide variety of user-level qualities.

Measurement of Manufacturer's View   Manufacturers are interested in obtaining measures of the following two different quantities:

- **Defect Count:** How many defects have been detected?
- **Rework Cost:** How much does it cost to fix the known defects?

Defect count represents the number of all the defects that have been detected so far. If a product is in operation, this count includes the defects detected during development and operation. A defect count reflects the quality of work produced. Merely counting the defects is of not much use unless something can be done to improve the development process to reduce the defect count in subsequent projects. One can analyze the defects as follows:

- For each defect identify the development phase in which it was introduced and the phase in which it was discovered. Let us assume that a large fraction of the defects are introduced in the requirements gathering phase, and those are discovered during system testing. Then, we can conclude that requirement analysis was not adequately performed. We can also conclude that work done subsequently, such as design verification and unit testing, were not of high standard. If a large number of defects are found during system operation, one can say that system testing was not rigorously performed.

- Categorize the defects based on modules. Assuming that a module is a cohesive entity performing a well-defined task, by identifying the modules containing most of the defects we can identify where things are going wrong. This information can be used in managing resources. For example, if a large number of defects are found in a communication module in a distributed application, more resource could be allocated to train developers in the details of the communication system.

- To compare defects across modules and products in a meaningful way, normalize the defect count by product size. By normalizing defect count by product size in terms of the number of LOC, we can obtain a measure, called *defect density*. Intuitively, defect density is expressed as the *number of defects found per thousand lines of code*.

- Separate the defects found during operation from the ones found during development. The ratio of the number of defects found during operation to the total number of defects is a measure of the effectiveness of the entire gamut of test activities. If the ratio is close to zero, we can say that testing was highly effective. On the other hand, if the ratio is farther from the ideal value of zero, say, 0.2, it is apparent that all the testing activities detected only 80% of the defects.

After defects are detected, the developers make an effort to fix them. Ultimately, it costs some money to fix defects—this is apart from the "reputation" cost to an organization from defects discovered during operation. The rework cost includes all the additional cost associated with defect-related activities, such as fixing documents. Rework is an additional cost that is incurred due to work being done in a less than perfect manner the first time it was done. It is obvious that organizations strive to reduce the total cost of software development, including the rework cost. The rework cost can be split into two parts as follows:

- **Development Rework Cost:** This is the rework cost incurred *before* a product is released to the customers.
- **Operation Rework Cost:** This is the rework cost incurred *when* a product is in operation.

On the one hand, the development rework cost is a measure of development efficiency. In other words, if the development rework cost is zero, then the development efficiency is very high. On the other hand, the operation rework cost is a measure of the delivered quality of the product in operation. If the development rework cost is zero, then the delivered quality of the product in operation is very high. This is because the customers have not encountered any defect and, consequently, the development team is not spending any resource on defect fixing.

17.2 MCCALL'S QUALITY FACTORS AND CRITERIA

The concept of software quality and the efforts to understand it in terms of measurable quantities date back to the mid-1970s. McCall, Richards, and Walters [6] were the first to study the concept of software quality in terms of quality factors and quality criteria.

17.2.1 Quality Factors

A *quality factor* represents a behavioral characteristic of a system. Some examples of high-level quality factors are *correctness*, *reliability*, *efficiency*, *testability*, *portability*, and *reusability*. A full list of the quality factors will be given in a later part of this section. As the examples show, quality factors are external attributes of a software system. Customers, software developers, and quality assurance engineers are interested in different quality factors to a different extent. For example, customers may want an efficient and reliable software with less concern for portability. The developers strive to meet customer needs by making their system efficient and reliable, at the same time making the product portable and reusable to reduce the cost of software development. The software quality assurance team is more interested in the testability of a system so that some other factors, such as correctness, reliability, and efficiency, can be easily verified through testing. The testability factor is important to developers and customers as well: (i) Developers want to test their product before delivering it to the software quality assurance team and (ii) customers want to perform acceptance tests before taking delivery of a product. In Table 17.1, we list the quality factors as defined by McCall et al. [6]. Now we explain the 11 quality factors in more detail:

> *Correctness*: A software system is expected to meet the explicitly specified functional requirements and the implicitly expected nonfunctional requirements. If a software system satisfies all the functional requirements, the

TABLE 17.1 McCall's Quality Factors

Quality Factors	Definition
Correctness	Extent to which a program satisfies its specifications and fulfills the user's mission objectives
Reliability	Extent to which a program can be expected to perform its intended function with required precision
Efficiency	Amount of computing resources and code required by a program to perform a function
Integrity	Extent to which access to software or data by unauthorized persons can be controlled
Usability	Effort required to learn, operate, prepare input, and interpret output of a program
Maintainability	Effort required to locate and fix a defect in an operational program
Testability	Effort required to test a program to ensure that it performs its intended functions
Flexibility	Effort required to modify an operational program
Portability	Effort required to transfer a program from one hardware and/or software environment to another
Reusability	Extent to which parts of a software system can be reused in other applications
Interoperability	Effort required to couple one system with another

Source: From ref. 6.

system is said to be correct. However, a correct software system may still be unacceptable to customers if the system fails to meet unstated requirements, such as stability, performance, and scalability. On the other hand, even an incorrect system may be accepted by users.

Reliability: It is difficult to construct large software systems which are correct. A few functions may not work in all execution scenarios, and, therefore, the software is considered to be incorrect. However, the software may still be acceptable to customers because the execution scenarios causing the system to fail may not frequently occur when the system is deployed. Moreover, customers may accept software failures once in a while. Customers may still consider an incorrect system to be reliable if the failure rate is very small and it does not adversely affect their mission objectives. Reliability is a customer perception, and an incorrect software can still be considered to be reliable.

Efficiency: Efficiency concerns to what extent a software system utilizes resources, such as computing power, memory, disk space, communication bandwidth, and energy. A software system must utilize as little resources as possible to perform its functionalities. For example, by utilizing less communication bandwidth a base station in a cellular telephone network can support more users.

Integrity: A system's integrity refers to its ability to withstand attacks to its security. In other words, integrity refers to the extent to which access to software or data by unauthorized persons or programs can be controlled. Integrity has assumed a prominent role in today's network-based applications. Integrity is also an issue in multiuser systems.

Usability: A software system is considered to be usable if human users find it easy to use. Users put much emphasis on the user interface of software systems. Without a good user interface a software system may fizzle out even if it possesses many desired qualities. However, it must be remembered that a good user interface alone cannot make a product successful—the product must also be reliable, for example. If a software fails too often, no good user interface can keep it in the market.

Maintainability: In general, maintenance refers to the upkeep of products in response to deterioration of their components due to continued use of the products. Maintainability refers to how easily and inexpensively the maintenance tasks can be performed. For software products, there are three categories of maintenance activities: corrective, adaptive, and perfective. Corrective maintenance is a postrelease activity, and it refers to the removal of defects existing in an in-service software. The existing defects might have been known at the time of release of the product or might have been introduced during maintenance. Adaptive maintenance concerns adjusting software systems to changes in the execution environment. Perfective maintenance concerns modifying a software system to improve some of its qualities.

Testability: It is important to be able to verify every requirement, both explicitly stated and simply expected. Testability means the ability to verify requirements. At every stage of software development, it is necessary to consider the testability aspect of a product. Specifically, for each requirement we try to answer the question: What procedure should one use to test the requirement, and how easily can one verify it? To make a product testable, designers may have to instrument a design with functionalities not available to the customer.

Flexibility: Flexibility is reflected in the cost of modifying an operational system. As more and more changes are effected in a system throughout its operational phase, subsequent changes may cost more and more. If the initial design is not flexible, it is highly likely that subsequent changes are very expensive. In order to measure the flexibility of a system, one has to find an answer to the question: How easily can one add a new feature to a system?

Portability: Portability of a software system refers to how easily it can be adapted to run in a different execution environment. An execution environment is a broad term encompassing hardware platform, operating system, distributedness, and heterogeneity of the hardware system, to name a few. Portability is important for developers because a minor adaptation of a system can increase its market potential. Moreover, portability gives customers an option to easily move from one execution environment to another to best utilize emerging technologies in furthering their business. Good design principles such as modularity facilitate portability. For example, all environment-related computations can be localized in a few modules so that those can be easily identified and modified to port the system to another environment.

Reusability: Reusability means if a significant portion of one product can be reused, maybe with minor modification, in another product. It may not be economically viable to reuse small components. Reusability saves the cost and time to develop and test the component being reused. In the field of scientific computing, mathematical libraries are commonly reused. Reusability is not just limited to product parts, rather it can be applied to processes as well. For example, we are very much interested in developing good processes that are largely repeatable.

Interoperability: In this age of computer networking, isolated software systems are turning into a rarity. Today's software systems are coupled at the input–output level with other software systems. Intuitively, interoperability means whether or not the output of one system is acceptable as input to another system; it is likely that the two systems run on different computers interconnected by a network. When we consider Internet-based applications and wireless applications, the need for interoperability is simply overriding. For example, users of document processing packages, such as LaTex and Microsoft Word, want to import a variety of images produced by different graphics packages. Therefore, the graphics packages and the document processing packages must be interoperable. Another example of interoperability is the ability to roam from one cellular phone network in one country to another cellular network in another country.

The 11 quality factors defined in Table 17.1 have been grouped into three broad categories as follows:

- Product operation
- Product revision
- Product transition

The elements of each of the three broad categories are identified and further explained in Table 17.2. It may be noted that the above three categories relate more to postdevelopment activities expectations and less to in-development activities. In other words, McCall's quality factors emphasize more on the quality levels of a product delivered by an organization and the quality levels of a delivered product relevant to product maintenance. Quality factors in the product operation category refer to delivered quality. Testability is an important quality factor that is of much significance to developers during both product development and maintenance. Maintainability, flexibility, and portability are desired quality factor sought

TABLE 17.2 Categorization of McCall's Quality Factors

Quality Categories	Quality Factors	Broad Objectives
Product operation	Correctness	Does it do what the customer wants?
	Reliability	Does it do it accurately all of the time?
	Efficiency	Does it quickly solve the intended problem?
	Integrity	Is it secure?
	Usability	Can I run it?
Product revision	Maintainability	Can it be fixed?
	Testability	Can it be tested?
	Flexibility	Can it be changed?
Product transition	Portability	Can it be used on another machine?
	Reusability	Can parts of it be reused?
	Interoperability	Can it interface with another system?

Source: From ref. 6.

in a product so that the task of supporting the product after delivery is less expensive. Reusability is a quality factor that has the potential to reduce the development cost of a project by allowing developers to reuse some of the components from an existing product. Interoperability allows a product to coexist with other products, systems, and features.

17.2.2 Quality Criteria

A *quality criterion* is an attribute of a quality factor that is related to software development. For example, modularity is an attribute of the architecture of a software system. A highly modular software allows designers to put cohesive components in one module, thereby increasing the maintainability of the system. Similarly, traceability of a user requirement allows developers to accurately map the requirement to a subset of the modules, thereby increasing the correctness of the system. Some quality criteria relate to products and some to personnel. For example, modularity is a product-related quality criterion, whereas training concerns development and software quality assurance personnel. In Table 17.3, we list the 23 quality criteria defined by McCall et al. [6].

17.2.3 Relationship between Quality Factors and Criteria

The relationship between quality factors and quality criteria is shown in Figure 17.1. An arrow from a quality criterion to a quality factor means that the quality criterion has a positive impact on the quality factor. For example, traceability has a positive impact on correctness. Similarly, the quality criterion simplicity positively impacts reliability, usability, and testability.

Though it is desirable to improve all the quality factors, doing so may not be possible. This is because, in general, quality factors are not completely independent. Thus, we note two characteristics of the relationship as follows:

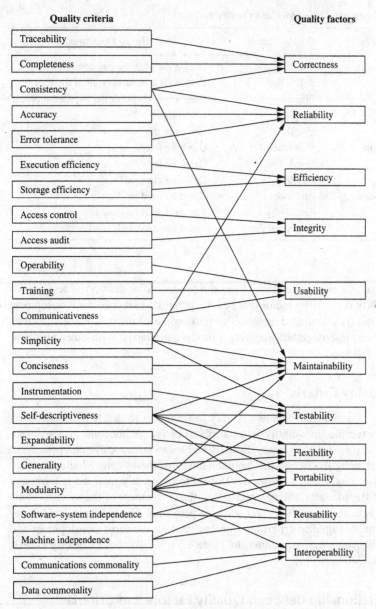

Figure 17.1 Relation between quality factors and quality criteria [6].

- If an effort is made to improve one quality factor, another quality factor may be degraded. For example, if an effort is made to make a software product testable, the efficiency of the software is likely to go down. To make code testable, programmers may not be able to write compact code. Moreover, if we are interested in making a product portable, the code must

TABLE 17.3   McCall's Quality Criteria

Quality Criteria	Definition
Access audit	Ease with which software and data can be checked for compliance with standards or other requirements
Access control	Provisions for control and protection of the software and data
Accuracy	Precision of computations and output
Communication commonality	Degree to which standard protocols and interfaces are used
Completeness	Degree to which a full implementation of the required functionalities has been achieved
Communicativeness	Ease with which inputs and outputs can be assimilated
Conciseness	Compactness of the source code, in terms of lines of code
Consistency	Use of uniform design and implementation techniques and notation throughout a project
Data commonality	Use of standard data representations
Error tolerance	Degree to which continuity of operation is ensured under adverse conditions
Execution efficiency	Run time efficiency of the software
Expandability	Degree to which storage requirements or software functions can be expanded
Generality	Breadth of the potential application of software components
Hardware independence	Degree to which the software is dependent on the underlying hardware
Instrumentation	Degree to which the software provides for measurement of its use or identification of errors
Modularity	Provision of highly independent modules
Operability	Ease of operation of the software
Self-documentation	Provision of in-line documentation that explains implementation of components
Simplicity	Ease with which the software can be understood.
Software system independence	Degree to which the software is independent of its software environment—nonstandard language constructs, operating system, libraries, database management system, etc.
Software efficiency	Run time storage requirements of the software
Traceability	Ability to link software components to requirements
Training	Ease with which new users can use the system

Source: From ref. 6.

be written in such a manner that it is easily understandable, and, hence, code need not be in a compact form. An effort to make code portable is likely to reduce its efficiency. In fact, attempts to improve integrity, usability, maintainability, testability, flexibility, portability, reusability, and interoperability will reduce the efficiency of a software system.

- Some quality factors positively impact others. For example, an effort to enhance the correctness of a system will increase its reliability. As another example, an effort to enhance the testability of a system will improve its maintainability.

17.2.4 Quality Metrics

The high-level quality factors cannot be measured directly. For example, we cannot directly measure the testability of a software system. Neither can testability be expressed in "yes" or "no" terms. Instead, the degree of testability can be assessed by associating with testability a few quality metrics, namely, *simplicity*, *instrumentation*, *self-descriptiveness*, and *modularity*. A *quality metric* is a measure that captures some aspect of a quality criterion. One or more quality metrics should be associated with each criterion. The metrics can be derived as follows:

- Formulate a set of relevant questions concerning the quality criteria and seek a "yes" or "no" answer for each question.

- Divide the number of "yes" answers by the number of questions to obtain a value in the range of 0 to 1. The resulting number represents the intended quality metric.

For example, we can ask the following question concerning the *self-descriptiveness* of a product: *Is all documentation written clearly and simply such that procedures, functions, and algorithms can be easily understood?* Another question concerning self-descriptiveness is: *Is the design rationale behind a module clearly understood?* Different questions can have different degrees of importance in the computation of a metric, and, therefore, individual "yes" answers can be differently weighted in the above computation.

The above way of computing the value of a metric is highly subjective. The degree of subjectivity varies significantly from question to question in spite of the fact that all the responses are treated equally. It is difficult to combine different metrics to get a measure of a higher level quality factor. In addition, for some questions it is more meaningful to consider a response on a richer measurement scale. For example, the question "Is the design of a software system simple?" needs to be answered on a multiple ordinal scale to reflect a variety of possible answers, rather than a yes-or-no answer.

Similarly, one cannot directly measure the reliability of a system. However, the number of distinct failures observed so far is a measure of the initial reliability of the system. Moreover, the time gap between observed failures is treated as a measure of the reliability of a system.

17.3 ISO 9126 QUALITY CHARACTERISTICS

There has been international collaboration among experts to define a general framework for software quality. An expert group, under the aegis of the ISO, standardized a software quality document, namely, ISO 9126, which defines six broad, independent categories of quality characteristics as follows:

Functionality: A set of attributes that bear on the existence of a set of functions and their specified properties. The functions are those that satisfy stated or implied needs.

Reliability: A set of attributes that bear on the capability of software to maintain its performance level under stated conditions for a stated period of time.

Usability: A set of attributes that bear on the effort needed for use and on the individual assessment of such use by a stated or implied set of users.

Efficiency: A set of attributes that bear on the relationship between the software's performance and the amount of resource used under stated conditions.

Maintainability: A set of attributes that bear on the effort needed to make specified modifications (which may include corrections, improvements, or adaptations of software to environmental changes and changes in the requirements and functional specifications).

Portability: A set of attributes that bear on the ability of software to be transferred from one environment to another (this includes the organizational, hardware or, software environment).

The ISO 9126 standard includes an example quality model, as shown in Figure 17.2, that further decomposes the quality characteristics into more concrete subcharacteristics. For example, the maintainability characteristic has been decomposed into four subcharacteristics, namely, *analyzability*, *changeability*, *stability*, and *testability*. The decomposition shown in Figure 17.2 is just a sample model—and not a universal one. The 20 subcharacteristics of Figure 17.2 are defined as follows:

Suitability: The capability of the software to provide an adequate set of functions for specified tasks and user objectives.

Accuracy: The capability of the software to provide the right or agreed-upon results or effects.

Interoperability: The capability of the software to interact with one or more specified systems.

Security: The capability of the software to prevent unintended access and resist deliberate attacks intended to gain unauthorized access to confidential information or to make unauthorized modifications to information or to the program so as to provide the attacker with some advantage or so as to deny service to legitimate users.

Maturity: The capability of the software to avoid failure as a result of faults in the software.

Fault Tolerance: The capability of the software to maintain a specified level of performance in case of software faults or of infringement of its specified interface.

Recoverability: The capability of the software to reestablish its level of performance and recover the data directly affected in the case of a failure.

Quality characteristic   **Quality subcharacteristics**

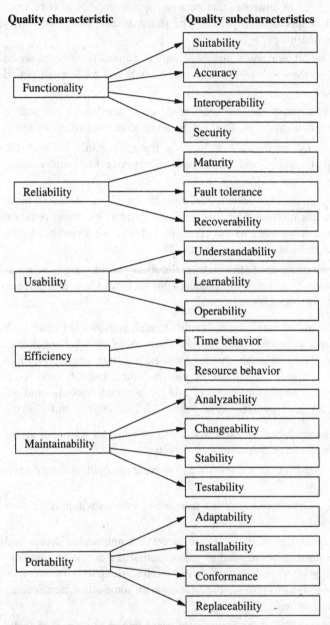

Figure 17.2   ISO 9126 sample quality model refines standard's features into subcharacteristics. (From ref. 4. © 1996 IEEE.)

Understandability: The capability of the software product to enable the user to understand whether the software is suitable, and how it can be used for particular tasks and conditions of use.

Learnability: The capability of the software product to enable the user to learn its applications.

Operability: The capability of the software product to enable the user to operate and control it.

Attractiveness: The capability of the software product to be liked by the user.

Time Behavior: The capability of the software to provide appropriate response and processing times and throughput rates when performing its function under stated conditions.

Resource Utilization: The capability of the software to use appropriate resources in an appropriate time when the software performs its function under stated condition.

Analyzability: The capability of the software product to be diagnosed for deficiencies or causes of failures in the software or for the parts to be modified to be identified.

Changeability: The capability of the software product to enable a specified modification to be implemented.

Stability: The capability of the software to minimize unexpected effects from modifications of the software.

Testability: The capability of the software product to enable modified software to be validated.

Adaptability: The capability of the software to be modified for different specified environments without applying actions or means other than those provided for this purpose for the software considered.

Installability: The capability of the software to be installed in a specified environment.

Coexistence: The capability of the software to coexist with other independent software in a common environment sharing common resources.

Replaceability: The capability of the software to be used in place of other specified software in the environment of that software.

Organizations must define their own quality characteristics and subcharacteristics after a fuller understanding of their needs. In other words, organizations must identify the level of the different quality characteristics they need to satisfy within their context of software development. Reaching an ideally best quality level from the present one is a gradual process. Therefore, it is important to understand the need for moving on to the next achievable step toward the highest level—the ideally best level.

At this point it is useful to compare McCall's quality model with the ISO 9126 model. Since the two models focus on the same abstract entity, namely, *software quality*, it is natural that there are many similarities between the two models. What is called *quality factor* in McCall's model is called *quality characteristic* in the ISO 9126 model. The following high-level quality factors/characteristics are found in both models: reliability, usability, efficiency, maintainability, and portability. However, there are several differences between the two models as explained in the following:

- The ISO 9126 model emphasizes characteristics *visible* to the users, whereas the McCall model considers *internal* qualities as well. For example, reusability is an internal characteristic of a product. Product developers strive to produce reusable components, whereas its impact is not perceived by customers.

- In McCall's model, one quality criterion can impact several quality factors, whereas in the ISO 9126 model, one subcharacteristic impacts exactly one quality characteristic.

- A high-level quality factor, such as testability, in the McCall model is a low-level subcharacteristic of maintainability in the ISO 9126 model.

Following are a few concerns with the quality models [4]:

- There is no consensus about what high-level quality factors are most important at the top level. McCall et al. suggest 11 high-level quality factors, whereas the ISO 9126 standard defines only 6 quality characteristics. Some of the quality factors in the McCall model are more important to developers. For example, reusability and interoperability are important to developers. However, the ISO 9126 model just considers the product.

- There is no consensus regarding what is a top-level quality factor/ characteristic and what is a more concrete quality criterion/subcharacteristic. These days many applications run on computer and communications networks. However, interoperability is not an independent, top-level quality characteristic in the ISO 9126 model. It is not clear why interoperability is a part of functionality. The absence of a rationale makes it difficult to follow a prescribed quality model.

17.4   ISO 9000:2000 SOFTWARE QUALITY STANDARD

There are ongoing efforts at the international level for standardizing different aspects of computer communications and software development. Standardization has been particularly successful in the field of computer networking and wireless communications. For example, the collaborative work of the Internet Engineering Task Force (IETF) has been the key to the proliferation of the Internet. Similarly, standardization efforts from the IEEE have led to the successful development of the local area network (LAN) standard, namely the IEEE 802.3 standard, and the wireless local area network (WLAN) standards, namely IEEE 802.11a/b/g.

In spite of the positive consequence of standardization in the field of communications, standardization in software development is met with mixed reactions.

On the one hand, the main argument against standardization is that it curtails individual drive to be innovative. On the other hand, standards reduce the activity of reinventing the same, or similar, processes for development and quality assurance. Repeatability of processes is a key benefit emanating from standardization—and repeatability reduces the cost of software development and produces a base quality level of software products.

The ISO has developed a series of standards, collectively known as the ISO 9000. The ISO was founded in 1946, and it is based in Geneva, Switzerland. It develops and promotes international standards in the field of quality assurance and quality management. The ISO 9000 standards are generally applicable to all tangible products manufactured with human endeavor, say, from spices to software—Even some brands of spice and rice used in everyday cooking are claimed to be ISO 9000 certified. The ISO 9000 standards are reviewed and updated from time to time, once every 5–8 years. The latest ISO 9000 standards released in the year 2000 are referred to as ISO 9000:2000. There are three components of the ISO 9000:2000 standard as follows:

ISO 9000: Fundamentals and vocabulary [7]

ISO 9001: Requirements [8]

ISO 9004: Guidelines for performance improvements [9]

At this point we remind the reader that ISO 9002 and ISO 9003 were parts of ISO 9000:1994, but these are no longer parts of ISO 9000:2000. ISO 9002 dealt with the quality system model for quality assurance in production and installation, whereas ISO 9003 dealt with the quality system model for quality assurance in final inspection and testing.

17.4.1 ISO 9000:2000 Fundamentals

The ISO 9000:2000 standard is based on the following eight principles:

- **Principle 1. Customer Focus:** Success of an organization is highly dependent on satisfying the customers. An organization must understand its customers and their needs on a continued basis. Understanding the customers helps in understanding and meeting their requirements. It is not enough to just meet customer requirements. Rather, organizations must make an effort to exceed customer expectations. By understanding the customers, one can have a better understanding of their real needs and their unstated expectations. People in different departments of an organization, such as marketing, software development, testing, and customer support, must capture the same view of the customers and their requirements. An example of customer focus is to understand how they are going to use a system. By accurately understating how customers are going to use a system, one can produce a better *user profile*.

- **Principle 2. Leadership:** Leaders set the direction their organization should take, and they must effectively communicate this to all the people involved in the process. All the people in an organization must have a coherent view of the organizational direction. Without a good understanding of the organizational direction, employees will find it difficult to know where they are heading. Leaders must set challenging but realistic goals and objectives. Employee contribution should be recognized by the leaders. Leaders create a positive environment and provide support for the employees to collectively realize the organizational goal. They reevaluate their goals on a continual basis and communicate the findings to the staff.

- **Principle 3. Involvement of People:** In general, organizations rely on people. People are informed of the organizational direction, and they are involved at all levels of decision making. People are given an opportunity to develop their strength and use their abilities. People are encouraged to be creative in performing their tasks.

- **Principle 4. Process Approach:** There are several advantages to performing major tasks by using the concept of *process*. A process is a sequence of activities that transform inputs to outputs. Organizations can prepare a plan in the form of allocating resources and scheduling the activities by making the process defined, repeatable, and measurable. Consequently, the organization becomes efficient and effective. Continuous improvement in processes leads to improvement in efficiency and effectiveness.

- **Principle 5. System Approach to Management:** A system is an interacting set of processes. A whole organization can be viewed as a *system* of interacting processes. In the context of software development, we can identify a number of processes. For example, gathering customer requirements for a project is a distinct process involving specialized skills. Similarly, designing a functional specification by taking the requirements as input is another distinct process. There are simultaneous and sequential processes being executed in an organization. At any time, people are involved in one or more processes. A process is affected by the outcome of some other processes, and, in turn, it affects some other processes in the organization. It is important to understand the overall goal of the organization and the individual subgoals associated with each process. For an organization as a whole to succeed in terms of effectiveness and efficiency, the interactions among processes must be identified and analyzed.

- **Principle 6. Continual Improvement:** Continual improvement means that the processes involved in developing, say, software products are reviewed on a periodic basis to identify where and how further improvements in the processes can be effected. Since no process can be a perfect one to begin with, continual improvement plays an important role in the success of organizations. Since there are independent changes in many areas, such as customer views and technologies, it is natural to review the processes and seek improvements. Continual process improvements result in lower cost of production and maintenance. Moreover, continual improvements lead to less differences between the expected behavior and actual behavior of products. Organizations need to develop their own policies regarding when to start a process review and identify the goals of the review.

- **Principle 7. Factual Approach to Decision Making:** Decisions may be made based on facts, experience, and intuition. Facts can be gathered by using a sound measurement process. Identification and quantification of parameters are central to measurement. Once elements are quantified, it becomes easier to establish methods to measure those elements. There is a need for methods to validate the measured data and make the data available to those who need it. The measured data should be accurate and reliable. A quantitative measurement program helps organizations know how much improvement has been achieved due to a process improvement.

- **Principle 8. Mutually Beneficial Supplier Relationships:** Organizations rarely make all the components they use in their products. It is a common practice for organizations to procure components and subsystems from third parties. An organization must carefully choose the suppliers and make them aware of the organization's needs and expectations. The performance of the products procured from outside should be evaluated, and the need to improve their products and processes should be communicated to the suppliers. A mutually beneficial, cooperative relationship should be maintained with the suppliers.

17.4.2   ISO 9001:2000 Requirements

In this section, we will briefly describe five major parts of the ISO 9001:2000. For further details, we refer the reader to reference 8. The five major parts of the ISO 9001:2000, found in parts 4–8, are presented next.

Part 4: Systemic Requirements   The concept of a *quality management system* (QMS) is the core of part 4 of the ISO 2001:2000 document. A quality management system is defined in terms of quality policy and quality objectives. In the software development context, an example of a quality policy is to review all work products by at least two skilled persons. Another quality policy is to execute all the test cases for at least two test cycles during system testing. Similarly, an example of a quality objective is to fix all defects causing a system to crash before release. Mechanisms are required to be defined in the form of processes to execute the quality policies and achieve the quality objectives. Moreover, mechanisms are required to be defined to improve the quality management system. Activities to realize quality policies and achieve quality objectives are defined in the form of *interacting quality processes*. For example, requirement review can be treated as a distinct process. Similarly, system-level testing is another process in the quality system. Interaction between the said processes occur because of the need to make all requirements testable and the need to verify that all requirements have indeed been adequately tested. Similarly, measurement and analysis are important processes in modern-day software development. Improvements in an existing QMS is achieved by defining a measurement and analysis process and identifying areas for improvements.

Documentation is an important part of a QMS. There is no QMS without proper documentation. A QMS must be properly documented by publishing a quality manual. The quality manual describes the quality policies and quality objectives. Procedures for executing the QMS are also documented. As a QMS evolves by incorporating improved policies and objectives, the documents must accordingly be controlled. A QMS document must facilitate effective and efficient planning, execution, and management of organizational processes. Records generated as a result of executing organizational processes are documented and published to show evidence that various ISO 9001:2000 requirements have been met. All process details and organizational process interactions are documented. Clear documentation is key to understanding how one process is influenced by another. The documentation part can be summarized as follows:

- Document the organizational policies and goals. Publish a vision of the organization.
- Document all quality processes and their interrelationship.
- Implement a mechanism to approve documents before they are distributed.
- Review and approve updated documents.
- Monitor documents coming from suppliers.
- Document the records showing that requirements have been met.
- Document a procedure to control the records.

Part 5: Management Requirements The concept of quality cannot be dealt with in bits and pieces by individual developers and test engineers. Rather, upper management must accept the fact that quality is an all-pervasive concept. Upper management must make an effort to see that the entire organization is aware of the quality policies and quality goals. This is achieved by defining and publishing a QMS and putting in place a mechanism for its continual improvement. The QMS of the organization must be supported by upper management with the right kind and quantity of resources. The following are some important activities for upper management to perform in this regard:

- Generate an awareness for quality to meet a variety of requirements, such as customer, regulatory, and statutory.
- Develop a QMS by identifying organizational policies and goals concerning quality, developing mechanisms to realize those policies and goals, and allocating resources for their implementations.
- Develop a mechanism for continual improvement of the QMS.
- Focus on customers by identifying and meeting their requirements in order to satisfy them.
- Develop a quality policy to meet the customers' needs, serve the organization itself, and make it evolvable with changes in the marketplace and new developments in technologies.

- Deal with the quality concept in a planned manner by ensuring that quality objectives are set at the organizational level, quality objectives support quality policy, and quality objectives are measurable.

- Clearly define individual responsibilities and authorities concerning the implementation of quality policies.

- Appoint a manager with the responsibility and authority to oversee the implementation of the organizational QMS. Such a position gives clear visibility of the organizational QMS to the outside world, namely, to the customers.

- Communicate the effectiveness of the QMS to the staff so that the staff is in a better position to conceive improvements in the existing QMS model.

- Periodically review the QMS to ensure that it is an effective one and it adequately meets the organizational policy and objectives to satisfy the customers. Based on the review results and changes in the marketplace and technologies, actions need to be taken to improve the model by setting better policies and higher goals.

Part 6: Resource Requirements   Resources are key to achieving organizational policies and objectives. Statements of policies and objectives must be backed up with allocation of the right kind and quantity of resources. There are different kinds of resources, namely, staff, equipment, tool, financial, and building, to name the major ones. Typically, different resources are controlled by different divisions of an organization. In general, resources are allocated to projects on a need basis. Since every activity in an organization needs some kind of resources, the resource management processes interact with other kinds of processes. The important activities concerning resource management are as follows:

- Identify and provide resources required to support the organizational quality policy in order to realize the quality objectives. Here the key factor is to identify resources to be able to meet—and even exceed–customer expectations.

- Allocate quality personnel resources to projects. Here, the quality of personnel is defined in terms of education, training, experience, and skills.

- Put in place a mechanism to enhance the quality level of personnel. This can be achieved by defining an acceptable, lower level of competence. For personnel to be able to move up to the minimum acceptable level of competence, it is important to identify and support an effective training program. The effectiveness of the training program must be evaluated on a continual basis.

- Provide and maintain the means, such as office space, computing needs, equipment needs, and support services, for successful realization of the organizational QMS.

- Manage a work environment, including physical, social, psychological, and environmental factors, that is conducive to producing efficiency and effectiveness in "people" resources.

Part 7: Realization Requirements This part deals with processes that transform customer requirements into products. The reader may note that not much has changed from ISO 9001:1994 to ISO 9001:2000 in the realization part. The key elements of the realization part are as follows:

- Develop a plan to realize a product from its requirements. The important elements of such a plan are identification of the processes needed to develop a product, sequencing the processes, and controlling the processes. Product quality objectives and methods to control quality during development are identified during planning.

- To realize a product for a customer, much interaction with the customer is necessary to understand and capture the requirements. Capturing requirements for a product involves identifying different categories of requirements, such as requirements generated by the customers, requirements necessitated by the product's use, requirements imposed by external agencies, and requirements deemed to be useful to the organization itself.

- Review the customers' requirements before committing to the project. Requirements that are not likely to be met should be rejected in this phase. Moreover, develop a process for communicating with the customers. It is important to involve the customers in all phases of product development.

- Once requirements are reviewed and accepted, product *design* and *development* take place:

   Product design and development start with planning: Identify the stages of design and development, assign various responsibilities and authorities, manage interactions between different groups, and update the plan as changes occur.

   Specify and review the *inputs* for product design and development.

   Create and approve the *outputs* of product design and development. Use the outputs to control product quality.

   Periodically review the outputs of design and development to ensure that progress is being made.

   Perform design and development verifications on their outputs.

   Perform design and development validations.

   Manage the changes effected to design and development: Identify the changes, record the changes, review the changes, verify the changes, validate the changes, and approve the changes.

- Follow a defined purchasing process by evaluating potential suppliers based on a number of factors, such as ability to meet requirements and price, and verify that a purchased product meets its requirements.

- Put in place a mechanism and infrastructure for controlling production. This includes procedures for validating production processes, procedures for identifying and tracking both concrete and abstract items, procedures for protecting properties supplied by outside parties, and procedures for preserving organizational components and products.

- Identify the monitoring and measuring needs and select appropriate devices to perform those tasks. It is important to calibrate and maintain those devices. Finally, use those devices to gather useful data to know that the products meet the requirements.

Part 8: Remedial Requirements   This part is concerned with measurement, analysis of measured data, and continual improvement. Measurement of performance indicators of processes allows one to determine how well a process is performing. If it is observed that a process is performing below the desired level, then corrective action can be taken to improve the performance of the process. Consider the following example. We find out the sources of defects during system-level testing and count, for example, those introduced in the design phase. If too many defects are found to be introduced in the design phase, actions are required to be taken to reduce the defect count. For instance, an alternative design review technique can be introduced to catch the defects in the design phase. In the absence of measurement it is difficult to make an objective decision concerning process improvement. Thus, measurement is an important activity in an engineering discipline. Part 8 of the ISO 9001:2000 addresses a wide range of performance measurement needs as explained in the following:

- The success of an organization is largely determined by the satisfaction of its customers. Thus, the standard requires organizations to develop methods and procedures for measuring and tracking the customer's satisfaction level on an ongoing basis. For example, the number of calls to the help line of an organization can be considered as a measure of customer satisfaction—too many calls is a measure of less customer satisfaction.

- An organization needs to plan and perform internal audits on a regular basis to track the status of the organizational QMS. An example of an internal audit is to find out whether or not personnel with adequate education, experience, and skill have been assigned to a project. An internal audit needs to be conducted by independent auditors using a documented procedure. Corrective measures are expected to be taken to address any deficiency discovered by the auditors.

- The standard requires that both processes, including QMS processes, and products be monitored using a set of key performance indicators. An example of measuring product characteristics is to verify whether or not a product meets its requirements. Similarly, an example of measuring process characteristics is to determine the level of modularity of a software system.

- As a result of measuring product characteristics, it may be discovered that a product does not meet its requirements. Organizations need to ensure that such products are not released to the customers. The causes of the differences between an expected product and the real one need to be identified.

- The standard requires that the data collected in the measurement processes are analyzed for making objective decisions. Data analysis is performed to determine the effectiveness of the QMS, impact of changes made to the QMS, level of customer satisfaction, conformance of products to their requirements, and performance of products and suppliers.

- We expect that products have defects, since manufacturing processes may not be perfect. However, once it is known that there are defects in products caused by deficiencies in the processes used, efforts must be made to improve the processes. Process improvement includes both corrective actions and preventive actions to improve the quality of products.

17.5 SUMMARY

The concept of software quality is very broad, and, therefore, it is useful to look at it from different viewpoints. In 1984, Garvin [1] analyzed the concept of quality—of products in general, not specifically software products—from five viewpoints, namely, *transcendental view*, *user view*, *manufacturing view*, *product view*, and *value-based view*. In the transcendental view, quality is something that can be perceived only through experience. The user's view concerns to what extent the product meets user needs and expectations. According to the manufacturing view, quality is perceived through conformance to a manufacturing process. According to the product view, good internal qualities of a product translates into good external qualities of products. The value-based view concerns how much a user is willing to pay for a certain level of quality.

It is useful to measure quality for three reasons. First, measurement allows us to develop baselines for quality. Second, since quality improvement has an associated cost, it is important to know how much quality improvement is achieved for a certain cost. Finally, it is useful to know the present level of quality so that further improvement can be planned.

Gilb's technique [5] for quality measurement, stated in the following, is useful in measuring quality factors which are not amenable to direct measurement: *The quality concept is successively broken down into its component parts until each component can be expressed in terms of some directly measurable attributes.*

Measuring the manufacturing view is easier. The two widely used metrics are *defect count* and *rework cost*. The first metric refers to how many defects have been detected, whereas the second metric refers to how much it costs to fix the known defects. A defect count can be analyzed to give us a better idea about the development process. For example, each defect can be traced to a phase of the software development process where the defect got introduced. Improvements should be made to the phases where a large fraction of the defects get introduced. Similarly, improvements should be made to the phases where critical defects are introduced. A second example of analyzing defect count is to identify the modules containing a large number of defects. A third example of analyzing defect count is separating defects detected during development from those detected during operation. If a large number of defects are found during operation, one can conclude that the test process needs much improvement. A fourth example of using defect count is to be able to compare different modules in terms of *defect density*.

Similarly, rework cost can be analyzed in two parts: prerelease rework cost and postrelease rework cost. The prerelease rework cost is a measure of development efficiency, whereas the postrelease rework cost is a measure of the delivered quality of the system.

Another concept of software quality, commonly known as McCall's quality factors, was proposed by McCall, Richards, and Walters in 1977 [6]. They studied the concept of software quality in terms of *quality factors* and *quality criteria*. A quality criterion is an *attribute* of a quality factor. McCall et al. identified 23 quality criteria. Some examples of quality criteria are modularity, traceability, simplicity, and completeness. In a nutshell, a quality factor represents a behavioral characteristic of a system, and McCall et al. suggested 11 quality factors: correctness, reliability, efficiency, integrity, usability, maintainability, testability, flexibility, portability, reusability, and interoperability. The 11 quality factors are categorized into three classes: product operation, product revision, and product transition. Product operation concerns correctness, reliability, efficiency, integrity, and usability. Product revision concerns maintainability, testability, and flexibility. Product transition concerns portability, reusability, and interoperability.

A global initiative for understanding the concept of software quality has been performed by experts around the world. Their collaborative effort has led to the standardization of the quality concept by the ISO in the form of documents ISO 9126 and ISO 9000:2000. The document ISO 9126 is about quality characteristics, whereas the ISO 9000:2000 document is a quality assurance standard. What is called quality factor in the McCall model is called *quality characteristic* in the ISO 9126 model. However, there are several differences between the two models. The ISO 9126 model focuses on characteristics *visible* to the users, whereas the McCall model emphasizes *internal* quality as well.

It is useful to note a few concerns about the quality models discussed in this chapter. There is no consensus about what high-level quality factors are most important at the top level. Moreover, there is no consensus about what is a top-level quality factor and what is a low-level, that is, concrete, quality attribute/subcharacteristic.

There are three components of the ISO 9000:2000 standard, namely, ISO 9000, ISO 9001, and ISO 9004. The ISO 9000 document is about fundamentals and vocabulary, the ISO 9001 document is about requirements, and the ISO 9004 document contains guidelines for performance improvements.

The ISO 9000 document is based on eight principles: customer focus, leadership, involvement of people, process approach, system approach to management, continual improvement, factual approach to decision making, and mutually beneficial supplier relationships. The ISO 9001 document deals with the following five kinds of requirements: systemic requirements, management requirements, resource requirements, realization requirements, and remedial requirements.

LITERATURE REVIEW

Several books and articles have been written about software quality assurance and quality models. The January 1996 issue of *IEEE Software* was devoted to software quality. The special issue presents a few papers addressing the following topics: contribution of standards to product quality, quality outcomes in terms of business value, support for quality-based design and inspection, software quality in consumer electronics, and a case study of early quality prediction in telecommunications systems.

In the book *Inroads to Software Quality* [10], Jarvis and V Crandall focus on two approaches to quality assurance. The first approach is to use quality-oriented methods such as total quality management, ISO 9000, and SEI CMM levels. Their second approach is based on the idea of building quality into deliverables at the outset and throughout product development.

In the book *Software Quality Assurance: Principles and Practice* [11], Godbole presents quality assurance principles and practice in a comprehensive manner. The book puts much emphasis on planning for quality assurance, product quality and process quality, software testing, inspection and walkthrough, and quality improvement models, such as the ISO 9000 and CMM models.

In the book *Software Quality Assurance* [12], Galin presents a comprehensive overview of software quality and software quality assurance (SQA). Additional topics covered in Galin's book are different components of a software quality assurance system, such as SQA architecture, preproject software quality components, SQA components in the project life cycle, software quality infrastructure components, and management components of software quality. For example, contract review and development and quality plans are preproject software quality components. Similarly, reviews and software testing strategies are project life-cycle components. Examples of infrastructure components are procedures and work instructions and staff training. Some management components of software quality are project progress control and software quality metrics. An example component of standards, certification, and evaluation is quality management using ISO 9000 and CMM.

REFERENCES

1. D. A. Garvin. What Does "Product Quality" Really Mean? *Sloan Management Review*, Fall 1984, pp. 25–43.
2. M. Paulk, B. Curtis, M. B. Chrissis, and C. V. Weber. Capability Maturity Model, Version 1.1. *IEEE Software*, July 1993, pp. 18–27.
3. M. Paulk, B. Curtis, M. B. Chrissis, and C. V. Weber. How ISO 9001 Compares with the CMM. *IEEE Software*, January 1995, pp. 74–83.
4. B. Kitchenham and S. L. Pfleeger. Software Quality: The Elusive Target. *IEEE Software*, January 1996, pp. 12–21.
5. T. Gilb. *Principles of Software Engineering Management*. Addison-Wesley, Reading, MA, 1987.
6. J. A. McCall, P. K. Richards, and G. F. Walters. *Factors in Software Quality*, Vol. 1, ADA 049014. National Technical Information Service, >Springfield, VA, 1977.
7. International Organization for Standardization (ISO). Quality management systems—fundamentals and Vocabulary, ISO 9000:2000. ISO, Geneva, December 2000.

8. International Organization for Standardization (ISO). Quality Management Systems—Requirements, ISO 9001:2000. ISO, Geneva, December 2000.

9. International Organization for Standardization (ISO). Quality Management Systems–Guidelines for Performance Improvements, ISO 9004:2000. ISO, Geneva, December 2000.

10. A. Jarvis and V. Crandall. *Inroads to Software Quality*. Prentice-Hall, Englewood Cliffs, NJ, 1997.

11. N. S. Godbole. *Software Quality Assurance*. Alpha Science International, Pangbourne, UK, 2004.

12. D. Galin. *Software Quality Assurance*. Addison-Wesley, Reading, MA, 2005.

Exercises

1. Briefly explain the five different views of software quality.

2. Briefly explain how one can measure the user's view of software quality.

3. Briefly explain how one can measure the manufacturer's view of software quality.

4. Briefly explain McCall's quality factors and quality criteria.

5. Briefly explain McCall's categorization of quality factors into three quality criteria.

6. Briefly explain the ISO 9126 quality characteristics.

7. Compare McCall's quality model with the ISO 9126 quality model.

8. State some difficulties in applying the McCall and ISO 9126 quality models.

9. Briefly explain the ISO 9000:2000 (Fundamental) document for quality assurance.

10. Briefly explain the ISO 9001:2000 (Requirements) document for quality assurance.

CHAPTER 18

Maturity Models

We are the product of 4.5 billion years of fortuitous, slow biological evolution. There is no reason to think that the evolutionary process has stopped. Man is a transitional animal. He is not the climax of creation.

— *Carl Sagan*

18.1 BASIC IDEA IN SOFTWARE PROCESS

The concept of a *process* plays an important role in today's software development. Without a repeatable process, the only repeatable results you are likely to produce are errors [1]. In the software engineering context, a process comprises a set of activities that are executed to develop software products. The activities find expressions in the form of methods, techniques, strategies, procedures, and practices. Those activities heavily rely on information repositories such as documents, standards, and policies. Different processes are driven by different goals and availability of resources. The concept of a process is applied not just to develop source code, but to other software-related products, such as a project plan, requirements document, design document, and user manual, as well. It is effective to follow a defined process because of the following benefits:

- The process can be repeated in subsequent projects.
- The process can be evaluated by using a variety of metrics, such as cost, quality, and time to deliver a product.
- Actions can be taken to improve the process to achieve better results.

A process for software development consists of several different processes for its different component tasks. For example, gathering the requirements of a system, constructing a functional specification of a system, designing a system, testing a system, and maintaining a system are different tasks to be performed in the life cycle of a software system. Those different tasks, which are quite different from each other, need different processes to be followed. A requirements gathering process is fundamentally different from a testing process. Similarly, a design process is very different from a testing process. However, some similarities between a maintenance process and a testing process cannot be ruled out because a maintenance task may involve significant changes to the design of the system as well as rigorous testing.

Software testing is treated as a distinct process because it involves a variety of unique activities, techniques, strategies, and policies as explained in the following:

- Testing is performed to achieve the following objectives:

    Reveal defects in software products

    Show the extent to which a software system possesses different quality attributes, such as reliability, performance, stability, and scalability

- Testing begins almost at the same time as a project is conceptualized, and it lasts as long as the system is in existence.

- Testing is carried out by people with differing responsibilities in different phases of software development. Those different levels of testing are commonly known as unit testing, integration testing, system testing, and acceptance testing.

- A number of techniques can be applied at each level of testing for generating test cases.

- A number of different testing strategies can be applied at different levels of testing.

- A number of metrics can be monitored to gauge the progress of testing.

- A number of metrics can be monitored to accurately reflect the different quality levels of a system.

- Testing is influenced by organizational policies, such as the level of quality to be achieved in a product, the fraction of the total budget for a project to be allocated to testing, and the duration of testing.

- Testing can be performed in a combination of manual and automated modes of execution of test cases.

To be able to improve a defined process, organizations need to evaluate its capabilities and limitations. For example, the *capability maturity model* (CMM), developed by the Software Engineering Institute (SEI) at Carnegie Mellon University, allows an organization to evaluate its software development processes. The model supports incremental process improvement. For an organization, it is more practical to develop a continuously improving process than find one which is "just right." By recognizing the importance of testing as a distinct process—much different from an overall process for software development—a separate model, known as a *testing maturity model* (TMM), has been developed to evaluate a testing process. In addition, for an organization to be able to improve its testing process, the *test process improvement* (TPI) model has been developed.

18.2 CAPABILITY MATURITY MODEL

In software development processes we seek three desirable attributes as follows:

1. The products are of the highest quality. Ideally, a product should be free of defects. However, in practice, a small number of defects with less severe consequences are generally tolerated.

2. Projects are completed according to their plans, including the schedules.

3. Projects are completed within the allocated budgets.

However, developers of large software products rarely achieve the above three attributes. Due to the complex nature of software systems, products are released with known and unknown defects. The unknown defects manifest themselves as unexpected failures during field operation, that is, when we know that the system was released with unknown defects. In many organizations, software projects are often late and over budget. Due to the business angle in software development, it is important for the survival of organizations to develop low-cost, high-quality products within a short time. In order to move toward that goal, researchers and developers are devising new techniques and tools. However, introduction of new techniques and tools into a process must be carefully planned to effect improvements in products.

While awarding a contract to an organization for a software product, the customer needs to gain confidence that the organization is capable of delivering the desired product. Such confidence can be gained by evaluating the capabilities of the organizations. The U.S. Department of Defense being a large customer of software systems, it wanted to evaluate the capabilities of its software contractors. The Department of Defense wanted to have a framework to evaluate the maturity of software processes used by organizations. In circa 1986, the SEI at initiated the development of a framework to evaluate process maturity.

The maturity level of a development process tells us to what extent the organization is capable of producing low-cost, high-quality software. Therefore, the evaluation framework is the CMM. After evaluating the current maturity level of a development process, organizations can work on improving the process to achieve the next higher level of process maturity. In the CMM framework, a process has five maturity levels. Before going into the details of different maturity levels, it is useful to have a glimpse of an immature process—an organization can be considered to be immature if it follows immature processes [2].

On the one hand, an immature organization may not have a defined process, and, even if there is one, the organization may not follow it. Developers and managers react to problems when they occur, rather than take preventive measures to eliminate them or reduce the frequency of their occurrences. In other words, product and process problems are resolved in an ad hoc manner. Estimates of cost, schedule, and quality are highly inaccurate due to the absence of a measurement program to gather process data. Hence, projects overrun cost and time estimates by a large factor. There is no measurement program to evaluate product or process quality.

On the other hand, a mature organization carries out its activities in a planned manner. Both process and product characteristics are measured to keep track of progress and quality of products. Estimates are more accurate due to following a rigorous measurement program. Employees are kept abreast of new developments through training. Continual effort is made to improve the quality of products while bringing down costs and lead times. Defined processes are continually updated to take advantage of new techniques, tools, and experience from past projects. As an organization becomes more and more mature, standards and organizational policies play key roles in product development. Organizations become mature in an incremental manner; that is, processes are improved in an evolutionary approach, rather than effecting drastic changes.

As an organization moves from one level to the next, its process capability improves to produce better quality software at a lower cost. The CMM defines five distinct levels of maturity, where level 1 is the initial level and level 5 is the highest level of process maturity.

18.2.1   CMM Architecture

First we explain the concept of a *maturity level* using Figure 18.1 followed by a detailed description of individual levels. Figure 18.1 can be read as follows:

- A maturity level indicates process capability and contains key process areas (KPAs). The KPAs for each level are listed in Figure 18.2.

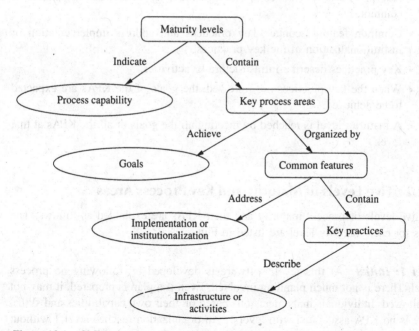

Figure 18.1   CMM structure. (From ref. 3. © 2005 John Wiley & Sons.)

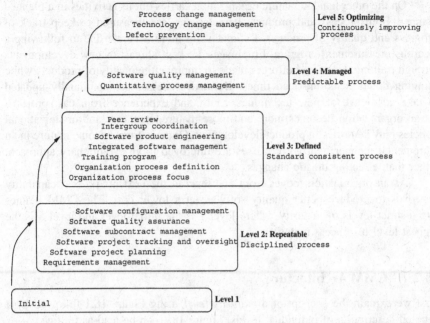

Figure 18.2   SW-CMM maturity levels. (From ref. 3. © 2005 John Wiley & Sons.)

- Key process areas are expected to achieve goals and are organized by common features.
- Common features contain key practices and address implementation or institutionalization of the key practices.
- Key practices describe infrastructure or activities.
- When the key practices are followed, the goals of the KPAs are expected to be achieved.
- A maturity level is reached by meeting all the goals of all the KPAs at that level.

18.2.2   Five Levels of Maturity and Key Process Areas

The five levels of process maturity and their KPAs are explained as follows. The KPAs for each maturity level are listed in Figure 18.2.

Level 1: Initial   At this level, software is developed by following no process model. There is not much planning involved. Even if a plan is prepared, it may not be followed. Individuals make decisions based on their own capabilities and skills. There is no KPA associated with level 1. An organization reaches level 1 without making any effort.

Level 2: Repeatable   At this level, the concept of a process exists so that success can be repeated for similar projects. Performance of the proven activities of past projects is used to prepare plans for future projects. This level can be summarized as being *disciplined* because processes are used for repeatability. All the processes are under the effective control of a project management system. The KPAs at level 2 are as follows:

- **Requirements Management:** It is important to establish a common understanding between the customer and developers. Details of a project, such as planning and management, are guided by a common view of customer requirements.

- **Software Project Planning:** This means creating and following a reasonable plan for realizing and managing a project.

- **Software Project Tracking and Oversight:** This means making the progress of a project visible so that management is aware of the status of the project. Corrective actions can be taken if the actual progress of a project significantly deviates from the planned progress.

- **Software Subcontract Management:** This means evaluating, selecting, and managing suppliers or subcontractors.

- **Software Quality Assurance:** This means evaluating processes and products to understand their effectiveness and quality.

- **Software Configuration Management:** This means ensuring the integrity of the products of a project as long as the project continues to exist.

Level 3: Defined   At this level, documentation plays a key role. Processes that are related to project management and software development activities are documented, reviewed, standardized, and integrated with organizational processes. In other words, there is organizationwide acceptance of standard processes. Software development is carried out by following an approved process. Functionalities and the associated qualities are tracked. Cost and schedule are monitored to keep them under control. The KPAs at level 3 are as follows:

- **Organization Process Focus:** This means putting in place an organizationwide role and responsibility to ensure that activities concerning process improvement are in fact followed.

- **Organization Process Definition:** Certain practices are useful irrespective of projects. Thus, it is important to identify and document those practices.

- **Training Program:** Individuals need to be trained on an on-going basis to make them knowledgeable in application domains and new developments in software techniques and tools. Training is expected to make them effective and efficient.

- **Integrated Software Management:** This means integrating an organization's software engineering and management activities into a common, defined process. Integration is based on commercial and technological needs of individual projects.

- **Software Product Engineering:** This means following a defined process in a consistent manner by integrating the technical activities to produce software with desired attributes. The activities include requirements elicitation, functional design, detailed design, coding, and testing.

- **Intergroup Coordination:** This means that a software development group coordinates with other groups, such as customers, the marketing group, the and software quality assurance (SQA) group, to understand their needs and expectations.

- **Peer Review:** Work products, such as requirements, design, and code, are reviewed by peers to find defects at an early stage. Peer reviews can be performed by means of inspection and walkthrough.

Level 4: Managed   At this level, *metrics* play a key role. Metrics concerning processes and products are collected and analyzed. Those metrics are used to gain quantitative insight into both process and product qualities. When the metrics show that limits are being exceeded, corrective actions are triggered. For example, if too many test cases fail during system testing, it is useful to start a process of root cause analysis to understand why so many tests are failing. The KPAs at level 4 are as follows:

- **Quantitative Process Management:** Process data indicate how well a process is performing. If a process does not perform as expected, the process is improved by considering the measured data.

- **Software Quality Management:** The quality attributes of products are measured in quantitative form to have a better insight into the processes and products. Improvements are incorporated into the processes, and their effectiveness is evaluated by measuring product quality attributes.

Level 5: Optimizing   At this level, organizations strive to improve their processes on a continual basis. This is achieved in two steps: (i) Observe the effects of processes, by measuring a few key metrics, on the quality, cost, and lead time of software products and (ii) effect changes to the processes by introducing new techniques, methods, tools, and strategies. The following are the KPAs at level 5:

- **Defect Prevention:** This means analyzing the root causes of different classes of defects and taking preventive measures to ensure that similar defects do not recur.

- **Technology Change Management:** This means identifying useful techniques, tools, and methodologies and gradually introducing those into software processes. The key idea is to take advantage of new developments in technologies.

- **Process Change Management:** This means improving an organization's processes to have a positive impact on quality, productivity, and development time.

18.2.3 Common Features of Key Practices

The key practices in every KPA are organized into five categories called *common features* as explained in the following. Common features are attributes of key practices that indicate whether the implementation or institutionalization of a KPA is effective, repeatable, and lasting.

- **Commitment to Perform:** An organization must show in action—not merely in words—that it is committed to process improvement. Upper management actions, such as establishing organizational policies and allocating resources to process improvement activities, give evidence that an organization is committed to perform in a better way. For example, management can formulate a policy to use established and enduring processes.

- **Ability to Perform:** The ability of an organization to realize a process in a competent manner is determined by the organization's structure, resources, and people to execute the process. Availability of adequately trained personnel and their attitude to change have a positive impact on their ability to perform.

- **Activities Performed:** These describe what needs to be implemented to establish the capability of a process. They include the roles and procedures required to realize KPAs. Typical activities performed to realize KPAs are making plans, executing the plans, tracking the work, and taking corrective actions to ensure that work stays close to the plan.

- **Measurement and Analysis:** Measurement is key to knowing the current status and effectiveness of a process. Measurement involves gathering data that can reveal the progress and effectiveness of processes. The gathered data must be analyzed to have an insight into the processes. Measurement and analysis must be performed to be able to take corrective actions.

- **Verifying Implementation:** After having policies and processes in place, it is necessary that activities be performed by complying with the standard process. Compliance with the standard process can be checked by performing frequent audits and reviews.

18.2.4 Application of CMM

For an organization to be at a certain level of maturity, all the goals of all the KPAs at that level—and all preceding levels too—must be satisfied. For example, for an organization to be at level 2, all six KPAs associated with level 2 must be satisfied. For an organization to be at level 3, the organization must meet all six KPAs associated with level 2 and all seven KPAs associated with level 3. The SEI provides two methodologies to evaluate the current capabilities of organizations: *internal assessments* and *external evaluations*. The SEI developed the *capability maturity model–based assessment internal process improvement* (CBA-IPI) to assist organizations for self-assessment. The CBA-IPI uses the CMM as a reference model to evaluate the process capability of organizations by identifying what KPAs are being satisfied and what need to be improved.

The SEI developed the CMM appraisal framework (CAF) to provide a mechanism for formal evaluation of organizations. The CAF describes the *requirements* and *guidelines* to be used by external assessors in designing CAF-compliant evaluation methods.

18.2.5   Capability Maturity Model Integration (CMMI)

After the development and successful application of the CMM in the software area, which is known as software CMM (CMM-SW), CMMs in other areas were developed as well.

The CMM for software, known as CMM-SW, was first released in 1991 as CMM-SW version 1.0, followed by CMM-SW version 1.1 in 1993. After its first release, many software organizations used it for self and external evaluations. The success of CMM-SW led to the development of CMM in other areas. Thus, the concept of CMM is not software specific. In order to appreciate the wide applicability of CMM, we remind the reader of the following: *A CMM is a reference model of mature practices in a specific discipline used to apprise and improve a group's capability to perform that discipline*. To name a few, there are several CMMs as follows:

- Software CMM
- Systems engineering CMM
- Integrated product development CMM
- Electronic industry alliance 731 CMM
- Software acquisition CMM
- People CMM
- Supplier source CMM

It is apparent from the above examples of the CMM that they are likely to have different characteristics. The CMMs differ in three ways, namely, *discipline*, *structure*, and *definition of maturity*. First, different CMMs are applied to different disciplines, such as software development, system engineering, software acquisition, and people. Second, improvements can be made continuously or in distinct stages. Finally, the definition of maturity is dependent upon the entity under consideration. It is obvious that *people* and *software acquisition* mature in different ways, and their maturity is defined in different ways.

As more than one CMM was applied in an organization, a number of problems surfaced because of the following reasons:

- Different models have different structures, different ways of measuring maturity, and different terms.
- It was difficult to integrate the different CMMs to achieve the common organizational goal which is to produce low-cost, high-quality products within schedule.
- It was difficult to use many models in supplier selection and subcontracting.

Therefore, a pressing need was felt to have a unified view of process improvement throughout an organization. Thus, evolved the idea of CMMI. The CMMI includes information from the following models:

- Capability maturity model for software (CMM-SW)
- Integrated product development capability maturity model (IPD-CMM)
- Capability maturity model for systems engineering (CMM-SE)
- Capability maturity model for supplier sourcing (CMM-SS)

The usefulness of the CMMI is readily recognized by considering the following facts. First, today's complex software systems are often built by using some subsystems developed by other parties. For example, a security module may be purchased from another vendor. Similarly, a communication module may be obtained from a vendor specializing in communication systems. There is a need for evaluating the maturity of the suppliers. Second, large systems often contain a number of diverse components, such as databases, communications, security, and real-time processing. Coexistence and interoperability of the diverse systems, which might have been developed by different vendors, are paramount to the successful operation of larger systems. Consequently, it is important to evaluate the maturity level of an integrated product development process. Third, in general, complex software systems often need to run on specialized execution platforms. For example, Internet routing software runs on specialized hardware and a specialized operating system, rather than the commonly used hardware platforms and operating systems. Those kinds of software need to be developed in the right system context.

18.3   TEST PROCESS IMPROVEMENT

A *test process* is a certain way of performing activities related to defect detection. Some typically desired test activities in software development are as follows:

- Identifying test goals
- Preparing a test plan
- Identifying different kinds of tests
- Hiring test personnel
- Designing test cases
- Setting up test benches
- Procuring test tools
- Assigning test cases to test engineers
- Prioritizing test cases for execution
- Organizing the execution of test cases into multiple test cycles
- Preparing a schedule for executing test cases
- Executing test cases
- Reporting defects

- Tracking defects while resolving them
- Measuring the progress of testing
- Measuring the quality attributes of the software under test
- Evaluating the effectiveness of a test process
- Identifying steps to improve the effectiveness of test activities
- Identifying steps to reduce the cost of testing

The nature of activities in a test process is wide ranging. On the one hand, a test activity can be a simple, straightforward activity such as reporting defects. On the other hand, prioritizing test cases for execution is a nontrivial task. A more complex task is to organize test execution into a few testing cycles by considering all test cases, or a subset thereof, in each test cycle. Similarly, identifying steps to improve the effectiveness of test activities is a nontrivial task.

Now we present a simple example of a test process for system-level testing. This test process is presented in the following steps:

- Categorize the features of a system into k categories.
- Design N_i number of test cases for feature category i for $1 \leq i \leq k$. The number N_i of test cases is denoted by the set T_i.
- Run $T_1 \cup \cdots \cup T_k$ to detect defects.
- Run $T_1 \cup \cdots \cup T_k$ after each defect fix until no more defects are found or it is time to release the system.

One can easily identify a number of deficiencies in the above test process as follows:

- Test tools have not been used.
- Test cases have not been prioritized.
- The entire test suite has been executed in each test cycle, rather than its selected subsets in the later test cycles.

Therefore, it is important to improve test processes, and it is advantageous to follow a defined model for their improvement. The idea of improving test processes by following a model, namely the TPI model, was first studied by Tim Koomen and Martin Pol. They have extensively discussed the TPI model in a well-written book [4]. A test process needs to be improved for three reasons as explained in the following:

- **Quality:** A better test process should give more insight into the quality characteristics of a system being tested. For example, after running all the test cases twice, we should have a good idea about the reliability level of the system. Here, the intention is not to have a better quality product—though that is always desirable. Rather, the intention is to have an improved test process that gives us better insight into the quality of the system being tested.
- **Lead Time:** A better test process saves testing time, and thereby gives more time to other areas of system development. For example, one can use

the idea of prioritizing the execution of test cases so that difficult-to-fix defects are detected as early as possible. Early detection of difficult-to-fix defects gives more time to the developers to address those defects, thereby shortening the development time.

- **Cost:** A better test process is expected to be carried out with a lower cost and thereby reduces the overall cost of system development. For example, one can judiciously select a subset of the test cases, rather than the entire test suite, for regression testing toward the closing stage of system-level testing during development. By carefully choosing a subset of the test suite, we can reduce the cost of system testing without compromising its effectiveness. Test cases can have a positive impact on development cost by influencing the processes of requirements gathering and software design. For example, while gathering software requirements we can ask the following questions:

  1. Are the requirements directly testable?
  2. If some requirements are not directly testable, can some other requirements be incorporated so that the original requirements are easily testable?

  Therefore, by considering the testability of requirements, it is possible to reduce the development cost. If a requirement is not testable, it is better to identify those requirements and discuss them with the customers early in the development phase. Essentially, what is being done is validation of requirements with test cases much before those requirements become a part of a design—or even a contract between a development organization and a customer.

It is apparent that a better test process gives us more insight into the quality attributes of a system, and it contributes to the development of software products at a lower *cost* in less time. An intuitive approach to improving a test process is as follows:

Step 1. Determine Area for Improvement: We identify an area of testing where we would like to see immediate improvements. For guidelines, we look at the three major areas for improvement, namely, quality, time, and cost, and focus on one precise aspect. Suppose that we want to have a good idea about the performance quality of the system as early as possible.

Step 2. Evaluate Current State of Test Process: It is important to know where we stand with respect to the chosen area for improvement. This is because it is likely to influence where we go next and how to achieve that. Referring to the example of having a good idea about the performance of the system as early as possible, we evaluate *when* the current test process lets us know about the system performance. Such an evaluation can be done by identifying the time when performance-related test cases are executed. If such test cases are executed toward the closing phase of system testing, there is a possibility that such tests are performed earlier.

Step 3. **Identify Next Desired State and Means:**   Once we know the current state of the testing process with respect to the desired area for improvement, we are in a better position to evaluate the extent of possible improvement. One must carefully identify the amount of improvement to be seen. Too much improvement in one state may require significant changes in the test process. Therefore, incremental improvements are preferred. Sometimes, a certain improvement may call for improvements in other, unselected areas. The type and extent of improvements one wants to effect must be carefully selected. For example, one can evaluate the performance of a system under different execution environments, such as a lightly loaded system, moderately loaded system, and heavily loaded system. Therefore, if we are interested in the early performance information in a lightly loaded environment, we can prioritize the performance-related tests to be executed before performing load tests. In the above example, *prioritization* of test execution is an example of the means necessary to effect an improvement.

Step 4. **Implement Necessary Changes to Process:**   Improvements, as identified above, are effected in the test process in a planned manner. Then, the effectiveness of the new test process is evaluated to verify whether or not the desired results have been obtained.

Though the steps of the above test process improvement model appear to be straightforward, their implementation is not. The steps, especially the second and third, are too general, and therefore it is difficult to achieve an agreement among test engineers. Consequently, there is a need for a reference model that can serve as a basis for test improvement. The TPI model of Koomen and Pol encourages and supports gradual improvement in a test process step by step. Too many changes in a test process may not be successful for two reasons. First, too many changes are likely to call for too much resources, which may not be available in one state. Second, people generally resist too many changes being effected at one time.

An important concept revealed in the intuitive test process improvement model of Section 18.3 is the idea of evaluating the *current status* of a test process. The current status of a test process is evaluated from different viewpoints, known as *key areas*—and 20 key areas have been identified. For example, use of *test tools* is a key area in a test process. Similarly, use of *metrics* is another key area. The status of a test process with respect to a key area is represented in terms of one of four *levels* of maturity—A, B, C, and D. The maturity level of a test process with respect to a key area ascends from A to D. In the following, we briefly describe the 20 key areas:

1. *Test Strategy*: A test process needs to detect critical defects early in the testing process. This, for example, can be achieved by prioritizing the execution of test cases. The test strategy needs to find defects at a lower cost. The test strategy should allow us to accurately map requirements with test cases for traceability purpose.

2. *Life-Cycle Model*: A test process can be a complex one involving many smallers activities and many persons and lasting for several months. Therefore, for micromanagement purposes, a test process can be viewed as having a clearly defined life cycle with distinct phases, such as planning, preparation, and execution. Each phase is characterized by a set of activities. For example, scheduling and cost estimation are planning activities. Similarly, designing test cases and setting up test benches are preparation activities. Each activity needs to have a clear structure in the form of objective, input, assumptions, process, output, constraints, dependencies, and tool support. A life-cycle model allows us to have a repeatable, and hence predictable, test process. Repeatability is a key benefit of a life-cycle model.

3. *Moment of Involvement*: Actual execution of test cases cannot start until code is written. However, the testing process can begin at any moment. For example, ideally, planning for testing should begin concurrently with requirements elicitation. This will allow us to verify the testability of each requirement. Sooner and closer interactions between developers and SQA personnel lead to better understanding of testing needs in terms of resources and challenges.

4. *Planning and Estimating*: Planning involves identifying and scheduling the activities to be performed, identifying the constraints, and identifying the resources. To prepare for the planned activities, it is important to be able to accurately estimate the quantity of resources needed. In the absence of a good plan and estimation, a project may run out of time and overrun budget. Thus, a test project needs to be carefully planned and its cost accurately estimated as early as possible.

5. *Test Specification Technique*: A test specification technique is one that allows us to derive test cases from an information source, such as the requirement specification of a system, design documents of a system, and source code of a system. Since there are multiple information sources of a software system, there is a need to identify multiple test specification techniques. Analysis of a test specification technique will tell us what kinds of test cases it will derive. In other words, by studying a test specification technique we will have a better insight into the quality and coverage of testing.

6. *Static Test Technique*: In a broad sense, there are two kinds of testing activities: *static* and *dynamic*. Dynamic testing involves actual execution of code, whereas static testing involves a variety of reviews, such as requirement verification, design review, and code review. The two forms of testing have their own advantages and limitations. However, what is clear is that there is a need for both forms of testing to be performed for the overall testing to be effective and inexpensive.

7. *Metrics*: It is well known that numbers give us a better insight into things—processes and products. The concept of measurement, represented

in the form of metrics, allows us to quantify the qualitative attributes of processes and products. One can easily identify a few quality attributes of a test process, such as productivity in test design, rate of test execution, rate of defect reporting, rate of defect fixing, and number of defects yet to be fixed. Test metrics allow us to track the progress of testing and help us get a handle on the quality level of the system under test. Metrics are also useful in evaluating the effect of process changes.

8. *Test Tools*: Tools can be used in a number of test-related activities as follows: test case generation, automatic test execution, and defect tracking. Test tools have the potential of reducing test design time and test execution time. Test tools can help in running more tests, thereby achieving more extensive testing. Tracking defects through a tool helps us in making the activity less error prone. Finally, tools make the testing tasks less monotonous for test engineers.

9. *Test Environment*: Ideally, system-level testing should be carried out in the system's operational environment. However, sometimes it is very expensive, or impractical, to set up an operational environment in a test laboratory. Therefore, test environments as close to reality as possible are realized in a test laboratory. Components of a test environment include hardware, software, communication equipments, and tools and techniques to emulate the interaction of the system under test with the outside world. For example, actual interaction with the outside world can be emulated by using a traffic generator. Different test environments are needed to perform different categories of testing. For example, we need one environment for performance testing and another environment for security testing. A test environment should accurately reflect the objective of testing. Without careful design of test environments, we will not be able to measure the quality attributes of a system under test. Moreover, if test environments significantly differ from operational environments, it is likely that a large number of new failures are observed during operation. Thus, test environments have a great impact on the delivered quality, cost, and timeliness of testing.

10. *Office Environment*: A well-organized office and timely available resources have a positive impact on test engineers. An office organization includes such elementary things as comfortable rooms, desks, chairs, and so on. A friendly work environment coupled with good human resource policies contributes to employee satisfaction. Satisfied test engineers in a good mood are likely to be more productive.

11. *Commitment and Motivation*: In a test project, several kinds of people are involved, namely, managers, test engineers, and technicians. Managers need to understand the importance of the task on hand and motivate others by providing them with training and resources. Test engineers are the people who design and execute test cases. Technicians provide support services. Even if software testing is not their preferred job, they need to be fully committed to their work. If test engineers stay in their position

in the company for a very short time, one can argue that they were not fully committed to testing.

12. *Test Functions and Training*: A test group needs to be composed of people with different kinds of expertise and training. Some people have management expertise, some are experts in the subject area of the system under test, and some are experts in testing. The test engineers need to have different expertise as well. For example, some test engineers are experts in performance test, some are experts in security test, some are experts in load test, and so on. If there is no right mix of people in a test group, some of them may be trained in some areas. Good interpersonal skills are also required for someone to be a successful test engineer.

13. *Scope of Methodology*: The core of a test process is the concept of a methodology comprising activities, procedures, techniques, regulations, and so on. Ideally, an organization uses one methodology but adapts it to different projects depending upon the special needs of the project. For example, one project may contain a large component of real-time processing, whereas another project contains a large component of the graphical user interface. The differences in project characteristics may require an organization to put different emphasis on test generation and execution techniques. But, essentially, the two projects can be adaptations of a generic methodology. The generic methodology should be flexible enough to lend itself to easy adaptation. On the other hand, it is highly undesirable to devise a new methodology for each new test project.

14. *Communication*: A test group communicates within itself and with the outside groups, namely, the developers, the marketing group, and the customers. Good internal communication is essential to working as a cohesive group with opportunity to keep oneself abreast of the happenings in the group. Communication with customers allows the test group to learn about customer expectations. Communication with developers is essential to understanding the design details of the system. The marketing group, by communicating with the test group, keeps track of the progress of system testing and the current quality level of the system under test.

15. *Reporting*: There are different kinds of reporting activities, such as internal reporting and external reporting, involved in a test process. Reporting defects is an internal activity. The quality of the system under test must be reported to the customers. Reporting to customers falls under external reporting. By giving useful reports to customers, it is possible to build a good relationship with them.

16. *Defect Management*: Test engineers report defects to be fixed by developers. However, the state of a defect is more complex than a fixed-or-not-fixed scenario. For example, a reported defect must be analyzed to understand if it is indeed a defect or a misunderstanding of the test engineers. A true defect is to be taken up for fixing by one or more developers. Therefore, a defect may stay in the open state for many weeks. Once

a defect is claimed to be fixed, test engineers must verify that the defect has indeed been fixed. Thus, it is helpful to follow a life-cycle model to manage defects. By managing defects by using a life-cycle model, we can easily identify the state and progress of testing as well as the quality level of the system under test.

17. *Testware Management*: The products developed during software development are used while testing a system. Such products are requirements specification, functional design specification, source code, a test plan, and a test suite. Since revisions are made to those entities on a need basis, it is possible that several versions of a product exist at the time of system testing. Therefore, the right version of each product should be used for efficient and effective testing. This can be achieved through proper use of testware management tools.

18. *Test Process Management*: Test processes are highly visible because everyone, including developers, marketing managers, and customers, is interested in knowing the progress of testing and the present quality level of the system and its trend. System testing occurs so close to the planned delivery date of the product that it attracts additional attention from all. Therefore, to be able to stick to the schedule and remain within budget, proven practices in management should be followed. An example of managing a test process in a defined manner is as follows: (i) Prepare a plan for the process, (ii) verify the plan, (iii) execute the plan, (iv) track the progress, and (v) take corrective and preventive measures.

19. *Evaluation*: Testing is just one aspect of quality assurance. The quality of an entire system can be improved by evaluating the quality of all the products, apart from source code, built during development. For example, it is useful to evaluate requirements and design documents, user manuals, and the different tools used in system development, including testing tools. The concept of test-related evaluation can be applied throughout the development process. By evaluating other products before carrying out execution-based testing, an organization can reduce the cost of software development. This is because evaluation of intermediate products allows for early detection of defects.

20. *Low-Level Testing*: The test processes in an organization cannot focus on system-level testing alone. Before an entire system is subject to the rigors of system-level testing, much testing, in the form of unit level and integration level, needs to be carried out by individual programmers and integration test engineers, respectively. Without a strong belief in unit testing and integration testing, it is merely a consequence that system-level testing will fall apart; that is, no meaningful system testing can be performed if basic things fail to work. The efficacy of low-level testing, namely, unit and integration testing, is derived from the fact that defects are detected and fixed much early in the development phase.

Levels of Maturity of Key Areas A test process is evaluated with respect to the 20 key areas explained above. Specifically, one is interested in knowing to what extent a certain key area has matured. All the key areas may not mature to the same extent because of the fact that an organization might not put an equal amount of emphasis on all. The maturity levels of the key areas are denoted by A, B, C, and D, where A represents the lowest level of maturity and D the highest level. The maturity of a key area increases as we move from A to B, B to C, and so on. Each level is better than its predecessor in one or more ways from the group of three desired parameters: quality, time, and money. Our intention to seek improvements in quality, time, and money (cost) is consistent with the previous discussion of the need to improve a test process in Section 18.3.

For a key area to reach a certain level, the key area must meet the requirements, called *check points*, associated with that level and all the levels below it for that key area. For example, a test process pegged at level C must meet all the requirements for levels A, B, and C. If a test process does not meet the requirements of level A, the process stays at an initial level below A. The requirements for each key area to reach a certain maturity level are given in Table 18.1. By analyzing Table 18.1, we make the following observations:

- All key areas do not have four maturity levels. For example, the key area test specification technique has two levels of maturity, namely, A and B, and B is the highest maturity level for this key area. For the key area test specification techniques, the two distinct requirements of importance are informal techniques and formal techniques, in that order. If test cases are never put in writing, then the maturity of test specification techniques remains at the initial level, which is below A. The number of maturity levels is determined by *all* the requirements a key area is expected to meet and how conveniently we can group those requirements in increasing order of strength so that progress from one group to the next results in a distinct improvement and a better test process. If there are not many requirements for a key area to meet, there is no need to have four levels of maturity.

- The highest maturity level of a key area need not be D. In the key area test specification techniques, the highest maturity level is B.

- There exist dependencies between maturity levels of key areas. In the given context, dependency means that for one key area to reach a certain level of maturity, some other key areas must have reached certain maturity levels. Now let us consider an example as follows. For the key area evaluation to be at level A, it is important that test specification techniques, communication, and defect management are at B. Thus, the maturity levels of all key areas do not improve in lock steps. The idea of maturity dependency calls for improvement in maturity levels of key areas in a *prioritized* manner. For example, we first raise the maturity level of defect management to B before we initiate a process to elevate the maturity level of key area evaluation to level A.

Based on the ideas of dependencies and prioritization, a test maturity matrix, as shown in Table 18.2, is constructed. The test maturity matrix

TABLE 18.1 Requirements for Different Maturity Levels

Key area	Level A	Level B	Level C	Level D
Test strategy	Strategy for single high-level test	Combined strategy for high-level tests	Combined strategy for high-level tests plus low-level tests or evaluation	Combined strategy for all test and evaluation levels
Life-cycle model	Planning, specification, execution	Planning preparation, specification, execution, and completion		
Moment of involvement	Completion of test basis	Start of test basis	Start of requirements definition	Project initiation
Estimating and planning	Substantiated estimating and planning	Statistically substantiated estimating and planning		
Test specification technique	Informal techniques	Formal techniques		
Static test techniques	Inspection of test basis	Checklists		
Metrics	Project metrics (product)	Project metrics (process)	System metrics	Organization metrics (more than one system)
Test tools	Planning and control tools	Execution and analysis tools	Extensive automation of the test process	
Test environment	Managed and controlled test environment	Testing in most suitable environment	Environment on call	
Office environment	Adequate and timely office environment			
Commitment and motivation	Assignment of budget and time	Testing integrated in project organization		
Test functions and training	Test manager and testers	(Formal) methodical, technical, and functional support, management	Test engineering	
			Formal internal quality assurance	

TABLE 18.1 (*Continued*)

Key area	Level A	Level B	Level C	Level D
Scope of methodology	Project specific	Organization generic	Organization optimizing, R&D activities	
Communication	Internal communication	Project communication (defects, change control)	Communication within organization about the quality of the test process	
Reporting	Defects	Progress (status of tests and products), activities (costs and time, milestones), defects with priorities	Risks and recommendations, substantiated with metrics	Recommendations have a software process improvement character
Defect management	Internal defect management	Extensive defect management with flexible reporting facilities	Project defect management	
Testware management	Internal testware management	External management of test basis and test object	Reusable testware	Traceability system requirements to test cases
Test process management	Planning and execution	Planning, execution, monitoring, and adjusting	Monitoring and adjusting within organization	
Evaluation	Evaluation techniques	Evaluation strategy		
Low-level testing	Low-level test life cycle (planning, specification, and execution)	White-box techniques	Low-level test strategy	

Source: From ref 4. © 1999 Pearson Education.

TABLE 18.2 Test Maturity Matrix

Key area	Scale													
	Controlled						Efficient					Optimizing		
	0	1	2	3	4	5	6	7	8	9	10	11	12	13
Test strategy		A					B				C		D	
Life-cycle model		A			B									
Moment of involvement			A				B				C		D	
Estimating and planning				A							B			
Test specification techniques		A		B										
Static test techniques					A		B							
Metrics						A			B			C		D
Test tools					A			B			C			
Test environment				A				B						C
Office environment				A										
Commitment and motivation		A				B						C		
Test functions and training				A			B				C			
Scope of methodology					A						B			C
Communication			A		B							C		
Reporting		A			B		C					D		
Defect management		A				B		C						
Testware management				A			B				C			D
Test process management		A		B								C		
Evaluation							A			B				
Low-level testing					A		B		C					

Source: From ref. 4. © 1999 Pearson Education.

shows that the overall maturity of a test process can be represented on a scale of 1–13. In the following, we classify the 13 scales of maturity of a test process into three distinct qualitative segments.

Maturity Levels of Test Processes The 13 scales of maturity shown in Table 18.2 are divided into three qualitative groups, namely, *controlled*, *efficient*, and *optimizing*, as discussed below:

- **Controlled:** The group of scales 1–5 is labeled as controlled. A test process executed in a controlled manner means that all component activities are planned, and those are executed in phases according to a planned strategy. In this group some key areas have achieved maturity level B, whereas the rest have achieved maturity level A.

- **Efficient:** After having established mechanisms to execute the component activities of a test process in a controlled manner (scales 1–5), more effort needs to be made to achieve efficiency in testing. The maturity levels of key areas falling on scales 6–10 emphasize efficiency. In this group of scales, all the key areas, except evaluation, are raised to at least level B with some being at C. For example, the key area moment of involvement is improved to levels B and C in the efficient group. A level C maturity of moment of involvement means involving a test process at the requirements definition phase. Such early thinking about testing of requirements allows the SQA team to design test cases that require less rework cost. By having the key area static testing techniques mature to level B, the cost of testing can be reduced by employing requirements reviews, design reviews, and code reviews.

- **Optimizing:** The three test process levels 11–13 fall in the optimizing group. In this group, all the key areas have reached their respective highest maturity levels. Optimizing a test process means performing testing tasks in the best possible manner from the standpoints of quality, time, and cost. As time passes, new techniques and tools may be available to solve testing problems. Therefore, a test process must evolve continuously to be able to take advantage of new technologies and tools. Organizations may apply the lessons learned from their past projects in order to do things to achieve better results in quality, while spending less money and less time on testing.

Applying the TPI Model In the following, we explain how to apply the TPI model to improve a test process.

- Analyze the current test process, using Table 18.1, in terms of the 20 key areas and give each key area a rating—A, B, C, or D—as applicable, depending on the maturity level of the key areas.
- Evaluate the current scale, between 1 and 13, of the test process by comparing the current status of the test process with the standard test maturity matrix of Table 18.2.
- Identify the goal of the organization in terms of the next scale, between 1 and 13, to be achieved by the organization. It is evident from the test maturity matrix in Table 18.2 that, in order to move from one scale to the next, one does not have to seek improvements in all key areas. For example, if we want to move from scale 5 to 6, we need improvements in key areas test strategy (A to B), moment of involvement (A to B), static test techniques (A to B), test function and training (A to B), reporting (B to C), evaluation ("initial" to A), and low-level testing (A to B). The other key areas remain at their current levels of maturity—these key areas need not improve to higher maturity levels because their impacts may not be useful at the test process scale 6. For example, too much detailed information concerning test metrics need not be collected if the test process is not going to use them, say, for optimization purpose, at scale 6.
- Finally, actions need to be taken to improve the key areas identified in the preceding step. Once again, Table 18.1 is used to identify the action items.

18.4 TESTING MATURITY MODEL

Similar to the concept of evaluating and improving software development processes, there is a need for a framework to assess and improve testing processes. Continuous improvement of testing processes is an ideal goal of organizations, and evaluation plays a key role in process improvement. This is because an organization must know its present level of maturity before it takes actions to move to the next level. Ilene Burnstein and her colleagues at the Illinois Institute of Technology pioneered the concept of the TMM to help organizations evaluate and improve their testing processes [5, 6].

The TMM describes an evolutionary path of test process maturity in five *levels*, or *stages*, as illustrated in Figure 18.3. The TMM gives guidance concerning how to improve a test process. Each stage is characterized by the concepts of

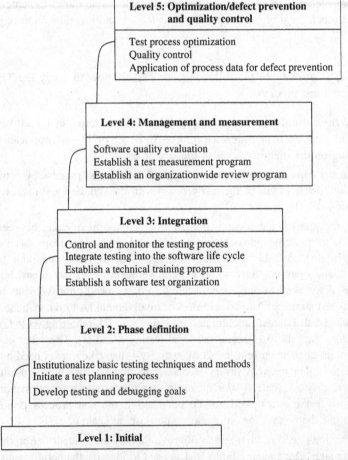

Figure 18.3   Five-level structure of TMM. (From ref. 5. © 2003 Springer.)

maturity goals, *supporting maturity goals*, and *activities, tasks, and responsibilities* (ATRs), as explained in the following:

- **Maturity Goals:** Each maturity level, except level 1, contains certain maturity goals. For an organization to achieve a certain level of maturity, the corresponding maturity goals must be met by the organization. The maturity goals are specified in terms of testing improvement goals.

- **Maturity Subgoals:** Maturity goals are supported by maturity subgoals. To achieve a maturity goal, it may be necessary to meet several, fine-grained subgoals.

- **Activities, Tasks, and Responsibilities:** Maturity subgoals are achieved by means of ATRs that address issues concerning implementation of activities and tasks. ATRs also address how an organization can adapt its practices so that it can move in-line with the TMM model, that is, move from one level to the next. ATRs are further refined into "views," known as critical views, from the perspectives of three different groups of people: managers, developers and test engineers, and customers (users/clients).

The maturity goals associated with the five levels of the TMM model will be explained in the following.

Level 1. Initial No maturity goals are specified at this level. The TMM level 1 is called the *initial* level. For an organization to be at level 1, nothing special needs to be done. Level 1 represents a scenario where testing is not performed in a planned manner. Testing begins after code is written. At this level, an organization often performs testing to demonstrate that the system works. No serious effort is made to track the progress of testing and the quality level of a product. Test cases are designed and executed in an *ad hoc manner*. Testing resources, such as trained testers, testing tools, and test environments, are not available. In summary, testing is not viewed as a critical, distinct phase in software development.

Level 2. Phase Definition At level 2, the maturity goals are as follows:

- Develop testing and debugging goals.
- Initiate a test planning process.
- Institutionalize basic testing techniques and methods.

(i) Develop Testing and Debugging Goals Separation of testing from debugging is an important growth in the maturity of a testing process. Unit testing and debugging may have some common features such as those being performed by individual programmers. However, their separation becomes more evident when we consider higher levels of testing, for example, integration testing, system-level testing, and acceptance testing. As we move away from unit-level testing to system-level testing, for example, test engineers are more interested in examining the higher level features of the system, and they do not focus on code-level details. On the other hand, debugging is primarily a code-level activity

that is initiated after a defect is detected in the software. The very nature of debugging dictates that it cannot be performed in a planned manner, except for getting ready to use tools in debugging.

Testing encompasses activities that can be carefully planned and executed. Responsibilities for testing and debugging must be properly assigned. Assigning responsibility for debugging is easier—the developer who writes the code for a unit or maintains it is in charge, by default, of debugging the unit. Similarly, assignment of responsibilities for unit testing is easy—the programmer of the unit performs unit testing. Assignment of responsibilities for integration testing, system testing, and acceptance testing is a nontrivial task because of the need for test personnel to possess different expertise. For example, some test personnel need to be experts in performance testing.

Some concrete maturity subgoals that can support this goal are as follows:

- Organizations form committees on testing and debugging, and those committees are supported with necessary funding.

- The committees develop and document testing goals. One example of a testing goal is to track a defect from its initial state of discovery to its final state of being fixed and verified.

- The committees develop and document debugging goals.

- The documented testing and debugging goals are widely used in the organization from managers to developers and test engineers. All the people in the organization are aware of the testing and debugging goals and strive to achieve those goals.

(ii) Initiate a Test Planning Process Planning is an indication of a certain level of maturity of any process. The exact extent of maturity depends upon the scope and execution of a plan. Test planning addresses the following:

- **Identify Test Objectives:** Identifying the objective of a test process is central to its success. Without explicit objectives it will be difficult to monitor and guide the progress of testing. Moreover, without explicit objectives it will be difficult to measure the amount of success achieved in testing. Two categories of objectives can be specified: software quality related and process related. One example of the former category of objectives is: Program units must pass all the unit-level tests before initiating integration tests. Another example of the software quality related objectives is: System-level test cases are grouped into functional test, reliability test, load test, security test, and so on.

    An example of a process-related objectives is: While system testing is in progress, the percentage of test cases passing should be monitored on a weekly basis. Another example is: System testing is reduced time by using multiple test beds.

- **Analyze Risks:** Factors that may adversely affect testing must be identified. An example of a risk in testing is that much emphasis has been put on the performance aspect of the system, but no test engineer is capable of designing and executing performance tests during system testing.

- **Devise Strategies:** Different kinds of strategies are involved in testing. For example, we can choose one among several integration testing strategies, such as top down, bottom up, and incremental, or a strategy that needs to be followed during the execution of system test cases as discussed in Section 12.7. In fact, every major testing activity requires a certain strategy to be followed.

- **Develop Test Specifications:** Individual test cases must be judiciously designed and documented. There must be an objective attached to the design of each test case. Next, a procedure outlining the steps of the test case is designed. Desired inputs and the expected outcomes corresponding to the test case are identified. The initial condition for executing each test case is also identified. Finally, a test case is properly documented for ease of use and accessibility.

- **Allocate Resources:** Resource allocation is an important task in any planned activity. A number of different kinds of resources are needed for software testing: test engineers with the right expertise, resources for setting up test environments, and resources for managing the testing process. In other words, for each test activity, personnel, funds, and time must be allocated.

The following concrete maturity subgoals can support the above goal at level 2:

- The organization assigns the task of test planning to a defined committee. The committee develops a framework for test planning.

- The committee develops a test plan template, and the template is well documented and made widely available.

- Proper tools are used to create and manage test plans.

- Provisions are put in place so that customer needs constitute a part of the test plan. In other words, customers are involved in the testing process.

(iii) Institutionalize Basic Testing and Methods   A number of basic testing techniques and methods are widely known in the industry. For example, unit-level testing can be carried out by focusing on the control flow and data flow aspects in a program unit, and a number of code coverage metrics are associated with those testing techniques. Coverage metrics associated with those techniques allow testers to quantify unit-level testing. Moreover, both white-box and black-box testing methods can be applied at the unit level. As testers move from a unit level to higher levels, such as integration and system levels, black-box testing becomes the norm as it is extremely difficult to apply white-box testing techniques to a large subsystem. One needs to apply one or more techniques to perform black-box testing: functional program testing, equivalence class partitioning, boundary value analysis, decision table, and error guessing. A requirement traceability matrix must be defined to maintain an association between requirements and test cases, that is,

what test cases cover each requirement, and what requirement is covered by each test case. By monitoring what test cases have passed, one knows what requirements have been satisfied so far by the system under test. The above maturity goal can be supported by the following subgoals:

- An expert group is formed to study, evaluate, and recommend a set of basic testing techniques and methods. The group also recommends a few tools to support those testing techniques and methods.

- Management must establish policies to ensure that the recommended techniques and methods are practiced and tools are used throughout the organization in a consistent manner.

Level 3. Integration   At level 3, as the name suggests, testing is fully integrated with the development process right from the project planning. Testing is not limited to an activity that starts after coding is over. Neither is testing considered to be solely execution based. Rather, different kinds of test activities are performed throughout the life cycle of a system, and some of those test activities are performed without executing code. At level 3, an organization creates a separate test group consisting of test specialists and test managers, their own resources, and a schedule to be able to inject a sense of quality into software products from project conception. For example, at the time of requirements specification, the test group can influence the process of requirements gathering by (i) confirming that all the requirements are testable and (ii) including their own requirements so that customer requirements are testable. The independent test group evaluates the system from the customer's perspective by directly interacting with the customers and incorporating their views into the test design process. By running independently, the test group focuses on quality-related matters, such as institutionalizing testing techniques and methods, evaluating testing tools, evaluating the testability of requirements, hiring and training test engineers by considering project needs, and defining test metrics. In other words, their objective is to perform test activities so that higher quality software is produced at lower cost and in a short time. The maturity goals at level 3 are as follows:

- Establish a software test group.
- Establish a technical training program.
- Integrate testing into the software life cycle.
- Control and monitor the testing process.

(i) Establish Software Test Group   Software testing is a highly specialized task at par with capturing requirements and designing a system. It has been widely recognized that testing activities must be initiated as soon as the planning for a project begins. Therefore, an independent test group must exist to carry out testing without any influence from the developers. The advantages of having an independent test group are as follows:

- The independent test group can develop the desired expertise in testing by hiring the right people and providing training to its members.

- The test group can have a positive impact on software quality by having its members participate in the meetings for requirements review in the requirements gathering phase of the software life cycle. The members from the test group ensure that the requirements are testable. Ensuring the testability of a requirement is important because without a concrete procedure to verify that a software system possesses a certain requirement, the organization cannot convince the customers that their needs are fulfilled.

- Testing involves a variety of specialized tasks, such as test planning, test design, test execution, test scheduling, following test-related standards, gathering and monitoring test metrics, maintaining test cases, and tracking defects. Therefore, scheduling those tasks and procuring the required resources are vital to the completion of system testing on time.

- The quality of a software product is independently evaluated without any interference from the development group. This independence is central to avoiding any intentional or unintentional bias that the developers may have toward their product.

- Customers feel much more confident about a product if it has been tested and evaluated by a test group which is independent of the development group.

Therefore, testing must be performed by an independent test group. Maturity subgoals which support the above goals are as follows:

- An organizationwide test group is formed with leadership, strong support, and funding from the management. The test group must be vested with authority to influence the quality of software products so that formation of the test group is not rendered as a mere exercise.

- The test group must be involved in all stages of the software development, and roles and responsibilities must be assigned to individual group members in appropriate phases of software development.

- Trained and motivated test engineers are assigned to the test group.

- The test group in an organization must communicate with the customers to get a feel for their needs so that testing can be carried out to meet the expectations of the customers.

(ii) Establish Technical Training Program   A technical training program is essential to maintaining a group of qualified and skilled staff for testing. Organizations tend to hire not so skilled staff for testing jobs because of general unavailability of sufficiently qualified test personnel in the industry. Therefore, organizations must make a sustained effort to train test personnel in the concept of quality, test planning, testing methods and techniques, standards, and testing tools. Test engineers learn the concepts and processes of various kinds of reviews, such as design review and code review, which are discussed in Chapter 3.

(iii) Integrate Testing into Software Life Cycle   In contrast to level 2, where testing is initiated as a distinct activity after coding is over, at level 3 testing is fully

integrated with a software development life cycle at the start of project planning. Therefore, test planning is initiated very early in the lifetime of a product. Early focus on testing allows the test group to participate in requirements gathering, design, and code reviews. Maturity subgoals to support the above goal are as follows:

- The test phase is partitioned into several activities, such as test planning, unit testing, integration testing, system testing, and acceptance testing, so that the distinct activities are easily performed at the appropriate times in the life cycle of a software product. Different kinds of reviews, such as requirements review, design review, and code review, are identified. All those testing and review activities are integrated into the V-model of testing.

- All the testing and review activities are integrated into an institutionalized V-model of testing, and the organization must ensure that the model is followed.

- The organization supports an effective mechanism for the test group to communicate with developers, customers, and the marketing group. As a result, test engineers learn about the requirements, design details, customer expectations, and marketing philosophy of the organization. The more the test group is knowledgeable about the product, the more it can influence product quality. The upper management of an organization must facilitate such communication.

(iv) Monitor and Control Testing Process Monitoring and control are important aspects of planning. Without monitoring it will not be known if a project is on course, and, consequently, no corrective measures can be taken to control the project. Level 3 concerns several test-related monitoring and control activities to provide visibility to the progress of a testing project. Management can take effective action for a test project to stay as close to the plan as possible when the progress of the project significantly differs from the plan. Progress of a test project can be measured as follows:

- **Amount of Testing effort:** This includes the number of test cases to be designed and the number of test cases to be executed.

- **Cost of Testing:** This represents all the cost in carrying out test-related activities.

- **Schedule:** This concerns the start and finish times of the test activities.

The following maturity subgoals are required to support the above goal:

- The organization develops policies and mechanisms to monitor and control test projects.

- A set of metrics related to the employed test process must be defined, recorded, and made available to all concerned test engineers.

- A set of potential corrective actions and contingency plans must be defined and documented. It may be used when the actual progress of a testing project significantly differs from the plan.

Level 4. Management and Measurement   At level 4 of the TMM, testing acquires a much larger scope and is not just another phase in a software development life cycle. The following are the maturity goals at level 4:

- Establish an organizationwide review program.
- Establish a test measurement program.
- Evaluate software quality.

(i) Establish Organizationwide Review Program   To augment the execution-based testing, a review program is established to detect defects early in the life cycle of product development and at a lower cost. All software products, such as requirements documents and design documents, are reviewed. Moreover, test plans, test cases, and test procedures are thoroughly reviewed. Thus, reviews are performed throughout the life cycle of a product. Maturity subgoals that support this goal are as follows:

- Management should develop review policies and ensure that those policies are rigorously followed.
- The test group should develop goals, plans, procedures, and recording mechanisms for carrying out reviews.
- Objectives must be clearly defined.
- Members of the test group must be trained so that their effective participation in review processes is ensured.

(ii) Establish Test Measurement Program   A test measurement program is established to measure productivity, progress, and quality of work associated with testing. For example, productivity in testing refers to the rate of test design in terms of number of test cases per person-day and the number of test cases executed by one person per day. The number of test cases reviewed by one person per day is another example of productivity in testing. Progress of testing refers to how much work has been completed with reference to how much is needed to be done. Therefore, one must measure at regular intervals all the quantities that represent progress. Some examples of measurable quantities are the number of test cases that have been designed and the number of test cases that have been executed. Quality of a software product is measured in terms of failure intensity, that is, the number of failures observed per unit time. Maturity subgoals that support this goal are as follows:

- Test metrics should be identified along with their goals.
- A test measurement plan should be developed with data collection and analysis.
- An action plan should be developed to achieve process improvement by considering the measured data.

(iii) Evaluate Software Quality An important goal of a software development process is to produce software products of the highest possible quality. A test group must measure the quality of a product to learn what quality a certain process can result in and take measures to improve the process with the objective of improving product quality. Therefore, the test group must identify the quality metrics, such as correctness, reliability, maintainability, and usability, for further improvement. The test group must evaluate the adequacy of a testing process for reliable assessment of the resulting qualities in a product. The maturity subgoals that support this goal are as follows:

- The organization should define quality attributes and quality goals for software products.
- Management should develop policies and mechanisms to collect test metrics to support the quality goals.

Level 5. Optimization, Defect Prevention, and Quality Control Optimization and defect prevention are the concepts at the highest level, namely level 5. Intuitively, optimization means spending less resources to achieve higher quality products, and defect prevention means taking measures throughout the development process so that products are largely defect free. At level 5, the maturity goals are as follows:

- Application of process data for defect prevention
- Statistical quality control
- Test process optimization

(i) Application of Process Data for Defect Prevention At level 5, organizations make a sustained effort to learn from experience to reduce the number of defects in a system. Defect prevention is an important characteristic of mature organizations. Test groups in mature organizations analyze defects and their patterns and perform root cause analysis to better understand the pattern of defects. To prevent the recurrence of common defects in future projects, action plans are developed and processes are improved. Mechanisms must be in place to ensure that the action plans are followed. Such mechanisms include formation of a defect prevention team that interacts with developers to apply defect prevention activities in the development process. Maturity subgoals that support this goal are as follows:

- Management should establish a defect prevention team.
- Defects identified and removed are documented in each phase of the development.
- Each defect is analyzed to get to its root cause.
- Managers, developers, and the test group should interact to develop an action plan to eliminate recurrence of commonly occurring defects.
- Management should put in place a mechanism to implement and track the action plan.

(ii) Statistical Quality Control   At level 5, organizations further improve the quality of software products by driving the testing process with statistical sampling, measurement of confidence levels, trustworthiness, and software reliability goals. This goal is stronger than the software quality evaluation goal at level 3. It may be recalled that the quality evaluation goal focuses on different kinds of software qualities, such as functionality, reliability, usability, and robustness. Automated tools are used for defect collection and analysis. Usage modeling is used to perform statistical testing, where a usage model is selected from a subset of all possible usages of the software. From statistical testing one can conclude the general operational performance of the software product. Subgoals that support statistical quality control are as follows:

- The test group establishes high-level measurable quality goals, such as test case execution rate, defects arrival rate, and total number of defects that can be found during testing.
- Managers ensure that the new quality goals form a part of the test plan.
- The test group is trained in statistical testing and analysis methods: Pareto analysis, cause-and-effect diagram, flow chart, trend chart, histogram, scatter diagram, and control chart.
- User inputs are gathered for usage modeling.

(iii) Test Process Optimization   Test optimization refers to all those activities which result in continuous improvement of the testing process. An essential element of test optimization is quantification of the testing process so that accurate measurements can be performed to find where further improvements are possible. Test optimization involves the following activities:

- Identify the testing practices that can be improved.
- Define a mechanism to improve an identified practice.
- Put a mechanism in place to track the practice improvement mechanism.
- Continuously evaluate new test-related technologies and tools.
- Develop management support for technology transfer.

Maturity subgoals that support test process optimization are as follows:

- Establish a test process improvement group to monitor the testing process and identify areas for improvement.
- Evaluate new technologies and tools to improve the capability of the testing process. There must be management support to establish policies and mechanisms for this purpose.
- A mechanism is put in place for continual evaluation of the effectiveness of the testing process.
- Test stopping criteria are based on quality goals, which are discussed in Chapter 12.

18.5 SUMMARY

The CMM is a framework for evaluating and improving the present capability of a software development company. As the name suggests, the CMM can be used to assess to what extent the capability of an organization to develop software systems has matured. The model allows one to give a rating to an organization on a scale of 1–5, where 5 represents the highest maturity level. The model allows one to evaluate an organization by examining its current practices. Basically, the CMM is a process improvement approach. In order to move to the next level of maturity, organizations need to adopt new practices relevant to the next maturity level. Level 1 is the *initial* level, level 2 is known as *repeatable*, level 3 is the *defined* level, level 4 is *managed*, and level 5 is the *optimizing* level. Each level is characterized by a set of *key process areas*.

It is useful to recall that the CMM focuses on the entire development process, whereas the TPI model allows us to focus on a test process alone. A test process is a certain manner of performing activities related to defect prevention and detection. Some examples of testing activities are identifying testing goals, preparing a test plan, and designing test cases. A test process needs to be improved for three reasons: (i) A better test process should give more insight into the quality characteristics of a system, (ii) a better test process should reduce testing time, and (iii) a better test process should cost less. Tim Koomen and Martin Pol [4] introduced the idea of improving a test process by proposing the TPI model. Intuitively, any approach to improving a test process consists of the following four steps: (i) Determine an area for improvement, (ii) evaluate the current state of the test process, (iii) identify the next desired state and the means to achieve it, and (iv) execute the necessary changes to the process. A test process is evaluated with respect to 20 key areas, such as test strategy, moment of involvement, planning, and metrics. The maturity level of a test process is assessed on a scale of 1–13. The 13 levels of test process maturity are partitioned into three broad qualitative groups, namely, *controlled*, *efficient*, and *optimizing*.

Finally, the TMM gives guidelines concerning how to improve a test process. In this model, the maturity of a testing process is evaluated on a scale of 1–5. Each of the five maturity levels is characterized by the concepts of maturity goals; maturity goals are supported by means of subgoals and activities, tasks, and responsibilities. The five levels of maturity are known as initial (level 1), phase definition (level 2), integration (level 3), management and measurement (level 4), and optimization, defect prevention, and quality control (level 5).

LITERATURE REVIEW

Numerous books and articles have been written about CMM and CMMI. A comprehensive article about CMM is by Paulk, Curtis, Chrissis, and Weber [2]—the first three authors are from the Software Engineering Institute. Two good books on CMM and CMMI are by Land [3] and Mutafelija and Stromberg [7], respectively. However, revisions are made to the CMM and CMMI documents from time to time. Thus, it is useful to refer to the main web page of SEI for timely information about CMM and CMMI: http://www.sei.cmu.edu/.

For additional information about the TPI model, the reader is referred to the book entitled *Test Process Improvement* by Koomen and Pol [4]. For additional information about the TMM, the reader is referred to the book entitled *Practical Software Testing* by Burnstein [5].

Another maturity model that is frequently adopted by organizations is known as the Six Sigma maturity model to address quality and customer satisfaction issues. Six Sigma was created by some of America's most gifted CEOs, people like Motorola's Bob Galvin, AlliedSignal's Larry Bossidy, and GE's Jack Welch. Six Sigma is a business-driven, multifaceted approach to process improvement, reduced costs, and increased profits. To achieve Six Sigma, a process must not produce more than 3.4 defects per million opportunities. The Six Sigma DMAIC methodology, consisting of the five steps define, measure, analyze, improve, and control, is an improvement system for existing processes falling below specification and looking for incremental improvement. The Six Sigma DMADV methodology, consisting of the five steps define, measure, analyze, design, and verify, is an improvement system used to develop new processes or products at Six Sigma quality levels. It can also be employed if a current process requires more than just incremental improvement. Interested readers are encouraged to read the following books for detailed discussions of this subject:

M. Harry, *Six Sigma: The Breakthrough Management Strategy Revolutionizing the World's Top Corporations*, Random House, New York, 2000.

T. Pyzdek, *The Six Sigma Handbook*, McGraw-Hill Professional, New York, 2001.

REFERENCES

1. R. R. Macala, Jr., L. D. Stuckey, and D. C. Gross. Managing Domain-Specific, Product-Line Development. *Software Practice and Experience*, Vol. 13, No. 3, 1996, pp. 57–68.
2. M. Paulk, B. Curtis, M. B. Chrissis, and C. V. Weber. Capability Maturity Model, Version 1.1. *IEEE Software*, July 1993, pp. 18–27.
3. S. Land. *Jumpstart CMM/CMMI Software Process Improvement*. Wiley, Hoboken, NJ, 2005.
4. T. Koomen and M. Pol. *Test Process Improvement*. Addison-Wesley, Reading, MA, 1999.
5. I. Burnstein. *Practical Software Testing*. Springer, New York, 2003.
6. I. Burnstein, A. Homyen, T. Suwanassart, G. Saxena, and R. Grom. A Testing Maturity Model for Software Test Process Assessment and Improvement. *Software Quality Professional*, September 1999, pp. 1–8.
7. B. Mutafelija and H. Stromberg. *Systematic Process Improvement Using ISO 9001:2000 and CMMI*. Artech House, Boston, MA 2003.

Exercises

1. Briefly explain the CMM architecture.

2. Briefly explain the five maturity levels in the CMM model.

3. Briefly explain the common features of key practices in the CMM model.

4. Briefly explain the idea of a test process.

5. Why is it important to improve a test process?

6. Briefly explain an intuitive approach to improving a test process.

7. Briefly explain how the current status of a test process can be evaluated.

8. Briefly explain the levels of maturity of key areas in the TPI model.

9. Briefly explain the main idea in the TMM.

10. Briefly explain the different levels in the TMM in terms of their maturity goals.

GLOSSARY

A man is born alone and dies alone; and he experiences the good and bad consequences of his karma alone; and he goes alone to hell or the supreme abode.
— *Chanakya*

1xEvolution-data optimized (1xEV-DO)   Communication standard for transmitting and receiving data frames over a wireless radio channel using CDMA technology.

Abstract Syntax Notation One (ASN.1)   Notation to formally define the syntax of messages to be exchanged among an extensive range of applications involving the Internet.

Acceptance criteria   Criteria a system must satisfy to be accepted by a customer and to enable the customer to determine whether to accept the system.

Acceptance test   Formal testing conducted to determine whether a system satisfies its acceptance criteria.

Access terminal   Can be a mobile phone, laptop, or personal digital assistant (PDA) with a wireless modem.

Accuracy   Degree of conformity of a measured or calculated quantity to its actual (true) value.

Adaptive random testing   In adaptive random testing, test inputs are selected from a randomly generated set in such a way that these test inputs are evenly spread over the entire input domain.

Adjacent domain   Two domains are adjacent if they have a boundary inequality in common.

Asynchronous transfer mode (ATM)   Cell relay network protocol which encodes data traffic into small, fixed-sized (53 bytes = 48 bytes of data and 5 bytes of header information) cells. A connection-oriented technology in which a connection is established between the two endpoints before an actual data exchange begins.

Attributes   Properties of the service delivered by the system to users.

Authentication   Process of verifying the claimed identity of someone or something.

Authentication, authorization, and accounting (AAA)   Network server used for controlling access to a network. An authentication process identifies the user. An authorization process implements policies that determine which resources and services a valid user may access. An accounting process keeps track of time and data resources used for billing and usage analysis.

Authorization   Process of verifying whether an individual has permission to access a specific resource.

Software Testing and Quality Assurance: Theory and Practice, Edited by Kshirasagar Naik and Priyadarshi Tripathy
Copyright © 2008 John Wiley & Sons, Inc.

Automatable Test case that is a good candidate for automation.

Availability Measure of the readiness of a system. Simply put, availability is the proportion of time a system is in a functioning condition.

Backdoors Mechanism created by a computer program that allows anyone with knowledge of its existence to gain access to the system.

Backup/recoverability test Verifies that a system can be recouped after a failure. It is done by backing up to a point in the processing cycle before any error occurred and reprocessing all transactions that occurred after that point.

Bad fix Fix causing collateral damage.

Basic interconnection test Verifies whether the implementation can establish a basic interconnection before thorough tests are performed.

Basic test Provides a prima facie indication that the system is ready for more rigorous tests.

Behavior test Verifies the dynamic communication systems requirements of an implementation. These are the requirements and options that define the observable behavior of a protocol. A large part of behavior tests, which constitutes the major portion of communication system tests, can be generated from the protocol standards.

Beta testing Testing conducted by potential buyers prior to the release of the product. The purpose of beta testing is intended not to find defects but to obtain feedback from the field to the developers about the usability of the product.

Big-bang integration Integration testing technique in which all the software modules are put together to construct the complete system so that the system as a whole can be tested.

Bit error test (BERT) Involves transmitting a known bit pattern over a channel and then verifying the received pattern for errors.

Black-box testing Also called functional testing, a testing technique that ignores the internal details of a system and focuses solely on the inputs accepted, outputs generated, and execution conditions.

Boot test Verifies that the system can boot up its software image from the supported boot options.

Bot Software agent in Internet parlance. A bot interacts with network services intended for people as if it were a person. One typical use of bots is to gather information. Another, more malicious use of bots is the coordination and operation of an automated attack on networked computers, such as a distributed denial-of-service attack.

Bottom-up integration Integration testing technique in which testing starts from the modules at the outermost branches of a module visibility tree and moves toward the modules making up the "main program."

Boundary inequality From a geometrical viewpoint, a domain is defined by a set of boundary inequalities, where each inequality defines a boundary of the domain.

Boundary value analysis (BVA) The aim of BVA is to select elements that are close to the boundaries of an input domain so that both the upper and lower edges of an equivalence class are covered by test cases.

Branch coverage Selecting program paths in such a manner that certain branches (i.e., outgoing edges of nodes) of a control flow graph are covered by the execution of those paths. Complete branch coverage means selecting some paths such that their execution causes all the branches to be covered.

Build Interim software image for internal testing within the organization. Eventually, the final build will be a candidate for system testing, and such a system may be released to customers.

Business acceptance testing (BAT) Undertaken within the supplier's development organization to ensure that the system will eventually pass the user acceptance testing.

Capability maturity model (CMM) Gives guidelines for improving a software development process. The model facilitates the evaluation of the maturity levels of processes on a scale of 1–5. Level 5 is the highest level of process maturity.

Capability test Checks that the implementation provides the observable capabilities based on the static communication system requirements. The static requirements describe the options, ranges of values for parameters, and timers.

Category partition method (CPM) Systematic, specification-based methodology that uses an informal functional specification to produce formal test specification.

Causal analysis A kind of analysis conducted to identify the root cause of a defect and initiate actions so that the source of the defect is eliminated.

Change request (CR) Formal request by a code reviewer to make a change to the code.

Characterizing sequence Sequences of the W-set of an FSM are called the characterizing sequences of the FSM.

Check-in request form For each fix that is checked into a build, a check-in request form is filled out by software developers and reviewed by the build engineering group.

Clean-room process Model introduced by IBM in the late 1980s. The process involves two cooperating teams—development and quality assurance teams—and five major activities: specification, planning, design and verification, quality certification, and feedback. The following ideas form the foundation of the clean-room process: (i) incremental development under statistical quality control (SQC), (ii) software development based on mathematical principles, and (iii) software testing based on statistical principles.

Closed boundary A boundary is closed if the data points on the boundary are a part of the domain of interest.

Closed domain A domain with all its boundaries closed.

Closure error Occurs if a boundary is closed when the intention is to have an open boundary or vice versa.

Collateral damage What occurs when a new feature or a defect fix in one part of the system causes a defect (damage) to another, possibly unrelated part of the system.

Combinatorial testing Test case selection method in which test cases are identified by combining values of several test input parameters based on some combinatorial strategy.

Command line interface test Verifies that the system can be configured in a specific way by using the command line interface.

Commercial off-the-shelf (COTS) components Software components produced by third-party vendor organizations that can be reused in a system. Often, these types of components are delivered without their source code.

Compatibility test Verifies that the system can work in the same manner across all platforms, operating systems, database management systems, and network operating systems.

Competent programmer hypothesis Assumption for mutation analysis, which states that programmers are generally competent, and they do not create "random" programs.

Compliance testing Also called conformance testing, the process of verifying whether a product meets the standard product specifications it was designed to meet.

Computation error Occurs when specific input data cause the program to execute the correct path but the output value is wrong.

Confidentiality Encrypting data by a sender such that only the intended receiver can decrypt it.

Configuration testing Reconfiguration activities during interoperability tests.

Conformance testing Process that verifies whether an implementation conforms to its specification.

Control flow graph (CFG) Graphical representation of the flow of control in a program unit.

Coordinated architecture Enhanced version of the distributed architecture, where the upper and lower testers are coordinated by a test management protocol.

Coupling effect Assumption for mutation analysis which states that if a test suite can reveal simple defects in a program, then it can also reveal more complicated combinations of simple defects.

Cross-functionality group In an organization the set of those groups that have different stakes in a product. For example, a marketing group, a customer support group, a development group, a system test group, a development group, and a product sustaining group are collectively referred to as a cross-functionality group in an organization.

Cyclomatic complexity (McCabe's complexity) Based on the graph theory concept and known as cyclomatic number, represents the complexity of a software module.

Data conversion acceptance criteria Used to measure and report the capability of the software to convert existing application data to new formats.

Data flow anomaly Sequence of "unusual" actions on a data variable, for example, two successive assignments of values to a data variable or referencing an undefined variable.

Data flow graph (DFG) Graphical representation of a program, where nodes represent computations and branches represent predicates, that is, conditions.

Debugging Process of determining the cause of a defect and correcting it; occurs as a consequence of a test revealing a defect.

Decision table Comprises a set of conditions and a set of effects. For each combinations of conditions, a rule exists. Each rule comprises a Y (yes), N (no), or—(don't care) response and contains an associated list of effects or expected results.

Defect Flaw in a software with a potential to cause a failure.

Defect age Period of time from the introduction of a defect to its discovery.

Defect density Number of defects per thousand lines of code.

Defect prevention Preventive measures that can be taken during the development of code to reduce the errors in the program.

Defect priority Measure of how soon the defect needs to be fixed.

Defect removal efficiency (DRE) Ratio of the number of defects discovered in an activity to the number of defects that should have been found.

Defect severity Measure of the extent of the detrimental effect a defect can have on the operation of the product.

Definition of a variable A variable is said to be defined if the variable's memory location explicitly gets a value.

Degraded node test   Verifies the operation of a system after a portion of the system becomes nonoperational.

Denial-of-service (DoS) attack   Flooding an information system, such as a server, with a large number of requests for service to the point where the information system cannot respond.

Design verification test (DVT)   Written and executed by the hardware group before integrating the hardware with the software system. Types of DVTs are diagnostic, electrostatic discharge, electromagnetic emission, electrical, thermal, environmental, acoustics, equipment packaging, safety, and reliability.

Deterministic finite-state machine   FSM such that its output and the next state are a function of its current state and the input that is applied.

Device under test (DUT)   Manufactured product undergoing testing.

Diagnostic tests   Verify that the hardware components of the system are functioning as desired. Examples are power-on self test, Ethernet loop-back test, and bit error test.

Digital signature   Encrypted message digest that is appended to the message. Producing a digital signature involves public key encryption and a hash function algorithm.

Distinguishing sequence   Input sequence which generates a unique output sequence for a state when the input sequence is applied to an FSM starting at the given state.

Distributed architecture   Test architecture where there is a PCO at the upper service boundary and another at the lower service boundary. The PCO at the lower service boundary is at the remote end of the $N - 1$ service provider to indirectly control and observe N ASPs and N PDUs. This allows the upper and lower testers to reside in physically separate locations.

Domain error   Occurs when specific input data cause the program to execute the *wrong* path in the program.

Dynamic unit testing   Execution-based testing methodology in which a program unit is actually executed and its outcomes are observed.

Element management system (EMS) test   Verifies EMS functionality, such as monitoring and managing the network elements.

Emulator   A software emulator allows computer programs to run on a platform (computer architecture and/or operating system) other than the one for which the programs were originally written. Unlike simulation, which only attempts to reproduce a program's behavior, an emulator attempts to model, to various degrees, the states of the device being emulated.

Encryption   Cryptographic technique used to provide confidentiality.

Engineering change (EC) document   Provides a brief description of the issues and describes what changes are needed to be done to the original requirement.

Engineering change order (ECO)   Formal document that describes a change to the hardware or software that is to be delivered to the customers. This document includes the hardware/software compatibility matrix and is distributed to operation, customer support, and the sales teams of the organization.

Entry criteria   Criteria to be met before the start of a testing phase.

Error   When an event activates a fault in a program, it first brings the program into an intermediate unstable state, called error, which, if and when it propagates to the output, eventually causes a system failure.

Error guessing Test design technique in which the experience of the testers is used to (i) guess the probable kinds and locations of faults in a system and (ii) design tests specifically to expose them. Designing test cases using the error guessing technique is primarily based on a tester's experience with code similar to the implementation under test.

Error seeding Process of intentionally adding known defects in a computer program for the purpose of estimating the number of defects remaining in the program during the process of testing and fault removal.

Equivalence class partitioning Divides the input domain of the system under test into classes (or groups) of test cases that have a similar effect on the system.

Equivalent mutant Mutant that is not distinguishable from the program under test. Determining whether or not a mutant is equivalent to a program is in general undecidable.

Exit criteria Criteria specifying the conditions that must be met before the completion of a testing phase.

Extended finite-state machine Extension of a finite-state machine (FSM). An EFSM has the capability to perform additional computations such as updating values of variables, manipulating timers, and making decisions. The Specification and Description Language (SDL) provides a framework for specifying a system as one or more EFSMs.

Extensible authentication protocol (EAP) Authentication protocol described in Request for Comments (RFC) 2284. For wireless LANs, the EAP is known as EAP over LAN (EAPOL).

Extreme point Point is a point where two or more boundaries cross.

Extreme programming (XP) Software development methodology which is self-adaptive and people-oriented. XP begins with five values: communication, feedback, simplicity, courage, and respect. It then builds up 12 rules/recommendations which XP projects should follow.

Failure Manifested inability of a program to perform its required function. In other words, it is a system malfunction evidenced by incorrect output, abnormal termination, or unmet time and space constraints.

Failure intensity Expressed as the number of failures observed per unit time.

False negative Occurs when a potential or real attack is missed by an intrusion detection system. The more the occurrences of this scenario, the more doubtful the accountability of the intrusion detection system and its technology.

False positive Commonly known as false alarm, occurs when intrusion detection system reads legitimate activity as being an attack.

Fault Cause of a failure. For example, a missing or incorrect piece of code is a fault. A fault may remain undetected for a long time until some event activates it.

Fault-based testing Testing technique used to show that a particular class of faults is not resident in a program. The test cases are aimed at revealing specific kinds of predefined faults, for example, error guessing, fault seeding, or mutation testing.

Fault (error) seeding Process of intentionally adding known faults in a computer program for the purpose of monitoring the rate of detection and removal of faults and estimating the number of faults remaining in the program. Also used in evaluating the adequacy of tests.

Fault injection Method by which faults are introduced into a program. An oracle or a specification is available to assert that what was inserted made the program incorrect.

Fault simulation Process of inserting faults in a program. The inserted faults are not guaranteed to make the program incorrect. In fault simulation, one may modify an incorrect statement of a program and turn it into a correct program.

Feasible path Path in which there exists an input to cause the path to execute.

Feature Set of related requirements.

First customer shipment (FCS) New software build that is released to the first paying customer.

Finite-state machine (FSM) Automata with a finite number of states. The automata changes its state when an external stimulus is applied. The *state* of an FSM is defined as a stable condition in which the FSM rests until an external stimulus, called an *input*, is applied. An input causes an FSM to generate an observable *output* and to undergo a state transition from the current state to a new state where it stays until the next input occurs.

Frame relay (FR) Physical layer data transmission technique for moving data frames from one computer/router to another computer/router.

Full polling Used to check the status and any configuration changes of the nodes that are managed by an EMS server.

Functional specification document Requirements document produced by software developers to represent customer needs.

Functional testing Testing in which a program P is viewed as a *function* that transforms the input vector X_i into an output vector Y_i such that $Y_i = P(X_i)$. The two key concepts in functional testing are as follows: (i) precisely identify the domain of each input and output variable and (ii) select values from a data domain having *important* properties.

Function point (FP) Unit of measurement to express the amount of business functionality an information system provides to a user. Function points were defined in 1977 by Alan Albrecht at IBM.

Gantt chart Popular bar chart to represent a project schedule.

Gold standard oracle Scheme in which previous version of an existing application system is used to generate expected results.

Graphical user interface test Verifies the look-and-feel interface of an application system.

Handoff Procedure for transferring the handling of a call from one base station to another base station.

Hash function Algorithm that takes an input message of arbitrary length and produces a fixed-length code. The fixed-length output is called a hash, or a message digest, of the original input message.

Hazard State of a system or a physical situation which, when combined with certain environmental conditions, could lead to an accident or mishap. A hazard is a prerequisite for an accident.

High-availability tests Verify the redundancy of individual hardware and software modules. The goal here is to verify that the system recovers gracefully and quickly from hardware and software failure without impacting the operation of the system. It is also known as fault tolerance.

High-level design document Describes the overall system architecture.

Ideal test If we can conclude, from the successful execution of a sample of the input domain, that there are no faults in the program, then the input sample constitutes an ideal test.

Implementation under test (IUT) Implementation subject to tests. An IUT can be a complete system or a component thereof.

Inappropriate action Calculating a value in a wrong way, failing to assign a value to a variable, or calling a procedure with a wrong argument list.

Inappropriate path selection If there is a faulty association between a program condition and a path, then a wrong path is selected, and this is called inappropriate path selection.

Infeasible path Program path that can *never* be executed.

Inferred requirement Anything that a system is expected to do but is not explicitly stated in the specification.

In-parameter-order (IPO) testing Combinatorial testing technique for the generation of test cases that satisfy pairwise coverage.

In-process metrics Monitor the progress of the project and use these metrics to steer the course of the project.

Input vector Collection of all data entities read by a program whose values must be fixed prior to entering the unit.

Inspection Step-by-step peer group review of a work product, with each step checked against predetermined criteria.

Installability test Ensures that the system can be correctly installed in the customer environment.

Integrity checking Verifying whether or not data have been modified in transit.

Internet Protocol (IP) Routing protocol used for moving data across a packet-switched internetwork. The IP is a network layer protocol in the Internet protocol suite.

Internet Protocol Security (IPSec) Network layer security protocol which provides security features, including confidentiality, authentication, data integrity, and protection against data replay attacks.

Interoperability test Verifies that the system can interoperate with third-party products.

Intersystem testing Integration testing in which all the systems are connected together and tests are conducted from end to end.

Intrasystem testing Low-level integration testing with the objective of putting the modules together to build a cohesive system. Intrasystem testing requires combining modules together within a system.

Ishikawa diagram Also known as a *fishbone* diagram or cause-and-effect diagram, shows the causes of a certain event. It was first used by Kaoru Ishikawa in the 1960s and is considered one of the seven basic tools of quality management: histogram, Pareto chart, check sheet, control chart, cause-and-effect diagram, flowchart, and scatter diagram.

JUnit Automated testing framework used by developers who implement program units and unit tests in the Java programming language.

Key process area (KPA) A CMM maturity level contains key process areas. KPAs are expected to achieve goals and are organized by common features.

Lean Methodology that is used to speed up and reduce the cost of a manufacturing process by removing waste. The principle to eliminate waste has been borrowed from the ideas of Taiichi Ohno—the father of the Toyota Production System. The lean development methodology is summarized by the following seven principles: eliminate waste, amplify learning, decide as late as possible, deliver as fast as possible, empower the team, build integrity, and see the whole. The lean process is a translation of the lean manufacturing principles and practices to the software development domain.

Light emitting diode (LED) test   Verifies the functioning of the LED indicator status. The LED tests are designed to ensure that the visual operational status of the system and the submodules is correct.

Lightweight Directory Access Protocol (LDAP)   Protocol derived from the X.500 standard and defined in Request for Comments (RFC) 2251. LDAP is similar to a database but can contain more descriptive information. LDAP is designed to provide fast response to high-volume lookups.

Lightweight Extensible Authentication Protocol (LEAP)   Cisco-wireless EAP which provides username/password-based authentication between a wireless client and an access control server.

Load and scalability test   Exercises the system with multiple actual or virtual users and verifies whether it functions correctly under tested traffic levels, patterns, and combinations.

Local architecture   Test architecture where the PCOs are defined at the upper and lower service boundaries of the IUT.

Logging and tracing test   Verifies the configuration and operation of logging and tracing functionalities.

Logic fault   When a program produces incorrect results independent of resource required, the fault is caused due to inherent deficiencies in the program and not due to lack of resource. The deficiencies are in the form of requirement faults, design faults, and construction faults.

Lower tester   Tester entity responsible for the control and observation at the appropriate PCO either below the IUT or at a remote site.

Low-level design document   Detailed specification of the software modules within the architecture.

Maintainability   Aptitude of a system to undergo repair and evolution.

Management information base (MIB)   Database used to manage the devices in a communication network.

Manufacturing view of quality   Quality is seen as conforming to requirements. The concept of process plays a key role in the manufacturing view.

Marketing beta   Beta testing that builds early awareness and interest in the product among potential buyers.

Mean time between failure (MTBF)   Expected time between two successive failures of a system. Technically, MTBF should be used only in reference to repairable items, while MTTF should be used for nonrepairable items. However, MTBF is commonly used for both repairable and nonrepairable items.

Mean time to failure (MTTF)   Mean time expected until the first failure of a piece of equipment. MTTF is a statistical value and is meant to be the mean over a long period of time and a large number of units. MTTF is a basic measure of reliability for nonrepairable systems.

Mean time to repair (MTTR)   Amount of time between when something breaks and when it has been repaired and is fully functional again. MTTR represents the amount of time that the device was unable to provide service.

Milestone   Major checkpoint, or a subgoal, identified on the project or testing schedule.

Mishap Also called an accident, an unintended event that results in death, injury, illness, damage or loss of property, or harm to the environment.

Missing control flow paths There is no code to handle a certain condition. This occurs when we fail to identify the condition and, thereby, fail to specify a computation in the form of a path.

Module test Verifies that all the modules function individually as desired within the system. The intent here is to verify that the system along with the software that controls these modules operates as specified in the requirement specification.

Mutation analysis Involves the mutation of source code by introducing statements or modifying existing statements in small ways. The idea is to help the tester develop effective tests or locate weaknesses in the test data or in the code that are seldom or never accessed during execution.

Network element Network node residing on a managed network and running an SNMP agent.

Network management station Executes management applications that monitor and control network elements.

New technology LAN manager (NTLM) Authentication protocol used in various Microsoft network protocol implementations. NTLM employs a challenge–response mechanism for authentication in which clients are able to prove their identities without sending a password to the server.

Nondeterministic finite-state machine FSM in which the next-state function is not solely determined by its present state and an input. An internal event too can cause a state transition. In addition, given an external input in some states, the next state of the FSM cannot be uniquely determined.

Off point Given a boundary, an off point is a point away from the boundary. One must consider a domain of interest and its relationship with the boundary while identifying an off point.

On-line insertion and removal test Verifies the individual module redundancy including the software that controls these modules.

On point Given a domain boundary, an on point is a point on the boundary or very near the boundary but still satisfying the boundary inequality.

Open boundary Boundary with data points that are *not* a part of the domain of interest.

Open domain Domain with all its boundaries open with respect to the domain.

Operational profile Set of operations supported by a system and their probability of occurrence. An operational profile is organized in the form of a tree structure, where each arc is labeled with an action and its occurrence probability.

Oracle Mechanism that verifies the correctness of program outputs. An oracle can be a specification, an expert, a body of data, or another program.

Original equipment manufacturer (OEM) Company that builds products or components which are used in other products sold by another company, often called a value-added reseller, or VAR. An OEM typically builds a product to an order based on the designs of the VAR. For example, hard drives in a computer system may be manufactured by a corporation separate from the company that assembles and markets computers.

Orthogonal array (OA) testing Combinatorial testing technique for selecting a set of test cases from a universe of tests and making testing efficient and effective. OA testing is based on a special matrix called a latin square in which the same symbol occurs exactly once in each row and column.

Orthogonal defect classification (ODC) Scheme for classifying software defects and guidance for analyzing the classified aggregate defect data.

Packet data serving node (PDSN) Provides access to the Internet, intranets, and application servers for mobile stations utilizing a CDMA2000 radio access network (RAN). Acting as an access gateway, a PDSN entity provides simple IP and mobile IP access, foreign agent support, and packet transport for virtual private networking. It acts as a client for an authentication, authorization, and accounting (AAA) server and provides mobile stations with a gateway to the IP network.

Pairwise coverage Requires that, for a given number of input parameters to the system, each possible combination of values for any pair of parameters be covered by at least one test case. It is a special case of combinatorial testing.

Pairwise testing Integration testing technique in which only two interconnected systems are tested in an overall system. The purpose of pairwise testing is to ensure that the two systems under consideration can function together, assuming that other systems within the overall environment behave as expected.

Parametric oracle Scheme in which an algorithm is used to extract some parameters from the actual outputs and compares them with the expected parameter values.

Pareto principle States that 80% of the problems can be fixed with 20% of the entire effort. It is also known as the 80–20 rule.

Partition testing Testing technique in which the input domain of the program is divided into nonoverlapping subdomains; next, one test input is selected from each subdomain. The basic assumption is that all the elements within a subdomain essentially cause the system to behave the same way and that any element of a subdomain will expose an error in the program as any other element in the same domain.

Path Sequence of statements in a program or a program unit. Structurally, a path is a sequence of statements from the initial node of a CFG to one of the terminating nodes.

Path predicate Set of predicates associated with a path.

Path predicate expression Interpreted path predicate.

Perfect oracle Scheme in which the system (IUT) is tested in parallel with a trusted system that accepts every input specified for the IUT and "always" produces the correct result.

Performance fault Causes a program to fail to produce the desired output within specified resource limitations.

Performance test Determines how actual system performance compares to predicted system performance. Tests are designed to verify response time, execution time, throughput, resource utilization, and traffic rate.

Ping Computer network tool used to test whether a particular host is reachable across an IP network. Ping works by sending ICMP "echo request" packets to the target host and listening for ICMP "echo response" replies. Using interval timing and response rate, ping estimates the round-trip time and packet loss rate between hosts.

Point of control and observation (PCO) Well-designated point of interaction between a system and its users.

Point-to-point protocol (PPP) Data link protocol commonly used to establish a direct connection between two nodes over serial cable, phone line, trunk line, and cellular telephone.

Power cycling test Verifies that a system consistently boots and becomes operational after a power cycle.

Power of test methods   Used to compare test methods. The notion of *at least as good as* is an example of comparing the power of test methods. A test method M is at least as good as a test method N if, whenever N reveals a fault in a program P by generating a test, method M reveals the same fault by generating the same test or another test.

Power-on self-test (POST)   Determines whether or not the hardware components are their proper states to run the software.

Predicate   Logical function evaluated at a decision point.

Predicate coverage   Exploring all possible combinations of truth values of conditions affecting a selected path for all paths.

Predicate interpretation   Symbolically substituting operations along a path in order to express the predicates solely in terms of the input vector and a constant vector.

Product view of quality   The central hypothesis in this view is: if a product is manufactured with good internal properties, then it will have good external qualities.

Program mutation   Making a small change to a program to obtain a new program called a mutant. A mutant can be equivalent or inequivalent to the original program. Program mutation is used in evaluating the adequacy of tests.

Protected extensible authentication protocol (PEAP)   Method to securely transmit authentication information, including passwords, over a wireless network.

Quality assurance (QA)   (i) A planned and systematic pattern of all actions necessary to provide adequate confidence that an item or product conforms to established technical requirements and (ii) a set of activities designed to evaluate the process by which products are developed or manufactured.

Quality circle (QC)   Volunteer group of workers, usually members of the same department, who meet regularly to discuss the problems and make presentations to management with their ideas to solve the problems. Quality circles were started in Japan in 1962 by Kaoru Ishikawa as another method of improving quality. The movement in Japan was coordinated by the Union of Japanese Scientists and Engineers (JUSE).

Quality control   Set of activities designed to evaluate the quality of developed or manufactured products.

Quality criterion   Attribute of a quality factor that is related to software development. For example, modularity is an attribute of the architecture of a software system.

Quality factor   Behavioral characteristic of a system. Some examples of high-level quality factors are correctness, reliability, efficiency, testability, portability, and reusability.

Quality management   The focus of a quality management group is to ensure process adherence and customize software development processes.

Quality metric   Measure that captures some aspect of a quality criterion. One or more quality metrics are associated with each criterion.

Quick polling   Used to check whether a network element is reachable by doing a ping on the node using the SNMP Get() operation.

Radio access network (RAN)   Part of a mobile telecommunication system. It implements a radio access technology. Conceptually, it lies between the mobile phones and the core network (CN).

Random testing   Test inputs are selected randomly from the input domain of the system.

Referencing a variable   A variable is said to be referenced if the value held in the variable's memory location is fetched.

Regression testing Selective retesting of a system or a component to verify that modifications have not caused unintended effects and that the system or the component still complies with its specified requirements.

Regulatory test Ensures that the system meets the requirements of government regulatory bodies.

Release note Document that accompanies a build or a released software. A release note contains the following information: changes since the last build or release, known defects, defects fixed, and added features.

Reliability test Measures the ability of the system to keep operating over an extended period of time.

Reliable criterion A test selection criterion is reliable if and only if either all tests selected by the criterion are successful or no test selected by the criterion is successful.

Remote architecture Architecture where the IUT does not have a PCO at the upper service boundary and no direct access to the lower service boundary is available.

Remote authentication dial-in user service (RADIUS) AAA protocol for applications such as network access and IP mobility.

Requirement Description of the needs or desires of users that a system is supposed to implement.

Reset sequence Input sequence that puts an implementation to its initial state independent of the state that the implementation is in before the reset sequence is applied.

Rework cost Cost of fixing the known defects.

Robustness test Verifies how robust a system is, that is, how gracefully it behaves in error situation or how it handles a change in its operational state.

Root cause analysis (RCA) Class of problem solving methods aimed at identifying the root causes of problems. The practice of RCA is predicated on the belief that problems are best solved by attempting to correct or eliminate root causes, as opposed to merely addressing the immediately obvious symptoms.

Safety assurance A safety assurance program is established in an organization to eliminate hazards or reduce their associated risks to an acceptable level.

Safety critical software system Software system whose failure can cause loss of life.

Sandwich integration Testing technique in which the software modules are integrated using a mix of top-down and bottom-up techniques.

Scaffolding Computer programs and data files built to support software development and testing but not intended to be included in the final product. Scaffolding code simulates the functions of components that do not exist yet and allow the program to execute. Scaffolding code involves the creation of stubs and test drivers.

Scalability test Verifies whether the system can scale up to its engineering limits.

Scrum Project management method for software development. The approach was first described by Takeuchi and Nonaka in "The New Product Development Game" (*Harvard Business Review*, January/February 1986). It is an iterative, incremental process for developing any product or managing any work.

Secure shell (SSH) Set of standards and an associated network protocol that allow establishing a secure channel between a local and a remote computer. SSH is typically used to log in to a remote machine and execute commands.

Secure socket layer (SSL) Protocol that provides endpoint authentication and communication privacy over the Internet using cryptography.

Security Branch of computer science which deals with protecting computers, network resources, and information against unauthorized access, modification, and/or destruction.

Serviceability Ability of technical support personnel to debug or perform root cause analysis in pursuit of solving a problem with a product. Serviceability is also known as supportability.

Shewhart cycle Also referred to as the Deming cycle after W. Edwards Deming, named after Walter Shewhart, who introduced the concept in his book *Statistical Method from the Viewpoint of Quality Control*, Dover Publications, New York, 1986. It is a continuous improvement cycle known as plan, do, check, and act (PDCA).

Shifted boundary Shifted boundary error is said to occur if the actual boundary is parallel to but not the same as the boundary of interest.

Shrink wrap Material made of polymer plastic with a mix of polyesters. When heat is applied to this material, it decreases in size so that it forms a seal over whatever it was covering. The shrink wrap provides a tamper-evident seal that helps ensure freshness and discourage pilfering. Shrink wrap is commonly found on CDs, DVDs, software packages, and books.

Simple Network Management Protocol (SNMP) Part of the IP suite as defined by the Internet Engineering Task Force. The protocol is used by network management systems for monitoring network-attached devices for conditions that warrant administrative attention.

Simulator Imitation of some real thing, state of affairs, or process. The act of simulating something generally entails representing certain key characteristics or behaviors of a selected physical or abstract system.

Six Sigma Set of practices originally developed by Motorola to systematically improve processes by eliminating defects. The term Six Sigma refers to the ability of highly capable processes to produce output within specification. In particular, processes that operate with Six Sigma quality produce at defect levels below 3.4 defects per (one) million opportunities.

Softer handoff Handoff procedure in which a user-level communication uses two sectors of a single base station simultaneously.

Soft handoff Handoff procedure in which a user-level communication uses two base stations simultaneously.

Software image Compiled software binary.

Software reliability Failure intensity of a software system operating in a given environment.

Specification and Description Language (SDL) High-level specification language which is built around the following concepts: *system*, which is described hierarchically by elements called systems, blocks, channels, processes, services, signals, and signal routes; *behavior*, which is described using an extension of the FSM concept; *data*, which are described using the concept of abstract data types and commonly understood program variables and data structures; and *communication*, which is asynchronous.

Spiral model Also known as the spiral life-cycle model, a systems development method (SDM) used in information technology (IT). This model of development combines the features of the prototyping model and the waterfall model. The spiral model was defined by Barry Boehm in his 1988 article "A Spiral Model of Software Development and Enhancement" (IEEE Computer, May 1988, pp. 61-72).

Spoilage Metric that uses defect age and distribution to measure the effectiveness of testing.

Stakeholder Person or organization that influences a system's behavior or that is impacted by the system.

Statement coverage Selecting paths in such a manner that certain statements are covered by the execution of those paths. Complete statement coverage means selecting some paths such that their execution causes all statements to be covered.

Static unit testing Non-execution-based unit testing. In static unit testing, a programmer does not execute the unit; rather, it involves formal review or verification of code.

Statistical oracle Special case of parametric oracle in which statistical characteristics of the actual test results are verified.

Statistical testing Testing technique which uses a formal experimental paradigm for random testing according to a usage model of the software. In statistical testing a model is developed to characterize the population of uses of the software, and the model is used to generate a statistically correct sample of all possible uses of the software.

Stress test Evaluates and determines the behavior of a software component when the offered load is in excess of its designed capacity.

Stub "Dummy subprogram" that replaces a module that is called by the module to be tested. A stub does minimal data manipulation, such as print verification of the entry, and returns control to the unit under test.

Sustaining phase Optimizing and refining software that is working and focusing much more solidly on customers and competitors to ensure that one does not lose what has been acquired.

Sustaining test engineer Test engineer responsible for testing the product in its sustaining phase.

System integration test (SIT) Testing phase in which software components, hardware components, or both are combined and tested to evaluate their interactions.

System resolution test Probes to provide definite diagnostic answers to specific requirements.

System testing Comprehensive testing undertaken to validate an entire system and its characteristics based on the requirements and the design.

Technical beta Testing conducted to obtain feedback about the usability of the product in a real environment with different configurations. The idea is to obtain feedback from a limited number of users who commit considerable amount of time and thought to their evaluation.

Telnet Network-based application that is used to provide user-oriented command line login sessions between hosts on the Internet.

Testability requirement Requirement that it is possible to construct a test objective which will determine if a system property has been satisfied.

Test adequacy Goodness of a test. If a test does not reveal any fault in a program, it does not mean that there are no faults in the program. Therefore, it is important to evaluate the goodness of a test.

Test architecture Abstract architecture described by identifying the points closest to the IUT at which control and observation are specified. The abstract test architectures can be classified into four major categories: local, distributed, coordinated, and remote.

Test automation Using test tools to execute tests with little or no human intervention.

Test case Pair of input and the expected outcome. A test case covers a specific test objective.

Test case design yield (TCDY) Commonly used metric to measure the test case design effectiveness.

Test case effectiveness Measure of the quality of test cases in terms of their fault revealing capability.

Test case escaped Sometimes defects are found in the testing cycle for which there are no test cases designed. For those defects new test cases are designed, which are called test case escaped.

Test case library Compiled library of reusable test steps of basic utilities that are used as building blocks to facilitate the development of automated test scripts.

Test coordination procedure Set of rules to coordinate the actions of the upper and the lower testers.

Test cycle Partial or total execution of all the test suites planned for a given system testing phase. System testing involves at least one test cycle.

Test data Element of the input domain of a program. Test data are selected by considering some selection criteria.

Test-driven development (TDD) Software development methodology in which programmers write unit tests before the production code.

Test driver Program that invokes a unit under test, passes inputs to the unit under test, compares the actual outcome with the expected outcome from the unit, and reports the ensuing test result.

Test effectiveness Measure of the quality of the testing effort.

Test effort Metric specifying the cost and the time required to create and execute a test case in person-days.

Test environment Setting in which system tests are executed. It is also known as a test bed.

Test event Atomic interaction between the IUT and an upper or lower tester.

Test first Software development methodology in which the programmers write unit tests before the code.

Testing maturity model (TMM) Gives guidance concerning how to improve a test process. The maturity of a test process is represented in five levels, or stages, namely, 1–5. Each stage is characterized by the concepts of maturity goals, supporting maturity goals, and activities, tasks, and responsibilities (ATRs).

Testing and test control notation (TTCN) Programming language dedicated to testing of communication protocols and web services. Up to version 2 the language was unconventionally written in the form of tables, and the language used to be called Tree and Tabular Combined Notation (TTCN) and was renamed to Testing and Test Control Notation in version 3.

Test management protocol Protocol used to implement test coordination procedures by using test management protocol data units (TM-PDUs) in the coordination architecture.

Test objective Description of what needs to be verified in order to ensure that a specific requirement is implemented correctly.

Test oracle Can decide whether or not a test case has passed. An oracle provides a method to (i) generate expected results for the test inputs and (ii) compare the expected results with the actual results of the implementation under test.

Test predicate Description of the conditions or combination of conditions relevant to the correct operation of a program.

Test prioritization   Ordering the execution of test cases according to certain criteria.

Test process   Certain manner of performing activities related to defect detection.

Test process improvement (TPI) model   Allows one to evaluate the maturity levels of test processes. The current status of a test process is evaluated from 20 viewpoints, known as key areas. The status of a test process with respect to a key area is represented in terms of one of four levels of maturity—A, B, C, and D. Level A is the lowest level of maturity, and maturity level ascends from A to D.

Test purpose   Specific description of the objective of the corresponding test case.

Test selection   Carefully selecting a subset of the test suites on the basis of certain criteria. A chosen subset of the test suites are used to perform regression testing.

Test selection criterion   Property of a program, a specification, of a data domain.

Test suite   Group of test cases that can be executed as a package in a particular sequence. Test suites are usually related by the area of the system that they exercise, by their priority, or by content.

Test tool   Hardware or software product that replaces or enhances some aspect of human activity involved in testing.

Test vector   Also called test input vector, an instance of the input to a program.

Tilted boundary   Error that occurs if the actual boundary intersects with the intended boundary.

Top-down integration   A kind of integration testing technique in which testing starts at the topmost module of the program, often called the "main program," and works toward the outermost branches of the visibility tree, gradually adding modules as integration proceeds.

Total quality control (TQC)   Management approach for an organization centered on quality and based on the participation of all its members and aiming at long-term success through customer satisfaction and benefits to all members of the organization and to the society. Total quality control was the key concept of Armand Feigenbaum's 1951 book, *Quality Control: Principles, Practice, and Administration*. Republished in 2004 as *Total Quality Control*, McGraw-Hill, New York.

Traceability matrix   Allows one to make a mapping between requirements and test cases both ways.

Transcendental view of quality   Quality that can be recognized through experience but not defined in some tractable form.

Transfer sequence   Minimum-length input sequence that brings an implementation from its initial state into a given state.

Transition tour   State transitions defined in an FSM specification are executed at least once by applying an input sequence to an implementation, starting from the initial state of the FSM. Such an input sequence is called a transition tour of the FSM.

Transmission Control Protocol (TCP)   Core protocol of the IP suite. Applications on networked hosts can create connections with one another using the TCP; data segments are transmitted over a TCP connection for higher reliability. The protocol guarantees reliable and in-order delivery of data segments. TCP supports many of the Internet's popular applications, including the World Wide Web, e-mail, and secure shell.

Transport layer security (TLS)   Provides endpoint authentication and communication privacy over the Internet using cryptography.

Tunneled transport layer security (TTLS)   Similar to the TLS protocol, but client authentication is extended after a secure transport connection has been established.

Undefinition of a variable   A variable is said to be undefined if the variable's memory location holds a value which is not meaningful anymore.

Unique input–output (UIO) sequence   Essentially an input sequence such that the corresponding output sequence uniquely identifies the state that an implementation was in before the UIO sequences was applied.

Unified modeling language (UML)   Standardized specification language for object modeling. UML is a general-purpose modeling language that includes a graphical notation used to create an abstract model of a system.

Unit   Program unit or module that may be viewed as a piece of code implementing a "low"-level function.

Unit testing   Testing a program unit in isolation. Unit testing is performed by the programmer who wrote the program unit.

Unit under test   Program unit that is being tested in the context of an emulated environment.

Upgrade/downgrade test   Verifies that the system software build can be upgraded or downgraded.

Upper tester   Tester entity that controls and observes the upper service boundary of the IUT.

Usability test   Means of measuring how well people can use some human-made object, such as a web page, a computer interface, a document, or a device, for its intended purpose.

Usage profile   Software profile that characterizes operational use of a software system. Operational use is the intended use of the software in the intended environment.

User acceptance testing (UAT)   Conducted by the customer to ensure that the system satisfies the contractual acceptance criteria.

User view of quality   Extent to which a product meets user needs and expectations.

Valid criterion   A test selection criterion is valid if and only if whenever a program under test contains a fault, the criterion selects a test that reveals the fault.

Validation   Process of ensuring that the software meets its customer's expectations.

Value-based view of quality   The central idea in the value-based view is how much a customer is willing to pay for a certain level of quality.

Verdict   A test verdict is a statement of pass, fail, or inconclusive that is associated with a test case. Pass means that the observed outcome satisfies the test purpose and is completely valid with respect to the requirement. Fail means that the observed outcome is invalid with respect to the requirement. An inconclusive verdict means that the observed outcome is valid with respect to the requirement but inconclusive with respect to the test purpose.

Verification   Process of ensuring the correspondence of an implementation phase of a software development process with its specification.

Virtual circuit (VC)   Communication arrangement in which data from a source user may be passed to a destination user over more than one real communication circuit during a single period of communication; the switching is hidden from the users. A permanent virtual circuit (PVC) is a virtual circuit established for repeated use between the same data terminal equipments (DTE). In a PVC, the long-term association is identical to the data transfer phase of a virtual call. Permanent virtual circuits eliminate the need for repeated call setup and clearing. On the other hand, switched virtual circuits (SVCs) are generally set up on a per-call basis and are disconnected when calls are terminated.

Virus   Software component that is capable of spreading rapidly to a large number of computers but cannot do so all by itself. It has to spread using the assistance of another program.

Walkthrough   Review where a programmer leads a review team through a manual or simulated execution of the product using predefined scenarios.

Waterfall model   Sequential software development model in which development is seen as flowing steadily downward—like a waterfall—through the phases of requirements analysis, design, implementation, testing, integration, and maintenance. The origin of the term "waterfall" is often said to be an article (Managing the Development of Large Software Systems: Concepts and Techniques, in Proceedings of WESCON, August 1970, pp. 1-9. Reprinted in ICSE, Monterey, CA, 1987, pp. 328-338) published in 1970 by W. W. Royce.

White-box testing   Testing methodology in which one primarily takes into account the internal mechanisms, such as code and program logic, of a system or component.

Worm   Software component that is capable of, under its own means, infecting a computer system.

W-set   Set of input sequences for an FSM. When the set of inputs is applied to an implementation of the FSM in an intended state, one expects to observe outputs which uniquely identify the state of the implementation.

Zero-day attack   Presents a new and particularly serious kind of threat. Developed specifically to exploit software vulnerabilities before patches are available, these attacks are not recognized by traditional security products: they enter a network undetected, giving absolutely no time to prepare for a defense.

INDEX

One of the great defects of English books printed in the last century is the want of an index.
— *Lafcadio Hearn a.k.a Koizumi Yakumo*

Software Testing and Quality Assurance: Theory and Practice, Edited by Kshirasagar Naik and Priyadarshi Tripathy
Copyright © 2008 John Wiley & Sons, Inc.